Lucks (Editor)   Transatlantic Mergers & Acquisitions

4 Professional Contributions

1 Introduction

This book seeks to convey three messages: The importance of transatlantic mergers and acquisitions, their poor success rate on average to date and the outstanding results that top players achieve. The U.S. and Germany are each other's most important investors. Diligence, experience management and knowledge management can considerably improve the success rate of acquisition projects.
They are thus key to tapping the tremendous potential for increasing value. The examples and articles in this book demonstrate how this can be achieved.

The economic role of TMA

Corporate mergers and acquisitions have become the hallmark of rapid economic change, particularly when it comes to the consolidation-based competition going on within Western industrialized countries. Companies seeking to establish themselves in mature markets cannot afford to engage in years of competition as a means of edging out their competitors. Instead, the acquisition of a national player has now become the method of choice for entering a market. Given the broadening scope of technological options and ever-shorter product lifecycles, acquisitions increasingly secure products and technologies that no single company would be able to develop on its own. These are the main factors driving transatlantic M&A activity today.

At $57 billion, the gross product generated by German affiliates in the U.S. (2002) is roughly the same as the revenues generated by subsidiaries of U.S. companies in Germany ($60 billion[1]). U.S.-German M&A projects are among the biggest deals worldwide (see the overview at the end of this book). At €65 billion, the volumes of U.S.-German M&A projects in both directions have been more or less equal over the last five years[2]. Most of the activity from Germany has been in the form of strategic engagements, with the volume showing a declining trend after the stock market hype in 2002. Americans are investing more and more in Germany, particularly equity investors.

---

[1] US Bureau of Economic Analysis: US-German linkages, gross product of majority-owned foreign affiliates

[2] According to Thomson Financials. Compare US Bureau of Economic Analysis: US Outflows to Germany 2000-2004 = $30.6 billion, US Outflows from Germany 2000-2004 = $63.5 billion

The markets

The structures of companies engaging in strategic acquisitions vary widely on the two sides of the Atlantic. German companies aiming to make the transatlantic leap generally already have a broad international presence in the European market. For them, entering the U.S. means tapping into the world's biggest single homogenous market. For budding transatlantic dealmakers from the U.S., on the other hand, the acquisition of a European company is aimed not only at achieving a leading position within the German market but also at establishing a broad presence in Western and Eastern Europe and developing a broad-based, multicultural management system to manage the diversity of markets and business entities there.

Given the dominance of the U.S. market and Germany's relative size within the European market, U.S.-German M&A activities are often among the most important strategic movements as the Western markets become more and more consolidated. Thus, the stakeholders on either side of the Atlantic often find themselves face to face with their strongest competitors. Once the M&A game has commenced in an industry, there is often a cascade of countermovements through M&A or organic defensive measures.

The limited number of candidates and the difficulties associated with trying to harmonize strategies and targets demands patience and endurance. It often takes years before a company's desired candidate becomes available, as was the case in the Siemens-Westinghouse example. And even then, the two companies may not always be a perfect match, as with Henkel and Dial. In such cases, buyers may have to settle for their second choice. If the necessary size increase is not achieved instantly, resources can be tied up for years, not only for integration but also for the subsequent organic development of the company's market presence. In many ways, Germany offers Americans the best platform for making a big entrance on the European markets. Germany is a leading location for industry and lies at the geographical center of Europe. It is home to strong players with holdings and relationships with low-cost suppliers in Eastern Europe, which is just a few hours' drive away.

Strategies

Until now, the markets for strategic investors (those seeking to achieve synergies) and financial investors (those primarily seeking to increase value through turnaround and by leveraging capital) have been largely separate. Increasingly, the massive financial resources available – particularly to U.S. funds – and the extensive portfolios managed by players like KKR are bringing the M&A markets together. Private equity firms are now also pursuing M&A strategies within their broad portfolios. Thus, they have also become serious competitors in the race for strategic targets and are now in a position to use their buying power to take on, take over and dissemble even large international players. Today, U.S. funds hold significant German assets that were previously in government hands.

For many companies, tapping into the huge market across the Atlantic is a top strategic and operative priority. A strong baseline position in the most important mature industrialized countries is often essential to developing the endurance needed for long drawn-out attempts to move into the new growth regions. New global players are rapidly emerging in the "BRIC" countries (Brazil-Russia-India-China). This makes transatlantic consolidation a must for companies that want to keep pace with the movement toward globalization in the decades ahead and to compete with newly emerging giants from the Far East.

What's different in the U.S. and Germany?

The differences between Americans and Germans lie in the goals they set, their structures and their tolerance for risk. For Americans, M&A is the method of choice for entering markets and developing technologies quickly. They are more likely to shy away from the inherent risks of tying up resources for long periods for organic growth, particularly when it comes to R&D endeavors. Americans tend to view the risks associated with M&A as part of doing business (see article by Matthiessen/ Daniel, chapter 4.2.1). By contrast, Germans tend to focus more on endogenous growth through research and development and consider external growth to be riskier. Consequently, the M&A market is less developed in Germany. Higher levels of spending on R&D and on serving heterogeneous national markets keep profit margins down, making the cost of acquiring these German companies comparatively low, and thus an appealing prospect for U.S. companies.

Success and complexity

However, this appeal is muted somewhat by the M&A success rate, a mere 30% – 50% on the whole, based on the relative development of share prices following acquisitions. Transatlantic M&A deals fare even worse on average. Large-scale transatlantic M&A projects have a particularly low success rate, destroying vast assets within national economies in their wake. The commonly expressed optimism that Germans and Americans are particularly close because of the special relationship that evolved from the post-war era's Marshall Plan, reconstruction and export ties – and that corporate mergers should therefore be easier – flies in the face of reality. According to analyses in several articles within this book, companies' overestimation of their own capabilities and underestimation of the challenges involved (compare my article on management of complex M&A projects, chapter 4.1.2) are the real cause of M&A failures. Large M&A deals – and particularly in transatlantic business, this is generally the case – are often driven by management egos. However, once ego takes over, barriers go undetected, general due diligence takes a back seat and the projects end in disaster. Even authoritative writings on M&A often don't take these considerations seriously enough. Many authors content themselves with merely enumerating situational snapshots of individual deals rather than systematically examining management problems. The American "way of M&A" is characterized by pragmatism and confidence in general management abilities. However, studies show that the expertise and skills that are critical for M&A are quite different from those needed to ensure continuity in ongoing operations. Companies with better baseline performance do not necessarily have better chances of success with M&A. I had to learn from experience in numerous integration projects that M&A is always a balancing act. Too much pragmatism can easily result in chaos, while a rigid, systematic approach can generate complexities and create new problems instead of solving them. All the textbooks in the world can't replace experience, which is something that can only be acquired through painstaking, often frustrating practice.

TMA: Out of the comfort zone

Along with poor performance there are also cases of abuse in which financial investors looking to make short-term gains ignore the long-term consequences of a transaction. They leave in their wake companies overburdened with debt and they destroy jobs. These cases should be denounced. In the months just prior to the release of this book, such "black sheep" triggered a political debate in Germany that did little to help the situation. I spoke with numerous fund managers while preparing this book and am now more convinced than ever that professional and successful investors are in agreement that there is a correlation between the success and the sustainability of M&A investments.

The effects of the bubble economy and stock market hype in 2002 are still being felt today. The findings of fraud and misrepresentations resulted in a wave of new legislation like the Sarbanes-Oxley Act in the U.S., and new codes of conduct on both sides of the Atlantic. Making executives personally accountable for any information which might affect the stock price led to their becoming extremely cautious in any of their public statements. This, in turn, has caused today's 'legal advisory hype' – a phenomenon which also impacted this book. Half a dozen top executives from U.S. companies were highly motivated to tell their M&A stories and had committed early on to contributing them. Some of their texts had been ready for months. But when these were put through a series of legal reviews, the result was last minute withdrawals. I am grateful for offers by these executives to contribute to a possible second edition; their assumption is that, by that time, an open discussion about effectively managing M&A projects will be more commonplace. Their optimism that this book might be more than just a one-time event is heartening. However, due to this reticence on the part of senior U.S. managers to tell their stories at this time, most of the first-hand top management reports are from German companies, while the U.S. case studies are generally presented by consultants.

The subject of this book is anything but "comfortable." Transatlantic success cannot be achieved through simple formulas. Yet it is impossible to deny that mergers and acquisitions are a necessity. Anyone who avoids M&A due to fear or a lack of expertise is bound to lose out in today's consolidation-based competition and will be unable to achieve success in the growth regions.

The idea behind this book: Knowledge transfer

The idea for this book goes back to the first German-American Mergers & Acquisitions Day, which took place in New York on October 21, 2004, at the initiative of the German Federal M&A Association. Under the auspices of Jürgen Weber, the Federal

Commissioner for Foreign Investment in Germany, and together with the German-American Chamber of Commerce, we invited German and U.S. businesspeople and M&A specialists to Deutsche Bank's offices on Wall Street to share their experiences. The meeting was a success, not only in terms of the subject matter. Discussions among the participants were lively, continuing until the last of the attendees had to leave for the airport. M&A is a business that sparks emotion and always needs an "owner" who identifies with a project. But a case can only promise success if it is supported by technical expertise. The workshop's leaders agreed to undertake follow-up activities, of which this book is the first. It seeks to relay the knowledge and expertise to a broader audience, our readers.

Fundamentals of German-American M&A relationships

There is agreement among business people and experts that the success rate of M&A is largely determined by experience, knowledge transfer and technical diligence. Studies support this thesis. In this book, large companies that make frequent acquisitions and specialists who have established the necessary expertise management report on success stories. Among the most important rules for success are ensuring that the management has gained personal experience through the planning and implementation of comparable projects and ensuring that the disciplines needed for M&A are managed by proven experts.

It is along these lines that this book is structured. The first part provides information about the basics of German-American M&A relationships. Jürgen Weber illustrates the central role that Germany plays in the European strategies of U.S. companies. Daniel Hamilton and Joseph Quinlan outline the significance and structures of German-American shareholding relationships from a U.S. perspective. Thomas Schwingeler and Stefan Griesser document the transatlantic M&A market and its prospects for the future. Marcus Schenck, Frank Richter and Karoline Jung-Sennsfelder write about the capital market as a lever for transatlantic deals. And Fritz Kröger points out the direction that global consolidation is taking and analyzes the need for improvement.

Learning from M&A cases

In the second part of this book, representative examples illustrate what drives M&A in various industries and how success has been achieved in individual projects. The articles cover the major industries, different "classes" of companies (from large corporations to medium-sized enterprises to small, specialized operations) and a variety of case categories (from "strategic" projects involving special integration challenges to equity investors). The cases described here involve efforts to cross the Atlantic in both directions. A wide variety of business types are covered, from equipment manufacture to products and services to IT and asset acquisitions. Because of its heavier weighting in strategic investments, Germany is more prevalent here, while articles on private equity illustrate U.S. involvement in Germany. The selection of authors, many of whom are corporate executives like Rüdiger Grube (DaimlerChrysler), Lothar

Steinebach (Henkel), Hermann Thiele (Knorr), and Klaus Zumwinkel (Deutsche Post World Net), highlights the diversity of perspectives. With George Nolen (Siemens Corporation) and Randy Zwirn (Siemens-Westinghouse), we also hear from senior executives of German companies operating in the U.S. Smaller players from the new economy (Dirk Hoffmann: Jamba!) and the IT sector (Ingo Möller, Ingram Micro) also share their insights. Strategists like Axel Wiandt / Rafael Moral y Santiago of Deutsche Bank and Barbara Jeremia and Konrad von Sczcepanski of Alcoa write about movements in various industries. Jörg Sellmann and Oliver Maier of Degussa explain broadly based portfolio movements within corporations. We have also included joint presentations by companies and their consultants (in the case of Dräger Medical, presented by Wolfgang Reim and Carsten Kratz) and collaborations between strategic buyers and their equity partners (in the case of Zeiss-Sola aided by EQT, presented by Michael Kaschke and Udo Philipp). The private equity scene is represented by big specialists and small cap investors (Gernot Wunderle, Volker Schmidt). Helmut Uder's account of the Onex Food case from the human resources perspective serves as the segue to the specialized articles that make up part three of this book.

Leadership and strategies

The specialized articles in the third part of this book discuss the field of M&A specialists who should be involved, whether in-house experts or external consultants. The order of their appearance reflects the order of the project phases in which they are involved. We begin with strategic considerations, leadership concepts and corporate governance, offering various approaches to overarching perspectives. This includes a comparison of leadership behaviors by Joerg Matthiesen, Allison Bailey and Jeanie Daniel Duck as well as my own concept for managing complex transatlantic projects. Gerhard Plaschka, Rohit Verma and Douglas Squeo focus on customer reactions, a topic that has been sorely neglected in M&A on the whole. Their quantitative measurement methods are among the most innovative areas of M&A. Jens Schädler and Reto Isenegger cover the broader field of (non-equity) partnership between companies.

Transaction and cultural change

The next section covers transaction-oriented disciplines relating to stock markets, finance, controlling, measurement, due diligence, taxes and anti-trust law. Here too, we cannot limit ourselves to easy-to-digest, "simple fare." The articles in this section describe numerous important and innovative products. These in-depth explorations seek to illustrate the amount of specialist expertise and experience necessary for success. I ask for your understanding that I cannot name each and every one of the authors here. We then come to the more or less "soft" factors involved in integration projects. The segue here is provided by an article by Alexander Geiser and Nikolai Juchem, in which the authors seek to establish a link between capital market rules and communication. Patrick Schmidt sweeps away some preconceptions in this regard and leads us deep into the realm of linguistic messages while Bettina Palazzo, Craig

DeForest and Bernhard Pelzer round out the book with a fundamental discussion of U.S. pragmatism and "German thoroughness."

Creating new enterprise organisms

Only a well-orchestrated ensemble can ensure success. Whether a selection of distinguished chamber orchestra musicians or a large marching band that can perform precision drills is needed depends on the case at hand. As we mentioned above, only experienced practitioners can determine which size of ensemble and which blend of (American) pragmatism and "German thoroughness" is needed. Americans and Germans can learn a great deal from each other, and a combination of the two cultures and approaches promises the greatest success. In a merger, the goal is not so much to equalize the existing cultures but rather to bring together the cultural and structural differences that are so critical to successful operation in different markets, and to thereby form a single organism.

Acknowledgements

I would like to express my deepest gratitude to all of the friends, authors, association colleagues and publishing house employees who have made this book possible. Although M&A is one of the toughest work environments, you have sacrificed your time to be a part of this endeavor. My special thanks go to the many teams of analysts, assistants and ghost writers, without whom these articles would never have been possible. To two of them I want to personally express my gratitude, namely to Andreas Richter who assisted me in organization and processing and to Gerhard Seitfudem for publishing of this book.

With the firm conviction that transatlantic alliances and mergers can regularly be brought to successful fruition, this book seeks to lend encouragement in undertaking the corporate mergers and acquisitions that are essential to the future of our nations – with competence, mutual understanding and enthusiasm for a new venture together.

Munich, October 2005
Kai Lucks

2 Markets and Structures

2.1 Going Where the Markets Are – M&A in Germany

Jürgen Weber

*The enlargement of the European Union in May 2004 brought
forth a single market of 454 million consumers offering major
opportunities for overseas investors. Germany presents itself as
a business location in the very heart of the union whose attraction
has appreciated considerably recently thanks to the country's drive
for greater global competitiveness.*

The essential questions when looking at capital investment overseas are similar to those facing a person when buying a home: The three most important things to consider carefully are – location, location, location.

Despite the popular conception of the "rising" economies of Asia and their big emerging markets, Europe and America continue to be the most powerful commercial players. They have the world's strongest markets, they provide high-grade jobs and they are the basis for considerable revenues and profits due to the wealth of their peoples. Take the three German states of Bavaria, Baden-Württemberg and North Rhine-Westphalia, for example: they alone have a higher GDP than the four Asian tigers – South Korea, Taiwan, Singapore and Hong Kong – taken together.

Within the European Union, Germany's attraction as a business location has appreciated over the past three years – structurally because of a new drive for economic and social reforms and geographically because the country has become the center of the European Union following EU enlargement in 2004. Today, you could not be more centrally based in Europe than in this continental heartland neighboring nine countries. Germany is the natural linchpin between East and West, North and South and EU expansion has dramatically improved its competitiveness.

Why should foreign direct investment be encouraged, and why is the integration of our economies of both sides of the Atlantic so important? At one time, companies would primarily invest in overseas production and service bases in order to seize fresh market opportunities. But now that all types of hedging strategies are vital for healthy balance sheets, foreign direct investment has become a key factor in guarding a company against currency fluctuations and regulatory restrictions. This effect has become known as "natural hedging."

Related party trade – that is, trade between parent and affiliate companies – offers an explanation as to why U.S. imports from Europe remained strong and continued to grow in 2003 despite a 20 percent appreciation of the euro against the dollar. And that also partly explains why Germany remained the world's leading export nation even in 2004, despite a very strong euro. Had we not invested in each other's economies, things would look much darker today. Indeed, an integrated economy is less vulnerable.

The M&A business and private equity serve as a powerful engine in this integration process. Acting on behalf of their private and institutional investors, M&A consultancy firms are on the constant lookout for business enterprises to buy and develop further.

We at "Invest in Germany" – the agency I represent as Federal German Commissioner for Foreign Investment – recognize three main factors that attract foreign direct investment:

1. The chance to open up new markets and develop existing ones
2. A low-priced production base, which is a very popular reason for going abroad
3. Natural hedging.

I mentioned natural hedging already. So, let's concentrate on points one and two.

Access to markets is a classic reason for going abroad. Even the very best intentions will get you nowhere if you are not familiar with your market and its people. Being on the spot enables you to analyze situations quickly, take decisions that are geared to local conditions and traditions and deliver your goods or services fast. The famous saying "When in Rome, do as the Romans do" is as valid as ever. It pays to have the know-how.

Germany is the leading economy in Europe. Eighty-two million people live there – that is 22 percent of the EU population. They create 23 percent of the Union's gross domestic product. So anybody who wants to win a market share in Europe can't get around having a presence in Germany.

The expansion on May 1 from the so-called EU 15 to EU 25 countries has created a single open market of 454 million consumers. Germany enjoys a prime geographical situation in this enlarged union. Goods can be delivered to and carried from Prague, Warsaw and the Baltic states just as easily as – say – to and from Amsterdam, Brussels, Copenhagen, Paris or Vienna. Distances are short and air services, in particular, are frequent and quick, with flying times usually less than an hour-and-a-half. Germany's hub airports in Frankfurt and Munich are the most central of their kind in Europe.

Also, there is an excellent network of fast highways and railroads radiating from Germany. That is an advantage no major company can afford to ignore when seeking a location for its regional activities in Europe. Another interesting point: Central Europe has become the most important trading partner of the EU during the past ten years – more important than Asia or Latin America. Germany, Austria and Italy account for more than three-quarters of total trade flows between eastern and western Europe. It is lucrative to tap into these trade flows. All these features are compelling reasons for investing in or buying companies in Germany. FDI in both directions keeps the continents of America and Europe alert and competitive and ensures that innovation finds its way to the markets quickly.

My second point is **the cost of labor.** A low-priced production base is not the first thing that comes to mind when you think of Germany. Because people automatically relate low cost to cheap labor.

Cheap labor certainly is not what attracts U.S. companies to Germany first and foremost. In fact, the political debate in Germany has permanently been revolving round the question as to how to cut labor costs in order to secure global competitiveness. So there must be other, more compelling reasons for investing in Germany.

When you take a more comprehensive look, a low-priced production base turns out to be a rather mixed basket of comparatively low wages, highly qualified local staff and management, and stable labor relations.

Here Germany can score on the salient points. Each spring the American Chamber of Commerce in Germany publishes a survey of their 100 biggest member firms. They continue to regard Germany as an ideal location for U.S. companies, specifically for headquarters serving the European area.

AmCham members cite the quality of highly trained labor as the second strongest reason for operating in Germany after the strength of the market. It is the excellent productivity and the flexibility of the workforce that they are so happy with. Skilled labor – the famous German *Facharbeiter* – is very versatile. He can fix things for you, an AmCham member told me, for which you would require another specialist in an American company if you want to avoid a borderline dispute.

I will not gloss over the fact that the recent expansion of the European Union has been used by industry to shift some of their production eastwards where labor is extremely cheap. This has put pressure on management and unions in Germany to adapt to a new environment. And, indeed, Germany has made astonishing progress in this respect.

Wage freezes, a partial return to the 40-hour week, lower entry wages and shop contracts that allow more flexible working in line with market demand – all this is happening and reflects the new realities. Codetermination at the shop-floor level works. You will find readiness on the part of local shop committees to reach tailor-made agreements. That would have been unheard-of only a couple of years ago. Germany is definitely moving with the times! Executives of big U.S. companies in Germany with whom I have spoken are impressed by the flexibility of their labor force and shop committees.

R&D is another quality factor in Germany's favor. Sixty per cent of U.S. corporate research and development conducted outside the United States is based in Europe. The UK and Germany are the biggest labs for U.S. companies abroad. Germans continue to register the highest number of patents in Europe. Companies like Ford and BP have moved their European research centers from the UK to Germany for that very reason. So, the comparative advantage of a location is based on a number of different factors. And Germany has strong plus points speaking in its favor.

There is one other, very recent argument for giving preference to Germany over other business locations in Europe – and that is money. Germany's comparative advantages in the euro zone have grown remarkably. A survey published by the British magazine "The Economist" revealed that the euro area may have a single currency, but it still has many different real exchange rates. That is stunning news.

When the single currency was born, Germany's unit labor costs were the highest in the euro area. But since 1999 they have fallen by ten percent relative to the average. In contrast, relative unit labor costs have risen by nine percent in Italy, Spain and the Netherlands. Economists at ABN Amro were quoted as estimating that Germany's labor costs are now lower than Italy's. Ireland and Portugal have also lost competitiveness. In the past five years, Germany has boasted faster growth in labor productivity than the euro area average.

The same analysts conclude that Germany's real trade-weighted effective exchange rate against the dollar has risen only 4 percent since early 2002. By the same token, France's real exchange rate has gone up by 9 percent and that of Italy and Ireland by 17 percent. Germany also has the lowest inflation rate in the euro zone. The economists argue that Germany's modest rise in the real trade-weighted exchange rate explains the country's success as the world's leading exporter – a result of a remarkable improvement in the terms of trade.

Also, Goldman Sachs, the investment bankers, stated in a report that Germany's competitiveness has improved dramatically and was now on par with the rest of the Union. Germany, indeed, is good for many a pleasant surprise!

A final word on how M&A and private equity are being viewed in my country. In contrast to a more skeptical view several years ago, the private equity business has gained a lot of respect in recent years. This picture has hardly been marred by political criticism recently.

Private equity is seen by trade and industry as an alternative to classical forms of financing a company. Particularly small and medium-sized companies – the backbone of the German economy – are confronted with two major challenges: They find themselves facing global competitive pressure and want to expand. But the new Basle Two credit regulations make it difficult for them to obtain the necessary credit facilities.

Most of these small and medium-sized businesses suffer from a lack of capital resources. While it is common for U.S., French or Dutch companies to have an equity ratio of 30 per cent, they only possess seven-and-a-half percent on average. As a result, only a few can afford to invest in new products or technologies, although they are highly innovative as companies. There are dormant potentials which only a few of them can realize. Also, many of those firms that were established in the fifties and sixties, when Germany was recovering from World War II, are now in need of a successor to their present owners. Private equity can help to solve problems of succession.

Major German groups are interested in PE because the pressure is on for them to concentrate on core activities. Many diversified groups are thinking of spinning off activities that do not fit the portfolio anymore, even though they are profitable. So, at a time when the whole country is debating reform and adjusting to new global chal-lenges, Germany has a lot of advantages to offer U.S. investors who are thinking of buying into local businesses.

By doing so, they will gain. They will obtain a footing in the EU or may help develop companies in their expansion drive. Whatever their objective may be, their activities will enhance transatlantic economic integration, produce results and secure jobs. A number of companies that are well known to German consumers have already become successful with the help of private equity: Gardena, the garden utensils manufacturer, for instance, or the Nordsee restaurant chain, the ATU auto repair chain, and Roden-stock glasses, to mention just a few.

Generally, the public is hardly aware of this fact. The lack of publicity is regrettable, but it could also be seen as a sign of normality in the transatlantic economy. And there are other, more spectacular cases, like that of the chemical giant Celanese or the purchase of Linde refrigeration engineering by United Technologies. A great number of M&A and private equity deals in Germany are real success stories. They bode well for a deepening of transatlantic economic relations.

Foreign direct investment in both directions will strengthen our respective position as global players. Let's always remain aware of that.

2.2 U.S.-German Relations: Will the Ties that Bind Grow Stronger or Weaker?

Daniel S. Hamilton and Joseph P. Quinlan

The economic interests and future prosperity of the United States and Germany have never been as interdependent as they are today. U.S.-German commercial interests are bound together by foreign investment – the deepest form of economic integration. The war in Iraq, and subsequent tensions between Washington and Berlin, served as a useful wake up call to policy makers on both sides of the Atlantic to the importance of the U.S.-German relationship. Now, however, the challenge for both parties is to renew their commitment to the relationship and forge ahead with new policies that will strengthen one of the most important bilateral relationships in the world.

With the end of the Cold War, and the receding threat of the Soviet Union, many parties on both sides of the Atlantic came to the conclusion that the United States and Europe were no longer strategic partners in need, that they were free to disengage from each other and free to pursue divergent interests. This view gained even more credence in the post-September 11th environment, when U.S. foreign policy shifted towards more pre-emptive strategies and unilateral initiatives, culminating in the U.S.-led war in Iraq.

The bitter division over the war in Iraq shook the transatlantic foundation to its core, notably the U.S.-German alliance. U.S. relations with one of its longest-standing European allies plunged to perhaps its lowest level since the creation of the Federal Republic of Germany. The war in Iraq fanned anti-Americanism across Germany, which, in turn, only served to stoke anti-European and German sentiment in the United States. Public opinion on both sides of the ocean turned decisively sour in 2003 and 2004. Against this backdrop, many observers began to think the unthinkable – the collapse of the transatlantic alliance in general, and downgrading of the U.S.-German partnership in particular, following decades of cooperation and prosperity.

Fortunately, the fashionable argument that the United States and Germany no longer need each other has begun to wane. In its place a new realism has emerged, one anchored in the belief that despite differences in other fields (security, climate change, Middle East policies), the economic interests and future prosperity of the United States and Germany have never been as interdependent and intertwined as they are today. U.S.-German commercial interests are bound together by foreign investment – the deepest form of economic integration – as opposed to trade – a well known yet rather shallow form of integration.

Interestingly, despite all the media hype about the emergence of China, the promise of India and the allure of the emerging markets, U.S.-German economic ties only grew stronger over the first half of this decade. However, the past is hardly prologue. Even a bilateral relationship rooted in foreign direct investment needs constant nourishment and reinforcing initiatives that deepen and strengthen the relationship. Today, U.S.-German linkages are among the strongest in the world. The question is whether or not the same will be true by the end of this decade and beyond.

U.S.-German commercial relations – the long view

In the aftermath of World War II, U.S.-German commercial relations were relatively shallow and underdeveloped. Given strong growth at home, U.S. firms were not aggressive foreign investors at the time, and what investment did take place abroad was directed at natural resources. Accordingly, mining and oil exploration were the principal sectors driving U.S. investment outflows; resource-rich Canada and Latin America accounted for roughly 70% of America's overseas investment position at the outset of the Cold War.

Europe's share of U.S. foreign investment was just 15% in 1950, with the United Kingdom accounting for nearly half of the European total. In the intervening decades, however, the motivations for investing overseas among U.S. firms shifted, as did the geographic composition of U.S. foreign investment. Access to markets, rather than raw materials, became the overriding determinant of U.S. firms' overseas expansion. As a result, Europe, which had lagged Canada and Latin America in the early 1950s, emerged as the most favored destination of U.S. firms in the ensuing decades, a ranking the region has never relinquished.

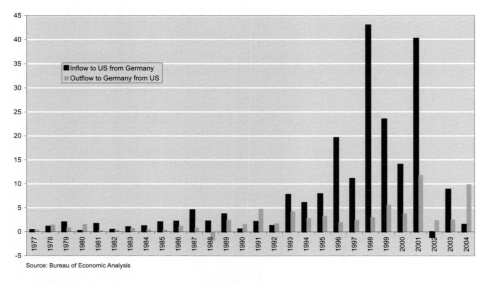

Source: Bureau of Economic Analysis

Figure 2.1 The Long View: U.S.-German FDI Flows (in US $ billions)

As Europe rebuilt and recovered from the ravages of war in the late 1950s, and moved toward the creation of a common market, U.S. firms were quick to seize the opportunities across the Atlantic. While U.S. foreign investment outflows to Europe averaged just $400 million (in nominal terms) annually in the 1950s, the annual average more than quadrupled in the 1960s, jumping to $1.7 billion. That represented nearly 40% of the U.S. global total, up from a 20% share in the 1950s. In the 1970s, Europe's share jumped to 47% of total U.S. FDI; in the 1980s, Europe easily accounted for more than half of total U.S. investment outflows.

U.S. foreign investment to Germany mirrored these general trends: over the 1950s, Germany attracted just $600 million of U.S. investment on a cumulative basis. Over the 1960s, as a European common market began to coalesce, and as Germany emerged as one of the most powerful economies in Europe and the world, U.S. foreign direct investment to Germany rose sharply. Indeed, over the 1960s, U.S. firms invested $3.4 billion on a cumulative basis in Germany, a near six-fold increase from the prior decade. In the 1970s, U.S. firms invested another $9.3 billion, more than two-and-a-half times the level of the prior decade. By the end of the 1970s, U.S. firms enjoyed a commanding position in Germany; U.S.-German investment flows were unbalanced by the end of the 1970s, with America's investment stakes in Germany, on a historic cost basis, roughly double ($15.4 billion) that of Germany's investment position in the United States ($7.6 billion).

The investment gap between the U.S. and Germany reflected the global economic conditions of the post-war era. Spared the destruction of war in their home markets, U.S. firms had the advantage of a healthy economy and the financial means to expand overseas. By contrast, the 1950s and 1960s were a period of rebuilding and reconstruction for most German companies. Before expanding abroad, many firms first had to resurrect their own facilities at home and reestablish their domestic market posi-

Table 2.1 FDI inflows

US foreign direct investment inflows from Germany (in US $ billions)

	US Inflows from Germany	US Inflows from Europe	Inflows from Germany as a % of Flow from Europe
1962-1969	0,5	3,3	14,9%
1970-1979	4,2	27,7	15,3%
1980-1989	19,4	216,3	9,0%
1990-1999	123,1	659,1	18,7%
2000-2004	63,5	502,4	12,6%

US foreign direct investment outflows to Germany (in US $ billions)

	US Outflows to Germany	US Outflows to Europe	Outflows to Germany as a % of Flow to Europe
1950-1959	0,6	4,2	13,3%
1960-1969	3,4	16,7	20,2%
1970-1979	9,3	57,9	16,1%
1980-1989	6,5	94,7	6,9%
1990-1999	31,8	465,3	6,8%
2000-2004	30,6	401,6	7,6%

Source: Bureau of Economic Analysis

tions. With the formation of the European Economic Community, German firms were initially venturing into neighboring nations rather than further abroad.

Over the 1970s, however, many German firms went on the offensive and made it a strategic priority to counteract corporate America's growing presence in Germany. Accordingly, after investing $4.2 billion in the United States over the 1970-79 time frame – up sharply from roughly $500 million over the prior decade – German firms dramatically increased their market presence in the United States over the 1980s. In fact, German firms invested nearly three times as much capital in the U.S. over the 1980s ($19.4 billion) as U.S. firms invested in Germany ($6.5 billion).

Over the 1980s, U.S. foreign direct investment overseas dropped sharply in part on account of the U.S. recession. Meanwhile, U.S. capital inflows from Germany and other nations soared, bolstered by a number of variables including favorable market attributes in the U.S., a wave of corporate restructuring that increased the number of domestic candidates for sale, and attractive incentives from many U.S. states and municipal governments. Shifts in U.S. tax laws related to accelerated depreciation schedules also lured record amounts of foreign investment. So did the dramatic depreciation of the U.S. dollar over the second half of the 1980s, with the weak dollar not only reducing the foreign currency cost of acquiring U.S. companies. The weak dollar also caused the dollar value of wages in other nations, notably Germany, to rise relative to U.S. wages, making it more difficult for German firms to export goods to the U.S. This made it all the more attractive for German firms to invest directly in the United States. And they did – by 1989, German investment in the United States, on a historic cost basis, was nearly 20% larger than corporate America's position in Germany, $28.4 billion versus $23.7 billion.

The 1990s and beyond – the bonds grow stronger, not weaker

When the economic history of the late 20th century is written, globalization will undoubtedly be invoked as the defining economic precept of the time. Like the initial period of globalization in the second half of the 19th century, the 1990s and beyond have been a time of robust and unfettered global capital flows, market liberalization measures and buoyant global trade. Global trade expanded by an average annual rate of 6.1% (in volume) over the 1990s, roughly double the rate of world GDP growth, and by a similar annual rate over the first half of this decade.

Global foreign direct investment (FDI) flows have expanded at an even faster pace, boosting the level of global inward FDI stock from $1.9 trillion in 1990, to $6.3 trillion in 2000, and to an estimated $8.2 trillion in 2003. At the start of the decade, there were over 60,000 transnationals with more than 820,000 affiliate spread around the world. From this global production base, the gross product of foreign affiliates totaled $3.7 trillion in 2003, with foreign affiliates employing over 54 million workers. Sales of foreign affiliates topped $17.6 trillion in 2003, versus $5.7 trillion in 1990, and were well above global exports of goods and services in 2003 – $9.2 billion.

Globalization's return has opened the untapped markets of central Europe, Latin America, and the Indian subcontinent. Free market reform has been the mantra of Poland, Brazil, India and a host of emerging markets for more than a decade, with these new markets providing new consumers, new resources to leverage and new opportunities to grow sales and revenues for the world's leading multinationals.

Yet despite all the hype associated with globalization, and notwithstanding all the excitement surrounding the emerging markets, notably China, one of the defining features of the global economic landscape over the past decade has been the increasing integration and cohesion of the transatlantic economy in general, and U.S.-German ties in particular.

American companies invested more capital overseas in the 1990s – in excess of $750 billion – than in the prior four decades combined. But the surge in U.S. foreign investment did not flow to the new and untapped markets of the developing nations. Rather, the majority of U.S. foreign direct investment in the 1990s, and the first half of this decade, has been directed at Europe. Of the top ten destinations of U.S. investments in the 1990s, five countries in Europe ranked in the top ten – the United Kingdom (ranked No. 1), the Netherlands (3), Switzerland (6), Germany (7) and France (8). Rounding out the top ten were Canada (2), Brazil (4), Mexico (5), Australia (9) and Japan (10).

In the first half of this decade (2000-04), six countries in Europe were among the top ten destinations of U.S. foreign investment. The United Kingdom, ranked first again, followed by Canada (2), the Netherlands (3), Switzerland (4), Mexico (5), Ireland (6), Germany (7), Singapore (8), Japan (9) and Italy (10). U.S. investment stakes in Europe have expanded sharply this decade, with Europe attracting nearly 56% of total U.S. foreign direct investment in the first half of the decade. The bias towards Europe runs counter to all the hype and angst associated with U.S. outsourcing to such low-cost locales like China and India, and the common belief that it is the low-cost destinations of East Asia that has attracted the bulk of U.S. investment.

To be sure, U.S. foreign direct investment to China and India has jumped dramatically this decade, notably U.S. investment to China. Total U.S. investment to China, for instance, surged to nearly $11 billion (on a cumulative basis) in the first half of this decade, nearly double U.S. investment flows to China of $5.9 billion over the second half of the 1990s. That represents a dramatic rise, although on comparative basis, U.S. investment in Germany over the same period ($30.6 billion) was nearly three times larger. By the same token, while U.S. foreign investment to India doubled in the first half of this decade, from just $1 billion over the 1995-99 period to $2.5 billion, U.S. investment in Germany was 12 times that level. In 2004, U.S. investment to Germany totaled nearly $10 billion, versus U.S. investment of $4.2 billion in China and just $1.2 billion in India.

Why such a disparity between U.S. investment in slow-growth Germany versus turbo-charged China and emergent India? At the end of the day, the motivations of multinationals to invest overseas are less about cheap labor and more about access to wealthy markets, to skilled labor and to the innovative capabilities of the host nation. The premium placed on these assets goes a long way in explaining why the U.S. and Germany are each other's most important foreign investors.

In addition, the size and the wealth of the U.S. economy has long been a key attraction for German firms, fueling a host of mega-acquisitions over the past decade. Chief among them were the Daimler-Chrysler deal and Deutsche Bank's purchase of Bankers Trust; the two deals helped to boost German inflows to a record $43 billion in 1998, equivalent to Germany's total investment in the United States over the 1980-94 period. German investment slipped to $23.5 in 1999, although the country still ranked second largest of foreign investors in the U.S. over the 1990s. Over the first half of this decade, FDI from Germany accounted for 9.4% of the U.S. total, making Germany the sixth largest investor in the United States.

Strong economic growth in the U.S. has been one propellant of rising capital inflows from Germany, with many German firms mindful of the fact that any truly global strategy dictates a presence in the U.S. This prompted both BMW and Mercedes-Benz to set up shop in the U.S. in the mid-1990s, bringing along many German suppliers as well. More recently, RWE, Henkel and Deutsche Post have all made significant acquisitions in the United States.

Other so-called push factors – created by local market and business conditions – have also been at work in promoting outward flows from Germany. These include high German wage costs, stifling corporate taxes, and inflexible employment practices, a lethal mix that has pushed many German firms abroad. The government has addressed some of these issues over the past few years, although change thus far has not be deep or radical enough to structurally change Gemany's low-growth-high unemployment environment.

Yet these issues aside, Germany remains an attractive market to U.S. firms. The allure of Germany lies with the nation's highly skilled labor force, research and development capabilities and first class infrastructure. The specialization and innovative capabilities of many small and medium-sized firms in Germany have also been notably attractive to U.S., particularly private equity groups. The latter, despite growing hostility in Germany, have been among the most active foreign investors in Germany lately, fueling greater cross-border M&A deals in Germany. Indeed, in the first half of 2005, Germany was among the most popular locations in the world for global M&A deals, with deals totaling $73 billion in the first half of this year, a 110% rise from the same period a year ago. Many of these deals have been initiated by U.S. firms.

The bottom line is that U.S. and German firms are stilled attracted to each other, and attracted to each other's home market, helping to sustain robust foreign direct investment flows in the first half of this decade – despite the transatlantic ill produced by the U.S.-led war in Iraq. In fact, over 2003 and 2004, German firms invested $10.4 billion in the United States, versus disinvestment of $1.1 billion in 2002. The latter was a result of the U.S. recession, which reduced affiliate profits and subdued new equity capital inflows from Germany. Over the same two-year period, U.S. firms sank $12.6 billion into Germany, up sharply from the $2.4 billion invested in 2002. In the end, while the politicians on both sides of the Atlantic were bickering over the war, is was largely "business as usual" regarding U.S.-German investment flows.

The eight ties that bind

The primacy of foreign direct investment in driving U.S.-German commerce is reflected in the robust infrastructure that links the United States and Germany. This

Table 2.2 U.S.-German linkages[1]

The Ties That Bind (US $ Billions, 2002)		
	U.S. Foreign Affiliates in Germany	German Affiliates in the U.S.
Gross Product of Affiliates	60,7	57,0
Overseas Assets of Foreign Affiliates	311,8	534,1
Affiliate Employment (thousands)	615,6	676,4
Manufacturing (thousands employees)	386,0	389,0
R&D of Affiliates	3,6	5,6
Foreign Affiliate Sales	205,7	290,4
Foreign Affiliate Income (Full Year 2004)	6,3	7,1

Source: Bureau of Economic Analysis

[1] Data from majority-owned foreign affiliates

commercial infrastructure has been under construction for over a half-century, but remains largely invisible to policy makers on both sides of the ocean. The following eight indices offer a clearer picture of the deep integrating force that makes the U.S.-German commercial link among the strongest in the world (Table 2.2).

Gross product of foreign affiliates

The total output of U.S. foreign affiliates in Germany ($60.7 billion in 2002) and of German affiliates in the United States ($57 billion) is rather sizable. Both figures, for instance, are equal or greater than the GDP of Bulgaria, Algeria, Peru, Morocco, New Zealand and many other nations. In Germany, U.S. foreign affiliates accounted for 3.1% of total German output in 2002, up from 2.7% in 1994. In the United States, the output of German affiliates has increased sharply over the past few years on account of rising German FDI in the U.S. In 1997, for instance, German-owned affiliate output in the U.S. totaled $37 billion, a figure that increased to $57 billion in 2002. Only British and Japanese affiliates in the U.S. produced more than German affiliates in 2002.

Overseas assets of foreign affiliates

America's overseas commercial presence, as measured by foreign assets of U.S. companies, is substantial, totaling over $6 trillion in 2002. The bulk of these assets, or 61%, are located in Europe, with the largest share in the United Kingdom ($1.5 trillion), the Netherlands ($508 billion) and Germany ($312 billion). While lagging the U.K. and the Netherlands, U.S. assets in Germany were greater than total U.S. assets in South America in 2002 ($117.8 billion), as well as many other developing regions, including Africa ($62 billion), the Middle East ($29 billion), Eastern Europe ($52 billion), and OPEC ($77.2 billion).

Total German assets in the U.S. – $534 billion – are among the largest of all foreign investors in the United States. Only the United Kingdom and Switzerland have a larger asset base in the U.S. than Germany. It is interesting to note that German assets in the U.S. are over 70% larger than U.S. assets in Germany, a factor related to the surge in German FDI in the United States over the past decade.

Affiliate employment

Thousands of workers in the United States and Germany are employed by foreign affiliates from each nation. Indeed, some 676,000 American workers were employed directly by German affiliates in 2002 – among the largest numbers of workers employed by foreign investors in the U.S. Only British firms employed more American workers in 2002. Roughly half of these U.S. workers were employed in manufacturing jobs, and concentrated in the Great Lakes region, as well as the southeast, where German affiliates are predominantly located. Although hard to quantify, many more American jobs are tied to U.S. exports to Germany.

In Germany, U.S. affiliates employed roughly 616,000 German workers in 2002, with nearly two-thirds of the total (386,000) consisting of manufacturing workers. So large was the manufacturing workforce of U.S. affiliates in Germany in 2002, that the number of manufacturing workers on the payrolls of U.S. foreign affiliates in Germany was 80% greater than the number of manufacturing workers employed by U.S.

affiliates in China in the same year. That said, however, U.S. foreign affiliate manufacturing employment in Germany is in decline, falling nearly 15% between 1990 and 2002. The job cuts reflect the migration of jobs to central Europe, where manufacturing employment of U.S. affiliates has soared over the past decade. Indeed, between 1994 and 2002, manufacturing employment of U.S. affiliates in the region rose from 63,000 workers to more than 190,000. The cut in manufacturing jobs in such high-cost places like Germany, however, has been offset rising employment among U.S service affiliates.

Research and development of affiliates

While R&D expenditures remain biased towards the home country, foreign affiliate R&D has become more prominent over the past decade as firms seek to share the costs of development, spread the risks and tap into the intellectual talent of other nations. Alliances, cross-licensing of intellectual property, and mergers and acquisitions – these and other forms of cooperation have become staples of the U.S.-German partnership.

Accordingly, of the $21.5 billion in R&D expenditures of U.S. foreign affiliates in 2002, roughly two-thirds was in the Europe, with the United Kingdom ($3.7 billion) and Germany ($3.6 billion) leading the way. Germany alone accounted for 17% of total global R&D of U.S. foreign affiliates in 2002, a reflection of Germany's skilled, innovative workforce and corporate America's penchant for leveraging skilled assets any place in the world. Conversely, America's highly skilled labor force, entrepreneurial culture and first-class universities have been key drivers attracting R&D capital from German firms. Indeed, in 2002, German affiliates in the United States invested more R&D capital ($5.7 billion) than another other foreign investor in the United States. German R&D expenditures in the U.S. accounted for 27% of the European total in the U.S. and just over one-fifth of the global total.

Intra-firm trade of foreign affiliates

Foreign affiliate sales are the primary means by which goods and services are delivered across the Atlantic. Trade is secondary, although the two modes of delivery should not be viewed independently of each other. They are more compliments than substitutes, since foreign investment and affiliate sales increasingly drive trade flows. Indeed, a substantial share of U.S.-German trade is considered intra-firm trade or related party trade, which is cross border trade that stays within the ambit of the company. It's BMW of Germany sending parts and components to BMW of South Carolina, for instance. Reflecting the tight linkages between German parent companies and their U.S. affiliates, roughly 62% of U.S. imports from Germany consisted of related party trade in 2004. Meanwhile, 32% of U.S. exports to Germany in 2004 represented related party trade.

Given the above, only after recognizing that almost two-thirds of U.S. imports from Germany are considered related party trade, can one begin to understand why U.S. imports from Germany have remained so strong over the past few years despite the sizable appreciation of the euro against the U.S. dollar since the beginning of 2002. Following such a large shift in prices or exchange rates, Economics 101 would have predicted or suggested a rebalancing of bi-lateral trade. Theory would have expected U.S. export growth to outstrip U.S. import growth, leading to an improvement in the overall trade balance. To the contrary, however, America's trade deficit with Germany actually widened in 2003, to $45 billion, and again last year, to $52 billion.

America's widening trade gap with Germany has confused many on both sides of the Atlantic. However, missing from most analysis is the simple fact that an unusually large percentage of U.S. imports from Germany are considered related party trade, and that parent-affiliate trade is less responsive to shifts in prices or exchange rates and more attuned to domestic demand. Accordingly, while a strong euro, in theory at least, would be associated with a decline in German competitiveness in the United States, the fact that many German multinationals produce, market and distribute goods on both sides of the ocean gives firms a high degree of immunity to a dramatic shift in exchange rates. Under this structure, trade flows are driven more by demand in the host nation. As such, with the U.S. economy among the most robust in the world, sales of German affiliates have remained strong over the past few years, which in turn, have generated more demand (a.k.a. imports) from the parent company for parts and components irrespective of exchange rate movements.

Foreign affiliate sales

Foreign affiliate sales are the primary means by which U.S. and German firms deliver goods and services to each other's respective markets. In 2002, for instance, U.S. foreign affiliate sales in Germany totaled $206 billion, well in excess of U.S. exports to Germany the same year, $42.2 billion. Similarly, German foreign affiliate sales in the United States totaled $290 billion in 2002 versus U.S. imports from Germany of $83.6 billion. In other words, foreign affiliate sales tell one story of U.S.-Germany ties, while trade tells another.

Based on U.S. exports, Germany ranked as the sixth largest market in the world for U.S. goods in 2004, well behind other nations like China, Canada, Mexico and the United Kingdom. From this vantage point, it's not hard to make the case that many emerging markets like China and Mexico are more important to U.S. commercial interests than Germany. That's not even half the story, however.

The story changes dramatically when considered foreign affiliates sales. Based on the latter, Germany ranks as one of the most important markets in the world for U.S. companies, with foreign affiliate sales of $206 billion in 2002 lagging only Canada ($336 billion) and the United Kingdom ($372 billion). In that a great deal of foreign affiliate sales in Canada represent exports to the U.S., Germany, for a practical purposes, is the second largest market in the world for U.S. companies. Relative to China, while U.S. exports and foreign affiliate sales to China have soared over the past decade, foreign affiliate sales of $42 billion in China were just one-fifth of U.S. affiliate sales in Germany in the same year. How important is Germany to corporate America? By the metric of affiliate sales, what U.S. foreign affiliates sold in Germany in 2002 exceeded the combined sales of affiliates in South America, Africa, the Middle East, and eastern Europe.

In the United States, it is a similar story: German affiliate sales in the U.S. in 2002 ($290 billion) were more than three times greater than U.S. imports from Germany – a striking statistic for Germany, a country commonly thought to be a classic "trading" nation.

Foreign affiliate income

In terms of profits, Europe easily remains the most important region in the world for corporate America. Over the first half of this decade, for instance, Europe's share of U.S. foreign affiliate income, a proxy for global earnings, actually rose to 54.6% versus a 53.1% share of the second half of the 1990s.

Germany's global share of U.S. foreign affiliate income fell from 4.8% over the 1995-99 time frame to 3.2% in the first half of this decade, a decline reflecting weak demand in Germany over most of this decade. However, thanks to the strong euro/weak U.S. dollar, U.S. foreign affiliates in Germany posted robust earnings in 2003 and 2004 – this despite the plunge in U.S.-German relations. U.S. affiliates tallied record profits in 2004, with affiliate income totaling $6.3 billion, more than double affiliate profits earned in China the same year.

Meanwhile, on account of strong U.S. demand, profits of German affiliates in the United States soared to a record $7.1 billion in 2004. For many German firms, strong demand in the United States has been a key offset to sluggish growth at home, helping to fuel earnings growth and solid gains in the stock market. In the end, Germany's prolonged economic slump has been quite painful for corporate Germany, although strong U.S. growth has been a critical offset.

Foreign affiliate sales of services

Following in the footsteps of manufacturers, service activities between the United States and Germany are becoming more intricate and complex. Indeed, foreign affiliate sales of services on both sides of the Atlantic have soared over the past decade, reflecting rising bi-lateral investments in such key service sectors as financial services, telecommunications, utilities, retail, insurance, advertising and computer services, to name a few.

In the 1970s and 1980s, firms delivered services primarily via trade. In the 1990s, however, foreign affiliate sales became the chief mode of delivery, helped by industry deregulation, falling communication costs, and the proliferation of the Internet. On account of these trends, sales of services by U.S. foreign affiliates in Europe soared from $85 billion in 1994 to roughly $212 billion in 2002. U.S. affiliate sales of services to Germany rose from $17.6 billion in 1995 to $24.5 billion in 2002, a near 40% increase. Over the same period, U.S. exports of services to Germany rose by nearly 26%. By 2002, U.S. affiliate sales of services were more than 50% larger than U.S. service exports.

Sales of services by German affiliates in the United States have also soared over the past decade. As Germany's investment position in services has expanded in the U.S., so have foreign affiliate sales of services in the U.S. The latter totaled $44.5 billion in 2002, representing a near four-fold increase from 1995, when affiliate sales of services amounted to just $11.9 billion. In 2002, German affiliate sales of services in the U.S. were nearly three times larger than service imports from Germany, highlighting the

Table 2.3 Sales of services

U.S. Sales of Services to Germany			German Sales of Services to the U.S.		
(US $ Billions)					
Year	U.S. Affiliate Sales of Services	U.S. Exports of Services to Germany	Year	German Affiliate Sales of Services in the U.S.	U.S. Imports of Services from Germany
1995	17,6	12,7	1995	11,9	7,5
1996	21,8	13,3	1996	17,0	7,9
1997	19,1	13,9	1997	22,2	8,2
1998	20,1	14,9	1998	27,4	9,5
1999	29,7	16,3	1999	29,5	10,5
2000	24,6	16,2	2000	42,0	12,6
2001	24,2	14,9	2001	42,2	12,8
2002	24,5	16,0	2002	44,5	15,6
2003	NA	17,5	2003	NA	16,4

Source: Bureau of Economic Analysis

role of foreign investment and affiliates as the primary means by which German and U.S. firms deliver services to each other.

In sum, these eight indices convey a more complete and complex picture of international economic flows than simple tallies of export and imports. Foreign direct investment represents the backbone of the U.S.-German partnership, with other variables like overseas assets, affiliate employment and sales, related party trade, services and others derived from the level and depth of investment linkages. That said, while U.S.-German commercial ties are deeply rooted, they are in need of a fresh impetus.

Wanted: a new impetus to deepen U.S.-German ties

U.S. and German commercial linkages are among the deepest in the world, with both parties benefiting greatly from over a half century of strong investment and trade ties. That said, however, the U.S.-German alliance needs a new catalyst to (1) prevent any erosion in the transatlantic partnership and (2) promote even thicker ties between the two parties.

The U.S.-led war in Iraq created a great deal of strain between both parties. More harmful to the relationship, however, is the increasing economic divergence of the United States on the one hand and Germany on the other. The embrace of free-market capitalism in the United States has never been stronger, helping to promote annual economic growth rates that have consistently outpaced growth in Germany. For its part, Germany not only remains an economic laggard of the developed nations, some elements of the German political spectrum have become more vocal in denouncing free-market capitalism. The backlash against private equity investment is the most recent evidence suggesting rising hostility toward what some call the "Anglo-Saxon" model of capitalism.

In general, the U.S. economy continues to outperform relative to its industrial peers like Germany, while Germany continues to underperform. The difference in economic paths could ultimately make it harder to build on the existing foundation of investment between the United States and Germany. Without policies designed to address labor rigidities, industry deregulation, and tax reform in Germany, U.S. multinationals might increasingly look elsewhere when it comes to investing in Europe and the surrounding region. How Germany handles its delicate immigration challenge, pursues environmental standards and reacts to its shifting demographics will also affect future U.S. investment flows.

In the United States, diverging regulations and technical standards, Sarbanes-Oxley legislation, and tightened security measures could act to halt or slow the pace of German investment in the United States. On both sides of the Atlantic, the potential for greater integration of various service activities is huge, although stiff regulations in both nations have prevented U.S.-German service activities from growing and becoming fully integrated.

In the end, the war in Iraq, and subsequent tensions between Washington and Berlin, served as a useful wake up call to policy makers on both sides of the Atlantic to the importance of the U.S.-German relationship. Now, however, the challenge for both parties is to renew their commitment to the relationship and forge ahead with new policies that will strengthen one of the most important bilateral relationships in the world.

2.3 Capital Market – Hurdle or Help in Transatlantic M&A

Marcus Schenck, Frank Richter, Karoline Jung-Senssfelder

According to a commonplace assumption, listed companies benefit greatly from having an acquisition currency in the form of their own shares. A secondary listing in the US is thus often seen as an important first step in preparing for external growth. While the financial advantages of such capital market based transactions in the context of transatlantic M&A are often pointed out, the associated disadvantages frequently go unnoticed. Specifically, the authors identify three factors, which may outweigh the potential benefits of a stock-for-stock transation across the Atlantic. First, shares originally paid as a purchase price tend to flow back into the home market, sometimes being the cause of substantial pressure on the acquirer's stock price. Second, different valuation levels and metrics may complicate negotiations and usually have an impact on how market

participants perceive the value of shares in the buyer. Third,
additional transaction risk may arise due to the incompatibility of
country-specific filing processes. Examining these issues in detail, the
authors set out to determine under which circumstances transatlantic
M&A is hindered rather than facilitated by capital markets.

Introduction

Exchange-listed companies are perceived to have a big advantage in managing mergers or acquisitions because they have an acquisition currency in the form of their own shares. These companies are not limited to financing acquisitions with cash, which to some extent may have to be raised in the markets. The purchase price for a company or asset will be paid by issuing new shares to the owners of the target company. The legal framework in Germany has been further developed to facilitate such transactions, e.g. by allowing the buyer to issue shares other than through a rights offering under certain circumstances. The result is similar in case of a merger between a company in Germany and another company in the US: If, for example, the shares of the US company are exchanged into the shares of the German company, the "selling" shareholders receive their proceeds in kind in the form of shares in the acquiring company (in our example the German company). Again, there is no need to raise money in the capital markets to finance such a transaction. Therefore, transactions using stock as an acquisition currency are perceived as fairly efficient, and the capital markets facilitate such transactions. As a consequence, it seems sensible to prepare companies that want to grow externally, e.g. by means of an exchange listing in the US in addition to a listing in their home markets. The company will thus get an acquisition currency, thereby increasing its strategic and transactional room for maneuver.

The benefits of such capital market based transactions are evident. However, they also have a cost. For example, if the selling shareholders are not interested or not allowed to hold the buyer's shares in their portfolio, a share-overhang will be created. In that case the shares received as a purchase price for the company or in exchange for other shares in a merger situation will most likely be sold in the home market of the buyer. This flow-back creates significant pressure on the buyer's share price and therefore has to be taken into consideration when planning such transactions.

Another important aspect is valuation. There are differences in market valuations in the US vs. Germany, e.g. in the utilities or the chemicals industries. The companies in the US trade at higher levels than the companies in Germany. In addition, the financial community uses different valuation metrics to assess valuation levels – e.g. P/E ratios in the US vs. EBITDA multiples in Europe. These differences often lead to complications in negotiations and may also influence the perceived value of the shares in the buyer. Managers who intend to engage in M&A discussions with their counterparts need to be aware of, and prepared to address, such valuation issues.

Finally, the legal requirements which define the process of stock offerings in the US are different from those in Germany or other European jurisdictions. The US requirements are more extensive and the processes take longer. This creates the need to manage the different time schedules according to local securities laws. Large timing gaps resulting from incompatible filing processes may lead to additional transaction risks.

These three aspects of capital market related M&A are discussed in more detail below. Many other aspects are relevant as well, e.g., corporate governance, taxation, and cultural issues. These aspects are dealt with in other parts of this book and are therefore not considered here.

Flow-back may lead to oversupply of shares in home markets

Can institutional investors be convinced to hold buyer's stock?

Certain institutional investors in the US invest only in US-listed companies. It is also possible that investors are not allowed to invest dedicated funds in stocks of non-US companies. The articles of incorporation of such funds define the investment strategies which the fund managers have to adhere to. Of course, larger investment management companies also have funds dedicated to international or European stocks. These companies are able to reallocate assets from a US-focused fund to an international fund. However, to do this the fund managers have to be convinced of the transaction and the overall equity story of the new entity. Experience shows that this is not always the case.

Additional issues arise if the buyer company is not included in stock market indices, either because they are not listed in the US or because of their size. Post transaction, the US target will no longer be listed and therefore eliminated from stock market indices which are tracked by institutional investors. In that case the question is whether the German company is included in any index of interest to the investors. The benchmark for inclusion in the S&P 500 is a market capitalization of $ 4 bn for US companies, whereby the definition of US companies used by the Index Committee depends on their legal and tax domicile, location of operations, corporate structure, accounting standards, and exchange listings. The benchmarks for other indices such as the Russell Index or the Wilshire Index are lower so that the listing requirement is the bigger hurdle.

The experiences of German companies with dual listings in Germany and in the US have not been very encouraging. The vast majority of trading volume still is generated in home markets, even for large companies like BASF, E.ON or Deutsche Telekom. Across a representative selection of companies, the median trading split is 93% domestic and only 7% US (Table 2.4).

Ways to mitigate the volume of flow-back

The trading split analysis shows that one cannot generally assume a strong interest of US institutional investors to keep the stock of German companies received in transatlantic transactions. The most important factors determining the level of flow-back, are the following:

- Strength of the equity story including the strategic rationale, expected synergy potential, and the anticipated impact on earnings per share
- Relative size of target versus acquirer

Table 2.4 Trading analysis of German US-listed stocks

Company	Trading Split[1]		Market Cap (€m)	US Exchange
	Germany	**USA**		
Qiagen	63%	37%	1,290	NASDAQ
SAP	79%	21%	40,562	NYSE
GPC Biotech[2]	86%	14%	317	NASDAQ
DaimlerChrysler	90%	10%	34,598	NYSE
Dialog Semiconductor	93%	7%	125	NASDAQ
Infineon	94%	6%	6,436	NYSE
Fresenius Medical Care	96%	4%	5,591	NYSE
Pfeiffer Vacuum	96%	4%	289	NYSE
Siemens	96%	4%	54,622	NYSE
Bayer	97%	3%	16,579	NYSE
Deutsche Telekom	97%	3%	64,016	NYSE
Schering	97%	3%	9,485	NYSE
Altana	98%	2%	6,599	NYSE
BASF	98%	2%	26,518	NYSE
Deutsche Bank	98%	2%	32,925	NYSE
SGL Carbon	98%	2%	540	NYSE
Allianz	99%	1%	32,778	NYSE
E.ON	99%	1%	43,271	NYSE
EPCOS	99%	1%	865	NYSE
Median	93%	7%		

Source: Bloomberg, Datastream, IFR

[1] Trading split adjusted for ADR gearing and based on US$-ADTVs over the last six months.

[2] Based on ADTVs since 1-Jul-04.

- Mix of consideration (cash vs. stock)
- Relative liquidity of both stocks
- Amount of index tracking money in acquirer's country and overall depth of domestic capital markets
- Acquirer's credibility and track record, including the support from target's management
- Place of incorporation

Clearly, it is of prime importance to the management of the acquiring company to convince investors abroad of the business prospects of the new entity created by the transaction. The flow-back will be reduced if investors "like the deal." To achieve this, concise communication and transparency are required. Also communication needs to be adapted to local standards and views. Size matters as well. Investors dislike relatively small companies with low levels of liquidity of their stock and limited research coverage. The credibility of the acquirer is also an important factor, which cannot easily be built-up just before a deal is considered.

Creating interest in and demand for the stock of the acquiring company in the US is important in limiting the amount of flow-back. Therefore, active marketing of the equity story even before any transaction and, clearly, at various steps of the transaction is important. Short-term oriented investors require tailored communication. Obviously, the buyer may also consider increasing the cash component of the consideration. (This is to say that capital markets may hinder rather than facilitate a transaction.) The buyer itself may absorb excess supply of its stock through a share buyback program. Under German law, this is possible for up to 10% of the share capital, subject to prior authorization by the shareholders' meeting. However, most of the larger German companies have this generic authorization in place anyhow. The company then can keep the stock and sell it in the markets afterwards over a longer period of time. The market may react cautiously to such a strategy, given the clear signal of a stock overhang and the expectation that the supply of stock will increase over time. The company may also consider reducing its capital by eliminating the shares it bought back. This, however, negatively impacts the capital structure and may not be desirable.

Challenges resulting from different valuation levels in the US and Germany

Differences in valuation levels as well as different perceptions of relevant multiples

Differences in relative valuations observed in capital markets are an additional source of challenges in transatlantic transactions. This is the case in particular if the underlying fundamentals in terms of expected growth and profitability do not differ too much. The phenomenon of different pricing levels despite similar performance characteristics can be observed in different industries such as utilities, chemicals, or automotive suppliers. Take, for example, the German OEM supplier Continental AG, which trades at Enterprise Value/EBITDA multiples of around 4.8x (based on 2005E EBITDA and July 2005 share price) and a P/E ratio of 10.9x. The median EBITDA multiples and P/E ratios of US automotive suppliers are 6.3x and 13.5x, respectively (Table 2.5). The question whether these companies are indeed comparable with each other, given their product mix etc., can be debated at length. However, one may as well take the view that the business and performance expectations for the German company are not worse than those for the average US supplier.

German buyers tend to focus more on "intrinsic" values, e.g., derived from Discounted Cash Flow valuation, rather than public market multiples. Their American

Table 2.5 Comparison of relative valuations in the automotive supplier industry

Company	Closing Price 12-Jul-2005	% of 52 Week High	Enterprise Value (€m)[1]	EBITDA Multiple 2005	P/E Multiple 2005[5]	5-Year EPS CAGR[2]
US OEM Suppliers						
Dana	$16.60	85%	$4,380m	7.0x	13.8x	5.0%
Eaton	61.77	85	11,416	7.4	11.8	12.5
Goodyear Tire & Rubber	15.58	97	7,506	NA	14.6	3.0
Johnson Controls	58.83	92	13,631	6.6	12.6	13.0
Lear	41.10	67	4,756	6.0	21.4	11.0
Magna International	74.35	81	7,744	4.3	10.3	14.7
TRW Automotive	25.13	100	5,113	4.8	16.0	9.0
American Axle	26.40	74	1,920	6.3	18.9	10.0
ArvinMeritor	18.79	83	2,821	6.3	11.2	7.0
BorgWarner	57.43	99	4,192	6.9	13.2	14.0
Dura Automotive	$4.94	45	1,150	6.4	NM	8.0
Mean		83	5,875	6.2	14.4	9.7
Median		85%	$4,756m	6.3x	13.5x	10.0%
European OEM Suppliers						
Autoliv	€38.27	90%	€4,204m	6.1x	12.9x	15.0%
Continental	59.30	93	9,963	4.8	10.9	5.6
Faurecia	58.10	79	2,975	4.5	9.1	3.0
ThyssenKrupp	14.36	83	9,258	2.9	8.1	5.0
Valeo	€35.94	96	3,625	4.1	16.9	5.0
Mean		89	5,115	4.6	11.8	7.4
Median		91%	€3,914m	4.7x	11.9x	5.3%

[1] Source: Latest publicly available financial statements with sufficient detail. Equity Market Cap based on fully diluted shares outstanding. Enterprise Value calculated using latest reported net debt and adjusted for minority interests, preferred equity and pro forma adjusted for recent M&A transactions

[2] Source: LTM numbers are based upon the latest publicly available financial statements. All projected sales, EBITDA, EBIT, and EPS estimates have been calendarised. Projected sales, EBITDA, EBIT, and EPS source: IBES median estimates.

counterparts concentrate on the facts obtained from the information in the capital markets. Any transaction involving these companies will be challenged by their investors if market-based valuations are not taken into consideration. In addition to this fundamental question, there are often different views on the right indicator for assess-

Table 2.6 Comparison of relative valuations in the utilities industry

Company	Closing Price 12-Jul-2005	% of 52 Week High	Enterprise Value (€m)[1]	EBITDA Multiple 2005	P/E Multiple 2005[2]	5-Year EPS CAGR[2]
Large US Integrated						
American Electric Power	$38.99	100%	$26,019m	7.4x	16.0x	3.0%
Dominion Resources	75.91	99	43,466	8.7	15.0	5.0
Duke	30.05	100	46,705	8.5	19.4	5.0
Edison International	41.18	100	22,352	7.3	16.5	6.0
Entergy	76.94	100	24,411	8.2	16.6	7.0
Exelon	52.94	100	50,112	9.6	17.2	5.0
FirstEnergy	49.52	100	27,708	7.2	17.4	4.0
FPL Group Inc.	43.81	100	26,895	9.3	17.2	5.0
PG&E	37.72	99	23,580	6.7	16.8	5.0
Progress Energy	45.63	99	21,360	9.0	15.0	4.0
PSEG	63.05	100	28,577	10.7	19.1	3.5
Southern	35.66	99	41,779	10.2	17.0	5.0
TXU	83.27	96	33,380	8.9	13.1	6.5
Xcel Energy	$19.53	99	14,883	7.9	15.6	3.0
Mean		99	30,802	8.5	16.6	4.8
Median		100%	$27,302m	8.6x	16.7x	5.0%
Large European Integrated						
E.ON	€74.13	100%	€79,157m	7.5x	12.0x	3.1%
Endesa	18.44	95	41,863	7.9	13.4	6.0
Enel	7.09	92	67,469	7.2	16.5	4.5
RWE	54.55	100	67,887	8.0	13.5	9.2
Suez	€22.56	99	54,574	8.5	15.1	2.0
Mean		97	62,190	7.9	14.1	5.0
Median		99%	€67,469m	7.9x	13.5x	4.5%

[1] Source: Latest publicly available financial statements with sufficient detail. Equity Market Cap based on fully diluted shares outstanding. Enterprise Value calculated using latest reported net debt and adjusted for minority interests, preferred equity and pro forma adjusted for recent M&A transactions.

[2] Source: All projected sales, EBITDA, EBIT, and EPS estimates have been calendarised. Projected sales, EBITDA, EBIT, and EPS source: IBES median estimates.

Table 2.7 Comparison of relative valuations in the chemicals industry

Company	Closing Price 11-Jul-2005	% of 52 Week High	Enterprise Value (€m)[1]	EV/ EBITDA 2005	P/E Multiple 2005[2]	5-Year EPS CAGR[2]
US Specialty						
Air Products	$60.10	92%	$16,647m	9.2x	18.7x	10.0%
Albemarle	37.20	92	2,555	8.9	16.2	10.0
Arch Chemicals	26.17	86	846	8.0	21.5	NA
Cabot	33.64	83	2,523	7.2	16.0	15.0
Cabot Micro	32.65	80	650	9.0	22.3	14.5
Cytec	40.94	75	3,641	8.5	12.2	10.0
Du Pont	44.15	81	49,611	8.8	15.9	10.0
Eastman Chemical	56.84	93	5,890	5.3	9.6	5.3
Ecolab	32.23	91	9,173	10.7	24.2	12.0
Engelhard	28.99	89	4,054	8.8	14.5	10.0
HB Fuller	35.74	100	1,171	8.1	20.5	9.0
Hercules	14.59	96	2,801	7.8	13.3	7.0
Lubrizol	42.78	99	4,628	NA	14.8	7.5
Monsanto	63.38	93	19,508	13.2	28.7	12.0
Nalco	20.55	100	6,414	10.3	34.5	10.0
Polyone	7.05	71	1,313	7.0	11.7	8.0
PPG Industries	64.49	87	11,894	6.5	12.9	8.5
Praxair	48.50	99	19,811	10.3	19.8	10.0
Rohm and Haas	45.63	92	12,589	8.2	16.6	10.0
Sigma Aldrich	58.12	90	4,410	9.9	16.1	10.0
Valspar	49.59	98	3,341	9.9	17.7	11.5
Mean		90	8,737	8.8	18.0	10.0
Median		92%	$4,410m	8.8x	16.2x	10.0%
European Specialty						
Ciba Specialty Chemicals	€48.60	84%	€4,441m	6.8x	13.2x	6.6%
Clariant	11.35	83	3,512	5.8	11.5	8.0
Croda International	5.63	97	797	8.6	16.2	8.0
DSM	58.35	99	6,887	5.7	11.4	16.9

Table 2.7 Comparison of relative valuations in the chemicals industry

Company	Closing Price 11-Jul-2005	% of 52 Week High	Enterprise Value (€m)[1]	EV/ EBITDA 2005	P/E Multiple 2005[2]	5-Year EPS CAGR[2]
Degussa	34.15	98	12,592	6.9	16.5	4.0
Imperial Chemical Industries	3.76	91	6,169	6.1	10.1	10.1
Rhodia	€1.50	78	4,640	8.1	NM	4.0
Mean		90	5,577	6.9	13.1	8.2
Median		91%	€4,640m	6.8x	12.3x	8.0%

[1] Source: Latest publicly available financial statements with sufficient detail. Equity Market Cap based on fully diluted shares outstanding. Enterprise Value calculated using latest reported net debt and adjusted for minority interests, preferred equity and pro forma adjusted for recent M&A transactions.

[2] Source: All projected sales, EBITDA, EBIT, and EPS estimates have been calendarised. Projected sales, EBITDA, EBIT, and EPS source: IBES median estimates.

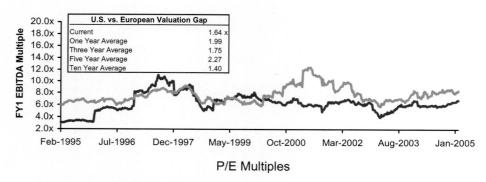

P/E Multiples

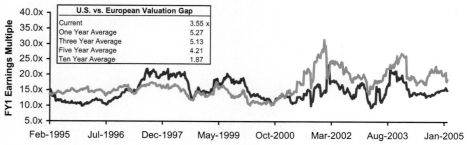

Source: Factset
European Specialty Chemicals Index includes Ciba, Croda, Degussa, DSM, ICI and Rhodia.
U.S. Specialty Chemicals Index includes Albemarle, Arch, Crompton, Cytec, Eastman, Ferro, Great Lakes, H.B. Fuller, Hercules, Lubrizol and Rohm & Haas.

Figure 2.2 Relative Valuations in the Chemicals Industry over Time

ing relative valuations. European companies tend to focus more on Enterprise Value/EBITDA multiples than on P/E ratios. In the example of the OEM suppliers, this would yield a difference in relative valuations of some 30%. On the other hand, stocks in the US tend to trade on earnings per share so that investors monitor P/E ratios. Given different histories of accounting standards and the perceived limitations of the relevance of net income numbers, the Europeans tend to disagree with the American view. In addition, differences in relative valuations might be different on a P/E basis.

The effect of diverging valuation levels is not limited to individual industries. Differences also occur in other industries like utilities or chemicals (Tables 2.6 and 2.7). Valuation differences are also not limited to the current market environment. In the chemicals industry, for instance, differences seem to be systematic and persistent over time (Figure 2.2). This raises the immediate question why such arbitrage opportunities are not being exploited and eliminated through transactions by profit-seeking investors. In fact, there are few examples of German companies being taken private and re-listed abroad, often after reorganizations and further improvements of the companies' positioning and operations. Such examples are rare because of the complexity of such transactions and the considerable efforts needed to complete them.

Challenges caused by diverging valuation levels

At least two sorts of issues arise from diverging valuation levels. First, such valuation differences make transatlantic stock-for-stock transactions expensive from the perspective of the foreign buyer, if it were to use its "undervalued" acquisition currency. It becomes difficult to agree on valuation, and negotiations sometimes boil down to the question which multiple is the "right" one. Second, the buyer company may be concerned about its own valuation in its home market after the transaction. In a perfect market the new valuation multiple of the buyer company should result from a combination of its (lower) multiple before the transaction and the (higher) multiple of the target company. But what if investors in the home market also assign the lower multiple to the target? The whole transaction might then appear less attractive, resulting in a potentially negative response of the share price. Thus, in many cases the capital market may hinder rather than facilitate an M&A transaction if the parties proposing a transaction on the one hand and the investors on the other disagree with the pricing levels generated by the markets.

Incompatible legal process requirements may create additional transaction risks

Cash merger: preferred transaction structure of foreign buyers

There are many different structures that can be applied by German companies in an acquisition of, or merger with, public US companies. These structures differ in terms of their complexity, filing requirements, and timing. It is neither our intention to review all of these structures nor to discuss all relevant legal aspects. The focus here is on managerial challenges that arise from certain legal process requirements. The issues that may arise can be illustrated by comparing a cash merger with a stock-for-stock merger.

A straightforward "friendly" approach is the cash merger: One company (typically through a wholly-owned Delaware subsidiary) acquires all of the stock of the target company in a one-step transaction. The target is merged with the acquirer's subsidiary and cash is paid to the stockholders of the target company. All of the target's shares issued and outstanding are converted into rights to receive cash. The transaction is voted on by the stockholders of the target company ("long form" merger), either by written consent or by means of an extraordinary shareholders' meeting, typically using proxy statements which have to be filed with the SEC. The period of time between signing of the merger agreement to closing of the transaction is around 2-4 months, provided that there are no material antitrust or "Exon Florio" issues. In order to execute a cash merger with a US company, the acquirer typically:

- conducts a due diligence review,
- negotiates the merger agreement with the representatives of the Board of Directors of the target (and/or a special committee of independent directors set up in connection with the merger negotiations),
- secures financing of the transaction and completes its duty-of-care process (e.g. by obtaining a fairness opinion),
- prepares the required filings and press releases,
- obtains approval from its own supervisory board (assuming that no shareholder approval requirement is triggered under German law either through the size of the acquisition (*Holzmüller-Gelatine cases*) or a fundamental change in the business not covered by the corporate purpose of the acquirer).

Within the process attention needs to be paid to a large number of details. However, it can be structured and managed to minimize transaction risks, provided that there is sufficient support from the target's shareholders.

Stock-for-stock merger, US listing and approval of capital increase

Let's have a look at the other end of the spectrum of potential deal structures. Things are considerably more complicated in a stock-for-stock merger. In a stock-for-stock merger one company also acquires all of the stock of the target company. Similar to a cash merger the target is merged with the acquirer or one of its subsidiaries. Shares in the acquirer are paid to the stockholders of the target. All of the target's shares issued and outstanding are converted into rights to receive a number of shares. This process requires more time than the cash merger as additional filings and a registration with the SEC have to be made. Registration of a transaction is time-consuming and less predictable from a timing perspective, leading to an overall time frame of (at least) some 3-6 months.

The transaction gets more complex if the acquirer's shares are not listed in the US. An offering of securities in the US requires registration with the SEC first. This means – loosely speaking – a process similar to an IPO of a German company in the US has to be managed in parallel. If the buyer were willing to register its shares, it would then be subject to the reporting and other requirements under US securities law. As a consequence, many non-US companies have preferred to acquire US companies for cash.

Complexity increases even more if, in addition, the German buyer has to obtain approval from its shareholders to increase its capital as a basis for issuing new shares to the target's shareholders. The amount of authorized capital that a company may have is limited to 50% of its current share capital. Thus, in larger transactions it may be necessary for the buyer to obtain the consent of its shareholders first, including certain litigation risks associated therewith. The management team will want to ask its shareholders for approval only if the likelihood of closing the envisaged transaction is very high. This, in turn, requires the consent of the target's shareholders, which, among other things, depends on the "quality" of the bid, including price, terms and conditions, and firm financing. This "chicken-and-egg" problem can be resolved only to some extent through parallel processing of the different flows of activity and by setting appropriate conditions precedent. Nevertheless, the time needed to prepare shareholders' meetings in different countries and the fulfillment of all legal requirements increases duration of the process and management efforts.

Transaction complexity, relatively long time periods until closing, approval requirements in different jurisdictions – these aspects should not be underestimated when assessing the likelihood of completing a proposed transaction. Even more attention needs to be paid to the issues associated with the exchange ratio for the transaction (fixed or variable, with or without collar, termination rights etc.). In addition, short-term oriented investors are encouraged to build up arbitrage positions by lending stock. This may make the stock prices more volatile, thus increasing uncertainty.

Summary

There are many facets to the question of whether it is helpful that two companies who want to merge are listed on stock exchanges. We have covered only three of them which have led us to the following conclusions:

- Capital markets facilitate transatlantic M&A transactions to the extent that the new entity attracts the interest of US investors. Even companies with proven and sound equity stories and a reasonable size may fail to attract such interest. As a consequence, non-US buyers need to take substantial flow-backs of shares into consideration, which will put pressure on their stock in their home markets.

- Although today's capital markets are interconnected, they do not form a single integrated market with single price levels for cash flows with certain growth and risk profiles. The depth of the regional market segments, their liquidity, preferences of investors etc. may well be different. As a consequence, valuations on both sides of the Atlantic may differ as well, also for longer periods of time. Such valuation differences, which cannot easily be justified by different fundamental performance indicators, are more of a hindrance than a help. They may create arbitrage opportunities for financial investors rather than strategic motivation for mergers between companies.

- Stock-for-stock deals have advantages which are often put forth when the benefits offered by capital markets for M&A activities are discussed. Realizing these advantages may well become a complex task or even impossible. The latter is true if different legal requirements lead to timing conflicts that create transaction risks beyond the control of the parties involved. Capital markets are helpful, but the help they offer may become too expensive.

Leveraging the opportunities of public companies in M&A situations is often a trade-off between financially optimal non-cash structures, which are sometimes tax efficient as well, on one hand and dealing with uncertainty resulting from heterogeneous, regionally regulated markets on the other hand.

2.4 Transatlantic M&A Market – Volumes and Dynamics

Stefan Griesser and Thomas Schwingeler

US and German companies have been important transatlantic M&A counterparties. Transaction volumes, direction and make-up have fluctuated over the last few years. This chapter examines these developments and looks at two important medium-term M&A trends, the return of the "strategic deal" between the two countries, and the ongoing importance of private equity in US-German M&A.

Germany has traditionally held strong economic ties with the US. This is reflected in the high number of M&A transactions between the two countries. It makes the US the most significant partner for German companies with respect to M&A transactions. M&A activity peaked in 2000 with German buyers acquiring US companies worth a total of over USD 46bn and 29% of all German M&A transactions involving US targets or buyers.

However, since then there have been a number of developments, affecting the M&A activity between the two countries: the accelerated process of "globalisation" redirecting a large portion of investment funds to Asia, the cooling off in US-German political relations subsequent to the Iraq war and in particular the considerable overall decrease in global M&A volumes during 2001 and 2002.

Against this background, how have US-German cross-border M&A transactions changed and what trends and dynamics have become apparent?

The sharp decrease in M&A activity after 2000 had a similar impact on both the US and Germany. M&A volume in both countries declined by approx. 50% in 2001 and by a further 30-40% in 2002. Whilst Germany experienced a decline in 2003 as well, US M&A recovered with growth rates of more than 33% in each of the subsequent years leading up to today. German M&A activity only returned to growth with some delay in 2004; if, however, volumes for the second half of 2005 were to reach those achieved in the first six months, this would constitute a doubling against the preceding

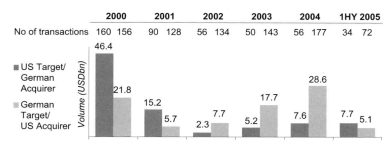

Source: Thomson Financial securities data

Figure 2.3 US-German cross border M&A acquisitions

year. In total, both countries would reach around 75% of their 2000 M&A peak volumes by the end of 2005.

In terms of overall cross-border M&A activity between the US and Germany, cross-border acquisitions are of much greater importance than disposals, constituting more than 80% of all cross-border transactions since 2000.

Figure 2.3 summarises the US-German M&A cross-border acquisitions development since 2005 in terms of transaction values and number of transactions based on Thomson Financial securities data.

Although the data used may contain elements of imprecision, e.g. missing information on transaction values that have not been disclosed, the figure allows for the following observations:

- The significant decline of German M&A interest in the US from 2000 to 2002
- The early recovery of US acquisitions in Germany in 2002 and the strong increase until 2004
- The more tentative rebound in German M&A volume in the US after 2002 combined with a stagnating number of transactions
- M&A volumes showing no correlation with the significant changes in the USD/EUR exchange rate over the period

German M&A acquisitions in the US

A closer look at German M&A transactions in the US puts the volumes in 2000 and 2001 into perspective. A few very large transactions dominate the overall statistics. In 2000, the acquisition of VoiceStream Wireless by Deutsche Telekom accounted for USD 29.4bn, an unprecedented amount for transactions between the US and Germany, without which the total volume would only have amounted to USD 17bn instead of USD 46.4bn. When looking at the year 2001 one has to take into account that the acquisition of American Water Works by RWE for a consideration of USD 7.7bn accounts for half of the total USD 15.2bn M&A volume. Thus, if volumes of the observation period are adjusted for the very largest transactions, the development of the German acquisition volumes in the US closely mirrors the M&A market development in both countries, with two exceptions: the still significant slump of volumes until 2002 and the number of transactions declining to well below the 160 transactions in 2000 or the 90 in 2001.

In 2002, there was no acquisition by German companies in the US larger than USD 750m; the fifth largest transaction had a volume of only USD 175m. Four of the five largest transactions were investments in real estate or real estate investment trusts. Only one of the five largest transactions can be qualified as truly 'strategic'. Also in 2002, German corporates even sold slightly more assets in the US than they acquired (in terms of volume).

In the same year, acquisitions completed, which had a US dimension, accounted only for 4% of all German acquisitions (domestic and cross-border), instead of a typical share of around 16% in recent years. In contrast, the share of German acquisitions which had a European dimension increased to 38% in 2002, which compares to a typical ratio of around 30%.

Therefore, this drop in 2002 seems to have been caused by US-specific parameters rather than just the general slow-down of M&A markets or a general reluctance to pursue cross-border acquisitions.

Most likely, the 2002 drop was a reaction of German investors to the terrorist attacks of September 11 and the subsequent slow-down of US GDP growth to a relatively low 0.3% in 2001. Based on our dialogue with many German clients we were left with the impression that the perceived US business risk increased significantly after 2001. Key concerns of clients included the uncertain impact of the US terrorist attacks on the further development of the US economy, a certain discomfort with the reporting requirements under the Sarbanes-Oxley Act and a wave of ex post criticism regarding a few prominent transactions by German companies in the US completed during the boom. This negative assessment was further marred by some corporate scandals in the US.

This experience underlines how important soft factors, such as business confidence, are in influencing M&A decision-making. At the same time, the focus of German companies shifted from transformational or strategic acquisitions to cost restructuring, debt reduction and export initiatives.

What have been and will be the drivers for German corporate decision-makers pursuing strategic deals in the US?

In recent years, most German companies implemented significant restructuring measures to cut costs and increase profitability. A weakened economy, intense international competition and high labour costs in Germany forced many large German corporations to shift production to low wage countries and negotiate cost concessions from their labour force. Management resources were focussed on internal operations aiming to take out additional costs and improve efficiency.

This has been accompanied by a steady rise in exports since 2000 with Germany's export ratio increasing from 29% in 2000 to 31% in 2003 as percentage of total GDP.

While in 2001, DAX30 companies (excluding financial institutions) achieved an average EBIT margin of 7.0%, they increased the average EBIT margin by more than one-third by 2004, to reach 9.7%. After focussing on improving their cost base and benefiting from success in export markets, corporate executives were able to reduce financial debt and improve their companies' balance sheets. By year-end 2004, the average DAX30 company had decreased financial debt by EUR 1.2bn on average and reduced its net debt/EBITDA ratio from 1.4x in 2001 to 0.7x. In addition, the average DAX30 company today has EUR 4.3bn in liquid assets. What to do with this financial flexibility? As dividend distribution is not tax-advantageous to shareholders and share buy-backs are limited to a certain amount, German corporates have to identify investments which generate returns above the cost of capital to create shareholder value, which includes strategic transaction initiatives.

After some years of economic stagnation, the German economy has regained some momentum. Although in recent years German GDP showed almost no growth, reaching a trough in 2003, it did record 1.6% growth in 2004, however almost exclusively led through net exports.

A combination of recovering equity markets, recovering profitability and a lower actual (or perceived) terrorism threat combined with the continuing globalisation process – and its associated liberalisation, growth and technology forces – are pointing towards a re-emergence of the strategically driven deal for German corporates.

In the meantime, US companies have not lost their economic attraction for cross-border business combinations. The US has recovered impressively from the economic slow-down in 2001 resulting in 2004 GDP growth of 4.4% which compares to less than 2% in Euroland on average, a gap which is not expected to change in 2005.

Today DAX30 companies generate 68% of their sales abroad. German corporates have increasingly de-coupled from their domestic market and now depend more than ever on the overall global economic environment. Besides Asia, the US has not only been the main pillar of global growth but also critically important to large German corporates.

Besides the higher confidence in US economic stability and solid growth expectations, the availability of good returns is another main factor driving German interest in strategic US acquisitions. Price/Earnings valuation ratios of S&P 500 companies, for example, have decreased from about 26x in 2000 to around 18x in 2004.

Furthermore, the relatively weak US Dollar does also support positive sentiment toward investments in the US. However, the currency impact should not be overstated, as a significant share of the revenues as well as the cost basis of large German corporates are denominated in US Dollars. Also, buying cheap US assets with a "Euro perspective" ignores the fact that the bought asset should be valued relative to its underlying cash generation potential, which is US Dollar based.

Against this background it is no surprise that approximately half of the largest strategic acquisitions announced by German corporates in 2004 and 2005 so far have targeted US companies.

US acquisitions in Germany

US investors already increased their acquisitions in Germany in 2002 and since then have outpaced German/US transaction levels. In 2004, US acquisitions volume in Germany was nearly four times higher than German/US M&A activity and even outpaced the boom year 2000.

During the same time period the USD/EUR exchange rate has developed unfavourably from a US perspective. As already mentioned, GDP growth expectations in Germany are also less attractive than they are in Asia or the US itself. And finally, Europe, and in particular Germany is still considered by some US strategic acquirers as a difficult regulatory environment for investments, with workers' co-determination raising the most frequent concerns. So which factors have been the drivers of this apparently counter-intuitive development?

US corporates' transatlantic deal flow is substantially driven by consolidation objectives and requirements of strategic fit. Compared to the US, many corresponding European industry sectors are still relatively fragmented despite a single European market having been in place for twelve years. On the other hand, US corporates frequently find themselves forced to meet shareholders' growth demands, which are difficult to achieve just through organic growth. Against this background a number of larger strategic acquisitions by US corporates have occurred over recent years, including the acquisition of Wella by Procter & Gamble to name the probably most prominent example. An analysis of transactions also shows US companies investing into German mid cap companies to round off particular product or R&D capabilities as well as brand and distribution assets.

However, corporate strategic deals do not fully explain the volume growth seen in 2003 and 2004.

A closer review of the industry sectors of the US acquirers shows that in terms of volume more than 50% of the US acquisitions in Germany in 2003 were made by private equity firms, and in 2004 this figure was even higher, reaching a level of 60%.

Private equity has become an integral part of the M&A landscape and corporate world in Europe. This development has been particularly pronounced in Germany, where LBOs accounted for over 30% of all M&A activity in 2004. This increase in activity has been fueled by a massive increase in funds raised by private equity firms. We estimate that collectively the private equity industry has funds of approximately EUR 50bn available for investment in Europe alone. The largest "financial sponsors," the now commonly used US expression for private equity funds, are still based in or stem from the US. As a consequence the biggest portion of private equity acquisitions in Germany are accounted for by US based financial sponsor firms.

Sources of the "deal flow" for financial sponsors in Germany can be grouped into four categories: Corporate spin-offs of non-core businesses (which is still the most significant category both by volume and number of deals), "Mittelstand" transactions (i.e. acquisitions of private companies from their owners), "public-to-private" transactions of listed companies, and last but not least "secondary LBOs" from other financial sponsors (which has become an increasingly important category, driven by the relative weakness of the IPO markets and the continued strength of the debt markets).

Transactions such as the acquisition of the GAGFAH housing portfolio by Fortress (USD 4.5bn), the disposal of Dynamit Nobel's specialty chemicals business to KKR and CSFB Private Equity (USD 2.7bn), the high profile acquisition of ProSiebenSat.1 Media by a group of financial sponsors and Saban Capital Group (USD 1.8bn) or the taking private of Celanese by Blackstone Group (USD 2.6bn) demonstrate the varied nature and substantial amounts of US private equity investments in Germany.

Obviously, the business model of financial sponsors relies on the optimisation of leverage and funding costs. European cost of debt financing is converging to US conditions. On average however, in 2004 pricing of European leveraged debt financings were still around 50 bps cheaper than comparable pricings in the US. On the other hand, the typical equity contribution for German financial sponsor deals is on average 5% points higher than in the US.

Even more importantly, US financial sponsors are finding lots of opportunities to invest in assets which are set for sale by German corporate groups due to a change of strategic focus and often also requiring a substantial amount of restructuring or strategic transformation. In this respect US financial sponsors have provided short term liquidity to German corporates, as well as to some public sector enterprises. The prospects for high returns as a result of successful restructuring as well as business development opportunities and the attractive funding from Euro debt markets seem to balance any potential disadvantages from the relatively weaker USD.

In particular the Blackstone/Celanese transaction serves as a good example of how financial sponsors can develop and reposition a company between German and US capital markets. Celanese combined most of the former Hoechst chemical activities after the spin-off in 1999. After the successful public tender offer for Celanese shares in 2004, Blackstone added strategic acquisitions totalling over USD 700m. The following year, in early 2005, Blackstone completed the IPO of the new parent legal entity Celanese Corp., headquartered in Dallas, Texas. Celanese is now a publicly traded corporation on the New York Stock Exchange and benefits from the valuation multiple differential between US and German equity markets.

We also expect other subsegments to receive considerable private equity attention. The real estate market will become a key focus of private equity activity over the next few years as illustrated by the GAGFAH/Fortress transaction already mentioned. Another asset category receiving considerable private equity attention in Germany are non-performing loans, as domestic banks restructure their loan portfolios. The US firm Lone Star recently acquired a portfolio of EUR 3.6bn of non-performing loans for an undisclosed amount from Hypo Real Estate, a spin-off from Hypo Vereinsbank. Furthermore, albeit often on a smaller scale, domestic and international funds focussing on corporate turnarounds have also emerged in Germany and are actively screening and acquiring assets.

Outlook for 2005 and beyond

The acquisitions of German corporates in the US during the first six months in 2005 amounted to USD 7.7bn, already reaching the level of the entire year 2004 and even outpacing US acquisitions in Germany in 2005. This has been mainly driven by the announced acquisition of Renal Care Group by Fresenius Medical Care (USD 4bn). This transaction as well as the acquisition of Sola International by a joint venture of Carl Zeiss and EQT Partners illustrate not only the growing confidence of German companies in pursuing strategic, growth-oriented transactions but also the feasibility of rather complex cross-border acquisition structures.

Still, the number of German acquisitions in the US is stagnating at much lower levels than before 2002. It may take some more time before mid cap corporates are also prepared to pursue active growth strategies and, possibly with some delay, are willing to take the "M&A leap" across the Atlantic.

Surprisingly, the volume of US acquisitions in Germany so far this year (USD 5.1bn) has been relatively low. However, we regard this as a short term distortion that does not point to a general change of the underlying trend of the last two to three years. This assessment is supported by the significant number of transactions accomplished during the first six months. Only 18% of the acquisition volume relates to private equity investments. However, there is no identifiable economic parameter from a US financial sponsor or corporate perspective that has deteriorated compared to recent years other than greater strategic interest displacing some private equity activity.

From a long term perspective, it remains to be seen as to how the importance of the US in German cross-border M&A will develop relative to European and other countries.

One noticeable obstacle for cross-border transactions between the US and Germany is the limited ability of financing transactions with stock. With very few exceptions (such as the already mentioned VoiceStream Wireless/Deutsche Telekom transaction) there has hardly been any German acquisition in the US in exchange for shares.

German companies which have shouldered the listing process in the US including the adoption to US GAAP standards and the onerous reporting requirements set by the Sarbanes-Oxley Act, often find themselves in a situation where trading liquidity and acceptance of shares by US investors have deteriorated to a very low level. In addition there is a growing number of investment funds, which are either "index-trackers" or bound by their investment specifications to hold exclusively US or German shares. As a consequence, if shares are used as a cross-border acquisition currency, the acquirer faces major flow back issues.

This stands in major contrast to the consolidation of European capital markets as well as the converging investment, legal and regulatory environment. Based on stock quotations in a common currency and the growing relevance of European stock market indices for asset managers in Europe, stocks have become a frequently used consideration for cross-border M&A transactions, such as the recent decision announced by the Italian bank UniCredit to acquire HVB Group, the second largest German private bank, for EUR 15.4bn all in the form of UniCredit shares.

The underlying drivers for transatlantic transactions between the US and Germany remain in place. Structural as well as cyclical factors should manifest themselves in continued transactions involving both, strategic and private equity investors.

2.5 Success and Success Factors of US-German Mergers

Fritz Kröger

*In the global merger environment US-German mergers really are
a different breed. Not only that success rates are significantly lower,
also global success factors do not apply. Only the complexity rule
is confirmed: In the integration, mergers of higher complexity are
correlated with lower success rate. This is an appeal to theorists and
practitioners to convert the high cultural affinities between the two
nations into a more successful merger reality.*

The strategic context of mergers

The merger endgames concept, based on the Value Building Growth (VBG) databank
of 29,000 companies over 15 years and covering 98 percent of the world market
capitalization, features the consolidation rate of industries and their change over time.[1]
The merger endgames curve plots global industries according to their actual position
in the consolidation game over a period of 25 years which describes the actual position and also predicts merger movements into the future.

According to the endgames concept, industries run through four consolidation phases:
The Opening phase, the Scale phase, the Focus phase and the Balance phase. The
Opening phase comprises young and de-regulated industries, coming out of a monop-

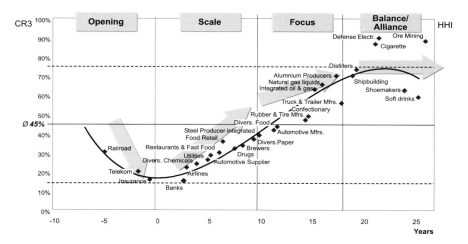

Figure 2.4 Merger endgames: industry consolidation follows a pattern through four phases

---

[1] Sources: Value Building Growth database; A.T. Kearney analysis

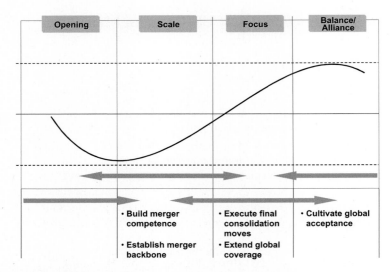

Figure 2.5 Each phase has its specific set of strategic missions

oly position, de-consolidating down to a minimum of 15 percent CR3.[1] The *Scale phase* holds fragmented industries that strongly consolidate over a period of eight to ten years until CR3 44 percent, which is the inflection point of the endgames curve. *The Focus phase* starts at the inflection point, at which the future market leader normally shows up. The focus phase holds two or three final mergers before the global leader finally reaches a dominant position.

In the *Balance phase,* the global leader shares the market with two or three smaller competitors. The leader dominates the market with accordingly high margins as long as he succeeds in defending his position against attacking followers.

In each phase, companies must fulfill specific strategic and operational missions to successfully "ride the endgames curve." This empirical-based theory implies that mergers are part of the regular strategy, inevitable to grow and to prevail long-term in the industry consolidation. It is simply a matter of when to start, which target to select, and how to integrate.

For example, the endgames concept and its missions explains why the German banking industry, the pharmaceutical industry and the brewery industry fell behind European and global competitors – the competitors moved much faster and were more successful in the industry consolidation.

---

[1] Compare Figure 2.4: CR3: Market share of the three largest companies of the total market based on Value Building Growth database (29,000 companies) – HR3 in accord with HHI: Hirschmann-Herfindahl Index corresponds to the sum of the squared market shares of all companies and is greater than 90%; the axis logarithmically plotted.

Success rate of mergers

According to widespread public opinion, two thirds of mergers fail or at least fail to create value. So, between the compulsion to merge (the merger endgame) and the disastrous failure rates of mergers, companies often find themselves in a Scylla and Charybdis situation – there are two monsters that have their own way of destroying ships.

But findings in a 2004 study of 1,037 mergers (companies above a transaction volume of US$ 500 million) between the years 1990 and 1999 reveals that we should revise the old bias of mergers being doomed to failure. For this study, a successful merger was defined as one that two years after the merger closed the new entity was beating the industry average in stock performance. An unsuccessful merger fell below the industry average in stock performance in the same timeframe. (This quantification and calibration was possible in running the 1,037 mergers against the 29,000 companies of the Value Building Growth databank.)

According to the findings, around 50 percent of all mergers are successful (Figure 2.6)! Clearly, in comparison to what happened in the past, companies had learned to cope with the merger risk, and the whole process had become more rational and even more automatized within the leading consolidators. Large teams of professionals had become specialists in identifying the right mergers, closing the deals, and integrating new partners into their business units.

The obvious question then is: Are there strategic patterns that can identify which mergers will be more successful than others? Based on the many studies performed to identify merger success factors, the answer is still not clear. However, the best explanation may be found in our study of the four phases of the endgames curve. We found that mergers in the first two phases – Opening and Scale – had a significantly higher success rate than those in the Merger and Balance phases (Figure 2.7). This makes

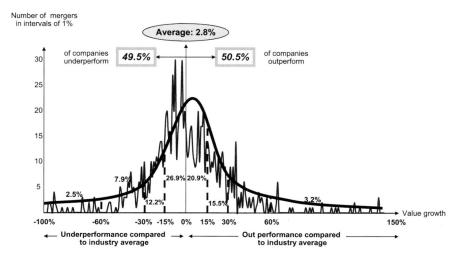

Figure 2.6 50 percent of all mergers are successful

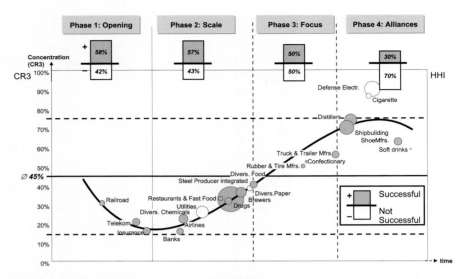

Figure 2.7 The four stages of industry consolidation redefine the pattern of merger success

sense, given that the Opening and the Scale phases are where companies face the highest pressure to obtain scale effects, nearly at any cost.

In the Focus phase, where the players are already well-established, it is much more difficult to realize the necessary synergies. In the Balance phase, where the merger success rate is a mere 30 percent, it is very difficult to buy at a reasonable price and then increase the combined stock price.

Therefore, on a global scale, the merger business is well under way with increasing success rates and newly revealed success factors.

US-German Mergers – a different breed?

We wondered whether these findings could be applied more specifically to US-German mergers? Because there is high cultural and business affinity between Americans and Germans, we expected the merger success rate to be even higher. To our surprise, the opposite was true (Figure 2.8). We decided to increase the sample, lowering the level of transaction volume down to US$2 50 million and changing the time span from 1995 to 2002, which resulted in a sample of 513 mergers. When the characteristics of the different samples were checked against the former 1,037 mergers, there were no major differences.

Yet when comparing the bell curve of transatlantic mergers with global mergers, the success rate of US-German mergers is quite different (Figure 2.9).

Of 513 mergers of which 359 were U.S. mergers into Germany and 154 were German mergers into the United States, only 35 percent were successful, accordingly, 65 percent were not. Obviously, the U.S. acquirers had a higher success rate of (37 percent) versus the Germans (25 percent).

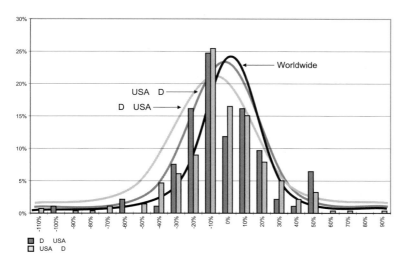

Figure 2.8 Transatlantic mergers score below global average

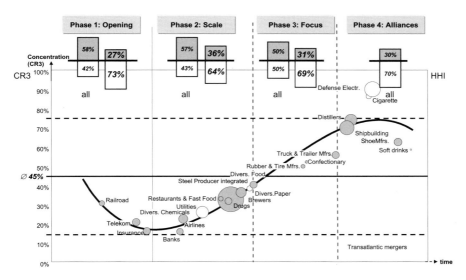

Figure 2.9 Transatlantic mergers do not follow the global success pattern

Armed with these results, we tried to identify the factors of success and failure in this sample, beginning with the endgames phases and plotting the U.S.-German mergers according to the phases in which they took place. Overall the results reveal that our U.S.-German sample again proved to be a different breed. The failure rate was even higher in the Opening phase, while in the Scale and Focus phases, the differentiation was not significant.

We then looked for an explanation in the type of industry where the mergers took place. We plotted them, according to the Dow Jones Sector Titan Index, into 17 major

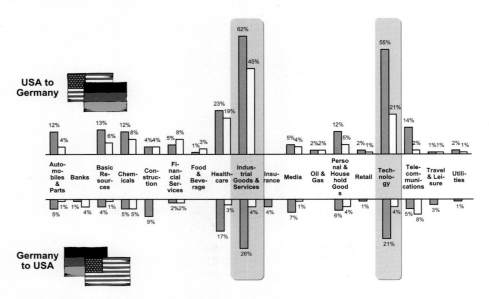

Figure 2.10 Most merger activities took place in industrial goods, technology industries

industries, again based on merger success and non-success (Figure 2.10). Overall, by far the most mergers took place in the industrial goods and services industries, in technology and then in healthcare. But again the success rate did not really differentiate, with a nearly equal distribution.

Therefore, the new sample did not provide a strategic rationale for the differences. None of those factors showed significant impact. With this in mind, we turned to the second major front of merger success: Integration.

It is broadly understood that 60 percent of merger success is determined by the integration of the candidates, depending on the methods, the processes and the toolbox used.[1] Different types of mergers have a strong impact on merger performance. Based on a broad scope of practical experience cases Kai Lucks uses a range of factors to describe the level of challenges for M&A integration cases. He distinguishes between factors relating to the size of the case, complexity drivers and level of restructuring, each broken down into 4 dimensions thus adding up to 12 "challenge indicators" (see chapter 4.1.2 on managing complex M&A projects in this book). Projects depicted in the resulting 12-dimension spider diagram can be distributed into different degrees of "challenge levels" ranging from "low challenge" (Cluster I) to "high challenge" (Cluster III).

Of the 12 dimensions, seven were identifiable in our 513er sample: sales volume of the acquirer and the candidate, number of the employees of the acquirer and the candidate, the number of involved countries, location and businesses. Due to the

---

[1] Habeck, Kröger, Träm: After the Merger. Seven Rules for Successful Post-Merger Integration. Edinburgh 2000

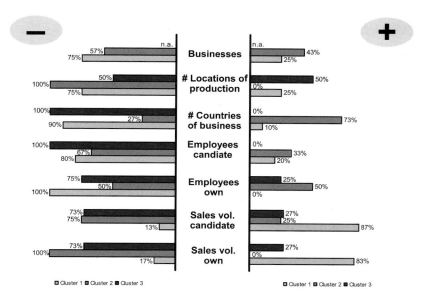

Figure 2.11 Complex mergers (Cluster II + III) have a higher failure rate

limited number of companies that had been acquired up to seven years ago, the sample was reduced to 48 candidates. Here we were able to track the numbers, and based on a small sample, we obtained a clearer score. Complexity drove merger success and the cluster III companies, which showed a higher degree of challenges, indeed proved to suffer from a higher failure rate (Figure 2.11). From our small sample specifically the quantity of employees and the number of countries involved in a merger gave an indication that higher challenges result in inferior M&A performance. The limited sample nevertheless does not permit further detailed interpretation

Overall, the findings in our study on merger success and success factors were disillusioning: The apparently high cultural affinity between Germans and Americans did not lead to a higher success rate than the global average. Although the U.S. companies had a higher success rate in merger drivers than German companies, none of the well-known factors of merger success had a significant impact on the results.

Ultimately, the major barriers to integration success come down to the people driving the mergers, their experience and the degree of complexity in integrating the two candidates.

3 Experiences from Industries

3.1 Automotive

3.1.1 The Post-Merger Integration Process of DaimlerChrysler AG

Rüdiger Grube

No merger in the last years has been so much discussed by the public than the one of Daimler and Chrysler. It was based on a detailed analysis of the situation of Daimler-Benz and Chrysler on the world's markets, showing that the two merger partners supplemented each other well. The principles and organizational structure of the PMI process had to be defined precisely, and a not too great number of PMI topics were to be identified and prioritized. Project management of PMI was based on three sources of information: one infobase for the Board of Management members and Issue Resolution Team (IRT) coordinators, one for the IRTs themselves, and finally the Project Infobase for the project employees. An essential aim of the merger has been for the individual brands to strengthen rather than weaken their positions in the market, therefore communication played a very important role in the PMI process, to keep enthusiasm high on both sides and on any hierarchical level.

Introduction

Although many corporate objectives, such as increases in effectiveness or improvements in competitive position, can also be achieved through organic growth, companies frequently opt in favor of inorganic growth in order to gain a time advantage. However, this is a goal that can only be realized if the new parts of the company are integrated with sufficient thoroughness and rapidity. In this respect, post-merger integration can be either a linchpin or a major stumbling block.

The post-merger integration process – as illustrated in Figure 3.1 – consists of three phases. First, there is the start-up phase, which is initiated before the closing (the point at which the contract is concluded and corporate responsibility is transferred) and involves the planning of integration activities. Secondly, there is the project implementation phase in which important integration topics, such as the integration of brands and products, are addressed and thirdly the transformation phase, where the results are transferred to the line organization.

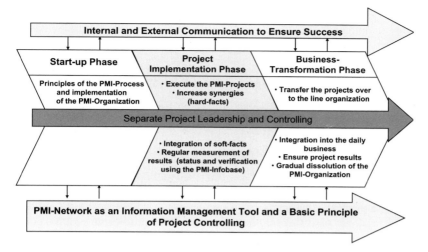

Figure 3.1 Post-merger integration process

Another important element is control of the overall process with the PMI network as an information management tool and a basic principle of project controlling. Based on these contextual phases and IT-assisted information gathering and processing, it is possible to differentiate between project management and project control. In order to ensure success these activities are complemented by targeted internal and external communications.

Opening status of the merger of Daimler and Chrysler

At Daimler-Benz, the merger decision was based on a four-step analysis aimed at strategic development. In the first step, the focus was on an analysis of the areas of current and future business development of the group in the framework of strategic business discussions, based on the current analyzed portfolio for further corporate development.

The growth analyses carried out in the second step led to the realization that investment should not be limited to new growth areas. This is the case, because many companies in growth industries generate no profit at all, while companies with long-standing core competencies in stagnating markets are capable of realizing outstanding results. The crucial factor, therefore, is not the sector or area – whether growing or stagnating – in which business is conducted, but rather how well the company is aligned in its core business divisions.

On this basis, a detailed portfolio analysis was carried out in the third step. By evaluating the then situation of Daimler-Benz and various drawn-up scenarios, it was possible to address the specific issue of the future growth strategy of the company. The following five challenges emerged:

- Volume disadvantages at Daimler-Benz as the 15th largest vehicle manufacturer

- Too little influence with the advance of market consolidation
- Limited growth potential since the alignment was mainly towards mature markets
- No second automobile base to fall back on, and therefore vulnerability in the premium segment
- Cost disadvantages in the amortization of R&D costs due to the small volume base.

The results of the analysis show that, in relation to the production volume and market requirements, the company is too small to be able to sustain a high level of earnings over the long term while ensuring its independence.

To reinforce its presence in North America, the company could either continue to grow endogenously or strive towards a merger with one of the big vehicle manufacturers in the US. The primary arguments for a merger were strengthening the market position in an increasingly consolidating industry, development towards a global company and the realization and utilization of synergies – in particular of economies of scale.

The Chrysler Corporation was particularly suitable as a potential merger partner. Prior to the merger (1996), Chrysler generated app. US$ 60 billion in revenues, and every sixth vehicle sold in the USA was a Chrysler. Despite the apparent saturation of the market, the net return on sales was six per cent. The corresponding figure at General Motors was four per cent, while the figure at Ford was not even three per cent. The rate of return on equity employed stood at 20 per cent over the same period. By comparison, the average for the automotive industry was 8.2 per cent, with the average for industry as a whole at 9.6 per cent. At the time, Chrysler had the lowest production costs and the highest margin of any vehicle manufacturer in the world. With liquid assets of US $ 7.5 billion, the view at the time was that there were no obstacles to future investments. The analysis also presented Chrysler with several challenges:

- Volume disadvantages at Chrysler as the sixth biggest vehicle manufacturer
- Potential takeover candidate with the advance of market consolidation
- Limited growth potential since the alignment was mainly towards mature North American markets (97%)
- Open to attack in the sports utility and minivan segment, insufficient presence in the premium segment
- Disadvantage in expertise due to only limited access to premium technologies.

Chrysler and Daimler-Benz supplemented each other well, as shown by the strategic and operational fit of the two merger partners. Figure 3.2 shows a comparison of the two companies.

Overall, however, the insufficient coverage of the Asiatic and Latin American markets could not be overlooked. The decision to merge with Chrysler represented the fourth step of the strategic analysis prior to the actual merger.

When the extraordinary annual meetings of the two companies were held on September 18, 1998, 99.9 per cent of Daimler-Benz shareholders voted for the merger, with a corresponding figure 97.5 per cent at Chrysler.

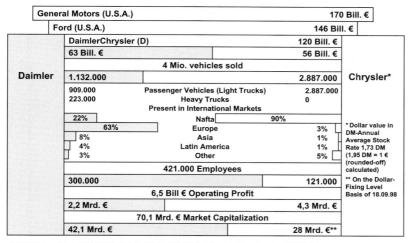

General Motors (U.S.A.)		170 Bill. €	
Ford (U.S.A.)		146 Bill. €	
DaimlerChrysler (D)		120 Bill. €	
63 Bill. €		56 Bill. €	

Figure 3.2 A comparison of the merger partners in 1998

It should be noted that the merger saw DaimlerChrysler emerge as a sizeable entity in the financial services sector. With a total financing portfolio of around €100 billion, DaimlerChrysler is the world's third largest OEM financial services provider behind GM and Ford. Neither Daimler-Benz nor the Chrysler Corporation could have achieved such a competitive position on their own.

Today, DaimlerChrysler is the world's foremost manufacturer of premium and luxury vehicles, number one in commercial vehicles over 6 tons, number 1 in buses over 8 tons, and in passenger cars it ranks number five in the world with a global market share of around 8 per cent.

Phases of the integration process

Start-up phase

The start-up phase can be subdivided into two parts (see Figure 3.3). The first part covers the definition of the PMI topics, their prioritization and establishing a PMI organization. The objective was to complete this part as far as possible prior to the closing.

Recognizing the necessity for the start-up phase and its good organization are crucial to the smooth operation of the overall merger process. For this reason, some important details of the start-up phase have been singled out for closer examination.

Identification and prioritization of PMI topics

PMI issues, that is to say the topics that are to be dealt with, are identified in the first sub-stage. It is important that the number of topics identified is not too great, because experience shows that a maximum of around 100 common topics lend themselves to

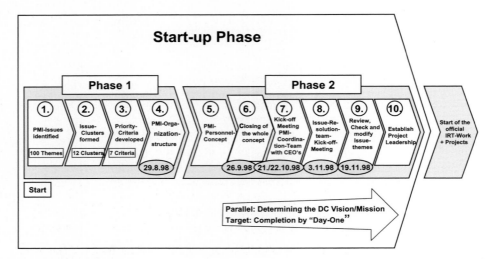

Figure 3.3 Start-up phase

proper organization. Anything beyond this figure may hinder appropriate control, assessment and direction.

During the merger of Daimler and Chrysler, the 100 topics identified were compiled in twelve clusters. In the third stage, criteria were developed to prioritize these topics. In the DaimlerChrysler merger an Issue Resolution (IR) team was assigned for dealing with each prioritized cluster.

The evaluation criteria consisted of the following:

1. *Signal effects*, both internal and external, were to be generated in the organization. In principle, a conservative approach needs to be adopted when it comes to determining the anticipated effects for the individual topic areas of the merger. This ensures that the figures on paper actually tally with the effects noticeable in reality.

2. The *influence* of the individual project *on profit* is the second criterion.

3. The savings and/or profit increases that can be achieved must be compared against the necessary *investments* for all measures introduced.

4. The individual measures to be introduced must be examined with a view to their strategic *influences and dependencies*. Above all, the issue of whether so-called *cannibalizing effects* may occur unexpectedly in other areas must be taken into account.

5. All measures and projects must be evaluated from the aspect of *time sensitivity*. This means that a check must be carried out to establish whether such measures and projects can only fully achieve their desired effect at a specific point in time or during a specific period.

6. Checking whether the *necessary personnel resources* are available for the implementation of measures before such measures are introduced is a further criterion.

7. Measures for which the anticipated level of effects can be high are evaluated critically if, prior to the merger, it is established that it would be virtually impossible to implement such a measure with the available personnel resources. From this perspective, and looking at the overall criteria, the *probability of success* is determined as a complement to the analyzed risk.

These seven criteria, which together determine the importance of the projects, were used to derive the level of decision-making and the reporting requirement. All projects, which are deemed to be 'value drivers' – and therefore designated as category "A" – are pivotal to the overall result and are presented for decision-making at Board of Management level. Decisions on category "B" topics may be made by the relevant leader of an Issue Resolution team, while decision-making in category "C" remains directly with the line organization. Topics in the lower-ranking "D" bracket are not pursued further at this stage; as topic areas, they may be brought back onto the agenda at a later point in time when the most important topics have been dealt with.

Under any other conditions, the Board of Management, in its dual function (line and PMI), would be confronted with too many individual topics.

On August 29, 1998, at the end of the first part of the start-up phase, the PMI organization structure was established based on the results of the project prioritization.

Implementation of the PMI organization

During the secret negotiations phase, only a small group of people are aware of the topics and conduct the negotiations. In the phases between announcement and closing, two independent companies still exist with two independent Boards of Management. In this phase, an equally appointed core team headed by members of the Boards of Management of the two companies is to be set up, with the subsequent merger managers already involved in the process. The core team controls the task forces that deal with the three key areas of the closing, relationship management (that is to say creating positive relations and atmosphere) and the conception of the PMI process. In this way, it is possible for the relationship management team to support the development of the formal and informal relations network even before the start of the PMI.

In the second part of the start-up phase, the organization structure established at the end of the first part was adopted by the Board of Management. The 100 topics were then checked, supplemented and remodified in collaboration with the IRT coordinators. Two objectives behind this fine screening were: first, to enable the coordinators to identify their topics better and improve the networking between the IRTs from the outset, and secondly, to subject all content to a critical examination by the commissioned experts. Thereafter, both top project management and sub-project management were institutionalized.

Since many problems have to be resolved during the course of day-to-day business, a contact person who can deal with issues as they arise is necessary on each side of the merger. In order to realize this in the context of the DaimlerChrysler merger, two representatives defined by the "plug-and-socket principle" were deployed as a dual infrastructure. The process continued at all times, uninterrupted by illness, leave or any other obstacle. According to the target objective, both partners were responsible for the joint implementation of the merger objectives. At DaimlerChrysler, there was not a single case of failed cooperation.

In addition to the dual PMI organization, therefore, there was also a dual control center, although at the outset this placed an added strain on the organization, and resulted in a considerable extra drain on resources. However, it paid off overall, because it served to confirm the equality of the partners from both the organizational and personnel aspects.

The closing was followed by the switch to an entirely new organization with just one board, a Board of Management and – at least in the medium term – a strategic alignment (see Figure 3.4). The aim is to create a non-bureaucratic, flexible PMI organization that can ensure a rapid response to events and be adapted to changing conditions at any time during the PMI process. This organization represents the institutional anchoring of the integration within the overall organization of the company.

As illustrated in Figure 3.4, the PMI organization consisted of five organizational units: The highest-level committee, and the first organizational unit, is the Board of Management with its 18 Board of Management members constituted from the two previous Boards of Management of Daimler-Benz and Chrysler, including the two CEOs, without any restructuring.

The second organizational unit was made up of the group of twelve Issue Resolution teams. The first block included the IR teams for development, production, sales and marketing, procurement and all global strategic topics in the automotive sector. The second block dealt with topics that do not belong directly to the automotive sector or which, in terms of priority, are at group level. Such a cluster, in accordance with the

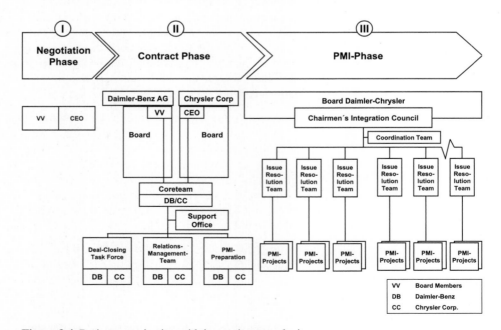

Figure 3.4 Project organization with increasing complexity

plug-and-socket principle, was always the responsibility of two Board of Management members – one German (formerly Daimler-Benz AG) and one American (formerly Chrysler Corporation).

The third organizational unit was the group of PMI projects where the operational processing of defined individual topics took place. At the time, there were a total of 1,273 such sub-projects, each with a project leader. In each case the responsibility for these projects was borne jointly by the relevant Board of Management member and the top-level project leaders.

The fourth organizational unit was also constituted in accordance with the plug-and-socket principle, and consisted of five special teams. One of these groups was the Integration Process Management & Communications group, which dealt exclusively with forecasting effects and monitoring the PMI process. It reported directly to the two heads of the PMI process. The other four groups were the cross-functional issue groups Strategy Integration, Business Culture, IT Strategy and Management Information.

The members of the core team, together with the IRT coordinators, formed the fifth organizational unit – the PMI Coordination team. These employees – about 45 in number – met in person once a month. There were also weekly video conferences. The two heads of this PMI Coordination team were assigned directly to the chairmen of the Boards of Management, symbolizing that the results of the PMI were of the highest importance.

Principles of the PMI process

At the so-called kickoff meeting, the Board of Management explained the following seven basic principles to the IRT coordinators:

1. *Only the best players for the PMI:* The object was to draft in only the best managers and staff from the existing organization for implementation of the project. Consequently, recruitment was by personal recommendation rather than by secondment through the relevant department. Each player remained in his or her line function at all times, and had to take on PMI tasks in addition.

2. *"Welding together" the project teams creates an ability to act quickly:* It is essential to build a team rapidly and to develop goals for every activity.

3. *Motivating project members through bonuses and career opportunities:* Successful collaboration in the PMI process was rewarded with financial bonuses and further opportunities for development within the group.

   What happened in practice was that each PMI participant received "half shares" in two phases. The first half was awarded at the beginning of their PMI work, and the second half at the end. The two sets of shares have since become a sort of status symbol. Even today, they are still on display in the offices of many of those involved in PMI. To have been part of this group – and be able to show it– was clearly a greater source of motivation than any pecuniary incentive.

4. *Achieving the personal commitment of everybody involved:* Based on these person-related and team-oriented principles, a direct and personal commitment to the desired goals was expected of each individual participant in the PMI process. As a

symbol, two flags bearing the DaimlerChrysler logo were chosen and signed by all of the approximately 100 people involved as a sign of their personal commitment. One of these flags was hung in the PMI room in Auburn Hills, USA, the other in Germany.

5. *Simultaneous realization of hard and soft success factors*: In post-merger integration projects of this nature, there is always a danger that consideration will only be given to the hard factors such as synergies or the development of new product and market segments. Such an approach is important, but is not sufficient.

With hard facts, it is particularly important to pay attention to synergies, mission, goals and core values, development of standard management, and multi-brand management. A further goal was to increase the room for maneuver in shaping the consolidation of the automobile industry. In addition, new product segments/regions were to be developed and the non-automotive business profitably expanded. When the subdivision is taken into account, some of the areas, such as Core Values, Management Culture and Brand Management, are at least close to the soft facts.

Soft facts include the following five areas: In *Culture*, what matters most is looking at and accepting various cultural attitudes and behavior without prejudice or negative associations. *Employees* of the newly created company have to understand each other, come together and develop informal networks. The primary consideration is therefore not how positions are filled according to competencies, but rather how attitude and conviction determine behavior. *Processes* are more part of the soft success factors as they involve not just a change to the procedural organization but also, and more particularly, a change to internalized patterns of behavior and decision-making processes. From the Board of Management down to the individual project member, a direct *commitment* is called for to achieve the personal goals aimed at within the context of the merger. There is always the danger that such commitments will just be paid lip service and the reality will be quite different. For this reason, additional specific tools such as balanced scorecards and target objectives must be applied, procedures run through, and defined milestones reached in order that the commitments are made "concrete" and comprehensible. The essence of a merger lies in the process of change, which calls into question – and clears away or changes – much of that which already exists. The very awareness of this can create an atmosphere of uncertainty that can only be countered through good, long-term *communication*.

6. *Avoiding gaps in communication*: The fifth soft success factor leads directly to the principle of avoiding gaps in communication – both internal (managers, employees and the works council) and external (in particular shareholders, customers, banks, suppliers and the public at large).

7. *Defining clear guidelines for the project leaders*: The guidelines include descriptions of processes and information about how new topics are generated and when a topic must be presented to the Board of Management. They are used as aids to orientation in the prioritization of day-to-day actions so that project leaders are afforded more security and independence when acting on a decentralized basis on their own authority. The crucial factor when setting up these guidelines is to limit their number to as few rules of behavior as possible.

① Continuation of the business during the PMI Phase

② More focus on the real value-drivers

③ Merger of equals

④ Quick decisions and quick implementation

⑤ All concerned to be made parties hereto (e.g. intensive integration of all Board Members)

⑥ Clear content definition, reaching deadlines and achieving project integration

⑦ Post Merger Integration is temporary and limited to a maximum of two years (earliest transfer to the line organization)

Figure 3.5 PMI guidelines in the DaimlerChrysler merger

The seven PMI guidelines set out in Figure 3.5 were summarized in the Daimler-Chrysler merger as a manual for each project leader so that not only the spirit and philosophy could be understood, but also specific guidelines for implementation of the projects given.

As illustrated in the last point of the PMI guidelines, the integration process at DaimlerChrysler was expected to take a maximum of two years. In practice, however, it was handed over to the line organizations – albeit with a range of tasks and problems still to be solved – after a period of only twelve months.

In this respect, it is necessary to distinguish between the different types of integration tasks. Integration of the essential features of tasks can be achieved in two years. Harmonization of Research and Development – and therefore of the new products – requires longer because of the corresponding product life cycles.

Project implementation phase

The start-up phase is followed directly by the project implementation phase with the carrying out of the PMI projects. Two objectives are pursued: the first of these is in hard facts, where synergies must be improved. Secondly, there must be integration of the soft success factors. In addition, provision must be made for a regular check of success, which enables status and control based on the PMI Infobase. This is directly connected to the PMI network. Based on the clear organizational regulations, clear rules and behavior patterns, it is vital that this process is rapidly controlled in a streamlined manner so that tangible results can be achieved relatively quickly.

The positioning of the topic of PMI on the agenda of the Board of Management represents an internal signal for both managers and employees. For this reason, PMI topics were top of the agenda from the aspects of both content and timing.

Brand strategy and information technology as central aspects of integration

The aim is for the individual brands to strengthen rather than weaken their positions in the market. It is only from this perspective that a brand "can be interpreted as a perception of a product or service that is distinctive and firmly anchored in the psyche of the consumer."

From the customer's perspective, however, the reality is often somewhat different. This is because, as far as the customer of one of the companies is concerned, the brand that he or she holds in high regard and has therefore bought in the form of the product, represents not only the promise of certain consistent quality, but also, above all, an "emotional comfort zone". When a merger occurs, customers not only frequently harbor doubts about the assurance of quality – they also feel that they have lost a part of their "emotional comfort zone." At the same time, this sense of insecurity increases the likelihood that such customers will consider switching their allegiance.

However, it is precisely these effects that are always counterproductive in relation to the original strategic and operational objectives of any M&A activity. It is for this reason that such effects should be actively counteracted at an early stage through communication and the adoption of selective measures, or even by foregoing integration opportunities. If action is not taken, brand management will become less clear, the essence of the brand will be less compelling and, in particular, the brand profiles conveyed will be less distinguishable.

It should also be borne in mind that the exertion of influence on a more heavily integrated product and brand policy will always depend on the life cycles of the individual products.

When products which were previously positioned as brands in very different sectors – and not just in the premium sector – are combined in the new company following a merger, the brand profiles must be kept quite separate.

There is one further important aspect. As far as the customer is concerned, it is not just the brand products of companies that come into play – the customer also identifies with the company itself. Viewed from this perspective, the company name – as a corporate brand – is afforded the character of a brand. Moreover, the identity-forming function of brands for the employees is often underestimated. If the company name, logo or well-known product brands of one of the partners are relinquished, and therefore disappear, during the integration, it is not uncommon for employees and managers to take this as a personal defeat. They sometimes try to hold on to their old name identity for as long as possible, and therefore have a negative attitude to further changes. In such a situation, employees can find it difficult to fulfill a specific brand promise to a customer and to represent the company in a manner befitting customer expectations.

By contrast, an IT integration – in the sense that it is a purely technical project – appears at first glance to be an altogether easier proposition. IT integration – through harmonized data and information flows that can be accessed jointly without the need for interfaces – is a fundamental step on the road to making the convergence process a reality.

In the first stage of IT integration, the communication platforms of the companies must be standardized and all the necessary measures taken to ensure the smooth running of day-to-day business. In a second stage, the previously worked out IT strategy can now be implemented, together with a decision about the scope of integration of the existing hardware and software. In parallel with the technical implementation, employees should be trained in using the new software. When one of the partners is newly introduced to the IT functions of the other company, there is an opportunity to at least move employees, so that, for a limited period of time, there is an "expert" available at every location. The technical implementation calls for special care – particularly in the area of migration of customer data, where it is essential to decide whether customers are to be informed of a change of customer number or, in the case of banks, account numbers.

Project management and control

Target- and results-oriented control of integration projects require that information has to be both complete and up-to-date, and that it can be accessed at any time at any required location within the new company. For the sake of clarity, the aggregate information must be clearly arranged and, if necessary, comprehensible down to the smallest detail. Evaluation of the project status also allows any delays or problems to be identified at an early stage and ensures a higher level of management attention for these projects.

There are three aspects that are essential to IT-assisted control of PMI projects:

- First, there must be a readiness to establish professional database management or expand existing IT systems for controlling M&A activities.
- Secondly, all PMI projects must be integrated into this database, though with clear differentiation between access authorizations according to function and hierarchy.
- Thirdly, a manageable number of criteria must be established according to which all projects will be evaluated and managed with a traffic light control system.

The architecture of the internal network used at DaimlerChrysler – the "PMI network" – was based on the organizational structure of the PMI process. It consisted of three work platforms: the PMI Infobase to provide information to Board of Management members and IRT coordinators, the IRT Infobase for the Issue Resolution teams, and finally the Project Infobase for the project employees.

Each of the three Infobases makes maneuvering through the more than 100 databases a simple process, while users have direct access to all project levels with the corresponding authorizations.

A standard design in all three work platforms facilitates orientation in the various Infobases. Especially important is the documentation function of the databases, which is guaranteed through standard allocation of documents to the corresponding project or subproject. It must therefore be possible to reconstruct accurately the whole course of the project during implementation, and also after its completion.

One essential process that is mapped using the PMI network is the PMI reporting process. Before the PMI phase began, management had decided that all reporting would be done within the PMI via the PMI network, and therefore exclusively in electronic form. The premises in the reporting process – such as a standard reporting form, simple processing and rapid access to clearly arranged information – require such an information network as a basis for process control.

It is the only way to make ongoing monitoring of key figures and project status possible. In addition to the improvement of synergies in a cluster, a so-called "degree of difficulty" was introduced and analyzed in the DaimlerChrysler merger in four stages. Degree of difficulty I means that the synergy has been achieved and recorded. Degree of difficulty II means that defined projects exist for the specified synergies for which a commitment has been made, though these defined projects have not yet been 100 per cent processed. Degree of difficulty III represents the residual commitments; the Board of Management has made a commitment for the level of this synergy, but has not yet defined precisely what measures are to be used to improve it. Degree of difficulty IV identifies extremely critical areas; here there is a deviation from the synergies for which the Board of Management member or project leader has entered into a commitment.

The qualitative components of the reporting process relate to the status of the content of the project. The contents ranged from a brief current status description through to a comprehensive description of the results achieved since the last status report and the representation of future core topics and milestones.

The current overall status of a project or the IRT can then be checked using the traffic light analysis. The aim of the traffic light analysis is to have a direct overview of the areas or criteria in which problems exist as identified by the yellow or red status of the traffic light. The basic idea for this approach arose from recognition that the high degree of complexity in a merger process can only be reduced if prominence is given exclusively to those topics that are critical in terms of their implementation and achievement of objectives.

This was realized with both project leaders, following feedback from the Controlling Department, having to enter the status of the project into the Infobase manually. Crucial to the particular traffic light change were the deviations or changes to the criteria of synergy contribution, qualitative objective achievement and adherence to the time schedule or milestones. The permissible deviations had already been established at the beginning of the PMI process in so-called "Ground Rules for PMI Status Reporting."

The Board of Management was kept informed daily on a "just-in-time" basis of all important PMI details, so that they were always aware of the current status of the increased synergies in each IRT cluster. When deviations occurred, the chairman of the Board of Management would regularly contact the relevant project leaders himself to discuss the background to any such deviations.

By the end of July 1999, half of the scheduled synergies had been achieved, with deviations and failures becoming fewer and fewer. To prevent any so-called "hockey stick effect" in which nothing happens for a long time and then suddenly at the end the required results arrive in a steep curve, two predetermined breaking points for the achievement of goals were introduced: 50 per cent of the synergies had to be achieved by July 1999, with 75% of all synergies by October 1999.

The PMI network proved its worth as a support tool in the DaimlerChrysler merger. In fact, it was so highly regarded by the employees in the projects that suggestions were made for its continued use in day-to-day line projects in the group as a whole.

Communication in the merger process

During the merger of Daimler-Benz and Chrysler in 1998, the press reported on a broad range of topics – from typical merger topics such as redundancies and structural changes through to research activities, planned integration and management. 60 per cent of the contributions made a positive assessment, with only ten per cent of coverage negative.

This was made possible through the meticulous planning of communication activities, setting up and expanding a constantly updated information platform for the communication experts, close contact with the communication departments in the planning phase in which the companies were still operating separately, and finally through a willingness to provide information and offer up-to-date information voluntarily to journalists with the maximum of transparency.

At DaimlerChrysler, the "PMI success stories" were published once a month in printed form so that all topics could be communicated accurately and fully, and over a period of two years copious amounts of information were generated within the company. This monthly report contained statements concerning each of the twelve clusters.

Nor were internal communications overlooked. As of day one, various events were held worldwide, the presentation at the New York stock exchange was transmitted live, and each employee received a small parcel in corporate colors containing a watch, a brochure entitled "One Company One Vision," and information about new corporate goals and the company itself. In other campaigns, 140,000 e-mails were sent, a personal letter from Jürgen Schrempp was sent to each employee on the German side, videos were provided, and a telephone interview with Jürgen Schrempp could be accessed by employees. Furthermore, a road show was organized at which the Board of Management members and the Chairman of the Board of Management informed in the individual plants locally about the current status of the merger.

The transfer of knowledge plays a particularly important role during the integration process. There had to be a guarantee that Daimler knowledge would come to Chrysler, and vice versa. This was achieved through an independent team, which called itself Global Sales and Marketing. The work began as early as the initial stage of the merger. In addition to formulation of the projects and organization of the meetings, its tasks included backup support in the identification and gathering of existing knowledge in the individual locations, as well as the establishment of benchmarks. This knowledge was then integrated into the PMI network already mentioned and was available to all those with access authorization.

In addition, numerous training sessions were held in a bid to highlight existing cultural differences and gain an understanding of the behavior of the other partner. It was especially important to recognize and understand the reactions of employees of the other new part of the company where there were particular cultural differences in terms of patterns of behavior.

Integration of the corporate cultures

Apart from the few cases in which a merger or acquisition can elicit unanimous long-term acceptance, or even enthusiasm, among managers and employees, even with a positive basic attitude such as that found with an acquisition or merger for growth it is by no means rare to see the sequence of phases set out below. Initial enthusiasm gives way to disillusionment as problems arise. In the case of an M&A activity where there is a need for rationalization from the outset, where major changes are involved the emotional process usually runs its course in three main phases:

Phase 1: shock and bemusement

Phase 2: suffering and

Phase 3: a willingness to find solutions.

It is apparent that this sequence corresponds to the normal pattern when serious problems of a general or personal nature occur. It is therefore understandable that such a sequence will also occur when there are far-reaching change management processes. Having acknowledged this, it is a case of management responding early and decisively.

In particular, when decisions about new structures and the associated staffing issues are taken relatively late, the existing lack of clarity causes a high degree of uncertainty and anxiety. This is because from the beginning, internal rivalry between the members of the two former companies arises in the form of competition for each individual newly created position. As a result, the future integration process is made more difficult – or even crucially impaired – right from the start.

Furthermore, there is the fact that the most highly qualified managers and employees from both companies do not want or have to expose themselves to this internal stress and competition. Therefore, they are most likely to apply to other companies and find themselves another job very quickly which meets their expectations. The process may be even easier. Headhunters recognize the problem and have a broad and lucrative field in which to recruit personnel. As a result, important knowledge is lost as managers and employees move to other jobs, while at the same time it is not just the level of qualifications and competence of the workforce that falls, but also the speed at which processes and structures are integrated.

The first thing that must be done is to form integration teams from both companies as quickly as possible. The inclusion of employees in the convergence process is an important measure for building trust. This is further strengthened if important decisions are disclosed and the reasons for them given, so that the process is made transparent. If the opinion formers from both companies play a role in these integration teams, they will be able to set and reinforce the integration message.

Efforts at integration will also be given a boost if well-directed incentives for active integration contributions are created in the particular sphere of influence of those affected, that is to say at their own place of work or in projects. This approach and behavior must not be either overestimated or underestimated in terms of its effect. It applies far less to the German mentality, for example, than it does to its American counterpart. A German will tend to see the negative aspects of change processes rather than developing positive aspects. Such cultural differences in attitude and behavior must, whatever happens, be taken into account in the control and shaping of an integration process.

Integration is therefore more than just harmonization – it is also an enriching experience.

In terms of the individual processes and players, this means that a cultural learning process involves a broadening of knowledge, which extends to values, attitudes and patterns of behavior.

At DaimlerChrysler, employees were informed about the amalgamation and integration at events and training sessions. These included seminars on the topics "Fit for DC," "Cross-Cultural Series" and "Global High Performing Teams." There were also exchange programs with children of staff in order to get to know each other's country and culture, and to make the parents more sensitive to and gain a better understanding of each other's culture by looking after the children of their counterparts.

Business transformation phase

In this the final phase of the PMI, the completed projects are handed over to line responsibility. Because of the different completion dates, this cannot be done simultaneously for each project.

At DaimlerChrysler, the business transformation phase centered on six main objectives. One of these was the transfer of the PMI results to line organization, while

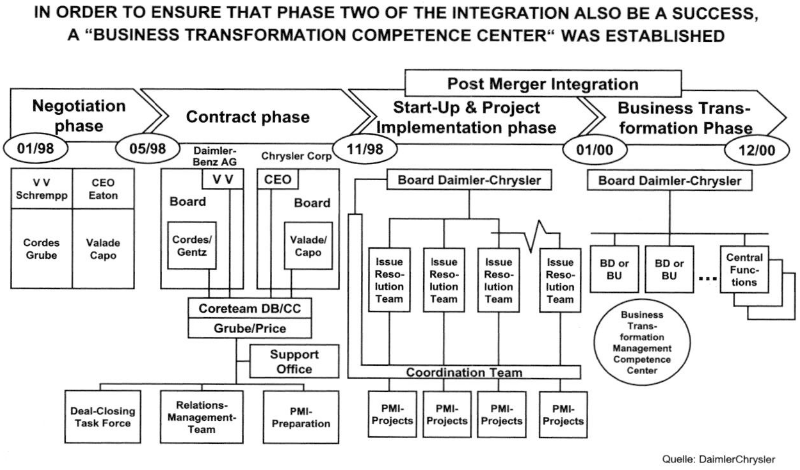

Figure 3.6
Reintegration of the PMI organization into the line organization in the DaimlerChrysler deal

others included the transfer of the main integration responsibility to the various businesses, business divisions and business units, integration of PMI responsibility into day-to-day business, and securing the same high level of process quality in operational day-to-day business as in the PMI implementation phase.

Another objective was the use of a small-scale coordination team – the "Business Transformation Competence Center" – to look after the transfer of the PMI organization to line organization (see Figure 3.6), where there are additional, and sometimes new, topics that have to be reviewed, pursued and resolved.

The knowledge acquired permanently and the experience gained must be safeguarded in a special knowledge database. In addition, it is the job of the coordination team to make this knowledge available to all those in the company who are actively involved in the transformation and reintegration into day-to-day business.

Further synergy improvements in the years ahead are of major importance in the business transformation phase. This issue was pursued and reconstructed very intensively at DaimlerChrysler in the implementation phase. When the PMI organization is disbanded and the pressure to increase synergies no longer applies as day-to-day business becomes more important, the opportunity to secure further synergies can soon be wasted.

Literature

A complete list of literature and references to this article can be obtained at Daimler-Chrysler's Corporate Development Department.

3.1.2 Transatlantic Mergers and Acquisitions: "Follow our customers"

Heinz Hermann Thiele

Due to multiple M&A steps the Group established a substantial footprint in the US commercial vehicle braking systems market. Key elements of this strategy have been focus on customer value added, creation of win-win potentials for all involved parties, respect for the differences in regional cultures and markets and highly motivated management teams on both sides of the Atlantic.

The Knorr-Bremse Group is the world's leading manufacturer of braking systems for commercial vehicles and rail vehicles. Knorr-Bremse has also established itself in the rail vehicle on-board systems segment and in the market for platform screen doors. In the commercial vehicle sector, vibration dampers for diesel engines are another field in which Knorr-Bremse has also attained worldwide leadership through it's brand Hasse & Wrede.

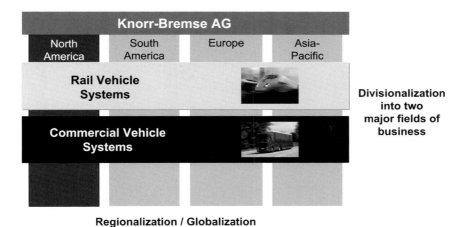

Figure 3.7 Matrix-structure of Knorr-Bremse Group

The regional structure of the Knorr-Bremse Group is based on the four major regions Europe, North America, South America and Asia-Pacific, each of which exerts a strong influence on the development of the Group's strategy (Figure 3.7). This organizational structure is designed to provide our customers tailor-made products and services for their regional market. We adopt therefore our product platforms to the specific technical customer and market requirements. Due to our global footprint we offer our customers, who operate on a regional basis, at the same time the benefits from globally tried-and-tested best in class systems and components. In addition to this technical localization of our products we design the full value chain, like sales, aftermarket, brand management and other functions with respect to the specific needs of individual markets.

Knorr-Bremse's business model and corporate strategy

Knorr-Bremse's business model relies on pillars like entrepreneurship, technology leadership combined with tight cost management, clear customer focus over the total product lifecycle including the service period and careful brand management. To address the aggressive growth targets of the group and to keep pace with the consolidation process on our customer side, the Knorr-Bremse Group requires a balanced mix of internal and external growth projects. As a consequence Mergers & Acquisitions have been for years a cornerstone of our corporate development. In the last decade we closed more than 30 deals.

In 2004 Knorr-Bremse closed several transactions. On the commercial vehicle sector Bendix, a 100% US affiliate of Knorr-Bremse, and Dana Corporation established a joint venture company, Bendix-Spicer Foundation Brake LLC, based in Elyria, OH. Bendix holds a majority stake and is responsible for operational management. This new joint venture marked the entry of Bendix and Knorr-Bremse into the conventional drum brake market whereas Knorr-Bremse has gained a leading position in disc

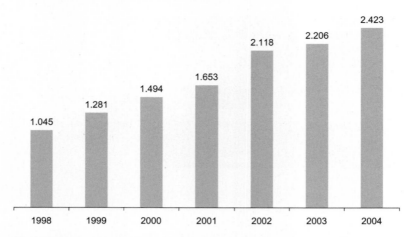

Figure 3.8 Turnover development Knorr-Bremse Group (in EUR millions)

brakes for trucks which has recently become the dominant technology in Europe. This deal will be discussed in more detail below. Other expansions on the truck brake side were the purchase of a controlling stake in a Spanish company and the formation of two joint ventures, one in China and one in India. On the rail brake side, a JV in Poland and two acquisitions were added.

In practice, the Knorr-Bremse Group is now well established on all major markets in the world, with own subsidiaries or majority owned joint ventures. The group has achieved a double digit CAGR and doubled the consolidated turnover in a 5 year timeframe (Figure 3.8).

Establishing a substantial transatlantic footprint in multiple steps

Overview

In our experience establishing a successful transatlantic footprint in North America requires a long-term strategic vision, persistence and sometimes a great deal of patience. It took twenty-five years of detailed corporate strategy, planning and execution in terms of laying the necessary groundwork and consistently pursuing the target step by step, to establish Knorr-Bremse's significant presence in both the North American rail and truck markets. This article focuses on the development of our US truck business through our acquisition of Bendix Commercial Vehicle Systems LLC, a process which has two decades of history, and which recently culminated in the formation of Bendix Spicer Foundation Brake LLC between Bendix and Dana.

This chapter describes the strategic rationale for Knorr-Bremse's entry into the North American commercial vehicle market and the milestones on the way to establish partnerships with existing American-based businesses. The chapter also addresses the lessons learned and identifies several critical success factors for creating and maintaining a viable transatlantic business activity. Knorr-Bremse's globalization has greatly enhanced its ability to serve its regional and global OEM customers, leveraging on global technological and worldwide applications and manufacturing capabilities.

The strategic landscape: Technology, market and customer trends in the US

Starting in the early 1980s, major steps of the transatlantic development of the commercial vehicle market have been the acquisition by Daimler-Benz of Freightliner Corporation, the acquisition of Mack in the US by the Renault – later Volvo – group and the acquisition by the US-based Paccar group of DAF in Europe (Figure 3.9). The Knorr-Bremse group also recognized the necessity for planning its own entry into the North American market to follow closely its customers.

Although the North American medium-and heavy duty vehicle market is approximately similar in size to the European market, the braking systems required on those vehicles are distinctly different, driven by regulatory requirements unique to each market, as well as end users' requirements and market practices.

One of the most significant technological drivers for the creation of a transatlantic presence among heavy-duty braking systems suppliers was the emerging opportunities in North America for antilock braking systems (ABS). ABS is an electronic system that monitors vehicle wheel speed and modulates braking forces in order to reduce or prevent wheel lockup. Vehicle stability and steering during braking on slippery surfaces or during emergency stops is dramatically enhanced. The first North American attempt for ABS regulation in the late 1970's failed, but the market acceptance was slowly evolving through the 1980s and early 1990s, creating opportunities for European suppliers. ABS had already begun to be widely installed on European heavy trucks by the 1980's.

Due to the huge research and development costs of these new ABS systems and the high manufacturing costs of the electronic components, major heavy-vehicle braking suppliers began forming transatlantic alliances to position themselves to support the developing market for ABS in North America. In the mid 1980s four companies

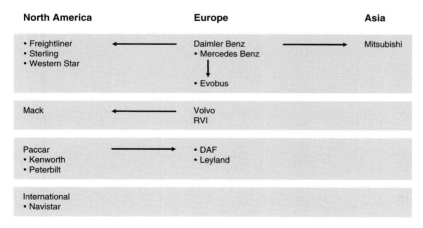

Figure 3.9 Consolidation of the global OE-Truck market

merged and pooled their resources to provide ABS for trucks and trailers, Midland Inc. (US), Graubremse (Germany), Berg and the air brakes controls division of Lucas Girling (UK), forming Midland-Grau. In 1990, German-based WABCO formed a North American joint venture with Rockwell Automotive. Then, in 1995, Robert Bosch formed an alliance with Eaton Corporation for the distribution of ABS products in North America. In 1997, ABS was finally mandated for all new heavy trucks made in the U.S.

The first step: Knorr-Bremse's initial joint venture partnership

At that time, Knorr-Bremse, which lacked a North American presence in commercial vehicles, developed its strategy for a global footprint. Discussions with AlliedSignal Automotive to form a transatlantic alliance or partnership in commercial vehicle braking were intensified in 1989. The initial intent was to acquire the global Bendix truck air brake business from AlliedSignal Automotive. However, due to strength and scope of the Bendix air brake business in North America, AlliedSignal was not willing to sell. On the other hand, the Bendix air brake business was small and weak in Europe due to its limited product and market scope, and AlliedSignal recognized that the business was in need of revitalization. Merger discussions continued off and on for a number of years. After each party carefully examined its relative strengths and weaknesses in Europe and North America, they finally reached agreement in 1993 on the creation of a global joint venture where AlliedSignal would in essence retain the majority of the shares and the business lead in North America and Knorr-Bremse would retain the majority of the shares and the business lead in Europe. This joint venture was a critical step for Knorr-Bremse to establish its North American presence in the commercial vehicle braking market.

Knorr-Bremse and AlliedSignal formed a partnership, named AlliedSignal Truck Brake Systems Company (ASTBS), in which Knorr-Bremse purchased a 35% interest for cash. AlliedSignal contributed its North American Bendix truck air brake business for a 65% controlling interest. As an additional inducement to obtain this North American foothold, Knorr-Bremse agreed to combine its well-established European truck air brake business with AlliedSignal's suffering European truck brake business. The two European businesses were contributed to a new entity known as Knorr-Bremse Systeme für Nutzfahrzeuge GmbH (KB SfN). Knorr-Bremse held a control-

	Knorr-Bremse	Allied Signal
US Market	35%	65%
	mirrored	
Europe Market	65%	35%
Latin America Market	65%	35%

Figure 3.10 Initial mirrored JV architecture and equity shares (in %)

ling 65% interest in KB SfN and AlliedSignal held a 35% interest. Two years later, in 1995, Knorr-Bremse and AlliedSignal combined their respective Brazilian truck brake businesses to form a truck brake Joint Venture in Brazil, with Knorr-Bremse holding the controlling 65% interest, and AlliedSignal holding 35% (Figure 3.10).

The second step: Further consolidation and taking full ownership control

Further consolidation occurred in 1999, when Robert Bosch GmbH contributed their European truck air brake business to KB SfN. This move did not affect the joint venture structure in North America and Brazil. In Europe, however, Knorr-Bremse's interest in KB SfN was reduced to 60%, while Robert Bosch GmbH and AlliedSignal each held a 20% interest in KB SfN.

Knorr-Bremse, Robert Bosch and AlliedSignal at this point had most of the fundamental pieces necessary to serve global truck brake customers. The product range was unmatched and, even more important, with the newly regulated ABS in the United States, the Knorr-Bremse, Bendix and Bosch combination was well-positioned to exploit this growing North America market opportunity.

In theory, ASTBS in North America and KB SfN in Europe, had established a platform for sharing technology and supporting global customers. However, the fact remained that the North American and the European entities were separate businesses, with different management priorities and different controlling share owners, and each entity retained and developed its own strategic priorities and financial metrics. Further both parties pursued different management cultures and practices in their own region. A further structural imbalance between the North American and the European perspectives came from the fact that the braking technology developed rather rapidly in Europe during that time. Electronic braking systems (EBS) gained market share from ABS systems and the pneumatic disc brake won over the conventional drum brake. All of these developments required tremendous development costs with no near term market acceptance on the North American market.

On the other side the market has meanwhile developed to a stage where the three big groups of truck manufacturers have supplied more than 70% of the North American demand and more than 50% of the European demand. Knorr-Bremse has therefore been convinced from the outstart that the technology which is available in Europe will also be adopted in North America. The consequence was obvious, there was no longer any justification for a distinction between the North American and the European side of the truck brake supplier. The mirrored majorities in Europe and North America were no longer in line with the market needs. The market required one uniform worldwide technical and management leadership.

Things started moving when, in 2000, AlliedSignal and Honeywell merged to form Honeywell International Inc., and after subsequent management changes and strategic repositioning at Honeywell, Knorr-Bremse was finally able to make a deal with Honeywell to assume of Honeywell's JV interests. In North America Knorr-Bremse finally held 100% ownership in the North American business, now known as Bendix Commercial Vehicle Systems LLC and was now able to offer the global solutions with local adaptations which the internationally active customer needed.

Lessons learned from the first steps of forming a global joint venture

The joint venture partners came to realize that inherent conflicts existed in the regional joint venture structure with mirrored regional majorities. The financial, operational and strategic focus of the North American truck brake business were driven by Honeywell, a publicly held, Fortune 100 conglomerate with a wide range of activities not only in automotive businesses, but also in aerospace, engineered materials, sensing and controls, and numerous other businesses. The truck brake operation was one of the many businesses within their portfolio. By contrast, Knorr-Bremse, a privately held company focused on braking systems, "lives and dies" on brakes and was willing to trade off short-term financial performance against the long-term market and technological perspectives.

Market differences also challenged the effectiveness of the joint venture structure. Unlike the more OEM-centred market in Europe, where system and component suppliers were OEMs typically set technological targets or negotiate technical advancements with their suppliers, the North American market was very much oriented towards strong national fleets and other end users which utilize their substantial buying power to specify preferred systems such as braking systems. The result of this North American structure are value based products and solutions, where the value is typically much more directly determined by the fleets and the other end users than under the typical European scenario. Whatever the primary driver of innovation may be, it has been not only Knorr-Bremse's experience that in the course of time superior technology will prevail with those sometimes substantial variations, however, as the local market demands.

Strategic background for the further steps to expand the North American footprint

Historically, air brake control systems were the main focus of the Bendix brake business in North America and the Knorr-Bremse SfN brake business in Europe. Foundation brakes, such as drum brakes or disc brakes, were the focus of other industry players.

In the 1980's, Knorr-Bremse recognized the distinct advantages for commercial vehicles that air disc brakes had over air drum brakes. In the 1990's Knorr-Bremse introduced its own design of an air disc brake for the European market. The benefits of this advanced design were soon recognized by European truck OEMs, and by the mid 1990's, Knorr-Bremse was at the forefront of the conversion of virtually the entire European foundation brake market to air disc brakes. In fact, Knorr-Bremse had become Europe's leading supplier of air disc brakes.

After successfully launching the air disc brake in Europe in 1996, it was a strategic imperative for Knorr-Bremse to expand this product offering to the North American market. This growth was needed in order to recuperate the enormous investment in product research, development and design as well as to reduce cost in the manufacturing process and to leverage volumes on a global basis. In order to successfully penetrate the North American market, Bendix needed to establish a value proposition addressed to the needs of the North American market. Because the fleet customers demand a demonstrated value for new products and technologies, Bendix focused on the "cost per mile" of vehicle operation utilizing the air disc brake compared to the widely used S-cam drum brake. Knorr-Bremse recognized that the conversion of the North American market from S-cam drum brakes to air disc brakes would be a more gradual process spread over many years. In order to manage the market transition effectively, the company needed to be in the foundation brake business. Developing an alliance or partnership with an established axle manufacturer was the desireable move which would facilitate fitting new air disc brakes onto the axle and to offer an optimized function between the product systems brake control, foundation brake and axle. The product optimization between foundation brake and axle is commonly referred to as "the wheel end solution."

The third step: Forming the joint venture with Dana

Beginning in the mid-1990's, Bendix and Knorr-Bremse held periodic discussions with Dana Corporation to form a cooperation in the foundation brake and wheel end business. Due to the already existing complexity of the Knorr-Bendix-Honeywell joint venture at this time, no acceptable transaction structure was ever found at that stage. However, once Bendix had become a wholly owned unit of Knorr-Bremse in 2002, Knorr-Bremse and Bendix reinstituted discussions with Dana concerning a potential wheel-end cooperation. The discussions finally concluded with the formation of Bendix Spicer Foundation Brake LLC, a new entity formed to conduct the wheel-end businesses of Bendix and Dana. Bendix Spicer Foundation Brake became operational July 1, 2004.

Bendix Spicer Foundation Brake combines Bendix's air disc brake, slack adjusters, brake actuators and other wheel end products with Dana's established S-cam and foundation brakes business. This move formed an unmatched product portfolio serving US and global customers.

Lessons learned

Knorr-Bremse learned numerous, valuable lessons from its experiences in creating its North American footprint.

Respect for regional culture

The overall guiding principle for Knorr-Bremse is the respect for the regional culture and the awareness of local specifics. The cultural considerations in a German-American partnership should be carefully addressed. At all times it was recognized by Knorr-Bremse that the vast differences in the market between North America and Europe required different strategic approaches, management styles and different market focus. Headquarters always focused on those cultural and market specifics and gave strong support for local management and leadership.

Leveraging the power of local management and brands

In acquiring Bendix, Knorr-Bremse took steps to ensure that existing Bendix management team stayed in place at Bendix and continued to operate the North American business and to bring the specific observations and demands forward which are crucial for their success. On the other hand, the Bendix management team recognized the benefits of a global approach to the globally active customer and to rely on a globally proven technology base. It has long been Knorr-Bremse's operating philosophy to empower local managers to run local businesses and to strengthen the local brand to explore the full customer potential in the regional market. Strong support of local leadership and brand management is a unique strength of Knorr-Bremse's global business. For example, during post-closing integration activities, global teams consisting of North American Bendix personnel and Knorr European personnel were formed to create integration teams, plans and strategies. Knorr-Bremse was careful to assure the Bendix management team that the North American Bendix business would continue to be run by Americans, not through Germany and at the same time strategic issues were commonly developed by the two management boards.

It is critical in any German-American partnership or any transaction or alliance where cooperation is essential for success, that each party is empowered and enabled to have its needs and objectives raised and considered. Many of the processes developed during the Bendix post-merger integration with Knorr-Bremse were refined and implemented during the Bendix-Dana joint venture negotiations and post-merger integrations.

When establishing transatlantic partnerships, each party must understand not only its own, but also, or maybe even more important, the other party's economic and strategic interests in the transaction.

Real win-win counts

A clear understanding of each party's strategic and financial needs in entering into the transaction is important. This will enable the parties to create a transaction structure that minimizes partnership conflict while maximizing the overall benefits to each party. Only a real win-win situation will bring the different interests of the parties together. Convergent interests are a prerequisite for a successful joint entity.

When establishing its joint venture with Dana, Bendix and Knorr-Bremse were careful to ensure that the financial and strategic objectives of all parties were adequately addressed in the transaction structure. From the Bendix point of view, it was essential that Bendix have the ability to offer customers a complete wheel end solution, having both air disc brake and S-cam brake and related components. Because the foundation brakes are mounted on the vehicle's axles, a strong alliance with a well established axle producer was an important ingredient in establishing Bendix Spicer Foundation Brake LLC.

From Dana's perspective, its core competency and strategic focus are in axle technologies. Rather than investing heavily in development of next generation foundation brakes, Dana chose to partner with a brake supplier and keep its focus on axles. However, Dana needed a strong alliance with a disc brake specialist in order to offer complete solutions to the customers as they move on to apply the upcoming brake technology. Since there will be an extended period of transistion from drum to disc brakes, it made sense for Dana and Bendix to combine their conventional drum brake and the upcoming disc brake competencies in a joint venture under the operational control of the brake specialist Bendix.

Guiding behavioural considerations

When Knorr-Bremse, Bendix and Dana were negotiating their wheel end business joint venture, they formed teams of working-level personnel that were responsible for conducting due diligence as well as developing and implementing post-merger integration planning. Since working-level teams were generally not familiar with the due diligence process, the Knorr-Bremse, Bendix and Dana corporate development and legal teams played an important role in guiding the working-level teams through this process. This upfront work proved to be a valuable investment, making the post-closing integration activities work more smoothly.

The parties developed the following guiding principles to build working level relationships centred on trust and respect between the parties. These principles included:

- *Transparency in all actions:* Building trusting and respectful working relationships requires that each party gets access to all necessary and appropriate information from the other party in order to conduct a thorough valuation, due diligence and to formulate practical and efficient PMI plans, for example, each party was pre-informed about the other party's reason why for forming the JV as presented in the respective board discussions.

- *Common goals, objectives and* vision: Creating a common vision statement for the joint venture and a common set of goals for each team will ensure alignment at all levels of the organization involved in the transaction.

- *No added bureaucracy:* Give clear guidance to PMI teams that new layers of management and resources will not be added to the existing combined businesses. Rather, efficiencies from the combined operations must be maintained.

- *Customer value add and seamless customer transition:* Always focus on the customer value add as the motivation of the deal and ensure no disruption to business or service results from the post-merger integration and transition activities. For example, the integration of foundation brake and axle to the wheel end solution and the coordination in terms of functionality with the brake control formed an unmatched sytem product offering for our customers.

- *Structure driven by business plan assumptions:* The joint venture transaction is built on a value creating business plan model which drives the financial/economic objectives of each party. All PMI teams must create transition plans that are in alignment with the deal's business plan assumptions to ensure both parties obtain the expected benefits of the deal.

Once Knorr-Bremse had completed the Bendix acquisition, the global truck brake group created a group vision shared by and pursued by both Knorr-Bremse and Bendix. Management review structures were established and global coordination team meetings in order to identify opportunities for technological or manufacturing synergies as well as customer and marketing opportunities.

Continuous learning

Today, successful businesses embrace and nurture an environment of continuous learning. Recognizing the cultural differences between European and American business is essential for successful PMI in transatlantic transactions. Identifying cultural differences through learning and bridging cultural gaps are essential steps for developing strong working relationships based on mutual trust and respect. These same principles can be applied even to transactions within the same continent where corporate cultures are often different. These principles were utilized by the Bendix and Knorr-Bremse teams when developing integration plans with the Dana teams for Bendix Spicer Foundation Brake LLC.

Recognize global impact

Finally, in a global environment, even regional transactions among companies headquartered in the same geographic area can have global implications. As a result, it is important to recognize the potential global consequences of a transaction. As well it is necessary at an early stage to form global teams to review and address those issues of global impact to minimize any risk that the parties are surprised down the road by unexpected issues. By giving early consideration to potentially global issues, new opportunities may be found for both parties to expand the beneficial scope of the originally envisioned transaction. When forming Bendix Spicer Foundation Brake LLC, Knorr-Bremse, Bendix and Dana were able to find broader areas of potential, global cooperation and mutual benefit.

Summary

Through strategic focus, perseverance and continuous learning, Knorr-Bremse has successfully expanded from a high technology, European focused braking system supplier to the leading air braking system and air foundation brake supplier in most of the global markets that it serves. Due to the multiple M&A steps Knorr-Bremse established a substantial footprint and extended significantly market presence and turnover in the US.

The mutual respect of regional different cultures, a cooperative working and management relationship as well as a highly motivated management team on both sides of the Atlantic have been the groundwork for this strategy. Its success in developing and implementing transatlantic partnerships and alliances as well as in practicing first class M&A and PMI skills have no doubt made an additional substantial contribution to the posture which Knorr-Bremse has achieved in the worldwide truck brake business.

Acknowledgment

The author would like to thank Dr. Thorsten Feix, Senior Vice President of Corporate Development of Knorr-Bremse AG and the Bendix and Bendix-Spicer management team.

3.2 Banking & Finance

3.2.1 Growing in the U.S. – Review of Deutsche Bank's M&A Strategy in North America

Axel Wieandt and Rafael Moral y Santiago[1]

Since the end of the last decade Deutsche Bank AG ("Deutsche") has transformed itself from an essentially European commercial and retail bank into a truly global modern universal bank with well established leadership positions in its client-focused Corporate and Investment Banking (CIB) and Private Clients and Asset Management (PCAM) divisions. This article reviews how Deutsche's North American M&A strategy involving multiple transactions contributed to continuous progress in the Americas and, consequently, to the overall transformation of the Group.

Strategic context at the end of the 1990s

Structural changes in the financial services industry

Deutsche as a major financial institution was faced with major challenges and opportunities in the late 1990s as the financial services industry worldwide underwent significant structural change. The significance of these trends was demonstrated as they continued through phases of international crises in the capital markets and beyond.

Globalization: Many businesses, especially those closely related to the capital markets were becoming increasingly global alongside clients, talent and competition. Regional home markets still accounted for the greater part of revenues at even the most global of institutions, but most firms found that leading market positions in the more global business areas could only be achieved and sustained with a global platform and execution capabilities. Without such platforms, even strong home market positions would slowly erode.

Consolidation: Most consolidation in the 1990s was domestic, the pace of which was similar in the U.S. and the E.U.: The number of financial institutions dropped by almost 40% between 1990 and 2002 and by more than a fifth between 1995 and 2002. Domestic consolidation in Japan also accelerated. Nevertheless, there was clearly some sizeable cross-border consolidation. Examples included HSBC (e.g. acquisition of Republic Bank of New York), Allianz (e.g. acquisition of PIMCO), and UBS (e.g. acquisition of Warburg). In addition to transatlantic transactions, Europe exhibited some cross-border activity, primarily in regional "clusters" such as Scandinavia and Benelux.

---

[1] The authors present their personal views.

Trends in issuer businesses: On the issuer side of the capital markets, where financial institutions satisfy clients' financing, transaction and risk management needs, businesses were becoming essentially global. A pervasive trend towards increased *concentration* of business within the first tier of investment banks – particularly in sales and trading – was observable. Furthermore, with the general trend towards *disintermediation* further evolving, many financial services firms recognized that significant competitive advantage could be gained from an integration of corporate and investment banking services. In turn, the *ability to provide credit* was revived as a source of potential competitive advantage and was further supported by the growing credit default swap market. All firms competing in this space engaged in relentless *innovation* of new products and services.

Trends in investor businesses: On the investor side, where financial institutions provide institutional and private investors with access to the capital markets in the form of investment opportunities, banking and insurance services, a much more regional business logic persisted with far more fragmented markets other than in institutional asset management and high end private banking. Asset management, life assurance and private banking businesses saw new opportunities as *pension reform, equification* and the formation of an *affluent population/segment* increased demand for new products. Simultaneously, most financial services providers moved to *multi-channel strategies* and the introduction of *third party products* better to match individual client needs.

The U.S. "imperative"

It was increasingly apparent that a strong presence in the U.S. was a strategic imperative for global universal banks. By the end of the 1990s, the U.S. market had undergone significant deregulation and liberalization. The profitability of the U.S. banking system increased markedly after 1991. Over the 1988-2001 period, the profitability of U.S. banks (as measured by after-tax return on assets) was consistently and significantly higher than that of E.U. banks. The U.S. was, and remains, the world's largest, most sophisticated and innovative capital market – home to many of the world's leading financial institutions and, in turn, attracting top industry talent. Thinking "global" requires "thinking U.S." with North America accounting for about one third of global financial services' revenue pools. It exhibits strong fundamental drivers of industry profitability such as high volumes of cross border investment activity and robust economic growth, partly fuelled by attractive demographics. Compared to other developed markets, its level of industry consolidation remains relatively low in several financial sectors.

Deutsche in 1998

In the mid 1990s Deutsche had been a broadly based *universal bank* and the creation of a global investment banking franchise was in its early stages. Deutsche's earnings still relied heavily on its German home market despite the existence of significant UK, Italian and Spanish presences. As part of Deutsche's Group Strategic Planning Process in 1998, a Group-wide portfolio assessment was undertaken and the following conclusions drawn:

1. Deutsche as a universal bank with a wide range of products had to define its portfolio of activities more clearly and focus on areas where it could add value for both shareholders and clients in the context of ongoing trends that were shaping the competitive landscape.

2. A new *"dual focus" strategy* was formulated. The basis of this strategy was to enable the Group to focus on those customer and product sectors in which it could become a leader and would have the potential to increase shareholder value while taking into account the different degrees of globalization to which the businesses were exposed. Important elements of Deutsche's "dual focus" strategy were the expansion of its Global Corporates and Institutions ("GCI") and Asset Management Divisions as well as its Private Banking business globally.

In line with the "dual focus" strategy the overall organizational structure of Deutsche underwent significant *"divisionalization"* in 1998 to enhance client focus, increase accountability, clarify responsibility, enable the creation of global/European platforms and to ensure a consistent strategy and execution.

It further became clear that, based on the planned growth rates, achieving GCI's goal of becoming one of the top five investment banks in the world would be a difficult task through organic growth alone. In terms of the competition, American investment banks were increasingly gaining market share both in the U.S. and in Deutsche's European home markets.

North American M&A strategy in three phases

Deutsche recognized that if it were to achieve its aspirations of being a formidable transatlantic force in investment banking and other global areas, there was a need to act and gain ground in North America in particular. A comprehensive M&A strategy was thus seen as a necessary condition to successfully strengthening its presence in this region. This strategy would comprise three phases (see figure 1): The first phase would consist of substantially *expanding Deutsche's U.S. presence* in its core businesses with global ambitions. The second phase would center on *re-focusing the enlarged business portfolio*. In the third phase Deutsche would complement the organic growth efforts of its increased and optimized U.S. platform with suitable *"add-on" acquisitions* to leverage further its competitive advantages, exploit new product and customer segment opportunities and enter potentially attractive white spots (Figure 3.11).

Phase one – Expansion

Phase one commenced with a detailed *screening* exercise of potential GCI targets involving quantitative (historical and forecasted financial performance analyses including synergies, discounted cash flow analyses, sum of the parts and market valuations, share price performance) and qualitative (strategic fit, management evaluation, business mix complementarity) factors. *Bankers Trust* scored highly and as a potential acquisition target promised to support Deutsche's "dual focus" strategy and accelerate the growth of the wholesale/global finance platform.

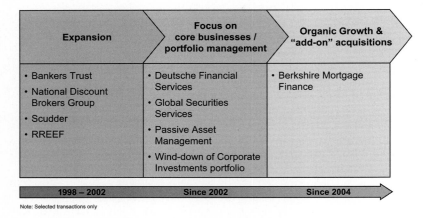

Note: Selected transactions only

Figure 3.11 North American M&A strategy in three phases

The acquisition of Bankers Trust's involved a purchase price of approximately USD 9.2 billion and was announced in November 1998. There was substantial *regional and product complementarity* between the two banks. The resulting combined organization would be a leading player with powerful transatlantic Global Markets and Global Equities platforms. Deutsche would gain strong M&A capabilities in selected industry groups. In addition, the combined organization would rank forth in the world in the profitable and stable Asset Management and Global Custody businesses with assets under management of USD 600 billion and USD 4 billion in custody assets. Finally, Deutsche would attain a leading global private banking franchise with a strong foothold in North America. The acquisition would provide an opportunity to leverage Bankers Trust's broad product platform and U.S. client base with Deutsche's global reach and relationships across all product categories.

Following the signing of the merger agreement, a *two-phased integration process* was established. This involved an *integration planning phase* until closing and a subsequent *integration/implementation phase*. Critical factors for the successful integration included the full achievement of deal synergies, communication to investors and analysts, the swift merging of businesses, keeping employees and customers informed in order to build confidence in the merger and monitoring results.

Initially, the market reacted with skepticism to the deal announcement. But Deutsche's share price recovered and appreciated by approximately 40% during the five months subsequent to reaching a low in April 1999. Deutsche's global peer group benchmark decreased by 7% in the same period.

In 2000 Deutsche further strengthened its Global Equities capabilities through the acquisition of National Discount Brokers Group ("NDB"), an S&P 600 Small Cap Index company which, among other things, was a market maker in over 4,000 NASDAQ and other OTC securities. The total purchase price was approximately USD 1.0 billion. For Deutsche, the transaction marked an important step toward enhancing its global equities capabilities: Upon the successful completion of the acquisition, Deutsche would be one of the leading NASDAQ market makers.[1]

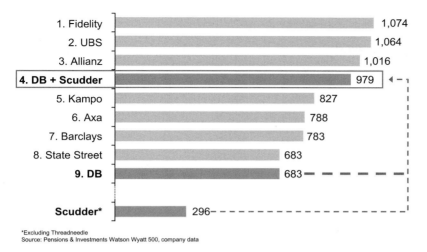

*Excluding Threadneedle
Source: Pensions & Investments Watson Wyatt 500, company data

Figure 3.12 Assets under management (end of 2000, in USD bn)

Following the Bankers Trust and RREEF acquisitions, at the beginning of 2001 Deutsche's earnings contribution had increasingly shifted to the capital markets sensitive global wholesale/global finance platform and especially GCI. With the other businesses trailing somewhat behind, Deutsche's strategy needed to aim at:

- *Profitably growing all businesses* – organically and through acquisitions – with the goal of reaching and sustaining leading global market positions in its two newly aligned client-focused Groups: *Corporate and Investment Banking (CIB)* and *Private Clients and Asset Management (PCAM)*; and

- Increasing the proportion of revenues attributable to the PCAM Group and *balancing Deutsche's earnings mix.*

Against this background and from a position of strength, Deutsche continued on the acquisition trail. The *Scudder/Herold* transaction, announced in September 2001, represented a logical step in this regard: Deutsche reached agreement with Zurich Financial Services ("Zurich") on the purchase of U.S. asset manager Scudder and of asset management companies in Germany and Italy for the equivalent of USD 2.5 billion. In return, Deutsche sold its Deutscher Herold insurance arm and its insurance activities in Spain, Italy and Portugal to Zurich.

Initially, Zurich had planned to sell only a minority stake in Scudder. But a minority interest would have failed to provide Deutsche with the necessary control to integrate Scudder. Deutsche set about structuring an *"asset swap"* whereby Zurich's longer-term interest in Deutsche's insurance arm could be satisfied alongside Deutsche's desire fully to integrate Scudder. The resulting deal offered the following key strategic benefits to Deutsche:

---

[1] In September 2001 Deutsche sold NDB's online brokerage business ("NDB.com") to Ameritrade Holding Corp. for approximately USD 154 million after deciding that NDB.com no longer constituted a core business of Deutsche.

- The *Scudder acquisition* significantly strengthened Deutsche's asset management business making it the world's forth largest player (as measured by assets under management; see Figure 3.12) with a leading U.S. franchise thereby contributing to a more balanced revenue and earnings mix for the Group. Additionally, Deutsche targeted sizeable cost synergies from integrating Scudder into its broader asset management platform.

- The *sale of Deutscher Herold* allowed Deutsche to increase the focus on its strategic core businesses as the production of insurance services was no longer regarded a core activity. A cooperation agreement with Zurich ensured that Deutsche would continue to offer its clients a broad spectrum of sophisticated insurance products following the deal.

The transaction's timing was challenging, with the envisaged acquisition being publicly announced two days after the terrorist attacks on September 11, 2001. Yet these tragic events did not negatively affect the fundamental transaction logic; on the contrary – with the Scudder acquisition Deutsche underlined its commitment to the U.S. market.

The capital markets' reaction to the Scudder/Herold transaction was positive: stock markets welcomed the deal, with Deutsche's share price appreciating by 5.1% (vs. DAX at 1.3%) post announcement and by 13.4% (vs. DAX at 6.6%) after disclosing the transaction terms. *Institutional Investor* named this complex international transaction *"Deal of the Year"* for 2001.

Deutsche's commitment to the U.S. was further emphasized in October 2001 when its stock was listed on the *New York Stock Exchange* and *U.S. GAAP* accounting standards were adopted.

In March 2002, i.e. about one month before completing the Scudder acquisition, Deutsche announced that it had agreed to purchase RoPro U.S. Holding, a holding company for the real estate investment manager RREEF for approximately USD 501 million. RREEF was a leading U.S.-based real estate investment manager with USD 16.2 billion in assets under management as of December 31, 2001. The acquisition of RREEF constituted another important step for PCAM towards its strategic goal of becoming a leading provider of investment offerings worldwide encompassing both traditional asset management products alongside real estate and other "alternative" asset classes. It would complete Deutsche's U.S. real estate investment management product offering and strengthen its position as a global asset manager by taking Deutsche to the number one position in combined real estate property and real estate equity securities globally with more than USD 36 billion in assets under management.

Phase two – Focus on core businesses/portfolio management

The year 2002 confronted Deutsche – and the entire financial industry – with external challenges as the difficult world economic environment depressed markets. A series of financial scandals shook investor confidence and the threat of terrorist attacks and possible military action caused ongoing uncertainty. Against this backdrop the lending environment continued to deteriorate.

In January 2002 Deutsche Bank aligned its top management structure to further enhance the execution of its strategy through the creation of a "Global Executive Committee" consisting of the members of the Group Board and the Global Business Heads. Three months later, Deutsche embarked on a medium-term program comprising four strategic initiatives aimed at raising the Bank's return on equity to a level comparable with its international peer group:

1. Focus on current earnings
2. Focus on core businesses
3. Improvement of capital and balance sheet management
4. Optimization of Private Clients and Asset Management Group Division

All four strategic initiatives were critical to the ongoing success of Deutsche's North American platform. The second initiative, Group-wide *focus on core businesses*, had particular implications for Deutsche's M&A strategy in the region. Achieving the goal of raising the return on equity involved focused investments in core businesses which, in turn, required the freeing-up of scarce resources utilized elsewhere including capital supporting and allocated against non-core businesses – phase two, the optimization of the enlarged U.S. business portfolio, became paramount.

To be regarded "core" a business had to be either a major value creating businesses with sustainable market positions in its chosen market or capable of achieving such positions. As a result of a global portfolio review several businesses failing to meet these criteria were identified. Accordingly, detailed plans were developed to ensure value maximizing exit strategies.

- In September 2002 Deutsche announced the sale of its U.S.-based Deutsche Financial Services' ("DFS") *commercial inventory financing* businesses to GE Commercial Finance for approximately USD 2.9 billion (including purchase price and funding repayment).

- Also in September 2002 Deutsche announced that it had entered into exclusive discussions with State Street Corporation in relation to the sale of substantial parts of Deutsche's *Global Securities Services* business including its domestic custody and securities clearing in the U.S. The purchase price was USD 1.5 billion subject to adjustments.

- Later that month Deutsche confirmed that it was planning to sell its global *Passive Asset Management* business to Northern Trust Corporation following the decision to concentrate all efforts on active asset management. Notwithstanding total assets under management of approximately USD 120 billion, the business was contributing less than 2% of Deutsche Asset Management's revenues and was sold for an initial payment of about USD 100 million and further payments over subsequent months.

- In November 2002 Deutsche announced that it had entered into a definitive agreement for the sale of DFS's *consumer financing businesses* to E*TRADE Bank for approximately USD 100 million plus repayment of debt.

Continuing the focus of resources on core businesses, Deutsche decided to wind down its EUR 27 billion *Corporate Investments'* ("CI") asset portfolio at the end of 2002.

At that time, CI's asset portfolio, comprising industrial holdings and alternative assets such as private equity and real estate holdings, represented 8% of the firm's risk-weighted assets and attracted an allocation of 21% of the Deutsche's average active equity.[1] Further, the exposure had contributed a significant element of earnings volatility.

As part of this wind-down, in February 2003 Deutsche announced the sale of its *late-stage private equity portfolio* through a management buy-out. The transaction was an important step in reducing Deutsche's exposure to private equity and represented the largest secondary sale of a private equity portfolio to that date. The portfolio (in which Deutsche retained a 20% interest) primarily comprised investments in the U.S. and Europe and was priced at EUR 1.5 billion. Subsequent Americas-related CI transactions included two divestments of private equity funds portfolios, the sale of asset backed securities to institutional investors, the securitisation of a private equity funds portfolio and the sale of 21 limited partnership interests in private equity funds.

Phase three – Organic growth complemented with strategic "add-on" acquisitions

By the end of 2003 Deutsche had successfully delivered on its strategic initiatives resulting in an underlying pre-tax return on equity of 13%. This did not go unnoticed – in 2003, Deutsche was named *"Bank of the Year"* by the industry publication International Financing Review, which referred, in glowing terms, to Deutsche's transformation. Also, recovering stock markets and an underlying feeling that corporates had started to clean up their balance sheets, contributed to a general mood swing in the capital markets. With a more positive outlook for the global economy there were undoubtedly countless opportunities for major financial institutions such as Deutsche.

The next phase of Deutsche's transformation strategy – which remains ongoing – focused on generating *profitable growth* with the financial goal of achieving a sustainable pre-tax return on average active equity before restructuring charges of 25% in 2005. This is being accomplished primarily through organic growth across all of Deutsche's chosen businesses and regions. For Deutsche in North America this means that its third M&A phase is centered on supporting the organic built-out of its core businesses with suitable "add-on" acquisitions.

In line with this commitment to invest in profitable high growth areas, the acquisition of *Berkshire Mortgage Finance* ("Berkshire Mortgage") announced in August 2004 represented an opportunity further to expand Deutsche's successful Real Estate Debt Markets franchise. Deutsche would acquire substantially all of Berkshire Mortgage's origination and servicing assets thus giving Deutsche a leading position in an important and very attractive market. Deutsche was already a market leader in the commercial real estate debt market, with expertise in originating, financing, structuring, securitizing and trading commercial real estate debt. Berkshire Mortgage would advance Deutsche's existing capital market presence in all of these areas being one of the largest privately held commercial mortgage lenders in the U.S., specializing in financing for

---

[1] Average active equity represents the portion of adjusted average shareholders' equity that is allocated to a segment pursuant to Deutsche's capital allocation framework.

multifamily real estate. Uniting these complementary businesses further strengthened Deutsche's position as a dominant player in the commercial mortgage markets.

The Berkshire Mortgage transaction represents the first completed acquisition in the context of Deutsche's third strategic M&A phase in North America. The Group continuously monitors the market for further opportunities to complement its North American growth efforts with attractive "add-ons." However, as with the Berkshire Mortgage transaction, any future acquisition would have to meet four criteria in order to be considered a viable project:

1. The target must operate in product areas key to Deutsche's strategy.
2. The target's business must exhibit high growth and value creation prospects.
3. The transaction must be capable of achieving strict financial hurdles.
4. The target integration must follow demanding timetables.

Deutsche Bank North America today

In 2004 Deutsche confirmed the robustness of its world-leading Group divisions, CIB and PCAM, with formidable growth momentum and a diversified global platform. In the first quarter of 2005 CIB was the world's largest corporate and investment banking franchise as measured by underlying revenues from loan and investment banking products and sales and trading. In the same period, PCAM ranked third among Deutsche's global competitor group as measured by invested assets. With a pre-tax return on average active equity of 33% in the first quarter of 2005, the Group has underlined its commitment to deliver on its sustainable 25% target.

Critical to Deutsche's leading global positions has been the ongoing success of its operations in the Americas. In 2004 they accounted for 26% of Deutsche's total revenues and have thus improved the firm's positioning vis-à-vis global revenue pools

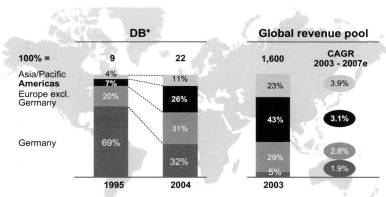

Note: Deutsche Bank figures for 1995 are based on IAS, 2004 on U.S. GAAP and are therefore not fully comparable; figures rounded.
1995 split based on total revenues before consolidation; 2004 split based on underlying revenues
*1995: total of net interest income, net commission income and trading profit; 2004: underlying revenues
Source: Boston Consulting Group, Deutsche Bank

Figure 3.13 Regional distribution of revenues (in EUR bn)

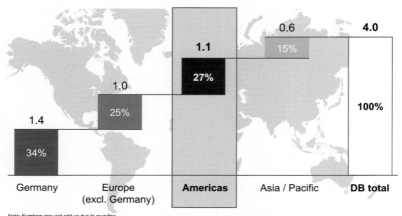

Figure 3.14 Regional distribution of income before taxes 2004 (in EUR bn)

in the financial services industry (see Figure 3.13). With approximately 12,000 employees Deutsche in the Americas contributed nearly 30% of the firm's global pre-tax income in 2004 (see Figure 3.14). Deutsche holds leading positions in both its Global Markets and Global Banking businesses: In the first five months of 2005 it ranked first in U.S. high-yield, second in U.S. asset backed securities, third in U.S. debt (excluding asset and mortgage backed securities), forth in USD clearing services and held a market share of approximately 9% in announced U.S. M&A. With Scudder it has one of the largest and most experienced investment management organisations in the U.S.

In autumn 2004, Deutsche streamlined responsibilities in the GEC and initiated a "Business Realignment Program" which includes the introduction of a reinforced regional management structure. This initiative will strengthen the regional dimension of Deutsche's management worldwide, including North America, and further improve performance for customers in a continuously changing environment.

Through the continuation of the organic build-out of all of its core businesses, comple-mented by potential value-enhancing "add-on" acquisitions, Deutsche is well posi-tioned to achieve its target of becoming an overall top five U.S. player in its chosen markets.

Lessons learned

While the three phases of Deutsche's North American M&A strategy have involved very different transactions – acquisitions and divestitures, large and smaller deals, CIB and PCAM – the following non-exhaustive list of common critical success factors emerges:

- *Clear strategic concept:* M&A activities must be consistent with the overall Group strategy. Each transaction executed in the context of Deutsche's North American

M&A framework has reflected Deutsche's corporate strategy and has been closely aligned with its organic growth efforts.

- *Determined decision-making:* Sustainable value creation via M&A requires taking calculated business, transaction and execution risks. Leading acquirers repeatedly identify, develop and execute on value creative M&A opportunities. A strategy, such as Deutsche's focus on core businesses demands brave decisions as to which businesses are "core" and determination to exit business when the strategic logic requires it.

- *Understanding of the counterparty:* Knowing the partner's motives is critical to value-maximizing M&A structuring. Understanding Zurich's strategic priorities, for example, allowed Deutsche to explore options to acquire 100% of Scudder and to tailor the transaction exactly to Zurich's strategic requirements to mutual benefit.

- *Disciplined pricing:* M&A must make both strategic and financial sense – over-paying or underselling risks turning a strategically viable transaction into a share-holder value destructive project. The ability to "say no" is critical. The effective price paid for Scudder amounted to only about 1% of Scudder's assets under management and serves as a good example.

- *Careful timing:* Specific assets or situations require optimal timing to crystallize maximum value. For example, the timing of Deutsche's exit from proprietary private equity needed careful management in order to optimize sales value and minimize negative earnings impact.

- *Swift execution:* Decisive and timely execution is critical to reducing transaction risk and utilizing windows of opportunity before they close. Deutsche, within approximately one year, successfully divested its commercial and consumer finance activities in North America, its global custody and passive asset management businesses and a large part of its private equity portfolio.

- *Clear communication:* Only continuous and open communication with customers, employees, the capital markets and regulators will ensure full support from all stakeholders. For example, Deutsche's regular updates on the progress of its focus on core businesses conveyed to the capital markets that its divestments were enabling it to reallocate its resources more efficiently.

- *Full exploitation of synergy potentials:* As in the case of the Bankers Trust transaction, the success of a given acquisition depends largely on detailed and realistic bottom-up evaluation of tangible synergies and the rigorous and continuous monitoring of their realization.

- *Stringent integration approach:* Particularly where acquisitions overlap with the acquirer's existing business model, thorough and early integration planning together with rigorous and expeditious execution are critical. For instance, following the signing of the Bankers Trust merger agreement a two-phased integration process was devised and its swift execution closely monitored.

- *Cultural and organizational evolution:* Sizeable expansion in non-home markets will likely require major cultural and organizational change. Deutsche has proactively facilitated and continuously managed this change. Its "divisionalization" in 1998, the creation of the CIB and PCAM divisions in 2001, the introduction of a

Global Executive Committee in 2002 and the ongoing Business Realignment Program have provided the right governance structure and organizational framework.

Conclusion and outlook

Deutsche has strategically repositioned itself and evolved organizationally in the late 1990s and at the beginning of this millennium in anticipation of, and response to, major structural changes within the financial services sector. It has systematically transformed itself into a truly *global modern universal bank* with well established leadership positions in its client-focused Corporate and Investment Banking (CIB) and Private Clients and Asset Management (PCAM) divisions.

Instrumental to this success have been Deutsche's inroads into the U.S., the world's largest, most sophisticated and innovative capital market. This accomplishment would not have been possible without a comprehensive and decisively executed *North American M&A strategy*, embedded into the Group's overall strategic framework:

- In the *first phase* Deutsche substantially expanded the U.S. presence of those of its core businesses that had global ambitions. The Bankers Trust and NDB acquisitions resulted in Deutsche's entrance into the "bulge bracket" in corporate and investment banking. With the acquisitions of Scudder and RREEF, Deutsche cemented its position as a leading global asset manager and took a significant step forward in the U.S. market to become the world's leading real estate asset manager.

- The *second phase* centered on re-focusing the enlarged business portfolio to free-up scarce resources utilized in non-strategic activities and contribute to a more efficient use of the Group's capital. Within approximately one year, Deutsche successfully divested its commercial and consumer finance activities in North America, its global custody and passive asset management businesses and a large part of its private equity portfolio.

- The *third phase* complements the organic growth efforts of Deutsche's existing U.S. platform with strategic "add-on" acquisitions further to leverage its competitive advantages, exploit new product and customer segment opportunities and enter potentially attractive white spots. The Berkshire Mortgage acquisition expands Deutsche's successful Real Estate Debt Markets franchise in line with its commitment to invest in profitable high growth areas.

The successful implementation of its North American M&A strategy has left a lasting mark on Deutsche as a whole. In 2004 the Americas contributed about one quarter of its global revenues and pre-tax income. It accounts for nearly one fifth of the Group's global employee base making it one of the largest employers on Wall Street. Through the continuing focused organic growth strategy complemented by potential value-enhancing "add-on" acquisitions Deutsche is well positioned further to strengthen its leadership status in North America to establish itself as an overall top five U.S. player in its core markets.

Literature

Deutsche Bank AG: Annual reports, 20 F filings with the Securities and Exchange Commission, company presentations and press releases (available on Deutsche Bank's investor relations website http://www.deutsche-bank.de/ir/en/)

Speyer, B.: US vs. EU banking market: the more integrated, the more profitable?, in: Walter N. (Ed.): EU Monitor No. 10: US vs. EU banking market: the more integrated, the more profitable?, Frankfurt 2003 (available on Deutsche Bank Research's website http://www.dbresearch.com)

Wieandt, A.; Blank, B.: Responses to structural changes in the financial services industry – the case of Deutsche Bank, p. 95, 96, 99, 108, in: Leser, H.; Rudolf, M. (Ed.), Handbuch Institutionelles Asset Management, Wiesbaden 2003

Wieandt, A.; Siemes, M.; Bachschuster, M.: Wechselwirkungen zwischen Strategie und Kapitalmarkt am Beispiel der Deutschen Bank, p. 243-246, in: Hungenberg, H.; Meffert, J. (Ed.), Handbuch Strategisches Management, Wiesbaden 2003

3.3 Consumer & Health

3.3.1 Henkel's Acquisition of The Dial Corporation, Scottsdale, USA

Lothar Steinebach, Steve Blum, Helmut B. Nuhn

A good strategic fit, the willingness of people involved to learn from each other and the concentration of management resources and efforts on core activities are the pre-requisites for a successful execution of any acquisition. For transatlantic mergers these approaches have to be accompanied by measures to bridge cultural differences and to establish a positive relationship with the key managers of the acquired company to make sure that the investment is value creating.

Introduction and overview

The purpose of this article is to describe and analyze transatlantic mergers and acquisitions based on the specific experience of a transaction where Henkel, via its affiliated company Henkel Corp., Gulph Mills (Pennsylvania), USA, in 2004 acquired 100% of the outstanding shares of The Dial Corporation, Scottsdale, (Arizona), USA. This transaction was for Henkel not only its most sizeable transatlantic deal, it was also the largest transaction in the company's nearly 130 year history.

Let us begin with some background about the Henkel Group. Founded in 1876, today the Group operates in more than 125 countries with 2004 net sales of 10.6 billion € and EBIT (before exceptional items) of 800 M€. Nearly 50,000 employees are on the payroll.

The operation of the Group is comprised of four business sectors i.e. Laundry and Home Care, Personal Care, Consumer and Craftsman Adhesives and Henkel Technologies. While the adhesives sectors (both for consumer and industrial applications) were already operating on a global scale and enjoyed leading market positions, the laundry and home care and personal care sectors were mainly European based. Therefore, we found ourselves facing a number of serious strategic challenges for these businesses as a result of the overall structure of competition, the position of our peer group competitors and the ongoing process of global consolidation in these industries.

In addition, Henkel had undergone a major re-shaping of its product portfolio as a result of selling its specialty chemicals business at the end of 2001, which had been carved-out and renamed Cognis. Furthermore, around the same time a 50% interest in a Joint Venture with Ecolab Inc., USA, in the institutional business in Europe was sold to Ecolab. These moves caused the financial community to ask for a clear indication of the future strategic course for Henkel and to question how Henkel would invest its "war chest" resulting from the proceeds of the two disposals and its subsequent increased financial capabilities.

Overall strategies of the acquirer

Henkel faced a number of strategic challenges in its laundry and home care and personal care (HPC) businesses. First, it had a high dependency on Europe where increasing pressure was coming from global competitors and private label was increasing its market share. The substantial investments in R&D, product and packaging development, marketing concepts and strategies coupled with the benefits from economies of scale in procurement, production and supply chain all require a broad production base to achieve competitive margins. This can better be realized on a global basis. Second, the Western European HPC markets where Henkel participates, are very mature, have low growth prospects and experience a high level of product, service and price competition from branded goods manufacturers on one side and the many private label offerings on the other side. Private label products have reached significant market shares in some European countries.

Although Henkel started very early to build positions in emerging markets in Asia Pacific, (China, India), in the Mediterranean rim of Africa (Algeria, Tunisia, Egypt) and in some markets in Central America (Mexico and Guatemala), these sales were not sufficient enough to offset the mature aspects of the European home markets. It was clear there were two huge market voids in Henkel's HPC businesses i.e. Japan and US. Entry into the Japanese HPC market did not move beyond the stage of co-operation in the fields of R&D and product development with some local partners. Therefore, the other big market, namely the US, remained the primary candidate for a strategic move.

There was another reason to choose the US market for future expansion and regional diversification: global key accounts. Henkel had started to build a relationship with the big US retail chains such as Wal*Mart, K-mart, Kroger and Target in its adhesives and personal care businesses. These positions, though, were vulnerable due to the limited market share and product breadth of its offerings. This resulted in costly efforts for

Henkel to defend itself against the market leaders as it fought for shelf space and facings.

So the clear messages were:

- to enhance and expand markets for the existing product portfolio and
- to leverage opportunities in adjacent categories.

These challenges had to be met under specific conditions. The first one was to maintain Henkel as a family controlled company, which basically meant to respect its capital structure. This meant business expansion by way of an acquisition had to be financed by a straight-forward cash deal rather than by using stock. A second constraint, given the size of the Group and its geographically dispersed activities, were the managerial resources that could be made available to run the acquired business successfully, particularly since stepping into the home market of one of its most powerful competitors could easily result in unpredictable counter-reactions. To meet these challenges, and at the same time develop and integrate a business, a very capable and loyal management team was of the utmost importance.

Table 3.1 gives a brief overview of key financial and economic data of Henkel compared to its global peers (2004 figures in MUSD).

Table 3.1 Financial data peer group

Company	Sales	EBITDA	Market capitalization
Procter & Gamble	51,400	11,600	139,500
Unilever	52,200	8,400	64,000
L'Oréal	18,900	7,000	48,900
Henkel (bef. Dial)	10,600	1,250	10,200

After identifying and analyzing the strategic challenges and geographic gaps it became obvious Henkel had to look for additional critical mass to benefit from economies of scale and to fulfil the requirements of its key customers. From a geographic perspective it became very clear that becoming a significant global player required Henkel to enlarge its presence significantly in the most important and most profitable single HPC market in the world, the United States. Three different routes and approaches had been identified and evaluated to reach this objective. The first was to accelerate organic growth and to increase market share by entering new markets (regionally or through new product categories) by way of a "green field approach." It immediately became obvious that this solution would take too long and showed the highest risk of failure. The second alternative was to team up with a partner who had already achieved a global presence in the relevant businesses but this did not fulfil the requirement to maintain Henkel as an independent family controlled company. So, consequently, it was the third route that was followed – to look for an acquisition candidate that met the strategic requirements to their maximum extent.

The acquisition case

Having outlined the strategic position of Henkel prior to the acquisition, it is similarly important to understand the situation at Dial prior to their being acquired by Henkel. Although Dial can trace its roots back to the 1850's, when it started as the Armour Brothers Food Company – a firm that revolutionized the meat packing industry, the Dial business Henkel acquired was originally the consumer products piece of a larger entity that was at one time engaged in a multitude of disparate businesses including: motor coach transportation, financial services, cruise ships, industrial catering and convention services. In 1996 what remained of this entity – coincidentally called The Dial Corporation – spun its consumer products businesses off from its remaining financial services businesses.

Up until the time of the spin off, the Dial consumer products businesses regularly suffered from a lack of management support and the resources necessary to compete in the highly competitive consumer products marketplace. In addition, the Dial brands were only recognized in North America and the Company lacked the infrastructure and resources needed to expand them into broader markets.

Although the consumer products company enjoyed some early successes following the spin off, attempts to expand into new markets and new categories heavily drained the financial resources of the Company. The situation rapidly deteriorated until August of 2000, at which time Dial's Board was forced to make sweeping management changes.

After a long period of assessment, that took place during some challenging times, the new management concluded that for Dial to survive long-term it had to gain greater scale. This could only occur through strong organic growth, acquisitions, merger and or being acquired. Since the first two options required greater resources than were readily available, the Board concluded and publicly announced that it thought it would be in the best interest of shareholders long-term if Dial were part of a larger organization. As a result, following this announcement all Dial employees, shareholders, customers, suppliers and communities were physically and emotionally prepared for Dial to be acquired. This, more than anything else, enhanced the success of the acquisition integration process.

Specific selection criteria

The Dial-Henkel transaction demonstrates that although individuals of different nationalities or national cultures were involved, and although the business models of the two companies were strikingly different (Henkel is a more marketing driven company in the classical sense, whereas Dial's focus is on sales and establishing and maintaining strong relationships with key customers) the decisive factor for the success or failure of such a transaction (whether it is Transatlantic or on the Continent), is that the acquisition or merger has a convincing strategy for both partners that grows the opportunities for the businesses and the people involved in them. It is essential to communicate this strategy over time to the employees and to encourage them to actively manage these changes.

Why this very partner?

Dial was for Henkel the perfect fit to overcome some of the previously outlined strategic gaps. First, Dial significantly strengthens the consumer business overall i.e. the proportion of the consumer business to total sales rose from 68% to 72%. It also increased Henkel's market position in the US by adding 1.3 billion USD in sales, increasing the US revenue share for the Group from 14% to 23% and consequently reducing the dependence on Europe accordingly.

Second, Dial was the best short-term option to enter the highly profitable (compared to Europe) HPC market in the US because of its leading market positions in the relevant segments, well-known brands and good financial performance. In addition, Dial gave access to some related categories Henkel was not involved in prior to the transaction (e.g. Air Care).

The most convincing aspect, however, was that the company had in place an excellent management team, good customer relationship management and offered all the other elements of an infrastructure necessary to enter a sizable market like the US.

Trade-off between strengths & weaknesses

Besides the driving factors for this transaction there were also some weak points that had to be overcome in the future.

Dial's price positioning in the value-for-money segment offers only limited opportunity for price increases and bears some risk of margin squeeze. One of the consequences of this is that the product offerings only have to be adequate i.e. have to match certain appropriate quality levels and in most cases do not have to offer additional value for the consumer. Pricing and maintaining a perceived adequate quality level and a high customer service level are the key elements for successfully competing in the marketplace against premium brands. On the other hand growth perspectives may be above average, assuming that the development in the US follows the European pattern where low price branded goods and private label products are gaining market share.

An inherent key performance indicator to maintaining satisfactory financial performance with such a business model is to establish a system of tight cost control and a high degree of cost consciousness among all employees. In this respect Dial has already served as an internal benchmark within the Henkel Group for critically reviewing cost structures in production, sales and administration.

One of the most important reasons for many acquisitions is the realization of synergies that add value and justify the premium paid. The Dial transaction has another objective, namely to serve as a platform for establishing Henkel's HPC business in the US. As a result, the whole organization and its existing infrastructure remained untouched which offered only very limited savings potential e.g. in procurement and by eliminating some redundant administrative functions such as Investor Relations, Internal Audit, Finance and Tax. To the extent add-on acquisitions in the future can be run with the currently existing resources and systems, financial performance is likely to improve significantly.

Improvement of market position through joining forces

Through the acquisition the Henkel Group immediately gained respectable market share positions in the US laundry detergent market with 14% in volume and in air fresheners with about 16% in value. In the personal care sector, Henkel's existing business in the US which was mainly in hair care will be enhanced with a sizeable Dial body care business that has an overall market share of 17% and a No. 3 market share position as measured by volume.

A significant improvement has been achieved in the relationships with key customers such as Wal*Mart, Target, and the various dollar stores with whom Dial has excellent relations. Prior to the acquisition Henkel was present on the shelves of these customers with only a limited product offering (hair care and adhesives). This is now enhanced by products in the laundry detergents, body wash, air freshener and canned food (sausages, chilli) categories. This helps to increase negotiating power vis-à-vis global accounts and leveraging the distribution platform.

Further opportunities are anticipated from expected product transfer in both directions. Dial will benefit from new product concepts and innovations such as a new category in body wash and tabs and gels as new forms of application for laundry detergents. Vice versa for Henkel with the adaptation of Dial's air freshener products for European requirements. Harmonization of product formulations and production processes are promising projects as are joint efforts in R&D and packaging development.

The overall process and phases of the project

The transaction can be split into three different phases:

- Screening of the candidate including due diligence and establishing a business plan
- Negotiating phase including decision on deal structure and process
- Fulfilment of conditions prior to closing.

The candidate's screening phase took a very short time because a good business relationship and personal contacts had been established between the two companies since 2000. Due to the positive attitude of the Dial management towards Henkel a detailed due diligence was conducted as the basis for a well-founded business plan including restructuring needs and synergy potential. The financial performance expected from this business plan was the basis for the valuation of the business and the price per share Henkel ultimately paid to the former Dial shareowners.

Because of the detailed insight Henkel gained during due diligence the negotiation phase ended with a merger agreement that was comparably short and could be agreed upon within 4 weeks. Since Dial was a New York Stock Exchange listed company most of the relevant data was publicly available. The representations and warranties of the company in this transaction were rather limited and basically concentrated on the fulfilment of legal requirements such as organization, warranties regarding capitalization, and compliance with laws including environmental and economic such as absence of material adverse changes since closure of the financial statements and covenants relating to the conduct of the business. The closing of the transaction was of course subject to anti-trust approval.

With respect to the practical aspects of the acquisition Henkel decided to go for a "Cash Merger" or "Merger by Proxy" process rather than launching a "Cash Tender Offer" procedure. This meant that following the signing of the merger agreement and announcement of the transaction, Dial had to prepare a proxy statement (this document provides Dial shareholders with notice of a special meeting to approve the transaction and other related information) for review and approval by the US Securities and Exchange Commission. After their approval was obtained the proxy statement was sent to Dial shareholders and a special meeting of Dial shareowners was convened. The whole process took about 3 and a half months. During this period the anti-trust approval was also obtained. The reason for following this route was that a "one step merger process" could be realized because once the shareholder approval was obtained all (even dissenting) shareholders had to deliver their shares under the conditions of the merger agreement. On the other side there is an "interloper risk" during the period between announcement and the general meeting. This risk was covered in the merger agreement and stated that the Dial management could not solicit other acquisition proposals during that time without the company having to pay a substantial termination fee.

In order to raise the level of confidence of Dial's shareholders its financial adviser for the transaction gave a fairness opinion stating the agreed share price to be received in cash was fair from a fiduciary point of view. Also the Dial Board of Directors determined that the merger agreement and the transaction contemplated by this agreement were fair and in the best interest of the company and its shareholders and recommended adoption of the agreement. On March 27, 2004 shareholders overwhelmingly voted their approval at a special meeting. The transaction closed on March 29, 2004.

The general integration process

As soon as the acquisition transaction closed the first phase of the integration process began with the CEO of Henkel coming to Dial's headquarters to address and welcome all Dial employees to Henkel and personally endorse the joining of the two companies.

In addition, a senior manager from Henkel headquarters, who had been part of the acquirer's acquisition evaluation team, was dispatched to Dial's headquarters to work with a senior Dial manager to:

- Begin constructive dialogue and build working relationships between the acquirer and the target company.
- Mediate and resolve any issues or disputes arising from conflicting or misinterpreted acquirer requests.

Dedicated acquisition integration staffing was purposely avoided at this stage of the process and every effort was made to minimize any unnecessary demands on Dial personnel as well as avoid any disruption to Dial's ongoing business. The Henkel logo was immediately added to all major facilities, business cards and letterheads to begin the new identity transition.

The first step in this phase of the integration process was to establish clear lines of responsibility for both the operations and the integration of the acquisition. This included:

- Responsibility for Dial's overall business performance which was assigned to the individual who had been CEO of Dial prior to the acquisition and who was retained to run the Company during the transition period.
- Responsibility for planning and executing the integration process which was assigned to a Henkel executive who was part of the acquirer's acquisition evaluation team.

Reporting relationships, from an operating standpoint, were not changed following the acquisition to allow both organizations time to better understand one another. Key functional teams were formed to start the learning and integration process. Each team was assigned integration objectives and had leaders at both Companies' headquarters that were responsible for coordinating the efforts of their teams and assuring their objectives were met. The teams included:

- Finance
- Purchasing
- Information Technology
- R&D
- Production
- Corporate Internal Audit
- Human Resources
- Sales
- Marketing Services

A "New" Dial Board, comprised of senior Henkel and Dial executives, was created to address operating as well as integration issues that may arise – assuring open lines of communications at the highest level of both organizations. The Board scheduled quarterly meetings to take place at both companies' headquarters as well as by videoconference.

The basis for the mutual understanding between the two companies with respect to the integration process and operating responsibilities was established in a "Code of Cooperation." In this Code it was acknowledged that the sales driven business model of Dial and its appropriate lean organizational structure should be retained. Henkel in turn was to provide the financial and technical capabilities and new technologies to launch new projects. The integration process during the transition phase was to be based on mutual respect and consideration for any cultural differences.

General objectives were

- to initiate a process of knowledge sharing and internal benchmarking to keep Dial's strengths and to make them also available for other businesses/areas of the Henkel Group
- to prepare the necessary organizational structures and resources to launch new projects

- to keep the current Dial senior management intact during the transition period (approx. 2 years after closing).

The Dial management retained responsibility for the business and made all decisions necessary to run the day-to-day operations e.g. sales, promotion and pricing policy, customer relationships, operations (except substantial investments), supply chain, HR policy (except senior management). In addition they agreed to manage the company in full compliance with all local and national legal requirements, apply for all necessary permits and authorizations and overall respect Henkel standards for safety, health, environment and quality.

Business decisions which required Board approval included the annual budget, the annual closing and the election of the auditor. In addition the Board retained its approval right concerning annual marketing plans including media spending, marketing plans for new products (launches of new products in addition to line extensions) and recruitment/termination of employment contracts for management, social benefit programs, incentive and bonus systems for senior management. The respective approval procedures and approval levels were outlined in detail.

Initial areas of full and immediate integration were Treasury and Corporate Finance (including cash management, FX management, bank policy and funding), Tax, M&A, Accounting and Financial Reporting (to assure a harmonized system within the Corporate Accounting Standards of Henkel).

To keep all people informed at the same level a "business reporting system" was established. During phone calls every other week the CEO of Dial and the heads of the Household Division and the Personal Care Divison of Henkel discuss top-level business issues and decide on any required "trouble shooting points." In a video-conference held once a month, a written business summary is presented by Dial marketing, sales and finance individuals. Those responsible from both companies then discuss business results and financial performance and any necessary actions to be taken.

The restructuring/team integration

The next step was to establish the objectives for this phase of the integration process. The number one short-term objective was to *drive acquisition synergies.* The initial focus was placed on the most obvious and easiest opportunities to achieve synergies.

These included:

- Cost savings from leveraging purchases of materials, supplies and services.
- Increased capacity utilization for underutilized manufacturing facilities.
- Technology transfer.
- New markets, customers and channels for existing products.

The second objective was to *assure the acquiree's organization remained focused and motivated.* Henkel achieved this by immediately endorsing Dial's Operating Plan and pledging any required resources to assure its success. The plan contained a comprehensive roadmap to keep the organization focused on achieving the strategic and financial goals for the integration year. Achievement of the plan also carried with it highly motivational financial and retention incentives. Additional demands of the organization relating to the acquisition integration process were purposely minimized, avoiding unnecessary distractions and making every effort to foster a "business as usual" atmosphere.

The third objective was to *introduce Dial to the Henkel culture and Henkel to Dial's culture*. The first phase of the integration process was launched with a celebration for all Dial headquarters employees. Henkel senior management attended and participated in the program. This was followed by a series of formal communications outlining Henkel's history and products. Each publication also included profiles of a cross section of Henkel people. The intent was to emphasize the similarity between the two companies and establish a high level of comfort by engendering familiarity. In addition, a consultant was hired to conduct a brief orientation of the German culture for all Dial headquarters employees. The biggest boost to cultural awareness, though, occurred when Henkel employees, specifically in marketing and product development, came to work at Dial headquarters and relocated their families to the area. These first ambassadors did more to promote cultural unity than could possibly have been achieved by any formal communications or culture consultant.

The fourth objective was to *continuously update and inform Henkel senior management*. This was achieved by initiating weekly telephone calls, monthly integration update reports and quarterly meetings of the previously described Dial advisory board. Since Dial management wanted as much as Henkel management for the acquisition to succeed, these calls and meetings almost exclusively addressed constructive issues relating to the integration.

The final objective of this phase of the integration process was to *promote close cooperation between Henkel and Dial*. From the start of the process cooperation was both close and sincere on the part of both parties. Dial enthusiastically endorsed the acquisition knowing as an independent company it did not have the resources necessary to compete long term in the highly competitive marketplace. Henkel on the other hand knew if the acquisition were to succeed it had to make sure Dial was aware and able to avail itself of Henkel's resources. This mutually beneficial relationship fostered and promoted cooperation.

When it was announced that Henkel was acquiring Dial, Dial employees were already emotionally prepared. The acquisition of Dial had been anticipated for quite some time. The only surprise was who the acquirer would be. When Henkel was announced as the acquirer relief and joy actually spread throughout the organization because it was widely felt Henkel was as interested in acquiring Dial's human resources as they were in acquiring its brands and physical resources.

This view was reaffirmed by Dial senior management's assurances that Henkel wished to keep the entire organization in place and wanted everyone to operate in the future as they had done in the past. This strategy was appropriate for the first phase of the integration process, allowing Henkel time to learn the specific roles and responsibilities of Dial's employees. Clearly, though, Dial was organized and staffed as an independent organization and had a fair amount of positions that would have to eventually be addressed as a result of integration into the Henkel Group. This aside, employees' viewed working for Henkel as a win-win situation because they saw the potential benefit from what Henkel, as a large and successful company, has to offer.

This first phase of the acquisition integration process took approximately seven months to complete and overall was a resounding success. The acquisition was well received by everyone involved. There was excellent cooperation at all levels. Morale remained high throughout the organization and a spirit of success was obvious at all Dial locations. All transition teams got off to a strong start and remained energized, cooperative and committed throughout the entire first phase of the process. There were a considerable number of early team successes – particularly in the purchasing area. Any issues that arose were resolved efficiently and always in the best interest of the combined businesses such as the immediate adoption by Dial of Henkel's template for their IT enterprise system even though Dial had just invested two years, a considerable amount of money and a substantial number of hours training employees on a different system.

The final organization, business process and management model

An organizational structure in a company is never final and business processes and management models have to be adapted continuously to meet the changing requirements of the marketplace. This is even more valid for Dial since it is a beachhead for Henkel's Household and Personal Care businesses that will be developed further. One of the first steps in this direction was an add-on acquisition in the household sector that closed in November 2004. Another step will be to bundle all household and personal care activities under one roof. As a result, a NewCo was established which currently holds all shares of Dial and will be the legal entity where the Personal Care activities will be transferred. This entity will also be supported by Henkel's North America Shared Services Organization.

Another aspect is the (foreseeable and planned) change in the top management of Dial. A number of key employees have already reached or will reach their retirement age shortly. A new CEO has already taken over responsibility as of April 2005. The basic challenge for the Dial management team is two fold. On one hand it is to defend the position the company and its brands have achieved in the marketplace. This is more a defensive approach as yet a number of top Dial people that had successfully managed the business turn-around in 2002 and 2003 are still "on board." On the other hand there is the increasing need to enter new markets and bring new products to existing markets. This is more of an "offensive" approach and requires different thinking in terms of investment and the hiring/training of new people who are able to exploit the market potential.

Basic differences between USA and Germany that have affected the project and how have they been overcome?

The project had been impacted very little by cultural differences between the USA and Germany except for some particularities in the acquisition process itself (e. g. the chosen "merger by proxy" approach does not exist in German law). The most important reason for this was Dial's and Henkel's strategies were complementary to each other. Dial management was aware that the company was too small to survive in a global marketplace with ongoing consolidation occurring in the US market. In addition it did not have the financial firepower necessary to realize an international expansion after its retreat from some ill-fated acquisitions in Central and South America in 2000/2001. Henkel on the other hand was well aware of the fact that on its way to becoming a global player in the HPC sectors, its position in the US market had to be significantly enhanced. For timing reasons and due to the high risk of a "greenfields approach" Henkel was looking to acquire a partner who offered all the elements for a successful entry into the US market. In addition, Dial's different management style and business model did not turn out to be a problem. Because Henkel was not at all present in the US laundry detergent market it adopted Dial's system and is very cautious but willing to adapt it, if needed, to realize the overall objectives of the acquisition.

Another contributor to the success in the initial phase of the integration was the similarity between the corporate cultures of the acquirer and the acquiree. Dial's corporate culture is built around the principle of people working together with a mutual respect for one another. Dial spells out how it expects employees to work together and how it intends to run its businesses in its Cultural Contract that includes:

- We treat people with dignity and respect
- We are open and honest with each other
- We regularly communicate with each other on important issues and developments
- We encourage and reward initiative and risk taking
- We make decisions that consider both the short-term and long-term needs of the Company

Henkel's corporate culture is very similar and is built around its unique and powerful family heritage as is embodied in its vision that includes:

- We strive for innovation
- We embrace change
- We are successful because of our people
- We are committed to shareholder value
- We are dedicated to sustainability and corporate social responsibility
- We communicate openly and actively
- We preserve the tradition of an open family company

Although the culture of the two companies is very similar, their personalities are quite different – primarily due to the differences between the scope and scale of Henkel versus Dial. This has nothing to do with one company being based in Germany while the other is based in America (too often we confuse country culture with corporate culture). Rather it is because Dial operated on a far smaller and considerably less complex scale than Henkel. It is about a tenth the size of Henkel, has only 2500 employees, operates almost exclusively in the US and gets more than 90 percent of its sales from the US and Canada. This contrasts with Henkel which is a global power-house with operations in 76 countries, sales in more than 125 countries and more than 50,000 employees. As a result, Dial was able to operate with a leaner, more informal organization in a more casual workplace and was accustomed to do things its own way – without the help or oversight of a parent.

Main lessons learned

The main lesson learned from the Dial/Henkel acquisition is that a good strategic fit (preferably for both parties) is key to success. This inherently leads to a friendly approach that should be accompanied by open mindedness on both sides and all managers involved seeing the long-term benefit. It is not always the acquirer who has the best ideas, the most capable people and the undisputed market knowledge. For the acquirer a friendly approach can achieve a number of advantages such as getting a better insight into the acquired company during due diligence and contract negotia-tions. With that the acquirer has a more reliable basis to build the business case for the future and to establish relationships with key managers while making assessments and finding ways acceptable for both sides to retain them when needed. It also makes post merger integration tasks more transparent and helps to achieve the necessary actions without losing momentum in the marketplace.

Acquiring a company and afterwards integrating the entity into an existing parent organization (even at a low level) always requires changes that have to be managed pro-actively. This is undoubtedly the task and responsibility of an integration manager and his team. Acting primarily as moderator and less as facilitator certainly reduces/avoids conflicts, however, this may not be beneficial to reaching the overall objectives – at least not in the shortest possible timeframe.

The best way to facilitate "learning from each other" is to exchange people between the two companies, more or less the day after closing, in those areas that are key to achieving the acquisition's objectives. If synergies in procurement, production and product formulations are seen as mandatory, bring these people together on a regular/constant basis to realize the information transfer and to set up the necessary rules, regulations and processes to make it all work. The most efficient way to achieve this is through a mutual transfer of people instead of establishing temporary working groups with members located at two different locations 12,000 km apart with 9 hours differ-ence in time. This also has the added benefit of facilitating networks across both organizations and of improving mutual understanding.

An exchange of people can also have a positive impact on realizing new projects (e. g. launching new products, re-formulations, new processes in production and administra-tion). It is undoubtedly true that American products and marketing concepts need to be adapted to meet European customer requirements. However, the already existing knowledge base should be used to shorten time-to-market instead of de facto re-inventing and testing of the whole concept from the very beginning.

In a sizeable share transaction very often some of the businesses acquired do not fit entirely into the product strategy of the parent company. To concentrate management resources and efforts on the core activities, soon after takeover non-core assets should be put up for sale even if for the time being they are absorbing cost and generating cash. This will help in giving a clear signal to the financial community that the company is proceeding according to the announced strategy and that a tight asset management is in place.

Outlook and future directions

The Dial acquisition was based on a sound strategic fit with clear objectives. The first phase was to maintain the position of the business in the market in spite of intense competition and to find bolt-on acquisitions to enhance and broaden its platform. This has been realized – although this will be an ongoing process. In addition, the transition phase of the management of the acquisition successfully started when the new CEO, who knows the home and personal care markets in the US very well, took over responsibility in April 2005. The next step is to complete the reorganization. This means consolidating HPC activities under the Dial roof and making it an integral part of Henkel's North American Shared Services Organization. In parallel new projects resulting from the different know how of both firms have to be launched and respectively implemented on "both sides of the Atlantic Ocean." Only this will reap the full benefit that was assumed when Henkel bought Dial in 2004 and write a new chapter of its worldwide business activities.

3.3.2 Carl Zeiss Vision – A Merger of the Carl Zeiss Eyeglass Division with Sola International, Inc.

Michael Kaschke and Udo Philipp

Carl Zeiss AG has been a traditional German mid-cap conglomerate generating sales totaling more than 2bn euros and owned by a special type of corporate foundation. The Eyeglass Division of Carl Zeiss and its largest US stock listed competitor Sola International, Inc. have been looking for a partnership for years. Using a financial sponsor, EQT, as a catalyst, Zeiss succeeded in acquiring Sola in March 2005. Zeiss and EQT now each own 50% of the merged business renamed Carl Zeiss Vision.

Introduction

The market for eyeglasses is large, profitable and growing nicely. Like in many other markets, until recently German midsized companies were highly successful in focusing on the high end segment of their home and nearby European market and almost felt no pressure to globalize.

This contribution will show that:

- the globalization of the market leader Essilor and the arrival of large international chains of opticians has changed a hitherto relatively cozy market
- different market conditions in Europe and in the USA have led to very different successful strategies of the leading local players, Zeiss and Sola
- both Zeiss and Sola needed to acquire a new set of strengths, and given their strong complementarities, a merger became almost a strategic necessity
- after some fruitless attempts to acquire each other, an innovative solution involving a private equity group as a catalyst was found
- combining the respective skills of an industrial group and a financial sponsor facilitated all aspects of the merger and made it attractive for both parties
- a well-planned integration setup will mitigate the inherent merger risk and will help to realize the high synergy potential.

The market for eyeglasses

The market for eyeglasses is very attractive. At the retail level it is a roughly 25 bn euro market growing at 3 to 4% p.a. 800 million eyeglass lenses are sold every year in the world. Almost 60% of people under the age of 45 need glasses. More than 90% of people over 45 find it difficult to read and need reading glasses. Most of these eyeglass wearers have to change their glasses every 2-5 years when they require a new lens prescription.

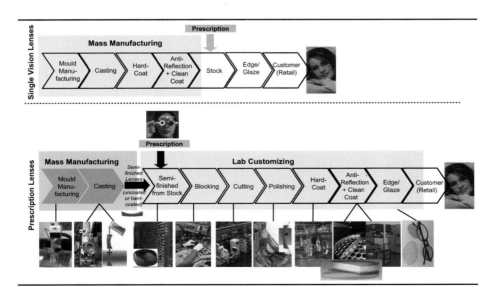

Figure 3.15 Production process for stock and prescription lenses.

The leading players in this industry are Essilor, Hoya, Sola, Rodenstock and Carl Zeiss. The EBITDA margins of the two public companies Essilor and Hoya have been nicely above 20% on an ongoing basis.

The production process is rather complex because of the large number of different vision defects that exist. The common eye deficiencies like myopia exist in very different degrees of severity and they can also be present simultaneously. Therefore, there are thousands of different possible individual defects that need to be corrected with specific eyeglasses. When combined with individual consumer preferences for different materials and coatings, this leads to so many different possibilities that a large portion of the market needs what are known as prescription lenses which can only be made to order. The production process for both prescription and standard (stock) lenses is shown schematically in Figure 3.15.

The eye is a very demanding, high precision instrument that does not tolerate low quality optical solutions. Until now, it has not been possible to introduce a technology that allows the production of these complicated optical designs in some form of automated casting or CAD/CAM aided carving process. The result has been fairly labor and capital intensive setups producing the individual lenses. Since these are in general prescribed by an ophthalmologist, these setups are called Rx labs.

Consumers, and also the opticians selling the lenses to them, are constantly becoming more demanding in terms of service and speed of delivery. Also, high quality expectations – especially with regard to more complicated products – have kept a fairly labor intensive production process in high cost countries close to the customer.

In order to somewhat reduce the complexity and high cost of producing these prescription and individually customized lenses, the industry has introduced a first production step where simple standard lenses and a couple of hundred semi-finished lenses are produced and then held in stock. These mass manufacturing sites can be set up at centralized locations further away from the customer.

US and European markets – two completely different market structures

In Europe, eyeglasses were subsidized by health insurance systems until recently. This, combined with high purchasing power, has led to a fairly large high-end market with a high penetration of high value added products. In Germany, for instance, close to 90% of all lenses feature an antireflective coating.

In order to fulfill this demand, the Rx labs have a need for expensive and difficult to handle capital equipment. This has led to a concentrated, industrialized setup of the Rx lab landscape. To be a leading player in the industry, it was necessary to be a successful Rx lab player.

In the United States, there is a significantly lower penetration of high value added products with, for example, only approximately 20% of all lenses being AR coated. This has allowed a completely different Rx lab structure. Whilst in Europe you find only a few labs producing less than 1000 lenses a day, in the US you see some several

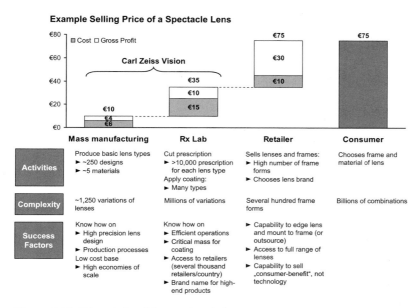

Example Selling Price of a Spectacle Lens

	Mass manufacturing	Rx Lab	Retailer	Consumer
Activities	Produce basic lens types ► ~250 designs ► ~5 materials	Cut prescription ► >10,000 prescription for each lens type Apply coating: ► Many types	Sells lenses and frames: ► High number of frame forms ► Chooses lens brand	Chooses frame and material of lens
Complexity	~1,250 variations of lenses	Millions of variations	Several hundred frame forms	Billions of combinations
Success Factors	Know how on ► High precision lens design ► Production processes Low cost base ► High economies of scale	Know how on ► Efficient operations ► Critical mass for coating ► Access to retailers (several thousand retailers/country) ► Brand name for high-end products	► Capability to edge lens and mount to frame (or outsource) ► Access to full range of lenses ► Capability to sell „consumer-benefit", not technology	

Figure 3.16 Value chain of the eyeglass industry

hundred labs with an average capacity of between 250 and 500 lenses per day. The function of these labs has been twofold: to customize lenses and to serve as a form of wholesaler between the lens industry and the optician.

A US and a German market leader – two very different companies

The difference between the two home markets has led to clearly adapted and different strategies of the two companies.

Until the end of the 1990s, Sola in the US were faced with a well functioning structure of small independent Rx labs serving the opticians. If Sola had short-circuited this wholesale channel and served the opticians directly, they might have strongly alienated their own wholesale customers. Since the Rx labs owned their customers, and since the simple, fully finished lenses and the semi-finished lenses that the Rx labs purchase from the industry are basically interchangeable commodities, the Rx labs might have changed suppliers if Sola had served the opticians directly.

Sola's strategy, therefore, was to be the best in class Rx lab supplier and focus all efforts on being a clear cost leader. In a heavy restructuring program Sola shut down all their high cost manufacturing facilities in the US and in most other high cost countries and built up highly efficient factories in Mexico, Brazil and China. This strategy was highly successful and Sola are now considered to be an excellent low cost manufacturer.

Carl Zeiss clearly adapted their strategy to the demanding and relatively rich German and Central European market. The Zeiss focus had been to excel in terms of high

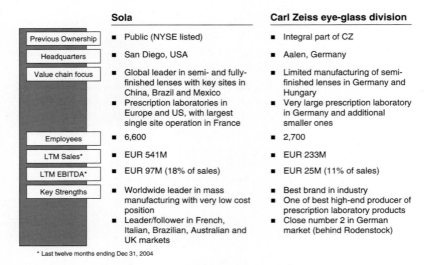

	Sola	Carl Zeiss eye-glass division
Previous Ownership	▪ Public (NYSE listed)	▪ Integral part of CZ
Headquarters	▪ San Diego, USA	▪ Aalen, Germany
Value chain focus	▪ Global leader in semi- and fully-finished lenses with key sites in China, Brazil and Mexico ▪ Prescription laboratories in Europe and US, with largest single site operation in France	▪ Limited manufacturing of semi-finished lenses in Germany and Hungary ▪ Very large prescription laboratory in Germany and additional smaller ones
Employees	▪ 6,600	▪ 2,700
LTM Sales*	▪ EUR 541M	▪ EUR 233M
LTM EBITDA*	▪ EUR 97M (18% of sales)	▪ EUR 25M (11% of sales)
Key Strengths	▪ Worldwide leader in mass manufacturing with very low cost position ▪ Leader/follower in French, Italian, Brazilian, Australian and UK markets	▪ Best brand in industry ▪ One of best high-end producer of prescription laboratory products ▪ Close number 2 in German market (behind Rodenstock)

* Last twelve months ending Dec 31, 2004

Figure 3.17 Complementary profiles of Sola and Carl Zeiss

quality, high value added products. They invested heavily in an efficient high quality Rx lab which is able to industrially produce the most sophisticated optical designs and complex quality coatings.

In actual fact, Carl Zeiss' production site in Aalen is, with a capacity of about 30,000 lenses per day, currently the largest Rx lab in the world. Being an Rx lab itself, the Carl Zeiss Eyeglass Division has always served opticians and retail chains, and only to a very limited extent other independent Rx labs as customers.

Building on their competency of high quality, high value added lenses and being helped by the very strong image of the parent company Carl Zeiss AG, a worldwide leader in optics, Zeiss enjoy the probably strongest optical brand with the consumer, the optician, and also with the retail chains.

New market dynamics leading to new challenges

In the late 1990s the worldwide market leader Essilor launched a bold move to attack Sola in its home market. Essilor decided to fundamentally change the industry structure in the US by massively acquiring Rx labs. Within a couple of years Essilor succeeded in buying more than 100 independent Rx labs and fully integrating them into their own structure. Essilor short-circuited the wholesale channel, now directly addressing the optician and no longer competing with low cost commodity products but with high value added prescription lenses.

At the same time, the retail market was changing dramatically. Some successful opticians successfully built up large national chains like Specsavers, and some large general retailers like Wal*Mart successfully established an optics line in their stores. While in the beginning these chains only competed on price, they progressively saw the opportunity to earn significant margins with value added products.

Therefore, both the tremendous quality improvement that Essilor introduced to their acquired Rx labs and the demand from the retail chains strongly accelerated the penetration of high value added products in the US. Today, almost 50% of lenses sold by Wal*Mart are AR coated (compared to a national average of 20% in early 2000).

Sola reacted by putting even more focus on operational efficiency. In a tremendous restructuring effort they dismissed more than 2000 employees and focused all production efforts on Mexico, Brazil and China. Efficiency and profitability rose significantly, but still the market share in the US was declining. Sola needed more competence in high value added products. The next move was to license a top consumer brand, Teflon, and together with DuPont develop an excellent AR and clean coating. Teflon has been a big success and is growing nicely, but would this be enough? Would Sola not need to establish a prescription lab network of its own, gain more expertise in running these Rx labs, develop other high quality coatings and ideally also possess a really strong optical brand name? How would Sola be able to acquire these competencies?

During the same time in Germany, a retail chain called Fielmann outpaced the market to such an extent that approximately 50% of all lenses sold in Germany today are sold in a Fielmann outlet. The enormous purchasing power of such a retail chain has forced even high end players like Zeiss to offer highly competitive, budget products.

Also, in two consecutive health care reforms the German government abolished the former system of subsidizing the purchase of glasses by consumers every other year.

The combination of both effects led to significant margin pressure at Zeiss, and a heavy restructuring program resulted in significant lay-offs, the closure of one of two German sites and the establishment of a small, low-cost site in Hungary. After this restructuring, Zeiss was reasonably profitable again, but from their position as number five in the world would they be able to compete in the long term against players with a significantly larger size, greater geographic reach, manufacturing sites in countries like China and Brazil? How would Zeiss be able to finally manage a breakthrough in the largest optical market, the USA? How would they manage to achieve efficient sourcing of stock and semi-finished lenses in low cost countries like China?

A catalyst finally facilitates the merger

The merger logic of these two highly complementary companies was so compelling that it almost became a strategic necessity. The merged company would all of a sudden solve the respective strategic deficiencies and would be among the top three players in the world. In 2000, discussions between the CEO of Sola and the Zeiss board member responsible for this business were intensified. Several studies quantifying likely synergies had been commissioned independently in both companies.

In 2003 Rodenstock, one of the main competitors of Zeiss, became owned by a large private equity group. If Rodenstock merged with Sola or with Hoya, Zeiss would end up in a very difficult position.

Zeiss tried to acquire a majority or controlling stake in Sola, Sola made an offer to acquire the Zeiss division, ideas were exchanged about merging the two businesses keeping Sola listed in the US and with Zeiss owning a minority position of a listed company, but none of these ideas was successful. Carl Zeiss did not want to sell their eyeglass division, nor was a minority position of a NYSE listed company very compelling. Sola's CEO and Chairman were convinced that they could create more value for their shareholders than by just selling to a small German competitor, or by accepting Zeiss as a quasi controlling minority shareholder of a listed company.

In 2004 profound reform of the legal structure of the Carl Zeiss Foundation resulted in the formation of the Carl Zeiss AG (with the foundation as the sole shareholder) which allowed, for instance, the carve-out of certain business divisions as daughter companies. This opened the door to more creative solutions hitherto impossible for Zeiss to pursue.

Therefore, Zeiss wanted to act, but could they financially afford it, could they bear the integration risk totally on their own and how would they be able to make an attractive offer to the Sola board without having to largely overpay?

This was when the Zeiss executive board member presented the consolidation opportunity to the private equity company EQT, with which previously contacts in other projects had been established. EQT, on their part, realized the potential of a leveraged buyout and proposed a first model to Carl Zeiss.

But, how do you convince the CEO of a NYSE listed company, enjoying all the freedom of this world – only tainted in a minor way by Sarbanes-Oxley – to sell his company – and himself – to a mid-sized German company, even if he were to keep his job and become head of one of 6 business groups of Carl Zeiss AG?

Gaining the support of the CEO, his management team, and with them also the support of the board, was of crucial importance. Doing an unfriendly transaction would have made this big transatlantic merger far too risky.

Unfortunately, speaking to the CEO and making him a clear job offer within the deal was not an option because the CEO would no longer have been considered to be acting in the best interest of his shareholders.

US rules concerning a takeover of a stock listed company are very strict and make sure that the CEO is not brought into a difficult conflict of interest. The main consequence of these rules is that the risk of litigation is significantly higher and in order to contain this risk, the board of a target company is more or less obliged to run a small auction of the company and cannot just recommend the one offer to the shareholders. For Zeiss and EQT this would have been an unbearable risk: nobody wanted to spend millions in due diligence costs and then loose the transaction. It was crucial to convince the board that the deal was in the best interest of their shareholders, get board recommendation and as a consequence some reasonable deal protection like customary break up fees.

After thorough debate with US legal council, Zeiss and EQT decided to play both the industrial and the private equity card in their approach to management. In summer 2004, in a period when the stock price had been under severe pressure and Sola was trading at 15-16 USD, Zeiss and EQT decided to approach the Sola CEO in a joint effort with a new proposal – an industrial leveraged buyout – which finally opened the doors to a due diligence and takeover of the company.

Zeiss would show the industrial logic and the attractiveness of Sola being strengthened by the high quality products and brand name of Zeiss. This was largely self-explanatory since the Sola CEO himself had been working on a takeover of the Zeiss Eyeglass Division. The charming part of this merger was that both companies were so complementary and that huge synergy potential was to be expected by cross-selling and not so much by restructuring and associated lay-offs in the Sola organization.

EQT was to explain in broad, but attractive terms the logic of a leveraged buyout. This was to be a 50/50 joint venture, i.e. an independent company with a board of independent directors, not just a division of Zeiss as it would have been in a 100% acquisition by Carl Zeiss.

Carl Zeiss already had a publicly listed company on the Frankfurt Stock Exchange which added credibility to the portfolio management strategy and governance model of Carl Zeiss AG.

EQT invests only in companies with excellent and entrepreneurial management teams. Management is always offered to become co-owners of the company on highly attractive terms. To be part of such a deal is the chance of a lifetime for every manager. Both Zeiss and EQT, without offering any jobs, clearly stated that the Sola management team had been doing a great job and that a merger could not be successful with Zeiss management alone. The Sola CEO could not be sure of being CEO of the merged entity. But he knew that the likelihood of being offered a highly attractive job, both in terms of industrial challenge and financial upside was reasonably high.

EQT would have to exit its investment again in approximately five years. This could lead, for instance, to a listing of the company on the Frankfurt stock exchange so that also the long term perspective would be attractive.

At the end, offering an attractive industrial logic helps to open the doors, but it is very clear that a CEO and a board of a US listed company has only one task and this is to act in the best interest of their shareholders. So Zeiss and EQT definitely had to offer a very compelling price with a high premium to the current share price.

A highly complex transaction process

When in early summer 2004 the Sola share price declined from 24 USD to 17 USD, Zeiss and EQT had already established a strong personal trust relationship which was vital for undergoing a complex and time constraint process.

In July 2004 Zeiss and EQT analyzed all publicly available material and ran their evaluation models. All indicators showed that it was possible to pay a premium to the current share price. At the end of July it was decided to approach the Sola CEO conveying the message described above. The CEO agreed to give some limited information to help finding a more solid indicative valuation.

In August, Zeiss and EQT hired top advisers, analyzed the limited set of information and came up with an indicative bid which, after very tough negotiations with the Sola board leading to a material increase of the offer, was accepted by the board. This opened the door to detailed due diligence and contract negotiation.

The process was particularly complex because not only had Zeiss and EQT to become comfortable with Sola's performance and market position but Zeiss also had to work on the carve-out of a fully integrated division and EQT had to get comfortable with a valuation largely based on management accounts. On top of this, there was not only a contract to be negotiated with Sola but also a contribution agreement of the Zeiss division into the joint venture and a shareholder agreement between Zeiss and EQT. And if all this was not enough, it was to be a leveraged buyout, i.e. about two thirds of the funds were to be provided by banks. Prior to going public with a bid, there had to be a firm bank agreement and the banks also had to perform their due diligence.

The process was steered by two small but highly experienced teams within the Zeiss organization, headed by the CFO and executive board member responsible for the division, assisted by a project team comprising a handful of very senior managers, all basically working full-time on the project. Within EQT a team of four investment professionals were fully devoted to the transaction. At its peak the working group list including all external consultants, accountants, M&A lawyers, tax lawyers, investment bankers, financing bankers, environment or pension specialists, etc. included more than 60 people.

All in all, it was four months of extremely intense work. Work proceeded in parallel work streams, and coordination was essential. Luckily, when the offer price of 28 $ per share was confirmed on Dec 6, 2004, the board signed a merger agreement and recommended the final offer to the shareholders who finally accepted it in January 2005.

High synergies are expected

Right after the signing of the merger agreement in December 2004, a structured process of post merger integration (PMI) was launched, but before the announcement basic PMI considerations were part of the transaction project and decisions were taken.

The main synergies result from the complementarities of the two companies.

Zeiss would be able to save significant costs by having their semi-finished lenses and simple, commodity type finished lenses produced in the highly efficient low cost manufacturing sites of Sola.

Sola would benefit from Zeiss' know-how in the operation of Rx labs. There is a lot of complexity in the processing of a prescription lens, and a lot of process know-how in the coating of these lenses. Just upgrading all labs to best practice status would save a high million euro figure.

The combination of these two items accounts for the main part of the cost synergies. Besides, there is a large potential in cross-selling the two complementary product lines. While Sola, for example, had a strong presence in the US but was unable to compete in the high end of the market, Carl Zeiss Vision will now be able to compete with a full product offering and the strong Zeiss brand.

All in all, the cost synergies initially calculated to be more than 5% of the combined total cost base have now been validated in a very detailed bottom-up process and have actually turned out to be a conservative assumption.

A well prepared integration set-up to mitigate risk

It is common knowledge that the odds are against merging companies, synergies are generally overestimated, the cultural clash and a long period of insecurity lead to a major loss of key talent. Focusing on internal problems reduces customer service. In a vain attempt to keep frustrated customers, cost synergies are given to customers through reduced prices. Disappointed shareholders force management to work on a never-ending sequence of new restructuring programs.

In this project, on top of these common problems, one of the largest perceived risks in the transaction was the potential cultural clash between a US stock listed company running a highly decentralized organization and focused on operational efficiency in large-scale manufacturing and best price position in commodities, meeting a German privately held company, running a centralized organization with a strategic focus on top quality, advanced technology and branded high end products.

Furthermore, there were some joint venture related risks: true 50/50 joint ventures do not have the best reputation. Is there not always a power struggle between the two shareholders, making tough or bold decisions generally impossible? Do shareholder differences prevent CEOs from receiving and taking clear strategic directions, and do such situations allow or even force CEOs to play the political games in order to exploit potential shareholder conflicts for their own personal benefit or pure survival?

When establishing the joint venture, Zeiss and EQT put a strong focus on achieving clear consensus on the vision and strategy for the merged business and also on key principles on how to accomplish this strategy. A relatively detailed strategy plan and a paper based on the merger rationale and the analysis of the strategic due diligence trying to precisely clarify each party's understanding of key issues and actions for the new company became an appendix to the shareholder agreement.

The corporate governance principles had been thoroughly thought through: the management team was to get full operational freedom to run the business without direct interference of the shareholders. The management was to be steered by a board of independent non-executive directors with highly relevant experience in this business and in the integration task. All important strategic decisions were to be approved by this board with only very large equity related issues to be decided by the shareholders. All relevant decision makers, i.e. top management and the independent board members were to invest significant amounts of private money into the equity of the new company. There was a clear mutual understanding on how EQT was to eventually sell its stake after approximately five years, with a listing on the Frankfurt stock exchange being one likely scenario.

There was a clear understanding that the best manager was to be selected for each job, irrespective of his or her previous company. An independent consultant performed a professional assessment of the top 25 managers of both companies. A "grandfather principle" was introduced so that each manager could select his team but had to discuss it and get it approved by his superior. As expected, there was ample talent in both organizations so that the team was well balanced between both companies.

The CEO position was given to the former CEO of Sola because he had more than twenty years international experience in the eyeglass industry. He had been responsible for the integration of a very large former acquisition of Sola, American Optical. As CEO of Sola, he had very successfully led a huge cost efficiency program. And last but not least, he was highly motivated by this professional challenge and highly respected not only in the Sola but also in the Zeiss organization. Funnily enough, he had started his career as a manager in the Zeiss UK organization.

Zeiss and EQT were able to motivate highly experienced top industrialists as non-executive board members. The chairman was a Carl Zeiss executive board member who not only was intimately familiar with the eyeglass and related medical industries but had also been responsible for the successful integration of another large US business into the Carl Zeiss organization and had himself worked for a couple of years in a US company. Vice Chairman and Chairman of the integration committee of the board was a former executive board member of ABB who had managed the merger of Asea and Brown Bowery and who had later been responsible for several very large transatlantic mergers. Further board members were:

- A former executive board member of Electrolux and Kodak because of his in-depth knowledge on steering an independent sales channel where consumers buy complicated products and mostly rely on the guidance of the retailer.
- The current head of Mercedes Car Group because of his personal experience managing the merger between Daimler and Chrysler, his restructuring knowledge and his brand expertise.
- A second Carl Zeiss AG executive board member with a McKinsey background and very strong experience in restructuring and operational excellence and international distribution.
- A partner of EQT Partners of the Munich office also with personal experience in large merger situations.

The board meets six times a year, but the individual board members serve more as ongoing consultants to top management in the areas of most critical importance to the company such as brand strategy and integration issues. The greatest focus was placed on integration. Therefore, the Chairman and Vice Chairman of the board formed an Integration Committee. They started their work during the due diligence phase of the transaction, i.e. many months prior to closing and had had very regular contact with management. As an example, they were deeply involved in the selection of the PMI consultant as well as the selection process of the top management.

Inside the company, two of the most talented top managers were nominated to be full-time integration managers working together with the integration committee. They are steering a very large group of special integration projects with their respective task forces.

The most crucial success factor in the integration was to reduce the natural insecurity in the organizations and to use the distinct window of change in order to quickly get the necessary restructuring measures executed and return to a market and customer oriented culture again. Therefore, sense of urgency was one of the most commonly used buzzwords. Directly after signing of the merger agreement between Zeiss and Sola, i.e. three months prior to getting antitrust approval and then being able to close the transaction, a detailed bottom-up process of preparing the post merger integration was started. There were several workshops lasting a couple of days between the top management of both companies, who exchanged the data that could be shared from an anti trust perspective and worked on concrete plans for the phase after antitrust clearance. Directly after the closing of the transaction, the top management team and the organization of the new company could be announced. Shortly afterwards, key account managers were selected so that the key customers knew who their contact was.

As expected, there was tremendous enthusiasm in these workshops. The managers saw enormous potential and the probable synergies almost exploded. In summer 2005, most of these ideas have now been planned in a very detailed manner. The level of probable synergies has come down to a much more realistic level again but, fortunately, there still seems to a cushion compared to the original plan derived on a top-down basis during the due diligence. So far it is too early to tell how much of this cushion will be needed to overcome the likely difficulties on the road to implementation.

With regard to the risk of a cultural clash between the two very different organizations, it is also still too early to tell if this will be successfully overcome. Such comments were often heard from the management team members who came from Sola: "We at Sola have a more 'Let's do it, the customer requires it' mentality. At Zeiss they seem to take more time, sometimes too much time, to analyze things. But I wish we had their long-term perspective." A typical remark from a former Zeiss manager was: "At Sola they really know how to cut costs and get things done, but it is difficult to see a clear process and a long-term direction. It all depends on certain people's decisions. The company is very focused on a few people."

When looking more deeply into the Sola organization, all that can be said is that it would be wrong to consider it as a purely American company just because it is US headquartered. Actually, the culture is very international with a management team coming from the UK, USA and Australia. The CEO is a Brit who, as already mentioned, had already worked for Carl Zeiss in the UK for many years and who had been living in the US for more than ten years. He clearly has the profile required to bring together a German/European and a US culture. But given the scope of the task, it was only natural that, as part of the PMI project, a cultural survey was started which was carried out with the help of a consultant and covered several hundred employees from both parts of the new company.

Main lessons learnt from this case

One of the main success factors allowing a consistent, speedy transaction process was the clear view on and mutual understanding of the strategic fit at the outset of the project. During the project it was important to carefully and repeatedly verify the strategic rationale also against strategic alternatives, different scenarios and antici-pated potential competitive reactions as a response to the deal.

If – as in this case – there is more than one shareholder with equal rights, it is absolutely essential to get very early alignment among the shareholders on the strate-gic directions, methods both for the pre- and post-merger phase. What was also extremely important was clear and communicable consensus on different exit scenar-ios or, for example, on the question how deadlock situations will be resolved.

From our experience in this case, we can only recommend that the process of starting to think about post merger activities can never start too early. During the strategy phase, systematically pick up considerations for the PMI process and translate them into postulates for the PMI planning. Last but not least, the future management has to implement the strategy. Therefore, their involvement in the strategy formulation as early as possible is very important, in the knowledge that the sequence of the process flow and the legal restrictions might be an obstacle. Some key lessons were:

- Find two ambitious top managers – one from each of the two units to be merged – to serve as full-time integration managers and steer the integration process.
- Define and announce the top management team and the organization of the new company as early as possible in order to reduce the risk of any disruption and management defection.
- Have a clear communication plan for all stakeholders with clear and consistent messages, in particular the request for information from employees in particular is high and a worldwide communication campaign needs intensive preparation.

A few comments should be made about the overall project or process management.

It was in our opinion essential that great attention and strong involvement of the key decision makers during the whole process was guaranteed. In addition, the permanent need for an efficient escalation required an escalation procedure again involving the key decision makers.

Throughout the project we assigned two very experienced teams (Zeiss and EQT), working full-time on the project and cooperating very effectively. The teams also realized early on that speed is critical. Highly efficient process management, use of first class consultants with clear briefings and directives was of key importance.

As always, transactions and integrations are all carried out by people. Consequently, the "Human Resource," cultural or so called soft aspect of such a project should not be underestimated. It may very well be that this is the decisive 5% one needs to turn a potentially successful or good project into a successful and great project. Our personal findings are again listed:

- Establish an atmosphere of trust: Personal trustful relationships between EQT and Zeiss on the one hand and with the CEO and Board of Sola on the other were of crucial importance.
- Candidness is key: Whenever concerns come up they should be discussed in an open and task-oriented manner. Critical issues should be discussed at top level directly, thus not affecting the atmosphere at the working group level.

- Firmness and consistency provide credibility and reliability: Do what you say and be in line with your guiding principles. When you have ultimately come to a point, where it is necessary to stand up and walk away – be serious and do it!

- Consistent communication: Timely, clear and coherent messages throughout the whole transaction process generate trust. This is especially important also for stakeholders in the approval processes.

- Enthusiasm is helpful: Since the merger logic was so evident, the management teams of both merged units were convinced and enthusiastic about the deal. Everybody saw the enormous potential. Build on such enthusiasm in the pre-merger project phase and keep the "fire burning" in the PMI process.

Outlook

At the time this contribution is being written, we have just completed the 3rd month of the merged company Carl Zeiss Vision. Obviously, it is far too early to speak about a successful merger. We can only state that it has been possible to carry over a large part of the enthusiasm and energy from the transaction phase into the post-merger phase. The company is performing largely according to plan, even though some adverse market environments (e.g. German post health care reform market demand) are impacting revenues. With a few exceptions, PMI projects are also on target and even more importantly, the company has received overwhelmingly positive reactions from customers.

Looking at the map of sites for CZ Vision (Figure 3.18), taking into account the management structure and composition, the expertise in the board, the shareholder structure and related attractive exit options and not forgetting the many loyal customers, this setup has all the ingredients to make CZ Vision a real success story.

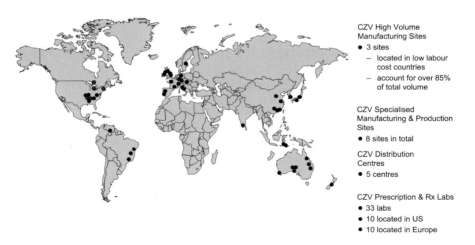

CZV High Volume
Manufacturing Sites
- 3 sites
  - located in low labour cost countries
  - account for over 85% of total volume

CZV Specialised
Manufacturing & Production
Sites
- 8 sites in total

CZV Distribution
Centres
- 5 centres

CZV Prescription & Rx Labs
- 33 labs
- 10 located in US
- 10 located in Europe

Figure 3.18 Carl Zeiss Vision's worldwide presence – a truly global company

Acknowledgment

We would like to thank to: Tomas Aubell, Andreas Eichelberger, Dr. Sumeet Gulati, Ulrich Hoffmann, Jürgen L. Hund, Andreas Huthöfer, Klaus Leinmüller, Dr. Michael Mertin, Dr. Christian Müller, Josef Riedel, and Werner Weber for their valuable contribution to the project.

Literature

Stevenson, Robert Louis; Sinatra, Frank: Project Management and Control, Wiley, New York 1964

L. Gordon Crovitz: Allianzen: Harvard Business Manager, February 2005, p. 12

Bamford, James; Ernst, David: Governing Joint Ventures. The McKinsey Quarterly 2005 special edition: Value and Performance

3.3.3 Air-Shields Integration into Dräger Medical: Experiences in the Medical-Equipment Industry

Wolfgang Reim, Rudolf-Henning Lohse, Carsten Kratz

This case study describes the process applied when the global Air-Shields business (US based) was carved out and integrated into the Dräger Medical Group (headquartered in Germany). The size of the business and the uncertain timeline of the antitrust approval process indicated a need to perform the carve out and integration quickly. The following approach was successfully used for two global carve-out and integration projects within the Dräger Medical Group. We believe this case study can provide helpful tips to readers to successfully accomplish their own integration.

Introduction: Company profiles and starting conditions

This section briefly describes the involved companies: Dräger Medical AG & Co. KGaA (Dräger Medical), a joint venture of Drägerwerk AG and Siemens AG, the buyer; Hill-Rom, a division of Hillenbrand Industries, Inc., the seller; and Air-Shields, the business that was carved out and integrated.

Dräger Medical is one of the world's leading manufacturers of medical equipment with a net sales volume of €1,023.4 million in 2004. As the largest division of Drägerwerk AG, Dräger Medical offers products, services, and integrated Care Area™ solutions throughout the patient-care process, including Emergency Care, Perioperative Care, Critical Care, Perinatal Care (particular products sold to neonatal intensive care units), and Home Care. With its headquarters in Lübeck, Germany, Dräger Medical employs nearly 6,000 people worldwide. R&D and production are located not only

decisions formed the initial point for defining the integration's top-down goals. In addition, important decisions with regard to the future setup of the perinatal service business were made. The workshops also established basic principles for addressing future organizational issues concerning the BU-PNC – for example, the operational start (Day 1), organization chart, and reporting structure. These boundary conditions formed the basis for the complete integration team's work in subphases 1 through 3.

A small team undertook the second component of subphase 0 – the Integration planning approach – using the results from the Strategy and Organization workshops. They defined the overall timeline, project organization, and roles and responsibilities (working mode). They also prepared the subphase's first event, the kickoff, and the 1st "Block Week" (which will be explained later) to bring the integration team up to speed in a short time. Another component addressed the Readiness of the BU-PNC to operate on Day 1 without customer-side or internal disruptions. Therefore, the important topics – which were responsible for Readiness on Day 1 – had to be identified (Readiness Topics) in order for the teams to be able to start working immediately on these issues during the kickoff and 1st Block Week. Additionally, the whole process for defining, managing, and controlling the achievement of Readiness was defined in detail (Readiness Topic lists, workplan templates, IT workspace, Readiness Cockpit). Due to the good preparation in subphase 0, the full team was able to start working immediately on the readiness topics during the kickoff and 1st Block Week. This preparation work in subphase 0 was absolutely necessary for conducting subphases 1 and 2 (carve out and integration) within the short time frame of approximately 12 weeks.

Subphase 1, which lasted four weeks, focused on Integration planning (some preparation had already been completed during subphase 0 to guarantee a quick start). The full integration team, composed of approximately 85 employees from the three involved companies (Dräger Medical, Air-Shields, Hill-Rom), started to identify and work on carve-out and integration topics. Subphase 1's main goals included setting up the joint teams and identifying tasks needing to be fulfilled by Day C to ensure the legal transfer of the Air-Shields business to Dräger Medical and by Day 1 to achieve Readiness. Based on a prepared Readiness Topic list – that covered all tasks to ensure a legal transfer on Day C and to achieve Readiness on Day 1, the Module teams defined Detailed Readiness Workplans with all prerequisites, tasks and actions, milestones, responsibilities, and start and completion dates. The team established such workplans for 100 Readiness Topics and identified possible transitional services Dräger Medical might need after Day C from Air-Shields' mother company Hill-Rom.

Creation of the new functional BU-PNC was the primary task of subphase 2, which lasted eight weeks. The integration team focused on carving out and transferring the global Air-Shields business to Dräger Medical on Day C and on setting up the new BU-PNC, which had to be ready to operate on Day 1 (work on Detailed Readiness Workplans). Subphase 2 also included preparing the Closing Week as well as defining PNC-BU's functional and organizational setup (e.g., processes, people, and positions). In addition, the integration team prepared all Dräger Medical internal prerequisites (e.g., IT infrastructure, payroll, communication processes, etc.) in order to integrate the new BU-PNC into the Dräger Medical organization without friction losses.

Subphase 3, lasting eight weeks, focused on two topics: Measure definition and Implementation and Controlling. The project-team size dropped to approximately 40 people because many tasks were handed back to the line organization and became part of the operative business. Measure definition concerned identifying a bottom-up concept precisely addressing how each top-down target set by Dräger Medical top management could be reached; it also meant deriving commitments from each responsible manager. Implementation and Controlling activities involved monitoring the integration efforts after Day 1, especially ongoing work on topics necessary for complete integration but not for being ready on Day 1 (e.g., aligning accounting issues).

In addition to defining the integration phases, organizing the project itself proved another key success factor for this high-speed integration. This topic is described in the next section below.

The integration organization: How to successfully manage the whole integration process

This section primarily focuses on describing the team setup during the Integration phases and major team events. In the following, we give you first a detailed insight into the overall organization and then present the major team events.

Overall organization and working mode

As mentioned in section 4, only a very limited number of Dräger Medical and Air-Shields employees – mainly top management – were involved in working on the two aspects of subphase 0. As a result, only a small project organization with three teams was established. The Executive Integration Team (EIT) was tasked with preparing the groundwork for obtaining boundary conditions in the Strategy and Organization workshops as well as setting up all necessary activities to quickly start subphase 1. During subphase 1 the team consisted of the Dräger Medical integration project leader and an external consultant. The Legal/Antitrust/Closing Team was responsible for preparing a high-level plan for Air-Shields' carve out from Hill-Rom and its subsequent integration into the Dräger Medical organization. This team was also tasked with determining the overall integration timeline and related activities. During subphase 0, the team was limited to the Hill-Rom carve-out manager, the Dräger Medical integration project leader, the Air-Shields site manager, and an external consultant. Both EIT and the Legal/Antitrust/Closing Team expanded for subphases 1 through 3, as described below in this article. A third team, the Steering Committee (SC), led the Strategy and Organization workshops and defined boundary conditions for the overall integration. Team members included Dräger Medical top management, the Dräger Medical integration project leader, and external consultants.

As subphase 1 began, the number and size of the teams grew considerably; as the actual integration work unfolded, the teams' tasks changed. Figure 3.21 outlines the organization in place through the end of subphase 3.

The SC was the only team (six members) that remained unchanged for the duration of the project. They held biweekly meetings to monitor high-level integration issues, make necessary (strategic) decisions e.g., nominating management positions for the new BU-PNC etc.), and find solutions to problems EIT could not solve (e.g., regulating compensation for Air-Shields employees, etc.).

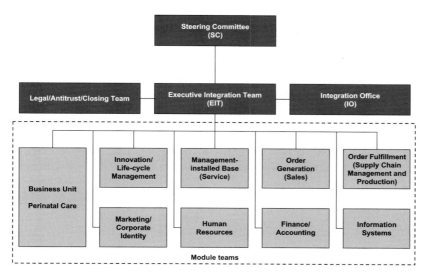

Figure 3.21 Organization of the integration

In subphases 1 through 3, EIT's composition changed: Dräger Medical and Air-Shields top management, the Dräger Medical integration project leader, all module team leaders (some modules were led by Dräger Medical employees, some by Air-Shields employees), employees from Dräger Medical's legal department, and external consultants – a total of 25 members, represented EIT. Their major task was to carefully monitor the integration process to ensure the Day C business transfer and Day 1 Readiness. This team had to define and decide on measures if issues came up that threatened to force the project off track ("troubleshooting list"). In addition, EIT provided overall guidance on module team work. EIT and Steering Committee members met on a weekly basis (conference calls); participation was mandatory.

The Integration Office (IO) was responsible for overall information, communication, and data-flow consolidation. The main tasks consisted of, developing the common business plan and preparing overall external and internal project communication, especially the EIT conference call. The main objective of internal project communication was a weekly report about the project status (Readiness Cockpit), therefore the team aggregated the status of the 100 Detailed Readiness Workplans on a weekly basis. The module teams continuously updated them according to their work's progress. The four-person team from Dräger Medical and Air-Shields plus external consultants held daily meetings.

The role of the Legal/Antitrust/Closing Team remained the same in subphase 1 as it was in subphase 0. They worked continuously on carve-out and integration issues, prepared the Block Weeks and Closing Week, finalized the Transitional Service Agreement, and took care of overall topics concerning the module teams and countries. The team was enlarged with internal and external legal support from Dräger Medical and Air-Shields and consisted of ten members. They held weekly conference calls.

The module teams carried out the actual work outlined in the Detailed Readiness Workplans to ensure Air-Shields carve out from Hill-Rom and its subsequent integration into the Dräger Medical organization. The module teams were set up in accordance with Dräger Medical business processes. The average team size totaled eight, with employees coming from Dräger Medical and Air-Shields as well as partially from Hill-Rom. As mentioned above, Dräger Medical employees led some teams while Air-Shields employees led others. The module teams held weekly conference calls and physical meetings locally during the Block Weeks.

For the overall Air-Shields integration, Dräger Medical involved only two external resources: legal and consulting. Legal support was required for negotiating with Hill-Rom, setting up the contract, and providing assistance during the antitrust process. The consultants brought experience with PMIs and processes as well as methodology know-how to the table.

Block Weeks

Below we outline one special meeting constellation as, in our opinion, it proved to be major factor in successfully realizing a rapid, smooth overall integration process. A core challenge for the whole integration was the limited time between the kickoff in mid-April 2004 and the BU-PNC's operational start on Day 1 (1 July 2004). Adding to this challenge was the problem that team members were located in two different countries, the United States and Germany. And compounding this problem was the difficulty that even team members from the same company might be located at different sites within these two countries. The compressed time and scattered locations meant that achieving broader alignment within and between the teams solely through conference calling was very difficult to achieve. Dräger Medical, Air-Shields, and Hill-Rom top management then decided to bring the teams together in one location for the crucial phases of the integration project by establishing the concept of Block Weeks. As outlined in Figure 3.20, three Block Weeks were executed during the integration, each taking place at the beginning of its respective subphase and each having a different focus. Block Weeks were held at the Air-Shields site in the United States, with participation from all integration team members except the SC. Alignment and synchronization within and between the module teams was secured to ensure that each team was working on the right topics and no topics were forgotten. In addition to that, interfaces between the Module teams and redundancies could be identified right from the beginning to save precious time.

The kickoff and 1st Block Week aimed to set up planning for the integration. Dräger Medical, Air-Shields, and Hill-Rom top management presented the overall integration setup, rationale for the integration and boundary conditions (which had been developed in the Strategy and Organization workshops), expectations for the coming weeks, and "dos and don'ts" during the pending antitrust process to align all integration team members. The module teams worked on two work streams: The first work stream involved setting up the majority of the 100 Detailed Readiness Workplans, including the identification of major interfaces and redundancies with other modules; and the second identified areas where transitional services might be necessary. Consequently, a lot of meetings between two or more module teams – as shown in Figure 3.22 for the service module team – took place during that week (cross-module meet-

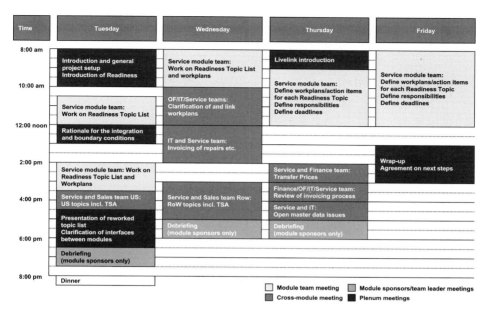

Figure 3.22 Schedule for kickoff and 1st Block Week for the service module team

ings). At the end of each day, all module team leaders met for a debriefing meeting to identify the major tasks for the single modules on the next day and to discuss cross-module topics.

The 2nd Block Week took place at the beginning of subphase 2. It was similarly structured as the 1st Block Week and also involved many cross-module meetings. The 2nd Block Week aimed to align the module teams' tasks with the "deadlines" unfolding over the next eight weeks for the new functional BU-PNC's creation (e.g., action items, interfaces, redundancies, responsibilities, and major milestones). The 3rd Block Week took place one week before the beginning of subphase 3 (Day 1) and directly after closing (Day C). One day after closing, as the first event of the 3rd Block Week, the CEO of Dräger Medical gave a presentation in Hatboro welcoming the new Dräger Medical employees. He presented Dräger Medical's overall strategy, outlined the goals to be achieved through the acquisition, and introduced the new BU-PNC management team. For the first time, Dräger Medical and Air-Shields employees could share all sensitive data. During that Block Week, all necessary tasks for ensuring Readiness on Day 1 were finished and all open issues were addressed and closed. As in the Block Weeks before, it was beneficial to have all module teams in one location because at lot of cross-module meetings took place to finalize open tasks.

Main lessons derived from the Air-Shields integration

All integration processes can carry numerous pitfalls, but we believe the ten lessons listed in table 3.2 can help avoid most of them. They are divided into two categories: preparing for the integration and executing the integration.

Main lessons

Preparing for the integration (initial phase)

1. As early as possible, integrate the integration project leader, who should play an important role in the future organization (candidate screening and due diligence).

2. Manifest the proposed integration approach and process in the purchasing agreement in as much detail as possible.

3. Name one lawyer to support the legal team for the entire duration of the project (from due diligence through closing) and use this resource as a knowledge pool for all potential future contract matters.

Executing the integration (integration phases)

4. Conduct a joint kickoff with the entire team and top management to facilitate identification with the project and "buy-in" from everyone – doing so guarantees a quick project start and sets the foundation for good cooperation later.

5. Cultivate a culture of trust by facilitating many cross-company team meetings from the beginning of the integration project on – trust can only be created if people know one other; a lack of trust hinders goal-oriented implementation.

6. Communicate the rationale for the integration (strategic logic) and define the top-down goals of the PMI at the beginning of the project – doing so is a prerequisite for operative management to break goals down into operative concepts and measures.

7. Recycle approaches from earlier integration projects (formats, processes, institutions – for example, EIT call) because (one's own) employees are used to them already.

8. Accomplish detailed "cross-functional checks" of the teams' working packages (e.g., Detailed Readiness Workplans) at the beginning of the integration project in order to identify interfaces with other modules as well as to eliminate redundancies and conduct Block Weeks to ensure broad alignment between all teams.

9. Outline the clean-team and data-room processes – if needed – as clearly as possible (one responsible person, simple processes, easy-to-use formats).

10. Do not stop the integration project after closing: monitor integration for at least two months following the closing day (e.g., continue with EIT calls) because the real problems come up when the operative business really starts.

Table 3.2 Main lessons from the Air-Shields integration

This case study can only offer a short overview of the topics touching this integration project as well as provide an idea of the many exciting challenges to be faced in a PMI situation. If you are currently considering a merger or acquisition, ensure that you are clear on the strategic logic at an early stage and set up the integration process accordingly. Consider what needs to happen during the PMI when negotiations succeed. Ensure that you are communicating the right signals and avoid well-meant gestures you will regret later. Above all, avoid compromises that lead to the lowest common denominator.

3.4 Electro & Electronics

3.4.1 Investing Locally to Grow Globally: Siemens M&A Strategy in the U.S. Market

George Nolen

For more than 10 years, Siemens has actively pursued an ambitious acquisitions strategy to grow its share of the key U.S. market. But the shifting economic climate and the rise of globalization required Siemens to adjust this strategy to stay competitive and profitable. The U.S. market remains an ever-important target of investment for Siemens and a linchpin of its global strategy.

Introduction

In the January 2005 issue of the influential *Harvard Business Review*, Dr. Heinrich v. Pierer noted how the U.S. market plays a central role in the growth strategy of Siemens AG. "Wherever it makes sense for us to do something in the United States, we do it," the CEO of Siemens told the editors of HBR. "It is still the biggest market in the world, and a very competitive market. Succeeding in the U.S. was critical to becoming more competitive as a company."

More than any previous CEO of Siemens before him, Dr. von Pierer, who is now Chairman of the Supervisory Board of Siemens, crafted a growth strategy that focused on tapping the huge potential for Siemens in the U.S. market. While in hindsight the strategy seems obvious, the stakes were high at the time and so was the risk. Though it operated in nearly every country, Siemens had yet to become a major player in the United States. The U.S. accounts for about 35 percent of the $4 trillion global electrical capital goods market. If Siemens was to succeed in its strategy of global expansion, it had to increase its share of the U.S. market and sustain long-term growth there. In short, we had to invest locally to grow globally.

Under CEO Heinrich von Pierer, who rose to the top job in 1992, Siemens followed a strategy that aggressively went after GE and other rivals on American turf. Breaking from a tradition that focused primarily on organic growth, Siemens went on an acquisition spree in the USA in the 1990s to fuel its growth there. The strategy succeeded initially and Siemens USA grew steadily, often at the expense of its rivals. The USA's share of global sales for Siemens went from 11 percent at the end of fiscal 1993 to 21 percent a decade later.

But there were inherent perils in such rapid growth. Would Siemens become a victim of its own success? When the Internet bubble burst and the U.S. economy spiraled into recession in the early years of the new century, it was clear that Siemens had to adapt this transatlantic M&A strategy to stay on the growth track. To analyze Siemens' M&A strategy in the U.S. market in this period, I have divided our activities in three chronological sections that trace the phases of our investment and growth.

Phase 1: Rapid expansion 1992 – 2001

In 1990, Siemens underwent a complete reorganization – its first in 20 years – that divided the company's large business units into smaller operations that would be better equipped to successfully compete in the steadily more complex and competitive global marketplace. With this more responsive corporate structure, Siemens sought to grow key elements of its communications and information technology, power generation, medical systems and lighting groups. These industry sectors formed the core of Siemens' plan to build its business and market share in the USA in the 1990s.

Siemens began its M&A push in the USA in 1992 by taking a controlling stake in the communications company Rolm. Formed originally as a joint venture between Siemens and IBM, Rolm provided Siemens an entrée into the then fast-growing market for private communications systems and enabled the German conglomerate to raise its profile as a leader in information technology.

A push in lighting came next when Siemens affiliate Osram bought the Sylvania lighting and precision materials businesses in North America from GTE in 1993. More than a century after Edison invented the light bulb and Siemens improved it, Siemens was competing head to head with GE in the lighting business. Today Osram-Sylvania is the second largest lighting materials company in the world, in large part due to this merger.

Perhaps the most hotly contested and coveted industry for Siemens in its competition with GE is in medical systems. In the mid-90's, Siemens revamped its strategy for its medical division, selling its dental-technology business to concentrate on the high-growth sectors of ultrasound and healthcare information technology systems (Daniela Decurtins, *Siemens: Anatomie eines Unternehmens*, 2002). The strategy took hold in the USA in 2000 with the purchase of Shared Medical Systems, a leader in the rapidly expanding market for healthcare IT services. In 2001, Siemens bought Acuson, a maker of ultrasound devices, boosting its market share and giving it critical mass with its healthcare customers.

Table 3.3 presents a short list of key acquisitions Siemens made in the USA from 1992 – 2005.

Table 3.3 Siemens key acquisitions in the USA

Fiscal year	Recent major U.S. acquisitions
1992	Rolm
1993	Sylvania
1998	Westinghouse Power Generation
1999	Unisphere
1999	Applied Automation
2000	Motorola Lighting
2000	Gardner Transportation Systems
2000	Moore Products
2000	Entex Information Services
2000	Shared Medical Systems
2001	Acuson
2001	Efficient Networks
2001	Security Technologies Group
2004	DaimlerChrysler Huntsville Facility
2004	USFilter
2005	CTI Molecular Imaging (to be completed in 2nd quarter/2005)

Siemens spent more than $8 billion in period from 1995 – 2001 (and a total of more than $10 billion to date) to acquire companies that fit its strategy and portfolio in the United States. It was a bold move on the home court of its primary adversary, GE. The decade of the 1990's was the largest expansion of Siemens in the USA, one of historic proportions. Siemens USA flourished from a tiny outpost in the 1970's's employing 650 people to a major contributor to Siemens growth and profit, employing 70,000 people and representing more than 20 percent of Siemens total world sales by the turn of the 21st century.

The assessment of our strategy has been positive for the most part. Discussing our M&A strategy in the medical area, investment firm Morgan Stanley wrote in a report dated August 31, 2004: "So have Siemens' steps in its medical division made sense? We think they have, in that Siemens has migrated away from simply being a supplier of medical imaging product; and gained local market (that is, US) leverage against its principal competitor in this segment, GE."

In addition to medical and other sectors, Siemens sought to grow in the U.S. power generation market. GE enjoyed dominance of the U.S. power market and a strong global position. In the 1980's, Siemens had only a minor stake in this sector. But with its 1998 acquisition of the power business from Westinghouse, Siemens leapt into a strong number two position behind GE in the U.S. domestically and globally. Kai

Lucks discusses the background and planning that went into this deal in his article in this volume on Westinghouse. Siemens Westinghouse CEO Randy Zwirn also provides key insights from the management perspective.

Of course, this growth came at a price – managing Siemens USA proved challenging and with the recession that accompanied the bursting of the Internet bubble in 2000 – 2001, it was clear that Siemens needed to revisit its growth strategy in the all-important U.S. market. Adding to the top line through acquisitions was one thing; ensuring that they contributed to the bottom line was a more difficult task.

Phase 2: Watch that bottom line! (2001 – 2003)

While much of this M&A activity in the USA proved successful for Siemens, the company had bitten off a large chunk of market share in diverse industries. Though the acquisitions fit our strategy and the portfolio, integrating companies as diverse as Westinghouse and Shared Medical Services under the Siemens banner proved difficult. Further complicating matters, the operating companies in the USA traditionally took their cues from their respective global corporate headquarters in Germany, reinforcing a silo mentality, discouraging cross-selling and diluting any synergies.

By 2001, with profits vanishing due to the recession in the USA, executives of Siemens Corporation, the U.S. holding company in New York, undertook a radical revamping of their operations. In 2001, the year that Siemens' shares began trading on the New York Stock Exchange, then-Chief Operating Officer Klaus Kleinfeld devised a new strategy, the U.S. Business Initiative (USBI), which aimed to trim the excesses of the M&A binge and improve the bottom-line performance of the company. Kleinfeld and his team formulated the USBI with two goals: improve the performance of the operating companies and their margins on the one hand and create more synergies and cross-selling among them on the other.

To boost profitability of the U.S. business operations, Siemens Corp. executives adapted a strategy that their rival GE devised under the aegis of CEO Jack Welch (be first or second in a given sector or get out). Siemens Corporation scrutinized the acquisitions of the operating companies and drew up a plan to fix, sell or close the unprofitable operations. "We'd made acquisitions where you questioned why they had been made," Kleinfeld told *The Wall Street Journal Europe* in September 2003. While the operating companies initially balked at having corporate look over their shoulder, von Pierer and management in Munich supported Kleinfeld and the USBI. By 2002, the number of money-losing businesses in the USA was reduced from 24 to 8. Kleinfeld, who became CEO of Siemens Corp. in 2002, also succeeded in cutting costs – upwards of $100 million annually – by creating a shared services organization that performed payroll, travel, IT, export-import and other non-core business functions for the operating companies. Within two years of the USBI's implementation, Siemens went from a loss of around $600 million to a profit of approximately $685 million.

The second programmatic element of the USBI was to coax the operating companies into more cooperation in order to tap the synergy and critical mass of Siemens. To encourage the operating companies to pursue business jointly, Kleinfeld and his team created *Siemens One*, a cross-company sales organization based in Atlanta but active

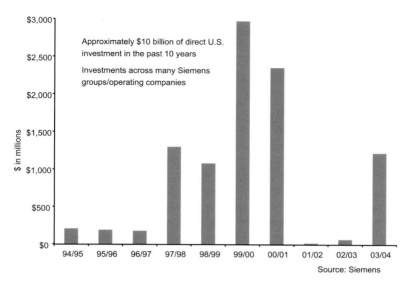

Figure 3.23 Siemens USA direct investments

nationally that spearheaded deals that involved more than one operating company. Presenting one point of contact to the customer, Siemens One helped sell and coordinate major deals in the U.S., including a joint project with Boeing for the Transportation Security Administration to enhance airport security and the construction of Reliant Stadium in Houston. From large infrastructure projects to information technology services such as help desk support, Siemens One continues to play an important role in helping the operating companies win new business.

By 2003, the U.S. economy had begun to heal and pick up. GE, Philips and other direct competitors were boosting sales but Siemens, while returning to profitability, seemed to be stuck in cost-reduction mode. Siemens operations were also picking up in key regions, notably in China and other parts of Asia. At the annual Siemens Business Conference in Berlin in October 2003, von Pierer said it was time for Siemens to pursue the twin goal of profit and growth. With about 80 percent of the company's revenue now coming from outside Germany, von Pierer said that Siemens would redouble its efforts in key markets such as the USA and China. "The U.S. is our biggest market – and also our greatest challenge, keeping us fit and innovative for the tough global arena," von Pierer said in a speech in Washington, D.C., in early November 2003. "We see a very bright future for our company in the U.S. We intend to keep investing in this great country. And we will continue to depend on our talented Americans to help keep us at the forefront of the industry."

Phase 3: Era of disciplined growth (2004 –)

The mandate from Munich to grow sales in a disciplined fashion is at the center of the third and most recent phase of Siemens in the USA since the launch of its growth by acquisition strategy a decade earlier. The mantle of leadership for this "profitable growth" phase fell to me, when I became the first American executive to lead Siemens in the USA. I succeeded Kleinfeld in January 2004 after more than 20 years of experience at Siemens in communications sales. Kleinfeld became CEO of Siemens AG in January 2005.

The U.S. Growth Initiative is designed to improve sales and revenue in the U.S. region by focusing on customer and market penetration, innovation and – in a nod to the successful strategy launched by von Pierer in 1992 – on acquisitions. Partnerships are also important in the U.S. market. For example, leveraging its long-standing joint venture in Bosch-Siemens Hausgeraete (BSH), Siemens completed in 2004 a $200 million expansion of its BSH manufacturing facility in New Bern, NC. This plant will turn out Siemens-branded consumer goods such as blenders and dishwashers for sale in places such as Best Buy. A print advertising campaign for these consumer goods is also underway to provide marketing support.

Our cross-selling engine, Siemens One, will continue to play a central role in boosting sales with public and private sector customers, including large government-financed infrastructure projects. Siemens One hit a milestone in 2004 of providing more than $100 million in incremental revenue. Our success in driving these inter-divisional synergies is being copied by our competitors in the U.S. market. I have also made it a priority to expand the Government Business Office of Siemens One based in Washington in order to concentrate on federal, state and local bids.

Under Kleinfeld, Siemens also clearly intends to continue to play, albeit carefully and strategically, the acquisition card to spur growth.

In fiscal 2004, Siemens acquired the Huntsville, Alabama-based electronic components manufacturing facility of DaimlerChrysler, which had put this non-core unit on the market to cut costs and focus on its primary manufacturing tasks. This strategic acquisition in 2004 will add about $1 billion in sales to Siemens VDO Automotive and keep about 2,000 jobs in that state. Equally important, our expanded presence in this region – known as "Detroit South" because of its concentrated number of auto manufacturers both domestic and foreign – will bring us closer to our customers and shorten the time-to-market of our next generation products. Siemens VDO Automotive has been active also in neighboring South Carolina, where it is building the North America headquarters for its Power train Diesel Systems Division and investing $25 million in a national R&D center for diesel technology that will result in nearly 100 additional high tech jobs.

The other major acquisition of 2004 was the deal for nearly $1 billion of US Filter, a leading water treatment firm in North America. With the water rapidly becoming the "oil of the 21st Century," this M&A deal signals that the U.S. market for Siemens remains central to its global growth strategy and that Siemens is committed to competing against GE in high growth sectors that are not part of its traditional portfolio. Solidly profitable, US Filter has revenues of $1.2 billion and 5,800 employees, making Siemens a big player in the world's largest water market. The integration of U.S. Filter into Siemens Industrial Solutions groups was completed smoothly.

The first major U.S. M&A deal of 2005 came in the medical arena with the announced acquisition of CTI Molecular Imaging Inc. Michael Reitermann, president of Siemens

Medical Solutions Nuclear Medicine Division in Hoffman Estates, Illinois said innovation and market share motivated the deal: "Molecular medicine will result in more individualized and more effective diagnosis and therapy. CTI Molecular Imaging has been actively engaged in next-generation molecular diagnostics research and the development of new imaging technologies and biomarkers. This acquisition will enable Siemens to strengthen and broaden our capabilities in molecular imaging, and define new standards within the industry."

Conclusion: Beyond M&A: Investing broadly for sustainable growth

In the last 10 years, it's clear that Siemens has successfully grown its business and market share in the U.S. through a strategy of aggressive acquisitions in key sectors. The strategy started in the early 1990's under Dr. von Pierer is continuing in the 21st Century under his successor, Klaus Kleinfeld. As Siemens moves forward in the U.S. market, our strategy of investing locally extends well beyond deals for companies. Our long-term approach to sustainable growth the U.S. market also encompasses investments in research & development, government relations and corporate citizenship. I would like to conclude my discussion by looking briefly at each of these pillars of our broader strategy.

R&D: Investing locally also guides our approach to research and development. Globally, Siemens dedicates about six billion dollars to R&D or about seven percent of sales. This makes us one of the largest supporters of corporate R&D of any company anywhere. In the USA, Siemens invests more than $800 million in R&D and has more than 6800 people dedicated to researching the next generation of products and services. Major original research is conducted our Siemens Corporate Research facility in Princeton, New Jersey. Siemens Corporate Research works with our business divisions on a tremendous scope of projects including medical imaging, industrial automation, communications networks, software engineering, security technologies, to name just a few areas. SCR also partners on projects with numerous universities and institutions of higher learning.

But in our globalized economy speed is everything. The pace of innovation is accelerating. Everybody is working on the next big thing. So how does a global company like Siemens stay aware of everything, especially in the research-rich and creative U.S. market? In several ways. Our Technology to Business Center in Berkeley California hunts for ideas and inventions that offer high ROI but represent high risk. TTB invests in a wide variety of start-ups and works with major research universities such as Berkeley, Stanford, the University of Michigan to name a few. Viable ideas are spun off as separate businesses or become part of the Siemens family and marketed globally to our customers. We have a $600 million venture capital organization with offices in Boston and San Jose that invests in companies – many in the U.S. – that can contribute products to our existing Siemens businesses. We are always on the look-out for ways to grow our business in the U.S. We look internally and externally for ways to meet the immediate needs of our customers' and their customers. We also keep an eye on the future to ensure we meet the needs of tomorrow's customers.

Government Relations: Much of our business, both here in the United States and worldwide, involves building or improving the infrastructure essential to the functioning of society, such as projects in the energy, water, communications spheres, to name a few. These projects are often public-private partnerships and de facto bring us into close contact with government at all levels. Government business in fact comprises a significant piece of our existing and potential business. Cultivating relationships with our government partners is a high priority for Siemens, whether it's a local chamber of commerce or meeting at the White House. Our message is simple and consistent: we're a reliable, financially stable partner who is investing in the U.S. market for the long term.

This message is more than about just making good business sense because in the globalized economy, government partners want to know that the companies involved in crucial infrastructure projects are in fact around for the long haul. We want all public policy officials and procurement decision makers to know this about Siemens. We want them to know we have 70,000 employees here – most of them American citizens. We want them to know we manufacture many of our products here and help make other companies competitive enough to grow their operations here.

Corporate Citizenship: While our research units and venture capitalists work to discover the next big thing, the Siemens Foundation in the USA sets its sights on those young people of promise who we hope some day will invent the next next big thing. We do this in a number of ways. You might have heard of The Siemens Westinghouse Competition in Math, Science & Technology. This program recognizes remarkable talent early on, fostering individual growth for high school students who are willing to challenge themselves through science research. Through this competition, students have an opportunity to achieve national recognition for science research projects that they complete in high school. The Siemens Foundation invests $1 million annually in the Siemens Westinghouse competition and other scholarship programs. These students are extremely bright, diligent and they represent the future of American leadership in science and business.

But there is a cloud on the horizon. The U.S. is not producing enough engineers and scientists as it used to. Our global competitors, such as China and Korea, are graduating many more students in the hard sciences and engineering. So the Siemens Foundation is responding with a couple of new programs that will support future instructors of math and science. Siemens is also dispatching its engineers into American grammar schools armed with some cool hands-on scientific experiments – and a few talking points of course about the importance of science for the future and what a cool job being a engineer is. Some of our divisions, in particular Building Technologies in Chicago, have been doing this for a few years with great success.

Community relations programs such as these are an integral part of our growth strategy of investing locally in the U.S. market. And these are only the national programs. Many of our 70,000 American colleagues volunteer in their local communities under our Siemens Caring Hands organization. We established this effort to help organize and provide resources to our employees around the country so we can have a positive impact in the communities where live and work. Relationships are everything in business. They require work and attention. It's not about a transaction or a contract.

Rising through the Ranks of a Changing Siemens USA

George Nolen is the first American CEO of Siemens Corp.

Like many of my colleagues at Siemens throughout the United States, I started my career at Siemens as part of an M&A deal for my employer. In my case, I was in sales at the telecommunications equipment company Rolm, which eventually became part of the Siemens communications division, ICN. From this vantage point in the key communications business segment, I was able to witness the transformation of Siemens over 20 years from a headquarters-controlled German holding company with a modest presence in the world's largest market to a powerhouse that grabbed market share in intensive competition with its American rivals.

To be in the communications industry in the 1990's – with the rise of the Internet and information technology – was to be at the center of forces that altered forever our business and societal landscape. It was exciting, but it wasn't always a walk in the park. At ICN, where I was sales executive and then CEO, we invested in the U.S. market with varying degrees of success. When the telecommunications industry crashed in the early part of the new century, we were confronted with a turnaround situation that required some tough and painful decisions. This was also true of Siemens' larger business in the U.S. These years were a test of the skills of our entire executive leadership, myself included.

During the course of this growth and then retrenchment, Siemens underwent a cultural change in the U.S. market. First, as we acquired large American companies, we increasingly – but not exclusively – turned to American managers to run these businesses. Second, to better integrate our companies and get better ROI from our investments, we adopted a variety of business improvement practices that required us to adopt a more American mindset that sometimes clashed with our headquarters view in Munich. Finally, our business evolved to include large infrastructure projects, often with government funding; thus, to succeed in the U.S. market, we de facto had to be perceived as not a German holding company, but an employer of 70,000 Americans and a first-rate and active corporate citizen.

As the first American executive to lead Siemens in the U.S., I can look back on two decades of growth and transformation in our U.S. operations that have had a positive impact on our overall business globally. As my colleagues and I grew Siemens business from a "German outpost" in the 1980s and early 1990s to the company's largest single market, we have contributed to Siemens' overall leadership in the electrical capital goods market worldwide. Our strategy of investing locally to succeed globally has paid off for Siemens in the U.S. market, and I will continue this approach for our business for the long term.

It's about trust, reputation and experience – things that can't always be imported. You have to build these blocks one at a time in front of your customers who can see you and build relationships with you.

Acknowledgment

George Nolen would like to thank Fred Pieretti, Senior Manager of Leadership Communication at Siemens Corporation, for his help with this article.

3.4.2 Siemens Power Generation – Transatlantic M&A in a Consolidating Industry

Kai Lucks

*The markets for fossil fuel power plants in the industrialized regions
are characterized by deregulation, consolidation and a cyclical
nature. And M&A projects do not always follow the textbook
examples. Nevertheless, through its unwavering pursuit of its
objectives and by leveraging opportunities, Siemens Power
Generation was able to move up from a weak position to the
No. 2 spot worldwide.*

Historical background

With 31,000 employees and annual sales of €7.5 billion, Siemens Power Generation (SPG) covers the entire field of fossil fuel-fired power plants, supplying the key components – gas and steam turbines and generators (Figure 3.24-3.26). SPG holds a minority stake in Framatome's nuclear power business and Voith's hydroelectric power business, and is active in the fields of fuel cell technology and wind power. SPG's current portfolio has a long history that dates back to four inventor-entrepreneurs from the earliest days of power generation: Werner von Siemens (1816-1892), who founded Siemens & Halske Telegraph Construction Company in Berlin in 1847, laid the groundwork for the power generation industry with his invention of the dynamo in 1866. George Westinghouse (1846-1914) was among the first to recognize the importance of three-phase current in the transmission of electrical energy. Based on this discovery, he founded Westinghouse Electric Co. in Pittsburgh, Pennsylvania. Sir Charles A. Parsons (1854-1931) invented the first steam turbine for practical use in 1884, founding his company in 1889 near Newcastle-on-Tyne, England. The Swedish

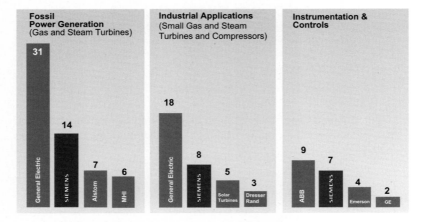

Figure 3.24 Siemens Power Generation global ranking (market shares %)

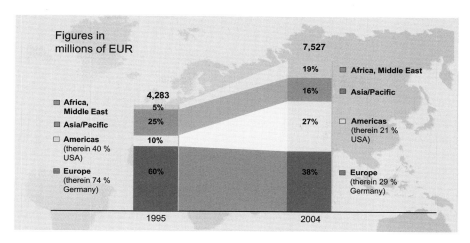

Figure 3.25 Siemens Power Generation sales by region

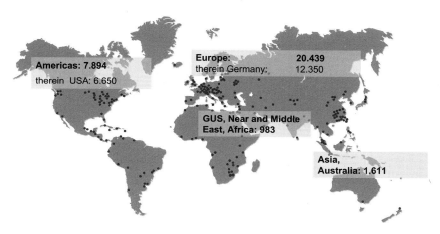

Figure 3.26 Siemens Power Generation worldwide presence 2004: 31 thousand employees

engineer Dr. Carl Gustaf Patrik de Laval (1845-1913) contributed substantially to the further development of the steam turbine, subsequently founding 37 companies.

Siemens signed its first partnership agreement with its U.S. competitor Westinghouse in 1924. After World War II, nuclear power technology moved into the forefront, along with fossil fuels. Siemens purchased a license for pressurized water reactors from Westinghouse in 1957, while its competitor AEG licensed boiling-water reactor technology from General Electric. The high cost of R&D, along with the tight market, made resource-bundling a necessity, prompting Siemens and AEG to merge their nuclear power plant activities in a 50:50 joint venture called Kraftwerk Union (KWU). AEG later pulled out of KWU. And in 1967, Siemens integrated KWU into the company, combining it with other businesses that focused on the power plant market, such as control systems. When Siemens listed on the New York Stock Exchange in

March 2001 and the Groups were given English names that reflected the sectors they served, KWU became Siemens Power Generation. Its U.S. subsidiary has operated under the name Siemens Westinghouse Power Generation since the 1998 merger.

Alliance with Allis Chalmers marks first inroads into the U.S.

The U.S. has always been one of the most important regional markets for power plants. Without a significant presence there, no company has a chance of surviving over the long term. The major U.S. competitors, General Electric and Westinghouse, were operating on both sides of the Atlantic. And the fact that the U.S. dollar was worth DM 4.20 in the 1970s – equivalent to €2.10 – made the U.S. a "low-cost region" from which companies could launch price wars in Europe. European companies without production facilities in the U.S. were at a disadvantage. Thus, U.S.-based manufacturing became a key strategic goal for KWU.

KWU focused on Allis Chalmers (AC), which had built the world's first 1000 MW turboset in 1965 before deciding to abandon the business when the U.S. market hit another slump. AC, headquartered in Milwaukee, spun off its plant there as West Allis Manufacturing Organization (WAMO). When another boom cycle hit the U.S. soon thereafter, AC began looking for an engineering partner. AC and KWU established AC Power Systems Inc. (ACPSI), a sales and service joint venture. However, the partnership with WAMO proved difficult. Employee turnover was high, and quality was inconsistent.

At a time when companies in the U.S. were moving from the unionized North to the less unionized Sun Belt states, KWU decided to detach itself from WAMO and build its own greenfield plant in Bradenton, Florida. Before the new plant was completed, the boom subsided again and it became clear that the facility would be far too large. The company found a solution that was right in line with the "Siemens One" concept: KWU built the plant for Siemens Energy & Automation (SE&A), keeping just one hall and an office complex for itself to provide service for the plants it delivered.

Now KWU also had to get out of its Milwaukee facility in a socially acceptable, cost-effective manner. A small group of employees was prepared to do a management buyout. Since the managers didn't have the money, KWU kept the assets and a 15 percent stake in the company. The rest was moved to Florida. Of course, many employees were lost, and the history of Siemens in Milwaukee could have ended here. But Bradenton limped along, suffered losses and had no work – even SE&A wanted to pull out. As the buyout in Milwaukee flourished, providing power plant service, it became clear that people are what make a business. KWU ultimately bought back the Milwaukee operations, closed the Bradenton facility and returned to Milwaukee. KWU put its trust in the management in Milwaukee and reentered the U.S. power plant market in a big way. But, due to errors on the part of management and a weak position within the U.S. market, the Milwaukee operation again incurred losses in many of its new business ventures.

Focus on fossil fuel power plants from 1985 onward

In light of the expected decline in nuclear power business, KWU systematically shifted its focus to new energy technologies and fossil fuel power plant technologies in the mid1980s. It pursued three technology paths: the transferability of technologies from the field of nuclear power; procuring new technologies through acquisitions; and R&D investments aimed at advancing KWU's leading position in fossil fuel power generation. The first path led to KWU's entry into solar, laser and marine technologies through its acquisitions of Rofin Sinar and Kongsberg Offshore Systems. However, the areas that were outside the power plant sector proved impractical for KWU from a strategic perspective. Thus, KWU successfully spun off Rofin Sinar on the stock market – after adding laser technology developed for the nuclear power sector – and Kongsberg Offshore was sold at a profit a few years later. In order to strengthen the hydroelectric power activities KWU in 1999 joined forces in a joint venture with a Voith majority stake who contributed hydroelectric turbines as a key component. At the same time, KWU transferred its nuclear business for a minority stake in the French company Framatome, where KWU was already involved in a joint venture focused on developing a new generation of nuclear power plants.

Deregulation and consolidation in the 1990s

By concentrating its strengths, Siemens KWU was able to hold its own in a period of dramatic consolidations and globalization in the fossil fuel power plant sector in the mid-1990s, a trend that was driven by the opening of national markets, dramatic price declines, increasing efficiency, increased regulation of emissions and falling transport costs.

The market was flooded with excess capacities. The major competitors engaged in price wars in an effort to maintain their market positions. Prices for combined cycle power plants plummeted more than 50 percent between 1993 and 1996. The biggest global players at the time were General Electric, ABB, Westinghouse, Siemens, GEC Alsthom and Japanese companies, particularly Mitsubishi Heavy Industries. All other providers were of secondary importance. GE and ABB were "first tier players," with far higher margins than the rest. Siemens and Westinghouse were "second tier players." Their insufficient market share, serious weaknesses in their regional presence (USA vs. Europe) and low margins all contributed to making their positions unstable.

In the mid-1980s, the U.S. market was depressed. The market for fossil fuel power plants in South America declined as many countries in the region were weakened by deregulation and privatization. The Southeast Asian market shrunk 30 percent in the wake of financial crisis and monetary instability. The Chinese market showed signs of saturation in the power generation market; and our home market of Europe was marked by weak growth in traditional utilities and the deregulation of the power generation sector. This cleared the way for a new customer group to emerge – independent power producers (IPPs). IPPs are investors and "brokers" who enter into contracts with fuel suppliers and power customers. They then manage construction of turnkey power plants, preferably financed by the power plant builder. And because – apart from technical expertise and global presence – power plant manufacturers now also needed financial muscle, the pressure to consolidate worldwide was heightened.

Examining strategic options in the 1990s, acquisition of Parsons

In this market environment and given the unstable development of its U.S. business, KWU management decided in 1992 to systematically examine all of its options, ultimately deciding to acquire Westinghouse's fossil fuel power plant business. KWU concentrated on the most important strategic components, namely the turboset consisting of gas turbines, steam turbines and generators. KWU had its eye on Westinghouse and Mitsubishi Heavy Industries. However, because the two competitors had already formed an alliance, it seemed that we had no chance of gaining either as a partner individually. A "global scenario" that remained an important option was a model calling for forced organic growth, with numerous regional stakes in India, Russia and China. However, this would not really have solved our main problem – a weak presence within the U.S. market. A strategy to strengthen our presence in the U.S. seemed of paramount importance – both because of its significance as the world's largest regional market and because our previous attempts had been too short-lived.

In order to probe our options, Siemens held talks with Westinghouse regarding a possible partnership in Power Gen (fossil) and Energy Systems (nuclear) in 1992. In nuclear, the time was not yet ripe. U.S. authorities looked askance at the idea of Siemens entering into Westinghouse's nuclear business since Westinghouse also provided submarine propulsion systems for the U.S. Navy. Only later was the British nuclear company BNFL able to take over Westinghouse's nuclear business unit. Siemens, meanwhile, had opted to work with Framatome as its partner. And because Frank Bakos, head of Westinghouse Power Gen, had already decided on the alliance with Mitsubishi Heavy Industries in the area of fossil power generation, we made no headway with Westinghouse.

At the same time, KWU had to develop the European markets that were now opening. The UK led the way to deregulation in Europe, opening its power generation market in the early 1990s. In the ten years that followed, the percentage of foreign supply grew from 20 to around 80 percent. In 1996, KWU was able to acquire the established British steam-turbine manufacturer Parsons, thus gaining access to a resource for turbine service and securing its market position by offering local content. Given the high level of technical stress that arises during operation and the long useful lives of turbines, measures for extending the lives of existing equipment are far more important than new business.

Preparing for the Westinghouse deal

Exploratory talks and forming the team

Further advances toward Westinghouse revealed that its partnership with Mitsubishi Heavy Industries (MHI) was not cemented for the long term. KWU saw its chance to make a move when the first signs of a technological split from MHI began appearing in 1995. In October, we established an internal team, code named 'Washington,' to examine our options with Westinghouse in the area of fossil fuel and the nuclear power business. After initial analysis, we decided to limit ourselves to fossil fuel power plants, given the political environment. We studied every conceivable scenario, even a three-way joint venture that included MHI. However, claims to leadership, the efforts involved in integration, technological diversity and cultural barriers made a three-way alliance impractical. We thus turned our focus to examining a partnership with Westinghouse Fossil Power Generation Business Unit (PGBU). We analyzed each stage of the value chain separately and developed various business models. The results were clear. Although a fully vertical merger that included the harmonization of the business model, product families and production presented the greatest integration challenges, it also promised the greatest strategic and financial leverage.

By now, Westinghouse had taken over the U.S. television broadcaster CBS. CEO Michael Jordan, who had come to the company from Pepsi-Cola, was focusing on investments that brought quick returns, a strategy incompatible with the long-term oriented policies of the industrial units. This opened the door for Siemens KWU, which was welcomed as a financially strong technology provider and strategic partner. At the initiative of Adolf Hüttl, president of KWU, the management of the two companies commissioned a small joint exploratory team in October 1996, operating in strict secrecy, to develop models for the merger of the power plant businesses. The team was headed by Siemens Corporate Strategy and consisted of five members from each company, one each in the areas of strategy, technology, production, sales and legal. After six weeks, the team recommended a full merger since this promised the greatest benefits. Apart from the synergies that could be derived from the technologies and complementary markets, the combined strength to compete against the powerful General Electric was a key motivation. Together, the companies would be able to break away from the field of other competitors and become a "first tier player," rising to the No. 2 position behind GE on the global market (Figure 3.27). Since Westing-

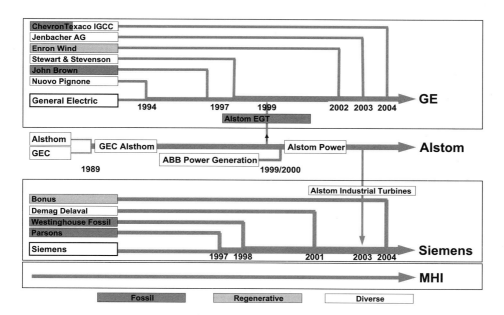

Figure 3.27 Consolidation in the power generation industry

house intended to remain active in the power plant business, the official premise of the talks was a 50-50 joint venture with Siemens having the casting vote. However, the clear intent of Siemens from the very start was to achieve a complete takeover. The Corporate Executive Committee had made this a precondition for its approval of the plan.

Expectations were dashed abruptly when Westinghouse decided to change its name to its recently acquired television subsidiary CBS and to divide into two areas – broadcasting and industry. The industrial areas, which included the Power Generation Business Unit, were to be auctioned off to interested parties from the respective industries. This blocked the road to direct negotiations for the time being. The joint exploratory team was so firmly convinced that the merger of the fossil power plant businesses was the right choice that two members from Westinghouse resigned, saying that they saw no better path for Westinghouse than a merger with Siemens.

Shortly thereafter, Westinghouse realized that an auction would be harmful to the business due to the tightness of the field of customers and interested parties. They thus pushed for a speedy resolution to enable the company to focus on broadcasting. This cleared the way for exclusive purchase negotiations with Siemens. Talks with the Westinghouse Industrial Division were initiated and jointly led by Corporate Finance and KWU's Chief Financial Officer. The contracts were ready for signing on November 14, 1997, after which the plan was filed with the anti-trust authorities.

The integration planning team

Following the signing, planning teams were established within KWU to work on the product portfolio and on restructuring production, with the assistance of external consultants. However, those who had hoped for quick approval of the merger were to be disappointed. The U.S. anti-trust authorities took a critical view of the fact that the oligopoly in an already highly consolidated market would lose yet another player. Siemens argued that it would have to pull out of the U.S. entirely if the merger was not approved, given the ongoing losses from our business there. The shear volume of documentation is a clear indication of how important the procedure was. Well over one million pages of documents were submitted, 700,000 of which had to be translated. For several months, the German-English specialized translators on both sides of the Atlantic worked pretty much exclusively on these documents. An entire suite of rooms was reserved for verification of the documents. Finally, on August 20, 1998, we had the approval papers in hand and could close the deal.

The merger of Siemens PG and Westinghouse

The challenge

Siemens had a broad range of experience with large-scale integration projects. In the U.S., these included the telecommunications equipment company Rolm, which we had acquired from IBM, and Sylvania, whose light bulb business was acquired by the Siemens subsidiary Osram (see George Nolen's article on Siemens' M&A strategy in the U.S.). Sylvania, in particular, was a successful example of a merger of two busi-

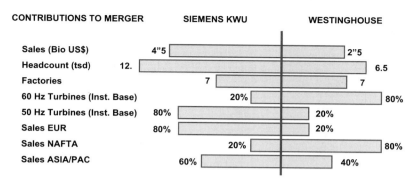

Figure 3.28 Merger contributions Siemens-Westinghouse Fossil Power 1998

nesses of comparable size. The involvement of management and key decision-makers from both sides in the shaping of the merger had a clearly positive impact. The strategic direction was also similar: In both cases, the company was trying to establish a strong second home base in the U.S. in order to build up a strong defensive position for when GE launched an offensive against us in Europe. Nevertheless, the merger of the power plant businesses presented a special challenge: We had to integrate two complex systems businesses whose product ranges had significant overlap (Figure 3.28). Technologically, the merger was difficult because it involved more than merely harmonizing the existing product families. Both sides were working on new generations of gas turbines at the time that promised significant efficiency improvements and thus major cost savings when combined with downstream steam turbines. These gains were offset by high development costs and problems in implementing the technology. In addition, excess capacities on the market had to be reduced and new performance classes for gas turbines had to be developed. Another obstacle was the dissimilar structures of the power plant markets in North America and Europe. The U.S. market was divided into component manufacturers for turbines and generators on the one hand and architect-engineers on the other. This sharp distinction did not exist in the European market, where the major power plant providers produced both components and complete turnkey power plants. Thus, Siemens Power Generation was a competitor not only to GE and Westinghouse but also to architect-engineers such as Bechtel and Foster & Wheeler. The Siemens-Westinghouse merger raised the question of which business model to use.

The merger's viability was examined in advance using extensive analyses and customer surveys to determine purchasing behavior and to assess the prospects of a market that had been depressed for some time. Scenario studies on the harmonization of the technologies and product families served a number of purposes, from estimating cost reduction potential to security questions and acquiring customers. These analyses, carried out before the takeover, formed the backbone of the project's long-term impact. The analyses proved correct. Immediately after the takeover, customers abandoned their coolness toward Westinghouse and the orders flooded in – a clear indication that the market rewards reliable players who focused on long-term relationships and results.

The merger

The integration was planned and implemented using a team of more internal and external consultants than Siemens had ever before employed for such a task. A change management team was responsible for harmonizing the companies' cultures and establishing a uniform structure that would apply worldwide. Management assessments were used to identify the best managers from each company. Leadership positions were filled based on an individual's performance, not which company they came from. The goal was to develop a culture and organization geared toward outstanding performance. After comparing the basic business models, Siemens decided to focus primarily on Westinghouse's component and services business and to limit turnkey plant construction, which had been KWU's line of business, to something done only on customer request. Joint management – Westinghouse Power Gen chief Randy Zwirn joined Siemens KWU's management board – further cemented the sense of cooperation.

The global business was split into two regional sales centers that were run from KWU headquarters in Erlangen, Germany, and from Westinghouse headquarters in Orlando, Florida. In addition to these two regional units, the product business for gas turbines/combined cycle, steam turbines/generators and services operated at the global level. These were then assigned to Europe or the U.S. or placed under globally coordinated management (Figure 3.29). Both sides worked together to optimize the processes and products, after which the two headquarters would be placed on an equal footing.

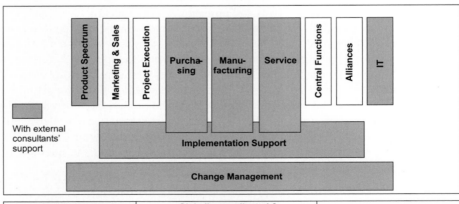

Figure 3.29 Siemens-Westinghouse team setup & regional responsibilities 1998

Post-closing integration

To support the integration planning, 11 post-closing integration teams were established (Figure 3.29, Figure 3.30). These teams – which focused on issues such as product lines, manufacturing, purchasing and service – included experts from the U.S. and Germany. Their job was to develop concrete suggestions for the future direction of the business. There were essentially four steps:

- October 1998: Reorganization of the business into five Divisions
- February 1999: Consolidation of the service locations in North America
- March 1999: Establishment of a global manufacturing alliance and combination of the service units, which had been separate until then
- June 1999: Redesign of plant engineering, project management and cross-company shared tasks.

KWU's Milwaukee site was abandoned, and the closure of other service locations in North America eliminated the only significant areas of overlap between the merged businesses.

Cost reduction programs were developed for each of the Siemens Power Generation Divisions. Implementation of the measures was tracked using a system based on degrees of implementation (DI). A total cost reduction target of $1.2 billion was set – and achieved (see article Randy Zwirn). The experience gathered during this merger was used as the main foundation for developing a standard framework for M&A projects and the Center of Competence for M&A Integration, established at Siemens' headquarters in 2000.

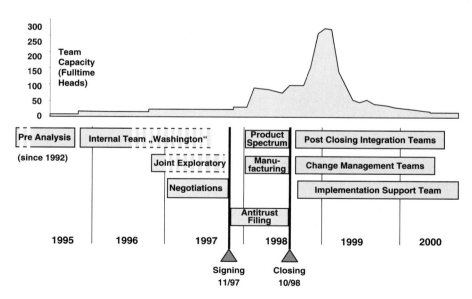

Figure 3.30
Siemens-Westinghouse fossil power generation merger: team capacities & timelines

Further developments and conclusions

Shortly after the deal with Westinghouse was concluded, the U.S. market picked up even more than the pre-signing customer analyses had forecast. Thus, Siemens was able to benefit fully from the boom in the fossil fuel power plant business in the U.S. In 2000, Siemens Power Generation acquired the Demag-Delaval Group for compressors through its takeover of the industrial activities of Mannesmann-ATECS. In 2003, Siemens took over Alstom Industriekraftwerke (see Figure 3.27). In a successful three-way merger, Siemens strengthened its industrial power plant business and increased sales from around €200 million to €2 billion (2004) within five years. In 2004, Siemens purchased the Danish company Bonus. This made Siemens a player in the systems business for wind power generation, where we had previously only supplied components from our Automation & Drives Group and project development services. The Westinghouse merger, however, remains the most important strategic move to date. Without it and the economic and social foothold it afforded us in establishing a second home market in the U.S., we would not have been able to achieve the stable position we now enjoy within the global market.

3.4.3 The Siemens-Westinghouse Case: Integration in the Eyes of the US Management

Randy H. Zwirn

The acquisition of Westinghouse Power Generation by Siemens AG was in many ways a landmark M&A transaction. In dealing with the coming together of two well renowned corporate presences, each with a storied background of over 100 years, one must recognize that to create a successful integration experience, many factors beyond merely combining operations come into play.

Initially, one may only think of the challenges confronted by combining two companies in the same industry, in context of the distinct differences in German and American business culture. However powerful these forces may be, and they are quite powerful, one cannot underestimate the impact that 100 years of corporate culture also has on an organization. In the end it is not clear which of these two represents the more significant challenge, but it is clear both require careful and thoughtful consideration in order to motivate both managers and employees to achieve the desired outcome. In this context the concept of "winners" and "losers" needs to be strongly avoided. A global organization can be a powerful competitive force, which can in many cases change the landscape of an industry resulting in further innovation and trendsetting behaviors. However, to achieve this balance and extract the value potential, it is vitally important that the diversity of the workforce be valued as an asset to be exploited, not a behavior to be controlled or changed.

In the 1980's and 90's the term "merger of equals" became an all too often catch all phrase for the integration of large organizations, typically for companies who were historical competitors. The concept was to give the organizations a sense of comfort that their value in the newly formed corporate structure would somehow be equally valued. However, in many cases it is my hypotheses that overuse of this term led to false expectations that were not reinforced by the integration strategy. It could have the intention of top management from 50,000 feet to create such an atmosphere. Setting such a vision is not difficult – implementing a disciplined integration process that supports this goal is a different story. It requires combining management skills to achieve business plans with a unique ability to get the newly formed team to accept a modified approach without resorting to a "winner and loser" mentality, which unfortunately is part of human nature. It requires an ability to communicate a common message to "listeners" who hear different messages whether because of language nuances, fear, anxiety about the future, or culture (whether national or corporate). It requires building a sense of trust in the process. This does not mean that everyone will like or agree with each decision or that all information can be freely shared, but instead that people believe the ground rules are fair, that a common set of values exist and that employees are given enough information to develop confidence in the future strength of the new organization.

What can be seen is when such a common vision and set of values can be established; the so-called insurmountable issues of cultural differences, language, and trust can in fact be leveraged as competitive advantages.

But how does one achieve this desired result. There cannot be a simple "cookbook" approach as successful integration is more "art" than "science." However, from my standpoint there are certain building blocks that establish the foundation of such complex cross-Atlantic transactions that then provide the management framework for success.

Starting situation

While Westinghouse and Siemens were considered to be major players in the same global energy markets there were some differences in each company's business model. For example, Westinghouse influenced strongly by its roots in the U.S. was predominately focused on 60-Hertz markets whereby Siemens with its European heritage was stronger in 50 Hz. This resulted in very few overlapping markets where both companies were strong, dominant players. This tendency toward relative market strength made the integration of the sales and marketing activities far less complicated than the product overlap where significant fixed costs and headcount resided. It provided also a unique competitive structure for a 'Dual Home Market" approach, whereby the new combined company could be seen as a truly global multi-national on both sides of the Atlantic, from the standpoint of culture as well as order acquisition and delivery.

Siemens strength was also inherent in its plant engineering capabilities, as it was quite common in its markets to offer customers complete turnkey solutions (EPC) for entire power plants. In the America's region, Westinghouse more typically was a component supplier to the utility and IPP industry, very often working through complementors such as an architect-engineer hired directly by the end user to consolidate the project.

Westinghouse with its large fleet of Steam Turbines in the U.S., was much more focused on the service business, viewing it as the "foundation" of the business model, whereas in Siemens it was viewed as an enhancement to the economics and image of the new plant business.

The early lesson was that even if you are in the same business, with similar products and categories of customers, you are different!

Post closing integration

In looking at a Post Closing integration plan there are certain key success ingredients as well as pitfalls to avoid. Most important, is to realize when you embark on such a complex integration, you are never finished. The risk of falling back is always present.

From my standpoint advance planning is critical to building a strong base to work from. From the outset leadership must come across as decisive, unified and with a clear direction. This does not mean that you must get each individual to agree with every decision. Clearly a plan to extract synergies or best practices from organizations that have overlaps will mean some difficult choices must be made that ultimately impact many employees. But the organization must get a sense that a plan for the future exists, that it makes sense and that a process to make decisions will be undertaken in a fair manner.

This requires establishment of a unified business strategy that includes visible goals and targets. Organization issues have to be gotten out of the way early. The new organization must strive for common corporate or group values – however, leveraging the diversity of the organization as a competitive advantage. As mentioned earlier, in

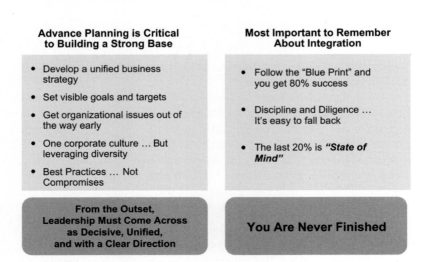

Figure 3.31 Key Messages for Integration

our case we wanted to maintain 'two home markets' to be seen by our customers as having local resources and a stronger competitive basis as a result of the synergies and best practices inherent in our new group. In that regard it is important to insure that best practices are relentlessly analyzed and implemented, avoiding compromises as a way for the organization to establish a cultural harmony, that potentially squanders large savings potential.

Equally important is the tracking of synergy affects. In our case we established a system of metrics to track the measures that would generate for us the desired cost savings. Filling our databank with ideas and regularly assessing them by Härtegrad (Hardness) on a scale of 1 (idea) to 5 (income statement relevant) gave us a scorecard to track progress. Regular audits were performed to check and insure that the measures did not languish under the weight of the day-to-day business. The leadership team signed off on these goals and they were regularly reviewed with employees. We targeted over $1.2 billion in savings!

Another vitally important lesson is to quickly communicate the 'story' about the integration. There is a need to quickly build momentum and excitement in order that uncertainty does not lead to anxiety. It is critical that the leadership not only communicate – but do so in person, being seen as on the frontlines and accessible. Even though we knew that the feedback would reflect the uncertainty of the workforce, we launched an Employee Opinion Survey to baseline the thinking within the organization and it became a vital integration tool. A group wide publication called 'Power Generation Live' was launched to provide people information on how we were progressing.

The global manufacturing network

Some of our early success stories such as the development of a Global Manufacturing Network were highlighted.

Harmonization of our factory network was clearly one of our most difficult tasks. Here we were dealing with large manufacturing sites on both sides of the Atlantic, involving substantial fixed investment, significant overcapacity, overlapping product lines serving common markets, and the largest number of our employees. As well there was a long proud heritage of product manufacturing and a sense of 'ownership' by the employees.

It was clear early on that we needed a common global manufacturing network incorporating all our locations. This would yield the most competitive product offerings, a merger of the two technology bases into harmonized product lines and possibly the most difficult and tough decision, a reduction in the overall size of the network.

In order to drive the investigation we formed joint teams for the major products, such as gas turbines, steam turbines and electrical generators. Each of them had representatives from both sides of the Atlantic as well as a representative from our outside consulting firm. The role of the consultant was critical in order to insure a rigorous evaluation that focused on best practice not compromise, particularly in light of the consequences of the decisions to be taken.

Two Success Stories:

Gas Turbine Network

- 250% increase in production
- Westinghouse GT's manufactured in Berlin
- Joint resolution of product problems

Steam Turbine Network

- One harmonized product line
- New product collaboration: The Best-in-Class-Generator
- Some tough decisions: reduction in network

Figure 3.32 The development of our global factory network

An early success was the integration of the generator product line. Here we had complete product and market overlap; full manufacturing capability on both sides of the Atlantic and a strong need for a harmonized product line.

The result was a new 'Best in Class' generator design (we actually named it B-I-C for best in class) that would incorporate the best features of each design into a new single product line. It was decided to manufacture this product in our North Carolina factory to supply all our global markets. However, we maintained the capability to service our existing generator fleet in both the U.S. and Germany, close to our customers, as service is time and transportation sensitive.

In the case of generators we were able to increase the electrical efficiency of the new design which is critical to the cost of generating electricity. Similarly, we recognized cost synergies from the ability to focus our engineering resources on a single common design and more efficiently leverage our purchasing and supply chain.

While the U.S. benefited from becoming the center of competence for generators, Germany became the global center for steam turbine manufacturing.

Although difficult, we took the necessary actions to optimize our manufacturing locations including the closing of a number of non-critical facilities. We introduced a common product line for both steam turbines and generators and created global centers of competence.

While only one example, the mandate to optimize the global manufacturing network was clear – as a next step we would also have to undertake insuring that we further leverage part of the network into 'low cost' countries. While not addressed in this contribution, this is an ongoing imperative that we remain focused on today.

The establishment of a global service organization was also a clear goal. Our combined operating fleet of turbines and generators exceeded 500,000 MW's and represented over 20% of the global generating assets. Unlike the sale of new units and power plants, service is a life cycle relationship with customers, representing a potential 'annuity stream' lasting over the 30-40 year potential life cycle of our products. It is an area of extremely high value to our customers as plant availability of their most

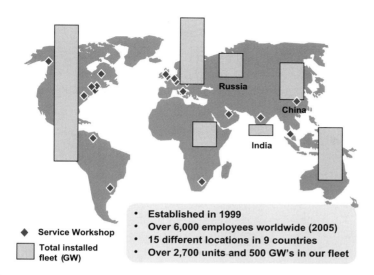

Figure 3.33 The establishment of a global service company

efficient power plants drives their primary source of revenues. Likewise, historically higher profit margins from service helps to 'flatten out' the cyclical peaks and valleys of new power plant construction, and thus enhance both the predictability and quality of our earnings.

We started out with an organization offering substantially different value propositions to our customers, and a wide range of organizational competence and capability. The newly combined division had over 3,000 employees, 15 different service locations in 9 countries, with responsibility for a fleet of over 2,700 units, comprising the afore-mentioned 500,000 MW's.

All this was brought together with a single common purpose – grow the Service Business. Our target was to more than double our service activities and achieve a goal of 40% of group sales derived from services while doubling our ebit margin into the 'high teens'.

We formed a global service headquarters to focus our activities irrespective of the original country or company that manufactured the product. Our challenge was to create excitement, to attract some of our best people to this field which had high profitability potential but lacked the 'glamour' of building new power stations. In particular, it was a challenge to attract the best people in our German organization, with its high reputation for 'engineering solutions' into an area that was not in the past considered to be the top of the professional career path. In this case we chose to build off the stronger service focus that existed in the U.S. and select an American manager located in the U.S. to drive the set up and operation of this business segment. For us it was critical to 'get this right' as service was to be a 'foundation of profitability' for our group.

Establishing a separate service organization with its own charter, profit and loss responsibility and global organization with regionally deployed resources, was a criti-

Aquiror vs Acquiree:
What's in it for Me

- Build momentum ... excitement (uncertainty = anxiety)

- Quickly communicate the story ... **In Person** !

- Employee Opinion Survey can be a very important integration tool ... if you can accept the feedback !

- *Power Generation Live* is our "Integration Newspaper"

Our People: A Big Reason
Behind Our Success

- Over 200 long term delegates bring cross cultural integration

- Celebrate the positive examples of best practice sharing

- Don't focus on differences *(build on the strengths / similarities)*

- Don't make everything the same... except for the game-plan *(homogenized PG is not the answer either)*

Let the People Know How
You Are Progressing

Don't Waste Time ... The
Enemy is Outside the Door

Figure 3.34 Key messages for partnering & people

cal step to culturally changing the mindset of our people as to the importance of this business. This segment through almost daily 'customer touches' is a powerful vehicle to enhance the customer focus of our organization, move our thinking from 'product and plant' to customer solution orientation and change our profitability profile. On paper it seemed logical, and while the implementation has been successful, it was far more difficult than initially imagined.

Today service has become a clear business 'driver' for us. Unlike the previous paradigm which saw us selling our services on an as needed 'a la carte' basis, today almost 80% of the new power plants we sell also include a Long Term Service Agreement that typically extends up to 12 years.

Cultural Alignment

From all of these examples there always seems to emerge the question of 'one culture or two'. In the end, despite having even more competitive products to offer customers, people clearly emerge as a big reason for our success. A clear lesson learned from our experience was that in addition to developing a unified business strategy with visible targets and goals, it is vital that one 'corporate' culture is established, however, leveraging the rich diversity of the organization. A true global player must celebrate diversity – it must resemble in its nature and values the differences associated with the vastly different global markets it serves. This means aligning common values and business processes, but not necessarily adapting to a homogeneous American or European approach. For us maintaining a 'dual home market' position that could address regional customer needs, under a common Siemens banner supported by consistent corporate principles and values was critical. We believed we could significantly differentiate ourselves from our competition which was far more home region 'centric' in their thinking.

team performed a headquarter staff evaluation and initiated a consecutive resource planning process with special focus on evaluating the potential of current and future leaders. Other tasks included the harmonization of all HR processes, establishing an incentive/target model for cross-staffing and giving Systematics employees access to the EDS University.

An interim organization was set up for the first year with an Integration Leader at the top responsible for integrating Systematics into the global EDS organization. The target organization was then introduced and completed during the following year, when EDS Systematics became partly integrated into Information Solutions and partly into E-Solutions.

The *Legal Workstream* covered all the normal legal requirements necessitated for an acquisition (preparation of contracts, company registration, etc.) and supported all other workstreams in legal matters. In addition, the team concentrated on two major topics: developing a proposal for future branding/names with all related contracts and preparing a detailed plan for the restructuring of the many legal entities within Systematics.

Whereas the importance of communication for the success of a merger is often underestimated, in this case it was set up as a separate workstream with a dedicated team assigned to it. Like the other workstreams, the *Communication Workstream* had to meet several critical milestones during a tightly scheduled eight-week period. The hot communication period kicked off with a high-level sales information and motivational event right after closing the deal. The next highlight were the "straight talk" sessions with the CEO of EDS at Systematics' headquarters in Hamburg followed by management road shows in the subsidiaries. These events clearly established an open communication process, which allowed employees to voice their concerns and get answers to many of their burning questions. Permanent information about the integration progress and any upcoming issues was achieved through management letters and

Merger Issues	Cross Cultural Issues
Decision control and information flow	Inter-personal communication
Differences in companies' history and traditions	Decision process differences and how to influence it
Style and capabilities of current management teams	Work habits (level of formalism, timelines,...)
Relative weights of engineering, manufacturing, purchasing	Communication styles (during meetings, internal communication, external to stakeholder)
"Superior" vs. "Inferior" (size, technology, cash situatio)	Traditional career paths stakeholders' weight (shareholders, unions, public,...)
Attack and defend (perceptions, resentment feelings)	Supplier relationship
Win vs. lose (staffing, rewards, gaps to objectives)	

"Soft" issues are critical to the success

Figure 3.38 Usual and cross-cultural merger issues

frequent employee newsletters. On the external communication side, new branding activities for the subsidiaries were initiated and new materials for events and trade shows were developed. Finally, once the entire communication structure in the combined EDS/ Systematics organization had been put in place, their first task was to develop a customer communication program to be launched just two weeks later.

On top of all these "normal" integration challenges, one major additional issue further complicated the situation with two former competitors – at least in certain areas – going together in a transatlantic merger. The *cross-cultural differences* were substantial between the self-confident, very successful American EDS with a background mainly in government and military and the German-style conglomerate of small acquisitions shaped during the ups and downs of the new economy hype and its aftermath. Through the composition of the integration teams, differences in decision processes, in work habits (more punctual and formal vs. more "laissez-faire"), etc., surfaced very quickly and served as a test case for the full roll-out of the integration. A combined effort of the Communication and HR teams was needed to deal with these issues. It was essential to develop a better understanding for each other and to achieve an adjustment of style and behavior. This was absolutely necessary to facilitate cooperation towards a common goal.

A look back: Outcome of the integration process

All integration activities were completed within the very ambitious timeframe and a well functioning organization was implemented for the combined entity. Almost 85% of revenue synergies and more than 100% of cost synergies were verified and several quick wins were realized already during the integration phase. Today the former separate organizations work together in a completely integrated way with common processes fully established. Some cultural integration issues, however, remain but a good understanding on both sides substantially facilitates the cooperation across the Atlantic.

3.5.2 German Roots, American "Drive": The Ingram Micro & Macrotron Case

Ingo H. Möller

When the U.S. company Ingram Micro Inc. acquired a majority interest in the former Munich-based Macrotron AG in 1998, the result was a unique type of merger. The following is a review of the lessons learned from the integration.

The success of any enterprise depends very much on the quality of its data and the correct interpretation of this data. It is what forms the basis for sound business decisions.

tion have fundamentally changed national and international trade markets. These days, goods and merchandise are transported under totally different conditions than they were just a few years ago. Customers no longer demand just pure transportation solutions. Today, they also expect integrated, time-definite value-added solutions at an international level. Only those companies that think and act globally can prosper in this competitive environment.

To fulfill these increasingly demanding requirements, companies need high-performance networks that enable them to offer their customers first-rate service anywhere in the world at any time. In a fiercely competitive market, organic growth alone can no longer produce these kinds of distribution and production networks. Often, business acquisitions are the only way to position one's own company in strategically important markets. In the logistics sector, mergers & acquisitions also have become part of a normal day's business. Following the sector's consolidation process over the past few years, the number of mergers has been declining. But acquisitions nonetheless remain a key strategic tool to tap new markets and to strengthen one's own competitive position.

Without mergers & acquisitions, Deutsche Post World Net also would not have become a true global player in such a short period of time in the past few years. From its strong domestic base in Germany, the group has continually advanced its position on international markets since the 1990s, partly through takeovers. Today, the company is present on all major mail, express and logistics markets. Its annual sales amount to about 43 billion euros, and its workforce totals more than 380,000 employees. Company takeovers like those of Danzas, DHL or Airborne, all of which are now integral parts of a global group, represent milestones in this development.

The acquisition of a company is just one side of the coin, its integration the other. The planned synergy effects may not be achieved because the integration of different corporate organizations is much more drawn out and complex than expected, and expected gains of market share remain a vision. And that will occur even though the transaction looked so inviting on paper and was so carefully prepared. So why do acquisitions fail? An important initial realization is that in many cases it is not economic factors or financial parameters that cause a planned merger to collapse – it is because the so-called soft factors were not given due consideration. Companies often forget that mergers are not just about facilities and IT systems. Above all, they are about the people who have to be integrated into a company. Such factors as communication, information, openness and motivation play a key role here. Mergers are likely to succeed only if companies are aware of the importance of these factors and duly consider them. I would like to give you an example that is still considered a model M&A deal for the logistics industry: the acquisition of the U.S. air freight carrier AEI by Danzas, Deutsche Post's logistics subsidiary at the time.

The actors

Until the mid-1990s, Deutsche Post had experienced dramatic growth. In just a few years, a formerly money-losing government operation had evolved into a modern service provider known for its high quality and strong customer orientation. Sales had nearly doubled from 1990 to about 16 billion euros, and the consignment volume had risen from 15.8 billion items to 24.9 billion items. The turnaround was achieved as early as 1997. Now, management could focus on the second strategic phase: the internationalization of a group that was generating only 2 percent of its revenues abroad in 1997. If the company wanted to prosper in international competition, it had to markedly boost this activity.

This process was kicked off in the same year, with the establishment of a powerful European express network. Investments in acquisitions, the purchase of corporate holdings and the establishment of own companies extended the network to more than 20 European countries in just 18 months. As early as 1999, Deutsche Post Euro Express was the market leader in the European express and parcel market with revenues of about 4.6 billion euros.

To fulfill customer demands for high-level integrated solutions, greater competence in the logistics area was needed. Here, the decisive move was made in March 1999 with the acquisition of the Swiss logistics group Danzas. The well-known company based in Basel had generated net sales of about 4.2 billion euros and EBITA of about 50 million euros in 1999. Virtually over night, Deutsche Post became a major player in the international logistics business that was active on most of the world's markets – with one exception: the United States, the world's biggest logistics market. In contrast to the express business, where the company found an ideal addition in the United States with the takeover of a 25 percent stake in DHL International Ltd. in March 1999, the group still lacked a strong North American pillar in the logistics segment. This, however, was urgently needed in order to keep our promise to the customer of offering a complete one-stop-shopping solution.

Executives at our headquarters in Bonn began to search for a suitable partner in this part of the world and soon focused on AIR Express International, or AEI. At the time, the company headquartered at Darien, Connecticut, was the biggest U.S. air freight hauler. It had about 7,700 employees and generated sales of more than 1.5 billion U.S. dollars in 1998 with customers like Caterpillar and Intel. The company was the global leader in integrated logistics, with a product line-up that ranged from multi-modal transportation through warehousing, distribution and customs management to IT-supported logistics services. AEI looked like the ideal complement to the group's logistics division – both in terms of size and products, but above all because of its firm roots in the North American market. In addition, the company apparently was not averse to the idea of a cooperative arrangement. This at least is the outcome of a market study that AEI asked Morgan Stanley to do in December 1998. The aim of this study was to find a suitable takeover candidate. However, nobody guessed at the time that this would be Deutsche Post.

Negotiations and takeover

Shortly before the two companies started initial negotiations, Deutsche Post completed two other deals that underscored its claim of being one of the world's leading logistics providers. In July 1999, the company acquired Nedlloyd, a Dutch logistics provider based in the Benelux countries. This company strengthened Danzas' euro-cargo and solutions business. Just four weeks later, the Scandinavian service provider ASG was acquired. Danzas closed the geographical gap that had existed in the north of Europe. After securing its position on the European market, Deutsche Post could concentrate fully on its expansion effort overseas.

The two acquisitions in the summer of 1999 not only extended Deutsche Post's own portfolio of services, but also sent out a key message to potential cooperation partners. These included AEI, whose takeover negotiations with an inner-American competitor collapsed just a few weeks earlier. Given both sides' strong interest in finding a powerful cooperation partner, it is not surprising that the talks that were started in summer 1998 and the subsequent negotiations were relatively brief. They were characterized by a high level of professionalism and a deep understanding among the people involved. The chemistry was right, as one of the lead negotiators stressed later – and even the discussions about the purchase price did not change this. In October 1999, the two partners announced the results of their negotiations to the public. These became official nearly four weeks later, on Nov. 15, 1999, when the two partners signed the takeover and merger contract. Under the agreement, Deutsche Post acquired AEI for 33 U.S. dollars per share. That corresponded to a total takeover price of about 1.14 billion U.S. dollars.

The agreement was extremely promising for both partners. While Deutsche Post gained the strong platform in the United States that it needed to keep the promise of offering one-stop shopping to its customers, the newly founded company Danzas-AEI immediately became the world's No. 1 provider of air freight services and one of the top 5 companies in the global sea freight business. As a leading provider of integrated logistics services, it could also strengthen its position in the United States and thus in the transatlantic and transpacific business. "The takeover of AEI has brought significant synergies and answers to our customers' desire for services from a single source," the logistics board member of Deutsche Post World Net said immediately after the contract was concluded. He was right.

At that point, though, the new partners had not yet overcome their biggest obstacle. AEI's shareholders still had to approve the deal. And that did not appear certain. Many members of AEI's management owned stocks and stock options in the company. They had helped return the company to profit following the crisis in 1985 and make it the United States' biggest air freight provider. They had to be convinced that it made sense to follow the board of management's recommendation and accept Deutsche Post World Net's offer. Apparently, these recommendations and arguments had an effect. By February 9, the deadline, about 96 percent of AEI's outstanding shares were offered to Deutsche Post. The agreement won the backing of U.S. officials. The European Commission then gave its approval on February 7, 2000, and cleared the way for the integration of AEI into Deutsche Post.

Organizational structures

As early as March 6, 2000, just under four months after the takeover announcement and only a few weeks after the launch of the Deutsche Post World Net brand, the new organization came into being. All previous AEI activities were integrated into Danzas'

Intercontinental (INCO) business division. A strong leadership team was put in charge of defending and expanding the company's newly gained leadership in the international air and sea freight business: It was led by Renato Chiavi, head of the Intercontinental business division and now Chief Executive Officer (CEO) of the newly founded company Danzas-AEI. The native of Switzerland first traveled the seas at 17, and now he was heading a company with more than 12,000 employees and annual revenues in the billions. He was assisted by Günter Rohrmann, previously CEO of AEI and now the new Vice Chairman of Danzas-AEI. His mission was to make the two companies' integration succeed, which was no easy feat. The other appointments to key functions at company, divisional, sub-divisional and country group level were also announced. All functions down to the country level had thus been transferred to the new executive leadership. The implementation of the new structure enabled executives to concentrate on the most important aspect of the acquisition: the integration of the roughly 12,000 employees, the two companies' networks and organizations and, above all, customers into the newly merged company Danzas-AEI.

At the time, the merger of Danzas and AEI was the sector's biggest marriage of companies. And this applied not just to the economic aspects of the deal. The agreement also allied two different partners: the all-American AEI, a strong player with regard to multinational clients that concentrated on a service-based volume business with a special focus, and the European Danzas, a traditional intercontinental logistics provider with a large customer base consisting of large, small and medium-sized companies. These customers were not supposed to sense any difference in their business relations with the newly founded company as a result of the two companies' integration.

"Speed is the name of the game." This also – and perhaps especially – applies to corporate takeovers. Of course, quality and customer service must not suffer as a result. Nonetheless, the goal is to complete the integration process as quickly as possible to ensure that clients do not lose faith in their service provider's performance strength. As a result, the group set up an ambitious timetable. In line with a three-step integration plan, all aspects of the merger were supposed to be wrapped up within 18 months. The plan included the following steps:

1. A concept to define the organization's top-tier structure as well as its goals, processes and principles.

2. Plans to determine details and structures for the headquarters and regional levels, to define products, goals and synergies, and to develop action plans for the third phase.

3. A strategy to implement programs and action plans. The new processes in the new organization were to become operational in this phase.

The first two phases of the integration plan were completed by the spring of 2000. By then, the company had finished its strategy development and set up new organizational structures. This created the foundation for the third integration phase, the longest and most difficult part: the practical implementation of strategic requirements. This is where it would become clear whether the decision to merge had been the right move.

Success factors

The integration of companies is an extremely challenging process. It takes the full commitment of all involved and their uncompromising willingness to work together to make this process a success. But it also takes the ability to meld people with different company and cultural backgrounds into one team. In this process, companies become melting pots of very diverse characters and cultures, not unlike large nations.

Successful company mergers typically have several fathers. But they are based on extremely complex, closely interwoven processes that depend on many individual factors. This also applies to our example. Here, the success of a company merger can be condensed into four core elements: the successful creation of transparent structures, the development of employees' trust in the new company, fast network integration and successful customer-relationship management during the integration phase.

Transparent structures

Communication is a basic precondition of mutual acceptance and joint action. If barriers to communication are too high, something that was meant in the right way is understood in the wrong way, and people will not be able to agree on a direction even if they share the same goals. For this reason, communication processes play a crucial role in the integration of two companies. In the case of AEI and Danzas, a stated goal was to actively include as many of the affected employees as possible in the integration process via a continuous dialogue, to initiate synergy formation, and to address and highlight the process as such.

This is why an "integration office" headed by Thomas Nieszner was set up in Basel. Its task was to manage and monitor the more than 1,000 individual projects. The 25 to 30 employees from both companies used an Integration Controlling System (ICS) to assess the quality and progress of the integration process, to compare results to plans and, where necessary, to introduce additional measures. Those affected were given the opportunity to have a direct exchange of views via regular face-to-face meetings and conference calls. This benefited both the project's organization and overall efficiency: Additional costs could be identified directly and controlled immediately.

Integration at the different locations, in turn, was implemented on site at the local level. Regional and functionally based integration teams were created around the world, supported by external experts and consultants. They sought to enter into direct dialogue with the employees to keep them informed about the integration dialogue and to answer questions. The company took a "bottom-up" approach to the integration of AEI. This was the only way to gain employees' support, a factor that was vital to the success of the process. Developments in the following months showed that the company was on the right track.

Getting employees involved

An integration process is about more than the flow of physical goods and funds. It is also about the people in the company, the indispensable basis of any business. It was all the more important, therefore, to convince employees in both companies that their company was making the right move, to dissipate fears and doubts, and to foster enthusiasm for the new company. Often, the announcement of a takeover fuels worries about the potential effects on the employees' own personal situations. These doubts, coupled with lucrative offers from the competition, usually entail a loss of valuable employees and thus crucial know-how to the competition.

To prevent this from happening, the management teams of Danzas and AEI pursued open and transparent communications from the start. The employees of both companies were informed about the progress of the takeover negotiations even while these were still being conducted in the early autumn of 1999. These meetings were then replaced by regular office meetings where employees learned about the progress of the integration process and could ask questions and express criticism.

"Top management must not leave local management hanging," Renato Chiavi demanded at the time. And it was a demand that was taken seriously. The top people in both management teams were informed about the process even before the takeover had been settled, and one-on-one meetings were set up as quickly as possible to discuss individual executives' personal futures within the new company. The 70 top managers globally were rated within a few days. A selection made on this basis was communicated as early as one and a half months after the takeover of AEI. The speed of this process and the introduction of incentive programs such as a loyalty bonus system helped avoid discontent and uncertainty among executives. At the same time, it took the wind out of the sails of competitors eager to lure away the best talent. This explains why only 15 out of 140 executives in North America left the company despite numerous wooing attempts by competitors – a sensational ratio that impressively testifies to the high level of acceptance and approval among the employees of both companies.

Network harmonization

The business foundation of any logistics service provider is its transportation and IT networks. They are the heart that keeps the company's business with goods, merchandise and services pumping. It was crucial, therefore, that the networks of both partners, Danzas and AEI, be dovetailed as quickly and quietly as possible. The companies' size alone meant that this was no easy feat: At the end of 1998, Danzas was already active in 49 countries, where it operated 585 offices, and had 324 warehouse and cargo-handling facilities worldwide. AEI, in turn, operated a network spanning about 700 branches in 135 countries in 1998 and was ranked among the top three air freight providers in many countries outside the United States, including Australia, the UK, the Netherlands and Spain. There were several locations where both partners had offices and others where none of the two companies was represented at all.

The fact that the two large networks could be harmonized relatively quickly is due mostly to the successful implementation of the IT system LOGIS, which was taken over from AEI. The system, which was subsequently used in the entire Intercontinental business division, was not only compatible with the systems used at Danzas, but was also comparatively easy to handle. That was a distinct advantage given the need to quickly establish LOGIS in the countries that were not yet or temporarily not linked to the network. For example, new offices had to be set up in a number of countries because both the Danzas and the AEI branches were too small to take on all employees.

Aside from the space and technology issues, the new colleagues at Danzas also had to learn the system. A comprehensive training program was developed for about 4,000 employees to teach them about the new system as quickly as possible. They were supported by "super users," that is long-time AEI employees with wide experience with LOGIS. This program not only provided the necessary basis for the urgently needed transfer of knowledge, but also promoted dialogue and mutual understanding among the new colleagues.

The magnitude of the IT integration made it one of the most difficult and most challenging elements of the integration process. In the United States alone, 52 different IT platforms had to be integrated under enormous pressure – alongside normal day-to-day business, that is without any safety net. But it worked: As early as July 2001, just one process and one IT investment sufficed to cover nearly 90 percent of the business.

Business as usual

From the perspective of Deutsche Post World Net's customers, the merger of Danzas and AEI offered excellent prospects. Thanks to the strong global presence of the newly created company, they could obtain services from a single source. One-stop shopping became a worldwide reality for them, no matter where they happened to be in the world. At the same time, this group watched the takeover of AEI with a critical eye because it knew from experience that companies often could not maintain their customary service quality during integration phases. To ensure that Deutsche Post World Net's customers did not lose the faith in the company that had been built up over years, the integration activities could not interfere with the scope and level of day-to-day business.

The fact that this was possible must be attributed not only to the external consultants who supported and relieved the operative staff during the integration phase, but also to the enormous dedication of AEI and Danzas employees. Despite the dual burden of integration and daily business, they showed a high level of professionalism and commitment, providing customers with the quality they expected of their service provider. Success proved them right. Despite intense efforts by competitors to capitalize on this phase of weakness, Danzas-AEI managed to tie all key customers to the company during this crucial phase and convince them of the value of this partnership. Not one of them switched to a different logistics provider during these critical months.

Summary

Looking back, Günter Rohrmann once described the integration of AEI as a mammoth task. Indeed, this move was a remarkable achievement on the part of all involved, and it even started to bear fruit during the implementation phase: Despite the "absorbing" effect of the integration, the results of the Intercontinental division continued to improve in 2000. By March 2001, 23 out of 31 countries had been integrated, and the integration process was largely completed by July 2001. The company managed to implement the integration process within the planned timetable, without a meaningful loss of know-how and employees, let alone customers.

Today, the former Intercontinental business division with the Danzas-AEI company has become the performance brand DHL Danzas Air & Ocean. It still holds the unchallenged No. 1 position in the worldwide air freight business and, as an important member of the group family, makes a major contribution to the success of Deutsche Post World Net. Thanks also to the achievements of this division, the Bonn-based group is on the cusp of becoming the world's premier logistics provider. The group intends to reach this goal by the end of 2005. It would be the preliminary high point of a development that few could have envisioned five years ago.

The acquisition and integration of AEI were important steps on this path, which have been followed by others and which will be followed by others. One thing is certain: In light of the increasing globalization of markets, economic success will depend far more on international partnerships in the future than it does today. Over the long run, only companies with an international network structure and strong global partners will be able to survive, let alone prosper in an increasingly tough competitive environment. Mergers & acquisitions will continue to play an important role in this process. Deutsche Post World Net demonstrated a successful corporate acquisition with the takeover of AEI. The secret of a successful merger is to acknowledge the significance of individual parts and components, to examine their complementing aspects and then to meld them into a sensible whole. This applies not only to networks and IT systems, but also and above all to employees. They form the foundation of any business, and their mutual commitment determines in the end whether a merger will succeed. This is how it worked in the case of AEI, and this is how it will work in the future.

3.6.2 How HR Contributes to Merger Success

A Case Example of Post-Closing Integration in a German-American M&A Transaction Confirms What Consulting Experience and Market Research are Telling Us

Ravin Jesuthasan and Helmuth L. Uder

M&A activity is undoubtedly complex, challenging and unpredictable. In this context people issues have proven to be the critical success factors in achieving the expected strategic objectives. Despite their importance, these people issues do not yet receive the attention they deserve. This article highlights the people-related challenges of cross-border mergers and describes a pragmatic way to tackle them successfully by considering the example of German-based LSG and US-based SkyChefs.

HR in M&A transactions: What is the market telling us?

Mergers and acquisitions are reemerging as a core business strategy for many organizations. Accordingly, the key question is whether the next wave of deals will prove more successful than many of those struck during the late 1990s. Recent research suggests the answer will be "yes" for many organizations, thanks in part to some hard lessons learned in past deals.

To understand what companies have learned from their M&A experience and how human resource professionals view their role in future deals, Towers Perrin surveyed HR executives worldwide. The results show that HR believes that it is well-positioned to meet many key M&A challenges, although respondents agree that the biggest issues still touch on people and culture. Responses suggest that companies are learning from past mistakes, and that they may be taking a more disciplined approach to deal-making overall, motivated in part by the current emphasis on fiscal restraint and corporate governance.

What has changed is that companies are paying more attention to these issues and are bringing HR into the process earlier, contributing to rising success rates in recent deals. The scope of the issues widens if mergers occur cross-border and between different cultures.

Another change has been the extent to which HR executives feel confident in taking on M&A challenges and the difference this readiness seems to make in getting results. While most HR executives believe that they are at least partially ready to address a range of M&A challenges, many doubt that the rest of their organization is at the same level of readiness. Significantly, this group reported better results than others in several key human areas, including productivity and motivation. More interestingly, there appears to be a relationship between the readiness to address M&A challenges and how well a merged company performs financially, as measured by total shareholder return.

HR is more qualified than ever as a business partner in M&A

One reason for the growing success is that HR now tends to get involved much earlier than before and can influence key decisions that affect the ultimate success of integration activities. At the end of the 1990s less than 40% of HR executives had any meaningful involvement in pre-deal or due diligence stages. Today, by contrast, close to two-thirds are involved in due diligence. And this number is expected to grow.

"Soft" issues remain the hardest ones

Despite these positive developments, no one has found a solution to the toughest issues in M&A: those involving people. At the top of the list are leadership, employee communication, talent retention and cultural alignment – particularly critical concerns in any situation of major organizational change.

Greater M&A readiness limits the duration and intensity of adverse employee reaction

Employee anxiety during the period between deal announcement and change of control is a key area where HR can make a difference. Managers who judged themselves ready not only reported less decline in morale and engagement following recent M&A activity, but also were more likely than other respondents to say morale had actually improved, resulting in retention of key talent.

Those fully ready for M&A do some things differently

Companies that view themselves as fully prepared for coming M&A transactions act differently. These companies:

- involve HR at board level in M&A discussions
- involve HR earlier in the process
- pay more attention to people issues
- have clearly defined objectives throughout their deals
- feel a greater sense of urgency in addressing difficult people issues in the critical three to six month period between announcement of the deal and closing.

The lesson here is that there are some actions that can help companies avoid some of the key pitfalls to successful corporate restructuring.

HR's role in due diligence is expanding

Traditionally, HR came to the party relatively late – typically after a deal was announced. It had limited, if any, involvement in pre-deal and due diligence stages – despite the fact that this is the stage where companies look at key pay and benefits issues, including the scale of potential liabilities they may be assuming. Today, HR executives have been deeply involved in due diligence for recent deals. One reason for the increasing involvement is the unsufficient financing of pension liabilities which have become a significant issue in a number of recent transactions.

However, due diligence is also the stage to begin addressing some of the other key people issues. Companies have much to gain from broadening the due diligence scope beyond a pure numbers focus to encompass these issues. In particular, this includes "securing the top team" and "managing the messages": telling a consistent story about the deal's potential benefits, practical challenges and why employees should want to be part of the new organization.

The M&A threat: Managing the decline of productivity and engagement

A major threat for the architects of any merger or acquisition is the inability to deliver on the transaction's value proposition and synergies, often not due to any miscalculation of the deal price, but to a decline in productivity and motivation. Restructuring of any kind is a major change event, and change triggers anxiety among the people involved – often reducing employee's level of engagement and willingness to deliver effort on the job.

To some extent, productivity gains are almost automatic after a merger or acquisition, due to elimination of overlapping functions and related economies of scale. Indeed, HR executives are much more likely to report productivity gains than losses following recent deals. At the same time, only 44% of them felt productivity had risen. Presumably companies may not be fully leveraging operational synergies or, worse, may be victims of the kind of behaviorally based performance declines that come about when employees are disengaged, too often absent (in body or spirit) or just performing at the minimum required level to do their job.

Turnover is another of those 'M&A facts of life', but the goal, clearly, is to minimize the loss of needed talent while maximizing the departure of redundant or low-performing individuals. However, this does not yet seem to be occurring to the desired degree. A quarter of our respondents reported increases in *unwanted turnover,* compared to a minority of 9% who saw it decline. Similarly, only a third reported increases in *desirable turnover.* In light of this it is no surprise that people issues remain the most critical area to address – throughout the process, but particularly in the initial three to six months of a deal. There are no substitutes or shortcuts when selecting and supporting the leadership team, implementing an effective employee communication program and retaining key talent. Cultural alignment, however, is the toughest issue of all.

When leadership, communication, retention and cultural issues are addressed early on, the new organization can invest more time in issues like integrating rewards, HR technology platforms and the HR function itself. These issues typically require more detailed technical analysis and longer lead times for effective implementation.

Key issues to be addressed and work streams to be conducted

While concerns about rising pension and other people costs may have prompted HR's original invitation to the table, the challenge now is to build on that advantage and expand the role it can play, particularly in critical situations like M&A transactions.

Being ready for M&A can make a significant difference in the outcomes of deals. In thinking about the readiness of an organization and its people, our experience suggests a fairly short list of actions that companies must get right to ensure deal success. Most of the work streams are derived from these merger issues:

- *Deal price and people risks:* For HR, this involves helping ensure that company leaders fully understand potential people costs and risks (e.g. pension liabilities).
- *Manage the messages:* Company leaders need to articulate the overall vision for the transaction and how the new strategy looks and how people are likely to be affected – this needs to happen fast.
- *Secure key talent:* It's critical early on to define retention programs for existing staff that support the key merger objectives.
- *Prioritize and manage activities:* Not all people issues have equal weight and urgency. Understanding the deal objectives helps to focus on those issues with the greatest potential impact.
- *Develop a workable change management plan:* Use a detailed merger integration process that incorporates change management techniques as well as cultural assessment tools and techniques.
- *Design and implement the right staffing model:* Staffing decisions do far more to signal the organization's values than formal communications.

- *Align total rewards:* Be sure to consider the strengths and weaknesses of both organizations' programs and use the opportunity of the new deal to make changes that better support the future business direction.
- *Measure synergies:* Be realistic about synergy targets and the effort required to achieve them. Then carefully track and communicate progress.

Critical success factors for cross-border transactions

In global and cross-border mergers, seamless working relationships are one ingredient for success. People can see how the future joint businesses work together effectively and respectfully. Global M&A teams such as external consultants can make a difference if they can demonstrate to their client how seamless global relationships work in practice. Very often they are seen as the "role model" for successful integration work.

The greater the cultural differences between countries and companies are, the earlier in the process turf battles begin, in particular if leadership fails to outline the strategy, structure and future direction of the entity. In this regard HR needs to work with the architects of the transaction on the picture of the new organization. Furthermore, it needs to develop a view on the people programs, such as total rewards, to acquaint people with the strategic framework and guidelines derived from the new deal, expressed, for example, in pay and benefit guidelines and processes.

Experienced organizations give this issue top priority in order to avoid behavior expressed as "let's first do the deal… afterwards we can talk about people integration." Different values of different corporate and national cultures need to be made understandable by using appropriate tools, such as cultural assessments, to be taken into account for integration plans and activities. Differences are by definition not a "bad thing" – rather they open up chances to combine strengths in the new organization or unit. Similarities very often can even increase turf battles due to increased competition.

In any case, cultural differences need to be addressed early in the process. Some companies with a successful M&A track record show that cultural assessment and so-called "soft facts" are part of a pre-deal due diligence and can even influence decisions on target selections.

In the following case study we address four critical factors for successful cross-border M&A transactions.

The case: LSG SkyChefs and its critical success factors

Like many mature industries, the airline catering business has long looked at increasing efficiency and productivity for margin enhancement with the recognition that growth will primarily be realized through either expansion of market share or diversification, or both. It was this goal of expanding share that led to the combination of SkyChefs and LSG.

SkyChefs began business in 1943 as a subsidiary of American Airlines and was sold in 1987 to a group consisting of its management and Onex Corp. In 1993, Lufthansa Airlines' subsidiary LSG acquired a stake in the food services company and established a global marketing agreement. LSG purchased the entire company in 2001, creating the world's largest airline catering organization.

From the outset, the organization had a clear vision of "One World, One Business, One Global Service Commitment." This vision extended to how the organization approached merger integration. The company began integration with a clear understanding of the current state at each organization and an awareness of existing practices at other leading companies, but integration activities were primarily driven by the organization's strategic priorities and the culture it wanted to create.

The terrorist attacks of September 11, 2001, hurt LSG SkyChefs like the rest of the airline industry. A 30% revenue decline led to a 35% reduction in the workforce, facility closures and consolidation and heightened the urgency of restructuring and finding innovative ways to create more value. Fortunately for LSG SkyChefs, the merger integration work – begun with quite a different purpose in mind – gave the organization a substantial head start over most other companies in adjusting to the unplanned business changes resulting from 9/11.

There were four people-related aspects to this transaction that both organizations had to focus on during and after integration to minimize disruption, retain key talent and realize merger synergies. These were:

- *Structure and Roles*: What is the optimal organizational structure for the newly merged organization? How different is this structure from the inherited structures? How will candidates be selected for various roles within this structure? How do we guard against bias and sending "unintended messages" via the selection process?
- *Culture*: What is the desired culture for the new organization? How does this compare with existing culture(s)? What are the risks associated with attempting to shift the culture?
- *Total Rewards*: How can we utilize rewards to retain key talent during the integration phase? What should the new "deal" look like as we exit the integration phase? How do we realize the value of rewards in aligning decision making and behavior to deliver on the merger value proposition?
- *Measurement and Alignment*: How will we measure whether we are on track to deliver merger synergies? Can we create a line of sight between key business priorities at each stage of the deal (from integration to implementation to operating as a new organization) and individual activities?

Structure and roles

In the context of the deal under discussion a coherent structure with clearly delineated roles was a prerequisite. Well before the deal was consummated, there needed to be a clear articulation of the structure required.

Beyond the obvious need to create a structure that was both efficient and customer-centric, it was essential to leverage the skills existing within both legacy organizations. This required a clear definition of the requirements of each position within the new structure: key competencies, definition of roles and responsibilities and specific understanding of the performance expectations for each position. Finally, came the most

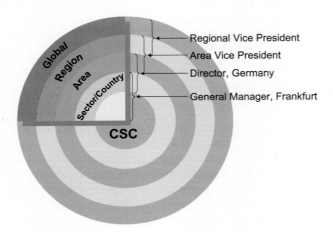

Figure 3.41 A combination of geography and functions: LSG SkyChefs' matrix organization (CSC = Customer Service Center)

difficult task of identifying candidates and filling the positions. Each candidate had to be assessed on four objective criteria:

- Job knowledge
- Experience
- Qualifications (technical or otherwise)
- Historical performance

When LSG SkyChefs merged, it created five organizational levels, from individual flight kitchens through countries, areas (aggregations of countries), regions (e.g. North and South America) and global. In this structure, functional responsibility meshed with geographic responsibility. The company ensured that executives at each level had the opportunity to participate in decision making at the next level up, thereby broadening their perspective. In addition, the company took a pragmatic view to sourcing talent, filling positions at each level with the best available candidate from either organization – or an external hire.

Culture

Widely acknowledged as the most challenging aspect of making this merger work was culture or, more precisely, bridging the existing cultural differences. As mentioned earlier, the seeds of M&A failure are often sown in the earliest stages of a transaction, the point when a deal looks good on paper, although the information available may be sparse. Even after an announcement, the exchange of certain data is restricted for antitrust reasons if the two companies are competitors. Yet, much can be gleaned at the preliminary stages that can compromise the deal in the long run if not addressed early on. Many of these differences are cultural.

If one company has a hierarchical culture and the other treasures a team environment with lots of divisional autonomy, the two will eventually clash. Better to recognize this and plan for reconciling the problem at the outset rather than postpone it.

The critical first step in bringing two organizations together involves getting a clear understanding of the differences between the two cultures and articulating what the desired culture of the new organization will look like. It is important that any target culture both seeks to build on the strengths of the existing cultures and introduces wholly new attributes. The key word here is "balance." There have been plenty of failed mergers where the merged organization tried to adopt the culture of one of the legacy entities.

In assessing the cultures of the legacy organizations, HR often uses a "culture map" to assess attributes like decision-making style, performance orientation, focus (cost, customer, etc.), work environment, etc. This allows decision makers to easily assess areas of commonality versus difference and plan for the steps necessary to move both legacy entities towards the desired culture.

In the case of LSG SkyChefs, this assessment took place, highlighting commonalities, strengths relative to the desired culture and gaps that would need to be bridged. The organization realized that differences between the two legacy cultures could actually provide the basis for a powerful new culture that would differentiate the new company in a highly competitive, rapidly consolidating market. Figure 3.42 illustrates the attributes associated with each of the two cultures and the future stage after successful merger and cultural integration.

The target culture was not an artificial product of workshops run by HR, but the result of moderated discussions between both senior leadership teams, based on a sound analysis of the status quo. It was derived from future business requirements and strategy. After this basic but important groundwork, the desired future culture was communicated by the leaders through media such as public meetings, one-on-ones, e-mail value statements etc. It was explicitly incorporated into the guiding principles of the rewards philosophy later in the process.

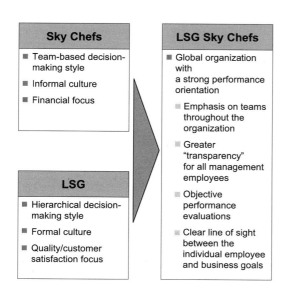

Figure 3.42
Two different cultures become one to support business principles and objectives

Interestingly, external advisors have a unique opportunity to act as role models to organizations in their search for an effective global culture. LSG SkyChefs engaged multiple consultancies for integration support. This required each consultant not only to deploy an integrated global team but also to cooperate with their own competitors to ensure seamless integration of the various work streams. Throughout the process, each firm brought the right talent to bear on their particular work stream, successfully blending global expertise with local knowledge. The keys to these successful relationships were a focus on ensuring the highest quality service to the client and mutual respect for the skills and capabilities of each firm or individual. These same basic tenets are the keys to creating a truly sustainable global culture.

Total rewards

An often overlooked element in any acquisition, an organization's rewards system, can be either one of the largest hindrances to cross-border integration or, if fully understood at the time of due diligence and appropriately integrated, a key mechanism for aligning behavior and driving the performance of the merged company.

When LSG and SkyChefs agreed to merge, the organization very quickly embarked on a process of inventorying its current reward programs. As previously discussed, the organization recognized the rewards system as a key enabler of (or barrier to) effective integration. This inventory did not merely look at differences in program design, but also assessed how the programs actually worked and the messages they sent to the organization. Not surprisingly, the very obvious differences between the two organizations were strongly reflected in how the reward programs worked. While they might have looked relatively similar from a design perspective, how the programs were interpreted and used to shape behavior was in fact quite different. For example, the

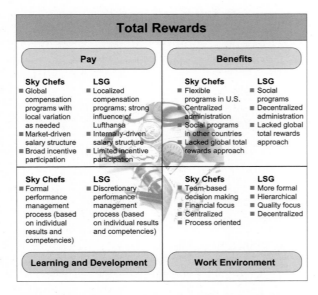

Figure 3.43 Differences in reward approaches: Sky Chefs and LSG

Rewards Philosophy

Global vs. Local Emphasis

- Ensure globally consistent program design for base salary, short-term incentives and long-term incentives
  - Global salary structure, with local ranges
  - Short-term and long-term incentives with consistent degree of "stretch"
- Use compensation elements (i.e., base pay, short-term incentives, long-term incentives) consistently across all locations down through the Regional Staff level

Pay for Performance

- Create direct linkages between pay and performance in base salary, short-term incentives and long-term incentives to increase differentiation
  - Base salary increases focus on individual performance (value-added competencies/behaviors and results)
  - Short-term incentives provide appropriate balance between financial, operational/customer and employee goals
  - Long-term incentives focus on value creation at the corporate level
  - Incentives are tied to rigorous performance metrics
  - Incentive payouts/goals are calibrated to balance return to shareholders with degree of risk to participant

Figure 3.44
A "Cut" of the new LSG SkyChefs reward philosophy as
a foundation for their rewards design elements

rewards system at SkyChefs was highly leveraged (i.e. greater percentage of variable pay), more structured in administration and yet informal in process while that at LSG was delivered more in fixed wages, was less structured in administration but more formal. Figure 3.43 illustrates some of the differences revealed by the inventory:

This inventory gave the merged organization a clear sense of the barriers that would need to be overcome. In combination with best practices data and a clear understanding of the business strategy and desired culture, the inventory was then used to formulate an overall rewards philosophy that would drive the integration of the two organizations. The philosophy clearly articulated the role of each reward element in driving performance, valuing work performed and supporting the creation of a new culture (figure 3.44).

Equally important was the process for ensuring the development and implementation of a robust rewards philosophy and design that was supported by multiple levels of the organization. The process involved engaging with three different groups of stakeholders:

- Design Team: This group consisted of senior HR and Rewards staff from both legacy organizations. This was the primary working group that reviewed the current status and formulated strategy, policy and design for the merged company. With the help of consultants, this group analyzed data, reviewed best practices, formulated and tested alternatives and developed implementation plans to ensure that the rewards system supported the business strategy.

- Challenge Team: The team was made up of line and staff managers from various countries. Their primary responsibility was to assess the effectiveness of the various program designs and communication materials that were developed from the perspective of a leader and a participant. This group helped ensure that program designs did not lead to unintended consequences and that communications were effective in shaping behavior.

- Review and Approval Team: This group comprised the Managing Board of the merged organization. Their responsibilities were both to approve the changes to the Total Reward system and to champion them in various forums with employees in each country.

Measurement and alignment

Most organizations do not have the systems or processes to systematically align organization goals and individual behaviors and track progress on an ongoing basis. This is even more challenging for newly-merged organizations, given the need to align employees of diverse backgrounds with short-term synergy goals and long-term performance objectives.

Achieving these goals and objectives requires organizations to have a robust infrastructure to assess progress toward to these goals and create accountability at various

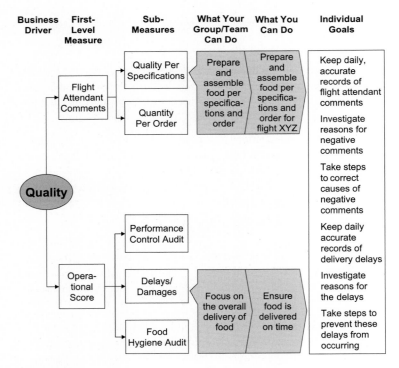

Figure 3.45
The linkage of business performance drivers with individual goals was ensured by building 'line-of-sight' and supported by training and communication

levels so employees have a clear line of sight between the goals and their individual activities.

The measurement infrastructure in a merger situation should track three things:

- Is the organization making progress in achieving the promised merger objectives?
- Is the organization managing operational risk (i.e. mitigating the impact of integration activities on various stakeholders like customers, suppliers and employees)?
- Are integration projects on track to realize their goal of building a sustainable organization?

However, it is insufficient to merely track these three categories of measurement. Employees in various roles need to have a clear line of sight between their individual activities and these measures. Figure 3.45 illustrates the framework LSG SkyChefs used to create a shared understanding of the key drivers of product quality. The organization leveraged the framework broadly into two key HR processes to ensure alignment between key business drivers and individual behaviors:

- *Performance Management:* The organization engaged employees at multiple levels to help them articulate how their individual goals and activities aligned with the drivers of quality, customer satisfaction and financial performance.
- *Annual Incentives:* The organization articulated an explicit policy of providing broad eligibility for annual incentives in order to align decision making at all levels. The objective was to engage and align employees at all levels in improving the key drivers of operating performance.

Key lessons from the case and other M&A transactions

The complexity and cultural challenges of cross-border transactions are very often underestimated, as is the reduction in employee morale and engagement. And the LSG Sky Chefs project shows that the earlier in the process senior management and HR work together to shape the merged entity and its goals, the greater the likelihood of success in a merger.

Successful, M&A-ready companies address these issues and do things differently. They incidentally tend to close more deals than other respondents. This highlights, again, that experience really does count, especially in cross-border deals.

Successful companies involve HR earlier in the process: Fully ready HR departments are more likely to report a high level of HR involvement in M&A activities. This finding underscores the advantages of involving HR from the very beginning.

Moreover, successful companies are more likely to have a growth agenda and clear objectives for their deals. Today, companies are far more likely to cite product, service or channel expansion as the key drivers of their M&A activity. They display less uncertainty about their M&A objectives. In our experience, it is critical for HR executives to have a clear understanding of the key business goals of each deal, including the marketplace and financial objectives as well as the people goals. This also helps them to gain credit for the HR function in general.

Successful companies are more likely to engage external HR advisors for help with multi-country due diligence and planning. This further confirms the benefits of experience in high-risk transactions where speed is essential and cross-border issues add additional layers of complexity.

Fully ready HR departments are likely to have an agenda of critical issues to address within three to six months of deal announcement – communication, staff retention, pay and benefits integration. This sense of urgency is consistent with our frequent advice to clients to follow the "100/80 rule" and be ready to accept the potential risks of acting 100% fast and 80% right. Good preparation – in terms of having established processes and tools for due diligence and integration planning – can make a big difference in helping organizations move quickly.

Also, they have a better appreciation of the challenges involved in doing key implementation activities right: Although it may seem counterintuitive, the experienced HR Director more likely than other HR managers can identify a number of core integration activities as challenging. Seasoned M&A veterans seem to have a more realistic view of the challenges they face in managing an effective communication effort, integrating pay and benefit programs, consolidating HR departments and helping middle managers play appropriate leadership roles. Managers who feel best prepared to support M&A take these key people-related steps very seriously and don't underestimate the difficulty of managing them effectively.

In short, these companies focus more attention and resources on the people issues early on and throughout the process, but also receive a faster payoff in terms of realigning the workforce to support the new business direction.

Although survey results tell us that we are realizing better results from our transactions and managers are more mindful of integration challenges, there are still significant differences in professionalism between the "new world" and the "old world." Anglo-Saxon leaders appear more aware that PEOPLE make or break M&A deals, not simply the deals themselves. Or, as a senior M&A architect argued: "Buying is fun, merging is hell."

Literature

"HR Rises to the Challenge: Unlocking the Value of M&A." Towers Perrin Track Survey 2004. New York, January 2005.

"The Role of Human Capital in M&A: A white paper based on the opinions of 132 senior executives worldwide." Published by Towers Perrin in co-operation with The Economist Intelligence Unit. London, October 2002.

"Making Mergers Work: The Strategic Importance of People." A Towers Perrin research jointly conducted with the Society for Human Resource Management Foundation. New York, October 2000.

"Reconnecting with employees. Attracting, retaining and engaging your workforce." The Towers Perrin European Talent Survey. London, October 2004.

3.7 Materials & Chemicals

3.7.1 Divestitures – How to Create Value from Shrinking the Portfolio

Barbara S. Jeremiah and Konrad J. von Szczepanski

With the financial markets rewarding growth companies, it is understandable that corporate divestitures may be perceived as not adding value – particularly if the strategic rationale and ultimate financial results are not achieved. Following a multi-year period of growth, driven largely by acquisitions, Alcoa Inc. conducted a regularly-scheduled strategic review of its portfolio of businesses and in 2003 embarked on a series of eleven simultaneous divestitures. These businesses represented approximately $1.3 billion of revenues, or 6% of total company revenue. The objectives were clear: focus on core businesses, reduce debt and maximize value for non-core assets. A three-pronged strategy was developed to ensure these objectives would be met.

Alcoa at a glance

Alcoa is the world's leading producer and manager of primary aluminum, fabricated aluminum and alumina facilities, and is active in all major aspects of the industry. Alcoa serves the aerospace, automotive, packaging, building and construction, commercial transportation and industrial markets, bringing design, engineering, production and other capabilities of Alcoa's businesses to customers. In addition to aluminum products and components, Alcoa also markets consumer brands including Reynolds Wrap® foils and plastic wraps, Alcoa® wheels, and Baco® household wraps. Among its other businesses are vinyl siding, closures, fastening systems, precision castings, and electrical distribution systems for cars and trucks. The company has 131,000 employees in 43 countries and has been a member of the Dow Jones Industrial Average for 45 years and the Dow Jones Sustainability Indexes since 2001. More information can be found at www.alcoa.com.

Context of divestitures

Between 1997 and 2003, Alcoa's revenues grew by 62%, with the majority of this $8.1B growth attributable to acquisitions. As shown in Figure 3.46, the major acquisitions included Alumax, which added approximately $3B in revenue; Reynolds Metals, at the time the world's third-largest producer of aluminum, which added approximately $4B in revenue; Cordant Technologies, which included Howmet Castings and Huck Fasteners; Siemens AG's automotive wire harness business; and Fairchild Fasteners and IVEX Packaging.

These acquisitions reshaped Alcoa's portfolio significantly. For example, between 1997 and 2003, revenues from U.S. operations grew from 54% of total company

191

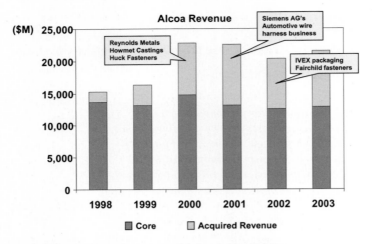

Figure 3.46 Alcoa's recent growth driven by acquisitions

revenues to 63%. Conversely, the share of revenue derived from operations in the Other Americas and Pacific regions declined from 16% and 13%, respectively, to 8% for each region. From a market perspective, packaging sales grew from 20% of total company revenues to 25% and aerospace sales grew from 6% to 9% of total company revenues between 1999 and 2003.

In 2002, Alcoa conducted a thorough portfolio review of its businesses and markets they serve. The review focused on two key parameters for all Alcoa businesses: financial performance, which included shareholder value creation and return on capital (ROC); and strategic fit. Strategic fit was rated high when the business held, or was able to attain, a leading market position (number 1 or 2), had a sustainable competitive

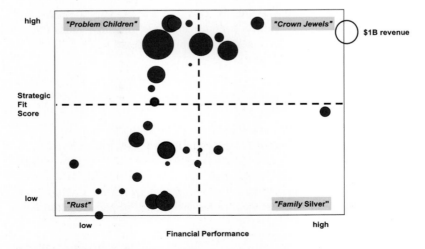

Figure 3.47 Alcoa's portfolio evaluation

advantage, and provided a platform for above-GDP growth. Figure 3.47 shows an illustrative example of Alcoa's portfolio, rated along the dimensions of financial performance and strategic fit.

Following the conclusion of its strategic review, Alcoa announced on January 8, 2003, its decision to divest a number of businesses that did not meet minimum levels of financial performance or strategic fit. The list of divestitures included the following businesses:

- Specialty Alumina Chemicals
- Packaging Equipment
- Architectural Products in North America
- Commodity Automotive Fasteners
- Certain fabrication operations in South America
- Aluminum foil operations in St. Louis, MO and Russellville, AR
- Minority equity stake in Latasa, a Brazilian producer of aluminum beverage cans

These businesses generated approximately $1.3 billion revenues in 2002, or 6% of Alcoa's total revenue.

Alcoa's three-prong divestiture strategy

The series of divestitures announced in early 2003 was the largest one in Alcoa's recent history. The company was able to conduct eleven divestiture processes, virtually simultaneously, and meet overall expectations on proceeds due to three key elements of its divestiture strategy:

1. Create a separate operating organization within Corporate Development
2. Dedicated divestiture teams
3. Deploy standard processes

Create a separate operating organization within corporate development

The first step was to create a "home room" for the businesses to be sold. A new Alcoa business unit, "Alcoa Diversified Products," was established, with an experienced operational manager as its leader, reporting to the Executive Vice President of Corporate Development. The main objectives of this organizational realignment were to prepare the businesses for sale and to sharpen the focus on near-term and sustainable performance improvement. The company was convinced that these objectives could be achieved to a higher degree if the businesses to be divested were separated from their historic reporting structures. In addition, this move eliminated potential conflicts of interest between businesses remaining with Alcoa and businesses to be divested. Corporate Development was now accountable for the overall financial outcome of the divestiture process, including both the performance of the businesses while still owned by Alcoa as well as the impact of the transaction itself, including proceeds. Consequently, decisions resulting in a trade-off between ongoing performance and overall value of the business could be made by a single organizational entity – Corporate Development.

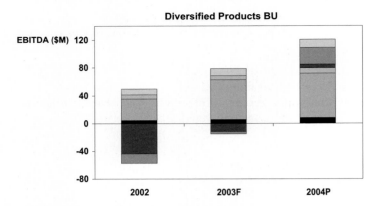

Figure 3.48 Focus on EBITDA Improvement

Preparing a business for sale involves many initiatives. For Alcoa, developing a sound business strategy for the period following the sale of each business, retention of key employees in the business, and maintaining the customer base rank at the top of the list of priorities.

As far as near-term and sustainable performance improvement is concerned, the leadership of the Alcoa Diversified Products deployed a combination of aggressive cost reduction and working capital management, and constrained capital expenditure to the bare minimum, while at the same time maintaining adherence to Alcoa's values such as focus on environment, health and safety. Management of both the Diversified Products group and the businesses to be divested kept a clear focus on EBITDA, rather than on the more complex ROC metric traditionally deployed within Alcoa. Importantly, management incentive compensation was aligned with this focus on EBITDA. Figure 3.48 shows the performance of the businesses to be divested from 2002 to 2004; in aggregate, EBITDA improved from a loss of $8M to a positive $64M in 2003, with a further improvement to $121M projected for 2004.

Dedicated divestiture teams

All transaction teams were led by experienced members of Alcoa's Corporate Development group. In some cases, investment bankers were engaged to support unique projects. Dedicated members of Alcoa's Resource Units – Legal, Human Resources, Accounting, Tax, Environment/Health/Safety, to name just a few – were assigned to each of the transaction teams and fully engaged in the divestiture projects from the start. This ensured continuity throughout each phase of the project, including post-closing matters. Further, by dedicating senior resources to each project the company was able to optimize seamless communications and transparency within the organization.

Deploy standard processes

Just as Alcoa focuses on standardizing production work under the Alcoa Business System (ABS), modeled after the Toyota Production System, the same principles were applied to the divestiture processes. The company's corporate development department defined a standard divestiture process and created a set of templates for the key transaction documents (e.g., teaser, confidential information memorandum, management presentation, process letters, confidentiality agreement and data room index) that facilitated information gathering, structuring, sharing, and presentation.

Another key element of standardization was to replace physical, i.e., paper-based, data rooms with virtual data rooms. A virtual data room is a secure website that allows all participants in the transaction process to access pertinent information online. Significant savings in time and dollars resulted from the ability to grant and remove access privileges instantaneously at the individual document level, irrespective of the physical location of the document or party involved. This proved especially helpful given the global scope and auction format of the divestiture projects.

In a typical transaction, a potentially interested party was contacted and granted access via the secure website to a teaser and a confidentiality agreement (CA). Once the CA was executed, the party received access rights to the confidential information memorandum on the same website. While the bidders evaluated the material, all data room material was uploaded to the web site simultaneously in the background. Second round bidders, following their selection, were granted access to the data room material, which was also accessible to their advisors. Due diligence questions and answers were posted to the online data room as well, accessible to all parties. As bidders were successively eliminated from the auction process, their access rights were revoked instantaneously.

Not only did the use of virtual data rooms save time and money for Alcoa, it was well received by virtually all potential buyers. For the buyers, access was available 24 hours a day, simultaneously, regardless of their physical location, and data room updates were instantaneous.

Lessons learned

As a result of employing the strategies described above, Alcoa met its overall expectations regarding proceeds and successfully completed the divestiture process for all but two of the businesses within the initially announced time frame. The company retained one business, which continues to perform well, and restructured one North American business, which is now part of a global architectural products business.

As discussed above, lessons learned included the importance of a separate organization to focus on performance, dedicated divestiture teams and standardized processes. Additionally, the company learned the importance of maintaining a competitive process throughout every step of the transaction. Finally, it is important to understand why and how to work with financial sponsors and to also conduct regular portfolio reviews.

Financial sponsors vs. strategic buyers

In addition to conducting several divestitures in parallel, selling to financial sponsors was a new experience for Alcoa as well. Attracting strategic buyers to a divestiture process remains an imperative to Alcoa, given that strategic premiums have averaged 25% over the past five years. However, an increasing share of U.S. carve-out transaction value, now approaching 40% or more in some sectors, is attributable to financials sponsors.

Contrary to what had been expected initially, Alcoa sold several of its businesses to financial sponsors. In the process, key lessons learned were:

- Financials sponsors seek to minimize risk, wherever possible. Expect requirements for long-term supply contracts and generous transition services in case of carve-outs (generally not the case with a strategic buyer).

- Valuations are fairly predictable, regardless of the sponsor, and are driven by last-twelve-months EBITDA and availability of bank financing (leverage).

- Financing procedures are vastly different between the U.S. and Europe, driving a different set of due diligence requirements. If the financial sponsor seeks financing in Europe, a Vendor Due Diligence (VDD) package, including certain guarantees, will be required in most cases. This VDD is largely not required if financing is obtained in the U.S. It is important to understand in detail the VDD requirements, and to allow for sufficient time and costs in the divestiture process.

Regular portfolio review

The 2002 portfolio review process was the first formal one Alcoa had conducted in several years with an eye toward potential divestitures. The lack of a regular process, combined with the intensive acquisition activity between the mid-1990s and 2002, resulted in a "divestiture backlog." By their nature, large acquisitions oftentimes bring with them some businesses or product lines that may not be of core strategic focus – and should be rationalized or divested. Alcoa has since established a regular portfolio review process, which is conducted annually. A regular process allows for improved timing of divestitures, fresh perspectives on core vs. non-core, and results ultimately in higher proceeds and shareholder value.

3.7.2 Degussa's Execution Experience with Transatlantic M&A Projects

Joerg Sellmann and Oliver Maier

Moving along the M&A process chain and drawing on the chemicals group's M&A practice, the article highlights US and German specificities as well as dos and don'ts relative to roadblocks and peculiarities.

Introduction

Degussa AG, currently considered the largest global specialty chemical group, is the result of several mergers between 1998 and early 2001, and a subsequent large-scale divestment program. During the first quarter of 2001 Degussa-Huels AG, Frankfurt and SKW Trostberg AG came together as a result of the combination of their holding companies, the utilities Veba AG, Düsseldorf and VIAG AG, Munich. At the same time, the publicly listed English specialty chemical concern Laporte also had to be integrated into the new Degussa AG. Shortly before, SKW Trostberg AG and Goldschmidt AG had merged to form SKW Trostberg, and Huels AG and Degussa AG were merged in parallel.

As a result, the new Degussa AG had revenues of €17 billion. Within months of the latest merger, however, a €6.5 billion revenue proportion was defined as non-core, and was to be divested, in an effort to strategically focus on specialty chemicals. The divestment program has now been essentially concluded as a result of the sale of 38 companies within about three years. Degussa AG has become, through these transactions, a focused specialty chemicals company with revenues of €11 billion in 2004 and roughly 44,000 employees as opposed to over 60,000 at the beginning of this transformation.

Obviously, various exit strategies were considered during this divestment process, including limited auctions, trade sales to industrial strategic players, management buy-outs (MBO/LBO), and an IPO notably for the pharmaceutical activities of Degussa. What is less well known to the market is the fact that the group also continued its active portfolio management vis-à-vis considering, and executing in part, acquisitions and joint-ventures. All in all, the M&A group has run more than 80 merger and acquisitions processes[1], and 48 transactions have been concluded since 2001.

As may be the case for a lot of chemicals players, a new Degussa focus is the growth through joint ventures, organic growth and acquisitions in the Peoples Republic of China. Degussa M&A has reflected this demand by positioning a sub-team on the ground in Shanghai. It has been discussed a lot lately that, despite M&A being a global business these days, some regional peculiarities are found and have to be dealt with when trying to execute transactions in China. This seems to be the new challenge in international M&A.

Elsewhere, cross-border merger and acquisition business should work seamlessly, should it not? After all, overriding aspects such as valuation technique and a sale and purchase agreement to complete the exercise should be alike everywhere in a world with truly trans-continental buyer's universes, especially in an industry which has become as globalized as the chemicals industry. There are hardly any language barriers, as English is the lingua franca in M&A; "even the French communicate in English on their own turf, especially when the properties they wish to sell are not the 'hottest ones'," as one US-based strategic player CDO recently remarked to one of the authors of this article. To put another spin on it, per a prominent Wall Street banker; "The Europeans understand now what a cash-and-debt free transaction means and do not necessarily work under the assumption of a balance sheet guarantee anymore."

This mirrors Degussa's recent own process experience: Of a total of 48, there have been 14 completed transactions for Degussa since 2001 with US party involvement

---

[1] M&A group only represents Degussa Group in transactions exceeding €25 million of value.

With the portfolio optimization towards specialty chemicals ...

Focus on Specialty Chemicals				
Construction Chemicals	Fine & Industrial Chemicals	Performance Chemicals	Coatings & Advanced Fillers	Specialty Polymers

... Degussa has acquired and integrated significant new activities ...

2001	2002	2003	2004	2005
Acquisitions				
• Laporte	• Genset Oligos	• *Midwest Lysine (50% JV Shares)*	• **Kyowa Hakko Feed Additives Business**	• *Cyro (50% JV Shares)*
		• Woermann Betonchemie		• Ratec
Joint Ventures				
	• Ausimont (JV)			• ENAX Japan and Degussa (Creavis) (50% JV)
				• Degussa-Cathay (51% JV)

... and has divested most of its non-core activities

2001	2002	2003	2004	2005
Divestments				
• AWD.pharma	• Degussa Bank	• Hythe and Barry	• Radebeul	• BDF+ Rotherham
• *Dental*	• Elbion	• Makroform	• SKW Metallurgy / Module Steel	• *Fruit Systems*
• *dmc²*	• Europeptides	• Methanova	• SKW Metallurgy / Module Stollberg	• *Proligo*
• German Remedies	• Gelatine Business	• *Polymer Latex*	• SKW Metallurgy / Module Foundry	
• *KWH*	• MainGen	• SKW East Asia		
• Oncology	• Persulphates Production	• Soderec SA		
• Phenolchemie	• SKW Piesteritz	• *Vitamine B3*		
• Prasfarma	• Textile Additives Activities	• *Oxo-C3 (JV)*		
• Southeast Asia	• *Viatris*			
• *Zaltbommel*	• *Zentaris*			
• Zeolithes	• Microparts (JV 15 %)			
• TFL (50% JV with Ciba SC)				

NAFTA Vendor/Purchaser/Partner

Figure 3.49 Overview of Degussa's transactions since 2001

(Figure 3.49). Three noteworthy Degussa transactions have been completed with US players in 2005 alone. Also worth mentioning is the experience with NAFTA players in almost every project, be it conclusive or not, including a partnering scheme with a major US private equity player on one of the largest recent acquisition attempts of Degussa which went rather seamlessly.[1]

---

[1] Joint approach with Blackstone in Bayer's Haarmann & Reimer auction.

In other words, with the speedy "locusts" feeding everywhere, and the allegedly slow-moving corporate Degussa being able to partner with one of them in a joint venture approach, attempting to harvest cooperatively, would it be time to draw a line and argue that the new challenge is indeed China relative to cross-border M&A, and thus to state that there are no differences in M&A deals in the western world anymore, at least from a process point of view? "Not quite so fast" is one of the mottos obviously of this book as well as of this article: There are still US and continental European characteristics which can indeed make or break a transaction at certain junctures of the process. The following is an attempt to throw some light on dos, don'ts, road-blocks and peculiarities that Degussa has come across just recently. These occur along the entire process chain, which is defined as the path from strategic decision to divest or acquire a business, through purchase or joint venture, to closing of the transaction. Given the vicissitudes of transatlantic mergers and acquisitions practice, the lack of available empirical data or the metrics by which to measure such data other than on valuation multiples and the like, this undertaking must necessarily rely primarily on anecdotal evidence, of course.

Observations derived from Degussa's transatlantic M&A experience

Generally, it is apparent that there are broad-brush commonalities of M&A processes as conducted on both sides of the Atlantic, especially in limited or fully-blown auction transactions. You will see that the seller has more or less carefully carved out the target, produced stand alone-financials; as a potential buyer you will be eventually presented with an Executive Summary, commonly called "Teaser," together with a Confidentiality Agreement. Next follows the Information or Offering Memorandum, and upon presentation of a meaningful indicative bid, the buyer will be invited to conduct due diligence consisting of four elements or modules: management presentation; data room; Q&A sessions and site visits. Thereafter, the potential buyers will be given precious little time to reflect upon the findings, to present an attractive final or confirmatory bid, and subsequently may be chosen to enter negotiations on the basis of a mark-up of a sale and purchase agreement. If successful, the parties would proceed to signing, and hopefully closing of the transaction.

Likewise, as a seller one would expect that the potential purchasers will have staffed their teams appropriately, thus showing seriousness by selecting and charging external advisors with certain tasks early in the process. Sophisticated, experienced buyers may also bring along post-merger professionals, and depending on the quality of the team and its decisiveness, the target management may be confronted with rather demanding questions, especially with regard to the viability of the business plan going forward, and other transaction-related issues like synergy potential or required capital expenditures. Most companies and M&A professionals comprehend and expect these elements. Resultingly one could easily argue that the tool box of mergers and acquisitions in Europe and NAFTA are by now identical, and that these are used not only by external professional advisors, but also by the players involved at the corporate level. In this context, it is often stated that this development is in part due to the wider application of skill sets of private equity buyers in Europe, which has become the norm in European transactions and strategic moves: After all, some US private equity houses are being called the "new strategics," in contrast to the "locust" remark earlier noted. The new strategics, such as Blackstone and KKR, conduct finely tuned buy-and-build strategies, often being one step ahead of the management of strategic chemical groups; financial investors are involved in the vast majority of public and private chemicals M&A deals. And the presence of financial investors has raised the awareness and competency of European strategic players with regard to the financial implications and methodology of M&A transactions. Resultantly, there appears to be a level playing field these days in the US and Europe.

However, we believe that there are differences, still. Obviously, these cases in point are derived from Degussa's recent execution experience only and do not represent an anthology; it was found, however, that some of them proved to be recurring, and drove Degussa to the guiding principle: "anticipation helps." The Degussa insights demonstrate that in each phase of a transatlantic M&A project, be it acquisition, divestiture or joint-venture, there are particularities along the way from strategic decision to pursue a project to closing that can be predicted and prepared for the sake of a successful project.

The preparation phase

Carve-out procedures

One observation of the Degussa team has been that due to the principle "economy of the deal" that may still have somewhat more grounding in the US, German buyers might often be disappointed, especially in non-auction transactions, that they will be shown a target whose lifelines have not been fully defined (let alone laid out by way of term sheets or agreements relative to its needs) with regard to seller's other entities. Often, the NAFTA seller may have made only allocations in this context. On the other side of the Atlantic, the trend would be that the European or German seller would have clearly delineated the demarcation lines of the target and documented same. Whilst this gap may have to do with "Deutsche Gruendlichkeit" or meticulous attention to detail, and structural thinking, this may actually generate an opportunity for a German buyer involved in a US purchase scenario. The potential purchaser might in fact create a "wish list of service contracts à la carte" rather than being confronted with mid-to-long term supply and service contracts set in stone with a negative impact on the economics of the deal.

Preparation of financials

An important part of the preparation phase, is course, a clean set of financials:

- When dealing with potential US buyers, a European Seller should know that especially publicly-listed companies are prone to take an exclusive US GAAP view. However, preparing financials in accordance with IFRS may be perfectly acceptable when seller and target apply IFRS; if looked at closely, the differences between the two accounting principles and policies even appear to be reasonably benign outside of really meaningful areas such as depreciation and amortization, goodwill issues, or clarification of contingent liabilities and assets. It might therefore suffice that the German seller using IFRS methodology to offer a handbook, describing the differences between its accounting approach and US GAAP. This may help an "IFRS" seller avoid the expense for a transaction services or other accountant group reconciliating audited IFRS balance sheets and profit and loss statements in a formal or pro-forma way to US GAAP.

The role of Memoranda of Understanding/Letters of Intent in negotiated trade sales/joint ventures

A customary early step to mark and define the cornerstones of a potential joint venture to be formed between two or more parties and on non-auction trade sales is the instrument of Memorandum of Understanding or Letter of Intent (MOU/LOI). Whilst the level of detail of these documents may vary, except for certain provisions, they are usually non-binding. The parties frequently lay out desired equity participations in joint ventures, or an indication of potential purchase price, contributions, governance issues, etc. Low and behold, using a good-faith approach, the parties entering into an MOU/LOI rarely deviate from the principles delineated in such document, unless there is a new set of facts presented or discovered in a later stage of the process. Alas, despite the lack of binding quality of the substantive provisions, these documents tend to be decisive for the further process. Therefore, the parties may be well advised to monitor as to what they agree to at this stage, in particular the less vitally-observed elements such as drafting rights for definitive agreements, choice of law, jurisdiction and the like.

The signed MOU/LOI versus the non-signed, "agreed" term sheet

An observation frequently made is the tendency that Germans often seek to have the comfort of a signed document. A signature "means something," the parties often believe that the agreement reached is more equitable or tangible, and "more good faith" is behind the parties' will. On the other hand, especially US-publicly listed companies generally have a phobia to sign anything before definitive agreements, but rather look to "agree" on a term sheet. They do not desire a situation where a deal had to be announced at a premature MOU or LOI stage, because a disposition material to the company would reside in the signed document, which shareholders have an immediate right to know. Generally, however, German parties need not worry about this distinction, as long as it is demonstrable that there is indeed an agreement on the non-signed term sheet, be that verbally or through acceptance by conduct i.e., by taking the next steps such as creating a data room. In this case, a term sheet is as valid a signed document as is a Memorandum of Understanding. The only caveat to be made in this context is that the party relying on the terms has to be able to prove that they had been agreed previously.

Most recently, though, the reluctance of US parties to execute a signed preliminary document has lessened, resulting from the announcement of the SEC that there is no obligation to publish such agreement as long as it is ensured in the document that just terms such as confidentiality are binding i.e., that the commercial terms are still preliminary, and would not, for example, have a definitive effect yet on a cash-out or similar arrangement at a later date.

Handling of deal breakers

Especially in the context of potential joint ventures between US and German parties, it has been the Degussa experience that the European player involved would look to focus on looser concepts that allow room for further structuring along the way to signing, but would be keen on clearly delineating governance and especially minority rights upfront. US parties like to cover fiduciary duties of the shareholders, and look to fix commercial terms at least on a preliminary, non-binding basis. This may serve as another example of American straightforwardness and their goal to keep a deal cost-effective; Germans, despite their general image that portrays them as detail-orientated and structured, may allow more flexibility to increase the chances of a deal materializing ultimately, and thus lean to be less confrontational at its beginning. This perception and approach delta has been observed in Degussa deals recurrently. By way of example, it has caused a large-scale, industry-reforming tripartite joint venture structure between two American parties and Degussa to collapse at term sheet stage, because of disagreements as to whether the joint-venture management should have fiduciary duties or not. However efficient the very direct and confrontational discussion may have been, it still took the parties involved approximately six months to call off the transaction. Nevertheless, a positive aspect was that, no significant external resource had been put to use. On another occasion the American party walked from a transaction, despite commercially beneficial terms having been laid out in a term sheet that was agreed. This decision was made due to the fact that reasonably complicated and resource-consuming steps were to be taken thereafter, first and foremost the construction of a multi-user site that the American party had no experience with. The related milestones were not clearly defined in the term sheet, and "surprised" the US party as the engineering concepts were presented.

Recently, though, parties on both sides of the Atlantic tend to address potential deal breakers in the term sheet or MOU/LOI stage already, it seems that German players have adapted to the concept that potentially significant differences should be bridged already at an early stage so as to avoid the unnecessary expense of resources.

Market phase through due diligence

As described before, standard elements one commonly finds in auction processes are management presentations, site visits, data rooms and questions and answer sessions.

Management presentations – "honest salesmen versus smooth operators"?

There is an observable delta between the US and Germany in terms of "selling the target" and the presenters themselves by way of the management presentation:

Whilst German management teams are perceived to present defensively, and share with advisors when preparing upcoming management presentations that they would not even conceptually elaborate on the target's "golden nuggets," in other words new product pipelines and projects and the like. This notion intends to protect the company's secrets more effectively, but often results in a more conservative presentation, and lesser price indications coming from potential buyers.

Americans are generally perceived as "born salesmen" that are usually optimistic about their business and have generally more exposure to presentations to larger groups as they grow up; additionally, they have a natural advantage in international M&A transactions which is the ability to present in their native language. Trial experiments where NAFTA presenters explain the same business as their German counterparts yield positive comparable results from their audiences through more positive and open presentations. This gap may be closed by careful coaching and several "dry runs" with presenters, a measure advisable especially in the case of great US buyer likelihood. The "typical" German approach is to present in a self-criticizing, negative "brooding mode." Presenting in this manner to positive, optimistic US investors can create a less than desirable result. A legitimate motif of the Germans may be to ensure that potential liabilities are avoided. These liabilities can arise, for example, by giving away carefully guarded company secrets that may be under confidentiality restrictions with customers or suppliers. Claims can also arise if the eventual buyer of a target is given ground to argue that too much and too detailed information has been shared with competing bidders or other parties, resulting in a devaluation of the business, as often happens when management is more open with one particular bidder competing for the asset. It is advisable to ensure a level playing field to avoid these pitfalls.

The diligence approach

Another culture clash may be seen in the multi-staged, or as some players call it, "onion ring," diligence approach often used in the US, in contrast to the traditional immediate "opening of the kimono"; i.e. almost full disclosure in a one-stage diligence drill which used to be the modus operandi for diligence information as offered by German sellers. This difference in approach can be explained by more anti-trust issue conscious US sellers who wish to refrain from disclosing sensitive information to competitors as long as they are not convinced that a transaction will indeed occur. Furthermore, the "economy of the deal" mindset that was discussed in conjunction with the treatment of carve-out issues earlier in this article may play a role. On the other hand, a one-stop detailed diligence can serve to make a potential transaction cost-effective, as it has been argued that the working team preparing the data and other materials for diligence would only have to make one stringent, collaborative effort, and could be "done with it" thereafter. The latter methodology has somewhat fallen out of fashion lately, though, as a tailoring of diligence phases via a focused deal team is possible once data has been collected and can accordingly be released in stages. It appears that there is a trend toward taking buyers through multiple milestones in order to better control the use of data, and also to see whether potential bidders are willing to make continuous efforts. Degussa is an example of that method in divestiture processes. This strategy may also work to keep the price from dropping in an "undeterminable fashion," by way of buyers stating that they have to reduce the price due to broad-brush findings from the entire diligence exercise, a black box for the seller. The staged-diligence methodology provides controls and valuation insights: specific potential risk and opportunity areas associated with the target can be presented in subsequent rounds, assessing the potential buyers' specific reactions.

The flipside of this difference in approach to diligence methodology is reflected by Americans generally appearing with smaller teams upfront, and bringing in specialists and external resource at a later stage of the process, versus the complete-team

203

approach often used by European buyers who would bring in their specialists rather early in the process which may result in management presentations with audiences in excess of 20 professionals. Whilst the latter could be a more economical approach to evaluating whether a transaction would be worthwhile at which price level, especially for a potential bidder with a lot of advance knowledge, it might be an easier facilitation of a deal to form a fast view on the crucial value-driving areas only by allocating the appropriate expertise, rather than to, as some US sellers put it, "look the ant in the eye" as of day one. However the case may be, it is advisable for a potential bidder who wants to bring in a complete team to ensure through a preview of the data room to ensure that there is adequate food for thought and meaningful analysis for a large team.

Negotiation phase through signing and closing

The drafting right

It appears to be common practice that, in a limited auction scenario, the drafting right for the purchase and sale agreement rests with the seller. Less well established across the Atlantic, but from a US perspective "clear," is the fact that in a negotiated, one-on-one trade sale, the buyer prepares the initial draft. This is generally explained by the buyer wanting to determine the final scope of the deal. This view might be in line with and a logical conclusion from US sellers' practice of refraining from carving out the target initially that was discussed earlier. According to the authors' sources, the opposite practice holds true in Germany where the seller would initially draft even in a negotiated trade sale scenario, as it has better knowledge about the target. It is hence advisable to determine the drafting party prior to jumping to conclusions, and investing resources without discussion.

Consequences flowing from the choice of law and "the parties being used to its regime"

Generally, corporate transaction sale and purchase agreements have structurally become more aligned recently, regardless of Common law or Napoleonic code law governing them. This is attributed to the "Anglo-Americanization" of the larger continental European law firms through the flurry of takeovers and mergers in the recent past. Most of them have been dominated by British or US firms, hence Common law standard forms "rule." There are, however, certain concepts that sometimes still create misunderstandings, or at least play a role in negotiations:

1. In case a German party agrees to US law in principle, it should be made clear and would find agreement by any sophisticated US transaction partner that the parties apply New York or Delaware law, as only in these single states the body of commercial, corporate, and transactional law and precedents is large and developed enough to provide the reliable substantive background for the parties to fall back on in case of a dispute post-transaction. To illustrate this: without available precedent, a judge or court could and would have to decide on its own on, e.g., a material adverse change scenario which may be poorly defined in the contract itself, possibly without significant experience in the given area, which may be disastrous to one or both of the parties involved. This risk would not be imminent

in a scenario where federal German law is chosen, as there is a large body of federal statutory law that would, when in doubt, be applicable.

2. A common negotiation complication is the fact that, although the divergence may be slowly eroding, Americans tend to seek more specific regulations and thus crave for more detail in sale and purchase agreements whereas the German players, as they are used to a large body of statutory law, may be satisfied with general principles to be explicitly spelled out. Although there may be no common recipe to match these positions, it might be advisable for the party foreign to the law applied in the transaction to listen to their own attorneys accustomed to the regime.

3. *Retroactive effective date:* A feature that German players often use and Americans do not, is the definition of a retroactive effective date with regard to the transfer of the commercial risks and rewards by way of the sale and purchase agreement. This concept can be easily agreed to under Napoleonic code law through an abstract transfer of rights or transaction in rem. Such a principle does not exist in common law, and US parties involved in an M&A transaction would normally find this a peculiar feature to be included in a contract. A senior partner in a major US law firm told Degussa M&A that he had only come across a retroactive effective date concept in agreements governed by New York law twice within 22 years of practice, and found this a difficult construct to comprehend. A retroactive effective date concept sought could prevail, if the requesting party has enough negotiation leverage to have the sale and purchase agreement governed by German law. Of course, this brings along a potentially complicating factor, in that seller and buyer would have to agree on a cash respectively debt level to be factored into the purchase price essentially by signing, as debt and cash accumulating after such retroactive effective date, would not be subject to adjustment. One convincing argument that can be used in favor of an retroactive effective date without adjustment is the fact that the often cost-intensive closing date accounting adjustment mechanism and subsequent potential dispute would most likely be avoided.

4. *Cash pools:* Whilst cash pools are common to many corporate groups these days, US parties tend to suggest that they be eliminated by the seller at closing, whereas German players would generally be comfortable with an assignment of shareholder loans. One way to persuade a US party of the latter approach is to point to the decreased administrative resource required under the assignment scenario.

5. *Structuring Flexibility:* Germans involved in corporate transactions often are not used to the flexibility of US corporate law and capital structures which even allow in certain cases negative capital accounts in a corporation versus the stricter bankruptcy code-orientated rules in German statutory law, which would under certain circumstances limit the amount of leverage allowed, a situation that is sometimes used to convince a German player of using US law.

6. *The US integration principle:* More complex, and often a deal-breaking issue, can be the so-called integration principle of common law, which US buyers try to introduce into an agreement even if German law is employed to govern the transaction. It is a principle often explicitly spelled out in the agreement that ensures that everything that has been discussed, presented and agreed before

concluding the sale and purchase agreement has been factored into it, except for cases of fraud in the inducement: the potential buyer, using the "snake in the woodpile" argument, is able to ensure that the knowledge it has gained through the diligence effort would not be attributed to it. In other words, whatever has been discussed in the management presentation or reviewed in the data room would hardly have any relevance, but serves only as to get the buyer more comfortable with the business and persuade him to enter the next stage. Under German law, different principles usually apply whereby the diligence efforts, at least to a certain degree, would be viewed as information that the buyer has knowledge of, including weaknesses of the business that were disclosed therein. As an antidote and a means to protect the seller, the US practice calls for enormous amounts of disclosure schedules. If the buyer has done diligence superficially, it will naturally concentrate on the information contained in the disclosure schedules. This, in turn may, depending on the findings, lead to the renegotiation of the sale and purchase agreement, as the buyer asks for more protection due to seller's disclosures. It would therefore not be advisable for a seller to seek Board approval for a transaction depicting a certain risk profile prior to the completion of the review of the most updated version of disclosure schedules by the seller. This methodology has recently found more followers in continental Europe, too, due to less uncertainty through the scheduling exercise.

7. *The "anti-sandbagging" clause:* Another US specialty, which should be amenable to a German party from a good-faith point of view, however, is the confirmation that the seller seeks of the buyer ascertaining the fact that the buyer has no knowledge of a breach of representations by the seller after having reviewed the disclosure schedules. In other words, at this stage the seller would try to make the buyer own up to at least a diligent review of disclosure schedules, and would like to avoid a scenario where the buyer would enter into the transaction in complete ignorance of the fact that it has been presented with valuable information. This point, according to Degussa's experience, is often a fiercely debated issue, because the buyer tends to argue that the seller is trying to reintroduce knowledge of the diligence information into the sale and purchase agreement, and especially that of the data room which, by way of the buyer representations requested, is now being attributed to him after all. A compelling counter-argument to insist on the buyer's representation, from the seller's perspective, is the fact that the seller, in case of a dispute, still has to prove that the buyer had positive knowledge of the seller's breach.

8. *Flexibility of asset deal structures in the US:* A feature that might help a US party to convince a German buyer to agree to US law in an asset deal scenario is the fact that the buyer may be allowed to renegotiate existing collective bargaining agreements with the Unions in the US, as opposed to the force of paragraph 613a German Civil Code and the force of multi-employer collective bargaining agreements, whereby the buyer practically has to step into the shoes of seller relative to the employees, and could hardly renegotiate more favorable terms and conditions for itself.

Further negotiation points

As has been discussed previously, there are a number of issues that a party used to its own system may not be accustomed to, and that in turn may give ground to discussion. To discuss a few:

Employee benefits

Generally, employee benefits are reserved but not funded under German plans; in the US, post-retirement plans are usually funded, and it may be a debatable issue whether the plan is adequately funded relative to the value of the assets at the time of transition. The aforedescribed employee benefit regime difference, however, often brings along serious discussion especially between parties that are not used to doing transatlantic corporate transactions. Lately, however, it has been more acceptable that non-funded plans in Germany are typically qualified as debt-like items, and that this would warrant a reduction of the gross purchase price.

The "post-Enron effect"

After the Sarbanes-Oxley Act was passed in the US, American companies have become more cautious and risk-adverse in general, and also with regard to M&A transactions. This phenomenon has brought along the inclination of US buyers asking for a number of representations and warranties which may or may not be applicable or meaningful to the transaction from the German perspective. In the context of one of the most recent Degussa divestitures, this translated into the buyer asking for: representations relative to seller confirming that the target had not traded in embargo countries, where the company clearly could not have traded to and from such countries; and also for, what was qualified by the team, as a "bathroom representation," where the buyer wanted assurance that the sanitary equipment of the target had been built and installed in a state-of-the-art-fashion, in locations where there was no such sanitary equipment. The explanation for these requests was that they were company "standard." Under German law, the statutory body of law would help avoid such extensive representations which would have no effect on the transaction. In such a scenario the seller might be well off to grant to the buyer such a reasonably meaningless representation, and seek for higher thresholds and de minimis clause in return.

As a general aside in regard to negotiation strategy, it may be useful for German parties involved in a transatlantic deal to remember that Americans are generally raised to have competitive notions, but also to win their games fairly: it might thus be advisable to give away certain "freebees" that do not have a major impact on the risk profile that the German party may be seeking. It has been frequently observed that the principle "you give one up, in return, you win one" often works in this context – horse trading may be put to use strategically, as the US principal would not make his German counterpart lose constantly in front of the teams.

Trading advice for upsides

In the context of a certain level of ignorance towards the other party's system, a similar device that sometimes pays off and builds trust is to inform the other side of certain administrative customs, and thus receive meaningful upsides relative to the transaction itself: Degussa, e.g., has recently had good experience relative to letting non-German buyers, who did not have professionals with detailed knowledge of German peculiarities on their negotiation teams, know for example, that it would be detrimental to the functionality of the target to revoke all powers of attorneys ("Prokura") registered in a commercial registry in Germany, as they would have to be reinstated at great expense and would be required to continue the business after closing. The buyer was also informed that the risk relative to such non-elimination of power of attorneys is rather limited. In exchange, the buyer was fair enough to give a commercially relevant point. Another example of voluntary display of detailed information would be the requirements of visa renewals upon closing.

The road towards closing

Anti-trust authority handling

Obviously, parties on both sides of the Atlantic are familiar with the importance of noiselessly clearing obstacles relative to approvals sought from anti-trust authorities. Generally, it seems to be the case, due to the tradition of drastic measures taken by the Federal Trade Commission in the past that American parties are somewhat more sensible in laying out a strategy with regard to anti-trust clearance early in the process. This is a process component that the attorneys of both parties can jointly try to ensure, so as to clarify the probability of a transaction closing soon. In more than one instance, it was stated that European buyer candidates were surprised and could not digest so-called "hell-or-high water provisions" in sale and purchase contracts whereby the seller aims to ensure that the buyer would even entertain non-economic measures to be able to close a deal such as forced partial target divestitures upon closing. Such a scenario could be avoided through a strategy towards anti-trust authorities that is synchronized between the parties: if same is pursued, the seller could hardly request that the buyer bears 100% of the regulatory risk. Not surprisingly, the number of joint-defense agreements according to which the parties' attorneys would collaborate to clear anti-trust obstacles has increased significantly.

Transaction announcements

Both German and US parties usually ensure that they have an agreed announcement strategy these days. What might still need better understanding in Europe is the adversity of US parties to joint announcements; they do not wish to be liable for projections, effects or forward-looking statements made by the other party by embedding the respective statements in its own press release. There are thus compelling reasons for separate announcements vetted by the respective other party.

Conclusion

As was attempted to highlight by way of the discussion of some examples along the process chain, despite the similarities relative to the M&A toolbox in NAFTA and Europe, in particular Germany, there are still differentiating aspects and issues that can and should be anticipated when trying to ensure a smooth transatlantic transaction. Degussa's experience is that most of these factors can be addressed already in the preparation phase. It might thus help a seller to take a close look at one's buyer's universe, and, from a German perspective, to realize early in the process that the most potent and likely partner for a transaction is a US one. As has been elaborated, this would most likely have an impact for the preparation of the data room, of the draft sale and purchase agreement, and may also assist to reflect numerous tactical issues in advance, so that pitfalls can be avoided, and opportunities seized.

3.8 Media

3.8.1 The Jamba! Case: US Investors in Germany – What They Bring, How They Do It (US/German M&A Experience from a German Perspective)

Dirk Hoffmann

The Jamba! case is a successful example of a recent foreign direct investment by a US-based corporation in Germany. Jamba! operates in (and has been one of the driving forces in Europe of) the fast-growing mobile internet services industry. The purpose of this article is to illustrate both partners' rationale for that transaction and to point out potential challenges and pitfalls that need to be considered and overcome to make such a deal successful. Key lessons learned are: To make it work, such a transaction needs to be looked at from a "teaming up" approach, rather than a US company simply acquiring a German target. The respective assets of both partners need to complement each other. It helps if – already at the outset of the deal – the key actors on both sides, while their companies' corporate cultures may be different, "tick" similarly in the way they look at the industry, they plan to grow the business and they handle day to day operational execution. Finally, the transaction is not finished with deal close – keeping the right balance on "integration" is critical.

About Jamba! and its industry

Jamba! (also trading under the brand name "Jamster") has been founded in 2000 and is today one of Europe's leading wireless consumer data services companies, focusing on mobile entertainment. The product portfolio consists of a wide range of entertainment products, from music, graphic, games, information services, videos, other software applications to online dating (under the "iLove" brand). These products can be ordered by SMS, WAP or through the web, downloaded to the customer's mobile handset and paid for via his mobile carrier phone bill. Jamba! covers the entire value chain to the customer – from content creation, packaging/aggregation to delivery, billing and customer service. Jamba! employs today more than 450 people and is active in over 15 countries. Jamba! has been acquired by US-based internet infrastructure and service provider, VeriSign, Inc., in June 2004.

The mobile internet services industry is fast-moving and requires a high degree of both speed and operational flexibility to succeed. Further advancement of network and handset technology requires a constant proliferation of the application base in all areas – a simple example for music content products has been the progression from monophonic to polyphonic ringtones to realtones to full-length downloads. At the same time, different geographical markets are in different stages of market development and "maturity" – both from a technological (handset, network/carrier availability) and a user adoption perspective, and therefore need to be managed differently. Customers request content in order to personalize and individualize their mobile handset – it needs to be "fresh" to be appealing, thus requiring a continuous update and expansion of the content portfolio. Content needs also to be "localized" to a certain degree to serve country-specific user preferences. The advertising needs to be targeted and tailored to the particular audience of the advertising medium, entailing a high degree of rotation of campaign elements such as TV spots, print advertisements etc. to always make the best and freshest available content library available to the customer and quickly react to customer preferences. Product and marketing decisions typically need to be taken on short notice in order to benefit from windows of opportunity in a certain market. Finally, the entire business model needs to be enabled by a powerful and scalable system architecture, including a mass-user-capable content administration and download platform and a flexible billing engine.

These company and industry characteristics help better understand the rationale for the partner selection as well as the particular challenges of the transaction and the subsequent integration.

Previous transactions with US involvement

Before teaming up with VeriSign in 2004, Jamba! and its founders, the Samwer brothers (Marc, Oliver and Alexander Samwer), had already gained experience with transactions involving US-based companies.

- The Samwer brothers had sold their first venture, the German internet auction site alando.de, to eBay in June 1999. The brothers stayed onboard and developed eBay Germany into the fastest growing and most successful of eBay's international operations. In the summer of 2000, they founded Jamba!.

- In 2003, Jamba!'s founding shareholders, the Samwer brothers plus a number of large industry partners from the German mobile communication retail / telecommunications industry, decided to sell 56% in Jamba! to an additional international strategic investor, US-based private equity firm Summit Partners.

It certainly helped that all members of the Jamba! senior management team had spent a considerable amount of time in the United States for study and/or work purposes and had already established quite a number of business contacts. Language or lack of awareness of cultural differences never were an issue or a barrier for such a transaction in the first place. The mindset and rationale from a US company's perspective to enter into such a transatlantic acquisition was also well understood.

Transaction rationale for VeriSign

From VeriSign's perspective, the main rationale to team up with Jamba! can be described by looking at the following factors:

- *Expansion of VeriSign's Communication Services platform:* Partnering with Jamba! enabled VeriSign to further expand their own coverage of the value chain from infrastructure, billing and payment into content services. It also allowed for VeriSign's Communication Services division to apply and expand their existing Communication Services platform and related product and service portfolio to an existing international Jamba! customer base.

- *Access to Jamba!'s relationship with tier 1 carriers:* Since inception Jamba! had been able to develop strong relationships with more than 15 tier 1 mobile operators in Europe that were attractive for VeriSign and complemented their traditionally strong US carrier customer relationships.

- *Unique billing engine technology:* One of Jamba!'s competitive advantages was and is their fully integrated, scalable and flexible billing engine that had been entirely self-developed on top of a few standard components of core database and application server software technology.

- *European presence:* The acquisition of Jamba! helped dramatically increase VeriSign's existing foothold in Europe in terms of geographical coverage as well as in-country human capital.

- *Opportunity for expansion of Jamba!'s business in the US and Asia:* The transaction was an opportunity for VeriSign to help take a proven successful business model to the US and Asia and help expand the entire content business from primarily European to truly global scale.

The combination of the assets that Jamba! had to offer (evidenced by an intensive due diligence process): a strong technology platform, a large existing customer base in more than 15 countries, well developed mobile carrier relationships, and last but not least, the know-how to successfully and profitably run a mass-market mobile entertainment business and the respective management team that had accomplished that, made Jamba! an attractive investment opportunity for VeriSign.

Transaction rationale for Jamba!

Acting from a position of strength given their proven business model, profitability and already initiated next-level growth trajectories, Jamba! was not "forced" into any kind of transaction but was able to select from a number of potential external growth options. The main reasons why the choice was made to join forces with VeriSign can be summarized as follows:

- *Fast decision making:* Both from a structural and a people perspective, VeriSign seemed to operate and act in their respective businesses relatively similar to Jamba! – allowing for flexible and fast decision-making procedures to act quickly in a high-tech market environment that changes at fast pace. It was communicated to Jamba! that also going forward with Jamba! being part of VeriSign this necessary speed of execution would still be possible, not slowed down by any on-top corporate processes not in line with local Jamba! business requirements. The fact that the transaction was pursued at all stages with highest and visible attention from the full VeriSign Executive Management Team rendered additional credibility to that commitment.

- *Availability of funds:* One of the main drivers for the Jamba! team to pursue an external growth option in the first place was to accelerate the growth and take the company to the next level with the goal of becoming a global leader in mobile entertainment services. A different financial resource base for further growth was required to achieve that goal, enabling international expansion into several markets in parallel and at high speed potentially including further acquisitions. This resource base was offered by VeriSign.

- *Entrepreneurial freedom for management team:* Founded in 1995, VeriSign itself had been built by entrepreneurs and is still led today by a number of their first employees. Both transacting parties understood that continuing or even accelerating the growth would only be possible if the Jamba! management team were able to retain their entrepreneurial freedom and act with as much independence and flexibility as possible (even more so due to the 9 hour time difference between the Jamba! central offices in Berlin, Germany, and VeriSign headquarters in Mountain View, Ca.).

- *Catalyst for US market access/expansion:* Jamba! valued VeriSign's assets and capabilities as a strong catalyst for Jamba!'s US market expansion that was being pursued at the same time anyway, independent of any external growth transaction.

- *Thought leadership in technology sector:* Finally, VeriSign is perceived as thought leader in a number of internet technology sectors (among others infrastructure, security, registry/domain services) – similarly as Jamba! has been a frontrunner and prime driver of the European mobile internet content services market. Therefore, it seemed to make a lot of sense to team up two companies that had already proven to be strong in further developing and shaping the technology that was the basis for their respective businesses – in order to join forces potentially also on the technology development side.

To summarize, VeriSign was favored by Jamba! as the best-positioned partner for their global growth strategy.

Key challenges of the transaction

Most important to note upfront is that a transaction of such size typically does not stop at deal signature or closing, nor are its key "challenges" overcome and resolved at that point in time. The more critical (and time-consuming) part comes with the "integration" of the acquired entity into the parent company's organization and processes.

For the Jamba!/VeriSign transaction, the key challenges that needed to be considered and managed can be illustrated as follows:

- *Retention of key management team and additional key employees:* Clearly, being able to retain the management team members as well as significant individual contributors was instrumental to the success of the transaction. This had to be facilitated by an attractive deal package and "currency" mix for the founders as well as different levels of incentives for the rest of the senior management team as well as certain contributors, that were all aimed at aligning the interests of both transaction parties also in the longer term.

- *Culture:* In general, the Jamba! culture could be considered similar to that of a Silicon Valley start-up, as VeriSign had once been one itself. A strong commitment had to be made to the Jamba! senior team, that despite the acquisition, VeriSign was willing to leave to Jamba! their management freedom to execute independently and flexibly on a day-to-day basis, also to keep the established company and brand name and other "visible" signs of the Jamba! culture. As mentioned before, the language and cultural awareness issue did not play a role for the management team, however it actually was an issue for a number of contributors below management level, requiring e.g. additional functional language training for teams that were in regular contact with the US headquarters.

- *Balance of corporate integration needs with local business requirements:* A number of operational integration projects (e.g. integration of accounting systems, IT integration) had to be carefully balanced with the Jamba! business requirements, in particular in such a period of high growth and constant change. Most likely this has been the largest challenge of all.

- *Sarbanes Oxley Act compliance:* A side effect of Jamba! then belonging to Veri-Sign, a NASDAQ-listed US corporation that is subject to the full SEC regulatory requirements (plus Jamba! representing a significant portion of VeriSign's consolidated revenues and income) was the necessary Sarbanes Oxley Act compliance. For Jamba! this meant a substantial amount of internal and external resources needed for process and internal controls documentation and testing over a very short time frame, prior to the auditor's attestation jointly with the 2004 annual financial statements review. Again, all this had to happen with minimal disruption of the operational business while the company continued to grow at rates of 20-30% per quarter.

- *Selection of right advisors:* Both a large degree of cross-cultural experience as well as global presence were required for this transaction and were delivered by the two selected partners.

One could summarize that going through these challenges the process became a "learning experience" for both sides – as the depth and relative importance of certain issues typically cannot be foreseen for an individual transaction.

Lessons learned

For this complex transatlantic transaction a number of factors clearly played in favor: the high level of mutual awareness of the own position and what the respective other party had to offer as well as the complementarity of the two partner's assets, the similar "mindset" of the key players involved in the deal, and finally the acknowledgment that the business could only continue to be successfully run on a day-to-day basis with a certain independence for the current local management. The right balance of corporate process integration and local business requirements had to be found – this is indeed critical to the overall long term success of such a transaction.

On a more general note, US corporations expanding internationally through acquisitions into different cultural environments, language areas etc., need to monitor carefully their approach and processes – a "US-centric" attitude would most likely become a barrier to successful transatlantic deals. If both partners see such a transaction from a "teaming up" approach rather than a simple "acquirer-target" setup, with respect for each other's contribution and concessions, this can actually turn into a "win-win" situation.

3.9 Private Equity Investments

3.9.1 US Private Equity in the German Property Market

Gernot Wunderle

The German real estate sector has been stagnating along with the rest of the German economy for several years. While property prices in the UK and France, together with Germany the largest economies in Europe, rose significantly, in Germany they barely changed and even fell in several areas. But since opportunistic real estate investors are seeking relative values, more and more Anglo-Saxon private equity funds are examining the country for undervalued assets. Since 2000, the market has seen a number of private equity players acquiring portfolios of residential property from both corporations and the government. Although many portfolios have already been sold, there is still a huge untapped potential. The following article gives an overview of the market and of the strategy underlying those investments and of the success factors for the execution of these transactions, including the specific aspects investors have to face when negotiating with public authorities in Germany.

With an estimated share of more than 20 per cent, private equity investments are an important component of the international and German markets for Mergers & Acquisitions. In the past, US financial investors specifically targeted the non-core assets of large German corporations, such as the sale of the DaimlerChrysler turbine manufacturer, MTU, to the private equity fund KKR, or the takeover of the former Hoechst subsidiary, Celanese, by the American financial investor, Blackstone. Private equity investors have now discovered the German property market and are positioning themselves alongside traditional investors, particularly in larger volume transactions.

Until now the German property sector has led a shadowy existence in the world of private equity. Although individual financial investors such as Terra Firma/Nomura or

Doughty Hanson Real Estate have been active in the German market for more than five years, only recently has the German property market enjoyed the undivided attention of the private equity sector: four of the ten biggest private equity transactions in 2004 targeted property companies; in terms of value these property acquisitions accounted for more than 60 per cent of the top ten transaction volumes. Particularly given the background of long-term unenthusiastic domestic demand and skepticism of local players, questions remain as to the motivation and successful execution of private equity real estate transactions: what are the goals of Blackstone, Fortress, Cerberus and Co.? What are the success factors in the execution of these large scale transactions?

German real estate market

Germany is by far the largest real estate market in Europe. The residential as well as the commercial real estate market differentiate substantially in terms of ownership compared to the USA. In the USA corporations traditionally hold only limited real estate assets, especially if those assets were not essential for its business. The opposite is true in Germany. German companies own a considerable amount of property, both essential and non-essential for core business. The property ownership of the DAX-listed German corporate groups is estimated at € 170 billion. Increasingly, these property assets are being sold by the companies to maintain liquidity or improve key balance sheet metrics. Additionally – and in contrast to other countries – the German central government holds a considerable amount of property assets consisting of residential properties and government-used or third-party used commercial properties. Public institutions are increasingly initiating plans to sell their property assets against a backdrop of depressed budgets. For example, the state of Hesse sold a substantial number of office properties in 2004 and the Hamburg Senate is going even further by preparing almost all its office and special properties for sale. A study and survey among German city treasurers carried out in the middle of 2004 by goetzpartners revealed that more than 500,000 apartments are forecast to be sold by 2007. Besides,

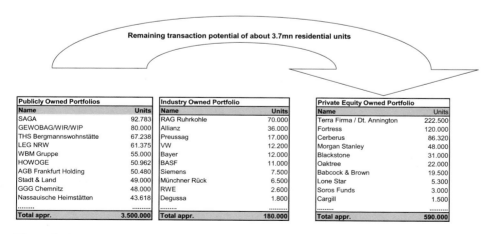

Remaining transaction potential of about 3.7mn residential units

Publicly Owned Portfolios		Industry Owned Portfolio		Private Equity Owned Portfolio	
Name	**Units**	**Name**	**Units**	**Name**	**Units**
SAGA	92.783	RAG Ruhrkohle	70.000	Terra Firma / Dt. Annington	222.500
GEWOBAG/WIR/WIP	80.000	Allianz	36.000	Fortress	120.000
THS Bergmannswohnstätte	67.238	Preussag	17.000	Cerberus	86.320
LEG NRW	61.375	VW	12.200	Morgan Stanley	48.000
WBM Gruppe	55.000	Bayer	12.000	Blackstone	31.000
HOWOGE	50.962	BASF	11.000	Oaktree	22.000
AGB Frankfurt Holding	50.480	Siemens	7.500	Babcock & Brown	19.500
Stadt & Land	49.000	Münchner Rück	6.500	Lone Star	5.300
GGG Chemnitz	48.000	RWE	2.600	Soros Funds	3.000
Nassauische Heimstätten	43.618	Degussa	1.800	Cargill	1.500
....	....	....	....	....	....
Total appr.	**3.500.000**	**Total appr.**	**180.000**	**Total appr.**	**590.000**

Figure 3.50 Ownership in German residential market

many of those have conducted internal analyses of the municipal properties comprising of office buildings, hospitals, schools, libraries to prepare privatization programes.

Private equity entering the German real estate market

This striking upward focus of private equity towards the German residential property market is illustrated by the transaction history. On the residential side the starting point was the sale of approximately 114,000 railway workers' association flats in 2000 by the German government. The buyer consortium was comprised by German housing companies and Deutsche Annington, a subsidiary of Guy Hands led Nomura Capital, today Terra Firma Capital Partners. After this acquisition in 2000, no billion euro transactions were recorded in the German residential property sector for three years. In 2004 the turning point was marked by the purchase of GAGFAH by Fortress, GSW by Cerberus/Whitehall, WCM apartments by Blackstone and Morgan Stanley Real Estate/Corpus' acquisition of Thyssen Krupp Immobilien: four transactions above the billion euro threshold (figure 3.51).

In numerical terms, the number of residential units purchased increased from approximately 20,000 in 2002 to more than 260,000 in 2004, and the number of total transactions rose from 2 to 13. Against the background of the most recent transactions, 2005 might set another milestone in terms of transactions and residential units purchased (figure 3.52).

As yet there is no sign of a decline in this trend. In 2005 the market has already seen Oaktree Capital's acquisition of the major Berlin housing company, GEHAG, the sale

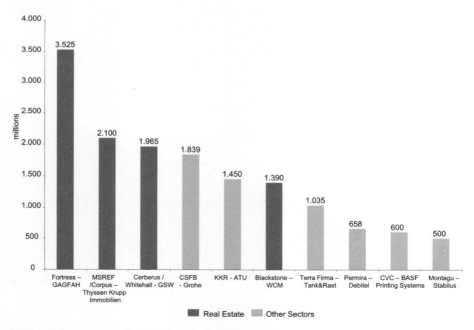

Figure 3.51 Top ten private equity transactions in Germany 2004

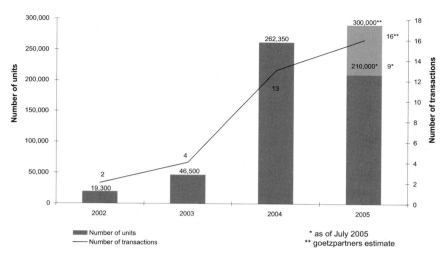

Figure 3.52 Private equity transactions in the German residential property sector 2002 to 2005

of Northern German real estate company NILEG, a subsidiary of state bank Nord/LB, with approximately 28,000 apartments to Fortress, and the divestiture of the largest private residential property company with approximately 138,000 apartments, Viterra, by energy supplier E.ON to a consortium of Terra Firma and Citigroup. Several other transactions are currently ongoing or being prepared.

In the commercial property market the share of private equity investments has risen substantially since 2003. Whereas open and closed property funds invest virtually only abroad, private equity investors are focusing on a diverse range of locations and commercial sectors. For example, GE Capital took over twelve hospitals of the Hamburg hospital operator, Marseille Kliniken AG, and Carlyle Real Estate acquired the UFA cinema complex in the Hamburg Gaensemarkt.

Many German players and real estate experts are surprised by the appetite of US private equity. Do the US players not see the problems of the German economy and the real estate market? It's true there are many economic and demographic hard facts which speak against an investment. Between 2000 and 2005 German GDP grew only by 1.1% per year [source: Statistisches Bundesamt], the unemployment rate rose from 7.2% in 2000 to 9.5% in 2005 [source: Eurostat] and the number of private insolvencies increased by a compound annual growth rate of ~70%. Besides the before mentioned macro-economic indicators the number of German inhabitants declined in 2003 and 2004. The economic and demographic development had a serious impact on the real estate sector: building of new flats decreased heavily and rents in the residential sector stagnated and decreased in the commercial sector.

An explanation for the rush of private equity into German real estate can be found in the general structural and market conditions in Germany. Historically attractive financing conditions, a reliable legal environment, low valuations (especially compared to international markets) and a virtually inexhaustible supply provided by privatization and company sell offs all create an investment climate which attracts financially, opportunity driven investors.

Table 3.4
Examples of private equity transactions in the German commercial property sector 2000 to 2005

Year	Acquired Properties	Buyer	Volume (€ m.)
2005	12 properties of Marseille Kliniken AG	GE Commercial Capital	100
2004	57 commercial properties of Frankfurter Sparkasse	DIC & MSREF	150
2004	109 German commercial properties of Deutsche Bank AG	Fortress	300
2003	51 European commercial properties of Deutsche Bank AG	Blackstone	1,000
2003	Commercial properties of Deutsche Telekom AG	Morgan Stanley/ Corpus	n/a
2003	27 Commercial properties of Deutsche Telekom	DIC	n/a
2000	Commercial properties of Holtzbrink	Doughty Hanson	n/a

Investment strategies

Unlike other large property investors in Germany, amongst them there are mainly to mention the open and closed property funds, private equity companies do not invest in individual long-term rented properties but rather in property companies and problematic properties in special situations. This strategy of investing in property companies is based on a goal of first increasing the cash flow and then the value of a property portfolio through professional management and exploiting overall economies of scale. Within the residential property sector, in addition to optimizing rents and cost structures, US investors' reliance is also placed in an active trading strategy, meaning the sale of individual apartments to tenants and capital investors as well as possible block sales to other investors.

In contrast to the future cash flows resulting from rental income, which can be forecasted comparatively easily on basis of the actual data, the second cash flow stream – meaning the cash flow resulting from an active trading strategy needs to be assessed very carefully. What percentage of the apartments in a building can be sold, over which period of time, what potential is already used, what sales prices could be achieved, how the sales are handled and many more issues have to be assessed. There are different sale routes: sale to tenants, sale of single apartments to private investors, sale of buildings or blocks of buildings to investors such as closed-end funds or family offices.

All of the above mentioned issues need to be assessed in coordination with specialists which have done such sales in the past and could be used to implement the adequate privatization strategy.

The second group of value drivers is the operational set screws of a property portfolio. In order to optimize the operational cash flows, a detailed modeling of rental growth, credit loss and vacancy rate development on the income side as well as a detailed modeling of the development of ongoing, periodic and top to bottom maintenance and refurbishment costs on the cost and capital expenditure side is necessary. Benchmark data of comparable operations is necessary to get a picture of what cost savings could be achieved. Last but not least, legal restrictions regarding rental increase and apportionment of modernization expenses have to be taken into account.

The combination of privatization strategy and optimized operational cash flows are illustrated in Figure 3.53.

Another difference between established German property investors and private equity investors is the way investments will be financed. For the latter a debt-ratio of 90% is not uncommon, especially when interest level is comparably low over time. After all, the development of the interest level is essential, since the financing will not be arranged for the long-term. Special clauses regarding the previous financing and contingent liabilities as well as warranties are also examples of issues that should be kept in mind.

Several questions also appear along the structuring of the transaction. The most obvious are cash repatriation and definitely the prevention of German real estate transfer tax, which will be triggered in an asset deal as well as in a share deal in case at least 95% of shares are acquired by one party. Other determinants of the deal structure are the available exit options and the time horizon of the investment. Tax issues have to be assed as early as possible to determine impact on valuation and develop efficient transaction structures.

To put it in a nutshell, the acquisition and due diligence exercise for large residential real estate companies is time and cost intensive as besides the operation and management, the properties need to be assessed legally, technically and financially. Limited experience in real estate M&A on the one and a sometimes vast number of contenders in auction processes on the other hand are two of the factors that make it difficult to

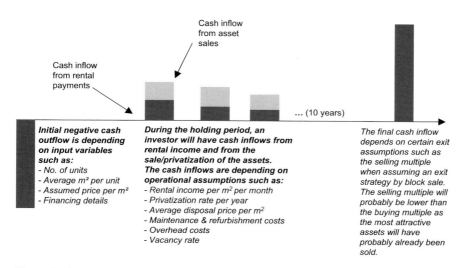

Figure 3.53
Possible business model for a residential property portfolio from an investor's point of view

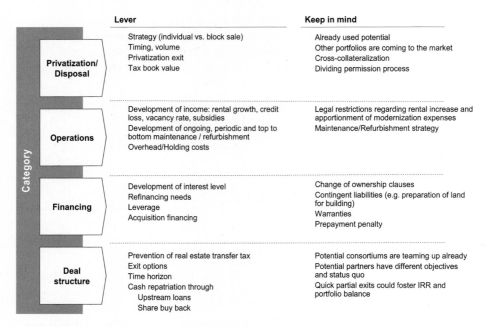

	Lever	Keep in mind
Privatization/ Disposal	Strategy (individual vs. block sale) Timing, volume Privatization exit Tax book value	Already used potential Other portfolios are coming to the market Cross-collateralization Dividing permission process
Operations	Development of income: rental growth, credit loss, vacancy rate, subsidies Development of ongoing, periodic and top to bottom maintenance / refurbishment Overhead/Holding costs	Legal restrictions regarding rental increase and apportionment of modernization expenses Maintenance/Refurbishment strategy
Financing	Development of interest level Refinancing needs Leverage Acquisition financing	Change of ownership clauses Contingent liabilities (e.g. preparation of land for building) Warranties Prepayment penalty
Deal structure	Prevention of real estate transfer tax Exit options Time horizon Cash repatriation through 　Upstream loans 　Share buy back	Potential consortiums are teaming up already Potential partners have different objectives and status quo Quick partial exits could foster IRR and portfolio balance

Figure 3.54 Value drivers of a residential property transaction

assemble the right acquisition team, which comprises financial advisors, lawyers, auditors, technical real estate advisors and appraisers.

As once more shown at a glance (in figure 3.54), the key value drivers which have to be assessed are privatization/disposals, operations, financing and deal structure.

Acquisition strategy and success factors

The German real estate opportunity created by the attractive investment climate and large scale sales by public and corporate property owners causes a rush of financial investors to Germany and as a result creates a highly competitive market. Almost all public, also for legal reasons and many corporate sales are handled as auction processes. The number of interested parties is high and still increasing. In the sale of NORD/LB's NILEG for example 42 investors handed in first stage bids, of whom 7 parties were invited to conduct due diligence. In front of huge transaction costs it is essential to get an in-depth understanding of the transaction situation and the objectives of the seller to develop a detailed bidding strategy.

Besides maximization of the purchase price, transaction security and social factors often play an important role in the selection of a buyer, especially in privatization processes. Privatization projects of public authorities are both commercial and political. They therefore follow the logic of the market and the rationale of politics at the same time. To supply every citizen with solid and cheap apartments is still believed to be one of the main achievements of the German welfare politics following the Second World War. Privatizations of housing companies are extremely sensitive for the gov-

Table 3.5

Selected partnering between foreign investors and experienced German real estate players

Investor	German Partner	Category	Assets
Morgan Stanley Real Estate Funds	Corpus	Real estate company	Residential, e.g. Thyssen Krupp
Morgan Stanley Real Estate Funds	DIC	Real estate company	Commercial, e.g. Grünhof Frankfurt
Oaktree Capital	HSH Nordbank	Public bank	Residential, e.g. GEHAG
GE Capital	HPE	Real estate company	Residential, e.g. Siemensstadt

erning party. For US investors it often appears very difficult to face the political issues and constraints. This led to a number of deals which collapsed in the last moment such as Terra Firma's failed acquisition of Cologne based GAG housing company. After successful winning an intensive auction including fully negotiated SPA, the deal failed because of one missing vote in the city council, the last body to approve the transaction. This happened although the sale was backed by the governing party. In fact many transactions like GAGFAH or GSW failed in the first attempt of privatization, the transaction processes were completely restarted and in most cases not a former bidder but newcomers made the race.

In order to save time and obtain credibility for the bidding process and instead of developing an own property management, partnering with an experienced German real estate player might be a successful strategy. Such a partnering might help to avoid triggering the German real estate transfer tax as well.

Recent acquisition history seems to approve this issue, since more and more private equity players are building up consortia with established players in the domestic real estate market.

Table 3.5 shows examples of partnering between private equity investors and German real estate players.

An exceptional success factor of every private equity investment is the well-planed exit strategy.

Compared to direct investments in individual properties, property companies offer a diverse range of exit alternatives. This is of utmost importance to private equity investors who work on the basis of investment periods of five to more than ten years. Given the ubiquitous current discussions about the launch of German Real Estate Investment Trusts (G-REIT), a listing at the stock market seems an especially interesting exit variation.

Conclusion

On their search for worthwhile investments, in the last years Anglo-Saxon and especially US-based private equity funds discovered the German real estate market, which

– within the European context – is considered to be undervalued. Transaction history demonstrates this increasing demand for German residential real estate assets, with the most recent acquisition of Viterra by Terra Firma/Citigroup marking another milestone.

Although macro- and microeconomic key factors indicate rather dismal prospects, there are many reasons for ongoing transaction activities. The main reason is the difference between the business models of established German property investors and private equity investors. Most notably, the last-mentioned try to increase cash flows by an active trading strategy that includes tenant privatizations as well as large block sales to other investors.

Since the interest in German property portfolios is still increasing, potential investors have to plan their strategy very carefully. In order to compete against a vast number of bidders the investor relies on an advisor which combines both expertise in the German real estate market and the political landscape as well as a strong M&A-transaction background.

3.9.2 Is Small Cap Private Equity an International Business? – Differences in the U.S. versus Continental Europe

Volker Schmidt

The Riverside Company is the largest private equity firm focused on the small end of the middle market and is one of the industry's most experienced leveraged buyout investors. Riverside specializes in premier companies with enterprise values of less than €80 Million, and partners with strong management teams to build companies through acquisitions and value added growth. Since 1988 Riverside has invested in more than 100 companies and currently operates out of offices in New York, Cleveland, Dallas, San Francisco, Budapest, Warsaw, Prague and Munich.

Based on our experience, we will first present how small cap private equity (PE) is further advanced in the U.S. than in Continental Europe and examine the implications. We will then show that European small cap private equity is much more international than is small cap private equity in the U.S. And finally, we will look at the pros and cons of taking an international approach to doing small cap private equity in continental Europe. While the emphasis of the initial comparison is on Germany and the U.S., we also include some references to our experiences in Scandinavia and Central Eastern European countries.

U.S. a more advanced market

Especially in the small cap segment, the U.S. private equity market is far ahead of Continental Europe's. The distinction "continental" is important here as the UK market is more similar to the U.S. than to its European counterparts.

On larger deals, the European market is dominated by Pan European or globally operating PE-houses, most of them headquartered in the U.K. or in the U.S. Here the sales process is run by global investment banks and the financing is syndicated to international banks. In the small and mid-cap segment, however, the market, on the advisory side as well as on the financing side, is still very much dependant on regional players. And in the small cap niche, the differences across countries seem to be much bigger.

Figure 3.55 points out some of the major differences between the U.S. and the German market. The same general observations apply across continental European markets, with an even more pronounced difference in less mature markets such as the Central and Eastern European countries.

Market size

Even though it has been growing recently the total value of all private equity transactions in Germany is still less than 0.12% of GDP, placing Germany about midfield within the Continental European context. In the UK and the U.S. the total value of all private equity transactions is almost 1% of GDP. In the small cap segment, the deal flow Riverside sees in the U.S. is more than 10 times that seen in our German operations. The infrastructure has developed accordingly. While in the U.S. we count about 3000 M&A advisory firms, that number is close to 200 in Germany.

Competition

In Germany there are probably 30-40 active private equity firms in the small cap segment, compared to about 500 in the U.S. Even though in the U.S. the PE-firms are

	U.S.	Germany
Market Size	(Riverside deal flow) >1500 deals/year	(Riverside deal flow) >150 deals/year
Competition	500 competitors	30 competitors
	EBITDA multiple on average one turn higher than Germany	EBITDA multiple on average one turn lower than U.S.
Process Standardization	High	Low
Sellers` Awareness and Understanding of Private Equity	High	Low - High

Figure 3.55 Comparison of U.S. and German small CAP PE-market

also chasing a larger number of deals, the number of competitors we see on a single deal tends to be significantly higher in the U.S. When we exit attractive companies in the U.S., we tend to get seven to eight "Letter Of Intent's (LOI)," a number that is typically somewhat lower in Germany.

Process standardization

In the U.S., even in the small cap segment, many aspects of transactions have become quite standardized:

For example, the content and quality of the information memorandum and the data room typically meet certain minimum quality standards in the U.S. In Europe, despite many equally professional advisers, the variation in quality of work is much higher.

On terms and conditions there tends to be a stronger understanding within U.S. PE-industry participants on what is considered market standard. In Europe we often find that issues need to be negotiated that would be treated as common practice in the U.S. Examples of common practice in the U.S. include a 1% "basket" for indemnification expenses which are the responsibility of the buyer and a 12 to 18 month limit on the indemnification period following the close for most representations and warranties.

Leveraged financing is also easier to obtain in the U.S. While at Riverside we never had a deal fail due to lack of financing, this has been much harder to achieve in Europe. In Germany, especially, the segment of financing deals with enterprise values between €10-25 Million is challenging. For the leveraged finance departments of the larger and more international banks, this size tends to be not attractive enough but on the other hand, this size is often too big for the corporate business departments of the local banks. We also find broad variations on financing terms and conditions. On a recent deal, we had a credit agreement that reached eighty pages while on another deal only two pages were required.

Seller's awareness and understanding of private equity

Even though in Germany the awareness of private equity is growing rapidly, the understanding of the asset class is still limited. A survey[1] on Management Buy Outs (MBO) done in Germany between 1999 and 2001 showed that more than 60% of the managers that participated in a buy out were not aware of the concept before they were approached by the private equity house doing the deal. At least among owners, this is changing quite rapidly now and in the last two years almost every Mittelstands conference also has included a discussion of private equity. But while in the U.S. it is quite common for buy outs to be initiated by management, we still find this rare in our European offices.

Most owners/CEOs of Mittelstands companies are not familiar with the cash flow-oriented valuation approach of financial investors, with the amount of due diligence required and with some of the representations and warranties needed. Still, some entrepreneurs are reluctant to hire the services of an experienced M&A firm to run the

---

[1] Nico Reimers: Private Equity für Familienunternehmen, Sept. 2004

sales process. Take the example of the founder/CEO of a very successful €60 million revenue firm who was represented in all negotiations by his 80+ year old tax adviser. While one might be tempted to believe that less sophisticated advisers on the seller's side would lead to more favorable deal terms, one needs to understand that it also drastically decreases the likelihood of getting the deal done. The reasons for this are twofold: 1) if the seller is not willing to pay for professional advice he is probably not "really" willing to sell but might just be testing his market value, and 2) Without professional advice, the typical Mittelstand seller will never get comfortable that the terms and conditions of the proposed transaction are indeed in line with market standards and prevailing industry valuations.

To encourage or even help the seller get professional advice is often also in the buyer's best interest since it increases the likelihood of achieving an outcome satisfactory to both parties; which in the end is the real requisite for getting a deal done.

But even with very sophisticated sellers we have found some significant differences in perspectives. When acquiring an add-on in Austria for one of our U.S. portfolio companies, Riverside found the seller (which had a lot of experience in buying and selling) much more balance sheet focused versus having the stronger focus typically seen in the U.S. on profit & loss statements and cash flow.

European small cap private equity is much more international

Small cap private equity in the U.S. is very much a domestic business. Most companies do the vast majority of their business in the U.S. and due to the size of the domestic economy, export is frequently not a big issue. In Europe the situation is quite different, as we will show in this chapter. In addition cross boarder transactions are more frequent in Europe than in the U.S.

Importance of export and international sourcing

Due to the size of the domestic market and logistical issues, U.S. small cap companies rely much less on export than their European counterparts. In Germany, Europe's biggest economy, about one in every six Euro earned by Mittelstands companies comes from export. In machine building, one of the domains of the Mittelstand, the export ratio is as high as 43%. In recent years increased export was the dominant driver of growth given the weak domestic demand.

Both the Riverside European and the Riverside U.S. funds focus on the same type of companies: profitable niche players with a leading market position and an enterprise value of up to €80 Million. An analysis of Riverside's deal flow in the U.S. versus Europe, however, shows significant differences regarding the international nature of the business (figure 3.56).

It becomes obvious that on our European deal flow a high export ratio is the rule, but in the U.S. it is instead the exception. Also in the U.S. out of fifty deals analyzed only seven had a foreign manufacturing site, and only four a fully-owned foreign sales subsidiary. In contrast, of the European companies we looked at, more than half had a foreign manufacturing plant or sales subsidiary.

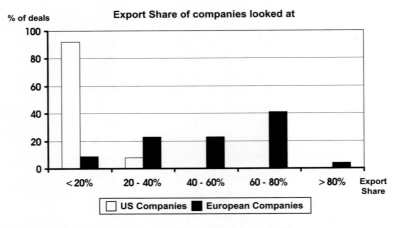

Figure 3.56 Analysis of Riverside US and European dealflow

Exits/cross boarder transactions

The more domestic nature of the private equity business in the U.S. also reflects itself in Riverside's exits. In the U.S., only two out of 17 Riverside exits were to domestic buyers, whereas in Europe all four exits have been to a foreign strategic buyer.

The number of cross border transactions in Europe has increased recently. For transactions ranging from 5 Mill. to 150 Mill. €, the total number of cross border mid-market deals involving European companies in 2004 was 1842, an increase of 29% over 2003[1]. The UK was by far the most active, accounting for 29% of all intra

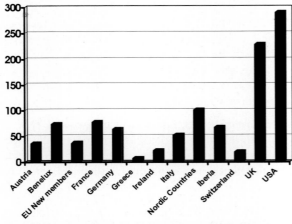

Source: Global M&A; Cross Border Deals Mid Market Review Based on Merger Market Deal Database

Figure 3.57
European cross boarder deal volumes by acquirer country

---

[1] Based on merger market database and analysis by global M&A

European and even 50% of all "outgoing" deals. The importance of transatlantic transactions is emphasized by the fact that North American companies acquired more companies in Europe than even the UK did. Figure 3.57 provides an overview of the volume of cross border acquisitions, in Europe by acquirer, including North America, which accounts for 76% of all acquisitions done in Europe by non European companies.

In the mid cap segment, North America still does more investments in Europe than the other way around (236 versus 212 completed transactions in 2004). At Riverside, we are also increasingly looking at transatlantic opportunities. Buying a company in Europe can turn a domestically focused U.S. player into a globally operating company as in the case of PPC, a company Riverside acquired in 1998:

> In 2001 PPC, a maker of porcelain insulators and #2 in the U.S. market, bought Austrian company CERAM, the leading player in Europe. The acquisition expanded PPC's market activities from one country to 50, and provided access to low cost production facilities that CERAM was operating in CEE countries. When competition from Asia aggressively entered the U.S. market, domestic plants were no longer competitive. Before the acquisition, PPC was a purely domestic company, both in sales and in attitude. Today PPC is run by the former CERAM CEO and the U.S. business has changed completely from being a manufacturer to being a sales and distribution company that is sourcing globally. Being acquired by a private equity investor on an international network and supported by the European add-on acquisition enabled PPC to pursue the vitally important international expansion strategy.

Local versus international approach to small cap private equity in Europe

While in the mid and large cap segment most of the PE funds are operating internationally, the majority of small cap funds maintains a local focus. As successful PE firms raise bigger funds, the tendency is to grow the size of deals rather than to expand internationally. Today only very few PE-firms in the small cap segment are following an international approach. Arguments can certainly be made to support either strategy. Ultimately the success of an international approach is driven by the balance of incremental value added on the one hand and increased complexity on the other hand (figure 3.58).

In the following we look at these points in more detail and provide some examples.

Supporting portfolio companies on international expansion

In a study commissioned by the European Venture Capital Association (EVCA) on the "Contribution of Private Equity to the Succession of Family Businesses in Europe" the average share of export sales of the 117 companies analyzed increased from 23.9% in the year before the MBO/MBI to 28.4% the year after.

Based on another study done at the European Business School[1] with financial investors as well as family business owners, more than 80% agreed that the importance of

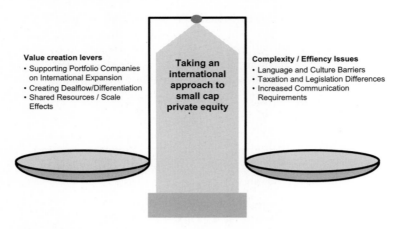

Figure 3.58
International approach provides additional value levers but also increases complexity

private equity will increase for family-owned businesses. When asked for the reasons, the entrepreneurs cited internationalization/expansion of the business as the main reason (60%), followed by the implications of Basel II (55%) and succession issues (45%) (figure 3.59).

This fits Riverside's European experience, where helping a company to grow internationally is one of the major levers for value creation a private equity firm can contrib-

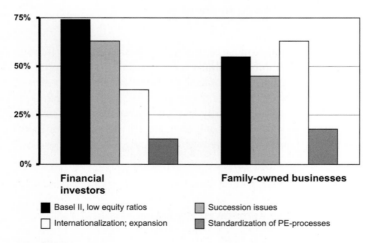

Figure 3.59
What will drive increasing importance of private equity for family-owned business

---

[1] MBO als Nachfolgelösung. F.A.Z. Institut für Management-, Markt und Medieninformationen GmbH; April 2002

4 Professional Contributions

4.1 Strategy

4.1.1 Strategic Alliances: Smart Alternatives to Mergers and Acquisitions?

Jens Schädler and Reto Isenegger

This article will explore the potential of strategic alliances as alternative to M&A in cross-Atlantic business relationships. In particular, the article will answer the following questions: 1. Reason for the momentum behind alliances; 2. Where to use alliances instead of mergers and acquisitions; 3. Which alliance model to choose; 4. How to manage alliances successfully. The article includes various case examples from different industries (including airlines, pharmaceuticals, Financial Services, Software, etc.).

The momentum behind strategic alliances

As recently as only two decades ago, competition was simpler and companies did not need to excel in all capabilities or participate across the globe – serving one major market region and offering one capability which made your business stand out was often enough. The pace of change of technology was modest compared to today, and industry had well-defined boundaries and mostly did not aspire to global reach. If you lacked a capability, you either took the time to develop it or you bought it through an acquisition. In today's dynamic environment, successful companies need to select, build and deploy critical capabilities which will enable them to gain competitive advantage, enhance customer value and drive their markets (figure 4.1). Competition is no longer for position itself, but for change in position. Positional assets such as facilities, market share and brand franchise are transitory, while capabilities are not.

The goal is to focus on the capabilities that the company can use to constantly renew and extend its position. Companies are facing several challenges in this new era of competition.

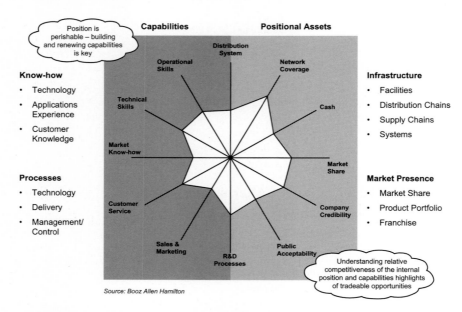

Figure 4.1 The search for advantaged capabilities

Challenges from new rules of competition

Filling single and multiple capability gaps

Capabilities are know-how leveraged by cost-effective, responsive business processes and systems for innovation and delivery of enhanced customer value. No company can afford to build advantaged capabilities against all aspects of the value-added chain any longer. Today's companies need to focus on their core competencies to protect their competitive advantage in the era of hypercompetition. Capabilities not required for improving core competencies have to be built up via teaming with potential partners.

Creating integrated products and services in the move from product- to solution-oriented supply

The product orientation of the 1980s has been replaced by a clear separation of business into two competitive fields. On the one side are the cost-focused commodities businesses, with low margins and experiencing fierce competition from low-cost countries. On the other side are companies offering integrated products and solutions to customers, allowing them to achieve higher margins. Companies that fail to transform their business model by moving towards an explicit solutions orientation will therefore be confronted with shrinking margins. Clients will shift to suppliers offering them greater customer orientation and integrated solutions.

Accelerating R&D and technology cycles

Moore's law, posited in 1965, states that data density on microchips will double every 18 months – this law still holds, and according to experts will hold for at least the next two decades. Indeed many companies in all kind of industries are facing the problem of shortening technology life cycles and the need for accelerated R&D activities to stay competitive. At the same time companies have to cope with increasing complexity, as they have to manage a growing number of products and R&D projects. Given their high R&D expenditures, pharmaceuticals companies in particular are challenged with the task of constantly filling their product pipeline with new blockbuster products.

Increasing globalization

In 1980, only 14 percent of revenues for the largest U.S. companies and 23 percent for the largest European and Asian firms came from offshore markets. With the opening of markets, business has expanded globally; now over one third of U.S. companies' revenues and nearly 50 percent of European and Asian companies' revenues are being generated outside their home countries. Markets did not only open in the comparatively young economic regions like the EU and NAFTA, but also in emerging markets like India, China and many states in south-east Asia, due to new WTO rules. As a result, companies need to focus on their core competencies and offer products that clearly differentiate them from the competition. In addition, companies need to enter different new markets, requiring significant investment and involving high market entry risks.

The allianced enterprise as a breakout strategy

To achieve their strategic objectives and to solve the challenges arising from the new rules of competition, companies are extending their enterprise beyond internal boundaries by teaming up with other companies in different ways. These relationships run from traditional transactional sourcing and service arrangements at one extreme to acquisitions and mergers at the other. Figure 4.2 illustrates an extended enterprise continuum, in which the vertical axis is a measure of commitment, ranging from traditional modest transactions up to permanent relationships. The horizontal axis is a measure of ownership, ranging from no linkage up to being wholly-owned. The term alliance can describe a broad range of the relationships that fall within these extremes, from short-term projects to long-lasting relationships between supplier and manufacturer and through to broad strategic alliances in which partners tap into and learn from each other's capabilities.

Clustered in the lower-left portion of Figure 4.2 are various modest relationships, often limited in both duration and scope, which we think of as transactional alliances. Among the many forms of transactional alliances are collaborative advertising or marketing, shared distribution, and cross-licensing. Examples for transactional alliances in the financial services sector are loan syndicates and fund supermarkets like the German 'Postbank Easytrade' which is offering third-party funds to its private clients. In this article we focus not on these relatively modest relationships but on the broader, deeper alliances – the middle ground between transactional alliances and acquisitions. These strategic alliances have the following distinct characteristics:

- A commitment for at least several years.
- A linkage based on equity or on shared capabilities.
- A reciprocal relationship with a shared strategy in common.

235

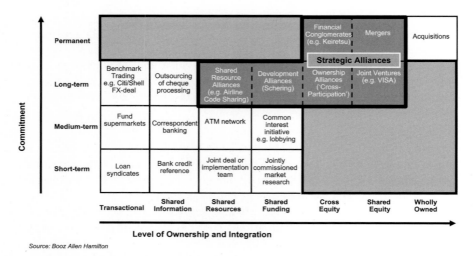

Source: Booz Allen Hamilton

Figure 4.2 Extended enterprise model

- An increase in the companies' value in the marketplace, exerting pressure on competitors.
- A willingness to share and leverage core capabilities.

Strikingly, many such alliances are now driven by industry agendas to cross national boundaries. Even more strikingly, many of the most successful alliances (e.g. in the airline and automobile industries) are between potential rivals.

The impact of strategic alliances

The number of alliances formed demonstrates their increasing importance for corporate managers as a strategic instrument. In the past two years, more than 20,000 alliances have been formed worldwide, with nearly 70% of them advancing beyond contractual relationships through an equity participation by the partners.

Alliances are generating a dramatically increasing percentage of revenues for companies worldwide (figure 4.3). While in 1980 alliances in the U.S. only generated less than 1% of revenues, they are expected to climb to 33% by 2005. IBM has recently stated that it expects alliances to contribute up to 50% of its total revenues by the end of this decade.

For the past ten years, strategic alliances by the 25 Fortune 500 companies most active in this area have produced a return on equity of nearly 17%. This is 5% points more than the average return on equity by all Fortune 500 companies. These results were confirmed by an analysis of 5,000 worldwide alliances conducted by Booz Allen Hamilton in cooperation with Prof. Dr. Pekar from the London School of Economics.

Another key finding of all our surveys on alliances is clear: financial results improve dramatically as a company gains experience of alliances. Indeed, companies experienced in alliance formation earn around twice the return on investment in their alliances compared to that achieved by inexperienced companies.

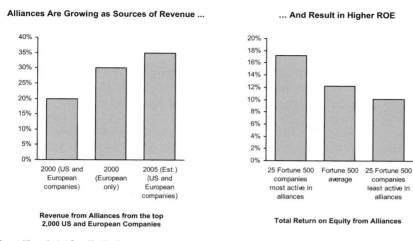

Source: Alliance Analyst, Booz Allen Hamilton

Figure 4.3 Alliances are growing as sources of revenue and result in higher ROE

Where to use alliances instead of mergers and acquisitions

As shown in the extended enterprise model, strategic alliances are – like mergers and acquisitions – a tool for companies to get access to important capabilities, so as to further improve revenues and profit. With more and more companies using strategic alliances to meet their strategic business goals, the key issue is knowing in which situations alliances have a competitive advantage compared to mergers and acquisitions. The following four key criteria for enterprise competitiveness reveal possible advantages of strategic alliances over mergers and acquisitions (figure 4.4).

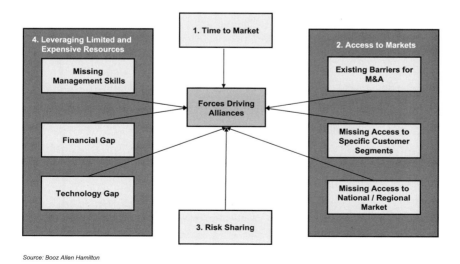

Source: Booz Allen Hamilton

Figure 4.4 Reasons for strategic alliances

Time to market

Especially in fast-moving industries, the possibility of implementing and dissolving alliances in a relatively short time is a competitive advantage compared to M&A deals. Companies increase their agility and flexibility, as old alliances can quickly be substituted by new partnerships. The management of several alliances gives companies the opportunity to react very flexibly to new customer requirements and changes in competitors' market strategies. For example, Siemens set up a strategic alliance with Microsoft in 2005. Both companies want to set up joint global sales and marketing activities in the area of enterprise communication and collaboration solutions, to respond to customer needs for a comprehensive family of applications for call conferencing, video conferencing, web conferencing and collaborations. Time to market is an essential capability in the telecommunications market, and a network of alliances is the only possible way to tie all major capabilities to the company even for the largest players like Siemens, Cisco or Microsoft – which all maintain an extensive network of alliances.

Access to markets

One of the most important advantages of strategic alliances over acquisitions and mergers is the opportunity of gaining fast market access to regulated markets. This has been key for the emergence of alliances in the airline and defense industries.

The airline industry is the most famous example of an industry tackling regulatory barriers with strategic alliances. As the acquisition of foreign competitors is difficult due to national regulations, companies need to establish alliances to use economies of scale, increase buying power and to exploit other synergies. A good example is the joint fuel purchasing company founded by Star Alliance members to reduce fuel costs by using economies of scale in fuel purchasing. Furthermore, in 2003 the members of the Star Alliance agreed to standardize their fleet of regional jets and jointly ordered 200 planes all complying with the new Star Alliance standards.

Gaining access to markets (especially in Germany) is a major issue in the financial services industry for US-based independent fund management companies too. In 2002 Invesco and Deutsche Bank announced a strategic alliance, with Deutsche Bank starting to sell third-party products from Invesco to their customers. Under this arrangement, Invesco gains access to about 8 million private clients in Germany, and Deutsche Bank can offer its clients a broader range of products and, therefore, is able to attract new customers.

Risk sharing

Strategic alliances are widespread in the pharmaceutical industry, as they are an opportunity to 'hedge your bets' in the risky area of R&D projects. The big players might be able to invest their money internally in R&D projects, but instead they decide to give research grants to several small biotechnology companies, at the same time securing licensing agreements and marketing rights for the developed products. An example is the $200 million alliance between Novartis and Vertex from May 2000, securing Novartis the worldwide distribution, development and marketing rights for eight drug candidates developed by Vertex. In November 2004 Vertex announced that

Novartis has selected the first drug candidate for the treatment of cancer to be transferred from Vertex to Novartis.

Leveraging limited and expensive resources

While buying another company is attractive because it confers total control, alliances can eliminate the huge up-front capital investments and premiums one has to pay for acquiring an attractive company. Strategic alliances require less capital than acquisitions and thereby provide access to international markets even for companies that are not well-funded. Small biotech companies like the Munich-based MorphoSys do not possess the capital either to set up their own distribution system or to buy the distribution system of competing pharmaceutical companies. Strategic alliances are the most efficient opportunity for them to get their products to the customer. MorphoSys has currently established ten strategic partnerships with leading pharmaceutical companies such as Pfizer, Bristol-Myers Squibb, Bayer, Novartis and Schering.

Additional advantages for MorphoSys arise from the fact that the big pharmaceuticals not only are supporting their R&D with significant financing, but with knowledge transfer as well.

How to manage alliances successfully

The burgeoning number and scope of alliances is creating challenges for executives trying to manage this complex activity – which is increasingly outside the direct control of the corporation. Companies are forming vast arrays of alliances that on the surface seem to be a collection of unconnected arrangements.

However, these alliances are increasingly becoming an interrelated tapestry of activities, linked in ways to gain competitive advantage and control the battlefield, rather than a series of discrete transactions. The need to adapt the organizational model is compelling.

Leading-edge companies are beginning to use alliance architecture models that are defined in terms of the role strategic alliances can play and their leadership structure. The key question is how should these alliances be governed, controlled and managed? It is worth considering that many of these alliances could dwarf the size of any one partner. Yet today, many of these highly dynamic and competitively strong entities have no definable business model of their own.

These entities cannot use a 'command and control' business model to span multiple partners. Rather, they require something more flexible and dynamic to reflect the market environment and the partnership structure. We see four models emerging for companies with multiple alliances: franchise, portfolio, cooperative and constellation models. Each of these 'pure tones' will have a different set of implications in terms of the appropriate governance model. These pure tone models are shown in Figure 4.5, and described on the following pages.

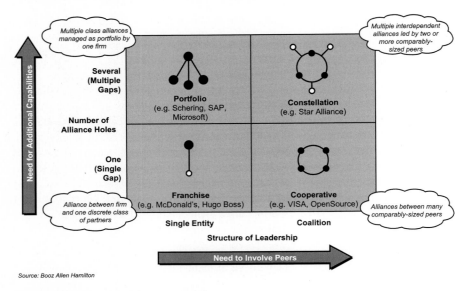

Source: Booz Allen Hamilton

Figure 4.5 Alliance architecture models

Franchise model: 'Reproduction'

This model is used by companies to fill a single critical gap in its value chain. But the needs in that gap area are greater than any one partner can fill. So the company develops a replicable alliance model for a class of partnerships.

For example, Hugo Boss is using a franchise model to fill a key capability need – the distribution of its consumer products via exclusive shops in top locations. Hugo Boss is positioned in the centre, closely controlling the activities of its alliance partners. As Hugo Boss operates a significant number of shops itself, it has a lot of knowledge that can be transferred to its franchisees. Hugo Boss wants to focus on its core competence, the design of branded clothes, and keep distribution in the hands of experienced franchisees.

The franchise model develops a single alliance role that can be refined and quickly replicated to create scale, thereby producing an alliance growth corridor for the initiator of the alliance.

Portfolio model: 'Hub and Spoke'

The portfolio model is a major step up from the franchise approach. Companies that adopt this approach are finding that the value-added chain contains far too many elements for it to command all the capabilities necessary to compete. However, instead of forming a number of single discrete arrangements to fill each gap (thus making itself vulnerable should a partner experience difficulty or if the market changes rapidly), the company decides to create multiple class alliances managed as a portfolio. These companies are still in the centre, but they are weaving together a portfolio of distinct and often unrelated partnerships. The external partners have little relationship to each other, but interact only with the company at the centre.

240

For example, Schering is trying to cover multiple gaps in key elements of the value chain – including basic research, development, distribution, marketing and production. In each of these areas, it has formed alliances with a variety of partners, although generally a similar class of companies (figure 4.6). It manages these classes as a portfolio, thus directing the arrangements to meet its strategic needs. Although Schering acts in consort with its portfolio partners, it never loses its sense of direction or co-opts its control of its future. By adopting the portfolio approach, it can move quickly within a class, adjusting its position or its partners. For Schering, the alliances with several small biotech and pharmaceutical companies offer the opportunity to invest into several options. With financial support from Schering, each company is trying to develop new drugs for different areas, with Schering normally having the exclusive marketing and distribution rights for these products. If just one partner develops a blockbuster product, the whole alliance portfolio has paid off.

An additional strength of alliances is the fact that they can be built as non-exclusive. Therefore small biotech companies like Munich-based MorphoSys can form an alliance with Schering and Novartis at the same time, creating value for both companies. This would not be possible if Schering had decided to buy MorphoSys. In this specific case the two portfolios of Schering and MorphoSys are filling gaps for the respective partners (R&D of new products, distribution) and creating a win-win situation for both.

Another famous example of the portfolio model is SAP, which committed itself to alliances with service, technology, hosting and software partners. Among their partners is Microsoft, which is itself a striking example of the power of alliances.

But many people do not understand the critical role that alliances have played in this evolution. Microsoft's first breakthrough was an alliance with IBM to develop the operating system 'MS-DOS' for personal computers. It followed this alliance with its second breakthrough, the emerging dominance in operating systems through 'Win-

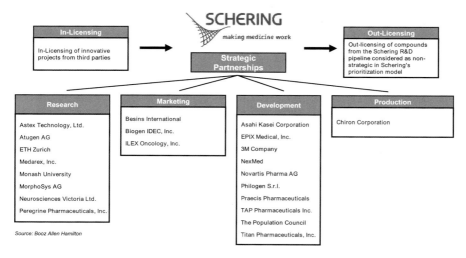

Figure 4.6 Portfolio model: Schering

dows' and its 'Wintel' alliance with Intel. The pace has never slackened. In the past years, the company announced on average two alliances per day.

The biggest advantage to the franchise and portfolio models is that the company forming the franchise or portfolio sits in the controlling position, directing and managing the interconnectedness of the arrangements. In the portfolio model, this company acts as the 'corporate core'. Through its actions it formulates strategic leadership and builds capability. It manages this process by forming and dissolving its alliances as its primary control mechanism. The more dominant the position of this partner, the easier it is to implement this model.

Cooperative model: 'Mutual Benefit'

With the cooperative model, the initiating partner moves from a central position to more of a cooperative role. The alliance is at the centre rather than one of the partners, and the customer relationship often shifts from the company to the alliance. Consider the examples of the credit card associations like VISA. One of the main reasons VISA has achieved such broad acceptance is VISA's partnership-driven structure. It is not a company in a traditional sense, but an industry association, owned and directed by more than twenty-one thousand member financial institutions world-wide.

Typically, we find that companies that have adopted the cooperative model do so to outflank the competition and substantially raise the competitive bar. The most distinguishing feature of the cooperative model is that no one company is in control – all work together to raise the competitive bar.

The cooperative model requires a different business model. While the relative size of the partners may differ, they are equals at the point of intersection (the specific product or service provided to the marketplace). All the companies are working towards the same goal; however the day-to-day running is not under direct control of any one partner.

There are also non-profit organizations following the cooperative model. One example is the Open Source Initiative dedicated to managing and promoting the Open Source Definition, specifically through the OSI Certified Open Source Software certification mark and program. Any programmer can have access to the source code of software and can thereby improve it, irrespective of whether this is a single private person or a larger corporation. As many people are working on improving the software at the same time, this leads to rapid advancement of the software, not possible if the source code were to be held by one single company.

Constellation model: 'Integrated Service Offering'

Companies that utilize constellations develop breakout strategies that leapfrog the competition and put industry competitors on the defensive. The requirements for global scale, standardization and substantial capital injections are forcing players to share leadership and equity with selected partners through migration to a constellation model. These constellations will mature as constellation partners discover new ways to work together to change the rules of the game. These constellations are initially comprised of a set of equity joint ventures and should naturally evolve into indepen-

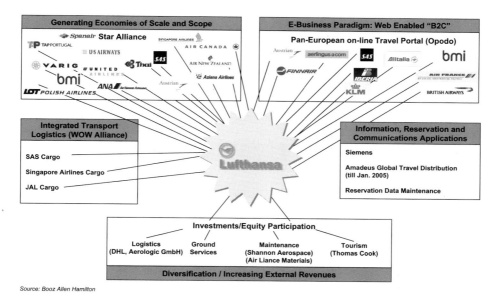

Source: Booz Allen Hamilton

Figure 4.7 Constellation model: Lufthansa and the Star Alliance

dent companies. They will have all the 'organization' required and be self-contained. They will be governed through board processes and create their own identity in the marketplace.

Probably the best example of a constellation is the Star Alliance network in the airline industry (figure 4.7). It is a network of networks, as each member airline has brought its own network of partners (e.g. for maintenance, marketing, IT, logistics, food) into the Star Alliance. The establishment of the Star Alliance in 1997 changed the whole airline industry, and indeed put all major competitors on the defensive. Member airlines can coordinate their schedules for rapid, more hassle-free connections, and frequent flyers are given recognition and special service even when they are far from home. Alliance members have the possibility of stimulating markets that no one carrier could have served effectively on their own – providing greater numbers of competitive offerings between medium-sized cities that were not aggressively marketed and sold under the more traditional interline relationships. The advantage recognized most by customers is the implementation of a joint loyalty program for frequent flyers and the installation of lounges in all major airports around the world. For the Alliance members, it is possible to provide world-wide solutions in transportation and logistics. And at the same time the Alliance offers new dimensions of economies of scale in all areas, e.g. sourcing (jointly purchased planes), maintenance (consolidation of the maintenance network), alignment of IT systems (one global platform) and in the core business of transportation. No airline would have been able to achieve this on its own, as acquisitions would have been too expensive and often prohibited by the local or anti-trust authorities.

Managing alliance models: The art of virtual coherence

Each alliance model described in the previous section has a different set of character-istics and governance issues and a different strategic focus, and this is one key reason why a new organizational model is necessary. Trying to manage these models under the old 'command and control' structure inhibits the formation and management of these models. In our experience, companies that form and manage these models successfully do not want to team up with companies that have not learned this lesson.

So what does the new organizational model look like? The answers differ depending on the type of alliance.

Franchise alliances are operational in nature, an extension of a specific part of a company, and that fact determines where and how they should be managed.

The *portfolio model* is, de facto, a new business model. Since it usually involves more than one primary part of the dominant partner, it is managed not by an operations group but by a business centre. That centre acts as the 'corporate centre' for the alliances. It must treat its partners as business units within a Centerless Corporation – adding value only where the businesses cannot (see Figure 4.8). It must focus on knowledge and people, and work diligently to build coherence internally and exter-nally.

The *cooperative model* is a shared business model that needs its own leadership, but with few 'owners', they need to work through some cooperative governance structure. The challenge with these models is to establish a set of operating/performance param-eters. This model is very similar to what firms do when they establish a shared services organization within the corporation, or rely on an outsourcing agreement.

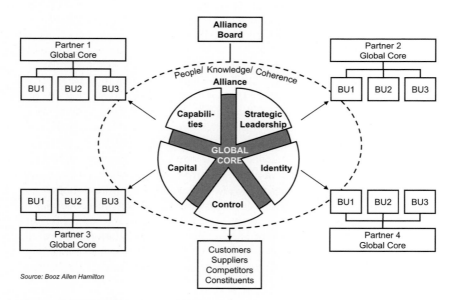

Figure 4.8 New business model for alliances

The *constellation* must be thought of as a new company. The constellation requires its own centre, one that is focused on creating value for the extended entity. The only areas where a corporate centre adds value are in strategic leadership, capability brokering, identity, control and capital. This holds true for a corporation and for a constellation.

Conclusion

The huge amount of transatlantic alliances established in the last few years shows that global industry has entered an unprecedented era of structural change. The old 'command and control' model that has worked successfully for nearly two centuries is now challenged by the 'Allianced Enterprise'. Leading edge companies are transforming their organizations and are reaping the benefits of this new business model. Peter F. Drucker has said that there is not just a surge in alliances but 'a worldwide restructuring' is occurring, in the shape of alliances and partnerships. In addition to the transatlantic alliances covered in this article, there are many more to come. Nevertheless we should bear in mind that alliances – especially international ones – are often described as unstable and complex to manage, therefore causing frustration among the partners. According to some critics, this makes alliances doomed to fail.

These observations concerning the challenges of building and managing a strategic alliance are certainly correct. But the conclusion is not. Our most recent survey involving 700 companies, 100 venture capitalists, 50 heads of corporate development and 50 investment bankers revealed a success rate for strategic alliances of about 60%, compared to 50% for acquisitions and 30% for venture capital investments. For those firms that have already developed alliance skills as a core competency, the success rate with their alliances is even higher, at 80%.

The false impression should not be given that a strategic alliance is in all cases superior to a merger or an acquisition. In cases of national consolidation of industries or in branches without legal and cultural barriers (where there is a higher probability of successful integration), mergers and acquisitions have advantages compared to alliances, due to the shorter negotiation time. Mergers and acquisitions also have advantages when two companies plan to merge with the aim of integration and restructuring of their core activities. Integration and restructuring can be accomplished much faster with a clear majority of votes and capital.

Strategic alliances are therefore no substitute for mergers and acquisitions, but they expand the spectrum of possible strategic alternatives to external expansion of a company. As we have seen in the cases of SAP, Lufthansa, Schering and others, alliances are a powerful strategic tool, especially in transatlantic business relations when regulatory barriers do not allow acquisitions and when market access, short time to market, or risk sharing is decisive.

To a large extent we are entering new territory in managing multiple alliances. As the word spreads and more companies seek alliances as a growth engine, the differentiator will shift from 'being able to form an alliance' to 'being able to manage one or multiple alliances'. Obviously, those in the game the longest have the most experience. However, the game is evolving and standards have to be set. We envisage a race to optimize the alliance business model over the next years. And, as with alliance formation itself, the early adopters will win big.

Literature

1) 'Strategic Corporate Finance – Unternehmenswertssteigerung durch profitables Wachstum' (Reto Isenegger, Alexander Frohne et al.; Ueberreuter; 2002)

2) 'Smart Alliances: A Practical Guide To Repeatable Success' (John R. Harbison; A Strategy & Business Book; 1998)

4.1.2 Management of Complex M&A Projects: Challenges in Transatlantic Deals

Kai Lucks

Professional experience management can significantly increase the success rate of merger and acquisition (M&A) projects. Project documentation and training are a relatively simple way to realize learning benefits from the medium-sized and small projects which occur frequently. Large projects are more rare and are marked by unique situations that require special attention. This makes these particularly challenging, especially when they are "breaking new ground." This document provides a toolbox that can be helpful in meeting these special challenges.

Introduction: Success rate, size and complexity

The most expensive corporate acquisitions are made by companies in the developed industrial nations. German-American transactions lead the pack in this regard. Specialists in the field estimate that the success rate for M&A worldwide is 30-50%. But when it comes to large-scale projects, the success rate is lower. All too often, these are driven by the egos of their protagonists, and their course is frequently determined more by internal politics than by the professional attention they actually require. The high visibility of blatant failures has shed a negative light on the entire M&A sector. Overall, transatlantic deals fare even worse than average, as Fritz Kröger demonstrates in chapter 2.5 of this book, using a comparative analysis of stock market trends. Weak performance is usually attributed to strategic mistakes or cultural problems. Shortcomings in management are rarely mentioned. But the fact is that well-managed M&A projects can result in considerable potential for improvement. That's why it makes sense to carefully consider fundamental approaches to managing M&A projects. The concepts for discussion presented in this workshop report are based on observations made during a large number of actual projects.

Companies that have accumulated experience, developed standardizable processes and used knowledge management – for capturing and transferring knowledge and thus continuous improvement – have consistently performed well in M&A. General Electric (GE) and Cisco in the United States and Siemens in Germany are good examples of such companies, though the approaches they follow differ. GE generally makes 100% acquisitions and transfers the entire management system of the parent company to the acquired company. Cisco, which specializes in telecommunications, fuels its growth primarily through the acquisition of technology specialists that complement its own areas of competence and offer potential for expansion through synergies. Cisco preserves the technological core of its acquired companies – usually start-ups, headed by their founders – by simply adding them to the Cisco organization under the leadership of the founder or chief technologists. The marketing, sales and administrative functions of these acquisitions, however, are dissolved and absorbed by the corresponding units of the parent company. Cisco has therefore zeroed in on a uniform, special acquisition model that it replicates with great success.

Siemens, a diversified and highly internationalized company with 80% of its sales outside of Germany, has chosen another course. This path is influenced by a number of factors: its businesses are multicultural, operating in many countries and there are major differences in the size, ownership and leadership structures of its acquisition projects. Thus, Siemens has developed an M&A system that allows uniform processes to be transferred into a variety of different project types. This is done through a framework concept composed of experience components, which is implemented in a uniform process structure.

Knowledge management is absolutely essential to improving the success rate of M&A. Regular buyers of medium-sized and similarly positioned acquisition targets can achieve real experience curve effects if they systematically document, process and share what they have learned. Large projects, which do not occur as frequently and usually vary from case to case, are a different story. To be consistently successful in this area, a company must take the time to uncover the fundamental risk drivers and the particular challenges. The following section presents an approach that can be used to define the degree of difficulty and the profile of complex M&A projects. Using this, project management elements can be derived which can be used to meet the challenges of large-scale projects.

Performance requirements

The difficulty of an M&A project can be examined in several dimensions. These include (a) the extent of the project's change goals, (b) the scope of the project, (c) the differences between the candidates that are to be merged and (d) the scope of action (Figure 4.9). These dimensions are not independent of one another; indeed, they are related in many different ways.

The demands placed on an M&A project (Figure 4.9, top) are measured by the *extent of its change goals*, particularly with regard to strategy (e.g. improving the company's competitive and technological position), structure (e.g. shifting value creation) and culture (bridging national and sector cultures).

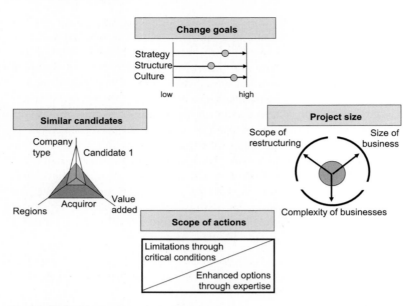

Figure 4.9 Determining project challenges

The pressure to internationalize often requires giant, rapid leaps, through the merger of very different organizations. This is particularly true when it comes to transatlantic M&A projects. The potential for improvement here is generally higher than in purely national mergers as there is more opportunity for complementary market access, products, and technologies. This benefit, however, is offset by higher hurdles in other areas – such as cultural differences, the effects of a foreign environment and the increased efforts and expense of combining different technologies. The *similarity* of the merger candidates is therefore an additional criterion for measuring the difficulty of M&A projects and can be examined in three dimensions: type of company, type of industry and country profile (Figure 4.9, left). The *project size* can be described by the volume of the businesses (sales, headcount, etc.), complexity (number of locations, value creation depth, etc.) and the scope of restructuring measures (Figure 4.9, right).

Another important indicator field for the performance requirements is the *scope of actions* for the project (Figure 4.9, bottom). If there are multiple options for action, the simplest way to achieve the objective will be chosen. Critical conditions can limit the options for action and force an M&A team to choose more difficult paths. A person with experience and skill can follow paths that would never occur to someone with less experience or that would be impossible for a less experienced person to master because of the many conflicts to be overcome. In other words, a high level of experience opens up pathways that remain closed to others.

"Total Project Management" as an approach to carrying out complex large-scale projects

Optimizing M&A objectives and minimizing risk means getting involved at all action levels – in the structures and processes in which the individual M&A projects must be embedded (described as *"Subsystem M&A"*), in the rules and standards which fundamentally govern the individual projects (*"project level"*) and in the levels of the individual *project elements* (Figure 4.10). The approach to "total project management" – outlined below and organized into levels – shows the levers and their interaction for optimum mastery of complex large-scale projects in M&A.

M&A subsystem

Experience management

Until now, little has been written about the role, use and effect of systematic experience management approaches in M&A. Experience from other types of projects – for example in the construction sector or in manufacturing – can, in principle, be applied to M&A. The following principles apply:

- Performance capacity increases greatly as experience is gained (experience curve effect).
- Leveraging similarities and consciously transferring experience from one project to another are crucial.

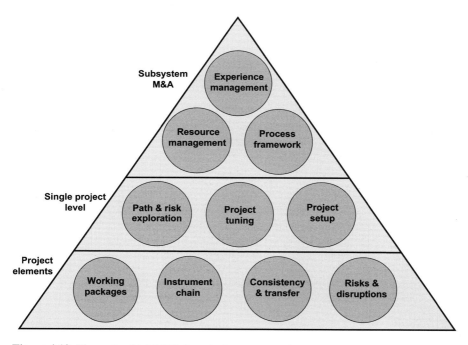

Figure 4.10 Elements of total M&A project management

- Accordingly, a new project should only "break new ground" to the extent that this can be mastered in the new project.

This means that, even in fulfilling large-scale objectives, one should pursue M&A projects and candidates that are as similar as possible. Performance requirements should only be increased gradually over time, and only to the extent that they can be mastered through the learning effects and transfer of experience from one project to the next. This concept is depicted in Figure 4.11. Ideally, this means that a subsequent project should focus on *either* developing another country *or* another technology *or* increasing one's size. Therefore, anyone who has ambitious goals on the other side of the Atlantic should proceed gradually, and should start with a project where he has a clear overview. This might mean entering into joint ventures first before acquiring a company (see chapter 4.1.1 by Jens Schädler). The poor performance of major transatlantic M&A projects described in the article by Fritz Kröger can be traced back to a lack of experience, scaling that was too steep and the resulting overestimation of competencies. Experience management therefore is not limited to documenting and sharing knowledge. It also includes influencing the progress and design of alliance projects.

One way to take the plunge into M&A competence management is to identify and measure the drivers of challenges in past and future large-scale projects. The main dimensions shown at the bottom of Figure 4.11 – size of businesses, complexity of businesses and scope of restructuring – are used as a basis for this article. These are broken down further, based on practical requirements: for example, individual contributions by the merger candidates with regard to sales and employees. To evaluate the difficulty of integration, it is very important to know whether the candidates are comparable or vary greatly in size. To achieve a balanced and graphically informa-

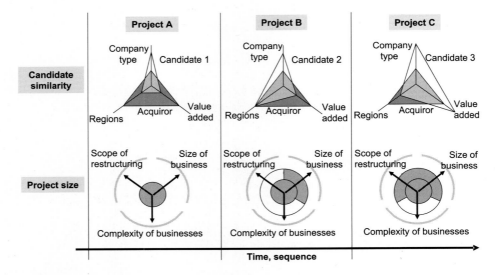

Figure 4.11 Ideal typical scaling of M&A projects

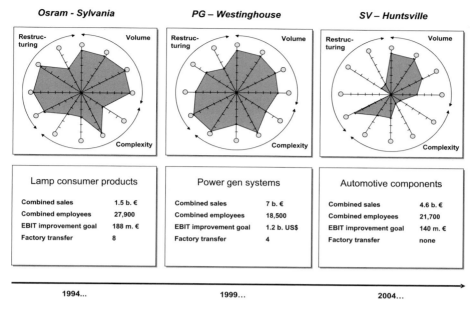

Figure 4.12 Scaling and experience effects in practice (Siemens)

tive presentation, the three main dimensions are each broken down into four sub-dimensions:

- Size: (1) own sales volume, (2) candidate's sales volume, (3) own employees, (4) candidate's employees
- Complexity: (1) number of countries, (2) number of locations, (3) number of businesses (each covering a significant portion of value contribution) and (4) coverage of value added steps ("value system")
- Scope of restructuring: (1) "dynamic" (= after baselining) EBIT delta between actual and goal to be reached in target year, (2) quantity of measures to be realized, (3) quantity of site relocations and (4) quantity of employees for relocations and outplacements (with the in-project-goal for finding new engagements)

Indices, in some cases linear and in some cases logarithmic, were formed for presentation on the axes of the spider diagram generated from this.

On that basis, Figure 4.12 of this report shows examples of actual experience at Siemens in managing major transatlantic projects. Both good and critical experiences in other large projects were systematically evaluated for the Westinghouse Power Generation project. The challenges arising during the acquisition of the Sylvania lamp business (see contribution by George Nolen in this book, chapter 3.4.1) were similar to those in the Westinghouse project. Where the Westinghouse case deviated from that of Sylvania was that the sector and business of the acquisition target were different. Given the lack of systematic knowledge management for major projects up to that point, and in order to play it safe, Siemens spent a relatively large sum on external consultants for integration and corporate restructuring (see figure 3.30 of my article on the Siemens-Westinghouse merger). The profile of the acquisition of Huntsville Automotive Electronic from DaimlerChrysler in 2004 looks completely different. This case was far less complex. Most of the risks of restructuring were excluded through the shaping of the purchase agreement. Those involved also had the benefit of learning effects from a series of other large projects, which were part of a professional system for M&A knowledge management that had been created in the meantime. Therefore, it was possible to considerably reduce the cost of resources, particularly with regard to reliance on external expertise. All three projects were extremely successful.

Resource management

Ensuring the use of (cumulative) experience by the acquiring company is directly related to the structure and the capacity of those individuals who have the expertise. During an M&A, the basic corporate staff functions involved are corporate planning and strategy, financial, legal, technology, human resources, communications and IT. While companies that only occasionally engage in M&A projects must turn to outsiders for assistance, it is worthwhile for frequent buyers to keep appropriate M&A specialists on hand within the company itself. The more frequent and the larger the projects, the more depth the in-house specialists within the M&A functional areas must have.

With a "closing frequency" of around 50 projects per year and an annual investment averaging around €2 billion over many years, Siemens has about 30 specialized departments that – exclusively or primarily – do the direct legwork for M&A projects. In-house employees have the advantage of being very familiar with the company and being "on call" (which works well since projects typically proceed erratically); they can be called upon at any time (including long after the completion of a project). As part of the breadth and depth of competence to be maintained in-house, these employees should also be able to manage external consultants and service providers.

Resource planning for M&A projects requires forecasts over the entire duration of the project. This is because the areas of emphasis can change radically during a project (for example, the transition from the advance phase to the transaction); or because additional specialized knowledge becomes necessary (this is particularly relevant in highly complex projects) and the capacity of the teams needs to be expanded considerably (during the transition from pre-closing integration planning to post-closing implementation). The main cause of failure is the vast differences between M&A partners and the environment on opposite sides of the Atlantic. Even a company that makes frequent acquisitions will not always have specialists available who are knowledgeable about the circumstances in all target regions for every single M&A function. Another task of the in-house specialized departments is therefore to be able to supervise outside specialists in the target regions. In the case of Siemens USA, for example, this is done by the U.S. holding company. A network of outside service providers delivers the additional expert resources that are needed to cope with major projects under particular local conditions. Anyone who has compiled and documented a great deal of experience will be able to use the model of the expense drivers to estimate the need for resources over the entire project, down to the level of individual working packages.

Process framework

A generally binding framework for project management must be developed in order to take advantage of the experience that has been collected. Process-based approaches have proven to be the best of the different management models for M&A projects. They are characterized by the (a) universality of tasks and responsibilities and (b) early establishment of objectives, which (c) rely on measurement programs with milestones to achieve the objectives and (d) are tracked by measuring the completion of objectives according to the milestones. Based on "generic" process approaches for M&A projects (whose core and support processes vary from one to the next), process approaches have been developed at companies like Siemens who engage in frequent M&A activity. These (a) are appropriate for complex large projects, (b) unify all necessary functional areas and (c) record the central project functions in core processes, thereby pooling experience and guidelines which are transferable from one project type to another and from sector to sector. A process outline for this is shown at the top of Figure 4.13.

The core processes it defines are (1) project management, (2) strategy-structure process, (3) the dealmaking process and (4) implementation & change management. The overarching *project management* ensures the consistency of the project as a whole from start to finish (goal definition relative to goal achievement) and ensures compatibility of processes or partial projects among themselves. The *strategy-structure process* is used to identify, determine the feasibility and evaluate the M&A path and its structuring after the closing. Because these activities are so closely intertwined, it is advisable to make this a universal process with universal responsibility. The *dealmak-*

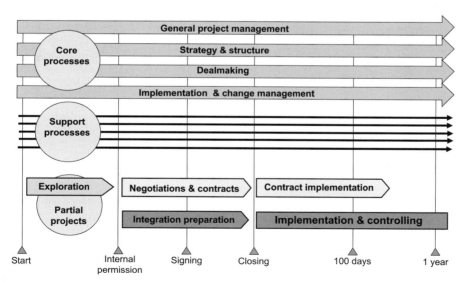

Figure 4.13 Processes vs. M&A partial projects

ing process includes all activities carried out as part of the transaction, particularly negotiation and writing the contracts. The main support processes linked to this core process are contract law, antitrust law, tax optimization processes and real estate and environment. *Management of implementation and cultural change* is assigned to its own core process in this model. The reason for this is the operationally strong differences vis-à-vis the aforementioned processes and the high level of importance assigned to change management. This core process is also closely related to special functional support processes, particularly the processes for communication and for human resources management.

The "support processes" include two categories, functional processes (such as human resources and IT) and cross-functional core processes. For example, the information acquisition process combines research in the strategic advance phase with the due diligence activities going on during the course of the transaction. All statements by management and all events and media must be coordinated in the communication process. Thus, this primarily serves the change and management process.

The single project

Path exploration

Given the variety of options for action, the large number of decisions to be made and in particular the great uncertainty about the outcome and success of the chosen paths which is so typical of M&A, it is best to give early consideration to potential activities and their implications for success. When doing so, a decision-making tree should be

Decision chain	Options for action, e.g.
Strategy	• Organic growth • Acquisition • Retraction
Candidate selection	• Company A • Company B
Business definition	• Business type • Make or buy
Transaction form	• Auction • Direct purchase • Carve-out
Business processes	• Business process definition • Process outsourcing • Partnering concepts
Integration model	• Leave separate • Add-on organization • Full merger
Legal structures	• Operative holding • Finance holding • Direct operating company
Governance structures	• Board types • Responsibilities • Governance contracts

= Options for action. Black arrow: selected path

Figure 4.14 Setting the basic direction for M&As

used to indicate at which points fundamental decisions must be made during the phases of an M&A project. These decision points should be thought out initially during the preparatory phases of the project, when the M&A strategy is being verified and the question about the candidate is still open. This allows the feasibility and repercussions of downstream options and requirements for action to be simulated and evaluated, rather than simply checking off the work phases as they occur later. Figure 4.14 shows a working model of this. The thorough analysis allows findings and contributions for all processes to be taken into consideration. Accordingly, aspects of the functional processes must also be considered, for example the model for tax optimization of structures, reporting and management models. The resulting overall "big picture" should be regularly updated and explored as the project progresses, particularly as the point of departure for the negotiations, due diligence and closing. By that time, the course should be set.

Project tuning

The size and complexity drivers presented here focus on the questions: "What problems will confront me?" and "What are the potential solutions?" These are the cornerstones of the project design. The question now arises about the optimum design for the project. Based on the main strategic objectives, the "management philosophy" of the project should then be specified. The "*project tuner*" (Figure 4.15) has been developed to help visualize this (Compare article on the Dräger case).

The strategic dimensions must first be specified. The profile for implementation is derived from them. The most important thing is to predefine the dynamic in the "strategy-structure" core process. Operative background conditions and observations on risk are also taken into account. Thus, the speed of integration is based on the timing of the strategic objectives, the degree of difference between the merging companies and the estimates of what resources are available for implementation. The "tuner" can be used to check the effect and consistency of fundamentally different management approaches. In particular, this involves the issue of the optimum speed and the resources to be deployed. Once the model has been selected, it is used as an overarching basic model for shaping the individual phases, processes and project sections.

Project setup

M&A projects are characterized by influences that are outside the control of the individual business. The consequences are surprise twists and turns, delays and high rates of abandonment. In addition, the character of the work during the project phases differs as the main protagonists change. The risk of abandoning transatlantic projects is greatest, for example, during the antitrust proceedings. The European Commission or the U.S. antitrust authorities may make a "second request" to clarify objections. This can take more than eight months from signing to approval, before they reach a decision. During that time, the merger candidates continue in full competition and may not take any steps to merge.

It is obvious that the entire project should be broken down into individual partial projects. This does not contradict the process approach, because the partial processes

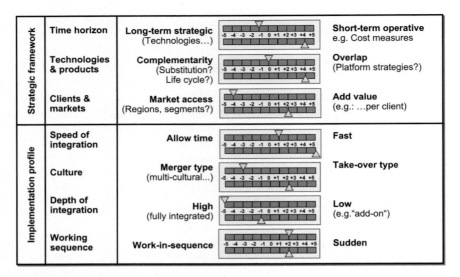

Figure 4.15 The "Project Tuner"

and people responsible for the project are chosen for the project as a whole. During a transition from one partial project to the next, having the same people responsible throughout ensures the continuity of tasks and objectives. What has proved successful in practice is an approach made up of three partial projects (bottom of Figure 4.13): the exploratory advance project driven by strategy analyses, the dealmaking project that focuses on negotiations and contracts, and the integration project which consists of preparation for the closing, detailed implementation planning and finally implementation after the closing. The transitional points of the partial projects are defined by major milestones.

Project elements

Development of standard working packages

An action framework for completion of M&A projects includes the definition of working steps in addition to the definition of processes and fundamental rules for forming (partial) projects. Because the processes represent the fundamental structural basis, it makes sense to divide them into performance packages. The objective of developing the performance packages is to put experience from projects into a structure that can be used directly as a model for future projects. An outline of the working packages of the core strategy/structure process is shown at the top of Figure 4.16.

Once there is sufficient project experience and the need for work has been evaluated according to the various project categories (size, complexity, extent of change, etc.), a time and capacity plan can be generated in advance at the level of the working packages. Naturally this must include additional considerations, e.g., the degree of the *a priori* definition of objectives and structures, the size and depth of the organization and the requisite cascading of individual tasks.

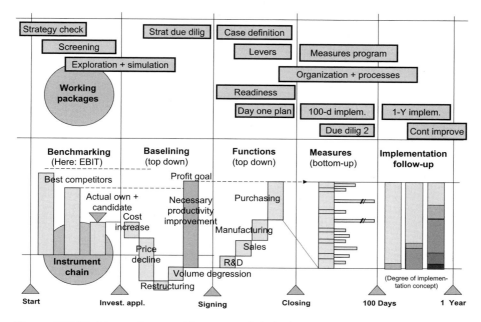

Figure 4.16 Working packages and instrument chain in the strategy-structure process

Linking methods and tools

Experience with the use of methods and tools is another prerequisite for protecting oneself against being overwhelmed and avoiding self-induced complexities. The bottom of Figure 4.16 shows the chain of methodical steps, along with the tools to be used for each of them, based on the example of the strategy-structure process.

In this case, the overall objective (the selected example is EBIT) of a company merger is derived top down, from a comparison with leading companies (benchmarking). A comparison with the static EBIT of the companies to be merged during the target year (baselining that factors out productivity assumptions in the previous business plans) provides the dynamized overall potential for improving profits. This must first be broken down by function (or product or location) from the top down. Once there is access to the acquired company after the closing, this can be verified from the bottom up. The levers for improving profits thus obtained must be backed by individual measures whose implementation is then tracked in a milestone plan, for example using the "degree of implementation" (DI) concept.

Consistency and transfer management

Assuring the goals above and beyond the level of partial processes and product phases ultimately results from having uniformity among the responsible individuals. The main drivers of the project change from phase to phase. The transitions between the phases or partial projects are particularly challenging. The transition that is most difficult to shape during an M&A integration is that of the post-closing measures. These involve transferring the goals and measures that were identified by the interim

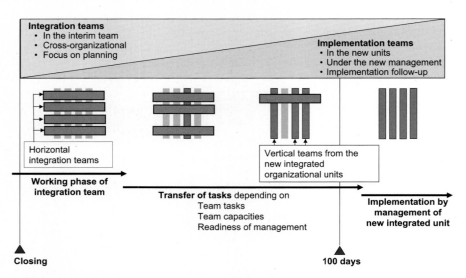

Figure 4.17 Tasks and transfers from team into the new organization

team and approved by the participants to the freshly named management of the newly integrated organization.

Transfer of the individual tasks should be done according to a uniform model. It is advisable to specify this transition in the "basic design" of the project even before the closing. Practice has proven a matrix structure to be the best of the available options. One dimension of the matrix is covered by the (interim) project team and the other by (future) management. This is shown in Figure 4.17 with "horizontal" (cross-topic) project teams and "vertical" organizational units (resulting from integration). The individual duties can be transferred from one project team to the corresponding new organizational unit when (a) the work of the project team has made sufficient progress, (b) the future organizational unit has been defined and (c) its executive management has been appointed. Because these prerequisites are fulfilled at different times in the individual units, tasks can be transferred progressively so that successive "horizontal" teams are dissolved and the individual operative units in the "vertical" part of the matrix begin to do the work instead.

Risk & disruption management

Systematic risk management has been proven to be an important contributor to ensuring a successful project. This includes all M&A-based levels (Figure 4.10). In detail, this includes:

- Evaluation of the paths of action for feasibility (Figure 4.14); identification and evaluation of substitute paths
- Identification and evaluation of disruptions (likelihood of occurrence, extent and effect of the disruption, such as sensitivity analyses concerning costs, time, etc.)
- Proactive management, such as timely decisions to follow a specific path in order to avoid anticipated risks

- Identification and evaluation of preventive measures to avoid disruptions in this path (resources, times, etc.)
- Turning to previously prioritized alternative paths when the agreed-upon main path proves not to be economically feasible
- Keeping completely different options open, such as placing a second candidate "on the back burner" as a fallback position, evaluation of optional paths
- Specifying limits for interrupting or abandoning the project
- Overall evaluation for an abandonment scenario and maximum project risk (such as "sunk cost" and limiting strategic options through lost time)

Risk management in M&A therefore includes more than just the "traditional" instruments and also requires shrewd thinking in order to steer clear of problems as much as possible. For example, experience has shown companies that M&A disasters can practically be eliminated if milestones for potentially backing out of the project are included in the plan.

Summary and outlook

The transatlantic pressure to consolidate will continue. Some sectors still have the greatest part of the journey ahead of them (see article by Fritz Kröger). In the future, combining forces through U.S.-European mergers will have to be evaluated from a positioning standpoint relative to the new giants from growth regions. Size competition and a multinational presence continue to set the pace for major mergers. The performance requirements for M&A will continue to increase. Knowledge management and control systems for permanent restructuring of the corporate structure will increasingly determine the ability of companies to survive as value creation is internationalized.

4.1.3 "Seen, but not Heard!" Predicting M&A Outcomes from the Customer Perspective

Gerhard Plaschka, Rohit Verma, Douglas Squeo

Irrespective of their industry, mergers are plagued with low success rates. This finding is surprising, given that all stakeholders (especially senior corporate executives) have vast experiences, credentials and significant vested interests. However, the voice of a very important stakeholder is often missed in a typical M&A discussion. This essential-but-ignored stakeholder – The Customer – probably makes the most significant decisions related to the present and future existence of the constituent corporate entities. In the frenzy of the typical M&A process, the impact of operational reorganization on future customer behavior is typically not considered systematically. By listening to, understanding, and incorporating present and future customer choices proactively in M&A processes, the probability of success can be increased to much higher levels. This chapter discusses state-of-the-the art tools for assessing customer choices in pre- and post-merger contexts.

Introduction

Why do 7 out of 10 mergers fail? The decades of research on M&A identifies the key determinants for successful mergers, such as, strategic vision and fit; deal structure and economic context; due diligence; planning and integration management. With great minutiae many articles have been written about overcoming the challenges in M&A transactions related to accounting, financial, legal, operations, personnel and organizational issues, and most recently on leadership and culture issues. Yes, the poor performance of mergers is quite surprising given that the majority of M&As are driven by scale, efficiency, cost cutting, and elimination of redundancies and typically take place in industries where excess capacity or R&D deficiencies exist, geographic expansions are desirable, industry boundaries convert or converge, or simply innovative product or service extensions are needed to remain competitive.

M&As are often doomed to fail whether they occur among equals, or involve acquisitions of smaller companies (with unique capabilities) into larger entities to create economies of scale or just a more efficient conglomerate. Perhaps the reason behind the low-success rate in M&A is simply the fact that choices and preferences of one of the most important stakeholders – *The Customer* – are intellectually and analytically sidelined during the entire pre-merger and post-merger activities. Rarely do any M&A processes mention, and never do they have, the customer as the epicenter of all the jotting and noting. The negligible contemplation on understanding customer choices is quite surprising because market-related effects are predominantly cited and communicated to the stakeholders as the key driver of M&A activity. In fact, 50% of all M&As fall into this category. (See also the article by Kruger, Fritz et al, "Success and Success

Factors of US-German Mergers.") So if five out of ten mergers are customer-induced M&As, why are executives not using suitable analytical tools in the deliberation and assessment process? Based on the authors' own observations during the typical pre-merger due diligence process and the immediate 'aftermath' of the post-merger integration, not many corporate executives think beyond the closing date and the following 100 days. On the other hand, when the authors ask, all executives believe that it is very important to think about the impact a merger will have on its customers and competitors during the subsequent 12 to 24 months. Thus it appears that we have an information gap about the available analytical tools for assessing customer choices and their applications within the merger process.

The following discussion will attempt to highlight tools, for both the pre- and post-merger phases, which allow for the discovery, quantification and prediction of latent (i.e. "hidden") customer choice mechanisms. The methods for assessing customer choices described in this chapter replace subjective assumptions about customer behavior with quantitative estimates of future corporate actions on market share, brand equity, and the value of product, service and experience drivers in the context of M&As.

The varying flavors of customer choices

When Deutsche Telekom acquired VoiceStream in 2001 it was instantly the sixth largest wireless service provider in the US and controlled anywhere between 5-6% market share. Deutsche Telekom offered originally approx. $22,000 USD per customer in the transaction which would require that each of the existing VoiceStream customers spend at least $75 USD per month for the next 25 years in order to achieve break-even. Deutsche Telekom had to not only operate outside its well known European territory but also maneuver in a deregulated oligopoly-like industry beleaguered by consolidation.

Like all wireless providers Deutsche Telekom was plagued by the industry phenomena that customers are 'very mobile'. In other words, customers cancel contracts and switch providers at the first sign of discontent (known as customer churn) causing a provider to replace anywhere between 20-35% of the customer base each year in order to maintain market share, which is even higher in any post-merger phase. Besides coping with the industry embedded 'macro challenges' the most difficult test in the post merger phase was to understand what truly drives the churn and migration rate within and across customer segments (e.g. residential versus business users). Are they driven by (a) the handset device desirability with its plethora of attention-grabbing features, (b) the constantly changing subscription, pricing and pre-paid plan offer, (c) the customer service and billing policies, (d) the telephone number portability, and/or (e) the network related performance and geographic coverage availability?

Though Deutsche Telekom AG has confounded critics by transforming the acquired company from a problem child to a wunderkind, it is rumored to be considering a sale of the U.S. unit due to the consistently required technology upgrades to keep pace with rivals, for as much as $30 billion USD, which is still well below the $38 billion USD paid in 2001.

Within the due diligence process, M&A managers routinely map the products, services, customers and markets from the acquisition target by size, segment, growth rate, competitive constraints, and profitability to their own product/market portfolio. But identifying the most profitable customers and mapping them to the management processes of both companies in a SWOT-like format is insufficient in today's environment of rapidly vanishing mass markets and proliferation of product and service offerings. Thus companies engaged in pre- and post-merger processes need to – even more quickly than 'non-merger active' firms – assess, redefine and execute their beloved business doctrine: 'Give customers what they want'. This argument holds true for Business-to-Business (B2B) and Business-to-Consumer (B2C) markets, for both mundane and involved decisions such as buying a bottle of shampoo, ordering a cup of coffee, choosing a health-care provider, or setting-up a totally integrated automation solution for an automotive manufacturer. Such decisions are becoming more and more complex because of the abundance of choices available to customers in the marketplace. This customer choice phenomenon is even further emphasized when a relatively small capital investment by the merger active firm suddenly controls a significant market share of previously 'unknown customers' within new geographic boundaries. Naturally disproportionate higher complexity occurs when the M&A transaction is between a firm operating in a mature industry and/or customer segment, and a firm operating in an emerging market, given that it can not be assumed that 'linearization' of the market and customer effects will take place. Such dramatic explosion and complexity of product and service offerings has ironically become a problem instead of a solution for both the M&A involved firms and their customers; given that quite often customers desire fewer alternatives than more choices. Given the paradox of choices and the resource constraints in a post-merger phase, it becomes virtually impossible for any firm to simultaneously excel in all aspects of product definition, innovation and service delivery (e.g. provide the highest quality, fastest delivery and most variety at the lowest price). However, common business acumen suggests that the further a company deviates from the defined 'home-base'[1], the harder it will be to have the appropriate knowledge and resources to understand and offer those customer choices which really matter. As a result, what might seem to be complementary products and service offerings to the 'home base' may turn out to be completely new (and different) offerings in the merged 'off-base' market.

The underlying problem in predicting customer choices resides much more in the fact that purchasing decisions are simultaneously made on the basis of many different criteria such as brand, quality, performance, price, service, features and channel. Optimization of product and service offerings, which is already a complex task for one firm, becomes exponentially harder for the company resulting from the merger of two or more firms. Therefore, firms contemplating M&A must make trade-offs on the basis of what they can do best in the future when their resources are pooled and match that with a precise understanding of what criteria matter most to their current and future customers. In addition, they must also include into their assessment process

---

[1] The term 'home-base' is used to refer to the group of existing customers of a firm irrespective of their geographic boundaries; 'off-base' customers are desirable customers but currently obtain products or services from other suppliers, use substitutable products or services, or not any such products and serves at all.

what their competitors are offering today and will be offering tomorrow. In order to create, capture, and maintain demand for their offerings within the merged entities, firms have to balance three key challenges when facing the 'new' customer:

Ambiguity – What do our current and future customers *really* want?

Companies that lack a clear understanding of customer choices often take a scattershot approach, hoping that at least one of their offerings will succeed. Such an approach is unfortunately neither efficient nor profitable for most firms operating in majority of industries today. As a result, markets often are flooded with products and services that have relatively little added value or significance for customers and that may cost businesses their entire bottom line.

Risk – Will our envisioned offerings be successful?

Managers face complex combinatorial problems when deciding which product-service bundles to offer in the marketplace. Potential product/service drivers (e.g. price or specific product-service features) can have several variants and a manager may use experience, benchmarking analysis or simply gut feel to decide what might or might not be of interest to the customers. On the one hand such "informed guessing" might lead to new and innovative ideas; but on the other hand it might also lead to depleted profits and chaos.

Conformance – Can we deliver what we promised?

While it is important for companies to understand market value drivers, they must also align those drivers with effective operations management. Even if firms succeed in identifying and delivering particularly attractive product-service packages, efforts to do so may prove futile unless they can efficiently deliver on their promises under resource constraints.

Within the new market dynamics, the likelihood of achieving a profitable and sustainable performance can be raised dramatically if the M&A team focuses on precise estimates of "what customers will choose" rather than imprecise indications of "what customers prefer." During the last few years, decision science-based marketing research has redefined a sophisticated and practical toolbox which is available for those companies who wish to accurately understand the drivers of customer choices. Such tools and methodologies now allow for the prediction of market performance parameters (e.g. market share) of new or existing product, service, or experience offerings with remarkable precision even for seemingly complex and erratic market conditions, irrespective if they occur in B2B or B2C environments. The original framework pioneered by Daniel McFadden (winner of the 2000 Nobel Prize in economics) focuses on both the economic reasons for individual choices and the ways researchers could measure and predict these choices. This theory, when applied within "real life" choice situations using multi-media and technology-driven data collection techniques, allows firms to accurately assess and predict customer product, service and experience choices in pre- and post-merger situations.

Demand side considerations in M&A processes

As we discussed earlier, while most merger-driven companies reason that the coveted 'value added' component usually falls within financial and operational areas, tapping the maximum 'value added' component requires a keen understanding of the customers and their reactions to the offerings of the "new company" within the constraints of competition, time and quality. Nevertheless, typically in merger situations the M&A buyer is driven by supply-side factors which implicitly suggest that, after the integration, the merged firms will immediately focus on leveraging and/or integrating the critical resources and capabilities that are possessed by the acquirer or target company.

For example, despite the obvious strategic fit between Chrysler and Mercedes, which was designed to significantly improve their position within the automotive industry through higher market penetration across customer segments, revenue and profitability based on cost savings and geographical fit was not only derailed through the clash of corporate cultures, but also by a limited understanding of the product, service, channel and brand drivers. On the other hand, despite the acquisition of Spiegel Inc. (Chicago/USA) by Otto GmbH & Co KG (Hamburg/Germany) and the post-merger challenges that arose, when it later acquired majority control in Crate & Barrel (Chicago/USA), Otto immediately leveraged its knowledge in the catalogue business and extended Crate & Barrel's business model. However, the merged entities failed to capture (in terms of market share, revenue and profitability) the changing and lasting shift in trends for more contemporary lifestyles in the household, furniture and accessory market. Thus losing the important market leadership position which now is shared with catalogue operators (and now also retail store operators) such as Williams-Sonoma, Pottery Barn, Sur La Table, Room & Board, Design within Reach and others.

When Deutsche Post AG's (Bonn, Germany), Brussels-based DHL Worldwide Express unit acquired Airborne Express (Seattle, USA) in August 2003, Airborne Express, then the 3rd largest player in the U.S. parcel delivery market, was primarily acquired as a means for DHL to gain inroads to the highly competitive US market. Although DHL ships more packages internationally than FedEx and UPS combined, its presence in the US market was scarce. When acquired by DHL, Airborne claimed approximately 6% share of the US market, while FedEx and UPS claimed nearly 80%. DHL increased its share of the US market to 7% in 2004, and industry experts predict that this could increase up to 18% by 2006. But how can such gains be realized without truly understanding the customer within a commodity-like market where pricing strategies are instantly matched? Or, phrased differently, how much larger a share could be gained if the customer was truly understood? Today firms in the parcel delivery business are 'attacking' on all fronts, from retail-based offerings (e.g. FedEx Kinkos, The UPS Store, DHL's alliance with over 5,000 retail outlets at Pak Mail, Office Max, etc.) to a highly fragmented customs 'delivery' brokerage industry to managing supply chains for just-in-time deliveries. So is a retail-strategy really the inroad to captivate the customer and market share under profitability constraints?

Though examples of Mercedes/Chrysler, Deutsche Post/DHL/Airborne Express, and many others (Other industry examples can be found in the articles by Steinebach L. et al, "Henkel's Acquisition of The Dial Corporation, Scottsdale, USA" and Kaschke, M. et al, "Carl Zeiss Vision – A Merger of the Carl Zeiss Eyeglass Division with Sola

International, Inc.".) provide some evidence as to why the focus on a supply-side perspective might have contributed to below-average M&A post-merger performance compared to the pre-merger expectations, the more important question of – *The Customer* – becomes evident: Can combined entities achieve a better M&A performance if in the due diligence process M&A managers include demand-side driven assessment mechanisms? Or asked differently: Why do M&A managers neglect the importance of demand-side concerns knowing that most M&A managers (a) overestimate or underestimate the value the customer inputs on the "new company's" offerings, and (b) often include in their M&A scenario-planning assumptions based on "market share illusions" rather than 'market share realities'?

Though analyzing the possible range of answers to the above questions is beyond the scope of this article, the typical due diligence process primarily maps the customer needs of the combined firms around a 'brand equity matrix'. (See also the article by Grube, Ruediger, "The Post-Merger Integration Process of Daimler Chrysler.") Given that it is widely accepted that brand is one of the most complex elements to assess, the majority of managers simply depend upon their own pre-conceived perceptions when assessing brand value and current brand positioning. However, if managers would truly measure the net worth of brands and evaluate the dispersion of brand equity across customer segments they would discover that the propensity to switch brands within and across customer segments varies widely when asking one of the following questions:

- What product and service offerings should the merged firm really offer in each market to maximize customer benefits?

- Can the brand equity really overcome the reluctance of customers to switch from their "old" supplier to the "new" merged supplier? Or, would they switch to a competitive supplier?

In the due diligence process companies rarely have mapped brand equity structures of the merging and third-party competitor entities. Thus managers typically will not discover the real value of customer choice drivers and how they can overcome the customers' embedded reluctance to switch. If a merger active firm cannot assess brand equity within and across its industry, it is not feasible to clearly understand the potential risk/reward relationship of customer choices within the more convoluted product, service and experience space.

Pre-merger assessment / measuring customer inertia

Hence, the core issue in pre-merger M&A situations is to understand the brand equity effects and its derived value in context of customers' reluctance to switch or inert[1]. This reluctance to switch (inertia) is the tendency for customers to stay with their

---

[1] Generally inertia can be caused by one or a combination of several factors including customer habit or preference for status quo ("don't like to switch"); satisfaction with current products and service offerings; lack of real or perceived alternatives; customer loyalty; alternative offers lack credibility, and so on. However, inertia does not account for lack of awareness; contractual limitations; ignorance of alternatives and paradigm shifts (e.g. product obsolescence).

current product-service provider, thus creating a positive or negative barrier for companies engaged in M&A activities. Understanding inertia is critical to determining what product and service offerings the merged company should offer to deter customers from switching to competitor offerings. Nevertheless, switching inertia has received relatively little attention among managers in developing a pre-merger customer-driven valuation, positioning or implementation strategy. Again, this is caused by the fact that it is probably easier to focus and control *supply-side mechanisms* rather than *demand-driven mechanisms* in the M&A due diligence and subsequent post-merger integration process.

To illustrate the importance of focusing on demand-side analysis in M&A scenarios, it is helpful to look at a typical pre-merger scenario from a challenger's (i.e. competitor's) perspective rather than argue its importance from the merged entity's perspective. It is obvious that simply seeking to imitate the resource capabilities of, in many cases, a superiorly endowed newly combined entity would be a short-sighted strategy for the challenger. It would amount to an unintelligent utilization of resources since such a strategy would at best bring about an approximate competitive parity between the challenger and the merged entity that would not suffice in the face of switching inertia. In other words, even if the challenger were able to imitate the merged entity, it may simply prefer not to do so due to poor returns from such a strategy. Certainly this effect also acts as a self-imposed isolating mechanism that becomes operational when a challenger does not have sufficient incentives to imitate the combined entity's value propositions (i.e. when there are inadequate returns to imitation). Thus switching inertia functions as a demand-side isolating mechanism and addressing the equally important issue: What if there are only minimal returns to imitation?

To conceptually illustrate how and why customers' switching inertia causes heterogeneity in value creation among the merged entity and the challengers, we adopt the widely accepted view that the essence of strategy is the search for competitive advantage. In this regard strategists make a distinction between operational effectiveness and strategic positioning. Operational effectiveness means "performing similar activities better than rivals" whereas strategic positioning means "performing different activities from rivals or performing similar activities in different ways." From an operational effectiveness standpoint, a challenger may benchmark and attempt to outperform the merged entity in offering customers a similar value configuration. However, assuming that the merged entity is in that position primarily because it performs a particular set of activities at the competitive frontier, any improvement by the challengers would probably not suffice to compensate for even a modest level of switching inertia. Moreover, seeking to outperform the merged entity following its activity configuration also has the disadvantage of competing with the merged entity on its own terms, and on terms which may depart from the challenger's own competencies.

On the other hand, strategic positioning refers to choosing a different activity configuration to deliver a unique mix of value. This may be more 'in tune' with a challenger's own competencies (or provide it with an opportunity to develop them) and would make it more difficult for a merged entity rival to respond. To restate the point, a firm must offer greater value to a customer to attain competitive advantage over rivals. This would be difficult through a strategy of operational effectiveness when switching inertia is present to a non-trivial degree.

Case snapshot: Customer value matrix[1]

To illustrate the effects of customer inertia we will use a simple customer-derived value matrix from an integrated cardiac IT and equipment solutions provider. For example, concern with comparative costs alone ignores quality. Ability to offer greater quality at the same cost, or same quality at lower cost, vis-à-vis other firms enables a firm to deliver superior value, which translates into competitive advantage. One can expand this concept into n-dimensional spaces, with each dimension representing one component of customer value (e.g. solution integration, flexibility, reliability and so on). Each component of customer value can then be drilled-down into further subcomponents of customer value (e.g. solution integration might be implemented across all hospital care & business units, within the cardiac unit only, etc.). Customer value can thus be conceptualized as a dynamic composite comprising an array of characteristics where the importance or relative weight (customer impact) of the various components or subcomponents in the mix is dependent on market conditions. Thus, this dynamic composite constantly shifts around depending on the particular operating environment of customers. For example, time to market may be very valuable in the computer industry but less so in the health care industry. The point is that various activities, or combinations of activities, enjoy differing levels of 'customer impact premium' in different M&A environments (or during different periods, maturity or geographic boundaries in the same industry environment).

Table 4.1 Customer value matrix in health care provider market

Core Market Driver	Solution Integration [A1]	Price [A2]	Clinical Performance [A3]	Operational Performance [A4]	Sum
Ideal combination	15	30	20	35	100
Merged Entity	10	25	18	25	78
Latecomer 1	11	24	16	33	84
Latecomer 2	12	22	16	25	75

Market Driver Extension Solution Integration [A1]	Across all hospital care & business units [A11]	Within Cardiac unit only [A12]	Limited integration with media breaks [A13]	Sum
Ideal combination	5	5	5	15
Merged Entity	3	4	3	10
Latecomer 1	5	2	4	11
Latecomer 2	3	5	4	12

[1] A more detailed discussion of switching inertia can be found at Li, S., A. Madhok, G. Plaschka, and R. Verma, "Switching Inertia: A Study of Demand Side Asymmetry in the Industrial Automation Systems Industry," working paper, David Eccles School of Business, University of Utah, June 2005.

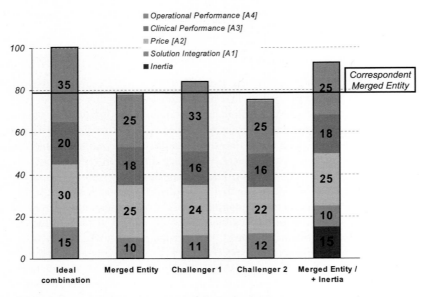

Figure 4.18 Optimal value configuration for merged entity

Suppose the firm's value proposition is comprised of particular customer value components such as solution integration (A1), price (A2), clinical performance (A3), operational performance (A4), with hypothetical weights of 15, 30, 20 and 35 percent respectively (adding up to 100). Each of these is comprised of sub-components of customer value. For example, solution integration (A1) may be comprised of subcomponents such as: solution integration across all care & business units (a1.1), solution within cardiac unit only (a1.2), limited solution integration within care and business units with some media breaks (a1.3), with the sum of the subcomponents' values adding up to the total value of the component (i.e. primary market driver).

In Table 4.1 we present the three mock firms' value structure matrices. One is the merged entity and the other two are challengers. The ideal value combination (i.e., the weight that is assigned to each attribute) is the most effective approach to satisfy buyers in this industry. In this mock market segment, we assume that buyers value the feature of operational performance most (i.e., weight 35 out of 100) and the market driver 'solution integration' least (i.e., weight 15 out of 100). In this example, the merged entity offers buyers 78 utilities out of 100. Challenger 1 outperforms the merged entity in operational performance, the most weighted market driver. However, although Challenger 2 is effective in solution integration, the least weighted market driver, this cannot give it enough leverage over the merged entity. Similarly the components of the customer value structure A can be divided into sub-market driver extensions as described for "solution integration." Table 4.1 further suggests that Challenger 1 outperforms the merged entity (84 vs. 78), thus the buyer could switch to Challenger 1.

On the other hand, the buyer would not switch to Challenger 2 because they do not provide superior value compared to the merged entity (75 compared to 78). This assessment of switching however assumes that the buyer has no or negligible switching inertia. If significant switching inertia exists then the buyer might not be motivated to switch to Challenger 1 even though the latter provides higher value. For example, let us assume that inertia is 15 units on the value matrix scale (Figure 4.18). Therefore, when considering switching to an alternate supplier, the buyer will compare the value provided by the merged entity + switching inertia which is 93 units (78 + 15). Since both challengers offer values less than 93, the buyer will perceive itself to be better off staying with the merged entity. This means that both the challengers will have to develop additional capabilities to overcome the inertia barrier before they can be seriously considered as an alternative to incumbent by the buyer.

From the challenger's point of view in particular, in the presence of buyer switching inertia, it will be better off establishing unique strategic positions than it would be in pursuing operational effectiveness. In this regard, even though a challenger's value creation capabilities may not be enough to overcome the overall switching inertia, variation across customer segments in the level of switching inertia, as well as in the value distribution across the various market drivers, provides opportunities for the challengers to selectively attack the merged entity to capture those customers with the lowest levels of inertia (highest propensity to switch), or the so-called 'low-hanging fruit'. This has direct managerial implications in assessing pre-merger situations: First, the future merged entities need to identify buyers' value structure(s) (i.e. buyers' 'hot buttons'), and levels of switching inertia within each customer segment and across the aggregated market in order to determine resource requirements. If possible, they also need to understand the differences between buyer groups (i.e. customer segments) in terms of value dimensions and switching inertia. Second, the acquirer and targeted entity need to examine their actual value creation capabilities and accordingly map their combined capabilities onto buyers' value profile(s). Third, the merged entities need to evaluate whether the potential value creation space that is not being currently occupied by the other competitors (i.e. challengers) is large enough to overcome buyer switching inertia. Fourth, the merged entities need to assess whether they are able (and willing) to put forward an alternative value bundle to buyers to attack the remaining competitors or more likely offer value bundles which allow them at least to maintain their anticipated market position.

Thus it is important in the pre-merger process to develop robust and reliable estimates of switching inertia and explore, whenever possible in computer simulated 'dry-runs', its impact on the newly established market equilibrium. Switching inertia can be easily derived from market-based customer choice models by forcing the target market's customers to choose in customer interviews between "current" and "new" product-service providers. Such assessment processes allow companies to easily derive, and clearly obtain, the value of "cash-like incentives," for example, to acquire customers. Of course, such processes also will minimize the "customer reversal process" to the customer's former 'home-base' if the merged entity's offering has no value above and beyond the initial inertia-breaking incentive (e.g. switching between wireless carriers for free phones, or replacing existing automation solution at no cost from an incumbent supplier in lieu of service contract from the newly 'merged' supplier).

Post-merger assessment/customer loyalty & experience assessment

A Smith Barney advertisement once stated, "A job well done is a job that's never really done." No matter how good a firm is in offering its products and services they all strive to get better because satisfying the customer is a never-ending process.[1] Understanding customers' relationships between the merging companies, and how these customer relationships enhanced or deteriorated over time, is critical to the long term post-merger outcome. Today's customers tend to be very well-informed and for the most part have at least several, and often many, choices in the marketplace. These choices need to be understood if the customer is to be 'captured' for the long-term. In simple economic terms a captured customer is typically referred to as satisfied and/or loyal customer[2] and considered a 'corporate' asset that yields future cash-flows and contributes to future growth. The impact of customer satisfaction has been linked to creating shareholder value and is correlated to increasing a firm's cash-flow. For example it is widely known among customer relationship executives that even very low increases of even 1-point (on a 0-100 scale) in satisfaction scores can increase net operating cash-flow considerably. In other words, the consequences of customer satisfaction result in an increased anticipated life of current customers, reduced operating costs, lower costs of future transactions, and delineated price elasticity. However, there are few managers that are intuitively keen as to what areas of the product, service, or customer experience require improvement, and this is even truer in M&A environments. Perhaps surprisingly, many customers who switch to a competitor report being satisfied by their current supplier at the time they switch to a new vendor (some studies report over 50% of customers who switch are satisfied). Satisfying customers is not enough, however, given that a loyal customer is not necessarily satisfied, and vice versa. For instance, a business traveler may be very satisfied with Lufthansa airlines, but when it comes down to choosing a carrier may only shop based on the lowest available fare thus not necessarily for Lufthansa or the carrier's alliance-based industry relationship (in this example Star Alliance). Therefore, the business traveler may be just as likely to fly with Lufthansa as he/she is to fly with American Airlines or Virgin Atlantic depending on their destination. On the flip side, a very loyal customer may not be satisfied at all with a particular supplier, but perhaps consistently chooses that supplier because of a variety of potential reasons, such as, experience, switching inertia, brand value or regulatory market conditions, which were for example extensively leveraged in the 1980s by AT&T during the post-deregulatory phase.

Consequently, loyalty must be motivated within customers because there is always another competitor in the market, or a new entrant, trying to offer more to customers. Loyalty is a core driver in achieving revenue growth, and is often misinterpreted as being the same as customer satisfaction[3]. While the obvious goal is to have the highest

---

[1] Smith, F. W., Chairman & CEO FedEx Corporation, November 13, 2000 at the J.D. Power & Associates Customer Service Conference, Santa Monica, CA, USA.

[2] Customer satisfaction can be defined as how fulfilled (pleased) a customer is with respect to a firm actually delivering on its stated promise to, and expectations of, customers, including the overall experience and perceived value received in transacting with a product or service provider. Economists define it simply as "a measure of the degree to which a product or service meets the customer's expectations."

In 2000, when Philips' medical business unit acquired ADAC Laboratories, a medical molecular imaging equipment supplier, the newly merged company realized a market share loss among their customers due to a different level of attention paid to customer satisfaction within each of the companies product and service propositions. ADAC imaging scanners achieved an extremely satisfied customer base among clinical technicians who operated their equipment in hospitals and clinics. Much of this satisfaction was derived via the technicians' interactions with ADAC's friendly, knowledgeable and competent service staff. According to the technicians, they were extremely loyal to ADAC equipment. ADAC had long-term relationships and repeat business with many customers and technicians who only wanted to work on ADAC imaging equipment. After the acquisition ADAC and technicians began seeing changes in the operations of the service units they interacted with in their facilities during scheduled preventative maintenance visits and emergency-repair situations. Technicians reported that post-merger service quality deteriorated greatly and quickly and that service did not appear to be a major focus within this 'new' company "they were now part of." In fact, dissatisfaction with Philips' services unit escalated to the point of overcoming the inertia created through the technicians' loyalty to ADAC equipment, and they switched to competitive equipment from suppliers such as Siemens and GE for their future nuclear medicine equipment needs.

satisfaction and loyalty scores possible, a less obvious goal is to use the gap in satisfaction and loyalty scores experienced across the two merged companies as an early warning system for successful merger integration from a customer's point of view. Thus in any post-merger situation it becomes quite important to instantly recognize customer problems and the ability to respond to them in the wake of the immediate post-merger implementation phase, particularly when the acquiring firm has lower loyalty and satisfaction scores than the target firm. This is based on the fact that satisfied customers, and loyal customers, are more insulated from competitors, less price sensitive and less likely to defect to competitors and are more open to cross-selling efforts. It thus becomes evident that the typical cross-selling initiative which often starts in the 'first post-merger days' would be much more likely to succeed if it were monitored through customer satisfaction mechanisms rather than in simple accounting and operating terms.

In summary, the inherent risks in post-merger situations can be summed up through the following simple illustration: Consider the PC market and some primary players a few years ago: Dell, Compaq and HP. When HP acquired Compaq their customers assumingly had no affiliation with or affinity to HP. What effect would the merger have on Compaq customers? Assuming that different value structures and 'rational' customer decision-making processes drove Compaq customers to choose Compaq over Dell and HP, how would HP incorporate Compaq's value proposition into its unique offering? And, would satisfied and loyal Compaq customers, turn to HP or Dell the next time around? The next time a former Compaq customer enters the market for

---

[3] Loyalty can be defined as the willingness of someone to make an investment or personal sacrifice in order to strengthen a relationship.

a new or replacement PC it cannot be assumed nor reliably implied that the Compaq customer will most likely turn to HP for its next purchase. The customer now has two alternatives, Dell or HP (assuming no other market participants exist), and the customer will choose between these two offerings based on which competitor is most closely aligned with his/her value structure. The resulting customer choice dilemma is even more elevated if neither of these two offerings, those of HP or Dell, were previously the most appealing one. This does not imply that the HP-Compaq merger was either a success or failure based on this particular factor. Rather it's to illustrate that while the M&A may or may not have been a success on some other levels (e.g. operational efficiencies, higher output capacity, combined R&D, etc.), it is highly probable that, if customer satisfaction assessment processes had been incorporated into the due diligence phase, the M&A success from the customer-retention perspective could have been very accurately predicted for the newly merged entity. Instead, valuable assets (i.e. former Compaq customers) were left to decide their next purchase on their own, if you will, without HP influencing that purchase by targeting the Compaq customers' "hot buttons" in the subsequent cross-selling strategy.

Measuring customer satisfaction and loyalty involves a tightly balanced mix of Art & Science. Post-merger integration managers must be cautious in using traditional and simple customer satisfaction mechanisms as customers are notorious for rating items very rapidly and similarly, using simplification heuristics to speed through the task. Customers often use only a limited range of the scale points, resulting in many "ties" across the tested product and service items. Some customers use just the top few boxes of a rating scale, some refuse to register a top score for any item, while others conscientiously spread their ratings across the entire range. To overcome these shortcomings, firms engaged in post-merger assessments have begun using Best-Worst choice analysis which enables development of more robust segment-level predictive choice models. This approach asks respondents to identify "Best" and "Worst" features presented on some latent (i.e. hidden) dimension (e.g. attractiveness, satisfaction). The ability to distinguish across items permits firms to uncover differences across customers very effectively. When a customer satisfaction and loyalty approach is combined with a customer relationship management data-mining technique, additional trends can easily and reliably be isolated and an even more accurate early warning system for the post-merger integration can be accomplished.

The future

We believe that customer inertia, customer satisfaction and loyalty approaches described in this chapter can yield valuable insights for market and decision science-driven M&A strategy and scenario development by revealing customer needs-based segmentation maps, by measuring the market share impact when modifying or repositioning the "merged" product-service offerings, or by simply accurately assessing the overall brand equity value in context of the customers' inertia indices. Moreover, the suggested customer choice and satisfaction approaches can reveal salient differences between managers' "armchair" *beliefs* about the customer's needs/wants and the customer's *actual* needs and choices. For managers eager to identify, *from The Customer's Perspective,* the value of the overall offering and the marginal product and service value differences compared to the available alternatives, the presented approaches offer a rigorous way to turn customer information into profitable and sustainable strategies for retaining or capturing market share and profitability when being engaged in pre-merger scenario planning or post-merger integration processes.

At the same time, customer choice processes, like other robust business tools and concepts, are subject to the 'garbage in, garbage out' principle (e.g., Black-Scholes option pricing models and its derivatives used in financial markets, Assan's efficient market theory simulations which guide hedge-fund investment decisions). They generate useful information only if the assumptions and understanding behind the selection of an industry's market drivers, the empirical design, analyses and data-collection methods are sound. In a number of projects conducted by the authors across various industries, such analyses have assisted managers to predict more effectively the outcome of pre- and post- merger opportunities. Given that it is always the objective of any company to have a rigorous way to turn knowledge and resources into profitable and sustainable customer-retention and customer-acquisition strategies, hence, *the customer must be also on the center stage of any M&A process.*

Acknowledgment

The authors are grateful to Brian Hanlon, Managing Consultant, MindFolio Chicago for his critical insights and editorial comments, especially for his contributions to the post-merger customer satisfaction and loyalty discussion.

Literature

Bonabeau, E. "Predicting the unpredictable," *Harvard Business Review*, 80, no. 3 (2002): 5-11.

Harding, D., S. Rovit,. *Mastering the Merger: Four Critical Decisions That Make or Break the Deal.* HBS Press Book (2004).

Reichheld, F., "The One Number You Need to Grow," *Harvard Business Review,* 81, no. 12 (2003): 1-9.

Schwartz, B., *The Paradox of Choices: Why More is Less*. HarperCollins Publishers. (2004).

Verma, R. and G. Plaschka, "The Art and Science of Predicting Customer Choices," *MIT Sloan Management Review*, 46, no. 5 (2005).

4.2 Leadership & Corporate Governance

4.2.1 The Impact of Management and Leadership Behaviors on German-American M&A

Joerg G. Matthiessen, Allison S. Bailey, Jeanie Daniel Duck

Why are cross-border M&A efforts so difficult and why do so many stumble? Differences in management perspectives and behavior do matter and often get magnified in a cross-border context. This article discusses the impact of management and leadership behaviors on German-American M&A and outlines what practitioners need to know in order to avoid potential pitfalls and improve their odds of success.

Introduction

The degree to which management and leadership behaviors influence the success of mergers and acquisitions is a source of long-standing debate. Few would argue, however, that the ability of executives to work together successfully is often a key determinant of whether a deal gets done, how fast it transacts, and ultimately the extent to which synergies are realized. This topic is of special interest to German and U.S. companies making cross-border acquisitions, where differing management perspectives can make working together more challenging. As one CEO of a U.S. industrial conglomerate said, "Let me get to know the management team and I'll tell you whether the deal will be successful."

Having advised both German and American companies throughout the deal cycle, we have seen firsthand the impact that differences in management styles can have on M&A. For example, U.S. executives are often surprised by the reluctance of their German counterparts to participate in more cross-border deals. They may fail to realize that German management's typical preference for organic growth and a relatively more conservative approach to risk means that any deals they consider must clear a very high threshold. In a similar vein, German managers frequently note the propensity of U.S. leaders to make decisions with what they perceive as limited information. They may be unaware that American managers' frequent use of the "80/20" rule stems from the high value they place on time and their strong preference for action over analytical certainty. Such differences clearly influence how managers negotiate deals, merge organizations, and ultimately work together to create value.

Our experience suggests that differences in three areas – strategic outlook, operating philosophies, and cultural norms – directly influence the way German and American executives work together throughout the M&A cycle. For example, a leader's strategic outlook directly affects which deals get done and how much is paid for them. A management team's operating philosophies often shape how well organizations come together after a deal is transacted. And, an organization's cultural norms influence how well executives deal with their differences – before, during, and after a deal is done

Figure 4.19 Elements of management behavior

(see figure 4.19). In our experience, practitioners involved in German-American M&A should pay careful attention to such areas to be more effective negotiators, mediators, and implementers and to improve their odds of M&A success.

Some background – The German-American M&A context

Overall, the U.S. and Germany have shown very different tendencies with regard to their cross-border M&A activity over the past decade. While German retrenchment has been both considerable and sustained after the "bubble," American firms since 2000 have shown a penchant to purchase German companies at an increasing rate (see Figure 4.20).

A major catalyst for this latest wave of American M&A activity in Germany has been investor groups. Despite a strong euro, American private equity firms have been lured by the prospect of German industry roll-up opportunities and are buying noncore

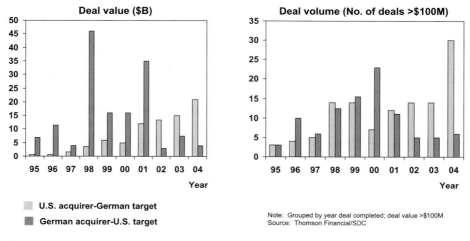

Figure 4.20 German-U.S. merger trends (1995-2004)

assets from conglomerates. For example, of the 58 "U.S. acquirer-German target" deals over $100 million executed between 2002 and 2004, a significant number (31%) were done by US-based investor groups. However, the strong euro and the weakness of the dollar have not yet resulted in a shopping spree by German firms in the U.S. In part, German management's risk aversion, combined with a hangover from the "bubble," has put off many firms. In addition, the challenges faced by many of the high-profile U.S.-German mergers of recent years (e.g., DaimlerChrysler) are still fresh in the minds of many German and American corporate managers. It is within this context that we analyze the impact of management behavior on German-American cross-border M&A.

Observations from the trenches

Having worked with German and American managers directly in a host of different M&A contexts, from target assessment to post-merger integration, we have seen that differences in management perspectives, behavior, and expectations matter greatly. While we recognize that no set of characteristics will be universally applicable, we have distilled those elements that we find generally hold true. Some of these differences confirm the traditional stereotypes of German and American managers, while others refute them. Below we discuss some of the most salient differences of interest to M&A practitioners who are likely to work with either German or American managers in cross-border deal situations.

Strategic outlook: Growth orientation, planning and investment horizons, and risk propensity

A company's M&A strategy is directly influenced by the executives' overall strategic outlook. It is impacted by the executive team's preference for internally versus externally generated growth, the length of its investment and planning horizons, and its desire to take on and manage risk. German and U.S. managers tend to show marked differences in their preferences across all of these dimensions.

Growth orientation

While both German and American managers understand the need for growth, they often pursue it very differently. U.S. managers generally feel very comfortable with generating growth externally (via M&A, joint ventures, and partnerships) and utilizing capital markets to "buy what they can't make themselves." In contrast, German managers tend to favor organic growth, believing that sustained investment in R&D is a better path to innovation and growth, especially in traditional industries. An analysis of the top 30 DAX and DJI companies reveals that German companies spend more on R&D than their U.S. counterparts in several key sectors. For example, German automotive companies spend on average 4.4% of sales on R&D versus 3.4% for their U.S. peers. Similarly, German diversified industrial companies spend 4.7% of sales on R&D versus 2.6% for their U.S. counterparts. This preference for internally generated growth is in part a historical legacy of relatively underdeveloped capital markets in Europe, but it also reflects a fundamental difference in what German and American managers believe is the best source of competitively advantaged growth.

This difference in growth orientation has significant implications for M&A, especially at the front end of the process. German management's bias in favor of organic growth means that any proposed deal has to clear a high hurdle before the executive team will even consider it. As a senior German executive remarked, "Given our focus on product innovation and internally generated growth, a potential technology deal really has to be compelling to get the engagement of our senior management." Furthermore, the level of scrutiny over potential deals, especially cross-border ones, is likely to be more intense and the decision-making process more protracted among German managers. Ultimately, this translates into German managers pursuing fewer cross-border deals than they otherwise might.

Planning and investment horizons

Most large U.S. and German corporations have in place well-developed planning processes and produce three-, five-, and even ten-year plans. However, German management typically places greater importance on long-term planning and investment than its American counterpart does. In some German organizations, senior executive compensation is directly tied to the outcome of long-term plans. This is in contrast to U.S. companies, where managers often equate three-year plans to long-term planning. Given the amount of U.S. executive compensation that is tied to short-term performance and the ongoing threat of job termination, it should come as no surprise that making the current year's numbers is paramount in the U.S. This is illustrated by the comment of one leading U.S. consumer goods executive: "You can talk to me all you want about strategic planning and making long-term investments to compete better against P&G, but if I don't make my numbers this quarter, I'm history."

The implications of different planning and investment horizons on M&A activity are significant. German executives are generally less sensitive to the vagaries of the financial markets and tend not to make M&A moves hastily in response to analyst opinions. Siemens Chairman Heinrich von Pierer noted:

"If we had listened to the financial analysts during the 1990s, we would have sold off most of the company by now. Even in the midst of a crisis, I know our medical business was stronger than they could know, so I didn't listen to them.... In that respect it was helpful to be a German company. Traditionally, German companies have been less responsive to the capital markets, which is often a weakness but in this case benefited us."

U.S. executives, on the other hand, focus more on the short term and often turn to M&A to realize their growth objectives. For example, GE's focus on being "number one" or "number two" in every industry, combined with modest R&D levels, has resulted in its heavy reliance on acquisitions to become the industry leader in many of its businesses. When GE built its services businesses between 1997 and 2000, it made 40 acquisitions in medical systems, 31 in power systems, and 17 in aircraft engines alone. This tendency toward externally generated growth means that American managers are often eager to execute M&A deals to meet their short-term objectives.

Risk propensity

U.S. managers are typically more comfortable managing risk than their German counterparts are. They are generally more willing to manage actively a corporate portfolio of assets and to take on financial risk. Many U.S. companies, following the GE philosophy of being an industry leader or exiting, have taken the risk of actively reinventing themselves through portfolio restructuring. IBM, for example, realizing that PC equipment margins were eroding, transformed itself through corporate restructuring into a high-margin "solutions" provider. By acquiring Price Waterhouse's consulting business and selling off its PC manufacturing business to the Chinese, IBM departed from its historic legacy position. Other U.S. corporations that have reinvented themselves through portfolio restructuring include Pepsi Co., ATT, Viacom, and HP. There are very few German companies, in contrast, that have been as aggressive in managing their portfolios of assets.

In addition, U.S. companies have become quite sophisticated in their approach to managing financial risk. Large U.S. conglomerates, like GM and GE, know how to evaluate and manage such risk and now derive a significant source of their profits from financing operations. GE's financing arm, GE Capital, represents more than 40% of the company's overall profits; similarly, GM's finance company, GMAC, is responsible for 104% of its profits. This is in stark contrast to German companies, where financing activities contribute much less to overall profitability – for example, financing activities at Siemens represent roughly 9% of overall profitability. As financing businesses increase in importance, German companies may want to consider whether they should engage more heavily in captive financing operations and take on additional risk.

German management's relatively more conservative approach to risk, together with a greater focus on organic growth, tends to lessen its interest in M&A and has the potential to create a vicious cycle. For example, a German management team that is risk averse and focused on organic growth is unlikely to consider many M&A opportunities. Its more conservative approach to risk also means that it tends to assign less value to potential deal synergies and is less likely to be the high bidder in any negotiations. The result is that it often loses deals, which leaves it in need of more organic growth; this, in turn, reinforces its perception that M&A cannot be relied on as a platform for growth.

Operating philosophies: Sources of advantage, process orientation, and focus on efficiency and execution

A management team's operating philosophies guide the way it makes tradeoffs during decision-making. In a cross-border M&A context, these philosophies especially influence the downstream steps of the process, such as post-merger integration. Differences in management operating philosophies often are not appropriately appreciated until problems have emerged, "us versus them" battle lines have been drawn, and implementation efforts have stalled. Therefore, M&A practitioners should actively manage such differences from the outset to avoid misunderstandings and prevent gridlock.

Sources of advantage

German managers and their American counterparts may differ in their operational philosophies about sources of competitive advantage. German managers are often seen as to be product-oriented and tend to believe that product innovation and engineering prowess are key determinants of business success. This is due, in no small part, to the fact that a significant percentage of German managers are originally trained as engineers. They can be quite skeptical of marketing and the value it brings to an organization. Americans, on the other hand, tend to believe more in marketing and services as sources of competitive advantage. As a former senior executive of IBM said, "We used to start with the product and add services and marketing to it in order to make the sale. In today's world, however, we are selling a solution that starts with marketing services and wraps product around it."

Differences such as these between German and American management philosophies have a profound impact on how managers work together, especially during integration efforts. During the merger of a U.S. technology company with a large German equipment manufacturer, differing beliefs about the value of marketing versus engineering caused a host of problems. The German managers felt that engineering was of the utmost importance and that marketing was largely a waste of time. The American managers felt that successful marketing was essential to growing their business. Because of their different beliefs, the German and American managers had great difficulty agreeing on anything – from the shape of a new solutions-based business model to where to place investment and how to realize potential revenue synergies. It was clear to all those involved that these radically different operating philosophies had led to gridlock, stalled decision-making, and sidetracked the overall integration effort. Had those involved in the merger been more cognizant of these biases up front, many of the differences could have been managed better.

Process orientation

Reinforcing a long-standing stereotype, German managers tend to be highly process-oriented. They generally want to define clearly structures, roles, and ways of doing things in order to reduce ambiguity and uncertainty in the corporate setting. For example, the German industrial conglomerate Siemens is run globally according to its "process house" model, which clearly states roles and responsibilities for several levels of the organization. For Siemens and many other German companies, this strong adherence to process is seen as a source of competitive advantage. In contrast, Germans tend to perceive American managers as much more entrepreneurial and freewheeling.

The impact of different levels of process orientation during M&A is significant. German managers are likely to have predetermined steps and processes for every phase of M&A and will be reluctant to deviate from them. During negotiations and "clean room" efforts, this means that any attempt to circumvent the process will be strongly resisted. American managers can perceive such a strong process orientation as intransigence.

While American managers generally believe that their greater flexibility is an asset during the M&A process, it can also lead to greater risk-taking (i.e., the "winner takes all" syndrome). As one U.S. senior executive remarked during the integration of a major consumer goods company, "If we had followed the process the Germans had suggested, we wouldn't have made such unrealistic calculations of the synergies and would have probably paid less for the acquisition."

Focus on efficiency and execution

In our experience, German managers tend to be more focused on efficiency and execution. They place a high value on managing the productivity of their assets (whether physical or human) and ensuring that performance does not deviate significantly from plan. As a result, monitoring and control mechanisms are extremely important at all phases of a process, and benchmarking is commonly used to measure performance compared to competitors. While American managers admire the German focus on efficiency and execution, they can frequently perceive German managers' monitoring and control to be excessive. In general, Americans believe that staying focused on the "end goal" is more important than tracking all the "means."

In an M&A context, the German focus on efficiency and execution generally translates into a high level of process control and diligent tracking of expected synergies. For example, at Siemens, all post-merger integration-related synergies (both cost and revenue) are actively tracked by an implementation control process, which requires managers to fill out and submit detailed forms with their realized versus planned synergies. While this approach increases the likelihood that deal synergies are realized, it can be perceived as "bureaucratic form-filling" and lead to frustration on the part of U.S. executives if not managed appropriately.

Cultural norms: Decision-making, expectations and motivations, and communication style

Decision-making, expectations and motivations, and communication styles are key determinants of management effectiveness and have a strong impact on the quality of executive interactions during M&A activity. While we recognize that there are more differences (and similarities) than can be discussed here, we have selected a few factors that deeply influence how German and American executives work together in M&A transactions.

Decision-making

The ability to make good decisions is one of the most important predictors of an executive team's success. The stereotype of German decision-making is that organizations are very hierarchical and that orders arrive from the top to be carried down. In contrast, American decision-making is typically thought to be more collegial and consensus-oriented. However, a closer examination of organizational structure and leadership behaviors in many cases reveals something far different.

Consensus in Germany has a long tradition and stems from a "social pact" between labor, business, and government. This results in a role for German business leadership that is far different from that of its American counterpart. As Siemens Chairman Heinrich von Pierer noted:

"A CEO in Germany is different than a CEO in the United States. A CEO in America can give instructions. A CEO in German is a member of the board. Nobody has to report to him – that's a big difference. So you need a lot of people supporting you, and this requires communication and negotiation, convincing people. You have to, as I say, emotionalize people – which contrasts with the more traditional command and control approach you find at many American companies."

The German desire for consensus also results in relatively slower decision-making. This, in turn, can frustrate many American execuves. For example, at one German conglomerate, during the integration of a U.S.-based firm, the appointment process for key management positions was slowed down considerably by the lack of approval from the German executive team. Each side, however, had a very different view of the integration delay. German executives saw themselves as securing organizational acceptance of new appointees, while the Americans perceived the delay as an indicator of the Germans' inability to make timely decisions. Such approval processes, including the oversight of appointments three and four levels below the business-unit CEO, seemed burdensome and unnecessary to the American executives, but were perceived by the Germans to be critical to consensus building. Such different perceptions of the same situation underscore the need to clarify and debate up front how decisions will be made during M&A efforts. Given the differing decision-making styles of senior leadership (i.e., consensus-oriented versus top-down), the risk of misunderstanding is considerable.

Expectations and motivations

While both Germans and Americans see themselves as ambitious, hardworking, and energetic, their expectations and intrinsic motivations are often different. Americans are influenced by their overarching belief in individualism and Germans by their sense of egalitarianism. We have seen this play out in several areas during integration efforts, including setting expectations around job security and pay structures. In an M&A context, managing these differences is critical to handling layoffs, retaining high-performing individuals, and harmonizing HR policies.

Because Americans place such a high value on the individual, there is a belief that developing and promoting one's personal brand is both legitimate and necessary. Paying attention to one's own career aspirations, especially in times of organizational transition, is considered not only smart but also necessary. Company loyalty has taken repeated hits in the U.S. as downsizing has become routine. Germans, on the other hand, feel a sense of duty and loyalty to the company and have more faith that their careers are, and will be, managed by the company to their advantage. It is typical for German managers to work with fairly standard employment contracts. In contrast, in the U.S. – the "land of litigation" – it is common practice for senior managers to have highly individualized employment contracts and even their own legal counsel. The need for this type of self-protection is borne out by differences in management tenure. The average tenure for a German manager at one company is eight years, compared to only three years for his or her American peer. Such differences directly impact managerial expectations of job opportunities when integrating organizations.

These differences are also reflected in the pay structures of German and American corporations. The star system in the U.S., where CEOs and other senior managers are routinely offered significant stock options and golden parachutes, has translated into U.S. executives earning significantly more than their German peers. For example, in 1998, at the time of the DaimlerChrysler merger, Chrysler CEO Robert Eaton's compensation was eight times greater than Jürgen Schrempp's of Daimler, and Detroit managers on average earned twice what their German counterparts made despite the similar size and complexity of the two organizations. At the same time, German workers generally expect a lot from management in return for their loyalty. While salary is important, quality of life counts a great deal and worker salary packages that include benefits like six weeks of vacation are the norm. This can translate into German workers earning significantly more than their American counterparts do. For example, during the DaimlerChrysler merger, German workers earned roughly $20.000 more per year than their American peers. These compensation inequities underscore the fundamental cultural bias of American individualism and German egalitarianism.

Such differences can lead to great difficulty during a merger, especially when trying to retain talent and harmonize pay structures. German managers will likely believe that higher worker wages, while not ideal, are the cost of social consensus and ensure dedicated employees. They will also be less likely to see the need for high retention bonuses to keep key managerial personnel. American managers, in contrast, are likely to insist on golden handcuffs to retain their stars and may balk at any increase in worker costs, even if that means more staff turnover. Ultimately, practitioners of German-American M&A will need to pay close attention to such differences when dealing with HR issues during integration efforts.

Communication style

As anyone who has operated in a cross-border context can tell you, communication is king. The overall way in which Germans and Americans communicate tends to be different reflecting differences in the way they approach problem-solving, value style versus substance, and make decisions. The risk of miscommunication and the potential to offend are high. All too often, this results in managers saying, "What you heard is not what I intended to say." Thus, being aware of different communication styles and of potential pitfalls is critical.

American and German communication styles tend to reflect their different approaches to problem-solving and reasoning. Americans tend to be inductive, while Germans are generally more deductive. This is exemplified by the preference of German managers for detailed analysis and well-argued recommendations, and by American managers' interest in deriving principles that can be broadly applied. Each can find the other's communication style troublesome. During integration efforts, for example, German managers sometimes feel that American managers are making decisions without understanding the true nature of the problem, and American managers often think that German managers get mired in details.

Germans and Americans also tend to place different emphases on how communication is delivered. Germans typically believe that a well-crafted argument drives the success of communication, while Americans often feel strongly that direct and confident delivery is critical. This is reflected in the observations Siemens Chairman Heinrich von Pierer made about his experiences on an investment banking road show:

"…So when I went on the road show in the U.S. and the analysts asked me a question, I would reply 'well you can see it this way or you can see it that way, but we will go in this direction.' This is how I think. You know, normally there are pros and cons to every issue – nothing is black or white….The American investment banker who accompanied me on the road show said 'Look, if you continue like this you will ruin the whole thing….You have to say, 'I've understood your question. These are our targets, this is how we will achieve them, and I guarantee it. Next question.'…"

In keeping with their focus on content, German managers tend to be more formal in their communication than their American counterparts. They frequently use formally scripted meeting notes and can exhibit a strong desire to stick to an agreed meeting agenda. It is quite common for the CEO of a German company to prepare extensively prior to an executive team or "town hall" meeting and to want all questions submitted in advance. American managers, in contrast, are more comfortable thinking on their feet. This often means a greater willingness to engage actively in brainstorming efforts and to make decisions in real time.

Understanding such differences in communication style can mean the difference between a healthy ability to work together and gridlock during M&A, especially during integration efforts. Ultimately, success rests on being able to iron out differences, which can only be done with strong communication. Keeping in mind the preferred communication styles of the parties involved can help practitioners avoid minefields and ensure that what is heard is what was intended. (For a more detailed discussion of communication style differences see Schmidt's article "Bridging the Intercultural Gap: Non-conventional Truths about American-German Business")

Conclusion

Typically, the purpose of M&A is to create something new and better. Clarity around the goals and challenges of any M&A effort can help guide negotiations, due diligence efforts, and the myriad decisions inherent in post-merger integration. However, at the outset, beyond examining the financials, leaders need to explore the perspectives of any potential candidate's management team – especially their strategic outlook, operating philosophies, and cultural norms. This means looking beyond pure business logic and considering intangibles when evaluating a deal prospect. As we have seen, differences in management perspectives and behavior do matter and can get magnified in a cross-border context. They influence which deals get done, whether synergies get realized, and, ultimately, whether value is created. Furthermore, the ability of two management teams to iron out their differences can often mean the difference between a deal's success and failure. If practitioners of German-American M&A are to extract the full value of their M&A efforts, they need to understand the important role that management behaviors play in determining deal outcomes and respond accordingly.

Literature

Ursula Glunk, Celeste Wilderom, and Robert Ogilvie, "Finding the key to German-style management," *International Studies of Management & Organization,* Vol. 26, No. 3 (1997), 99.

Patrick L. Schmidt, *Understanding American and German Business Cultures* (Düsseldorf: Meridian World Press, 2005), 55.

Thomas A. Stewart and Louise O'Brien, eds., "Transforming an Industrial Giant," *Harvard Business Review,* February 2005.

Jack Welch, *Jack: Straight from the Gut* (New York: Warner Business Books, 2004), 321.

4.2.2 US and German Corporate Governance Issues and Their Implications on M&A Transactions

Lutz Angerer and Christopher Winckler

Corporate governance issues are in relevant of consideration for M&A transactions on both sides of the Atlantic. We discuss some of the issues which regularly come up in the course of mergers and acquisitions below. The first part of this article covers US, the second part German corporate governance aspects, in both cases preceded by a brief overview of the relevant legal framework.

Overview of corporate governance in the United States

US companies must comply with rules on corporate governance enacted pursuant to federal statute, applicable listing rules, relevant state statute and common law. Since the passage of the federal Sarbanes-Oxley Act in 2002 ushered in sweeping reforms to the US corporate governance environment, US public companies are required to modify and in many cases formalize their corporate governance guidelines. In addition, the reporting and certification requirements of the Act have immediate impact on corporate governance implications of an M&A transaction involving a US company.

Meaning of the term "corporate governance" in the United States

While there are multiple characterizations for what constitutes "corporate governance" in the United States, one general definition is that corporate governance is the system by which corporations are directed and controlled. The corporate governance structure specifies the distribution of rights and responsibilities among different participants in the corporation, such as the board of directors, officers/managers, shareholders and other stakeholders, and spells out the rules and procedures for making decisions on corporate dealings. By doing this, it also provides the structure through which the company objectives are set, and the means of attaining those objectives and monitoring performance. Set out below is a description of some of the more noteworthy of these rules.

Rules on corporate governance

Federal regulation of corporate governance is a new development in the United States and means that U.S. public companies must now comply with rules on corporate governance enacted pursuant to federal statute, or by any national securities exchange or association on which they are or propose to be listed, or pursuant to relevant statute in any state in which they are organized and common law.

Federal statutory provisions

The Sarbanes-Oxley Act of 2002 and the U.S. Securities and Exchange Commission ("SEC") rules that were adopted under it apply to all companies with securities registered under, or otherwise required to file reports with, the SEC pursuant to the Securities Exchange Act of 1934, as amended (the "Exchange Act"). Annual report filings are required pursuant to Section 404 of the Sarbanes-Oxley Act to contain a report by management on the adequacy of the company's "internal control over financial reporting." Exchange Act rules were adopted pursuant to the Sarbanes-Oxley Act which require that a company's periodic reports filed under the Exchange Act contain certifications by the principal executive and financial officers as to the truth and fairness of the company's reports and the adequacy of internal control over financial reporting.

In addition, pursuant to the Sarbanes-Oxley Act the rules of the US national securities exchanges and associations must prohibit the listing of any security of an issuer unless the issuer's board of directors and key committees are comprised in a manner that is designed to provide an objective oversight role and directors and management adhere to high standards of conduct.

New York Stock Exchange rules

While each exchange or stock market in the US will have its own requirements, the NYSE rules will be focused on here.

Independence of majority of board members

The NYSE Manual requires the board of directors of each listed company to consist of a majority of independent directors. Pursuant to Section 303A(2), no director would qualify as "independent" unless the board affirmatively determines that the director has no material relationship with the company. The NYSE rule tightens the definition of independent director by prohibiting many relationships that otherwise could impair the independence of directors, such as employment, business, financial, and family relationships.

Application to foreign private issuers

NYSE Section 303A permits NYSE-listed companies that are foreign private issuers to follow home country practice in lieu of the new requirements, except that such companies are required to: (1) have an audit committee that satisfies certain home country listing or legal provisions (as further described in Rule 10A-3); (2) notify the NYSE in writing after any executive officer becomes aware of any non-compliance with any applicable provision; and (3) provide a brief, general summary of the significant ways in which its governance differs from those followed by domestic companies under NYSE listing standards. Listed foreign private issuers are permitted to provide this disclosure either on their website (provided it is in the English language and accessible from the US) and/or in their annual report as distributed to shareholders in the US in accordance with the NYSE Manual.

Compensation / nominating / corporate governance committees

In addition to a compensation committee, each listed company is also required to have a nominating / corporate governance committee composed entirely of independent directors.

Audit committee

Each NYSE-listed company must have a minimum three-person audit committee composed entirely of directors that meet the independence standards. In addition, each member of the audit committee must be financially literate and at least one member of the audit committee is also required to have accounting or related financial management expertise.

Corporate governance guidelines / code of ethics

The NYSE Manual also requires each listed company to adopt and disclose corporate governance guidelines. These are to address director qualification standards; director responsibilities; director access to management and, as necessary and appropriate, independent advisors; director compensation; director orientation and continuing education; management succession; and annual performance evaluation of the board. Each listed company must also adopt and disclose a code of business conduct and ethics for directors, officers and employees, and promptly disclose any waivers of the code for directors or executive officers.

CEO certification of corporate governance listing standards

The CEO of each listed company must certify to the NYSE each year that he or she is not aware of any violation by the company of the NYSE's corporate governance listing standards. This certification is required to be disclosed in the company's annual report. In addition, the CEO of each listed company must promptly notify the NYSE in writing after any executive officer of the listed company becomes aware of any material non-compliance with any applicable provisions of the requirements.

Nasdaq rules

The Nasdaq rules are largely similar in scope and effect to those of NYSE.

State law requirements – Delaware

State statute and common law play a very significant role in determining the corporate governance rules applicable to a particular US company. Since many companies are organized in Delaware due to the ease of organizing in Delaware and the developed corporate law there, such law is described below. The Delaware General Corporation Law (the "GCL") sets forth powers and responsibilities for boards of directors. GCL Section 141(a) provides that the business and affairs of every company shall be managed under the direction of the board of directors, except as otherwise provided in the company's certificate of incorporation.

Implications on M&A transactions

Sarbanes-Oxley Act implications

The Sarbanes-Oxley Act does not explicitly mention M&A transactions but it is expected that the Act will nevertheless change the way most public companies engage in mergers and acquisitions. While the full extent of the changes may not yet be appreciated due to the novelty of the new regulatory framework, the certification and reporting requirements of Sections 302 and 404 will be of immediate consequence as they apply to the entire company, including acquisitions. As described above, Section 404 requires most public companies to certify annually that their internal control system is designed and operating effectively and Section 302 requires quarterly certifications of the financial statements and disclosure controls and procedures by CEOs and CFOs. The practical effect is that companies will have to include acquired entities in their Section 302 assessment beginning with the first quarter in which the acquisition closes and in their 404 assessment beginning at the first year-end after acquisition.

The corporate governance implications of the rules enacted under the Sarbanes-Oxley Act affect M&A strategy in these ways:

- The timing of the Section 302 and 404 certification and reporting requirements may cause the postponement of closing on deals that otherwise would have been ready to close; and
- Failure of a company to properly coordinate its response to Sections 302 and 404 or to assess and correct a weak control environment could jeopardize the credibility of management and could also negatively impact share price or lead to enforcement actions by the SEC.

Obligations in a takeover situation

As described above, state statutes, court decisions and US federal laws and regulations as well as rules of any applicable national securities exchange or association delineate certain specific obligations for directors. The generally accepted duties of directors according to Delaware common law are fiduciary duties of care and loyalty.

Duty of care

In the M&A context, where decisions are necessarily significant to the company, the time devoted to establish that the duty of care was applied is increased and substantial diligence is required. Due care requires directors to inform themselves of all reasonably available material information prior to making a business decision and to act in good faith to make prudent, considered and informed choices.

Duty of loyalty

Directors also owe the company and its stockholders a duty of loyalty to give higher priority to corporate interests than to personal interests in making business decisions. If a director has a personal interest in a matter, it must be fully disclosed and that director will likely need to abstain from voting on or participating in discussions of the matter.

Business judgment rule

Under the business judgment rule, which is applied by courts to most decisions made by directors, the decisions of disinterested directors are presumed to be appropriate absent evidence that the directors did not act in good faith or were not reasonably informed, or that there is no rational business purpose for the decision that promotes the interests of the company or its stockholders. One way for directors to show they exercised due care and should get the benefit of the business judgment rule is for them to obtain a fairness opinion by a reputable third party that a transaction is fair to the company and its stockholders from a financial standpoint.

Corporate governance procedures in M&A context

The Delaware GCL provides that the board of directors of each corporation which desires to merge or consolidate must adopt a resolution approving an agreement of merger or consolidation and must declare its advisability. The agreement must then be submitted to and approved by a majority of the stockholders of each constituent corporation. Note that a Delaware company may specify in its certificate of incorporation or by-laws a requirement for a supermajority vote (typically requiring the affirmative vote of 66 2/3% of stockholders) for a merger or asset sale.

Major differences between public and privately held company

The negotiation of a public deal involves fiduciary and disclosure considerations that are inapplicable to a private setting. Traditionally under state law, the directors' main fiduciary duty is to shareholders. In the noteworthy case *Revlon Inc. v. MacAndrews & Forbes Holdings*, the court described the role of the board of directors as that of a price-oriented neutral auctioneer once a decision has been made to sell the company. This has the effect of limiting a board's ability to favor one buyer over another that would not apply to most sales of private companies. In addition, unlike the sale of a public company, the structure, timing, financing, and negotiation of a private company sale is not affected by the federal and national securities exchange or association regulations. Further, most material aspects of a proposed transaction involving a public US company quickly become public information.

Overview of corporate governance in Germany

Meaning of the term "corporate governance" in Germany

There is no generally accepted view as to the exact meaning of the term "corporate governance." Different explanations stress different aspects of its meaning. However, it is widely accepted that good corporate governance is a legal and practical organizational framework which leads to responsible corporate management and control aimed at creating long-term added value.

Rules on corporate governance

Statutory provisions

International investors often complain about the lack of transparency of German corporate governance. It is indeed true that the German corporate governance rules are scattered about numerous acts and are not always easy to find in these acts.

The basic rules for the two most important legal forms of companies can be found in the Stock Corporation Act (*Aktiengesetz*) and in the Limited Liability Company Act (*GmbH-Gesetz*). Rules on accounting and auditing are set forth in the Commercial Code (*Handelsgesetzbuch*). The Securities Trading Act (*Wertpapierhandelsgesetz*) contains rules concerning insider trading and the disclosure of insider information, the Takeover Act (*Wertpapiererwerbs- und Übernahmegesetz*) duties for management boards in takeover situations, and the Stock Exchange Listing Ordinance (*Börsenzulassungsverordnung*) as well as the stock exchange rules set out additional disclosure requirements. Other statues set forth further corporate governance rules.

Another major criticism leveled from the international community against German corporate governance is the two-tier system of management board and supervisory board for stock corporations. However, it could just as easily be argued that separation of the supervisors from the supervisees is a good idea.

Corporate Governance Code

As a response to the criticism of the German statutory rules on corporate governance, Germany introduced a Corporate Governance Code in 2002. The code sets out the main statutory corporate governance provisions in one document. Also, it contains recommendations and suggestions on good corporate governance practice.

The code was drawn up by the government commission "German Corporate Governance Code" chaired by Gerhard Cromme. Its recommendations and suggestions are not binding, but only "soft law." However, the Stock Corporation Act requires the yearly disclosure of all recommendations of the code which are not being complied with by listed stock corporations.

The German Corporate Governance Code is regarded by the German government as a success and the listed stock corporations follow its recommendations to a substantial extent. Each year the Cromme Commission reviews whether it is appropriate to amend the code.

Implications on M&A transactions

Restrictions for due diligence reviews

If target is a stock corporation

Due diligence reviews at stock corporations raise several legal issues. One problem is whether the management board may permit a potential acquirer to conduct a due diligence review of the company although the management board is bound by a statutory confidentiality obligation on behalf of the company. Since the management board can be held personally liable and might even be subject to criminal prosecution if it breaches its confidentiality obligation, this becomes a difficult issue.

The prevailing view is that the due diligence must not only be in the interest of the shareholders but also in the interest of the company and that the members of the management board have to weigh the pros and cons of the sales process. An interest of the company could be strategic, e.g. becoming part of a larger group of companies, or financial, e.g. gaining access to a source of equity.

It is in any event required to take safeguards to ensure that the information about the company is kept confidential as far as possible. Thus, a confidentiality agreement with the potential buyer is mandatory. Also, the management must assure that there is no uncontrolled dissemination of information to the potential buyer. Rather, a data room should be set up and there should be a data room supervisor present in the data room who procures that the documents in the data room are not removed or copied.

Further, the potential buyer needs to be seriously interested in the acquisition. Normally, the signing of a letter of intent is required to substantiate this. The management board should pass a unanimous resolution approving the due diligence. If appropriate, it is also a good idea to procure the approval of the supervisory board.

A due diligence review at a listed stock corporation also raises insider trading and ad-hoc publication issues (as discussed below).

If target is a limited liability company

Due diligence reviews at limited liability companies are less problematic. Here, it is sufficient that the interests of the selling shareholders prevail over the confidentiality interests of the company. It is advisable for the managing directors, however, to procure a shareholders' resolution approving the due diligence.

Obligations in a takeover situation

In the event of a takeover offer regarding a listed stock corporation, the management board and supervisory board of the target must submit a statement commenting on the offer. This is supposed to help the shareholders to make an informed decision whether they wish to accept the offer.

In general, the management board may not take any actions which could frustrate the success of the offer following its public announcement. There are some statutory exemptions to this rule: the managing board may (i) take actions in the ordinary course of business, (ii) search for a competing bid (a "white knight"), and (iii) take measures which the target's supervisory board or the target's general meeting has authorized.

The corporate governance code suggests that the management board convenes in appropriate cases an extraordinary general meeting at which shareholders can discuss the takeover offer and decide on defensive measures.

Required participation of shareholders

General rules

As a rule, the shareholders of a stock corporation do not participate in the management of the company. The management board alone is in charge of running the business.

However, the articles of association or the rules of procedure for the management board can and regularly do provide that the management requires the approval of the supervisory board in certain M&A scenarios, e.g. the sale of a business unit or a subsidiary.

Also, the board may request that the shareholders of the stock corporation decide upon a transaction. Given the costs involved in calling a general meeting, in particular if the company is listed, such requests should be and are kept to a minimum.

In a landmark decision of 1982 (*Holzmüller*), the German Supreme Court held that there are certain transactions affecting shareholders' rights in such a substantial way that the management board has to obtain the approval of the shareholders although the management is formally empowered to act on its own.

In subsequent decisions in 2004 (*Gelatine*), the court clarified the highly debated quantitative criteria of the test if such approval requirement exists. Fortunately, it strengthened the rights of the management by clarifying that cases in which the shareholders have to be asked for their consent are extreme exceptions. This has made conducting M&A transactions in Germany easier.

With respect to limited liability companies, the situation is different. Here, shareholder approval is required for all major transactions. This is, however, normally not an issue since a limited liability company typically has only one or a few shareholders.

Mergers, share and asset deals

The German Transformation Act (*Umwandlungsgesetz*) requires that the shareholders of companies which are parties to a merger agreement approve the merger with a majority of 75%.

The articles of association of a limited liability company may restrict the transferability of the shares in the company so that a share deal can only be executed if the company approves it. In addition, a shareholders' resolution might be required. This is a typical due diligence item.

Shareholder approval is further required if a company wants to enter into an agreement to sell all or almost all of its assets. This is obvious for the limited liability company because such transaction is necessarily a major one, but shareholder approval with a majority of 75% is also required for the stock corporation. The Stock Corporation Act contains an explicit provision to this extent.

Insider trading and ad hoc-publications in connection with M&A transactions

In October 2004, the German rules on insider trading were tightened. Now, more facts and more persons are subject to the insider trading rules.

The term "insider information" is defined in the Securities Trading Act as specific information on facts which are not in the public domain, which refer to issuers of listed securities or listed securities and which is capable of influencing the market price of such securities considerably.

The issuer of listed securities is required to publish insider information pertaining to it without undue delay (so-called "ad-hoc publication"). The issuer can decide to postpone an ad-hoc publication (i) if this is in its legitimate interest, (ii) if the public is not mislead, (iii) as long as the issuer can assure that the insider information is kept confidential, e.g. by a confidentiality agreement, and (iv) if the issuer publishes the information as soon as it is no longer in its legitimate interest to keep it confidential.

If the issuer or a person acting on its behalf discloses insider information to a third party which is not bound by a confidentiality obligation, an immediate ad-hoc publication is required and there is no exception to this rule. All persons which are in the possession of insider information have to refrain from using it for the acquisition or sale of the securities to which the information relates, from recommending to others the acquisition or sale of such securities and from disclosing such information to third parties.

These rules are in several ways relevant for M&A transactions:

- If a company plans to acquire the shares in or assets of a listed company, this plan is already insider information. The acquisition in the pursuit of this plan is nevertheless permitted although the wording of the insider trading rules might suggest a different result. However, if the buyer changes its plan in light of the due diligence results, e.g. now wants to acquire more shares or assets than originally planned, this can be unlawful insider trading.

- The same is true if not the buyer itself but a person acting on its behalf acquires the shares for the buyer (so-called "warehousing"), provided that the actual buyer has no economic benefit from such acquisitions.

- If a buyer performs a due diligence review, it might discover in the course of such due diligence insider information. Is it now necessary for it to refrain from the acquisition? Again, the wording of the rules might suggest this. However, if the seller has the same information and the buyer acquires the assets or shares in a face-to-face transaction, it is not appropriate to qualify such transaction as insider trading.

- The management of the target does not violate the insider trading rules if it permits the buyer to perform a due diligence review, even if this means that the buyer will acquire insider information, provided that a confidentiality agreement is signed.

- Since the planning of an acquisition is a longer process, the question arises at which point in time a listed buyer has to issue an ad-hoc publication if it plans to acquire another company. In general, this is already the case if its managing board has decided to pursue the transaction, regardless of the supervisory board's approval. However, it should normally be possible to postpone the disclosure as explained above.

- If a listed company learns that it will be the target of a hostile takeover, an immediate ad-hoc publication is required. In the event of a friendly takeover, the target has also the duty to issue an ad-hoc publication if it is not possible for the target to delay such publication based on a legitimate interest.

If there are already rumors in the market regarding an imminent takeover offer, both bidder and target (if listed) are required to issue an ad-hoc publication.

4.3 Stock Markets

4.3.1 Application and Impact of U.S. Capital Markets Law on Public Tender Offers Under the Security Purchase and Take-over Act

Stephan Oppenhoff and Dirk Horcher

This article deals with the question to what extent U.S. capital markets law applies to German takeover offers. Afterwards, the principal requirements of U.S.-American law regarding such a tender offer are illustrated and relief available under U.S. law is described. Finally, the article discusses in which cases U.S. shareholders can be excluded from the public tender offer according to Sec. 24 WpÜG.

Tender offers under the German Security Purchase and Take-over Act (Wertpapiererwerbs- und Übernahmegesetz, hereinafter "WpÜG") with a German target company and a German offeror are no longer a domestic matter ruled only by German law. On the one hand, the globalization of financial markets has led to an increasingly internationally diverse shareholder structure of German companies. On the other hand, the announcement of tender offers and the publication of the offer document on the Internet make the offer accessible around the world. The German tender offer, therefore, will almost inevitably be affected by foreign legal systems.

Application of U.S. law

U.S.-American securities law may apply to capital market transactions of foreign issuers where American interests are concerned. The extensive application of U.S.-American capital markets law and the far reaching authority of the U.S. Securities and Exchange Commission ("SEC") is heavily influenced by the wish to protect U.S. shareholders. In general, German commentators resign to the view that public tender offers made to shareholders located in the United States are subject to the U.S. capital markets law, even if the target company is based abroad and its shares are listed on a foreign stock exchange.

Whether such an extensive application of U.S.-American law to extraterritorial facts can be justified under general conflict of laws' provisions is not given consideration by the SEC. The so-called "Final Rule: Cross-Border Tender and Exchange Offers, Business Combinations and Rights Offerings"[1], which was adopted by the SEC and became effective in 2000, does not mention this matter, although the release deals with the topic of cross-border tender offers. The release (hereinafter "Cross-Border Rule") instead tries to reduce the requirements set by U.S. law with regard to such tender offers by establishing exemptions.

---

[1] Securities Act Release No. 7759, available at: www.sec.gov/rules/final/33-7759.htm

According to the principles of U.S.-American case law, U.S. securities laws are applicable exterritorially if an action in the United States is not only of preparatory nature for other actions abroad, the so-called "conduct test," or if conduct outside the United States has had a substantial adverse effect in the United States, in particular on American investors or securities markets, the so-called "effects test." U.S. courts have not yet proposed any clear guidance as to what constitutes as a "substantial adverse effect" in terms of the "effects test" which is – as a rule – the main link for German public tender offers. The conduct test's requirement that the action has a close relation to U.S. territory should be an exception in case of German public tender offers.

A "substantial adverse effect" was assumed in case of a placing of shares of a Canadian company that was listed on a U.S. stock exchange to the French majority shareholder significantly below value, in the case of a take-over bid of a Luxembourg bidder concerning shares of a British company in which U.S. shareholders had invested in 2.5% of the capital with a market value US$ 120 Mio. in form of shares and American Depositary Receipts (hereinafter "ADRs"), as well as in the case of a fraudulent securities' placing of a Canadian company in which 22 U.S. shareholders purchased a total of 41.936 shares despite being expressly excluded from the offer.

A "substantial adverse effect" was rejected in the case of a public tender offer of a Canadian offeror concerning shares of a Canadian company under exclusion of U.S.-shareholders who had invested in 12% of the shares, in the case of a public tender offer of a British offeror for a British target company in which U.S.-Shareholders who held 1.6% of the capital in form of ADRs were excluded six days after the announcement of the offer as well as in the case of the subscription of a capital increase of a Bahamas domiciled company by a Luxembourg investment fund in which 300 U.S.-Americans had participated with 0.5% of the fund's capital, worth 3 Mio. US$.

In light of these precedents it is fair to say that under the "effects test" U.S. Security laws will not apply if U.S. shareholders are completely excluded from the offer which is from a U.S. perspective a foreign offer for a foreign target company. In case of fraudulent conduct, however, the U.S.-American anti-fraud rules, that as a rule apply more extensively, would still apply. As the U.S. Court of Appeals case "Bersch v. Drexel Firestone" illustrates, the exemption of U.S. shareholders from a tender offer does not always lead to an exclusion of U.S.-American law.

On the other hand it is unclear, to what extent U.S. capital markets law may otherwise apply. The term "substantial adverse effect" can be interpreted to mean that not every small participation held by U.S. shareholders should be sufficient, but only those that are of a certain absolute or relative significance. Nevertheless, some legal uncertainty remains.

Requirements set by U.S. law for public tender offers

U.S. Federal law, in particular Federal Securities Laws are applicable – as opposed to State regulations – if a transaction involves the use of the mail or other means of communication in interstate commerce. The use of such "US jurisdictional means" is generously assumed if security holders of the target company are domiciled in the United States.

Sec. 14(e) of the Securities Exchange Act (1934) and Regulation 14E[1] as released by the SEC are always applicable regardless of the consideration offered to target company's shareholders and whether the target company's shares are listed on a U.S. stock exchange:

The offeror shall hold the tender offer open for a minimum of 20 business days. The public tender offer also has to remain open for at least further 10 business days after amending the scope of the offer, i.e. an increase or decrease of the number of securities covered by the offer, or of the consideration offered. Furthermore, the extension of the tender offer period shall be published no later than 9 a.m. of the business day following the scheduled expiration date of the offer. The consideration has to be paid promptly after the acceptance period has expired. In addition, the offeror may purchase, or arrange to purchase, shares of the target company only as part of the tender offer from the time of its public announcement until its expiration. The offer document does not, however, have to be filed with the SEC before its public announcement. Finally, the target company shall no later than 10 business days from the date the tender offer is first published issue a statement in relation to the tender offer.

If the offer is aimed at the purchase of so-called "registered securities" the additional requirements of Sec. 14(d) of the Securities Exchange Act (1934) and Regulation 14D apply. The offeror is in particular obliged to file Schedule TO with the SEC no later than the day of the offer's public announcement or any other disclosure of the offer. The Schedule TO has to contain an offer document which is distributed to the target's shareholders. The SEC's practice requires that the offeror's annual accounts have to be included in the Schedule TO unless (a) the only consideration offered is cash, (b) the offer is not subject to any financing condition and (c) either (i) the offeror is a public reporting company under U.S. disclosure provisions or (ii) the offer is for all outstanding securities of the target company. All written communications relating to the tender offer, from and including the first public announcement, are filed with the SEC under cover of Schedule TO. Sec. 14(d)(5) of the Securities Act (1934) gives the shareholder the right to withdraw from its acceptance of the offer within seven days of the offer documents being published. Rule 14d-7 extends this right to withdraw to any period during which the offer remains open. Rule 14d-10 determines that the tender offer shall be open to all security holders of the class of securities subject to the tender offer and that the consideration paid to any security holder pursuant to the tender offer shall be equal to the highest consideration paid to any other security holder during such tender offer. Finally, the target company shall provide the SEC with a statement regarding the offer including Schedule 14D-9 within 10 business days and shall distribute this statement to the shareholders.

In the case of an exchange offer, the provisions of Sec. 5 of the Securities Act (1933) also have to be observed. This rule provides for the preparation of a registration statement which is submitted to the SEC for audit. On the basis of SEC's previous audit practice, the procedure can take up to 3 months and the registration process can lead to serious delays.

---

[1] All U.S. acts, regulations and rules mentioned in this essay are available at: www.law.uc.edu/CCL/xyz/ sldtoc.html

4.3.2 Delisting – the US and the German Perspective

Robert Ripin and Volker Geyrhalter

Where there are companies listed on a stock exchange, there will be strategic reasons for the company to consider delisting from the exchange. Typically, delisting is not an end in itself, but is a step in a process to achieve a particular management goal. This article analyzes recent developments in both Germany and the United States regarding delisting. In Germany, delisting has been the focus of an important court case impacting the requirements of a formal delisting. In the last several years Germany has seen a number of going private transactions initiated by majority shareholders, in particular, private equity investors, after the acquisition of a majority stake in a listed company for strategic and legal reasons. In the United States, delisting has been focused on recently in the context of non-US companies looking to withdraw from the US trading market following the enactment of the Sarbanes-Oxley Act of 2002 and the resulting additional burdens on non-US companies in complying with US securities laws.

The US perspective

Given the access to capital enjoyed by companies with a US public listing, one might ask why it might be preferable to delist prior to or contemporaneously with a contemplated M&A transaction where a non-listed, non-US company merges with or acquires a company with a US listing. While the US listing requirements are not particularly onerous, due to the regulatory burdens that attend US reporting and corporate governance required in connection with an ongoing listing, there are many circumstances under which a non-US company might want to be delisted from a US national securities exchange or NASDAQ and, following the delisting, to remove itself from the reporting requirements of the US Securities Exchange Act of 1934, as amended (the *"Exchange Act"*). Set forth below is a discussion of the regulatory overlay and practical process of delisting and de-registering in the United States.

US securities laws

Any company that has a class of securities listed on a national securities exchange (such as the New York Stock Exchange (the *"NYSE"*)) or quoted on NASDAQ, which for this purpose, will be referred to as a listing, must register that class under the Exchange Act and thereafter comply with US reporting requirements under the Exchange Act. The Exchange Act also imposes a separate registration requirement on companies whose equity securities are widely-held in the United States, even if the securities are not listed on a US exchange. As described in greater detail below, under the Exchange Act, if a non-US issuer's equity securities are held of record by 500 or more persons worldwide (and more than 300 in the United States) and it had total assets exceeding US$10 million on the last day of its most recent fiscal year, the issuer must register the class of securities. For this purpose, an issuer will have to look through the holdings of banks, brokers, dealers or nominees for any of them to determine the number of US holders.

Implications of Sarbanes-Oxley

While there can be significant benefits to being listed on a US stock exchange or quoted on NASDAQ, there are significant costs and burdens associated with the related reporting and corporate governance requirements under the Exchange Act. The adoption of rules under the Sarbanes-Oxley Act of 2002 has led to dramatic increases in the costs and burdens of having a listing in the United States. Strict new reporting and certification obligations have been imposed on public companies in the United States. The Sarbanes-Oxley Act also required the implementation of rules regulating internal corporate organization and procedures for US publicly traded companies, including non-US issuers. Previously, the US Securities and Exchange Commission (the "SEC") had left the internal regulation of corporate practices and procedures to local state regulation (for US companies) and non-US regulation (for non-US companies). Some of the obligations imposed on publicly traded companies pursuant to Sarbanes-Oxley include:

- Requirements for assessment of internal control over financial reporting;
- Requirements for a CEO/CFO certification of documents filed with the SEC;
- Requirements for a bonus and incentive compensation (including trading gains on shares) forfeiture when financial statements are restated due to misconduct;
- Prohibitions on insider loans;
- Prohibitions on improper influence on audit activities;
- Requirements on the composition of the audit committee;
- Requirements for a code of ethics for financial executives and audit committee financial expert (comply or disclose reasons for not doing so);
- Enhanced financial reporting requirements, including disclosure of off-balance sheet arrangements; and
- Restrictions on executive trading during pension fund blackout periods applicable to US employees.

While the SEC attempted to take the concerns and local practices of non-US issuers into account when enacting the rules implementing the Sarbanes-Oxley Act, many non-US issuers have felt that the rules are still excessive and burdensome. This is particularly true of non-US issuers who did not voluntarily choose to enter the US public market, but, through a merger with a company listed on a US stock exchange or on NASDAQ, now find themselves with a US listing that they believe has little strategic benefit. Non-US companies who find themselves in this position due to mergers with a listed non-US company may seek to delist from the US market. What these companies often find surprising is that they will remain subject to most of the Exchange Act/Sarbanes-Oxley Act requirements even when they have delisted in the United States.

The costs of complying with the Sarbanes-Oxley Act can be high, both in monetary terms and in terms of the man-hours required to comply. One issuer which recently delisted from the NYSE and deregistered under the Exchange Act estimated that its compliance costs in relation to its US listing would be approximately $7.75 million in its first year and approximately $5.6 million annually thereafter. Perhaps more troubling is the amount of management time taken up with Sarbanes-Oxley matters, time which some companies would argue can no longer be devoted to building shareholder value. One of the SEC Commissioners indicated a concern that the Sarbanes-Oxley Act might cause companies to put business initiatives on hold due to the management time required for compliance. Although one can not draw a direct line between the burdens of compliance with the US securities laws following the enactment of the Sarbanes-Oxley Act and the trend of non-US issuers either avoiding the US market or exiting the market, one Commissioner noted that as of the end of 2003, over 1,200 non-US companies from 57 countries filed reports with the SEC. This number is three times the number of non-US companies that filed reports in 1990, but is down nearly 100 from a year before. The number of issuers from Germany fell from 28 to 24 in the same time period.

Delisting

Delisting from a US stock market is a fairly simple process. In order to delist from the NYSE, an issuer's board of directors (equivalent to a German company's supervisory board for this purpose) must approve the delisting and the issuer must furnish a certified copy of the relevant board resolution to the NYSE.

Delisting from NASDAQ is even more easily accomplished. An issuer may voluntarily terminate its quotation on NASDAQ upon written notice to NASDAQ from an executive officer of the Company which should be received at least 48 hours prior to the time of the desired delisting.

Deregistration

As mentioned earlier, although delisting is a relatively simple process and will end a company's obligation to comply with those corporate governance requirements imposed by the stock exchange or stock market as mandated by the Sarbanes-Oxley Act, delisting will not exempt a company from the ongoing reporting requirements under the Exchange Act or the corporate governance requirements imposed directly through the Rules under the Exchange Act. To avoid these requirements, an issuer must not only delist its securities, but must also deregister the class of securities under the Exchange Act, which is a much more difficult process.

A non-US company with a security registered under the Exchange Act may terminate the registration by filing with the SEC a certification that the relevant class of securities is held of record by either (a) less than 300 US residents or (b) less than 500 US residents where the total assets of the issuer have not exceeded US$10,000,000 on the last day of each of the issuer's last three fiscal years. The company's duty to file reports under the Exchange Act is suspended immediately upon its filing the certification with the SEC; however, if the certification is later withdrawn or denied, the company must file all reports which would have otherwise been required within 60 days after such withdrawal or denial.

The options in the M&A context for companies that wish to de-register but have too many US holders to immediately de-register is for the registered company to undertake some form of transaction or procedure, such as a tender offer, reverse stock split, or court or administrative procedure, in each case aimed at reducing the number of security holders overall or reducing the US ownership in a targeted manner. However, these procedures may be time consuming and expensive for a company and, in the end, do not have the certainty of success that a company may want. This has frustrated various non-US companies and may act as a disincentive for non-US companies who are considering a listing in the United States. The SEC has signaled to the market that it is currently considering liberalizing the ability of foreign private issuers to de-register. The then-chairman of the SEC publicly stated in early 2005 that relaxation of the 300-shareholder rule is under "serious consideration." While the SEC has not yet put out a proposal on this subject, one is expected by or before 2006. The proposal will likely be a balance between non-US companies' ability to come into and go out of the US market as they wish and the SEC's desire to provide adequate shareholder protection by ensuring that those companies with a significant market presence continue to report and comply with the Sarbanes-Oxley Act provisions.

The German perspective

Reasons for delisting

A delisting in Germany is typically pursued by listed companies and/or their majority shareholder for the following reasons:

- Certain publication and notification obligations, i.e. for ad hoc publicity (see § 15 of the German Securities Trading Act), only apply to listed companies and the delisting of a company limits the transparency and disclosure obligations;

- Costs are incurred by the listed company in relation to the listing and such costs could be saved by a delisting;

- Only German companies organised in the legal form of a stock corporation (*Aktiengesellschaft*) or a partnership limited by shares (*Kommanditgesellschaft auf Aktien*) qualify for a listing. Certain corporate restrictions only apply to these companies but not e.g. to a GmbH. This applies for example to the following restrictions impacting LBO transactions: (i) on the grant of upstream securities and (ii) the access to the cash flows of the company, which are in both cases more restrictive for companies organised as stock corporations (see § 57 of the German Stock Corporation Act) than for a GmbH. In addition, the change of legal form can create tax benefits in certain situations. The decision of the majority shareholder to change the company's form can also form a reason for a going private transaction.

- Only listed companies fall within the scope of the German Takeover Act (*WpÜG*). Thus, a delisting could serve as a protective action against a hostile takeover by a new investor. This could be a reason to apply for a delisting in cases in which the stock price does not reflect the actual value of the company and the company has no realistic chance to raise further capital by way of a secondary issuance.

Methods of delisting

A German listed company may go private in one of two ways:

- a "formal delisting" from the stock exchange which requires that the listed company applies to be delisted in a formal administrative procedure under the regime of the stock exchange, or
- a "cold delisting" which involves using a "squeeze-out" procedure or measures under the German Reorganisation Act (*Umwandlungsgesetz*), including a going private merger or a going private conversion, the effect of which is to end up with a corporate vehicle which does not qualify for a listing.

Formal delisting

If a "formal delisting" is sought, an application for withdrawal from the relevant stock exchange is filed with the admission office of the relevant regional stock exchange which is obliged to take into account possible investor protection concerns. However, the eight German regional stock exchanges have each implemented the investor protection provided for in Section 38 (4) of the German Stock Exchange Act (*Börsengesetz*) in a different way. In March 2002 the Frankfurt Stock Exchange ("FSE") introduced a special procedure making it possible for a company to withdraw from the FSE without making a cash offer. It was considered sufficient if the shareholders have a certain time period (six months) to dispose of their shares on the FSE after the notification of the pending delisting. This amendment was aimed at making the procedure for delisting from the FSE much simpler and faster. The Munich Stock Exchange ("MSE") implemented a similar rule. The other German regional stock exchanges did not follow suit and continue to permit a delisting only if a cash offer has been made based on the average price of the shares for the previous three or six months respectively.

Partial delisting

The foregoing does not apply to cases in which only a partial delisting is sought by the issuer, e.g. in which a listing at another German or recognised foreign stock exchange continues. In this case the investor protection rules do not apply as the shareholders could still trade their shares at the remaining stock exchange. The same is true for a change of the trading segment.

Impact of the Macrotron decision

In the "Macrotron" judgment issued in February 2003 the Federal Supreme Court ruled that in the course of a delisting it is imperative that the minority shareholders are offered a cash payment based on the company's actual value. It ruled that neither the time limits stipulated by the FSE and the MSE nor the compensation payments required by the remaining German regional stock exchanges provided adequate investor protection and were therefore insufficient. The Federal Supreme Court maintained that the FSE's and the MSE's procedures were inadequate because their stipulated time limits do not allow shareholders to realise their investment since a company's share price usually falls immediately after notification of a pending delisting. The same applies to the provisions of the other German regional stock exchanges. According to the Federal Supreme Court, a cash offer linked to the average share price does not grant sufficient investor protection because the average share price does not necessarily reflect the actual value of the company. The Federal Supreme Court has therefore ruled that adequate investor protection exists only if a mandatory cash offer based on the company's actual value is made either by the company or by the majority shareholder. Where the average share price is higher than the compensation derived from the independent valuation, the average share price is used.

Reaction by the regional stock exchanges

Although the Federal Supreme Court ruled that none of the investor protection provisions of the eight German stock exchanges offers sufficient protection, none of the German stock exchanges has amended its rules to comply with the judgement. The procedure for a "formal delisting" is an administrative procedure and the Federal Supreme Court does not have jurisdiction to declare the rules of the German stock exchanges null and void. Only the administrative courts are entitled to challenge their rules. Currently, no case challenging the rules of the German stock exchanges is pending so the existing rules of the German stock exchanges are still applicable. The Federal Supreme Court's jurisdiction is limited to determining the corporate requirements for a "formal delisting" which does not have a direct impact vis-à-vis the respective stock exchanges. Recent information received from some of the German stock exchanges indicates that the procedure for a "formal delisting" is still being considered by the stock exchanges on the basis of the existing rules. It would still be possible, therefore, for a "formal delisting" to be concluded even if the requirements set forth in the "Macrotron" judgement are not fulfilled. As the procedure for a "formal delisting" is an administrative procedure, the German stock exchanges are not concerned to check whether the corporate requirements for the delisting are met. It is not clear whether the (minority) shareholders are entitled to challenge the delisting decision of a German stock exchange in an administrative procedure on the grounds that the corporate requirements for the delisting have not been met.

Obligations of management

The management board of a listed company is, however, obliged to act in compliance with all applicable corporate rules. If the management board of a listed company applies for a "formal delisting" and the corporate requirements set forth in the "Macrotron" judgement are not met, this could be considered a breach of the management board's obligations and entitle (minority) shareholders to damage claims.

Methods of a "cold delisting"

A "cold delisting" is a corporate reorganisation of a listed company with the effect that it ends up in a corporate form which does not qualify for a listing. With the consummation of such reorganisation the listing of the company ends automatically. Following is a discussion of the various methods to achieve a cold delisting.

Going private conversion

Pursuant to a shareholder meeting a listed company can resolve with a majority of 75% of the votes to change the legal form into i.e. the legal form of a GmbH or a GmbH & Co. KG (limited partnership). The majority shareholder has to offer the minority shareholders cash compensation for their shares based on an independent valuation of the company (not necessarily identical to the average stock price during a certain time period) payable in the event the minority shareholders decide to surrender their shares. The conversion becomes effective with its registration in the commercial register and upon such registration the company is automatically delisted. Upon the effectiveness of the conversion the minority shareholders who have not accepted the cash offer become shareholders in the GmbH or limited partners in the GmbH & Co. KG, as the case may be.

Going private merger

The merger of a listed company into another company can also lead to a delisting if the acquiring company is not listed. The merger requires a shareholder resolution of both involved legal entities to be adopted with a majority of more than 75% of the votes. Further, the majority shareholder has to make a cash offer which is subject to the same requirements set forth above. The merger becomes effective with its registration in the commercial register and upon such registration the listed company ceases to exist and all assets of the listed company are transferred by virtue of law to the acquiring entity.

Squeeze-out

The right to conduct a squeeze out procedure was introduced on 1 January 2002 into the German Stock Corporation Act. If a majority shareholder owns 95% or more of the share capital of a listed stock corporation he is entitled to initiate a squeeze out procedure. The majority shareholder has to offer cash compensation to the minority shareholders for their shares based on an independent valuation. Again, the squeeze out becomes effective with its registration in the commercial register and, upon such registration all outstanding shares are transferred by operation of law to the majority shareholder.

Going private liquidation

A further method to carry out a "cold delisting" is that (i) the listed company sells and transfers all of its assets in an arms' length asset deal transaction to a new company fully owned by the majority shareholder and (ii) thereafter resolves on the liquidation of the listed company. A transaction under which the company transfers all or substantially all of its assets requires a shareholder resolution with a 75% majority (§179a German Stock Corporation Act). After the expiration of a waiting period of one year the remaining assets (the purchase price received) are distributed on a pro rata basis to the shareholders. Upon the consummation of the liquidation the company no longer exists and is therefore no longer listed. The disadvantages associated with this method are that (i) the purchase price needs to fully reflect the value of the business and, thus, any potential hidden reserves need to be activated and (ii) the transfer of any real property, if any, would trigger real estate transfer tax.

Legal redress of minority shareholders

If a minority shareholder challenges the shareholder resolution, this constitutes a suspension for the registration and, thus, could delay the procedure. Challenging actions of minority shareholders are typically based on breaches of procedural rules or information rights. They cannot be based on the inadequacy of the cash compensation. Any dispute on the valuation will be considered in a special appraisal procedure (*Spruchverfahren*), which does not prevent the consummation of the measure. In case the challenging action is obviously unfounded and it is in the best interest of the company that the reorganisation is carried out without undue delay, the court can

Table 4.2 Length of going private transactions in Germany

Company	Method	Duration
Friedrich Grohe AG	Conversion	1 month
Honsel AG	Conversion	2 months
Rolf Benz AG	Conversion	2 months
Spinnerei und Weberei Momm AG	Conversion	4 months
BSU Beteiligungs AG	Conversion	8 months
Aesculap AG	Conversion	11 months
FPB Holding AG	Conversion	14 months
Schaerf AG	Conversion	16 months
Pfersee-Kolbermoor AG	Conversion	38 months
Average duration of going privates by way of Conversion		11 months
MAN Roland Druckmaschinen AG	Squeeze-out	2 months
Tempelhofer Feld AG für Grundstücks-verwertung	Squeeze-out	2 months
Anneliese Zementwerke AG	Squeeze-out	2 months
Entrium Direct Bankers AG	Squeeze-out	3 months
SPAR-Handels Aktiengesellschaft	Squeeze-out	3 months
SinnLeffers Aktiengesellschaft	Squeeze-out	4 months
GEA Aktiengesellschaft	Squeeze-out	9 months
debitel AG	Squeeze-out	9 months
Baden-Württembergische Bank AG	Squeeze-out	22 months
Average duration of going privates by way of Squeeze-out		6 months

decide upon the application of the company in a fast-track proceeding that a registration shall occur prior to a final decision in the litigation. It can take years before a final decision has been issued in litigation cases. In practice, the litigation on challenging actions is often settled amicably by payment to the minority shareholders. On average the duration for the consummation of the "cold delisting" from the date of the shareholder meeting until the registration in the commercial register can take up to one year. Table 4.2 gives a brief summary about the length of going private transactions carried out in Germany in the last years.

Conclusion

There are two recent major trends regarding going private transactions in Germany:

- Companies which were in financial difficulties and the share price of which have dropped to the level of penny stocks have decided that a listing was no longer of any commercial benefit. This applies in particular to companies which were listed on the former Neuer Markt. A delisting of these companies was often carried out as a "formal delisting" in particular pursuant to the provisions of the FSE without launching a cash offer. This applies e.g. to the going privates of Brokat Technologies AG, PixelNet AG, Bio Tissue Technologies AG, CompuGroup Holding AG and Saint Gobain Isover G + H AG.

- There have been a number of private equity driven LBO transactions in Germany, in which financial investors have acquired a majority stake in listed companies, thereafter launched a statutory cash offer and then conducted a "cold delisting" of the listed company. The preferred route was until the introduction of the squeeze-out the conversion of the listed company into a GmbH & Co. KG. Examples include the delisting of Honsel AG by Carlyle or the delisting of Grohe AG by BC Partners. Since the introduction of the squeeze-out and provided that a 95% ownership is achieved, the squeeze-out has become the preferred route.

After the landmark "Macrotron" decision the legal framework for the requirements for a "formal delisting" are rather unsettled. No major delisting transaction has been carried out since that date by way of a "formal delisting." All major going privates have been effected by way of a "cold delisting" usually done by way of a squeeze-out. As the requirements of a squeeze-out are clearly set forth in the German Stock Corporation Act, this procedure provides a relatively high transaction certainty and a quicker implementation compared to other methods.

4.4 Financing & Controlling

4.4.1 High Yield Bonds: A U.S. Product for German Financing Purposes

Raymond J. Fisher and Fabian Ehlers

The article is designed to familiarize the reader with the core principles of high yield financings as a vehicle for German medium-sized to large companies who do not have an investment-grade rating and who want to raise at least €100 to €150 million in debt financing. Such companies should have a relatively stable business model that will allow them to become locked into the covenants with little realistic possibility of refinancing for a four to five-year period.

Introduction

High yield bonds present a financing option for merger and acquisition transactions that should not be quickly overlooked. Sometimes misunderstood as "capital markets instruments with bank covenants," high yield bonds require the issuer to agree to restrictions on its business that will shape its growth until the bonds mature (7 or 10 years bullet maturity) or until the bonds can be repaid economically (four to five years). Unlike bank loan transactions, high yield bonds presuppose a certain level of independence from investors, an understanding that, as long as the issuer complies with its agreements under the notes, it is unlikely to require any direct contact with its investors. This understanding is fundamental to the structure of high yield covenants and their differences from covenants in bank lending transactions.

The term "high yield bonds" is generally used in contrast to investment grade corporate note offerings. In both the European and U.S. markets, investment grade companies can offer debt instruments on the capital markets with relative ease, especially when already known to the markets through an equity listing. These issuers benefit from a relative absence of covenants that will shape the way they conduct their business. But there is a broad range of worthy companies that find themselves unable to access this investment grade market. In particular, many companies that are newly merged or are in the process of being reshaped by a new investor will find it much easier to access the high yield market.

High yield's reputation as an American product no longer reflects the reality in Europe. Most recent German high yield bond offerings were conducted with little or no placement in the United States. Nonetheless, to ensure the most liquid secondary market possible, the documentation for these transactions is in English, and the governing law is New York. These bonds are typically listed in Luxembourg or Ireland.

Documentation

While high yield bonds offer the advantage of minimal ongoing investor contact, the initial offering is somewhat document-intensive. The key documents that are drafted and negotiated include the following:

- A "trust indenture" or "indenture," which is the New York-law document under which the bonds are issued. The indenture contains the detailed covenants and the other terms and conditions of the bonds. The indenture also sets out the responsibilities of the "indenture trustee" or "trustee," who is a passive agent of the bondholders and who is the channel of communication between the issuer and bondholders. Any guarantees of the bonds by subsidiaries or other related companies are also contained in the indenture.

- An "offering circular" or "prospectus," which is used to market the bonds. This detailed disclosure document contains, in addition to three years of financial statements and a detailed description of the bond terms, a detailed description of the business of the issuer, its management and shareholders, a textual explanation of its financial results and financial condition and a detailed discussion of the risks involved in purchasing the bond. It is, in scope and detail, very similar to an offering circular or prospectus used for IPOs and other equity capital-markets offerings. Since disclosure of material negative facts is required under the securities laws of most countries, the offering circular or prospectus functions as both a selling document and a document used to protect the company against investor claims of inadequate disclosure.

- A "purchase agreement" or "underwriting agreement." Following the marketing process, the managing banks will agree with the issuer on a price at which the bonds can be placed with investors. At that moment, the managing banks will sign an agreement with the issuer in which it agrees to purchase the specified amount, subject to certain conditions. Perhaps more importantly, the issuer agrees to indemnify the managing banks for claims that they may face under applicable securities laws for allegedly faulty disclosure.

The governing law for high yield documentation has traditionally been the law of the State of New York. Within the United States markets, New York law is widely trusted for strictly enforcing agreements between companies and their investors or lenders, with a minimum of judicial second-guessing of the intent of the parties. This level of investor trust in New York law seems to have become the norm in Europe as well; recent European high yield transactions that were marketed and sold wholly within Europe are nonetheless governed by New York law. English law, though less common, has been used successfully in some European transactions.

Nature of the relationship with investors: "Hands-off" is preferred

High yield bondholders, as passive capital-markets investors, typically hold and trade a large portfolio of bonds. They will often have no relationship to the issuer and may indeed be wholly unknown to the issuer. Ideally, the bondholders' monitoring role will be limited to reviewing the quarterly and annual financial statements and "compliance reports" that are distributed by the issuer and confirming periodically that the credit rating of the bonds has not been downgraded. In addition, bondholders are generally active participants in the quarterly investor call with the company. This arrangement implies a certain level of trust in the issuer, whose reports and annual financial statements are nonetheless reviewed and confirmed by its external auditors. It also implies that, once this trust is broken, it can be extremely hard or impossible ever to restore.

The bondholders in a high yield transaction are represented by the indenture trustee. So long as the company is in compliance with its obligations under the bonds, the trustee's role will be quite passive and will consist of little more than receiving reports from the issuer and passing them along to investors (generally simply through delivery to the appropriate clearing system) and facilitating any negotiated amendments to the indenture. Following a breach under the indenture that results in an "event of default," however, the role of the trustee changes; it is required to become a more assertive representative of the bondholders' interests. But even following an event of default, the trustee will generally only act at the instructions of the bondholders. Upon the occurrence of an event of default, bondholders holding a specified portion of the bonds (often 25%) will have the right to "accelerate" the bonds, or require immediate repayment, and the right to request the trustee to seize any pledged collateral. Certain insolvency events lead to automatic acceleration.

An issuer that encounters difficulties in complying with its covenants and meeting its other obligations under the bonds may find it difficult to communicate directly with investors. Since high yield bonds are nearly always held in book-entry form through either US or European clearing systems, determining the identity of the bondholders can be difficult and expensive. Even if key bondholders can be identified, issuers should be cautious about conveying information to some bondholders that it does not convey to all bondholders. This is especially true if there is a liquid or semi-liquid trading market for the bonds.

Balancing the rights of bond investors and bank lenders: Structuring of high yield transactions

A key role of the financial advisor in a high yield transaction is recommending a transaction structure that is acceptable to the issuer, the bond investors and the issuer's existing bankers. By "structure" we mean:

- whether the bonds are issued by a holding company or by one of the operating companies;
- the extent to which the issuer's various subsidiaries and/or parent companies are required to guarantee the debt;
- whether bank indebtedness is permitted to rank senior in right of payment to the bonds (or in fact does rank senior as a structural matter); and
- whether the bank indebtedness is permitted to be secured by pledges of shares and assets if bond holders do not benefit from the same security.

The structure of a transaction will be crucial to the rating assigned to the transaction by the rating agencies, which has a direct impact on the interest rate that investors will require to buy the bonds.

The crucial question in choosing a transaction structure is the relationship with the issuer's banks. Conventional bank lending arrangements prohibit a borrower assuming significant new indebtedness without the banks' consent, and some European bank lenders were historically hesitant to modify their standard arrangements to allow the borrower to become still more leveraged. Early European high yield transactions attempted to resolve this problem by issuing the bonds out of a holding company, rather than having them be direct obligations of the operating companies. As a structural matter, bonds issued out of a parent holding company have the same priority upon a liquidation of the company as do equity holders of the company – that is, the bank lenders and other direct obligors will be paid off first, and any remaining amounts will be distributed to the parent holding company as equity holder, who must use those amounts to repay the bondholders. Given that the bond obligations were "structurally subordinated" to the bank obligations, bank lenders had little ground to object to financings carried out on this basis.

Bonds offered under these structures were generally offered to specialized high yield investors in the United States, who were accustomed to other structures and whose appetite for bonds issued under this "European" structure was predictably muted. Under the traditionally "American" structure, the bonds and the bank indebtedness were both incurred at the operating-company level. Bank lenders, however, were generally secured while bond investors were not, giving bank lenders a de facto priority in the event of insolvency. Alternatively, the bond investors might be secured but rank junior to the bank lenders.

Today's market has become far more sophisticated about these issues. European banks operate in a different environment than 5-7 years ago; among other things, they must acknowledge the impact on their lending business imposed by Basel II, competitive pressures within Europe (especially Germany), the loss of state support in the case of some German banks and the increasing trend of banks to securitize their loan portfolios to reduce risk on their balance sheets (which sometimes leads to greater standardization of loan arrangements). At the same time, European banks have become more sophisticated in understanding the high yield product and the possibilities for addressing their intercreditor concerns through a variety of structural mechanisms. Many European banks now recognize the potential fee income to be earned from alternative products such as high yield bonds and actively steer their customers to consider such alternatives.

Today, high yield structures on both sides of the Atlantic are likely to involve guarantees by all significant operating companies. There is likely to be some element of subordination of the bond indebtedness and the bond guarantees vis-à-vis the bank indebtedness. Most typically, this subordination will be set out in the terms of the bonds and the guarantees ("contractual subordination") rather than being structural. If the bonds are secured, they will typically be secured on a junior basis (that is, the bank lenders have a first claim to the secured assets). But today's market sees a wide range of transaction structures that are tailor-made to reflect the particular situation of the issuer.

Exiting the high yield transaction:
Prepayment and refinancing possibilities

High yield transactions have a stated maturity of between 7 and 10 years but are generally structured so that the issuer is locked into the arrangements for an initial period of four to five years. In some transactions, there is a blanket prohibition on repayments during the initial period. In other transactions, prepayment during that period is possible only with payment of a "make-whole premium" that is designed to allow investors to reinvest their funds and realize the originally planned yield at then-current interest rates. More specifically, the make-whole premium is calculated as the excess of (i) the stated principal amount outstanding over (ii) the net present value of all scheduled payments on the bonds, using a discount rate that is equal to the then-current market Bund rate plus a small spread (often 50 basis points). Depending on the movements in interest rates between the time of issuance and the desired time of redemption, the make-whole premium can be little to nothing, or it can be quite prohibitive.

Following the fourth or the fifth year, prepayments are possible with the payment of a premium above outstanding principal amount. The prepayment price is typically set out in a schedule and reduces annually, reaching 100% in the last years or years prior to scheduled maturity. The initial premium will often equal half of the stated annual interest rate.

In addition, early repayment of the bonds is possible in two further scenarios:

- Under standard high yield arrangements, issuers are responsible to gross up interest payments for withholding taxes that are required to be made by the applicable taxing jurisdictions. An issuer is permitted to request early repayment (at par) in the event of a change in tax law that increases the issuer's withholding-tax obligations above a certain specified amount.
- In the event of an IPO or similar share placement, the issuer is often permitted to use a portion of the share proceeds to prepay a certain portion of the bonds (often limited to 35%) with the payment of a premium.

There are, in addition, two scenarios in which the issuer can be forced to refinance the bonds by granting bondholders a put right. First, bondholders receive a put right at 101% following a change of control of the company. While the precise definition of "change of control" can be highly negotiated, the put right is often triggered by shareholders other than the existing controlling shareholders acquiring more shares than the existing controlling shareholders (and in any event acquiring at least 35% or 50% of shares). In addition, following a significant asset disposition, if the company has not applied the asset proceeds in the manner required in the covenants, it can be compelled by bondholders to use those proceeds to redeem the bonds.

Agreeing guidelines for future behavior:
Covenants and events of default

As discussed above, bond investors normally expect only passive involvement with issuers. For high yield bonds, the price of this passive investor relationship is a level of detail in covenants that most issuers initially find surprising. Most aspects of the issuer's business are implicated – not only fundraising and payment of dividends, but also permissible lines of business, divestitures and transactions with affiliated companies, among others. Although these covenants follow a fairly standardized formulation, each covenant is adapted to the needs of each issuer through a series of exceptions or "carve-outs" that seek to allow the issuer to conduct and expand its business in a reasonable manner.

The covenants encompass not only the issuing entity itself, but also most companies that are part of the group, and in particular the important operating subsidiaries. Specifically, the covenants restrict the behavior of the issuer and a group of "restricted subsidiaries" that is defined by the issuer. Issuers generally are motivated to make this list of restricted subsidiaries as inclusive as possible, because their flexibility under the financial covenants is generally increased if the core "credit group" is larger, and because interactions with subsidiaries that are not restricted subsidiaries is subject to the same restrictions as transactions with non-group affiliated companies.

The covenants generally fall into one of the following four categories:

- covenants that control the payment of cash outside the credit group, principally limitations on indebtedness and limitation on dividends and other restricted payments;
- covenants that protect the credit group's continued generation of cash and the availability of that cash to repay the notes, including restrictions on lines of business and prohibitions on cash ring-fencing arrangements by subsidiaries;
- covenants that guard the assets of the credit group, principally limitations on sales of assets, limitations on liens, guidelines for affiliate transactions and limitations on mergers and consolidation; and
- information covenants that ensure that investors have access to a predictable flow of information about the credit group.

We discuss some of the key covenants in the coming pages. This discussion, however, does not cover all covenants, but rather only those covenants that we believe issuers will be most focused on.

Covenants that control the payment of cash

It is predictable that investors in a highly leveraged company want to ensure that the company's debt payment obligations do not exceed its ability to pay. Likewise, investors wish to ensure that cash does not get siphoned out of the company by its shareholders to an extent that jeopardizes repayment of the company's debt. Investors are also concerned to know that new investments by the company bear a reasonable relationship to the company's cash flows and indebtedness levels.

These obligations cannot be governed in too rigid a manner. In bank lending transactions, the covenants might be very rigid, but the company will rely on being able to call and negotiate with its relationship banker in the event of any difficulty. Thus, financial covenants in a bank lending transaction are generally "maintenance covenants," which means that, if the borrow fails to maintain its financial ratios at certain levels, an event of default will occur and the banks will have the right to require early repayment of the loan. In practice, difficulties are resolved through renegotiation with the banks.

The capital-markets structure of high yield bonds requires a more flexible approach, since routine one-on-one discussions between issuer and investor are neither expected nor desired, and the mechanics for negotiating changes to the documentation are considerably more bulky. For this reason, bond transactions rely on "incurrence" covenants, meaning that additional debt can only be incurred, and restricted payments can only be made, if immediately thereafter the issuer continues to be in compliance with the target financial ratios set out in the covenants. Failure of the issuer to have its financial ratio fall within the agreed parameters does not lead to an event of default but rather to increased limitations on the conduct of the issuer's business.

The ratio most often used in high yield transactions is EBITDA to debt service. That is, the issuer must maintain a ratio of cash flows for the previous four financial quarters that exceeds its scheduled interest payments on debt by a specified multiple. In European transactions, this ratio tends to vary between 2.0:1 and 2.75:1, depending on the strength of the issuer.

Limitation on indebtedness

Indebtedness is permitted to be incurred by a high yield issuer under one of at least three alternatives:

- The issuer can incur "ratio" indebtedness, meaning that it can incur debt if, after doing so, its financial ratio will still fall within the agreed parameter.
- The issuer can incur "basket" debt. The carve-outs to the indebtedness covenant include one or more categories of debt that can be incurred up to a specified amount. Thus, even if the financial ratio is not within the agreed parameter, so long as the "basket" for that category of debt is not "full," further indebtedness of that category can be incurred.
- The issuer can incur "permitted indebtedness" of certain specified types without limitation on amount and without reference to whether the financial ratio is within the agreed parameter. These typically include subordinated intercompany debt and debt incurred to refinance existing debt.

In negotiating the limitation on indebtedness, the company and its bankers will need to have a clear understanding of the company's cash needs over the next four to five years, as well as a clear understanding of what its sources of liquidity will be. The limitation on indebtedness may not be so restrictive that the company is unable to meet its foreseeable cash needs.

A company negotiating the limitation on indebtedness will also need to focus carefully on which entities are permitted to incur which types of debt. It is not unusual for the covenant to be drafted so that most future debt is only incurred by the issuer and the subsidiary guarantors.

Limitation on restricted payments

The term "restricted payment" is defined to capture a variety of discretionary cash outflows. In the first instance, this term encompasses distributions to shareholders, whether in the form of dividends, subordinated debt repayments prior to stated maturity or repurchases of stock. The term "restricted payment" also includes a variety of investments that the company might make, unless they fall within a defined category of "permitted investments."

Restricted payments are not absolutely forbidden. Among other things, it is expressly foreseen that an issuer whose business is healthy will continue to pay dividends to its shareholders and to invest in its business. The company is permitted to make restricted payments if all of the following conditions are met:

- after making the restricted payment, the company's financial ratio is still within the agreed parameter;
- after making the restricted payment, the issuer is in full compliance with the other covenants, and no other breach under the indenture has occurred under the indenture has occurred; and
- the amount of the restricted payment falls within the amount permitted under a "basket" whose size is tied to the company's consolidated net income. Specifically, in most cases, the total amount of restricted payments made since the issuance of the notes cannot exceed 50% of the company's cumulative consolidated net income over that period. This basket is typically increased by the size of any IPO proceeds.

In addition to the carve-outs contained in the definition of "permitted investments," there are a number of other general carve-outs and exceptions to the restriction on limited payments that are negotiated as part of every transaction. These carve-outs should always specify whether the amounts paid under the carve-out are to be included in the cumulative restricted payments used to calculate the size of the available "basket" described above.

A company negotiating the limitation on restricted payments will need to be clear on its investment plans and will need to negotiate adequate investment flexibility to develop in accordance with its business strategy. Limitations on distributions to shareholders will need to be considered in light of the expectations of the shareholders, any applicable laws and any requirements set out in the issuer's organizational documents.

Covenants that protect the continued generation and availability of cash

High yield investors not only are focused on limiting competing uses of cash, they also seek to ensure that the company continues to generate cash and that the cash is made available to the issuer for bond repayments.

Limitation on changes to the line of business

Investors in the high yield issuer will have made their credit decisions based in part on their assessment of the company's line of business and its prospects for success in its current market. Accordingly, companies are generally not permitted to change their lines of business to a material extent. Any change to this covenant would require the consent of bondholders holding more than 50% of the outstanding bonds. Accordingly, any planned or probable additions to the issuer's line of business will need to be discussed with the banks. Any such additions should be reflected in the covenant and the disclosure to investors.

Prohibition on ring-fencing: no limitations on subsidiary distributions to issuer

When a company consists of a holding company and numerous subsidiaries, it is not unusual for the operating subsidiaries to take out bank loans. These bank loans will often contain "ring-fencing" language, or provisions that restrict the subsidiaries ability to dividend the cash it generates up to its parent.

These ring-fencing arrangements are prohibited in high yield transactions, along with any other restrictions on a subsidiary's distributing cash to its parent. To the extent that pre-existing loans are not refinanced by the high yield offering, there will generally be an exception for the pre-existing loan covenants.

Covenants that guard the assets of the credit group

An investor's credit analysis rests not only on the company's ability to generate cash and use that cash for bond repayments, it also considers the value of the company's assets in the event of a liquidation. For that reason, bondholders are concerned to know that the value of the company's asset base will not diminish over time.

Restrictions on sales of assets

High yield issuers and their restricted subsidiaries are free to sell assets at any time, provided that they follow the guidelines set out in the high yield covenants. These include the following requirements:

- the company must receive fair market value for its asset sale;
- most of the funds must be received in cash or cash equivalents (75% for many high yield companies);
- the funds must be used for a permitted reinvestment or for a repayment of senior debt or the high yield bonds; and
- the funds must be applied as permitted within a specified period (often nine months or one year).

For large dispositions (often €10 million to €30 million for mid-sized European issuers), the issuer may be required to deliver an independent appraisal of the fair market value of the asset being sold.

Limitations on asset sales differ in the length of time permitted for application of the funds, as well as in the range of permitted investments that is foreseen. In addition, in some transactions the "cash" compensation is permitted to include replacement assets, and the scope of the permitted "cash equivalents" can differ. When negotiating these provisions, issuers should have clarity on which asset sales are likely, what form of compensation they can expect to receive for those assets and how they expect to reinvest any proceeds.

"Negative Pledge": Limitation on liens

Investors require clarity, at the time they make their investment decision, on how their claims against the issuer and the guarantor will rank in the event of an issuer insolvency. In high yield transactions with no competing bank lenders, investors will insist that companies not incur liens on their property or assets unless the high yield bonds are secured by those liens to the same extent as other creditors. Where there is independent bank financing that ranks senior to the bonds, the investors will sometimes insist on receiving a subordinated lien on the same property. Such a subordinated lien may, of course, be of limited practical value. Alternatively, liens to secure senior bank debt might be unrestricted, with other liens being permitted only if the subordinated bonds are secured to the same extent as those other non-senior bank creditors.

Affiliate transactions

High yield investors do not generally seek to monitor or second-guess the business decisions of the company, nor do high yield covenants give them any power to do so. An important exception to this general principle is transactions with "affiliates." Affiliates include (i) direct or indirect controlling shareholders of the issuer, (ii) subsidiaries controlled by the issuer, directly or indirectly, and (iii) sister companies that are, together with the issuer, under common control by the same shareholder or group of shareholders.

Affiliate transactions are required to be at least as beneficial to the company as what would have been negotiated with unrelated third parties "at arm's length." Board confirmation of the arm's-length nature of the transaction is required for transactions above a certain size (often €5 million for mid-sized European companies). For much larger transactions, the issuer is typically required to obtain an independent confirmation of the arm's-length nature of the transaction. For mid-sized European companies, such an independent confirmation is often required for transactions with a value of above €15 million.

Information covenants

Even if the issuer need not expect extensive one-on-one contact with investors, it is generally required to provide them with a high level of information on an on-going basis. This includes, most importantly, annual financial statements (which must be audited) and quarterly financial statements (which generally need not be audited). With the delivery of the annual financial statements, the issuer must provide confirmation of compliance with the covenants (or details about any non-compliance).

The issuer must also provide, annually, an update of key sections of the offering circular or prospectus shown to investors. This includes, most significantly, updates of the business description and of the textual description of the company's financial results and financial condition.

Finally, the issuer is required to give the trustee prompt notice of any breach of its obligations under the indenture.

Events of default

If the company does not make prompt payment on the bonds, or does not comply with its covenants, an event of default will occur under the indenture. With most covenants that can be cured, the issuer is given a "grace period" (often 30 days after notice from the trustee) to cure the default. With other specified covenants, the event of default can be declared immediately upon the trustee becoming aware of the breach. In addition, the issuer typically has a grace period of 30 business days to cure any non-payment of interest.

A bankruptcy or insolvency of the issuer or a subsidiary guarantor also will constitute an event of default, as will a payment default (or an acceleration of the indebtedness) under the company's other significant debt or credit facilities. Likewise, a failure to pay significant monetary judgments that have been awarded by a court will constitute an event of default. Additional events of default may be negotiated for a particular transaction.

Upon the occurrence of an event of default, bondholders holding a specified portion of the bonds (often 25%) will have the right to "accelerate" the bonds, or require immediate repayment, and the right to request the trustee to seize any pledged collateral. Events of insolvency or bankruptcy lead to automatic acceleration.

Modifying the covenants and other indenture provisions

As discussed above, gaining the approval of the bondholders to any changes to the indenture can be difficult and expensive, in particular because the identity of the bondholders is unknown. In recognition of this difficulty, potential changes to the indenture are divided into three categories, which differing requirements for the changes becoming effective:

- Certain changes become effective with the signature of the trustee and the issuer, with no requirement for investor consultation and approval. These include corrections of inconsistencies and obvious errors in the indenture, the addition of security arrangements for the benefit of the bondholders and other changes that are not adverse to the bondholders. The trustee generally has the right to require the issuer to deliver a legal opinion that the change is permitted without investor consent.

- Certain changes require unanimous investor consent. These include principally changes in repayment terms, including the interest rates or the payment dates, as well as any changes to the amendment provisions themselves. In some European Transactions this unanimity requirement is replaced with a super majority requirement, often holders of 90% in value of the outstanding bonds.

- The remaining changes are generally possible with the vote of bondholders holding a simple majority in value of the outstanding bonds.

Given the difficulty of getting holder consent, it is especially important that the issuer be well informed and well advised in its negotiation of the covenants and events of default, and that it in particular has adequate flexibility to conduct its ongoing business according to plan.

Particular issues involving German companies

As noted above, payment of principal and interest on the high yield notes are usually guaranteed by key operating subsidiaries of the issuer. German law, like the law of some other European civil-law jurisdictions, places restrictions on a subsidiary's ability to guarantee obligations of its parent; guarantees that require payment in violation of these restrictions may not be enforceable. Under the indenture, the obligations of subsidiary guarantors are drafted to reflect the limitations on enforcement set out in applicable law.

The extent of these limitations on enforcement in Germany differ depending on the legal structure of the company granting the guaranty. In the case of a German limited liability company, or "GmbH" (a typical structure for closely held companies), no direct or indirect payment of any kind may be made by a GmbH to its shareholders that would jeopardize its stated share capital (*Stammkapital*). The term "payment" is generally construed broadly to also cover all types of commercial benefits, including the provision of security for payment obligations of the shareholders. The stated share capital of the GmbH is jeopardized if its net assets fall below the amount of its stated share capital.

The consequences of making a payment in contravention of this requirement can be harsh. The GmbH has a repayment claim against the relevant shareholder that cannot be waived. More significantly, the managing directors of the GmbH may be held personally liable for the payments made and any additional damages incurred by the GmbH resulting from the payments and may even face criminal charges. The same principles apply for a similar partnership-like structure, the GmbH & Co. KG.

The protection of the stated share capital is even stronger if the subsidiary guarantor is either a share corporation, or "AG," or the subsidiary of an AG. Except for the distribution of dividends and certain other statutory exceptions, an AG must not make any payments or grant other benefits which are made with a view to the payee's position as shareholder of the AG. Unlike with GmbHs, the German Stock Corporation Act protects not only the stated share capital but rather all assets of the AG. Payments or benefits which are granted in violation of this provision of the German Stock Corporation Act are void, and the AG has a claim against the shareholder who obtained the prohibited payment or benefit.

An AG or a subsidiary of an AG may thus only act in very limited circumstances as guarantor. Specifically, it can comfortably guarantee the issuer's obligations if the proceeds of the bonds are on-lent to the guarantor, the payment obligation under guarantee does not exceed the amounts so on-lent and the guarantor would not otherwise be able to obtain funds at equal or better terms. Given the difficulties of building these restrictions into the indenture provisions, it is preferable (where it is feasible) to have subsidiaries other than AGs provide the guarantees.

As already stated, these limitations are incorporated into the guarantees included in the indenture. They are also disclosed to investors in the "risk factor" disclosure in the offering circular or prospectus and are considered by investors in assessing the strength of the structure and the collective creditworthiness of the issuer and the guarantors.

Is a high yield bond offering right for my company?

High yield transactions offer a number of concrete benefits compared to traditional syndicated bank loans or other bank credit transactions. These include the following:

- *Long maturity dates.* The 7-10 year maturity of typical high yield transactions is longer than what is typical in the bank market.

- *Independence from creditors.* The self-monitoring nature of covenant compliance may be viewed by many companies as an advantage.

- *Flexible and tailor-made covenant structure.* Even though the covenants are complex and detailed, the issuer is generally given significant latitude in negotiating tailor-made solutions that take its particular business plans and legal situation into account.

- *Availability to companies with limited financing options.* As discussed in the opening paragraphs of this chapter, there are a wide range of worthy companies who may not meet the criteria established by traditional bank lenders and who may not yet be ripe for the equity markets. High yield often presents these companies with a financing option.

- *Flexibility to offer on a subordinated or unsecured basis.* If arrangements with existing bank lenders are such that incurring additional senior or unsecured debt is not possible, issuers may find that the high yield bond market is willing to purchase their obligations on an unsubordinated and/or unsecured basis.

Notwithstanding these advantages, high yield bonds are not the appropriate solution for all companies with financing needs. The initial transaction costs for high yield bonds are quite high, much more similar to the cost of an IPO rather than the cost of a bank lending transaction. This cost means that high yield is not appropriate for smaller fund-raising activity. This high cost is principally driven by the need to produce a detailed disclosure document, which must be signed off on by the lawyers involved, and also by the cost of negotiating the covenants. The sheer complexity of the covenants – and the fact that they are drafted in rather opaque legal English that cannot be easily translated – is another disadvantage of high yield transactions. While the relative lack of investor contact may be seen as an advantage, the difficulty in establishing direct investor contact may seem like a disadvantage in a distressed scenario or following a significant change in the issuer's circumstances, particularly if modifications to the indenture arrangements are desired.

In short, high yield bond financing is likely to be appropriate for medium-sized to large companies (in Germany, the mid-sized to larger *Mittelständler*) who want to raise at least € 100-150 million in debt financing and who do not have an investment-grade rating. It is also important that such a company has a relatively stable business model that will allow it to become locked into the covenants with little realistic possibility of refinancing for a four or five-year period. For a company meeting those criteria, high yield bonds represent a financing possibility that may merit careful consideration.

4.4.2 Tracking Stock – A Smart Concept for Acquisitions in Diversified Businesses

Kirsten Girnth

The purpose of this article is to focus on a specific aspect of doing M&A transactions in Germany by introducing a technique which may have the potential to become a trend in the German market for investors who are interested in specific parts of diversified businesses: investing into these businesses by acquiring tracking stock.
The attractive aspects of a tracking stock acquisition is that the investment does not require the legal separation of business sections and therefore has no impact on the target's legal structure.

Investing in the profitable part of the business – a case study

Under an actual case a foreign utilities company intended to expand its business into other European countries; its own business was – due to historical reasons – restricted to its own local market. Together and in close cooperation with a strong German partner such foreign investor ("Foreign Investor") intended to get a foot in the German market by acquiring a participation in a local utilities company. The German partner ("German Investor") identified the Utilities Company of a German municipality ("Municipality"). It had been evident from the very beginning of the transaction process that solely acquiring shares in the Utilities Company would not have made any sense since the public transport business also run by this company was unprofitable.

Originally, the Municipality was the sole shareholder of the Utilities Company which is incorporated as a stock corporation; the shares, however, were not listed. Having finalized the due diligence it was apparent that a participation would have made sense only with respect to the electricity, heating, gas and water activities of the local Utilities Company.

Not only for the two investors but also for the Municipality the question came up whether to create two separate entities either by way of an equity carve out or by way of a spin-off under the German Transformation Act. Both steps would have resulted in separate entities for the different sectors, one consisting of the transportation sector and the other comprising its water, electricity and energy activities. Such separation, however, would have resulted in the Municipality being a shareholder of two separate entities, which would not only have been a very sensitive political issue. Besides political aspects, a separation would have meant to cease synergy and subsidy effects between the different activities but also at least a partial loss of influence over the management group.

Terminology and definitions

A strategic investor who intends to invest in a single business line rather than in a diversified company may feel uncomfortable when investing into a company with different lines of business that are far away from being homogeneous. In order to attract strategic investors companies or their shareholders, respectively, think about offering a participation only in a specific business that is for example supplementary to the investor's current fields of business; and a possible way of doing so is to offer tracking stock.

Tracking stock which is also known as "targeted stock," "letter stock" or "alphabet stock" stands for an interest in a legally dependent division of a commercial enterprise, the so-called "tracked unit." The concept of a tracking stock enables an investor to economically hold shares only in certain legally dependent divisions of a company, the tracked unit, although, from a legal point of view he holds shares in the whole company. One may also think of other varieties of tracking stock such as e.g. "subsidiary shares" which grant a participation in profits of a subsidiary company.

Necessarily, the scope of tracking stock is extended to the whole company as shown in Figure 4.21: By issuing tracking stock all previously issued common stock automatically becomes tracking stock, however, now representing the result of all other business lines. Whereas in the U.S., the concept of tracking stock is well known, European companies are rather hesitant issuing tracking stock. In the U.S., General Motors, AT&T and Sprint – amongst others – have issued tracking stock for their individual business areas, whereas in Europe only Alcatel as a major player has issued tracking stock for its optical items division ("Optronics"). In Germany, several municipal utility companies have issued tracking stock due to the fact that their public transport business in almost each city is unprofitable and investors are generally interested in the water, electricity and energy supply activities only. Whereas Alcatel's tracking stock is traded on a stock exchange none of those of the German utilities is yet listed.

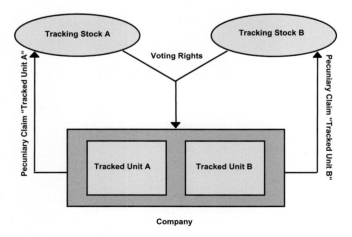

Figure 4.21 Structure of tracking stocks

How to implement a tracking stock structure in Germany

As a matter of principle, tracking stock may be issued either (i) by changing the company's articles of association in order to adapt and differentiate the rights related to the shares already issued (see below) or (ii) by issuing new shares by means of a capital increase (see also below).

Conversion of stock already existing

An extension of the tracking stock model to the complete stock of shares already issued requires the modification of the company's articles of association. There are mainly three ways to convert already existing shares into tracking stock:

- Although permitted by section 60 para. 3 German Stock Corporation Law ("AktG") the conversion of the existing stock by only *amending the articles of association* accordingly requires either an unanimous resolution by all current shareholders (which is practically almost impossible especially in case of a listed company); or all shareholders must be offered shares of the newly created type which usually contradicts the purpose of the tracking stock, i.e. the participation of one investor in a specific line of business.

- The mainly practical disadvantages of the above-mentioned concept are prevented by *splitting existing shares*. For each share the current shareholders receive new shares ("Stock Units A," "Stock Units B," etc.) reflecting the different lines of business. As the shareholders' rights are not impaired no unanimous resolution of the shareholders' assembly is required.

- If a splitting of shares is not possible (i.e. because the splitting value would be less than one Euro) the company may, under certain conditions, solve the problem by a *capital decrease* and *a subsequent capital increase*. As both steps are legally independent from each other there is a risk that shareholders leave the company after having received the reimbursement for the capital decrease.

Issuance of new shares

Tracking stock may be issued by either increasing the company's capital without using the company's own resources or by creating new shares as so-called preferred shares:

- Because of section 216 para. 1 sentence 1 AktG the issuance of tracking stock generally may only be affected by means of a *capital increase* using contributions.

- Alternatively, the company may issue *preferred stock*.

The process chosen in the case study

In the case study mentioned at the beginning of this article the common stock granting unrestricted rights to all divisions of the Utilities Company was renamed in "Stock Class A." Such Stock Class A tracked all profits and losses generated by the entity in its entirety after distributions made to stockholders of Stock Class B (namely the tracking stock shareholders). Stock Class A was to be hold exclusively by the Municipality.

Stock Class B – the tracking stock – was created both by (i) the conversion of common Stock A into Stock Class B which was then sold and assigned to the Foreign Investor and (ii) by means of an increase of the share capital of the Utilities Company, such stock subscribed by the German Investor as shown in Figure 4.22. The Stock Class B tracked a certain percentage of all profits and losses generated by the Utilities Company in the tracked unit (B) as it was set forth in the side agreement and also reflected in the Company's articles of association.

After conclusion of the sale and assignment of Stock Class B to the Foreign Investor and the subscription of Stock Class B by the German Investor the structure looked as shown in Figure 4.23.

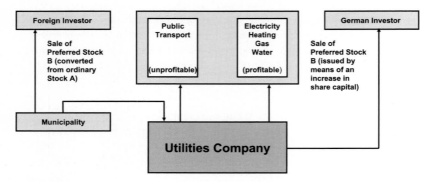

Figure 4.22
Implementation of the tracking stock structure by means (i) of conversion of common stock and sale and assignment to the foreign investor (ii) by increase in share capital and subscription by the German investor

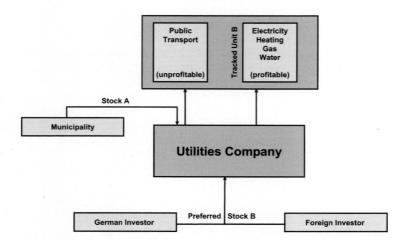

Figure 4.23
Final Structure, i.e. German and foreign investor only participating in the profitable tracked unit B

An alternative to the increase in the share capital and the conversion of shares would have been the splitting of existing shares by means of a modification of the articles of association. For each existing share, the Municipality would have received new shares (i.e. "Stock Class A" and "Stock Class B") reflecting the different business lines. As shareholders' rights were not impaired, no unanimous resolution of the shareholders' meeting would have been required.

Further practical aspects of the issuance of tracking stock

As already mentioned, tracking stock does not require the legal separation of business sections and therefore has no influence on the target company's legal structure. In addition, the management will not be separated which means that the general shareholders' influence will stay at the same level as it was before issuing tracking stock. The influence of the tracking stock shareholders, however, will certainly be limited to the management of the tracked unit which is usually set down in an additional agreement between the shareholders – such agreement binding the partners to exercise their voting rights in a pre-described manner with regard to topics which have an impact not only on the tracked unit but also on the remaining divisions of the company. It will also be easier for both, the shareholders and the target company itself, to raise money for the unprofitable (or less profitable) division as it would be if the unprofitable division was a separate legal entity because – then – the profitable division may serve as additional security.

In order to determine the dividend to be paid to the tracking stock shareholder(s) the company has to draw up a special balance sheet only with regard to the tracked unit. This, of course, requires additional efforts with respect to cost allocations and a model how to allocate overhead costs. All this is usually set forth in the company's Articles of Association that are to be revised in the course of the tracking stock transaction, anyhow. The same procedures apply to any tax burden or tax benefit to be allocated to the tracked unit: The tax burden or tax benefit, as the case may be, must be determined on a fictitious basis under the condition that the tracked unit is an independent entity which raises additional questions that should be dealt with by the investors' tax advisers.

Advantages of the issuance of tracking stock

Besides some potential drawbacks arising from the specific structure of tracking stock there are the following advantages:

- Tracking stock is a *flexible alternative* for raising equity capital with respect to specific divisions of a company. The investor will only participate in the division he deems worth for an investment and the issuer is not required to initiate a time and money consuming reorganisation of the company.

- Tracking stock may be used as *consideration* in connection with an acquisition or cooperation; for the former shareholders the concept of tracking stock offers the opportunity of keeping shares in their "old" company indirectly and at the same time realizing synergy potentials from the occurred merger.

- The issuance of tracking stock may result in an *increase of shareholder value* in the case where a stock evaluation is linked in a disproportionately strong manner to a less successful business unit and where a spin-off will not be an option. As the introduction of tracking stock makes additional information available due to a detailed analysis the issuance of tracking stock may result in a "correct" evaluation of all other divisions of the respective company.

- Unlike a spin-off, the issuance of tracking stock allows the continued use of those *synergy effects* that may only be realized within a single entity or at least within a closely allied group of companies. Thus, the result achieved within one entity or within an allied group may be higher than the added individual results of business units that have become legally independent, e.g. due to the central handling of administrative tasks which are equal or similar for all business units. Further cost advantages are based on the fact that, contrary to a spin-off or equity carve-out, only one board of directors is required.

- Another advantage is the *flexibility* of the tracking stock structure: The tracked unit may be spun-off or otherwise transformed at a later date without the requirement of taking major restructuring actions prior to such transformation.

- In connection with the issuance of tracking stock an existing system of *incentives* could be modified so that bonuses are linked to the performance of the shares of such business unit for which a manager is responsible. The motivation generated hereby may be significantly higher than linking the remuneration to the performance of all divisions.

Drawbacks of the issuance of tracking stock

Also, the potential drawbacks are quite evident:

- It's obvious that the investor who invests in tracking stock does not only take the *financial risk* of the failure of the tracked unit but the risk that also other divisions of the company have to bear losses which may – as a worst case scenario – result in an insolvency of the whole company which also sweeps away potential profits of the tracked unit.

- Closely linked to this financial risk is the fact that – due to losses in other divisions – tracking stock investors may only receive a *minor or no dividend* at all even if profits were achieved in the tracked unit and could be distributed.

- Despite the chance of synergies there is also the risk of a *collision of interests* and "selfishness" of divisions – e.g. in decisions on investments, allocations and evaluations.

There is, however, a chance to overcome the potential drawbacks, mainly by a side agreement to be concluded by the tracking stock shareholders. In the case introduced at the beginning of this article, specific concessions by the major shareholder (i.e. the Municipality) were conceived:

In a side agreement *("Konsortialvertrag")* between the old shareholder and the new investors the old shareholder agreed to the new investors' right to enforce a spin-off of the tracked unit in case of a crisis of the whole entity. In order to facilitate the anticipated spin-off process this requires to collect all consents required for a transformation of the company or at least to oblige all other shareholders to consent to a spin-off in a situation and under circumstances where the spin-off itself has not become real at all. However, the tracking stock shareholders must be aware that even if the conditions of the spin-off have already been agreed, the implementation of such spin-off will take some time. Further, in order to ensure the payment of dividends investors should require a guarantee of the major shareholder to pay dividends assignable to the tracked unit, even if other divisions only generate losses which usually results in a lack of liquidity required to pay dividends. To prevent the company from the situation of over-indebtedness the tracking stock shareholders should also enforce a contribution of the major shareholder to the company's capital reserves in an amount sufficient to service the potential dividends to be paid to the tracking stock shareholders.

Rights of employees

If municipalities or other public authorities are – either directly or indirectly – affected by a tracking stock transaction usually, a work place guarantee is requested by either the municipality itself or by the unions involved. The term of the work place guarantee may easily exceed a time period of ten years which may prevent potential investors from investing into a tracking stock model as the company will not be in the position to terminate any employee even if this is required for operational reasons. Usually, unions have a strong position in companies that are owned or operated by municipalities. Thus, besides the request for a work place guarantee, the side agreements to be entered by the former shareholder and the new investor(s) normally cover the obligation to accept and fully support the co-determination structures that are already in place at the respective company.

Beyond such demands which intend to protect the status quo of the target company unions from time to time also request to strengthen the future position of the company by asking for the development and establishment of concepts regarding the future economic growth of the company and the promotion of employees. However, usually the provisions covering those obligations are soft and difficult to enforce.

Pre-emptive rights and take-along clauses

To strengthen both, the new investors' and the old shareholder's position, the shareholders of the company usually grant each other pre-emptive rights which means that each shareholder who intends to sell his participation must as a first step offer his shares to the remaining shareholders (usually on a pro rata basis). Further, in order to protect the new investors' position the old shareholder usually has to grant the new shareholders a so-called take-along right: If the old shareholder intends to sell his participation he is not only obliged to offer his shares under the pre-emptive right but also to find a third investor that does not only acquire the old shareholder's shares but also the shares of the new investors if the new investors waive their pre-emptive right but exercise the take-along right granted.

Literature

Nippel, Peter; Mertens, Raphael: *Tracking Stock*: Ein Beispiel für Risiken und Nebenwirkungen komplexer Strukturen in der Unternehmensfinanzierung. Kiel 2003

Prinz, Ulrich; Schürmer, Carl Thomas: Rechnungslegung bei Tracking Stock-Strukturen in Deutschland. Grundfragen und Gestaltungsüberlegungen; *DStR* 2001, S. 759 ff.

Prinz, Ulrich; Schürmer, Carl Thomas: Tracking Stock und Sachdividenden – ein neues Gestaltungsinstrument für spartenbezogene Gesellschaftsrechte? *DStR* 2003, S. 181 ff.

Sieger, Jürgen; Hasselbach, Kai: "Tracking Stock" im deutschen Aktienrecht; *Betriebsberater* 1999, S. 1277

Tonner; Martin: Zulässigkeit und Gestaltungsmöglichkeiten von Tracking Stock nach deutschem Aktienrecht; *IStR* 2002, S. 317 ff.

4.4.3 Thin Capitalization Rules in Germany and the United States

Ruth Zehetmeier-Müller and Ingmar Doerr

The main purpose of the so-called "Thin Capitalization Rules" is to restrict the debt financing, especially loan funding of a domestic corporation by a (foreign) shareholder. To limit the loss of tax revenue at the level of the borrowing corporation for the respective State the deductibility of interest will be limited by Thin Capitalization Rules, particularly in the case of foreign shareholders. Both Germany and the United States apply such provisions, although in different ways.

Intra-group financing can be structured in different ways. The parent company may elect to finance its subsidiary by means of equity or loan. In the former case, the parent company will receive its return by way of a dividend, whereas in the latter case it will receive a return by means of interest payments. On the level of the related company the tax consequences of such payments will vary: while interest payments are – under normal circumstances – tax deductible business expenses, dividends are not.

Where related companies are resident in different jurisdictions with different tax rates, the group might try to maximize its tax efficiency by financing a related company through a loan. In an ideal world, this would enable the borrowing company to deduct the interest payments as business expenses and thus lower its taxable income, while the lending company is located in a jurisdiction in which the interest payments are not taxable at all or are only subject to a tax rate which is lower than the tax rate applicable in the jurisdiction of the borrower.

In order to avoid these unfavorable tax consequences, national tax authorities apply special rules to companies which are "thinly capitalized," where – inter alia – the level of shareholder lending exceeds the financing the company would be able to raise from third parties. In Germany, these rules are referred to as *"Gesellschafter-Fremdfinanzierungsregelungen"* and in the United States ("US") as *"Earning Stripping Rules."*

German Thin Capitalization Rules

Introduction

German Thin Capitalization Rules have a long tradition. They were first introduced by a letter of the German Federal Ministry of Finance in March 1987 as a kind of anti-abusive measure. After this letter was found to be unlawful due to a lack of legal authorization by the German Federal Tax Court in 1992, Sec. 8a Corporate Income Tax Act ("KStG," Körperschaftsteuergesetz) was introduced in 1994. Almost a decade later, Sec. 8a KStG was substantially amended as the former Thin Capitalization Rules had been found to be invalid by the European Court of Justice, which held that the German Thin Capitalization Rules then in force were in violation of the right of freedom of establishment under the EC-Treaty (12 December 2002, case C-324/00, Lankhorst-Hohorst). As a consequence, the rules could no longer be applied with respect to EU shareholders. Instead of abolishing the discriminatory rules, however, the German government decided to widen their scope and apply them in the future also to domestic shareholder debt financing. With effect for fiscal years commencing after 31 December 2003, new Thin Capitalization Rules apply in Germany. For the application of the Thin Capitalization Rules in Germany in particular the letters – dated 15 December 1994 and 15 July 2004 ("July Letter") – published by the German Federal Ministry of Finance are of relevance. German Thin Capitalization Rules do not address the transfer pricing regime with its arm's length-test. Both regimes apply independently.

Legal requirements

German Thin Capitalization Rules apply, in principle, if all of the following requirements are met.

- A shareholder, which is either a resident or non resident, individual or corporate shareholder, holds more than 25 percent of the share capital of the German or foreign corporation ("substantial shareholder").

- The corporation or a subordinated partnership in which the corporation has a substantial interest is debt financed. The funds are provided by way of a loan, with a fixed or variable rate of interest, including loans which are regarded as deemed equity ("eigenkapitalersetzend"), or a typical silent partnership, a loan with profit participation ("partiarisches Darlehen"), a participating bond ("Gewinnschuldverschreibung") or participating-rights capital ("Genußrechtskapital").

- The debt financing is granted by the substantial shareholder, a party related to the substantial shareholder, or a third party (especially banks) with recourse against the substantial shareholder or the party related to the substantial shareholder.

- The debt is not a short-term liability, which is assumed if it has a term of more than one year.

- The interest payments on the loan exceed € 250,000 ("de minimis threshold") per fiscal year. If the € 250,000 threshold is exceeded by € 1, the full interest amount falls within the scope of the Thin Capitalization Rules.

- In cases where the remuneration for the loan is determined by fractional interest, i.e., a fixed interest rate or a non-profit dependent interest rate, the permitted debt-to-equity ratio of 1.5:1 ("safe haven") is exceeded at any point of time during the fiscal year ("tainted debt") and the test that the loan would have been granted by a third party ("third party test") under the same conditions fails. If the shareholder loan exceeds the safe haven (as determined on the basis of the equity at the end of the previous fiscal year of the corporation) the rules will apply to the interest on the excess debt. In this context, equity means in principle the equity of the borrowing corporation according to German GAAP.

The safe haven and the third party test are not available for the financing if the rate of interest is contingent upon the profit generated by the company.

A checklist is presented in Figure 4.24 in order to assist in determining whether German Thin Capitalization Rules apply.

Tax consequences in Germany

In cases where Thin Capitalization Rules apply, one has to distinguish between the tax consequences on the level of the debt financed company and on the level of the substantial shareholder.

Taxation on the level of the debt financed company

The application of the Thin Capitalization Rules leads to the non-deductibility of interest expenses, to the extent that they are paid on the portion of tainted debt at the level of the borrowing company, which results in a higher taxable income of the domestic corporation for both corporate income tax and trade tax purposes.

The taxable income of corporations in Germany is currently subject to a corporate income tax rate of 25 percent plus a solidarity surcharge on the corporate income tax of 5.5 percent, totaling to approximately 26.4 percent. Moreover, corporations are subject to German trade tax, the amount of which is dependent upon the municipal multiplier applicable in the municipality in which the corporation is carrying on its business. The aggregate tax rate, including corporate income tax and trade tax, should currently amount to approximately 38 percent in the average.

Taxation on the level of the substantial shareholder

At the level of the substantial domestic shareholder being subject to German income tax, the interest payments are reclassified into constructive dividends, which are 100 percent tax exempt in Germany if the domestic shareholder is a corporation, whereas 5 percent of the dividends are treated as non-deductible business expenses. Consequently, from an economic standpoint, 95 percent of the constructive dividends are tax-exempt. In the case of a substantial individual shareholder resident in Germany, 50 percent of the constructive dividends are subject to income tax in Germany (at progressive tax rates, with a maximum income tax rate of currently 42 percent plus solidarity surcharge).

A US shareholder will normally be taxed in the US on its (full) interest income, because the US tax authorities will not reclassify the interest as dividend income. A

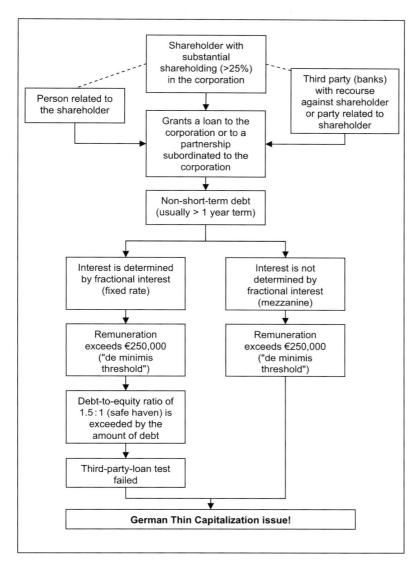

Figure 4.24 Checklist for German Thin Capitalization Rules

withholding tax of 20 percent plus solidarity surcharge of 5.5 percent, totaling to 21.1 percent, has to be withheld by the German debt financed corporation on the constructive dividends (unless a certificate reducing the withholding tax rate to 5 percent, according to Art. 10 of the German-US Tax Treaty 1989, has been provided). It is questionable whether the US tax authorities will grant a tax credit for the German tax withheld at source, because the US authorities will probably not reclassify the interest income into dividend income under the US tax laws. If such a qualification conflict leads to a de facto double taxation of the US shareholder, he should apply for a mutual agreement procedure pursuant to the German-US Tax Treaty 1989.

Example

X-GmbH, resident in Germany, is the sole shareholder of the domestic Y-GmbH. The equity as defined in the German Thin Capitalization Rules amounts to €100,000. X-GmbH grants a loan of €5 million to Y-GmbH at a fixed interest rate of 10 percent p.a. The interest rate complies with arm's length terms.

Variant: The shareholder of Y-GmbH is resident in the US.

Result: The interest payment of €500,000 p.a. exceeds the de minimis threshold of €250,000. The safe haven of 1.5:1 would allow a loan in the maximum amount of €150,000 which is exceeded by an amount of €4.85 million. Therefore, 10 percent interest of €4.85 million (€485,000) are not allowed to be deducted as interest expenses and thus increase the taxable income of Y-GmbH. X-GmbH receives, in addition to a fully taxable interest income of €15,000 (leading to a corporate income tax of €3,750 plus solidarity surcharge and trade tax thereon), a constructive dividend of €485,000, which is 95 percent tax exempt and results in a taxable income of €24,250 for X-GmbH and a corporate income tax of €6,062 (plus solidarity surcharge and trade tax thereon).

In the variant, the US shareholder receives a payment of €500,000, fully subject to US corporate income tax. Withholding tax in an amount of 20 percent of €485,000 plus 5.5 percent solidarity surcharge thereon, i.e. €102,335, must be withheld by Y-GmbH at source unless a certificate reducing the withholding tax rate, according to the German-US Tax Treaty 1989, has been provided.

Third party financing & guarantees

The German Thin Capitalization Rules also apply to third party loans, such as bank loans, where the third party has recourse against the substantial shareholder or a party related thereto (through a legal claim or security in rem), provided that e.g. the third party loan is a "back-to-back" financing. Financing with recourse is assumed, where the interest payments for the third party loan are connected to remunerations for interest bearing deposits, or other long term cash deposits or capital commitments, which the substantial shareholder or a related party thereto has in particular with the lender. In a most recent letter by the German Federal Ministry of Finance dated 22 July 2005, the tax authorities take the view that, for example, a back-to-back financing is, in principle, assumed, if the substantial shareholder has an interest bearing bank account that will be pledged as collateral for the loan granted by the bank to the borrowing company. However, the Thin Capitalization Rules will not apply to such third party loans with recourse if the borrower can prove that there is no connection between the interest payments for the third party loan and the remunerations for the interest bearing deposits of its substantial shareholder or related party thereto.

Holding structures

Special rules apply to holding structures even after the implementation of the new Thin Capitalization Rules. There is still an advantage in being a holding company, because the equity of a holding company will not be reduced by the book value of the shares of subordinated companies when calculating the available safe haven. A holding company, under Thin Capitalization Rules, is defined as a corporation the principal activity of which is to hold and to finance participations in corporations, or the assets of which consist to more than 75 percent of its balance sheet total in participations in other corporations. According to the July Letter, only a corporation subject to German taxation, whether resident or non-resident, can qualify as a holding entity within a corporate chain. Inter-company financing of entities below such a holding entity, e.g. by the ultimate parent, has to be routed through such holding entity, as otherwise the lower tier entity would have no safe haven of its own.

Intra-group debt financing within a fiscal unity

Thin Capitalization Rules do not apply within a so-called fiscal unity ("Organschaft"), because the income of the debt financed subsidiary is allocated to its lending shareholder. A group relief presupposes that (i) the parent company holds directly or indirectly more than 50 percent of the voting rights in the subsidiary; (ii) both companies are subject to unlimited income taxation in Germany; and (iii) both companies have concluded a profit and loss transfer agreement for a minimum term of five years. The disadvantage of a fiscal unity is the obligation of the parent company to pay for the losses of the subsidiary and to be bound by the profit and loss transfer agreement for a period of five years. Apart from that, the fiscal unity is an interesting model to avoid the negative tax consequences resulting from German Thin Capitalization Rules. However, this concept is not available for companies resident abroad.

Outbound financing

The new Thin Capitalization Rules had been hastily drafted, resulting in unintended tax consequences. Under certain constellations, the application of Thin Capitalization Rules might lead to tax advantages within a group. This could apply in a scenario where the interest payments for a loan are tax deductible on the level of the subsidiary abroad and where such interest payments are reclassified in dividends on the level of the lending German parent company, with the consequence that they are 95 percent tax exempt in Germany.

The German tax authorities are trying to close this loophole, which opens tax planning opportunities within a group, by taking, in the July Letter, the view that the reclassification of interest income into dividend income only occurs if the corresponding interest payments have been disallowed as a tax deduction at the level of the foreign subsidiary. Whether this view will be supported by a German court or the European Court of Justice will be seen in future.

US Thin Capitalization Rules

Introduction

There is a set of rules concerning intra-group debt financing in the US. As a general rule, Section 163(a) of the Internal Revenue Code (IRC) provides that a deduction shall be allowed for all interest paid on indebtedness. An instrument will be treated either as debt or equity for US federal income tax ("US tax") purposes, dependent upon the economic substance of the transaction. There is no clear definition of debt and equity. For determining whether funds received by a corporation represent debt or equity for US tax purposes, both objective and subjective evidence of the taxpayer's intent are considered and given weight, in light of the particular circumstances of a case. The US Courts have introduced various criteria for the determination of debt and equity.

If the preliminary question, whether the capital granted qualifies as debt or equity, is answered in favor of debt, then IRC Sec. 482 provides an arm's length standard, known as the transfer pricing rules. Where two or more taxpayers are owned or controlled by the same interests, the Internal Revenue Service may reallocate income and deductions in order to prevent tax evasion or to reflect clearly the income of the respective businesses. Thus, IRC Sec. 482 applies in situations, where, for example, the income of a US corporation will be diminished by granting a loan to its shareholder on terms which are not arm's length, e.g. non-interest bearing loans.

Earning stripping rules

A further set of rules limits the amount of deductible interest expenses, and these are comparable to the German Thin Capitalization Rules: IRC Sec. 163 (j), the so-called "*Earning Stripping Rules.*" These provisions only apply to a US borrower when interest paid to the lender is not completely subject to income tax or withholding tax in the US. In contrast to the German Thin Capitalization Rules, the US provisions are generally limited to cross-border debt financing. The Earning Stripping Rules are supplemented by IRC Sec. 267 (a) (3), which generally allows a payer of interest to deduct such payment only when the corresponding income is includible in the income of the payee.

Legal requirements

Interest paid by a US corporation to a "related person" on whom no US federal tax (either withholding or income tax) is levied with respect to such interest is deemed to be "disqualified interest." A person is a related person if it is financially connected with the corporation, which is the case if it holds more than 50 percent of the corporation's stock or voting rights. Pursuant to Art. 11 para 1 of the German-US Tax Treaty 1989, interest income of a German lender is exempt from US tax and is, therefore, disqualified interest under IRC Sec. 163 (j). The related person who grants the debt financing can be a related corporation, individual, or partnership. In contrast to the German Thin Capitalization Rules, the US Earning Stripping Rules do not apply to loans between related US persons unless they are tax exempt US organizations (such as non-profit organizations).

A checklist is presented in Figure 4.25 in order to assist in determining whether Earning Stripping Rules apply.

Tax consequences in the US

The application of the Earning Stripping Rules results in the non-deductibility of disqualified interest. IRC Sec. 163 (j) applies when a US corporation pays disqualified interest and fails both the debt-to-equity test and the ATI-test (Adjusted Taxable

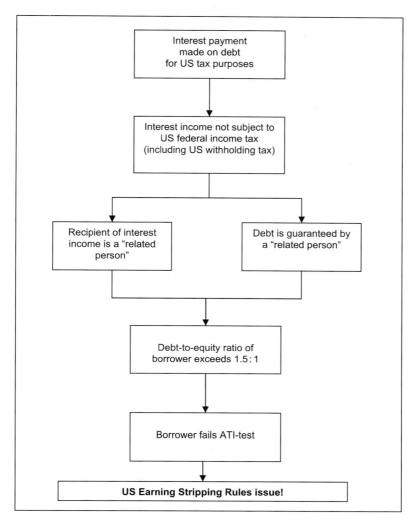

Figure 4.25 Checklist for US Earning Stripping Rules

Income). Firstly, it is necessary to examine whether the corporation exceeds the debt-to-equity ratio of 1.5:1 (safe haven), and secondly, whether it has so-called "excess interest expense" (ATI-test). The debt-to-equity test compares the borrower's total indebtedness (with certain adjustments) to its equity (total assets minus total liabilities at tax basis value).

The ATI-test fails if a corporation has interest expenses in excess of the sum of (i) 50 percent of the "adjusted taxable income" and (ii) any "excess limitation carry forward." Adjusted taxable income means the taxable income of the taxpayer for the tax year prior to deductions for net interest expense, net operating losses, depreciation, amortization or depletion, etc. "Excess limitation" is assumed when 50 percent of the adjusted taxable income exceeds the net interest expense. That excess can be carried forward in the three subsequent fiscal years to increase the threshold for the ATI-test.

Unlike the German Thin Capitalization Rules, IRC Sec. 163 (j) does not influence the tax treatment of the lender receiving the interest payments as the Earning Stripping Rules generally apply in cases where the lender is not taxable in the US. The US Earning Stripping Rules also do not have a special set of rules for holding companies.

Example

X-GmbH, a German holding company, owns 100 percent of Y-Inc., a company resident in the US. X-GmbH grants a loan to Y-Inc. and receives an annual interest payment of $ 30, which meets arm's length standards. Y-Inc. has the following balance sheet.

Assumptions:			Limitation of Interest Expense:
Assets (fair value)	=	$ 1400	∅ Debt-to-equity ratio < 60:40 < 1.5
Assets (tax basis)	=	$ 1000	✗ no, as 700 / 300 = 2.3
Liabilities	=	$ 700	(safe haven not met)
Equity	=	$ 300	∅ Excess interest expense (ATI-test)
Interest expense	=	$ 30	✗ none, as 30 < (90 x 50% = 45)
Depreciation	=	$ 20	∅ Result: interest of $ 30 is fully tax
Adjusted taxable income	=	$ 90	deductible
Excess limitation carry forward	=	$ 0	

Third party financing & guarantees

Disqualified interest includes interest payments to an unrelated person if and to the extent a disqualified guarantee is granted by a related non-US person (e.g., a German corporation) for the financing (e.g., of the US subsidiary) by a third party (e.g., non-US bank), if the interest payments received by such a third party are not subject to US tax. A guarantee includes any arrangement under which a person assures the payment of another person's obligation under any indebtedness, commitment to make a capital contribution to the debtor to maintain its financial viability, or any arrangement according to a comfort letter, regardless of whether this comfort letter is legally enforceable.

Intra-group debt financing within an affiliated group

Under the Earning Stripping Rules, all members of an "affiliated group" are treated as one entity. In this context an affiliated group is defined as one or more chains of US corporations connected (directly or indirectly) through stock ownership and voting rights of at least 80 percent. Members of an affiliated group generally combine their income, expense and carry-over items, etc. with those of other members by filing a consolidated return. The debt-to-equity test has to be applied on an adjusted basis of the assets and debts of the consolidated group resulting in intra-group stock and debt (that is, stock of or debt from a fellow member of an affiliated group) held directly or indirectly being eliminated in the debt-to-equity test for the members of an affiliated group.

Deemed dividend rules

In respect of collateral granted by a controlled foreign corporation (CFC), e.g., a German subsidiary, in support of a loan obligation of its US shareholder the so-called "deemed dividend rules" of IRC Sec. 956 are to be considered. A non-US corporation will be deemed a CFC if more than 50 percent of its capital or voting rights is owned by US persons, each of whom owns at least 10 percent of the voting rights of the CFC. If a CFC guarantees the repayment obligation of a US shareholder or pledges its assets to secure such repayment, the US shareholder has to include a certain amount as deemed dividend equal to the lesser of (i) the outstanding amount of the loan and (ii) the earnings and profits of the CFC – as calculated under US tax law – in his taxable income. If deemed dividend rules apply, the US shareholder has to pay tax without actually having received a dividend from the CFC.

Conclusions

The difference between the US Earning Stripping Rules and the German Thin Capitalization Rules lies in their scope of application. In contrast to the US provisions, the German Thin Capitalization Rules are also relevant to domestic shareholder debt financing. The minimum ownership requirement of at least 50 percent in the US under which Earning Stripping Rules come into play differs from Thin Capitalization Rules in Germany where those rules already apply to a shareholding of more than 25 percent. The regimes in both countries employ special rules in regard to the financing by third parties. Both regimes might result in a de facto double taxation within a group. In order to avoid the application of the German Thin Capitalization Rules or the US Earning Stripping Rules a thorough tax planning as well as constant control of the intra-group financing is required.

4.4.4 Share Pledges in German/US Mergers and Acquisitions

Russell J. DaSilva

Share pledges are common in German/US mergers and acquisitions,
but when shares of companies in the United States are involved,
these pledges may be laden with complications. This article focuses
on issues that may arise in the due diligence process, in the
determination of applicable law, in the granting or release of
security interests, and in the steps taken for perfection.

The lenders that provide financing for transatlantic mergers and acquisitions transactions often require the acquiring party to pledge the shares of stock or other equity interests in all existing and future subsidiaries of the target company in order to secure repayment of the acquisition credits. When those subsidiaries are in the United States, complications can arise in the closing of the transaction, the taking of security, and the maintenance of security throughout the life of the credit facility.

Due diligence

The first step for a German acquiror and its lender is to identify those companies in the United States whose shares will be pledged. It is essential to know:

Name

The precise name of each company (a "doing business" name is not sufficient).

Type of business organization

Until relatively recently, most companies in the US were organized as business corporations, but today limited liability companies are nearly as common. In addition, some subsidiaries with the word "Company" in their names may in fact be organized as limited partnerships. The method for pledging the equity interests in each of these types of business organization may differ.

Jurisdiction of organization

While term sheets from European lenders often identify US subsidiaries as being organized "under the laws of the USA," in fact corporations, limited liability companies and partnerships are entirely creatures of state law, and each of the fifty states has its own statutory and common law regime governing these entities.[1] Moreover, European acquirors and their lenders typically assume that a company in the United States

---

[1] Corporations can be formed under certain United States federal laws, but with the exception of national banks, few are likely to be business corporations that will be the target of an acquisition. This is a notable difference between the United States and Canada, for in Canada business corporations may be chartered under the laws of a province or territory or under Canadian federal law.

is organized under the laws of the state in which the company is headquartered or principally doing business, but that often is not the case. A corporation or limited liability company organized under the laws of one state may well have its headquarters or principal production facilities in one or more other states. Delaware is a particularly popular jurisdiction for incorporation, even if the company has no business operations there.

Statutory background

Pledges of shares of company stock are a type of security interest in personal property and are governed by state law, not US federal law. Virtually all jurisdictions in the United States have adopted the Uniform Commercial Code ("UCC"), and most secured transactions involving personal property (as opposed to real estate) are governed by Article 9 of that statute. In addition, when the collateral is shares of stock, Article 8 of the UCC also is relevant. Variations in the UCC and its interpretation do exist from state to state, but many concepts and terminology are close to universal.

Steps for granting a security interest

Article 9 of the UCC contemplates four critical steps in a secured transaction.

Attachment

When a security interest has "attached" in favor of the secured party, it is enforceable against the pledger (called the "debtor" in the UCC). "Attachment" occurs when the debtor has rights in the collateral, value has been given, and the debtor and secured party have entered into a written security agreement.

Perfection

The procedure by which the security interest becomes enforceable against third parties is called "perfection." Article 9 provides for several methods of perfection of security interests, depending on the nature of the collateral. In the case of shares of stock, perfection is governed by Article 8 of the UCC, and, as further discussed below, the method of perfection depends in part on whether the shares are evidenced by share certificates and, if so, where the share certificates are located.

Priority

For many types of personal property serving as collateral, it is possible for more than one secured party to claim a perfected security interest. The third step of any analysis of a secured transaction, therefore, is "priority." Article 9 of the UCC typically provides that the priority among perfected secured parties is based on timing, and "first in time" is "first in right." However, the UCC also makes a distinction between different methods of perfection. In the case of pledges of shares of stock, perfection by possession or control takes priority over other methods of perfection. This, too, is discussed further below.

Enforcement

This is the secured party's exercise of its remedies in the collateral. A full discussion of the procedure for enforcement of security interests is beyond the scope of this contribution, but it is worth noting that the secured party's typical remedy upon enforcement is a public or private sale of the collateral to a third party and application of the proceeds of that sale to the repayment of the secured obligation. Secured lenders in Europe often assume that they will be permitted to accept ownership of the collateral in lieu of payment of all or a portion of the secured claim. Article 9 of the UCC does contemplate the possibility of this remedy (often referred to by lawyers in the United States as a "strict foreclosure"), but it is subject to limitations, including a requirement that the debtor consent to the strict foreclosure *after* the secured obligation has gone into default. Moreover, certain other parties may have the right to receive notice of and object to a strict foreclosure. So as a practical matter this remedy may not be available.

Methods of perfection

When the shares of a US subsidiary are in "certificated" form (as most commonly will be the case for wholly-owned subsidiaries), the UCC says that perfection is achieved when the secured party or its representative takes physical possession of the share certificates together with the debtor's indorsement of those share certificates in blank by an effective indorsement. The indorsement typically is set forth in a one-page document called a "stock power," which is signed by the debtor but not otherwise filled in.

In the unusual circumstance in which the shares of a subsidiary are "uncertificated," the UCC provides that perfection occurs either when the uncertificated security has been "delivered" to the secured party (i.e., when the issuer of the security registers the secured party as the registered owner of the security) or when the issuer of the security agrees that it will comply with instructions originated by the secured party without further consent by the registered owner.

For both certificated and uncertificated securities, the UCC also provides a second method of perfection: the filing of a UCC-1 financing statement. A financing statement is a simple document that identifies the name and address of the debtor, the name and address of the secured party, a description of the collateral, and some other very basic information. It is filed by one of the parties (typically the secured party) in the office of the Secretary of State or comparable office of the appropriate jurisdiction in the United States. If filing is made by the secured party, the filing must have been authorized by the debtor. Under Section 9-509(b) of the UCC, a debtor that signs a security agreement is deemed to have authorized the filing of a UCC-1 financing statement, but lenders often provide for a specific authorization in the security agreement.

Lenders would be ill-advised, however, to rely on a filed UCC-1 financing statement as the sole method of perfection for securities, because any other secured party who perfects by possession or control will have priority over the secured party who perfects only by filing. This is an exception to the "first in time, first in right" rule of priority described above.

Applicable law

The UCC does not specify what law will govern a security agreement, so the parties are free to select it in their contract. It is not necessary that it be the state of incorporation of the company whose shares are being pledged or even of the company that is the pledgor. There is no reason, for example, why the shares of a Delaware corporation must be pledged under a security agreement governed by Delaware law. It is far more common for lenders in the United States to select the law of the state in which the particular lender is located or of another state, such as New York, with which lenders tend to feel comfortable.

At least in theory, the parties could select a law outside the United States, such as German law, to govern a security agreement. Nevertheless, if enforcement of the security interest will be taken in the United States, use of a non-US law security agreement may give rise to procedural complications. For example, a court in the United States may, at the very least, require that the secured party prove that the terms of the German-law document are sufficient to create a "security interest" and that the security interest "attached" within the meaning of Article 9 of the UCC. In an extreme case, a court in the United States might even require the secured party to present a judgment of a German court as to the validity of the German-law pledge, or perhaps even an order of foreclosure from a German court.

The law governing attachment of a security interest in shares of stock is not necessarily the same as the law that governs perfection. While the parties may select the law that governs their security agreement, the UCC determines what law governs the perfection, the effect of perfection or non-perfection, and priority of the security interest. According to Article 9, for certificated securities, the law of the jurisdiction where the share certificates are located governs perfection by possession. This means that a non-US lender would be well advised to hold the collateral at a branch in the United States or with a custodian located in the United States. A non-US lender that intends to take the share certificates back to its home office outside the United States should consult with counsel there and make sure that all steps under the law of that jurisdiction have been taken to ensure perfection there. As a practical matter, this means that the securities are likely to be pledged twice, under parallel documents governed by two different laws.

Perfection of a security interest in an uncertificated security in most cases is governed by the law of the jurisdiction of organization of the company whose shares of stock are being pledged.

Finally, perfection of a security interest in any security, whether certificated or uncertificated, if made by filing of a UCC-1 financing statement, is governed by the law of the place where the debtor is "located." For most corporations organized under a law in the United States, this is the jurisdiction of incorporation of the pledgor. On the other hand, a debtor that is a company organized outside the United States is deemed to be "located" in the jurisdiction of its organization only if that jurisdiction generally provides for perfection of security interests by a filing, recording or registration system, presumably along the lines of a UCC-1 financing statement. All other organizations are deemed to be "located" in Washington D.C., and filings would be made there.[1]

Limited liability companies

A common misconception is that the membership interests in a limited liability company are treated in the same way as shares of stock of a corporation for purposes of the granting of a security interest, but that is not necessarily the case. The limited liability company is a very flexible form of business organization and its members have considerable leeway to structure the company according to the unique needs of the parties. The "limited liability company agreement" or "operating agreement," which is the principal organization document of an LLC, may contain an election for the membership interests to be treated as securities, and may even provide for the issuance of certificates evidencing those membership interests. If that is the case, a security interest in those membership interests will be treated under the UCC as a certificated or uncertificated security, as the case may be, and perfection will be achieved as provided above for corporations. On the other hand, if the limited liability company agreement or operating agreement for an LLC does not contain a securities election, then the membership interests in that LLC are likely to be considered to be "general intangibles" under Article 9 of the UCC, and the security interest in them is perfected by the filing of a UCC-1 financing statement naming the member as "debtor." For that reason, experienced counsel in the United States should review the limited liability company or operating agreement of each LLC to evaluate the proper characterization of its membership interests.

Limited partnership interests

A limited partnership interest most likely will be characterized as a "general intangible" under the UCC, and perfection will be achieved by the filing of a UCC-1 financing statement. Here, too, however, counsel in the United States should be asked to review the limited partnership agreement to see what other consequences there may be. If the goal of the secured lender (or its transferee in foreclosure) is to step into the shoes of the pledger and become the limited partner, the lender should be aware that limited partnership agreements typically limit the type of person or entity that can become a substitute limited partner. This is because the change of limited partners can give rise to consequences under laws relating to taxation, investment companies, securities and employee benefits. At the very least, the purchaser of a limited partnership interest will need to be approved by the general partner, and a substitute general partner will, in all likelihood, require the consent of all other parties to the limited partnership agreement. It is doubtful that these consents can be obtained in advance, when the identity of the substitute limited partner or general partner is not yet known. Accordingly, limited partnership interests should not necessarily be considered liquid.

---

[1] Special rules apply to limited partnerships that are not required to be registered in the state of their organization, and general partnerships.

Steps for closing

The steps for closing a secured transaction in which shares of US subsidiary serve as collateral in theory require little more than the due execution and delivery of the security agreement, and delivery of the original share certificates and stock power, and in some cases, the filing of a UCC-1 financing statement. Once again, however, the process doesn't end there.

Share certificates

It is not uncommon for companies that are to be acquired to discover that they are unable to locate all of the original share certificates for their subsidiaries. There are procedures under most state statutes and corporate by-laws by which shares certificates can be reissued, but the corporate secretary of the issuer in question may need at least a few days to go through the corporate formalities. Borrowers frequently ask if share certificates can be delivered on a post-closing basis, but lenders need to be careful that they do not put at risk the perfection or priority of their security interest.

Existing pledges

The shares may already be pledged to an existing lender, as security for debts that will remain outstanding until the closing of the acquisition. In that case it is likely that the existing lender has physical possession of the share certificates. They also may have a UCC-1 financing statement on file that includes a reference to the shares or to "all personal property." It would be optimal if the existing lender were to release its security interest in the shares and deliver the share certificates back to the debtor and terminate UCC-1 financing statements in advance of the closing of the acquisition, but that rarely is feasible. Existing lenders typically insist on being paid out in full before they will release any collateral. In these circumstances, attorneys in the United States frequently set up a closing in escrow. The share certificates, pay-off letters, releases and other similar documents are delivered to one of the attorneys in escrow, with instructions to release them to the appropriate parties only when all steps for the closing have been completed and the funds are being transferred.

Termination of existing liens

One of the important documents in connection with this type of closing in escrow is a written authorization by the existing lender to file UCC-3 "termination statements" terminating the existing lender's security interest of record in the pledged shares. While the termination statement could be filed either by the existing lender or by the debtor, filing on behalf of the existing lender provides greater certainty to future secured creditors that the termination of the security interest was authorized by the existing lender. For that reason, an authorization by the existing lender in favor of one of the other parties (or their counsel) to file the UCC-3 termination statement should expressly authorize filing it on behalf of the existing lender.

4.5 Valuation & Due Diligence

4.5.1 Differences in Valuation Methods – A Comparison of Income Approach Valuation

Manfred Bögle and Rainer Bätz

The purpose of this article is to illustrate the general differences in valuation methods and models used in Germany and in the U.S. The comparison will focus on income approach valuation. The differences will be highlighted by using examples.

Introduction and overview

In Germany and in the U.S., professional valuation experts have to follow national valuation guidelines that set out the requirements for professional valuation. The standards in Germany – for chartered accountants – are set by the Institute of Chartered Accounts (IDW). U.S. valuation professionals need to comply with General Accepted Valuation Practices guidelines, which – compared to German standards – are much more general.

In Germany as well as in the U.S., the Discounted Cash Flow method is typically used to determine the value of a company. In Germany, the Earning Value (EV) Method (Ertragswertverfahren) is also common.

Both methods are based on the concept of calculating the present value (PV) of future cash/income streams by using an appropriate discount rate. Whilst the EV uses the net income (after interest) as a basis for calculating the present value, the DCF method distinguishes between calculation of an equity or an entity value by using pre-interest or post-interest cash flows. These streams are income or cash flow streams to equity and thus have to be discounted at the cost of equity. The DCF method based on pre-interest cash flows needs to discount these streams using a discount rate that includes the cost of equity and the cost of debt. The relevant discount rate – based on the CAPM model – reflects a weighted-average cost of capital (WACC) and leads to an enterprise value including equity and debt values. When using the DCF entity approach, one needs to deduct the fair value of the debt to arrive at the equity value. In principle, all of these methods should lead to the same equity values.

In Germany as well as in the U.S., professional valuation standards require that the results of any valuation be benchmarked with the results obtained by using other valuation techniques (e.g., market approach methods like multiples, etc.). The purpose of the benchmark analysis is to check the valuation results for plausibility.

In the case of legally motivated valuations in Germany, the actual share price is the minimum value of the company per share, according to the Federal Constitution Court[1]. No such stipulated minimum exists in US valuation practice.

German valuation standards

The standard issued by the IDW is relevant to legally and non-legally motivated valuations. Legally motivated valuations are mainly performed because they are required by the German Stock Corporation Act (AktG). Specific instances include:

- Control agreements acc. to Section 304 of the AktG,
- Integrations acc. to Section 319 of the AktG,
- Squeeze-outs acc. to Section 327a of the AktG

Such valuations are also required by the Transformation Act (UmwG). Specific instances include:

- Carve-outs acc. to Section 123 of the UmwG
- Mergers acc. to Section 60 of the UmwG.

Whereas non-legally motivated valuations are not limited in their choice of the valuation model used (e.g. Discounted Cash Flow, Earning Value, Multiples, etc.) nor in the composition of the underlying income or cash streams (e.g. inclusion/exclusion of synergies), legally motivated valuations must follow a predefined valuation model that leads to the fair value ("Objektivierter Unternehmenswert") of the company.

Professional valuation standards for accountants in Germany have significantly changed in recent years. Until 2000, a pre-tax valuation model according to IDW HFA 2/83 was used. One of the reasons for modifications of the valuation standard was an extensive makeover of the German tax regime. Until 2001, corporate taxes were allowable against personal income taxes of the shareholder for dividends received ("Anrechnungsverfahren"). For the shareholder, corporate income tax was a pre-payment on his income tax. This means that ultimately a company's distribution was only burdened with trade tax and each shareholder's personal income tax.

From a shareholder's point of view, the discount rate – which represents the return on the alternative investment – is also burdened with his personal income tax. Under this tax regime, corporate income tax or a shareholder's personal income tax is not relevant to valuation because the tax position – without trade tax – can be eliminated as follows:

- Present value = Profit x $(1 - s)$ / discount rate x $(1 - s)$
- Present value = Profit before tax / discount rate before tax

When IDW S1 (2000) and its updated version, IDW ES 1 (2004), were implemented, a shareholder's tax position became part of the valuation model. As mentioned above, Germany's tax regime has significantly changed. Now corporate income tax can no longer be set off against personal income tax. Retained profits are now subject to corporate income tax and trade tax, and distributed profits are additionally taxed with personal income tax. The basis for income tax calculation is 50% of the dividends received (half-income taxation method or "Halbeinkünfteverfahren").

---

[1] Cp. BVerfG, Decision dated April 27, 1999 – 1 BvR 1613/94, in: DB 1999, p. 1693 ff.

Usually, a company's stock is held by a variety of different shareholders whose personal income tax rates vary. Therefore, IDW S1 is based on what is assumed to be a typical shareholder's tax position. Based on statistical analysis, the average income tax rate in Germany is 35%. Thus, when fair value ("Objektivierter Unternehmenswert") is calculated, a 35% tax rate is applied.

In accordance with the principle of equivalence, the required return on the alternative investment should also reflect a shareholder's individual tax position. Therefore, the Tax-CAPM is used to determine the appropriate discount rate (WACC). This has two major implications:

- Relevant cash flow is after corporate income tax and personal tax
- The discount factor is after personal tax

Whereas HFA 2/83 and IDW S1 assumed a complete distribution of net income or the available free cash flow, the new standard requires assumptions about the distribution policy since the tax position for distributed and retained profits is different.

On average, the above changes in valuation methods have resulted in enterprise values that are approximately 20% to 30% lower than those under HFA 2/83.

For non-legally motivated transactions IDW S1 stated that the individual position (including the tax position) of the transaction partners should be considered.

IDW ES1 assumes that retained earnings will not be used to repay interest-bearing debt but will be reinvested in the company at a rate of return that equals the cost of equity.

U.S. valuation standards

In contrast to the relatively strict regulations of the Institute of Chartered Accountants in Germany that apply to fair value calculation, U.S. valuation professionals are required to follow Generally Accepted Valuation Principles which do not stipulate any specific method. The AICPA (American Institute of Certified Public Accountants) has issued an exposure draft that seeks to introduce Standards for Valuation Services[1]. According to this exposure draft, three valuation approaches should be considered:

- The income approach (earnings and DCF method)
- The asset-based approach or cost approach
- The market approach (the public company method and the transaction method)

The exposure draft specifies what should be included in a valuation report and discusses the steps that, at a minimum, must be performed to be able to adequately value a company. The exposure draft does not give any guidance on what to include in the discountable cash or income streams (e.g. taxes), nor does it say how a discount rate should preferably be calculated.

---

[1] Cp. AICPA, Exposure Draft "Proposed Statement on Standards for Valuation Services: Valuation of a Business, Business Ownership Interest, Security, or Intangible Asset"; March 30, 2005

Depending on the level of company information available, DCF valuation models are typically used to calculate company value. The result is benchmarked against the results obtained by using other valuation techniques (e.g., market valuation). As in Germany, there are legal circumstances that require independent valuation. Such legally motivated valuations are regularly performed during squeeze-outs, mergers etc. The main difference from the German legal environment is that such legal requirements may vary from state to state.

In contrast to Germany, there is no nation-wide valuation organization that issues recommendations for the application of valuation techniques or the actual levels of risk-free rates or risk premiums that should be applied when calculating fair value. This lack of uniformity requires the particular circumstances of each valuation to be scrutinized.

Each appraiser is responsible for how he or she decides to calculate the appropriate discount rate. There is no predefined approach that defines the elements of such discount rate. Depending on the individual circumstances, the discount rate might be calculated as a WACC or an industry-specific IRR. The actual values chosen (e.g., for the risk-free rate or market risk premium) were usually obtained or derived from generally accepted valuation books (e.g., the Ibbotson "Cost of Capital Yearbook") that annually analyze such parameters.

For the purpose of calculating cash compensations for minority shareholders, a minority interest discount is usually deducted from the equity value, reflecting the inverse of the idea of a control premium that must usually be paid when acquiring a majority of a company's voting rights. This discount may be based, e.g., on the "Control Premium" issued by the annual Mergerstat Review.

Examples

All of the examples are based on the following key financial figures:

in USD thousand	2006	2007	2008	2009	2010	Terminal Value
Sales	1.100	1.200	1.300	1.400	1.500	1.515
Expenses	650	700	750	800	850	859
EBIT	450	500	550	600	650	657
Interest	200	200	200	200	200	202
Taxes (corporate and trade tax)	93	112	131	149	168	170
Net income	157	188	219	251	282	285

in USD thousand	2006	2007	2008	2009	2010	Terminal Value
Change in WC	0	0	0	0	0	0
Depreciation	20	20	20	20	20	20
CAPEX	20	20	20	20	20	20
Free Cash Flow (after taxes)	357	388	419	451	482	487
Distribution quote	50%	50%	50%	50%	50%	50%

For simplification purposes it is assumed that an increase in sales will not affect working capital.

Germany

The calculation of the discount rate used to determine fair value is based on the Tax-CAPM[1] model originally created by Brennan in 1970. Since the return on the alternative investment – which is reflected in the WACC – will affect personal income tax, calculation of the cost of equity is modified as follows:

- The risk-free rate – reflecting an investment in government bonds – has to be adjusted for the personal income tax rate (which is 35% because interest income is fully taxable); as announced by the IDW's Valuation Board (Arbeitskreis Unternehmensbewertung "AKU") in July, 2005, a risk free rate of 4.25% should be used. This recommendation is based on empirical analysis of the yield curves of long-term German government bonds;
- The market risk premium reflects the after-tax excess return (return in excess of the risk-free rate) of an investment in a diversified stock portfolio. The Valuation Board recommends using a post-tax market risk premium in the range of 5.0% to 6.0% to calculate fair value ("Objektivierter Unternehmenswert") or a pre-tax market risk premium in the range of 4.0% to 5.0%. This recommendation is based on empirical studies of the return rates of diversified stock portfolios over the last 50 years. The market risk premium includes an adjustment to reflect expectations of future volatility.

For the calculation of subjective values, using WACC as a discount rate is one of the potential possibilities. The discount rate usually reflects the individual circumstances of the investor. Depending on the purpose of the valuation, the individual IRR (internal rate of return) of an alternative investment, interest rates for the repayment of debt, or an individual WACC may be chosen as an appropriate discount rate.

---

[1] Cp. Jonas/Löffler/Wiese, WPg 2004 (Fn. 28), p. 904.

For the purposes of the German earning value method, the discount rate for fair value valuation is calculated as follows:

	Discount rate
Risk free rate	4.2500%
income tax on risk free rate	
− (35% for the typical shareholder)	−1.4875%
	2.7625%
+ Risk premium	
Market risk premium (pre tax)	5.0000%
× Beta	100.0000%
	5.0000%
Discount rate	**7.7625%**

To arrive at terminal value, using a growth rate should be considered. Normally a growth rate of 1% is used. When calculating terminal value, one would thus use a discount rate of 6.76%.

When the DCF equity approach is used, the discount rate is calculated in the same manner.

When using the DCF entity approach, one needs to consider the cost of debt. The discount factor equals the weighted average cost of capital (comprising equity and debt), WACC, and is calculated as follows:

	WACC
Risk free rate	4.2500%
income tax on risk free rate	
− (35% for the typical shareholder)	−1.4875%
	2.7625%
+ Risk premium	
Market risk premium (pre tax)	5.0000%
× Beta	100.0000%
= Cost of equity	**7.7625%**
Pre-tax cost of debt	7.0000%
Tax rate (company tax rate + typical income tax on 50% on after tax interest)	48.2800%
= After-tax cost of debt	**3.6204%**
Debt weighting (fair value of debt/equity value)	53.1100%
WACC	**5.5626%**

As debt weights will vary from period to period, WACC will be slightly different each period.

To calculate terminal value, growth rates should be used both for the cost of equity and the cost of debt. A growth rate of 1% is common. Thus, the WACC used for the calculation of terminal value equals 4.77%.

Based on the above example, application of two different valuation methods yields the following values for the main valuation parameters:

						Terminal value	
in USD thousand	2006	2007	2008	2009	2010	Distributed	Retained
DCF entity approach							
Free cash flow (after taxes)	357	388	419	451	482	487	
- Interest	-200	-200	-200	-200	-200	-202	
= Free Cash flow to equity	157	188	219	251	282	285	
Distribution quote	50%	50%	50%	50%	50%	50%	
= Retained profit	78	94	110	125	141	142	
Tax shield on interest	75	75	75	75	75	75	
Distributed cash flow (= free cash flow – retained profit – tax shield on interest)	204	219	235	251	266	269	142
+ Income from retained earnings	0	6	14	23	34	40	
= Total distributed cash flow	204	226	249	274	300	309	
- Personal income tax on 50% of total distributed cash flow	-36	-40	-44	-48	-53	-54	
= Net cash inflow	168	186	205	225	246	253	142
DCF equity approach and EV approach							
Free cash flow	357	388	419	451	482	487	
- Interest	200	200	200	200	200	202	
= Net income	157	188	219	251	282	285	
Distribution quote	50%	50%	50%	50%	50%	50%	
+ Income from retained earnings	0	6	14	23	34	40	
Total distributed income	78	101	124	149	175	182	
- Personal income tax on 50% of total distributed income	-14	-18	-22	-26	-31	-32	
Income	65	83	102	121	142	148	142

in USD thousand	2006	2007	2008	2009	2010	Terminal value	
						Distributed	Retained
Discount basis							
Earning value	65	83	102	121	142	148	142
DCF equity	65	83	102	121	142	148	142
DCF entity	168	186	205	225	246	253	142
Discount rate							
Earning value	7.7625%	7.7625%	7.7625%	7.7625%	7.7625%	6.7625%	6.7625%
DCF equity	7.7625%	7.7625%	7.7625%	7.7625%	7.7625%	6.7625%	6.7625%
DCF entity	5.5624%	5.6118%	5.6570%	5.6983%	5.7355%	4.7689%	4.7689%

Equity value	
Earning value	3.357,2
DCF equity	3.357,2
DCF entity	3.357,2

U.S.

Calculation of the discount rate for purposes of determining fair value is based on the CAPM model.

The risk-free rate typically used is based on empirical analysis of the yield curve of twenty-year U.S. treasury bonds. Actually, a risk-free rate of approx. 4.55% is used.

The market risk premium reflects the excess return (return in excess of the risk-free rate) of an investment in a diversified stock portfolio. The premium used is before income tax and is based on empirical studies of the return rates of diversified stock portfolios[1] over the last 80 years. The risk premium will typically be adjusted to reflect the appraiser's estimate. Usually, the market risk premium is adjusted as follows:

- *Price-to-earnings (P/E) ratio adjustment:* The P/E adjustment is intended to reverse the average annual appreciation in the P/E ratio included in the reference stock index over the measurement period (1926-2004)[2]. The reference stock index in this example is the Standard & Poor 500 index. The rationale for the adjustment is that in an efficient market the best estimate of the future S&P 500 P/E ratio is the current ratio – there is no reason to expect sustained expansion or contraction of the P/E ratio. Thus, in projecting the future market risk premium, the contribution to the realized market risk premium of the historical S&P 500 P/E expansion is reversed since it is not expected to recur.

- *Volatility adjustment:* The volatility adjustment is made to refine historical market risk premiums to reflect current expectations of future market risk premium vola-

---

[1] Cp. for example: Ibbotson & Associates; Stock, Bonds, Bills & Inflation, 2005

[2] Cp. Ibbotson & Associates; Stock, Bonds, Bills & Inflation, 2005, p. 95, and Roger Ibbotson & Peng Chen; Financial Analysts Journal, January/February 2003

tility.[1] The historical arithmetic-average market risk premium is partly a function of its volatility over the measurement period (1926–2004). The refinement truncates the historical period of market risk premium variance to measure only the trailing 50 years of variance. The rationale for the adjustment is that the better estimate of future market risk premium volatility is thought to be that of the trailing 50 years rather than the longer period, because there were incidences of market risk premium volatility in the early years of its measurement period that appear anomalous, that have not recurred in the last 50 years, and that are thought more likely not to recur in the future than to recur.

On the basis of a raw market risk premium of approx. 7.2% and the adjustments made for the P/E ratio (-0.9%) and for volatility (-0.67%), the adjusted market risk premium equals approx. 5.6%.

When the DCF equity method is used in the U.S., the discount rate is calculated as follows:

	Discount rate
Risk free rate	4.5500%
	4.5500%
+ Risk premium	
Market risk premium (pre tax)	5.6000%
× Beta	100.0000%
	5.6000%
Discount rate	**10.1500%**

When using the DCF entity approach, one needs to consider the cost of debt. The discount factor equals the weighted average cost of capital (comprising equity and debt), WACC, and is calculated as follows:

	WACC
Risk free rate	4.5500%
	4.5500%
+ Risk premium	
Market risk premium (pre tax)	5.6000%
× Beta	100.0000%
= Cost of equity	**10.1500%**
Pre-tax cost of debt	7.0000%
Tax rate (company tax rate)	37.3125%
= After-tax cost of debt	**4.3881%**
Debt weighting (fair value of debt/equity value)	56.6800%
WACC	**6.8842%**

[1] Cp. Triumph of the Optimistics: 101 Years of Global Investment Returns (New Jersey: Princeton University Press, 2002)

As debt weights will vary from period to period, WACC will be slightly different each period.

To calculate terminal value, a growth rate should be used both for the cost of equity and the cost of debt. A growth rate of 1% is common. Thus, the WACC used for the calculation of terminal value equals 6.24%.

Application of two different valuation methods yields the following values for the main valuation parameters:

in USD thousand	2006	2007	2008	2009	2010	Terminal value Distributed	Retained
DCF entity approach							
Free cash flow (after taxes)	357	388	419	451	482	487	
- Interest	-200	-200	-200	-200	-200	-202	
= Free cash flow to equity	157	188	219	251	282	285	
Distribution quote	50%	50%	50%	50%	50%	50%	
= Retained profit	78	94	110	125	141	142	
Tax shield on interest	75	75	75	75	75	75	
Distributed cash flow (= free cash flow – retained profit – tax shield on interest)	204	219	235	251	266	269	142
- Personal income tax on 50% of total distributed cash flow	0	8	17	29	41	50	
= Net cash inflow	204	227	253	279	308	319	142
DCF equity approach							
Free cash flow	357	388	419	451	482	487	
- Interest	200	200	200	200	200	202	
= Net income	157	188	219	251	282	285	
Distribution quote	50%	50%	50%	50%	50%	50%	
+ Income from retained earnings	0	8	17	29	41	50	
Income	78	102	127	154	182	193	142

in USD thousand	2006	2007	2008	2009	2010	Terminal value	
						Distributed	Retained
Discount basis							
DCF equity	78	102	127	154	182	193	142
DCF entity	204	227	253	279	308	319	142
Discount rate							
DCF equity	10.1500%	10.1500%	10.1500%	10.1500%	10.1500%	9.1500%	9.1500%
DCF entity	6.8842%	6.9713%	7.0506%	7.1219%	7.1849%	6.2398%	6.2398%
Equity value							
DCF equity	2.726,1						
DCF entity	2.726,1						

Summary of valuation discrepancies

In principle, the methodology used when valuations are performed in the U.S. is no different from the German methodology. In cases where legally motivated valuation is required, fair value ("Objektivierter Unternehmenswert") varies significantly from the values obtained in similar U.S. valuations.

The main differences include the following:

- In the U.S., a shareholder's tax position is not included (neither in the income or cash streams nor in the discount rate);
- Control premiums are included in the U.S.; German valuation practice does not account for such premiums;
- Due to the IDW S1 methodology and the recommendations of the Valuation Board ("AKU") regarding the risk-free rate and the market risk premium, German valuation practice is much more standardized than U.S. practice.
- Measured U.S. market risk premiums are adjusted to reflect the actual P/E (price-to-earnings) ratio and expectations of future volatility. In Germany, the risk premium is also adjusted to reflect expectations of future volatility.

4.5.2 Cross Border Due Diligence and Beyond

Georg Christopher Schweiger

The substantial number of transactions confirms that merger and acquisition activity has become an established part of the strategic tool kit for corporate development and portfolio management. Conducting a thorough analysis of the target company may seem to be the obvious course of action. Differences in culture, access to information and corporate governance create disparate policies and expectations on both sides of the Atlantic. Learning from due diligence can help to mitigate the uncertainties and imperfections of any transaction.

Buying and selling a business has become an established part of corporate life. Mergers and acquisitions have initiated considerable debate in board rooms, among policy makers and within the academic community. Numerous aspects have been discussed and complex models have been considered to explore the merger and acquisition *phenomena*. Media coverage of large and often cross-border transactions as well as the increasingly prominent role of private equity have shown that acquisition success and failure often traces its origins back to a detailed understanding and better management of the *processes* by which acquisition decisions are made. In the highly charged environment of international capital markets (often characterised by the constant search for stakeholder value and the resulting real or perceived pressures for speed and secrecy) many executives and specialists engage not only in a complex routine of analysis and evaluation, but also in a process of internal selling and negotiation. The outcome of these deliberations are not only parameters such as price and financing, but also a much more multifarious assessment of how the transaction will be justified. The cautionary advice for the impatient executive and his eager advisers should always be the ancient rule of *caveat emptor*: let the buyer beware.

Acquisition decision making is often presented as a clear and logical step-by-step process where every move is analytically laid out and following clear milestones. In North America this process has deep roots in corporate governance principles and a legal system incorporating rules such as *discovery* (cf. table 4.3). Furthermore, a greater appreciation of principles such as public accountability and transparency have created a greater need to ensure a general and specific duty of care on every company executive. For many German companies, merger and acquisition activity tended to be conducted without any external assistance. Different inhouse departments were charged with gathering information on the prospective target and *Hausbanks* (often represented on the company's supervisory board) were happy to provide substantial and often unsecured acquisition finance without the need for any external due diligence. Increasing regulatory pressure (e.g. Basel II), greater competition and insufficient returns have led over recent years to substantial changes in the traditional role of the *Hausbank*. Many German banks have decided to dispose of their sometimes extensive shareholdings in public and private companies. However, they are still repre-

Table 4.3 Due diligence culture

North American principles	German principles
Well established and codified corporate governance rules setting out duties of management towards shareholders	Less precise management duties and limited ability for shareholders to seek recourse
Strict adherence to written and unwritten rules and codes of conduct (strong reliance on capital markets)	Fewer requirements for public disclosure of information (strong reliance on private funding)
Discovery based legal system	More codified disclosure rules
Open culture of public accountability, corporate transparency and information disclosure (high reliability and quality of filings)	Tradition of restrictive disclosure based on minimum requirements (minimum and sometimes vague filing information)
Results-orientated management style with culture of give and take, own initiative and personal achievement	Greater emphasis on formalities and corporate hierarchy resulting in more complex decision making processes

sented on the supervisory board in the large majority of DAX companies and hence still play a crucial role in the *gentlemen's club* which administers German corporate governance.

The due diligence process generally commences with agreed acquisition objectives, a target search through a systematic screening of the market place and a strategic evaluation of the agreed target list, followed by a due diligence on the target company, hopefully leading to successful negotiations and a timely closing of the transaction. The outcome of the acquisition process is meant to secure an acquisition of the desired target company at a justifiable price. In the real world however, and on both sides of the Atlantic, both the intention, circumstances and the true nature of acquisitions are much more multifaceted. At the heart of the increasingly intricate acquisition master plan lies the due diligence process with its key task to assess the assets and the liabilities of the target company. In this process extending to and entailing aspects such as financial, technical, legal and environmental matters as well as cultural considerations, the purchaser seeks to obtain all relevant facts of the past, present, and predictable future of the business to be acquired.

Due diligence plays a decisive role in any transaction process and has over recent years also found its way from a more abstract academic discipline into actual German corporate deal-making. The term not only relates to a structured set of inquiries but also describes the overall duty of care and review to be exercised by executives and professional advisers in connection with public offerings. The lack of proper due diligence and a disregard of its findings have long been known and are generally considered to be leading causes of poor acquisition performance and a major cause for post transaction litigation.

The due diligence process usually commences from the moment a buyer is seriously getting interested in a possible acquisition opportunity. This interest may originate from internal sources or may be presented to the buyer from third parties. The buyer evaluates the most pertinent information about the target company that is readily available at this early stage. The intention of every executive to make sound judgements about potential acquisitions is often dealt an early blow because the information available on the potential target may be fragmented, ambiguous in nature, in a different language, and sometimes hampered by the buyer's lack of own resources. Hence developing meaningful acquisition justifications on a cross border or trans-continental basis can be a substantial challenge for every executive in its own right. Whilst North American executives tend to consult at an earlier stage external advisers such as investment bankers, lawyers and other transaction specialists, German corporate executives have a far greater tendency to use and rely upon information provided by in-house departments. Hence, there is a risk that the information on the target company might be tainted at an early stage by internal considerations.

Irrespective of the quantity and quality of the available information, every potential acquisition should contribute to the acquiring company's strategy and establish or secure a competitive advantage that leads to financial performance. For many German companies, the overall financial performance is often only a secondary consideration. Technical, product or market leadership are sometimes regarded as more important than superior financial returns. Hence, contributions to earnings per share and other shareholder value attributes (usually validated by external advisors and the focus of capital markets) often rank behind or are seen as the result of technical assessments undertaken by in-house resources. These differences in priorities sometimes support the impression that whilst North American companies are run by accountants and lawyers for the exclusive benefit of their shareholders, German boards tend to be managed by engineers with a strong emphasis on product quality and for the benefit of the company itself.

After sufficient information has been obtained on the target company and an adequate acquisition justification has been developed to arrive at a tentative value range for the transaction, every buyer should engage experienced professionals to conduct a thorough study of the target company. Acquirers can never start this process too early attempting to discover where the strengths and weaknesses of the target company lie. Compared to domestic transactions, structured and reliable information gathering is often neglected in cross border transaction, because buyers often unfamiliar with local market practises and cultural peculiarities do not want to cause offence to potential sellers at an early stage. This reluctance to ask or inability to obtain detailed information about the target company is sometimes accompanied by a human phenomenon where a general euphoria and often publicly stated desire for a successful transaction abroad displaces the natural caution more ubiquitous in domestic deals.

To investigate the entire background of a company's past and present standing, the international cross border due diligence process should more often than not commence with a detailed search on present and previous corporate names as well as trade names, trade marks, and trade registrations. International transactions are much more likely to miss out on negative aspects of corporate history simply covered up by changes to company names. Whilst North American companies are much more used to the needs and requirements for the full and regular disclosure of financial and other corporate information and where future corporate prosperity centres around a competitive market position, their European counterparts are much more restrictive with providing sensitive company information and where a "need-to-know" disclosure culture seeks more to protect the status quo (table 4.4).

How far a buyer wishes to go in the due diligence process and at what stage, largely depends on how much time the buyer wishes to spend on the investigation. For many acquirers, this question is also related to how many internal and external resources the company is willing to invest at an early stage. Experience to date seems to suggest that the resource allocation for early stage enquiries for international transactions is almost the same as for domestic deals. The search, screening and investigation of potential target companies has increasingly become the domain of deal initiators such as investment banks, industry insiders and other specialist advisers where the provision of often free upfront information on potential acquisition targets is considered the entree ticket for more lucrative business (e.g. buy side advisory, valuation, due diligence, financing, etc.).

The amount of information available on potential target companies will also depend to some extent on the status of the seller in the national or industry community. Other factors also include years in operation, whether the target company has been audited and/or banked by major firms, whether it operates nationally or internationally, if executive turnover is low, and other factors that would establish the basic stability of the firm, such as long-term customer retention and ownership structure.

Many German sellers discourage or even restrict the due diligence efforts of the potential acquirer. Such sellers commonly also seek a reduction in the representations and warranties based on the argument that the buyer is free to visit all relevant parts of the target company's operations. Experience tells that buyers and their advisors should utilise such opportunities to get their own impression of the target company's operation, especially as financial statements and other company record may not truly reflect the current state of affairs. On the other hand, such friendly gestures should not tempt the buyer to relieve the seller of any possibility of misrepresentation. For an increasing number of transactions in Germany, mainly accompanying auction processes, sellers

Table 4.4 Information policies

North American perspective	German perspective
US-GAAP based on more uniform requirements of SEC (e.g. Forms 10-K, 10-Q, 8-K)	Accounting principles provide greater ability to interpret rules and regulations
Provision of decision relevant information for shareholder	Closer link to other information requirements such as tax filings
High emphasis on correct accrual and comparability with previous financial statements	More emphasis on correct structure of statements, greater ability and tendency to smooth out results
Principles of "substance over form" and "fair presentation"	Less detailed information in director's report, greater emphasis on form rather than substance
Strict adherence to tax filings and other formalities	Numerous filing procedures and formats

are providing potential buyers with access to due diligence information prepared by the seller and their advisors. Such vendor due diligence may reduce the workload for the due diligence of the buyer and accelerate the disposal process, it does however not relieve the purchaser of its duty to make its own independent investigations as to the quality of the information provided and should not be used as an undue bargaining tool by the seller not to provide reasonable representations and warranties to the buyer. Due to the high costs involved in obtaining vendor due diligence, most buyers should expect German sellers able and willing to provide only limited (past) information. Requests for additional (forward looking) information are regularly viewed with suspicion and refused on the grounds of confidentiality.

For North American companies, representations and warranties of the seller are a crucial part of the transaction process. Depending on the legal environment of the seller and the bargaining power of the buyer, such representations and warranties may extend from a few paragraphs to many pages in the sale and purchase agreement. Given the different natures of the legal systems in North America and Germany, the general willingness to seek recourse via litigation, the cost of litigation and the size of potential damages are not only reflected in the different formal understandings and negotiating stances on representations and warranties, but they show a fundamentally different approach to contracting and dispute resolution.

Table 4.5 Due diligence focus

North American approach	German approach
Detailed enquiries about incorporation and legal status of company, corporate documentation and ability to represent and contract company	Detailed enquiries about legal nature and structure of company (e.g. private company, public company, partnership, mixed partnership, etc.), greater reliance on codified documentation and rights to represent company
Emphasis on pending and potentially forthcoming litigation, assessment of potential future costs and claims (compensatory and punitive damages)	Emphasis on pending litigation, assessment of potential costs (limitation via mitigation, insurance coverage, etc.)
Focus on specific employee matters such as worker compensation (e.g. accident liability, third party compensation claims, etc.) and discrimination (e.g. minority rights, sex discrimination, etc.)	Focus on employee matter such as protective employment, trade union representation, pension and other benefits
Focus on national and local/state legislation, especially environmental matters (e.g. Clean Air and Clean Water Act, etc.)	Mainly national legislation, few local/state legislation
Common use of definitions in contracts to limit ability for interpretation by all parties, great emphasis to regulate in advance future "eventualities"	Stronger reliance on codified law for interpretation and eventualities
Drafting and negotiation through or with aid of third party legal advisors	Increased reliance on and use of in-house legal department

In many markets and with most transactions the seller will be clearly concerned about the confidentiality of its operations and its financial affairs and hence will often require the prospective acquirer to enter into a separate confidentiality agreement. Such confidentiality agreements are now an established feature in most merger and acquisition transactions and contain terms and conditions under which and in which way the seller discloses documents to the buyer and the degree of confidentiality that will be given to them. Many German companies are despite extensive confidentiality agreements naturally unwilling to disclose confidential company information in fear of releasing information to potential competitors. In such circumstances, potential buyers should seek at an early stage the personal contact with the senior management of the German seller to convince them of their need for and the extent of the additional information requirements. These trust building meetings can help to facilitate not only the due diligence but also the entire transaction process. North American buyers should not be surprised if these meetings are very formal affairs where the senior German executive is not able or willing to provide answers to detailed questions but delegates the task to a member of his staff.

In the same manner as due diligence should be completed swiftly, the due diligence process efforts should also extend up to, be practised throughout, and reach beyond transaction closing. The discipline imposed by the due diligence process and its findings, dealing with the realities and imperfections of daily business life, should never be abandoned, and it is a rare transaction which does not trigger, on the closing day or soon after, some chances to the acquisition agreement because of unfinished or vague items of the original due diligence inquiry.

The due diligence efforts going beyond the closing of the transaction have on both sides of the Atlantic two significant considerations. First, individuals from the seller and the buyer have with their hands-on involvement in the due diligence process usually a detailed insight into the field or area of operation which they have managed or investigated. For this reason, they may be called upon during the post-acquisition and integration phase to answer questions or provide guidance for the management of the combined new operations. International transactions more often than comparable domestic deals have items of unfinished or unresolved financial, technical, legal or other issues that have come to light during the due diligence process. Many open issues require a speedy resolution after closing. Given the reluctance of many German companies to disclose all confidential information during the due diligence process, a number of post closing issues might need to be settled swiftly. These can range from competition authority approvals, the appointment of new senior executives to the establishment of new financial and other reporting requirements. Second, if any material disputes arise between the buyer and seller after closing, their respective claims and counterclaims may go back to a due diligence issue. The question then quickly arises whether one party has disclosed or made available to the other the documents or pertinent facts to the other. For this reason, experienced due diligence professionals know that it is essential to maintain complete and detailed written reports on all due diligence findings.

The post-acquisition and integration phase aims to overcome the imperfections discovered during the acquisition process and exploit known and untapped synergies and other future value potential.

Table 4.6 Due diligence cycles of learning

North American approach	German approach
Emphasis on client driven business integration	Emphasis on swift legal and financial (internal) integration
Willingness to make early changes to structure and running of business to achieve synergies and other potential	Longer willingness to accept the status quo
Greater emphasis on internal and external communication	Communication largely through hierarchical structures
Establishment of mainly (North American) cultural identity and value system throughout entire company	Expectation to accept different domestic cultural identity
Results orientated management style with emphasis and greater recognition own initiative and personal achievement	Greater emphasis on formalities and corporate hierarchy

To ensure a lasting union and making mergers and acquisitions work, due diligence provides a considerable opportunity for organisations to learn and swiftly getting behind the scenes of the target company (table 4.6). Due diligence can through its own unique language clarify uncertainties and provide the missing link between transactions from different markets, industries and nationalities. Most of all, thorough due diligence can help many transactions move with mutual confidence from pre-merger idea to post-merger reality. Learning from the findings of previous transactions, individual experience and organisational learning can help many firms overcome integration problems. The North American continent is and will remain for many German companies a desired market place where corporate fortunes can be made or lost to this day. For many North American market participants, acquiring a German company can provide direct access not only to the largest consumer market in Europe but also serve as a springboard to other markets in Central and Eastern Europe.

Literature

Berens W. and J. Strauch (2002) Due Diligence bei Unternehmenstransaktionen – eine empirische Untersuchung, Frankfurt am Main

Brush T. H. (1996) Predicted Change in Operational Synergy and Post-Acquisition Performance of Acquired Business, Strategic Management Journal, 1/1996, pp. 1-24

Coley S. C. and S. E. Reinton (1988) The Hunt for Value, The McKinsey Quarterly, Spring, pp. 29-34

Hubbard G., Lofstrom S. and R. Tully (1994) Diligence Checklists: Do They Get The Best Answers?, in Mergers & Acquisitions, September/ October, pp. 33-38

Lawrence G. M. (1995) Due Diligence in Business Transactions, Law Journals Seminars-Press, New York

Marten K.-U. and A.G. Köhler (1999) Due Diligence in Deutschland – eine empirische Untersuchung, Finanz Betrieb, 11/1999, pp. 337-348

4.6 Tax

4.6.1 German and US Tax Aspects of Private Equity Funds

Susanne Schreiber, Julianne Reynolds, and Carolina Perez-Lopez

The article summarizes certain recent developments under German tax law that should be considered in order to structure a private equity fund in Germany. In addition, the article describes in general terms the taxation of US private equity funds and its investors from a US tax perspective.

Introduction

An increasing number of M&A-transactions in the German market have been led by international private equity firms in recent years.

The classification of the activity of a private equity fund organized as a German partnership has been clarified recently by the German tax authorities. This development has clearly had a major impact on the private equity market for funds established in Germany. The following article gives an overview of this recent development in German tax law and compares the tax consequences in Germany with the US federal income tax ("US tax") treatment of private equity funds.

The first part of this contribution explains the general structure of German private equity funds and the requirements to avoid a trade tax liability for such funds established as German partnerships.

The second part of the article summarizes the taxation of US private equity funds and the taxation of both US and non-US investors in US private equity funds under US tax law.

Taxation of German private equity funds

Private equity funds can be established in Germany as corporations or, more commonly, as partnerships.

Corporations

German corporations are subject to the German trade tax and the German corporate income tax, regardless of their type of activity. The corporate income tax rate in Germany is currently 25% plus a solidarity surcharge of 5.5% (computed on the corporate income tax), that together result in an effective rate of 26.375%. The effective German trade tax rate depends on the municipality where the German corporation carries on its business. The aggregate tax rate including corporate income tax and trade tax currently averages around 38%.

Partnerships: Asset management versus trading

Most German private equity funds are established as partnerships in Germany. One reason for this is that, depending on their activities and legal structure, German partnerships are not subject to trade tax – an important cost factor for investors.

German partnerships (or limited partnerships, *Kommanditgesellschaft – KG*) are transparent for German income tax purposes. Income of the partnership is allocated to the partners in accordance with their profit participation. This allocated portion of the profit will be part of the partner's income in order to compute his or her individual or its corporate income tax liability in Germany. The utilization, i.e., the set-off of losses allocated to limited partners, is subject to certain restrictions under German tax law.

If the partnership is only engaged in asset managing activities, it will generally not be subject to German trade tax, whereas German partnerships engaged in trade activities will be subject to German trade tax. Trade activities are defined as independent and sustained activities that happen in the "common economic market place" (i.e., generally offered to the public) with the intention to derive profits, that are not otherwise independent (i.e., free-lance) activities and that are not mere asset management.

If a German private equity fund is organized as a partnership that is subject to German trade tax, only individuals as partners subject to taxation in Germany may be entitled to credit that German trade tax liability against their income tax liability. That credit will not be available for corporate partners or for individuals not subject to tax assessment in Germany (i.e., non-resident individuals whose income derived from Germany is taxed through the mechanism of withholding).

The difficulty of avoiding trade activities

Most German private equity funds are set up as limited partnerships with a limited liability company as the general partner (GmbH & Co. KG), as the general partner's unlimited liability is reduced due to its legal form in this case and such partnerships can avoid a trade tax liability under certain conditions.

In addition to receiving trading income if the fund actually carries on a trade, a partnership may be deemed to be carrying on trade activities in two circumstances. For German tax purposes, a partnership may be presumed to be engaged in trade activities by virtue of its legal structure or due to a so-called "business infection."

- According to Sec. 15 para. 3 no. 2 Income Tax Act, where a limited partnership has corporations as partners (such as a GmbH), it will be regarded as running a trade business (*gewerbliche Prägung*) if it is managed only by a general partner that is a corporation or by a person who is not a partner. Private equity funds will usually ensure in the partnership's agreement that a limited partner of the fund is also always granted managing authority in order to avoid a classification as trade business by virtue of the legal structure.
- Investments in partnerships that are themselves engaged in trade activities (or deemed to be engaged in trade activities) can result in a "business infection" of the top-tier partnership that itself would otherwise be regarded as a non-trade partnership. For example, with respect to a partnership that invests in another partnership

that carries out trade activities, those activities of the subordinate partnership that will be attributed to the parent partnership result in a re-classification of all income of the parent partnership as trade income (with the consequence of a potential trade tax burden for this parent partnership). Under its decision of 6 October 2004, the Federal Finance Court (*Bundesfinanzhof – BFH*) held that participation in a trade partnership will not result in the "infection" of all the income of the parent partnership as trade income. The BFH ruled that the "business infection" rules only apply if the parent partnership carries out, at least in part, a trade activity of its own. However, this decision, which would be a relief for private equity funds investing in trade partnerships, is not applied by the German tax authorities. Thus, the participation of an asset-managing partnership in a partnership that carries out trade activities will lead, despite the decision of the BFH, to all of the income of the parent partnership being regarded as trade income by the tax authorities. It remains to be seen how the German legislator or the tax authorities will react in future to the BFH's decision.

Requirements for asset management activities

Due to the adverse German tax consequences for a partnership that is treated as engaged in trade activities, the activities of the fund must be carefully structured to ensure that its activities are mere asset management activities. The BFH established some guidelines in its decision of 25 July 2001 to characterize the activities of a company as asset management activities, but there was still uncertainty with respect to how to characterize those activities in relation to private equity funds.

To resolve that uncertainty, the Federal Ministry of Finance (*Bundesfinanzministerium – BMF*) issued a decree on 16 December 2003 establishing a set of guidelines to classify the activities of a private equity fund as asset management activities. Under these guidelines, a fund generally qualifies as an asset management fund when its activities are purely making and holding investments, executing shareholders' rights, and increasing the value of the assets held.

Consequently, according to these criteria and to the BFH's judgment of 25 July 2001 defining trade activities, a fund organized as a partnership is not considered to be engaged in trade activities if:

- The fund finances the acquisition of interest in a portfolio company with the equity investments of its partners. In contrast, financing the acquisition of portfolio companies with debt is regarded as a criterion for trade activities. The view taken in the decision of BFH of 20 December 2002, according to which debt-financing does not lead to trade activities from the sale of shares, is not applicable to the activities of private equity funds in the opinion of the tax authorities. The fund is treated as debt-financing its acquisition if the investors in the fund (e.g., banks) grant shareholder loans to the fund instead of capital contributions.

- If the fund provides collateral with respect to the indebtedness of any of its portfolio companies (or guarantees any of its liabilities), the private equity fund will be treated as engaged in trade activities rather than in asset management activities.

- The fund does not maintain an extensive organization of its own in order to manage the fund's assets. It is not detrimental if the fund runs its own office and has only a few employees, because this does not exceed the normal scope of dealing with extensive private assets. The volume of the assets under management does not by itself constitute a trade.

- The fund does not operate for the account of others in using its own professional experience. In the opinion of the BFH, the use of relevant professional know-how for one's own account does not establish a trade activity. The limited partners authorized to conduct the business management often use their know-how and knowledge of the industry when reviewing potential investments. This is, however, similar to the conduct of a private investor who has an extensive portfolio of assets to manage and, therefore, is not detrimental.

- The fund does not offer interests in portfolio companies to the general public nor does it act on account of third parties. If the portfolio company goes public or the fund's investments are sold, however, this is still considered a management activity of the fund, if it relates to the fund's own investments. The use of the limited partners' know-how, as persons authorized to conduct the management functions,[1] does not imply that the fund is also acting for the account of others, because the activity of the limited partners is directly attributable to the limited partnership fund with respect to its own activity.

- The fund holds its interest in the portfolio companies for a medium term, i.e., for three to five years. Indeed, an objective of obtaining the benefits from the intrinsic value of assets cannot be presumed from short-term investments. In order to determine the average holding period, all investments of the fund need to be evaluated. The sale of an investment prior to the expiration of the average holding period does not automatically make the fund engaged in trade activities. Nevertheless, the average holding period of the total capital invested in portfolio investments is decisive. Syndication, i.e., splitting the invested amount among various funds for risk diversification after a portfolio investment has been acquired, is treated as a disposal. Syndications will not be taken into account for the determination of the average holding period if (i) the syndication takes place within 18 months after the acquisition; (ii) the syndication partner is a fund managed by the same initiator; and (iii) the interests are sold for a purchase price which comprises an amount of the acquisition costs plus the customary interest.

- Proceeds from the sale of the underlying investments are distributed among the partners and may not be reinvested. It is permitted, however, to reinvest such proceeds into portfolio investments to the extent that expenses and management fees have previously been paid out of capital contributions. This rule also permits the reinvestment of proceeds of up to 20 percent of the total capital commitment as "follow-on" investments into portfolio companies in which the fund partnership already holds an interest.

---

[1] At least one limited partner of a fund in the legal form of a German limited partnership will usually be authorized to manage the fund in addition to the general partner. This is necessary in order to avoid the qualification of a limited partnership having only corporations as general partners as running a trade business by virtue of its legal structure.

- The fund is not actively involved in the management of its portfolio companies. However, the exercise of certain supervisory board functions in the corporate bodies managing the portfolio companies is allowed. As a general rule, the retention of a catalogue of management actions that require approval by the board is allowed. However, that general rule does not apply if the retention of such a catalogue does not allow the management board of the portfolio company to exercise entrepreneurial discretion. The latter situation would be an indication that the fund is engaged in trade activities.

The above criteria, issued by the BMF, establish a quite clear guideline for private equity funds as to how to structure their organization and their investment in order to comply with the requirements for an asset managing partnership under German tax law.

Taxation of US private equity funds

Private equity funds organized in the United States can be established as corporations or, more commonly, as pass-through entities. Under current law, most legal entities other than state law corporations qualify for pass-through treatment, either by default or on an elective basis, as discussed below. If treated as a pass-through entity, a fund would be regarded as a partnership for US tax purposes. Thus, the fund itself would not be subject to US tax but rather the partners would be treated as earning their pro rata share of the fund's income directly. The character of that income as ordinary income or as capital gains would flow through to the partners. In addition, private equity fund partners generally would be entitled to receive tax-free distributions of cash or property from the US private equity fund.

Classification of the private equity fund for US tax purposes – Check-the-box election

In 1996, the Treasury issued regulations under Internal Revenue Code ("Code") section 7701 that set forth rules governing the classification of business entities for US tax purposes (the "Regulations"). The Regulations classify a business entity as either a "corporation per se," in which case it is always treated and taxed as a corporation, or as an "eligible entity," in which case the entity is entitled to elect its classification for US tax purposes. The Regulations adopted a five-step mechanism for the classification of entities for US tax purposes, as follows:

- First, it is necessary to determine whether a separate entity for US tax purposes exists. The Regulations clarify that not every joint undertaking constitutes a separate entity and, therefore, a mere co-ownership arrangement, sole proprietorship, branch, and certain entities formed under local law will not be treated as separate entities for US tax purposes. The Regulations do not provide, however, clear guidelines for the determination of whether a separate entity exists in a particular case and, therefore, that determination should be made according to pre-existing guidelines developed by the courts and the Internal Revenue Service.
- Second, an organization that is recognized as a separate entity for US tax purposes is classified as either a trust or a business entity.

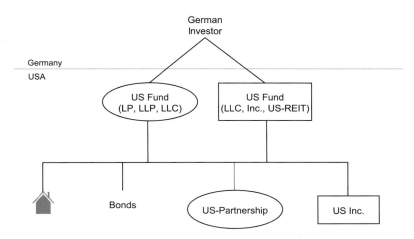

Figure 4.26 Basic structure of investments in US Funds

the investor's income from investments in US opportunity funds must be ascertained, and in each case a determination must be made whether and to what extent Germany is entitled to collect tax in accordance with the double taxation treaty (DTT) with the United States. Finally, the issue of whether the income of the fund or the target is subject to the German CFC (controlled foreign corporation) regime must be decided in accordance with the provisions of the German Foreign Tax Act (*Außensteuergesetz*).

Priority application of the Investment Tax Act

Scope of applicability of the Investment Tax Act regardless of legal form

In the case of an investment in a US fund, the priority from the German tax perspective is to examine whether the fund is considered a so-called "foreign investment fund" (*ausländisches Investmentvermögen*) to which the special tax regulations of the Investment Tax Act apply. The Investment Tax Act follows the material, or economic, investment concept for foreign funds (Section 1 (1) No. 2 of the Investment Tax Act in conjunction with Section 2 (8), (9) of the Investment Act (*Investmentgesetz*). According to this concept, foreign investment funds are basically defined as (i) all funds subject to foreign law, (ii) that invest directly or indirectly in certain assets (e.g., securities) in a risk-diversified manner, and (iii) regardless of their legal structure (legal form). Contrary to the letter of the law, the German tax authorities express the opinion, that foreign partnerships (in this case, US partnerships) should not fall under the provisions of the Investment Tax Act. Nonetheless, foreign partnerships can hold equity investments in other companies that are in turn subject to the Investment Tax Act (Sub-section 6 of the Introductory Circular (*Anwendungsschreiben*) to the Investment Tax Act, dated 2 June 2005 – "BMF InvStG").

The economic investment concept – Investment in accordance with the principle of risk diversification

Assets invested in accordance with the principle of risk diversification

The issue of whether the assets of the foreign target fund are invested in accordance with the principle of risk diversification therefore takes center stage. If the fund invests in "a large number of assets" with the aim of safeguarding the capital value of its assets by balancing profit opportunities and risks, then the fund is considered to be risk-diversified. It is not possible to specify in figures the minimum number of assets necessary for a fund to qualify as this type of risk-diversified investment. A decision must instead be made on a case-by-case basis about whether the risk-diversified investment of capital is the objective business purpose of the fund, or only a secondary objective of another, primary business activity. Risk diversification does not have to be practiced directly by the foreign investment fund; an indirectly risk-diversified investment (e.g., via downstream real estate companies) is also sufficient.

No risk diversification in the case of business influence

According to the practice of the Federal Banking Supervisory Office (*Bundesaufsichtsamt für das Kreditwesen* – BAKred), which is now the Federal Financial Supervisory Authority (*Bundesanstalt für Finanzdienstleistungen* – BAFin), an investment is in particular not considered to fall under the principle of risk diversification if investments are made with the intention of limiting the autonomy of the objects of the investments (target companies) and of intervening in their corporate decision-making processes and responsibilities. The following factors in particular indicate this type of business influence:

- *Most acquisitions are strategic equity investments:* The US fund has a controlling influence, or at least a significant influence under corporate law, over its portfolio companies via its equity investments.
- *Active or advisory capacity in respect of target companies:* Fund representatives are represented in the management and supervisory bodies of the portfolio companies or act in some other active or professional advisory capacity at the executive level in the target companies.
- The investments are preceded by an in-depth audit of the relevant investment object that covers all areas relevant to the company.
- The fund focuses on just a few companies.

This means that funds, including private equity funds in particular, that are not already structured in the legal form of a partnership (see exception for foreign partnerships due to Sub-section 6 BMF-InvStG), typically do not fall under the scope of the Investment Tax Act.

Risk diversification at real estate companies

Furthermore, BAKred has stipulated that a fund is classified as a risk-diversified investment in real estate if the fund invests directly or indirectly in more than three properties via property companies. In contrast to equity investments in other portfolio companies, BAKred assumes that investments in real estate companies always require active real estate management. The result is that even if business influence is exerted over the real estate company, it is always classified as an investment under the principle of risk diversification.

Basic principles of taxation where the Investment Tax Act applies

If the fund falls within the scope of the Investment Tax Act, then the fund is classified as a "foreign investment fund." In this case, German investors are subject to a special tax regime. According to this regime, taxation of German investors depends materially on the extent to which the fund fulfills reporting requirements in accordance with the provisions of the Investment Tax Act. A distinction is drawn between three types of investment funds for this purpose:

- *Non-transparent investment funds:* Funds that provide no information about circumstances affecting tax liability. Their shareholders are therefore subject to penalty taxation at a flat rate under Section 6 of the Investment Tax Act. According to this regime, distributions, along with 70% of the surplus difference between the first and last redemption price calculated in the calendar year, but not less than 6% of the most recently calculated redemption price, are treated as taxable income.

- *Semi-transparent investment funds:* Funds that provide no information about the basis for taxation favorably affecting the taxable amount. Their shareholders are therefore in particular ineligible for (i) tax exemptions in accordance with Section 8b of the Corporate Income Tax Act (*Körperschaftsteuergesetz*) according to which dividends and capital gains on the sale of shares in corporations are 95% tax-free or for (ii) tax exemptions in accordance with DTT.

- *Transparent investment funds:* Funds that provide complete information about the basis for taxation. For tax purposes, their shareholders are therefore treated as they would be if they held a direct investment (particularly regarding the application of Section 8b of the Corporate Income Tax Act).

The reporting requirements can generally be met with a reasonable effort, and the US fund qualifies as a fully transparent investment fund. However, this requires that the German investors be able to force the fund or the fund's management company to meet reporting requirements. Experience shows that this approach is only successful if the German investors hold a significant investment in the fund and/or are willing to bear the not insubstantial costs of implementing a reporting system. From the German tax perspective, it is essential for German investors to arrange for the corresponding provisions in a side letter to the investment agreement.

The reporting requirements are accomplished by the fund calculating the composition of its distributed income (particularly dividends, capital gains, rental and interest income) and reporting it to its investors. In addition, retained income is allocated to the investors as "deemed distributed income" (*ausschüttungsgleiche Erträge*). This approach has the following specific tax consequences:

- To the extent that the distribution or deemed distributed income includes dividends, German corporate income is 95% tax-free for investors. According to the view of the tax authorities, which misses the mark in our opinion, the provisions of the trade tax participation exemption (*gewerbesteuerliches Schachtelprivileg*) are not applicable in respect of dividend income. The result is that the German investor is subject to trade tax (*Gewerbesteuer*) on the full amount of dividend income realized by the fund (regardless of the size of the shareholding). If the investor is a natural person, the so-called half-income-taxation regime (*Halbeinkünftever-fahren*) applies, i.e., half of the dividend income is free of tax.

- If the distributions include capital gains on the disposal of shares in portfolio companies, then 95% of the distributions are also free of corporate income tax and trade tax. Losses are not tax-deductible. For natural persons, no tax is levied on distributed capital gains on the sale of shares in incorporated portfolio companies.

- If the distributed income or deemed distributed income contains income that would have been tax-exempt in accordance with US DTT if the German investor had held the investment directly (particularly rental and leasing income and capital gains from the disposal of real estate located in the United States), this income is also tax-exempt. If the investor is a natural person, the exemption-with-progression method (*Progressionsvorbehalt*) applies.

- German investors are regularly liable for tax on the full amount of other distributed or deemed distributed income of the fund (particularly interest income).

Taxation of investments in funds not subject to the Investment Tax Act

Classification of the foreign fund

German investors with an unlimited tax liability are generally liable for German personal and corporate income tax on their entire worldwide income, including possible income from investments in foreign funds. If the US fund does not fall within the scope of the Investment Tax Act, taxation of the income from an investment in this company depends on how the fund is classified for German tax purposes. The fundamental distinction that must be made is whether the fund is an independent taxable entity in the United States, or if it is considered a pass-through entity, and whether this classification is also acceptable from the German tax perspective.

The US fund is classified for purposes of German taxation, i.e., it qualifies as a US corporation or partnership including application of the US DTT, solely in accordance with German domestic tax law based on a comparison of the company's structure. On the one hand, this classification is important for determining whether the fund is eligible for application of the US DTT. On the other, this classification determines the income that an investor domiciled in Germany receives from the foreign fund (dividends, capital gains, interest income, etc.). The decisive factor is whether an entity set up under US law (i.e., the fund) is comparable to a German domestic corporation (*Körperschaft*). In particular, the following criteria can lead to qualification of the fund as a German corporation: centralized management and representation (third-party participation in executive bodies (*Fremdorganschaft*)), limited liability, free transferability of shares, resolution on distribution of profits to be adopted annually, raising of capital, unlimited duration of the company, profits distributed proportionally to number of shares held, formal formation requirements.

4.7 Merger Control

4.7.1 Pre-Nuptial Puritanism for Corporate Marriages – Antitrust Limits on the Pre-consummation Relationship Between Merging Parties

Thomas W. Wessely

Once a corporate marriage has been agreed upon, the two partners still have to abstain from moving under one roof and living their alliance until it has been blessed by the competent competition authorities. The present article looks into the practical implications of this waiting period for the merging parties. It explores the limits of permissible cooperation and discusses the (mostly unpublished) case law.

The European Merger Control Regulation (ECMR) prohibits the parties from implementing a transaction before it has been approved by the European Commission (so-called „gun-jumping"). A similar prohibition is to be found in the US Hart Scott Rodino Act and in the merger control rules of most other jurisdictions (there are some notable exceptions such as the UK, Hungary and Brazil). Infringements of this suspensory obligation are subject to stringent sanctions. In the EU, the European Commission may impose fines of up to 10% of the parties' annual worldwide group turnover. The US antitrust authorities may fine both the merging parties and individual officers, directors or partners of the merging parties. In addition, the merging parties are subject to the general antitrust rules prior to the implementation of the merger. Accordingly, any pre-consummation cooperation between the parties may fall under the general antitrust prohibition for competitors to coordinate their market behaviour.

Scope of the prohibition

The primary purpose of the suspension obligation is to prevent the transaction from being consummated before it has been cleared. The formal closing of a transaction prior to the antitrust approval or even prior to notification is therefore clearly illegal. In the past, the European Commission has thus imposed fines on Korean electronics company Samsung for notifying the acquisition of AST only 14 months after it had been completed (in 1998) and on Danish company A. P. Møller for omitting to notify three different transactions (in 1999).

The suspension obligation however also covers other and more limited forms of premature implementation of the transaction. It is clear from the case law both in the United States and in Europe that any measures of partial implementation of the merger or any coordination of the market behaviour of the merging parties is also caught by the prohibition to implement. This is illustrated by the following cases:

The Gemstar case

The 2003 Gemstar decision represents the highest ever fine in respect of gun-jumping, where the defendants (Gemstar and TV Guide) agreed to pay $5.7 million. The merging parties had agreed not to market their products in competition with one another and had allocated customers between themselves. Furthermore, Gemstar had acquired a right to approve TV Guide's customer contracts whilst TV Guide acted as an agent to Gemstar in customer negotiations and settlements. In addition, the parties had shared substantial information about prices, marketing strategies and capacity. The Department of Justice ("DoJ") filed a complaint alleging that these practices constituted the unlawful *de facto* acquisition by each merging party of the assets of the other party in violation of US merger control law.

The Computer Associates case

In 2001, the DoJ brought an action against a merged entity for practices which were undertaken by the merging parties (Computer Associates and Platinum) prior to the approval of the transaction. The DoJ complained that during the completion of the merger, the acquisition agreement prevented the merging parties from competing effectively against each other and provided Computer Associates with effective management control of Platinum. In particular, Computer Associates had authority to approve any Platinum agreement to offer discounts greater than 20% off list prices, vary the terms of customer contracts, and to offer longer term, fixed price contracts and other services. In addition, Computer Associates was alleged to have altered the manner in which Platinum recognised revenues, have reviewed competitively sensitive information and have made numerous day-to-day management decisions. The DoJ alleged this conduct constituted gun-jumping and price-fixing. Computer Associates was ordered to pay $638,000 as a penalty.

The Bertelsmann/Kirch/Premiere case

In *Bertelsmann/Kirch/Premiere*, the Commission sent letters to the parties warning them and requesting that Premiere should stop marketing Kirch's decoder boxes for digital channels on the grounds that it constituted the "partial anticipation" of the proposed concentration. The Commission also required the parties to "correct the impression created with consumers by their marketing campaign" that the jointly marketed digital decoder had become the market standard in Germany. The Commission furthermore threatened the parties the imposition of fines if they did not comply with its request (though no fines were imposed).

Practical guidelines

As a general guiding principle, the merging parties are expected to continue to conduct their market activities as „normal competitors", i.e., in the same way as they were acting before the merger project. This means in practice:

1. The acquirer is prohibited from exerting influence on the management of the target company. It would therefore be illegal for the acquirer

   • to appoint members of the board of the target company;

- to have its own executives involved in the management of the target company;
- to request the target company to have its investments, R&D activities, new product launches and other types of competitive strategic decisions approved by the purchaser; or
- to interfere otherwise with the business decisions and market conduct of the target company.

2. The merging parties also may not take any measures that would amount to a premature de facto implementation of the transaction. It is therefore not permissible for the parties

- to jointly market their products (e.g., through joint customer contacts, joint trade fair presence, joint contact persons or joint account managers for common customers);
- to integrate their IT systems;
- to combine their R&D activities or their production; or
- to start the coordinated implementation of business activities which are based on the merger agreements and would not have been pursued in the absence of the transaction.

3. Thirdly, the merging parties have to abstain from any coordination of their market conduct and the exchange of commercially sensitive information. In particular, they must refrain from

- coordinating the setting of prices, pricing strategies, discounts and other terms of sale, or otherwise implementing any joint selling or joint purchasing practices beyond those used in the past;
- exchanging information on customers, prices and bid opportunities;
- allocating customers, geographic markets or product markets, or telling customers that the other party will withdraw from certain markets in the future;
- agreeing to delay customer negotiations until the completion of the transaction („slow-roll" agreement);
- coordinating the phasing-out of products or the introduction of new products; and
- disclosing technical know-how.

Permissible actions

It is however recognised by the antitrust laws that a transaction requires certain information exchanges, a certain degree of coordination between the parties and certain restrictions on the seller.

Due diligence

US case law has expressly confirmed the parties' right to conduct a reasonable and customary due diligence prior to closing the transaction. Two situations have to be distinguished in this respect.

In the first case, the two parties do not have any competitive relationship with each other. This is for example the case where a pure financial investor is bidding for an industrial company. In this context, the full disclosure even of competitively sensitive data will normally not raise any competition issues since there is no competitive relationship between the two companies that could be affected by the information exchange.

In the second category of cases, the two parties are (actual or potential) competitors or there are vertical or conglomerate links between the parties. Under these conditions, general antitrust law prohibits the parties from exchanging competitively sensitive information (i.e. data on prices, customers, sales, capacities, marketing strategies etc.). However, to the extent that this is necessary to conduct a reasonable and customary due diligence, the merging parties are exempted from this prohibition. They are nevertheless expected to limit the disclosure of information to the data which are objectively required by the prospective purchaser for the purposes of preparing his bid. Customer names and sales prices for individual customers normally do not fulfill this condition. Where competitively sensitive information is exchanged, the parties are required to enter into a non-disclosure agreement which obliges them to use the information only for the purposes of the transaction and to keep the information confidential vis-à-vis employees who are involved in the marketing, pricing or sale of competing products.

Ordinary course of business obligation

Pending the merger review of the transaction, the purchaser may legally oblige the seller to conduct the business of the target company "in the ordinary course of business consistent with past practice." This has been explicitly recognized by the US Department of Justice in the *Computer Associates* case. The DoJ also confirmed that it was possible to oblige the seller "not to engage in conduct that would cause a material adverse change in the business." Thirdly, it was clarified in the same case that the purchaser may contractually oblige the seller to abstain from offering and/or granting payments or extended rights to customers conditional upon the acquisition of the target company by the purchaser.

The DoJ's Competitive Impact Statement for the settlement also made clear that many other customary covenants in merger agreements will not be deemed inconsistent with the suspension obligation or the general antitrust rules, such as limiting the seller in its ability

- to declare or pay dividends or distributions of its stock;
- to issue, sell, pledge or encumber its securities;
- to amend its organizational documents;
- to acquire or agree to acquire other businesses;
- to mortgage or encumber its intellectual property or other material assets outside the ordinary course;
- to make or agree to make large new capital expenditures;
- to make material tax elections or compromise material tax liability;
- to pay, discharge or satisfy any claims or liabilities outside the ordinary course; or
- to commence lawsuits other than routine collection of bills.

There are however limits to the restrictions the buyer can impose on the seller in the interim period between signing and closing. *Computer Associates* was found to have infringed the suspension obligation by requiring the target company not to grant rebates of more than 20% (although such rebates were customary in the trade), not to deviate from an agreed-upon standard service contract in its offers to customers, not to offer fixed prices to customers for service contracts running over a period of more than 30 days and not to enter into "Y2K" contracts with customers. The DoJ concluded that these restrictions went beyond reasonable and customary restrictions.

Integration planning

While the parties must not prematurely implement the transaction, they remain allowed to *plan* and *prepare* the consummation of the merger and the integration of the parties' businesses. The integration planning activities should take place in a „clean team" which inter alia should not involve employees who are at the same time responsible for the marketing of products competing with those of the other party.

An open issue: Premature transfer of the business and antitrust risk

Frequently sellers attempt to pass on the antitrust risk (i.e., the risk that the transaction is prohibited by the antitrust authorities) to the purchaser. In a leading case concerning the acquisition of a Union Carbide business by Atlantic Richfield (ARCO), the DoJ concluded that this could amount to illegal gun-jumping. In that case ARCO had paid the full „non-refundable" purchase price on the day of the signing of the purchase agreement. The agreement provided that Union Carbide was „required to operate the business in the ordinary course and in accordance with its existing business plan" until consummation. ARCO „was required to cover liabilities from the continued operation" of the assets and would benefit from any gains during the waiting period. The parties had furthermore agreed that, if the antitrust authorities prohibited ARCO from acquiring the Union Carbide business, a trustee would have to sell the target business with the proceeds to be paid to ARCO. The DoJ took the position that this arrangement eliminated Union Carbide as an independent competitor since it reduced its role to that of a mere caretaker for ARCO, thereby effectively implementing the transaction.

The decision has been criticized by US commentators. Also, it is influenced by a specificity of US law (the „beneficial ownership" test). It remains untested whether the European Commission would take a similar position. It is submitted that, under European law, it is not necessarily excluded by the suspension obligation to transfer the antitrust risk to the purchaser – provided that the parties choose the right structure and take the necessary measures to ensure that the target business remains an independent viable competitor.

Special rules for public bids

EC merger control law provides for special rules applying to acquisitions by way of public bids. The particular dynamics of public bids and the applicable stock exchange rules or securities regulations normally do not allow for lengthy waiting periods in which the bidder would be prevented from acquiring the shares in the target company. The EC Merger Regulation therefore enables the bidder to implement the bid even before antitrust clearance.

The bidder is however prohibited from exercising the voting rights attached to the shares acquired by him. Exceptionally, they may be exercised with express permission of the European Commission and, if this is necessary, for the preservation of the full value of the investment. In *Nestlé/Perrier*, Nestlé asked the European Commission for permission to vote on certain matters prior to clearance of the transaction. The Commission permitted Nestlé to exercise its voting rights in the annual shareholders meeting of Perrier in order to approve the accounts and to discharge the board for the past business year. The Commission however rejected Nestlé's application to vote on the appointment of new board members since this would have allowed Nestlé to influence the management of Perrier and would thus have gone beyond the mere preservation of the value of its investment.

The same principles apply for staggered acquisitions of shares in a company via the stock exchange. The Merger Regulation does not explicitly deal with share purchases outside of the stock exchange. It is however reasonable to assume that where such private share purchases serve the purpose to improve the chances of success of a public bid, they are also covered by the more lenient suspension obligation applicable to public bids.

Derogation from the suspension obligation

Under European law, the parties may at any time (even before notification of the merger) request a derogation from the suspension obligation. In deciding on this request, the Commission takes into account inter alia the effects of the suspension obligation on the parties and on third parties and the threat to competition posed by the merger. It will also review whether the measures taken by the parties could be reversed in case of a prohibition of the transaction. The Commission may make the derogation subject to conditions and obligations with the aim of protecting effective competition.

In practice, the Commission considers the grant of a derogation as an exception and is prepared to release the parties of their duties under the suspension obligation only in exceptional circumstances. The parties must normally show that respecting the waiting period would inflict considerable damage on either of them. This damage must go beyond the normal risks resulting for all merging parties from the suspension obligation. General claims that the uncertainty of the interim period between signing and closing may result in customer losses, may negatively affect sales or may lead to the resignation of employees are therefore normally not sufficient to justify a derogation.

The Commission's practice of granting derogations is relatively intransparent since derogation decisions are not published. From the Commission's statistics, it can be gathered that derogations are granted in less than 5% of all cases (including those where no application for a derogation has been made). In its past practice, the Commission has been prepared to grant derogations in particular in the following circumstances:

- *Bankruptcy or financial distress of the target company:* The Commission has released the acquirer from its duties under the suspension obligation in several cases where the target company has been in insolvency proceedings or in financial distress. The latest such example is the acquisition of parts of *Walter Bau* by *Strabag* in 2005. At the time of the acquisition, Walter Bau was already in receivership. Strabag had agreed with the receiver to acquire certain parts of Walter Bau including a significant number of construction projects (both existing ones and ones under negotiation). In order to avoid that the property developers terminate the agreements underlying these projects based on Walter Bau's insolvency, Strabag required the Commission's approval to negotiate with the property developers on behalf of Walter Bau. There was also a need to provide financial support to Walter Bau in order to prevent suppliers from stopping their deliveries. The Commission concluded that these were exceptional circumstances which justified a derogation from the suspension obligation. Strabag was thus permitted to provide its support to the management of Walter Bau. Similar decisions were taken by the Commission in a number of other cases.

- *Significant financial losses caused by a delay of the deal:* In a few other cases, the Commission has granted derogations against the background that a suspension of the transaction would have resulted in significant financial damage for the parties. In the *German Toll Collect* case, for example, the parties argued that the joint venture had to be set up by the end of the year since changes in the German tax regulations and the terms of the financing of the JV would otherwise result in two-digit million euro losses for the parties. In addition, the parties were subject to strict deadlines for ensuring operability of the new highway tolling system. They risked to miss these deadlines and to be liable to daily damage payments if the creation of the JV would be suspended until after the end of the ongoing in-depth competition investigation. The Commission approved the setting-up of the JV and the start of its operation, but maintained the suspension obligation for certain telematic services in relation to which it perceived potential competition problems.

- *Legal deadlines imposed on the parties:* Besides the German Toll Collect case, legal deadlines also were the basis for a derogation decision in *Omnitel*. The Commission released the JV parties from the suspension obligation since the JV, a start-up mobile telecoms provider, would otherwise not have been able to meet the strict deadlines imposed by the telecoms licence.

- *Competitive bid situation:* In a number of cases, parties have attempted to obtain a derogation on the basis that the possibility of immediate closing of the deal would increase their chances in a competitive bid situation. Typically this argument is brought forward where the other bidders are not subject to suspension obligations under EU or any other national regimes. The Commission is reported to have accepted this reasoning in the acquisition of *London Electricity* by French energy giant *EDF* as well as in its decisions in *Cinven/Angel Street, SEB/Moulinex* and *Morgan Grenfell/Whitbread*.

Where the parties need to take only certain limited steps ahead of the clearance of the merger it is often advisable to have informal discussions with the Commission in order to obtain their tacit acquiescence rather than submit an application for a formal derogation.

Conclusion

The suspension obligation remains a costly burden for the merging parties. In the case of an acquisition, the target company is exposed to a period of uncertainty over its future direction, which may lead to losses of sales, customers and key employees. Business decisions that need to be taken urgently are being postponed. In the case of the creation of a JV, the entry of the JV into the market or (in the case of the combination of existing business activities) the realization of efficiencies are being delayed. It is therefore to be regretted that, at the occasion of the reform of the European Merger Control Regulation in 2004, the Council rejected the Commission's proposal to give the Commission the power to declare the suspension obligation inapplicable for certain types of mergers (i.e. those which do not raise any perceivable competition concerns). To a certain degree, however, the damages associated with the waiting period can be minimized by early notification of the merger. This is made possible by the amended Merger Regulation which now expressly foresees that a transaction can be notified on the basis of a letter of intent (and not only after signing the definitive merger agreement). This road is however not available for parties who want or need to keep a transaction confidential until final agreement on it has been reached.

4.7.2 The Role of Third Party Interveners in Merger Investigations before the Competition Authorities and in Judicial Review Proceedings

Martin Sura

Unlike in the U.S., where the competition agencies tend to be sceptical of competitor complaints about a proposed merger, active intervention by competitors seeking to interfere with a rival's merger project is commonplace under both the European and German merger control rules. The two forums for such an intervention are the merger investigation by the competition agency, or subsequent court proceedings that aim to challenge a merger clearance decision handed down by the agency. Telling recent examples of successful competitors' complaints are the E.on/Ruhrgas merger, where intervening competitors managed to keep the largest German merger in the energy sector in limbo for more than six months, and the SEB/Moulinex merger, where a competitor was partly successful in obtaining the annulment of the merger clearance decision before the European courts. This article describes the main prerequisites of competitor complaints about a proposed merger under both the European and German merger control rules.

Importance of third parties for merger investigations

When investigating a proposed merger, competition agencies rely on more than just data provided by the merging parties. In order to adequately assess the impact a proposed merger will have on competition in the relevant sector, the agencies will also contact a broad group of interested parties, such as competitors and suppliers or customers of the merging parties. These third parties can (and, if formally requested by the agency, must) provide input on topics as diverse as market definitions or size, market shares, past and expected future development of the market(s) under scrutiny, recent and planned market entries of new competitors, the importance of intellectual property rights on the relevant markets, financial strength of and strategic behavior by certain players. Quite often this information will be relied upon by the agencies in their decision of whether or not to oppose a proposed merger. If the agency finds that a proposed merger may harm competition in a relevant market, rather than to oppose the merger altogether, it may also decide to make its consent conditional upon remedies (such as the divestment of certain assets or businesses) that solve the competition concerns identified during the investigation.

Beyond purely "passive" involvement in merger investigations as a result of invitations or formal requests by the agencies to provide information and/or make comments, third parties may have an interest in proactively challenging a merger. Proactive challenging is most obvious for competitors who may often be keen to block a merger contemplated by a rival, or, failing that, to at least have remedies imposed, which may present them with the opportunity to acquire what their rivals have to divest in order to obtain clearance for their merger.

Limited scope for challenge of mergers by competitors in the U.S.

Whilst the approach taken by both the European Commission ("Commission") and the German *Bundeskartellamt* (Federal Cartel Office – "FCO") allows competitors to influence the outcome of an investigation, the U.S. agencies tend not to consider competitor complaints about a merger. The U.S. agencies reason that, very often, a competitor will object to a merger if it expects the merger to lead to a decrease in sales prices, but not if it expects prices to rise after the merger, since that might be beneficial for the competitor itself. A decrease in sales prices, however, is an indication that a merger is pro-competitive and, ultimately, beneficial to the consumer. A competitor complaint will have credence in the U.S. only in very specific circumstances, e.g., if it is argued that a merger would restrain the supply of inputs available to rivals of the merging parties and thus result in raising their costs.

The circumstances under which third parties may file suit against a merger are also limited in the U.S. Such a suit would be directed against one or more of the merging parties and aim for damages or injunctive relief. The thresholds for establishing both standing and antitrust injury are arguably higher than the prerequisites for successful court actions against a merger under both the European and the German rules.

Third party interventions in the EC and Germany

Jurisdiction. Whether a merger comes under the jurisdiction of the Commission or the FCO (or of other national agencies of EC member states) depends on the turnovers of the parties to the merger. Large transactions involving parties with an aggregate annual worldwide turnover of more than €5 billion and EC-wide annual turnovers of more than €250 million are normally dealt with by the Commission. Below these thresholds, the FCO has jurisdiction over mergers that involve parties with an aggregate annual worldwide turnover of more than €500 million, if at least one party has achieved an annual turnover in Germany of more than €25 million.

EC investigations. The Commission's merger investigations generally take 25 working days in simple cases (so called Phase 1) and generally an additional 90 working days in complex cases (so called Phase 2).

German investigations. Merger investigations by the FCO can either take up to one month in simple cases (so called Phase 1) or up to four months in complex cases (so called Phase 2).

Interventions during the agency's merger investigation

Publicity given to investigations. Both the Commission and the FCO publish the fact that a merger filing has been submitted within a few days of receipt of the filing. The Commission publishes a notice in the Official Journal (online at http://europa.eu.int/eur-lex) and invites interested parties to submit comments. Comments should be made within ten days from the date of the publication.

The FCO publishes the fact that a notification has been made on its website (www.bundeskartellamt.de). Third parties can intervene until the FCO has issued its decision on the proposed merger.

Prerequisites for granting intervener status. When filing a merger with the Commission, the parties are usually requested to provide the contact details of their most important competitors, suppliers and customers. In more complex cases, the Commission sends requests for information to these competitors, suppliers and customers. This is the primary way in which third parties contribute to the Commission's merger investigations. However, the Commission also welcomes unsolicited information and comments from third parties – including actual and potential competitors – on the proposed merger. As a general rule, the Commission has discretion whether or not to hear a third party before making a decision on the proposed merger. The Commission must, however, hear any person who demonstrates a *sufficient interest,* i.e. an adverse effect of the proposed merger on the economic or legal interests of the third party. Members of the administrative or management bodies of the merging companies or the recognized representatives of their employees as well as consumer associations are presumed by the law to have a sufficient interest. With respect to shareholders, the European courts held that shareholders in a company generally do not have a sufficient interest because their shareholders' rights are not changed by the Commission's merger clearance decision.

Natural/legal persons and associations can apply to the FCO to be formally admitted as a party to the merger investigation. Applicants need to show that the decision affects their interests. Even a potential competitor may be admitted. As a general rule, it is in the FCO's discretion to admit the applicant to the merger investigation, which will normally require that the applicant is likely to offer input which is of added value to the investigation.

Status given to interveners in the proceedings. The Commission informs intervening third parties in writing of the nature and subject matter of the proposed merger, and invites them to submit their comments. There is no enforceable right to full access to the files. However, the Commission generally provides third parties with non-confidential versions of important documents, e.g., the decision to initiate an in-depth procedure, or the statement of objections. At a later stage in the merger investigation the Commission can ask the third party to participate in formal oral hearings. Third parties do not have the same procedural rights as the parties to the transaction. In particular, the Commission is not obliged to hear the third party on all objections raised during the merger investigation before making its final decision.

Any intervener who has been formally admitted as a party to the merger investigation led by the FCO must be heard before any decision is made. The intervener can make oral and written statements, receives copies of all correspondence and is given access to the file. Business secrets of the merging parties will, however, be kept confidential.

Subsequent challenges of a merger in court proceedings

Third parties may also appeal a merger clearance decision in court. If merger clearance was granted by the Commission, the competent court is the European Court of First Instance ("CFI") in Luxemburg. If merger clearance was granted by the FCO, the competent court is the Higher Regional Court of Düsseldorf ("Higher Regional Court"). The court proceedings are administrative proceedings directed against the agency that handed down the merger clearance. Under European and German competition law, mergers cannot be challenged with civil law proceedings.

Court challenges of EC merger clearances. Both the clearance decisions rendered in Phase 1 proceedings and rendered in Phase 2 proceedings can be challenged. The legal remedy is an action for annulment before the CFI. The statutory time limit is two months either from the publication of the merger clearance decision or from when the applicant is notified of the merger clearance. The fact that a merger clearance was granted is published in the Official Journal (http://europa.eu.int/eur-lex). In order to have *standing,* the applicant must demonstrate that the merger clearance decision is of direct and individual concern to him. As a general rule, a merger clearance decision is always of direct concern to the third party intervener since the clearance decision authorizes the immediate closing of the proposed merger and leads to a direct change of the competitive situation on the markets. It is more challenging to demonstrate individual concern. According to established case law, third parties must show that the Commission's decision affects them in a similar way as the addressees of the decision, either because of certain characteristics which are particularly relevant to them or because of circumstances which differentiate them from all other persons. Individual concern requires that the third party participated actively in the Commission's merger investigation. Indications of active participation are that the third party was contacted by the Commission, took part in telephone conferences and meetings with the Commission or participated in the formal hearing. A potential competitor can have standing, if the merger takes place in an oligopolistic market which is characterized by high entry barriers. Even applicants who are active in a neighboring market or in an upstream or downstream market may have standing, if the contested merger leads to the strengthening of a monopoly on the market directly affected by the merger.

The CFI can annul a clearance decision by the Commission either completely or in parts (e.g., relating to certain products or geographical markets). If a clearance decision is annulled in part, the case will be reviewed a second time by the Commission since the court cannot make a final decision as to the compatibility of the transaction. Decisions by the CFI can be appealed to the European Court of Justice in Luxemburg.

Filing an action to the CFI for annulment of a clearance decision does not have a suspensive effect, and the parties to the merger can therefore consummate the contested merger while the court proceedings are ongoing. In theory, third parties can request the CFI to issue an interim measure ordering a suspension of the merger. In practice, however, there have been no successful requests for interim measures ordering such a suspension.

Court challenges of German merger clearances. According to established case law, third party interveners can only challenge merger clearance decisions issued by the FCO in Phase 2 proceedings. Furthermore, the applicant can only apply for the annulment of the clearance decision, but not for the additional endorsement of conditions and obligations. The appeal must be lodged either with the FCO or directly with the Higher Regional Court within one month of service of the decision to clear the merger.

A third party intervener will only be entitled to appeal a merger clearance decision if it was formally admitted by the FCO as a party to the merger investigation. This excludes third parties who have only informally submitted comments to the FCO during the merger investigation or have answered questionnaires issued by the FCO.

In order to have *standing*, the third party intervener must demonstrate both formal and substantive concern. Formal concern requires that the FCO did not follow and implement all of the intervener's requests in the merger clearance decision. To demonstrate substantive concern, the third party intervener must show that the clearance decision has a negative impact on the competitive conditions on both the product market and the geographical market on which the intervener is active.

If the Higher Regional Court decides that the clearance decision by the FCO was unlawful, it will annul the entire merger clearance decision. The Court is not entitled to annul only parts of the merger clearance decision. Furthermore, the Court can only annul the merger clearance decision of the FCO, but it is not competent to issue a final decision on the proposed merger. Rather, the case will be reviewed a second time by the FCO. Decisions of the Higher Regional Court can be appealed to the German Federal Court of Justice.

Third parties can apply for an interim court order to suspend the effect of the FCO's clearance until the Court makes its final decision. In the past, the Court could issue such an interim order if it had serious doubts as to the legality of the merger clearance decision. As of 1 July 2005, an additional condition must be satisfied: Third parties must be able to credibly demonstrate that the contested merger clearance decision infringes their individual rights. This condition was introduced because there was a perception that competitors could misuse the possibility to request an interim order. For example, in the *Trienekens Case*, the waste disposal company Trienekens intended to acquire a waste incineration plant. A competitor appealed the merger clearance decision and obtained an interim order. While Trienekens was prevented from acquiring the plant during the ongoing court proceedings, the competitor used the opportunity to acquire the plant itself. In the *E.on/Ruhrgas Case,* E.on intended to acquire control over Ruhrgas. A number of companies, mostly small utility companies, appealed the FCO decision clearing the merger and successfully applied for interim orders, effectively preventing E.on from completing the transaction during the subsequent court proceedings which lasted more than six months and could be terminated only by way of a settlement between E.on and the intervening parties, who eventually withdrew their complaints.

Summary

- Both the Commission and the FCO are more receptive to interventions by actual and potential competitors than their US counterparts, the DoJ and FTC.
- In complex merger cases the competent merger authority will contact the merger parties' most important competitors, customers and suppliers of its own initiative. However, third parties should not rely on this, but should, if they are interested in the outcome of a given proceeding, contact the Commission or the FCO on their own initiative.
- A third party will only have standing to challenge a merger clearance decision to the CFI or the Higher Regional Court if it actively participated in the preceding merger investigation led by the FCO or the Commission.

4.8 HR & Pensions

4.8.1 Effective People Management in US-German Mergers

Ulf M. Tworeck

This section addresses the specific context for business model integration, synergy management, integration management and leadership transition issues as they relate to German acquisitions by US organizations. In each section relevant advice for Germany is provided backed up by an actual case example. US organizations planning German acquisitions will find these references essential for planning their transactions.

In most transatlantic mergers the cultural integration aspects were severely undervalued during the transaction planning stage during the past 10 years (Mercer Consulting Group Study: Transatlantic Mergers – 2003). Germany with its structured legislation is an excellent market for systematic synergy management related to M&A. In over 80% of transactions that we have tracked, people cost-related synergies were realized exactly against plan whereas other cost synergies emerged later than anticipated (Mercer Management Study: Effective Mergers – 2004). The key barrier to effective synergy management was rooted in different perceptions by US and German management of the future joint business model that the newly merged entity would operate under in the post-closing phase. US acquirers often shy away from German acquisitions due to perceived legislative and works council barriers.

Business model integration

German leadership teams operate differently to US leaders when defining the deal logic or integration planning. This is rooted both in legal and cultural differences, the main difference being the consensus-driven decision-making environment in Germany. However, this approach has significant advantages in driving the merger process through its various stages to combine business models, reposition the merged entity and accelerating the merged business to further top-line growth.

The key tenets that require clarification early in the transaction between the senior leaders of both sides include the following:

1. Operational structure: Decision-making authority related to changes in business model and operating structure.
2. Management model: Selection of key business leaders for the future merged structure, citing objective and rational criteria for making choices.
3. Financial management: Significant differences exist between the German and US perceptions of financial management, in particular cashflow-related measures.

4. Synergy management: German management must first be convinced of the rationale underlying any synergy plan in 1-on-1 sessions before being committed to implementation.

5. Scope of changes: Early lack of clarity on scope of organizational changes leads to misalignment of expectations (hence frustrations) of German management and works councils.

6. Management meeting culture: A key difference to US management meetings is the need for the merged management team to adhere to a set agenda during the initial monthly meetings to overcome cultural differences.

Case example: A US-based global chemicals division acquired a German competitor of equivalent size (several €BN in revenue) and made the following mistakes related to the business model integration:

1. The US senior team did not share their view of the future integrated business model with their new German colleagues. The Germans proceeded to run their European business as if no change in ownership had occurred. Cost synergies were attained on time and the operational integration appeared to be on plan. 12 months later it emerged that the biggest of 4 operating divisions had not changed its business model at all – it was merely shedding excess resources through the synergy exercise. It was only when the German division leader was ousted that the division returned to profitability.

2. The US acquirer had sent one of their most experienced senior executives to run the division. As this individual went through the process of understanding the acquired business he emotionally sided with the German senior leadership. Not only did this make the transition to the new business model impossible but also caused a serious performance rift within the US leadership team. This resulted in an unintended organizational redesign into 2 global centers: North America with rapid integration and Europe with slow integration.

3. The initial management meetings included European representatives from both organizations. The internal competition for the key jobs was significant leading to substantial deviations from plan as personal agenda items began to control meetings. The management meetings only returned to schedule after the new European leadership group was announced and installed. This led to a significant loss of momentum in the integration process costing 60% of operational synergies planned for year 1.

Synergy management

A key consideration of any transaction in Germany is the need to recoup part of the price premium through synergy extraction after closing. Germany, with its system of works councils, is ideally placed to manage the extraction process on a systematic basis. The majority of synergies (Figure 4.27) come from Full Time Equivalent (FTE)-related savings in the G&A and sales areas. Our experience shows that with the support of a strong legal team and a well structured synergy plan negotiations can

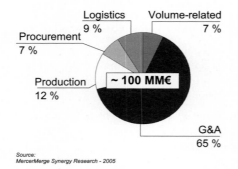

Figure 4.27
Synergy management:
100% of typical synergies from
year 3 after closing (before tax)

commence within 8-12 weeks after closing. Typically, a 3-step process is adopted to ensure the buy-in of all parties:

1. Review of planned synergies by senior management of acquired business to confirm operational assumptions and develop the synergy plan for the works council presentation
2. Presentation and selling of synergy plan to a sub-team of the works council formed to negotiate a reconciliation of interest (ROI) and social plan (SP), with adjustment to the synergy plan to settle on a compromise
3. Refinement of negotiated synergy plan with operational management to attain buy-in and commitment for implementation

A well orchestrated plan would be negotiated in 3-5 months (depending on scope and severity) and then be immediately implemented with cashflow savings emerging 18 months after starting the negotiations. The process may encounter several roadblocks

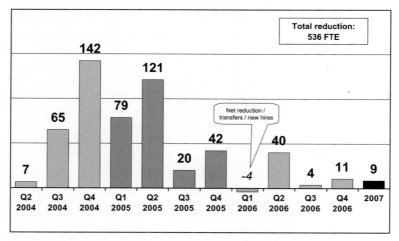

Figure 4.28
FTE synergies: Full time equivalent (FTE) reduction by quarter over a 4 year period

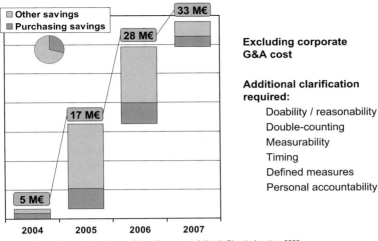

Source: MercerMerge – Other Synergy Plan – German acquisition in Chemical sector - 2005

Figure 4.29
Non-FTE synergies: Synergy plan (non-FTE) for German integration over a 4 year period

as each phase is completed by the integration team but it also guarantees management and works council buy-in during the 3-phased approach.

The typical implementation of FTE-related savings is depicted in Figure 4.28. A significant wave of employees leave early in the process with defined critical groups leaving at a later stage. The exact exit dates are typically negotiated with the works council. The advantage to the acquiring entity: Once the reconciliation of interest is signed it is almost always guaranteed to be implemented as laid out in the signed document.

The non-FTE synergies in our experience take longer to extract from the merged business (Figure 4.29) and typically lead to savings later than expected. The reasons often include:

- Difficulties when planning exact operational savings of target organization (e.g., procurement, IT)
- Delays with the integration of systems (e.g., ERP complexity, process re-engineering delays)
- Delays in defining a new joint business model as a platform for synergy management

The synergy planning process in Germany is contingent on the quality and assumptions of the integration master plan.

Case example: A US financial services group acquired a German retail banking operation. The German branch structure was three times larger than that of the acquirer. The US acquisition team had developed a structured integration plan, leading to synergies of approximately 40% of the FTE across the German branches. The detailed plan was delayed due to 2 significant mistakes:

1. Although the high level restructuring plan was discussed with the top 2 German leaders, the German works council was not informed about the plan on a timely basis. Subsequently details leaked from the works council of the US financial services group in Germany to the newly acquired entity's works council. The unions were involved by the works council leading to the publishing of derogatory headlines in the German financial press. Next the employees in a large German city branch marched through the streets, waving signboards against the planned changes.

2. German management was approached by the local Federal State government to appease in the public confrontation. This enhanced the conflict even further. It was only when management began to hold offline meetings with both union and works council representatives and struck a mutually acceptable deal that both sides began to work together at resolving the employee grievances and restoring order. Although wildcat strikes in Germany are not permissible, in the worst case employees can elect to stop working (resulting in a loss of pay). A better approach would have been to involve the works council at an early stage in the assessment of the synergy plans, giving them some scope to influence the measures.

Integration management

The success of changing the business model in a German M&A context depends on the structure of the integration plan. Typically integration management covers 3 work streams simultaneously during the first 3-6 months after closing (Figure 4.30):

1. Integration of the senior and middle management teams: Selection and allocation of leaders to new roles, managing dual structures (acquired and previously owned business) during the selection process and defining a new governance framework for the new management team after migration to the new operating model. Clarity in the redesign of the future organization and redefinition of roles and responsibilities for the new functions is key for an accelerated integration process.

2. Synergy management: Kick-off of the negotiations with the works council to reach agreement on the synergy realization process, culminating in a reconciliation of interest and social plan. This effectively provides the roadmap for the transformation of the merged business operations.

3. Hive-off or organizational changes to comply with German/EU anti-trust rulings: This typically requires a rapid carve-out of the businesses to be exited in terms of the rulings. As it involves employee selection and transfers it requires the consent of each side's works council, often requiring to a rapid negotiation process to protect staff transferring to new owners.

Case example: A US manufacturer acquired a German-based market leader for automotive components at a high EBITDA multiple. The transaction was approved by the EU anti-trust authorities on the basis that defined business units in Germany had to be divested in an auction process. The carve-out covered both defined customer-centric regions and product lines across Germany. The acquirer appointed an interim management team under the supervision of a trustee to prepare the carve-out for the divestiture process. The following roadblocks had to be overcome:

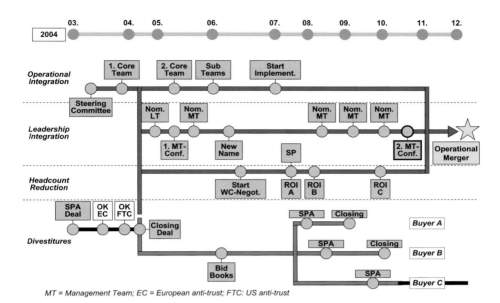

Figure 4.30 Integration management

1. The leadership team had to be split between the divested and retained businesses based on rudimentary information. In particular, the decision pertaining to the CFO was difficult. As a highly recognized contributor to the acquirer's business, allocating the CFO to the carve-out was a difficult decision. Yet the divestiture of the carve-out should result in a comparable EBITDA multiple to the initial transaction to meet analysts' expectations. The decision was made to transfer the CFO as a key business leader to the business units for sale with an option to return if the subsequent buyers did not require the services after closing (strong German management team with future acquirer).

2. An additional measure that required rapid resolution for the divestiture process was the FTE loading of the businesses for sale. By allocating the minimum number of employees possible the projected financials would be improved to achieve the desired EBITDA multiples. The surplus headcount could easily be restructured as part of the synergy measures that the acquirer had planned for the German operations. It was essential not to share this information with the works council bodies. To conceal this optimization approach the departing employees of the carve-out were awarded a "blanket" social plan to define their severance entitlement in case the new owners decided to reduce headcount in future.

Leadership transition

To transform the merged organizations through implementation of new processes, governance structures and interaction between the leadership groups will require several steps to change the incumbent behaviors during the initial 3 months of ownership after closing.

As sponsors of the integration process, the newly appointed leaders are accountable to implement the relevant integration projects. This should not have a counter-productive impact by leading to a low level of consensus between both former teams of leaders.

A common vision of the desired business model is required to instal a "new way of thinking" amongst top team members. A common language must be developed to cover simple operational tools such as budgeting, capital requests, monthly reporting, cost allocation and managing customers.

The new leadership organization should be in place by the end of the first 8 weeks to ensure the subsequent rollout of new processes, working methodologies and behaviors to start generating the planned integration synergies. The top level team should be announced within 1 week of closing, the first management level within the first month and the next critical level/roles within the first 2 months. Often decisions will not be made because of the need to arbitrate between feuding parties. In our experience decisions are not improved by waiting longer – rather be prepared to remake an appointment after the initial 12 months if the wrong candidates were nominated. Appointed leaders should prove their value contribution within the first year – if they do not match the performance expectations of the acquiring organization they should be replaced.

This immediate post-closing phase should include the engagement of the senior leadership group, their buy-in and shared understanding of managing the merged business and of their individual roles or behaviors as they migrate to the new organization structure.

This will require a consistent governance framework at the German level, defined operating processes and a structured change management program. Our experience highlights that not waiting for a minimum level of momentum amongst the new leadership members regarding their future roles in business management would be a counter-productive to rapid integration. A key success factor in this phase is a minimum set of agreed and shared guidelines. This phase is typically very sensitive and difficult to manage as it will initiate a period of "dual organization and management," bringing additional uncertainty and therefore two additional risks:

1. Businesses have to be kept running under pre-closing processes and decision-making modes, within an old governance framework
2. The new organization has to be reengineered to comply with proposed guidelines and principles, within a new and untested governance framework.

Most leaders will have dual responsibilities throughout this period.

Case example: A US-based multinational listed on the NYSE completed another acquisition in Germany. The business unit was part of the sell-off of a DAX 30 organization that had previously merged with an European competitor. The acquired management team was nervous but had also been newly appointed in the top 2 roles. Senior managers had been transferred into their German roles from Asian subsidiaries during the 18-months' period leading up to the sale. Anxiety was high as these relatively inexperienced leaders were confronted with the US senior leadership team during the first integration workshop in Orlando.

- Transfer of full legal ownership of the trust assets to the Pension Trust
- Use of the trust assets exclusively to fulfill the secured pension liabilities
- Limitation of the re-transfer of the trust assets
- Limitation of termination possibilities in accordance with the purpose of providing security
- Definition of the shortfall and the secured pension liabilities
- Determination of ranking of security

The special requirements placed on the contents of the Trust Agreement in respect of insolvency law are dealt with later in this contribution (see "Protection against Insolvency").

The Pension Trust in the legal form of a Registered Association (*eingetragener Verein*)

Registered Association as suitable legal form

The Pension Trust is usually established in the legal form of a registered association. Alternatively however, other legal forms are possible, such as for example the establishment of a limited liability company (GmbH). But comparatively, the legal form of a registered association is the least complicated and therefore most preferable option. For example, a GmbH would have to be provided with a respective minimum amount of capital and the question would also arise as to who shall hold the shares in the GmbH. The sponsoring company is out of the question as shareholder because according to international accounting regulations (IFRS), the trust assets must be transferred to an organization which is legally independent from the sponsoring company in order to be recognized as *plan assets*. All these issues do not arise for a registered association, provided that its members are at an adequate distance from the sponsoring company.

Legal statutes of the Pension Trust

The legal statutes (*Satzung*) of the Pension Trust have to conform to the minimum statutory contents (Sec. 57, 58 BGB) concerning the following subjects:

- Name and seat as well as the fact that the association shall be registered
- Purpose
- Entry and withdrawal of members
- Creation of the board of directors (*Vorstand*)
- Requirements and form of convening of the members' assembly as well as adotion of resolutions
- Responsibility of the board of directors vis-à-vis the members' assembly
- Membership dues

In addition, when structuring the legal statutes, in particular it must be ensured that the requirements for qualification as a non-profit association are fulfilled, the autonomy of the association is assured and protection against insolvency is guaranteed.

Non-profit association

The Pension Trust can be qualified as a non-profit association (*nichtwirtschaftlicher Verein*). Hence, registration in the Register of Associations is sufficient to achieve legal capacity (*Rechtsfähigkeit*) (Sec. 21 BGB).

The Pension Trust is not a commercial association (*wirtschaftlicher Verein*) and therefore does not require a license (Sec. 22 BGB) in order to achieve legal capacity. Such an association within the meaning of Sec. 22 BGB only exists if the purpose of the association is based on commercial business operations (*wirtschaftlicher Geschäftsbetrieb*), i.e., the association operates as a provider on a market on a routine basis and for remuneration. The exclusive purpose of the Pension Trust, however, is to manage and protect the trust assets in a fiduciary capacity. The Pension Trust does not pursue any commercial interests and only receives reimbursement of expenses for the pursuance of the purpose of the association. In principle, membership dues are not levied. No services are provided to outside parties or members against payment, i.e., insofar the situation of a provider on a market is absent.

Assurance of association autonomy

It has to be ensured in the provisions of the legal statutes of the Pension Trust that the autonomy of the association is assured and that therefore the capability of the association to be registered in the Register of Associations is guaranteed.

A prerequisite for the assurance of the autonomy of the association is that the association possesses the minimum requirements of a corporate organization, especially in respect of third-party control. According to some court decisions extensive third-party control from outside over internal operations of the association may be inconsistent with the character of an association and may thus result in the refusal to register the association in the Register of Associations. If the association is already registered, the respective provisions of the legal statutes would be void and there is the risk of the association being deleted from the Register of Associations by way of an official deletion from the register (*Amtslöschungsverfahren*).

Labor law effects

No consent of the pension plan beneficiaries required

The consent of the pension plan beneficiaries is not required for the establishment of the Pension Trust or for the conclusion of the CTA as the relationship between employer and employee remains unaffected by the establishment of a CTA. There is no change in the type of pension scheme implemented. The direct pension commitment made initially by the employer remains in effect and its contents remain unchanged.

No entrepreneurial co-determination

There are no co-determination rights according to the Co-determination Act (*Mitbestimmungsgesetz*), the Co-determination Act for the Coal, Iron and Steel Industry

(*Montan-Mitbestimmungsgesetz*), the Co-determination Amendment Act (*Mitbestimmungsergänzungsgesetz*) or the One Third Participation Act (*Drittelbeteiligungsgesetz*) apparent.

No co-determination of the works council

There is no co-determination right of the works council set forth in either Sec. 87 (1) No. 8 Works Council Constitution Act (*Betriebsverfassungsgesetz* – BetrVG) or Sec. 87 (1) No. 10 BetrVG.

The prerequisites set forth in Sec. 87 (1) No. 8 BetrVG are not fulfilled because the Pension Trust is not a welfare service (*Sozialeinrichtung*) within the meaning of this provision. The decisive factor in this respect is that the Pension Trust (in any event prior to the insolvency of the sponsoring company) does not and shall not provide any direct services to the personnel. When a CTA is established, the employer (as long as it is solvent) remains responsible for the pension liabilities. To this extent, the Pension Trust is only an economic means of protection (*wirtschaftliches Sicherungsmittel*).

Also a co-determination right according to Sec. 87 (1) No. 10 BetrVG does not apply. The formation and separation of trust assets is not a question of the wage structure (*Lohngestaltung*).

Protection against insolvency

Insolvency resistance of the CTA

In terms of the German Insolvency Code (*Insolvenzordnung* – InsO) which came into effect on 1 January 1999, to date no supreme court decisions have been handed down concerning the question of whether a two-way trust arrangement provides protection against insolvency for the pension plan beneficiaries. However, in a decision based on the previous Bankruptcy Act (*Konkursordnung* – KO), the Federal Supreme Court (*Bundesgerichtshof*) confirmed the insolvency resistance of a two-way trust arrangement.

The Federal Labor Court (*Bundesarbeitsgericht*) also stated in an *obiter dictum* that in principle insolvency resistance of the trust arrangement developed in the literature and in practice can probably be presumed.

The bodies participating in the legislative procedure also proceed on the assumption of insolvency resistance of the two-way trust arrangement as is documented in the legislative intent of Sec. 8a Old-Age Part-Time Act (*Altersteilzeitgesetz*) (the two-way trust arrangement is cited here as being suitable as protection against insolvency).

Yet, Sec. 115, 116 InsO, the general reasons for invalidity pursuant to Sec. 134, 138 BGB and the facts and circumstances justifying avoidance pursuant to Sec. 129 et seq. InsO can be in contradiction to insolvency resistance.

Sec. 115, 116 InsO

Pursuant to Sec. 115, 116 InsO, a contract for services (*Geschäftsbesorgungsvertrag*) for the debtor or a contract order (*Auftrag*) placed by the debtor, which concerns the assets belonging to the insolvency estate (*Insolvenzmasse*), expires upon commencement of the insolvency proceedings. For the two-way trust arrangement, in any event this situation affects the Management Trust, meaning the trust relationship between sponsoring company and Pension Trust.

On the other hand, according to the opinion voiced in prevailing literature, the Security Trust relationship existing between the Pension Trust and the third-party beneficiary remains in effect and is not changed even if the Management Trust expires. The insolvency receiver (*Insolvenzverwalter*) has no right to dispose of the security agreement set forth in the Trust Agreement and the third party beneficiary contract (*Vertrag zugunsten Dritter*) based on this agreement. In this respect, prevailing literature focuses on the court rulings concerning Sec. 23, 27 KO because these mainly correspond in terms of content with Sec. 115, 116 InsO.

General reasons for invalidity

The literature assumes that invalidity pursuant to Sec. 134 or Sec. 138 BGB is excluded for security trust agreements with normal contractual structure.

In some isolated cases it is opined that the provision of security rights pursuant to Sec. 138 BGB is invalid on account of unconscionability (*Sittenwidrigkeit*) if this provision is only carried out for cases of insolvency. In contrast, the prevailing literature states that the fact that the pension plan beneficiaries shall not have a right to their own due claims for payment against the Pension Trust until the occurrence of a shortfall (*Sicherungsfall*) does not change the immediate effectiveness of the provision of security (*Sicherheitenbestellung*). Furthermore, the deferred security in case of insolvency does not burden the creditors any more than the immediately effective.

Invalidity pursuant to Sec. 134, 138 BGB on account of disadvantage of creditors (*Gläubigerbenachteiligung*) is excluded because third-party creditors can easily see that the separated assets shall be reserved for satisfaction of pension claims. Therefore, other creditors are not misguided to an erroneous impression of the financial standing of the sponsoring company.

Right of avoidance

As concerns the question of right of avoidance (*Anfechtungsrecht*), there are various possible legal transactions which can be avoided. In particular, the following transactions could possibly be avoided:

- the conclusion of the Trust Agreement,
- the transfer of the security trust assets (*Treugut*) from sponsoring company to Pension Trust,
- all subsequent transfers of further trust assets from sponsoring company to Pension Trust,
- the benefits for the beneficiaries within the scope of the Trust Agreement and
- payments by the Pension Trust to the pension plan beneficiaries.

All these legal transactions lead to a reduction of the insolvency estate to the detriment of the insolvency creditors and therewith to a disadvantage of creditors within the meaning of Sec. 129 InsO, so that in principle, a risk of avoidance pursuant to Sec. 129 ff. InsO exists:

- Avoidance according to Sec. 130 to 132 InsO is possible if the legal transaction to be avoided was carried out three months prior to the filing for the commencement of insolvency proceedings. If the legal transaction has been accomplished within this time period, avoidance depends on the individual circumstances and cannot be excluded.

- Pursuant to Sec. 133 (1) InsO legal transactions can be avoided which the debtor carried out within the last 10 years prior to the filing for commencement of insolvency proceedings with the intention of placing his creditors at a disadvantage and the advantaged creditor was aware of this intention. However, even if the employer intentionally placed his creditors at a disadvantage, this fact is usually doomed to failure due to the advantaged creditor not being aware of this intention.

- As a rule, avoidance pursuant to Sec. 133 (2) InsO is also excluded. Pursuant to Sec. 133 (2) InsO, a contract against payment (*entgeltlicher Vertrag*) concluded by the debtor with a person in close relationship (*nahestehende Person*) within the meaning of Sec. 138 InsO can be avoided if it directly puts the insolvency creditors at a disadvantage. The Pension Trust is not deemed to be a person in close relationship with the sponsoring company. The Pension Trust is neither a member of a representational or supervisory board of the sponsoring company nor does the Pension Trust hold more than 25% of the capital, Sec. 138 (2) No. 1 InsO. Furthermore, the Pension Trust does not have the opportunity to obtain information on the financial situation of the sponsoring company by way of a corporate-law relationship with the sponsoring company or based on a service contract (Sec. 138 (2) No. 2 InsO). This is not changed by the fact that persons act for both the sponsoring company and the Pension Trust in respective functions because only the legally granted opportunity to obtain information is decisive, not an opportunity which is available due to the factual situation.

- Avoidance pursuant to Sec. 134 InsO is unsuccessful because the voluntary provision of securities for ones own debt is not an avoidable gratuitous service.

Exploitation right of the trust assets

Although the transferred assets legally belong to the Pension Trust, the sponsoring company remains the economic owner. Therefore, upon commencement of insolvency proceedings concerning the assets of the sponsoring company, the transferred assets belong to the insolvency estate. In this respect it is unclear whether the Pension Trust has

- a right of separation pursuant to Sec. 47 InsO (*Aussonderungsrecht*), meaning a right of separation of the specific object, or

- a right of separate satisfaction pursuant to Sec. 49, 50, 51 InsO (*Absonderungsrecht*), meaning the right to exploit the asset and prevailing satisfaction from the exploitation proceeds.

According to case law, in any event the Pension Trust has a right to separate satisfaction if the trust serves the purpose of securing claims of a third party (here the pension plan beneficiary). This results from a comparison of the two-way trust arrangement with the assignment of a claim for security (*Sicherungszession*) and the transfer of property by way of security (*Sicherungsübereignung*).

Insofar as the assets which have been transferred to the Pension Trust are movable assets, which are not in the possession of the insolvency receiver, the Pension Trust is authorized to exploit the assets within the scope of a right to separate satisfaction, Sec. 166 (1) InsO. On the other hand, if the assets are in the possession of the insolvency receiver, then he has the right to exploit the assets. The insolvency receiver is also authorized to realize accounts receivable which have been assigned to the Pension Trust as security for a claim (Sec. 166 (2) InsO).

In case of an exploitation by the insolvency receiver 4% of the received gross proceed has to be discharged to the insolvency estate as costs of determination (*Festellungskosten*) and 5% of the received gross proceed as cost of the disposition (*Verwertungskosten*). Possibly VAT has to be retained and discharged according to Sec. 170, 171 InsO.

As regards the right of separation there is currently a discussion whether IAS 19.7 requires a right of separation instead of a right of separate satisfaction. The prevailing literature is of the opinion that the right of separate satisfaction fulfills the requirements set forth in IAS 19.7 and that therefore a right of separation is not necessarily required. On the other hand, models are discussed which exclusively provide for rights of separation. These models, though possible, may however contain risks in several ways, in particular with regards to a possible avoidance.

Statutory insolvency insurance

Pursuant to Sec. 7 (1) and (2) Company Pensions Act (*Betriebsrentengesetz* – BetrAVG), the Pension Sicherungs Verein aG (PSV) is obligated to secure certain (vested) pension rights against insolvency (obligatory statutory insolvency insurance). Sec. 9 (2) sentence 1 BetrAVG stipulates that these secured pension rights and accessory collateral rights (liens, mortgages) shall transfer to the PSV in the event of a shortfall. This means:

- Insofar as PSV must not grant insolvency protection, no transfer takes place.
- If PSV must grant insolvency protection in the full amount, the pension entitlements to be secured and (accessory) collateral rights transfer to PSV.
- If only part of the beneficiaries' pension rights is provided with statutory protection against insolvency, the PSV shall accordingly be entitled to a partial transfer under Sec.9 (2) sentence 2 BetrAVG only.

Presently there is no established case law which confirms this. However, in regard to pledging of pension plan reinsurance (*Rückdeckungsversicherung*), this corresponds with the opinion of the PSV. The PSV considers itself to be obligated in this respect to release securities in favor of the pension plan beneficiaries to the extent that the pension plan beneficiaries do not receive satisfaction from PSV.

According to opinions contained in the literature, this also applies to the two-way trust arrangement and it is effective, possible and even recommendable to firstly provide security by way of a priority rating which has been established in the Trust Agreement for those pension entitlements for which there is no statutory insolvency protection through the PSV. Thereby, the PSV can – in case of a shortfall – only claim the transfer of those assets which are not required in order to satisfy the unsecured beneficiaries. However, it must be pointed out that there are no supreme court rulings or PSV opinions in this respect.

Literature

This article is based on the relevant technical literature and case law available at the time of writing, in particular the Commentary on the German Company Pension Act by Reinhold Hoefer and publications by Bode/Bergt/Obenberger as well as Küppers/Louven. A detailed list of the used technical literature and case law can be obtained from the authors.

4.9 Communications & Culture

4.9.1 Key Factors for Successful M&A Communications in Germany

Alexander Geiser and Nikolai Juchem

Cross-border M&A transactions – be they friendly or hostile in intention – are among the most complex of capital-market-related tasks. Alongside the legal specificities of the respective country, the difficulty of compiling valid feasibility studies, and not least determining the right price, it is primarily the challenges at the communications end that need to be tackled strategically in order to minimize execution risk. In this chapter, the focus is initially on the importance of transaction communications in general as a value driver. The authors then address special aspects of M&As in the German market, going into detail on the different groups targeted by communications and their respective expectations in light of the gradual emergence of a mature market in German. The chapter concludes with a presentation of a study of the P&G/Wella case in order to visualize the impact of professional transaction communications.

Strategic communication as a value driver

Recent years have seen a lively discussion in Germany on the role and importance of corporate communications. The greatest challenge continues to be to find a way of quantifying the value generated by successful communications on the one hand, and determining the value destroyed by inadequate or misleading communications, on the other. Communications professionals are experiencing ever greater pressure from management to prove what ROI their budgets achieve. Beyond dispute at both the theoretical and practical levels is the fact that communications functions as a key value driver. The academic literature on the subject contains countless models that focus on identifying and maximizing this contribution to value, without, as said, being able to quantify it with any precision. We shall focus below on aspects of this topic relating to financial/transactions communications in order to visualize the value-adding importance of professional communications.

Rising impact of financial communications in everyday business

In recent years, the transparency requirements that companies face worldwide have risen considerably. The United States has been the trailblazer here, and Washington's introduction of the Sarbanes Oxley Act made for even stricter regulation and supervision of the capital market. In Europe, efforts are underway to create a uniform legal framework in order to protect investors more effectively following the considerable share-price deterioration over the last few years. On both sides of the Atlantic, penalties for violations of communications provisions have been raised dramatically, in particular with regards to the personal liability of management in the US. Media interest in IPOs and M&A deals is also higher than ever before; in fact, it is safe to say that the crises and scandals of recent years have boosted it. In short, at the corporate end the risks associated with poor communication and/or the potential for enhancing value through financial communications have climbed considerably. Parallel to this, the reputation a company has in the capital markets plays an ever more crucial role. After all, publicly-listed companies with a global focus are not only competing at the operational level with their peers. They are likewise competing for institutional investors, who in turn set clear criteria for future investments. In this context, a company's communications track record and its reputation in the capital market is of critical significance, as this lays the foundations for trust and thus for a long-term investor/issuer relationship. By contrast, communicative "errors" are not infrequently punished in the form of a loss of trust and considerable share-price markdowns. It often takes years for a company to recover the ground lost by thoughtlessly permitting its reputation to be dented. And during that time, valuation distortions can occur in relation to the peer group, something that attracts investors interested primarily in making a short-term profit and thus increases the volatility of the share. Moreover, a negative reputation in the capital markets also tends to reflect on other stakeholders such as staff or customers, who then feel uncertain as a result of the critical media coverage. The question then often arises whether a company that misleads its investors does not also do likewise with the groups with whom it interacts. Put differently, financial communications is far from being a niche discipline in which only a handful of experts are interested. Rather its impact and thus the possible influence it has on value determine everyday life in the company, albeit to differing degrees and in differing ways.

A one-voice policy: Reducing risk and creating value

In light of the above remarks, laying the foundations professionally for communications is especially important precisely in the case of "mission critical," such as M&A transactions. All possible scenarios need to have been thought through and the communications side to them prepared, in order to minimize execution risk. For example, it would be negligent not to be prepared to counter possible leaks, as a dynamic opinion-formation process gets triggered both in the media and the capital market and once set in motion it is hard to control. Rampant speculation can send the market price of an acquisition target sky-high and thus threaten any deal being done. In such a case, in the absence of intensive prior preparation, the deal team will hardly be in a position to turn a purely reactive into a proactive role and get a handle on the matter. Be it leak communications or planned announcement: the message must be one and the same! Although core statements must be specifically tailored to the particular target group or possibly the specific culture of the country in question, the substance must always be the same. The challenge here is to speak to the different addressees, such as investors, media or staff in terms of the level of information they have, while preparing the data to be conveyed to them in such a way that the added value derived from the transaction becomes clear for all. It is thus obvious that preferential treatment of individual target groups must be clearly avoided. Not only does the legal framework set the goal posts in this regard, but information asymmetries nurture speculation or can give rise to protests, which in turn impact negatively on the course of the transaction and/or the company's reputation.

A communicator's view of corporate Germany: Myths, facts and trends

Only about ten years ago, Germany was still relatively underdeveloped with regards to major cross-border M&A deals (find more details in chapter of Stephan Leithner). There were so many different levels of cross-ownership between the major DAX-listed corporations that larger takeovers from the outside were nearly impossible. In 1995, the entire transaction volume in which German companies participated ran at only EUR 38.7 billion and the average deal volume was a mere EUR 17 million or so (Thomson Financial, see figure 4.32). By international comparison, the stock-market and equity culture was still in its infancy, and the legal framework and market regulators equally underdeveloped. Professional German financial communications only evolved slowly in the form of investor relations owing to pressure from national and international investors. Concerning media relations, given the relatively low media interest there was very little depth to the facts dished up. In short, while being decidedly interesting for investors, German corporations were considered anything but transparent. In what follows, we briefly sketch the mushrooming of the German capital market, the media scene and corporate culture, as this will help shed light on the current role and future development of financial communications, and specifically give foreign investors an idea of the challenges in this field.

Evolution of the German capital market and its constituents

In Germany, it is not that many years since there was no culture of the capital markets in terms of Anglo-American standards. Traditionally, German institutional and private investors alike focused more on classic investment vehicles such as bonds or real estate. Moreover, conservative forms of saving money, such as S&L plans, or life-insurance-based pension provisions played the decisive role influencing private inves-

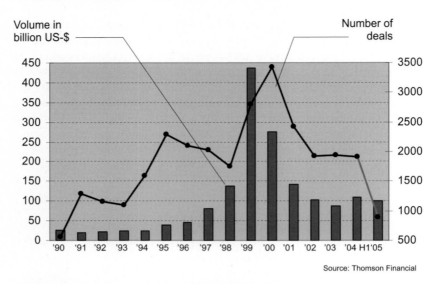

Figure 4.32 Development of M&As: Values & volumes Germany 1990-2004

tor behavior. In 1990, the total amount committed to equity funds in Germany came to a mere EUR 7.8 billion (BVI, German Bundesbank). Indeed, DIRK, the German professional association of investor relations managers, was firstly founded in 1994. Prior to that, almost nobody in Germany was familiar with this side of capital market communications. It was not until the Deutsche Telekom IPO in 1996 and the immense PR drive deployed to back it up, that real life was breathed into the stock market, kindling a culture of investing in equities. This trend was buttressed above all by the bull-market toward the end of the last millennium. Thus, the assets committed to equity funds had soared to just short of EUR 213 billion by 2000 (BVI, German Bundesbank). At the same time, investor relations became increasingly more important for publicly-listed German corporations. Initially founded as an organizational addendum to established company PR or Finance sections, today IR departments have a firm place in German companies and as a rule are a key central function reporting direct to the CEO or the CFO.

Trends in the German financial media

The German media were a real driver in the expansion phase of the financial markets. While prior to 1996 corporate and financial market reporting was very descriptive and quantitatively limited, the capital market became the focus of daily coverage in both the print media as well as TV and radio at the latest with the foundation of Neuer Markt in 1997, the stock-market segment for young growth and technology corporations. The number of specialist media truly exploded and, given the high short-term profits to be reaped on the exchanges, a very subjective sense of a "gold rush" spread among the general public, climaxing in spring 2000 after Vodafone took over Mannesmann. Owing to the strong qualitative and quantitative demands for corporate and financial information, an increasing number of journalists established themselves as experts in the field and started assessing companies more carefully, evaluating corporate strengths and weaknesses, and bombarding corporate press officers with firm questions on business figures or deal synergies. As a strand in reporting on the capital markets this critical and frequently investigative journalism, with its pronounced focus on fact gathering, gained an even sharper edge after the stock-market bubble burst in 2000 – when it became clear that the lion's share of the synergies targeted during the wave of mergers would not happen owing to the inflated prices paid for the shares. However, the editorial desks at the major newspaper did not themselves emerge from the crisis unscathed. For example, since 2001 the eight largest German business papers have fired a large part of their own staff.

Internationalization, professionalization and regulation

The boom years on the German capital market were characterized first and foremost by the strong growth in the number of transactions. There were 321 IPOs in Germany in 1999 and 2000, alone – and 6,225 M&A transactions with German involvement, accounting for a total volume in excess of EUR 700 billion (Thomson Financial). The growth was also spurred by greater activity by foreign investors, with the portion of German equities held by non-Germans rising from 11% in 1991 to 16% in 2000, (Institut der deutschen Wirtschaft) and these investors focusing in particular on Neuer Markt growth stocks.

However, the dynamic growth was so rapid that it was not possible to put a due regulatory legal framework in place at the same pace, and thus ensure appropriate investor protection. In the crisis years 2001-3, these shortcomings became apparent, with an awareness of them rising not least in the wake of international scandals such as Enron, Worldcom or Parmalat, and a new era of capital market regulation commenced in Europe, with companies having to meet communications and transparency duties that had a far greater reach and a stronger emphasis on the international side to reporting. German lawmakers have taken the translation of the corresponding stringent EU directives very seriously and have frequently even gone one step further. What are now complex communications regulations, have become the subject of controversial debate among capital market players. In particular, publicly-listed companies bemoan the meager "everyday viability" of some laws and the fact that they need to have a large part of external communications checked by lawyers prior to release. At the same time, the sanctions for deficient, misleading or overdue communications have been given even sharper teeth with enactment of AnSVG, the German Act Enhancing Investor Protection, in 2004. Nevertheless, these regulatory measures and the public discussion on corporate governance standards triggered professionalization and an international gearing of corporate communications in Germany especially as regards investor relations. This may also be proof that following the crisis of confidence in 2001-3, foreign investors are starting to come back into the German market, which, moreover, many international stock-market pundits consider comparatively under-valued.

This trend is being bolstered not least by the fact that today many CEOs of the German blue chips are of a younger generation, as many of the new men at the helm have excellent international track records and are intimately familiar with customs in the various different capital markets. Frequently, however, there is still insufficient awareness of the international side to media work, something that has become significantly more demanding owing to the greater expertise of journalists and the swiftness of coverage. Highly reputed, opinion-leading formats such as "breakingviews" or the "Lex Column" have in recent years increasingly focused on German corporations, and the electronic dissemination of their news has appreciably speeded up the pace of reporting. By contrast, communications officers in Germany often still concentrate overwhelmingly on their domestic market and on nurturing their local networks, thus neglecting to foster contact to opinion leaders outside the country. Yet precisely the latter are crucially important in the case of cross-border M&A transactions, if the core messages and background to a transaction are to be conveyed swiftly and lock into existing investor confidence. Since such networks can only meaningfully be established locally, and many companies shy away from the costs of a foreign press desk, there is an increasing trend to rely on the expertise and networking of international communications consultancies specifically in the case of major transactions. Specialists in this segment have garnered experience from numerous M&A transactions and can function as a pivotal interface between the deal team and the in-house communicators during the different phases of a deal, as the in-house officers have in the course of their professional lives rarely, if at all, provided the communications backup to such transactions. In other words, making use of outside expert services can considerably lower execution risk.

M&A communications in Germany: Challenges and best practice

No deal team without communicators

While the greatest possible discretion is one of the critical factors for the potential success of any an M&A project, mandatory disclosures and over and above them, carefully focused information for the capital market play an equally important role for publicly-listed corporations. Therefore, in an optimal team structure the corporate IR and PR functions, both reporting directly to the Board, constitute central management functions for gathering and disseminating information. In the M&A process, the key communicative abilities must come to the fore in communicating with the financial media, on the one hand, and with investors and analysts, on the other. Depending on the size of the company involved, as well as on the scope and structure of the M&A transaction, classical PR/advertising can also contribute to the deal being closed successfully. Finally, there is internal communications, during the transaction phase as a means of information providing and increasingly during the control phase, as it is of crucial importance for integration processes, for the realignment of the company, and as a source of staff motivation.

The key tasks handled by the expanded project team are information procurement and forwarding. In the case of publicly-listed corporations, the success of M&A deals depends to a great extent on the quality of the external and internal communications effort. The latter has an overarching pivotal function in the pre-merger and post-merger processes. The challenges facing interface management as regards communications can be optimally mastered by a clear team structure that includes external communications experts.

Disclosure duties and voluntary information during the M&A process: The challenges for a one-voice policy

In Germany, the wide-ranging basic mandatory disclosure requirements for M&A transactions were in part first put in place after the Vodafone/Mannesmann deal – in the form of WpÜG, the German Act on Securities Acquisition and Takeovers, which came into force in 2001 and thus established a legal framework. Together with stricter ad-hoc disclosure regulations gradually established by EU legislation, which had a strong investor thrust, the standards for communications relating to transactions involving German publicly-listed corporations have risen incisively. To summarize, the rule of thumb is: there are countless complex and time-critical mandatory disclosure elements to be considered by both the bidder or the company targeted. Delivering

Table 4.7 Financial communications during M&As – mandatory and voluntary measures

Mandatory		Voluntary
Ad-hoc disclosure pursuant to section 15 WpHG	Immediate publication of insider information that is of such a nature it could considerably influence the stock-exchange share price	• Personally inform shareholders and analysts by email • Compile additional press release with background information
Disclosure duties pursuant to sections 21 ff. WpHG pursuant to sections 20, 21 AktG	Communication by the buyer to the target company and publication by the target company once the shares have been acquired 5%, 10%, 25%, 50%, 75% for all companies listed in first and second-segment trading 25%, 50% for all joint-stock corporations	• Conference call • Ad campaign • Personally refer key contact persons to the news posted on the Internet • Summarize key aspects of the bid, e.g., in the form of a press release or presentation
Bidder's viewpoint: Decision to submit an offer pursuant to sections 10, 34 WpÜG	Immediate publication, prior publication at exchanges, the BAFin and target company	• Prepare a newsletter for private shareholders • Set up call center to respond to questions from private investors
Bidder's viewpoint: Achieve control (≥ 30 % voting rights)	Immediate publication, at the latest seven days after control has been obtained	• Hold road shows to discuss the M&A transaction / company strategy with investors and analysts
Bidder's viewpoint: Bid documents	Immediate publication after approval granted by BAFin and forwarded to the target company	
Target company's view: Statement on the bid with mandatory elements "Status report" pursuant to section 23 WpÜG	Immediate publication after release of the bid documents Publication of the respectively current voting blocks	

convincing voluntary information as part of a focused communications strategy is usually only possible if the project team pulls together to an above-average degree and external coaching is at hand. In the case of a hostile bid, the quality of the communications strategy pursued specifically by the communications team in the target company depends utterly on the time factor and the ability to offset bottlenecks and a lack of specialist knowledge by considerably broadening the resources available.

The key legal regulations for M&A transactions relating to publicly-listed corporations are encoded in AktG, the German Stock Corporation Act, WpHG, the German Securities Trading Act, and WpÜG. The German Stock Exchange Act, the Stock Exchange Rules and Regulations, and the disclosure regulations for sales prospectuses all help define an additional regulatory regime covering transfers of title to stock. Important key elements for all transactions are: ad hoc disclosure requirements, insider trading laws, reporting duties, the information rights/duties set out in the Stock Corporation Act, and the duties stipulated in the same that the respective Executive Board must discharge, such as ensuring equal treatment of all shareholders and the unconditional preservation of the company's interests.

In the case of public takeovers, the key factors for success are the communications strategy and the tactical deployment of the dynamic factor of time. A convincing communications strategy is also required in the case of larger-scale disinvestments or spin-offs by publicly-listed corporations, as these transactions as a rule need a qualified majority at the respective General Meeting. Table 4.7 presents the sequence of legal stipulations applying to takeover bids and outlines what voluntary measures can be implemented.

Evidently, legal requirements, the need to convincingly present strategic and business arguments as well as the restricted time available are very closely related in the case of public takeovers. At the same time, the process is accompanied by great internal and external attention. Adherence to the one-voice policy, namely strict and unwavering communication of the same key arguments and content to all target groups, is imperative in such a context. Practically speaking, this means a successful transaction is only feasible on the back of very close consultation and coordination of the Legal, Strategy, and Accounting/Controlling departments with Corporate Communications and IR. Moreover, during the integration phase a key focus should also be on precise information being provided for the staff, not to mention the other stakeholders such as clients and suppliers.

Many questions – target group expectations

In general, every M&A transaction impacts on the stakeholders of the company/company sections involved: staff members, clients, commentators and capital backers. The latter group includes the owners of the company, i.e., private shareholders and institutional investors. Credit institutes are the main outside capital backers. Precisely larger deals repeatedly tend to attract the attention of politicians, who tend to vehemently champion the interests of the particular location and thus their electorate. Good examples of such political intervention were to be seen in the case of transatlantic deals involving Germany when Liberty Media tried to take over Deutsche Telekom's cable network, when Saban Capital Group acquired ProSiebenSat.1 or when Blackstone bought out Celanese. It therefore bears carefully considering the possible political relevance of any potential deal.

In the public phases of a deal the company must actively communicate with all target groups, although with different emphases. During the transaction phase it is decisive that the owners be persuaded that the measure be carried out – or, in the case of repealing a hostile bid, that they be convinced to reject the bid, in the integration phase communication with staff members and clients and financial backers becomes increasingly important.

Any communications strategy gains greater weight if the opinion multipliers, i.e., the media and analysts, are professionally and proactively addressed and informed. In practice, what is always decisive here is personal contact to the individual representatives of the newspapers, journals, trade publications, news agencies, TV stations and research houses. Figure 4.33 offers an overview of the major thematic complexes that the various target groups want to hear answers to, of the possible communications tools and the meaningful media to address to respective groups.

To summarize: an incisive one-voice policy impacts effectively on the target groups, by specifically addressing the different parties concerned. The same content must be presented in different ways. Institutional investors, analysts and financial journalists are addressed in person and in an individualized manner. Successful transactions communications is a management task with a pronounced person focus and is first and

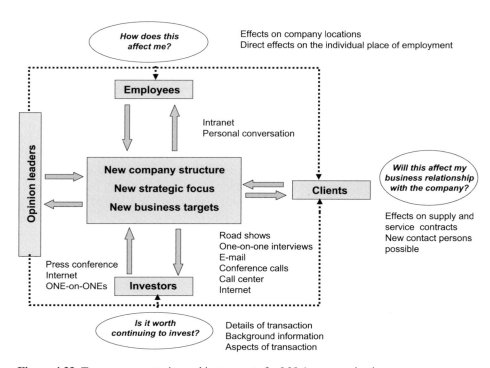

Figure 4.33 Target groups, topics and instruments for M&A communications

foremost based on disciplined core messages, an exact knowledge of target groups and a comprehensive scenario analysis.

Dealing with transatlantic M&As: The P&G-Wella case

Over the last three years there have only been three acquisitions of publicly-listed companies in Germany that had a market capitalization of at least EUR 500 million and were taken over by a US bidder.[1] However, precisely these larger cross-border takeovers entail the greatest risks as regards communications owing to the strong public interest, the frequently different legal regulatory framework and the cultural differences.

In what follows we will closely examine Procter & Gamble's (P&G) acquisition of Wella AG in 2003 from the viewpoint of communications. There are three main reasons for this: first, the transaction volume was over EUR 5 billion and by far the largest of the three transatlantic deals; second, the specificities of German takeover law led to massive activism on the part of minority shareholders and to a retrospective increase in the bid; and third a lack of intercultural due diligence significantly complicated integration of the two corporations. In a nutshell: the P&G/Wella case visualizes how important professional transactions communications are precisely in the phase of the public announcement.

Deal summary: Facing shareholder activism (external view)

On April 18, 2003 P&G announced it had acquired a 77.6% stake in its German competitor Wella, which at this time was still family owned. Under German takeover law, this transaction triggered a mandatory offer to all other shareholders; it bears mentioning in this context that the vast majority of the free float of the non-vote-bearing preferred stock was traded on the exchanges. Owing to the trading liquidity, this share category was included in the MDAX, the German mid-cap index. P&G offered the family and all owners of the ordinary stock EUR 92.25 per share, and initially bid only EUR 61.50 per preferred share, something that prompted great protest on the part of holders of the preferred stock. A special characteristic or rather a gap in German takeover law formally permitted this spread, whereby the interpretations of it have been unique in how widely they differ. In the official bid documents, P&G thereupon raised the bid price for the preferred shares to EUR 65 – which still amounted to a spread of just under 30 percent. After expiry of the acceptance period in September 2003 about 20 percent of the capital stock, but only slightly less than two percent of the voting rights were still owned by the minority shareholders. Headed by several institutional investors, including hedge funds, the public's attention was then deliberately drawn to an "unjust treatment of the small shareholders," thus putting P&G and the Wella Board under pressure.

Shareholder associations supported this criticism and termed the offer an "disadvantaging of the holders of preferred shares." After talks between institutional Wella

---

[1] For the details: Saban Capital Group-ProSiebenSat.1 (2003), P&G-Wella (2003), Blackstone-Celanese (2003)

investors and P&G broke down, in fall 2003 DEKA, one of the largest mutual fund managers in Germany, joined the ranks of the investors who were on the attack. Since the spread between the ordinary and the preferred shares was legal, the minority shareholders then pointed to violations against German law covering conglomerates. According to this, the majority shareholders, if holdimg less than 95% of the capital stock, may only intervene in the conglomerate's structure and the operating business of the target company if a so-called domination agreement has been concluded. The share price for the Wella preferred shares had meanwhile risen to considerably higher than the bid price of EUR 65.

Supported by professional communications consultants, the actions the minority shareholders opted for included a consistent newsflow to the key financial media on implementation of their own informative Web site (http://www.wella-minderheitsaktionaere.de) and placing ads, not to mention a careful sponsorship program at the local level. The deliberate goal was to emphasize clear facts and thus focus public attention on the takeover process and thus generate greater momentum in reporting. At the same time, opinion was to be moved into a position backing the minority shareholders. In December 2003 they finally succeeded in compelling Wella to convene an extraordinary general meeting in which, among other things, the plan was to appoint a special auditor to assess the legality of the entire process. In a fiery and very protracted debate there, the minority shareholders tried to bombard the Wella management with questions, provoke them and thus get them to make mistakes. Although P&G fielded its majority votes against all the points on the agenda at this EGM, the minority shareholders raised further demands and complaints, all in pursuit of the main goal of getting P&G to conclude a domination agreement. Once reputed legal experts had publicly sided with the minority shareholders, P&G gave in. The domination agreement was actually signed in April 2004 with reimbursement for all outstanding shares

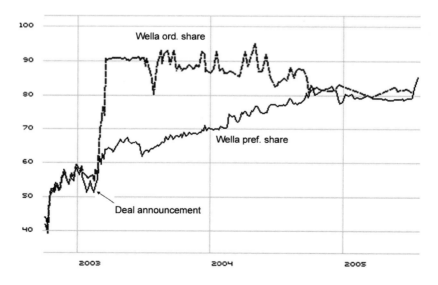

Figure 4.34 Shareprice development of Wella's ordinary and preferred shares

of EUR 72.86, meaning P&G footed a bill of about EUR 100 million more than it had wanted. As a consequence of the control agreement being signed, the date for the next AGM, which had to decide among other things on approval of the agreement, had to be put back from May 13 to June 8, 2004. This was greeted with an uproar, as June 5, 2004 was the final deadline by when P&G had to pay a higher cash sum to the shareholders who had already tendered their shares. The market was still hoping to see the cash reimbursement raised further, and the price of a Wella preferred share had reached over EUR 80.00 by the time this book goes to press (figure 4.34).

Internal affairs: Facing the cultural differences (internal view)

Each and every takeover inevitably entails a change process, above all in the company bought out. For most staff members, the process starts with the announcement of the transaction. At Wella, the staff was informed of the planned takeover by P&G by a communication from the Board at the same time as was the general public. A staff meeting followed, broadcast live to the company's subsidiaries outside the country. In the further course of the processes, however, the number of internal updates dwindled, and the staff members primarily relied on outside sources of information, without for example being informed of the background to the nascent debate on the price differential between the two types of shares and the resulting actions taken by the minority shareholders. The surge in fluctuation among top management also engendered uncertainty. Thus, the CFO and some of his management staff quit during the first integration phase. In the absence of information, staff and the general public were left guessing as to the reasons. The cultural differences between the corporations were, however, more decisive for the emerging frictional losses during the integration phase. On the one hand a very American and very focused P&G with numerous unwritten behavioral codes that govern employment, promotion cycles and how the company saw itself. On the other, Wella albeit an international player but was still very traditional, more consensus-focused and with staff members with strong roots in their company. Since the communicative bridge between these two cultures simply had not been built at the beginning of the integration phase, countless Wella staff members felt frustrated, specifically as regards how they would identify in future with the new overall conditions. And with no internal information forthcoming, others relied on books to find out what P&G was like and double-guess what the parent company's next step might be. Precisely the system of job rotation, as good as obligatory at P&G where managers move to a new field after three years and are frequently posted in the process to a new country, caused waves at Wella, where this strongly contradicted the mindset and mid-term plans for their lives that many of the German managers had. At the same time, P&G staffers were probably astonished by how sedentary their Wella counterparts seemed to be and how they concentrated in the long-term on one and the same task. This may have confirmed them in believing they needed to impose the P&G culture even more swiftly on Wella, which led to the front lines hardening even further. The result: many strong achievers at Wella left, although they were urgently required to achieve the synergies P&G targeted in justifying the takeover. This was something that went against the grain of the P&G creed and was as good as inconceivable – after all P&G prides itself on its extremely low fluctuation rate and lives by the rule: "At P&G you never quit." Yet a large number of the remaining Wella staff felt misunderstood and increasingly started focusing more on themselves than on the good of the company. As a result, P&G closed the first year without having achieved the desired synergies and thus came under pressure from its own investors.

Key Learnings: Focusing on intercultural aspects

The P&G-Wella case shows emphatically how important it is to concern oneself closely with the stakeholders affected by an M&A transaction and their PROs and CONs. Precisely in the case of cross-border deals, macro-level differences in legal and economic regimes, in capital market and media practices, in codetermination and other national idiosyncrasies all need to be borne in mind. Then, at the micro-level, there are all the various facets of different corporate cultures that need to be harmonized if you do not want to endanger the overall success of the transaction.

Questions such as "Will a spread in the bid price of just under 30% between ordinary and preferred stock trigger activism among the shareholders?" need to be asked and processed in a scenario analysis before the deal gets announced publicly. Possible legal "loopholes" opponents may exploit, such as the purported need for a domination agreement in the case of an acceptance rate of less than 95% of the capital stock need to be discerned in advance and factored into the strategy and into communications. Precisely US corporations should be very familiar with shareholder activism in all its different colors, as it is part of everyday life on the stock market there. Deal processes need to be examined well in advance as to the potential innate delays – above all with a view to steering investor expectations and communicating tight timelines in order to achieve specific transaction synergies. A strong offense, with premature communication of the "best-case scenario" can very swiftly trigger profit warnings, slash confidence in management, and deal a hefty blow to the share price and with it the company's reputation.

In this context, ignoring staff sensibilities can often push the company off the ideal course. Studies back in the boom days of M&A transactions at the turn of the millennium highlighted insufficient internal communications and ignoring HR management focused on integration as key factors in companies falling short of various synergy benchmarks (Towers Perrin Research 2000).

Careful inclusion of staff in the integration process, an emphasis on future prospects and their careful familiarization with the respectively other corporate culture are generally accepted crunch factors in successfully maintaining staff motivation levels and productivity and limiting fluctuation. Protracted uncertainty among employees on their own future in a new company leads to 12 times the fluctuation normally encountered. Specifically the high-flyers in mid-management tend to feel excluded in the first phase of the integration processes and follow with frustration how top executives initially focus on their own positioning and ignore the needs one rung below them on the ladder. Specifically the high-achievers are the first to quit if an info vacuum emerges and no future prospects are highlighted for them, resulting in a significant loss in human capital and the related potential. At the end of the day, those have upped and left who were expected to generate the added value for the merged company and its shareholders. In the pre-merger process, it is highly advisable not only to formulate an external communications strategy for clients, the capital market, media, the politicians and other interest groups, but also an internal communications strategy for the integra-

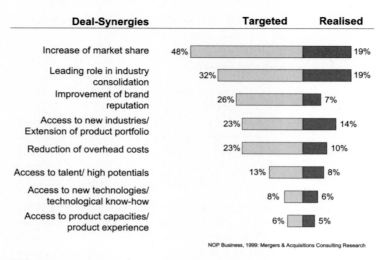

Deal-Synergies	Targeted	Realised
Increase of market share	48%	19%
Leading role in industry consolidation	32%	19%
Improvement of brand reputation	26%	7%
Access to new industries/ Extension of product portfolio	23%	14%
Reduction of overhead costs	23%	10%
Access to talent/ high potentials	13%	8%
Access to new technologies/ technological know-how	8%	6%
Access to product capacities/ product experience	6%	5%

NOP Business, 1999: Mergers & Acquisitions Consulting Research

Figure 4.35 Expected and realized synergies following M&As

tion process. One recommendation would be to rely on external consultants and coaches, here, as their experience enables them to identify the critical fields swiftly and thus take the sting out of them. Cultural due diligence should then be undertaken to spotlight cultural and potentially critical differences between the companies concerned. On this basis, suitable measures can be initiated as part of communications and HR policymaking to avoid a clash of cultures that would impact negatively after a done deal. Key learning must therefore address identifying the persons in each transaction who are critical to its success and nurturing them with a view to that goal. Only in this way can forecasts on synergies and value-added be translated into real figures. Noticeable learning effects were to be seen when Blackstone took over Celanese. Although well-organized minority shareholders again took the stage, with the swift conclusion of an agreement, the control process moved forward far quicker and smoothly than in the P&G/Wella case. As a consequence, Blackstone was able to restructure the way it wanted, relocate the head office to Dallas, and opt for an IPO on the NYSE worth USD 800 million. Moreover, Blackstone's investors profited from a dividend disbursement totaling USD 1 billion – a considerable and realized added value.

Conclusion

In other words, in order to generate long-term added value for the stakeholders through M&A transactions you need to consider far more than just a figures-focused due diligence process. Precisely in the case of transatlantic deals there are any number of "soft" factors to be taken into account, that can at the end of the day actual decide whether the transaction is successful or not. A precise knowledge of the target groups in the countries concerned and their communications needs, detailed scenario planning, and disciplined implementation of the resulting communications strategy both inside the company and to the outside world can appreciably enhance general acceptance of the deal and its consequences, thereby significantly reducing execution risk.

Professional M&A communications thus makes a decisive contribution to the desired success of the deal done.

Literature

Feldmann, M. L.; Spratt, M.: Speedmanagement für Fusionen. Gabler: Wiesbaden 2000

Hering, R.; Schuppener, B.; Sommerhalder, M.: Die Communication Scorecard. Haupt: Bern, Stuttgart, Wien 2004

Rolke, L.; Koss, F.: Value Corporate Communications. Books on Demand: Norderstedt 2005

Uder, H.L.; Kramarsch, M. H.: Mergers & Acquisitions durch erfolgreiche Integration der Human Resources, published in: Jansen, S. A.; Picot, G.; Schiereck, D.: Internationales Fusionsmanagement – Erfolgsfaktoren grenzüberschreitender Unternehmenszusammenschlüsse. Schäffer-Poeschel: Stuttgart 2000

4.9.2 Due Diligence for M&A Communications

Christoph Walther and Roland Klein

Since the end of the last decade, companies and transaction activities have come increasingly under the spotlight. While one eye of the public is still on product, the other has shifted towards the companies themselves, and the way they operate. With increasing regulation on transparency, corporate governance and of brand valuation, companies are required to be more accessible to a critical public than in previous times. The perceptions of a company's stakeholders are also becoming a decisive factor in determining a company's scope for action. And when planning a transaction, the perception of a company shifts from being a "soft" factor to a "hard" asset. In the US, the assessment of perception issues has been an integral part in the acquisition strategy for many companies for years now. For corporations like General Electric or Cisco, a diligent check of soft issues has been common practice for some time.

Three key areas of communications due diligence

Communications play an essential role during due diligence in a transaction. In the initial preparation phase, management consultants, lawyers and investment bankers prepare the implementation of the transaction. Their recommendations determine if further procedures are necessary and if so, which ones. Typically companies underestimate the value that communications professionals can bring to the process and are only called for as negotiations begin. However contributions from experienced communications experts can, for example, result in operational changes to enhance value within the company. Particularly in cross-border transactions, PR issues can determine success or failure, its management can facilitate acceptance or decline of a deal. When

425

Siemens acquired the British telecommunications company Plessey in the 80ties through a contested bid, it offered no profile for anti-German PR from the defender because it chose to bid together with a UK ally, GEC. When Nestlé tried to take over Rowntree at about the same time, it had to overcome a heavy public battle as the producer of the Kit Kat chocolate bar was seen by the public as an ultra-British icon.

Communications professionals should be requested to perform due diligence in three areas:

1. The reputation of the sector
2. The reputation of the acquiring company
3. The reputation of the company to be acquired

The reputation of the sector

If the acquiring company operates in a different sector from the company to be acquired, sector-specific attributes must be taken into account. When John Malone, the US media mogul, tried to acquire Kabel Deutschland in 2001/2, he did not take into account that everything he presented – his approach, his strategic intentions, his way to appear in public – was perceived by German authorities and the general public as culturally unacceptable – and the deal was turned down. If the acquirer is a private equity firm, for example, reputation can be the decisive factor in a competitive bid, in winning over management, shareholders and other stakeholders. In 2005, the public debate in Germany focused on one-sided Anglo-Saxon capitalism that is perceived in many quarters as hostile for the long-term-oriented German way of company strategies. In this situation, it is important for the private equity company to be recognised as a genuine alternative to a partner within the sector and to traditional methods of corporate finance, and not as a last resort.

The reputation of the acquiring company

The perception of the acquiring company among its own shareholders, those of the company to be acquired and other stakeholders is of vital importance to the transaction. Careful positioning of the company is the only way to avoid being labelled with the attributes common to its sector, should the perception of that sector turn for the worse.

When Haim Saban prepared to acquire German TV company ProSiebenSat.1 communications was an integral part of his strategy. Saban Capital Group was completely unknown in Germany and foreign ownership of one of Germany's leading media companies seen as a threat by many. A carefully crafted programme addressed these concerns both with regard to the media and to the public affairs audiences on a local, regional and federal level. After initial criticism perception shifted and Saban was widely portrayed as the most competent buyer.

Media coverage of the company should be analysed from the perspective of the objectives of the transaction. But more important is analysis of perceptions of key opinion-formers, through interviews of a panel weighted according to the importance of their respective stakeholder group (perception study). A SWOT analysis of the results of the perception study highlights the strengths and weaknesses of the company from the external point of view, and identifies potential opportunities for the presentation of the transaction, as well as relevant issues that could arise, before they have become public.

The reputation of the company to be acquired

An analysis of the reputation of the target company has two objectives: to identify its perception among stakeholders at a particular point in time, as well as the drivers of those perceptions. A company's internal organisation, its product range, the quality of the management and a convincing strategy, of course, all contribute to an excellent reputation. However, experienced PR managers will add that the image of a company, its credibility and its ability to present its image externally in a way that is sustainable, are all the result of a variety of intertwined decisions and processes in which communications, and the management of communications, play an essential role.

How can one be sure that there are no negative issues lying dormant in the system? How does the company deal with unpleasant truths? Does it open up to its problems, or shut up shop? How effectively is the external presentation of the company co-ordinated? To what extent do statements on markets, products and goals coalesce? How seriously is corporate social responsibility taken? How seriously are the concerns of pressure groups taken? Where can external considerations beyond the bottom line, blow that bottom line? And in particular, does the economic rationale of the transaction pass the test in the market or the broader public?

Only with satisfactory answers to these questions is it possible to judge the sustainability of current reputation, and to evaluate how it might influence the success or failure of the transaction. Early and systematic inclusion of communications should be a touchstone of the due diligence process, creating the best environment for success. Recent experience demonstrates that companies with serious acquisition experience include a comprehensive communications evaluation in their repertoire. Even when

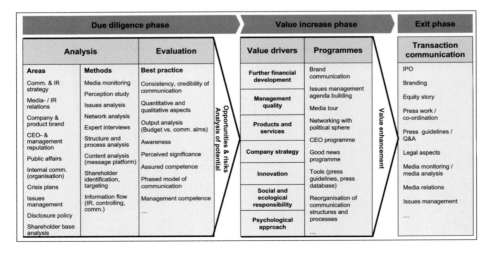

Figure 4.36 Value enhancement through strategic communication

this relates only to "soft" factors, there is no lack of quantitative or qualitative analyses that can be drawn from it. They simply have to be applied consistently and systematically.

The Communications Toolbox (see figure 4.36) illustrates the systematic process designed to identify the time-bombs in any transaction. This process should not be limited to analysis of past newspaper articles to locate the warning signs. The ability of the company to manage difficult issues, in a systematic way, and with foresight, will determine the reputation of the company in the future, and thus, in the case of a transaction, public acceptance of the company's activities. Where public contracts are concerned, this should include analysis of political acceptance.

In the due diligence phase, communications analysis of the target company provides the necessary information for more effective and targeted decisions. It also provides a solid foundation for the post-acquisition/-merger phase and the opportunity to remedy shortcomings, both in terms of internal processes and external perception, in an equally systematic manner. The benefits of a commitment to communications management are two way.

Internally, the process uncovers deficits in value drivers and indicates how these can be overcome. The ill-fated acquisition of Columbia Pictures by Sony in 1989 was fraught with internal communications challenges and led to five years of cultural and perceptual misunderstanding. The complexity of communicating across long distances and culture proved a major stumbling block and ultimately resulted in a $3.2 billion write down.

Externally, the reputation of the company will be improved because communications will better reflect both value drivers and the demands of the market. Where two companies collide, i.e. not in a private equity scenario, the benefits can be seen through the entire organisation. When going to a private equity company the focus normally remains on the acquired company. Only then it is possible to present an optimal market exit, e.g. through an IPO.

Reputation has a value in, and of, itself. In a transaction, reputation management permits a company to assure its perception of reliability and ensure a level of public trust. To maintain a good reputation, it is therefore vital to include communications in the due diligence process. As recent history has shown, realistic and sustainable communications are key to a successful transaction; and their absence can lead to embarrassment, and hasten the end of even the highest-flying career.

4.9.3 Bridging the Intercultural Gap: Non-conventional Truths about American-German Business

Patrick Schmidt

American and German business is thought to be culturally close. But as this paper will show, the communication styles and work habits of the two groups are almost diametrically opposed.

Globalization has led to remarkable changes in the way we conduct the world's business. As more and more companies are offering similar products of similar quality worldwide, businesses are being forced to rethink their strategies. To gain the competitive edge, language training needs to expand beyond verbal communication, so that intercultural competence is included in its curriculum. Heightened awareness of the power of culture – and of the skills that promote understanding between colleagues from different countries – has thus become the new business mantra.

Unfortunately, most people think this pertains only to "exotic" cultures. Articles and anecdotes remind us not to wrap a gift in white paper in China (the color symbolizes death) or to sit with your ankle across your knee in an Arabic country (showing the sole of your foot is considered an insult). American-German teams, on the other hand, are thought to be culturally close. That Germans often speak English fluently only strengthens the misconception. But the communication styles and work habits of the two groups are almost diametrically opposed – something many companies learn the hard way. It has cost Wal*Mart in Germany over a billion dollars![1]

Denial of differences

Many executives and managers involved in American-German joint ventures have come to appreciate the need for intercultural training. Ironically, however, even those who understand how cultural "soft factors" can make or break a deal usually don't believe American and German business styles are all that different. At least, not at first.

One CEO told me, "I've spent a lot of time in the U.S. and I speak English almost as well as I do German. In terms of philosophy, I know all about 'burning the midnight oil' and being 'lean and mean'. I'm not sure you have much to teach me." What he was describing is called the trap of similarity. It's the most popular mistake in U.S.-German business relations.

Germans share many characteristics with Americans. Anglo-Saxon roots lead the two to view problems monochronically (i.e., one thing at a time). Both cultures place a high value on being punctual, direct and honest. Both are future-oriented, competitive and practical. Still, many subtle – and not-so-subtle – differences are to be found

---

[1] Wolfgang Hirn "Wal*Mart: Der US-Handelsriese hat in Deutschland fast alles falsch gemacht," *Manager-Magazin*, Januar, 2002, 58-66

beneath this veneer. And their effect is all the more damaging because they're unexpected. When a person, or group, underestimates the degree to which values and assumptions differ in the other culture, misunderstandings are guaranteed.

Wal*Mart's dilettantish approach to the German market is only one example. Volkswagen's spectacularly unsuccessful attempt to set up a Rabbit assembly plant in the U.S. cost almost as much. G.M.'s "over-americanization" of Opel is also a textbook case of how not to do things. I'm tempted to smile when a corporation decides a two-day workshop would be "too time-consuming, too expensive." The losses from fiascos like those above are measured in millions, if not billions.

Another oft-repeated, albeit specious claim is, "We bankers" – CFOs, CEOs, managers, etc. – "are the same all over the world!" Or even "I've watched enough 'Dallas' and 'Miami Vice' and 'Law and Order' to know Americans."

Sometimes there's an outright refusal to acknowledge that cultural differences matter at all. An American entrepreneur who'd just bought a mid-sized German company said to me, "We don't need any of this intercultural training stuff. The best way to create a merger is to fight out the issues!" But his facial expression indicated frustration and he later admitted being "perplexed by the way the Germans react to things."

Foreign cultures present a huge challenge; comprehending and confronting patterns that seem strange is genuinely difficult. Many try to avoid the issue, hoping that any cross-cultural conflicts will somehow resolve themselves. In fairness, what sounds like ignorance may also be "informed fatalism." It's not that managers don't want to spend time on sociological issues, it's just that they're already overloaded with more immediate tasks. All too often, intercultural awareness is placed at the bottom of the list.

Time for training

These same managers, being pro-active by nature, don't let fatalism influence the need to solve problems as they occur, including cross-cultural misunderstandings. If, as happened in a company near Düsseldorf, the R&D department resigns en masse four months after an American takes over operations, company bosses act quickly. "There's obviously a clash of cultures at work here. What do we do about it?"

Siemens and Bosch both provide a three-day intercultural workshop for employees going abroad. This is considered the minimal amount of training necessary to achieve "intercultural competence." While it's obviously better to prepare before leaving, our American friend in Düsseldorf could probably make a new start by taking the same course (instead of being sent home in disgrace and replaced, which is both expensive and disruptive for all concerned).

Nonetheless, an American personnel director in South Carolina, who prides himself on being "time efficient" and pragmatic asked me if, instead of three days, we couldn't offer "a mini-session, say two or three hours. You could give a list of the do's and dont's." Except that reducing complex concepts to checklists doesn't result in real awareness, let alone skills. Rather, it's like fast-feeding the participants junk information, creating a false sense of intercultural security. Successful overseas adaptation is not so much about "learning the new culture" as acquiring a better understanding of your own background. Knowing your mental software is a prerequisite to understanding other peoples' ways and habits.

I feel a seminar has been successful when a German or an American comes up to me at the end and says, "Mensch, ich wusste nicht, dass ich so deutsch war!" / "Gee, I had no idea I was so American!" This sort of transformation can't be condensed into three hours.

Sprechen Sie Deutsch?

Another important element in attaining intercultural competence is widening one's linguistic horizons. So much of how we think goes into how we say it, style and content being hopelessly intertwined. Learning foreign phrases, proverbs, even jokes, provides a fascinating window on the society in question.

Ideally, a U.S. manager going to work in Germany would learn German. But the vast majority of executives work 55 to 60 hours a week; most don't have the time or mental energy left over to devote to effective language study. I've seen the results first-hand, having coached German managers in English for over 15 years.

Almost all of them had studied the language from the age of ten and spoke well enough, if rather simply. Taking it to the next level, however, proved extremely hard. Basic pedagogical tools, such as reading assignments or the writing of short essays or stories, went out the window. These executives – most of whom ran entire divisions – would sheepishly tell me, "I'm very sorry but I didn't have time to do my homework." Our English training was normally limited to a weekly hour and half of one-on-one conversation and exercises.

In the U.S., where it's likely a manager has absolutely no German to begin with, the company's decision is usually to skip language classes altogether. "Don't worry," the departing employee is told, "they all speak English over there!" Even if this were true, which it most certainly isn't, it's an attitude that virtually guarantees cross-cultural conflicts.

If an American really wants to learn German, experts recommend a minimum of three months' intensive study, the first two in a group setting and the last on a one-to-one basis. It's a full-time endeavor and means being relieved of all other work. The cost, while high, is certainly not prohibitive in the context of a multinational corporation's budget. More to the point, it's a policy designed to avoid foreseeable problems, which can be very expensive in the long run.

Skills for overseas success

When asked about the skills necessary for international work, both American and German personnel managers list common-sense attitudes such as empathy, openness, communicativeness, flexibility, perceptiveness and so on. It sounds logical and they base their selections on it.

On the other hand, Robert Kohls, former director of the Washington International Center and author of *"Survival Kit for Overseas Living"* (considered a classic among intercultural consultants), says that there are three important traits which are rarely mentioned.

The first is a *sense of humor*. No matter how well you're prepared for your assignment, there will be moments of anger, annoyance, discouragement and embarrassment. The best defense is the ability to laugh things off.

Being less task-driven is another suggestion. Managers are chosen for foreign assignments because they're the company's stars. They set extremely high goals for themselves and those they supervise. The same behavioral traits may not work in the new culture and certainly not in the same way. "Unspoken rules" must first be learned, then mastered. Expatriates less concerned with winning at all costs tend to be more effective and better able to enjoy their experience.

Closely related is the *ability to tolerate failure*. The executive selected to go abroad has normally gone from success to success in the corporate world. But anyone who's been overseas for a few years will tell you that nobody comes back with a perfect record. Setbacks are part of the adaptation process, as is a certain amount of frustration.

These "unorthodox" ideas almost always encounter some resistance in my seminars, especially from those in personnel. Once we bat them around, however, initial critics usually become the biggest supporters. Many of the savvier companies and institutions are now adding "a sense of humor" and "the ability to fail" to their selection criteria.

Different ways of saying

Both German and American executives tend to assume that a German who's fluent in English will be a competent communicator in the U.S. Nothing could be further from the truth. Understanding a foreign society is less about language than deciphering cultural values. Without going into a long discourse on the nature of communication, a few principles need to be pointed out.

Communication is the process of conveying, i.e. encoding ideas, information, feelings and symbols, so that it is recognizable to the receiver. Communication, therefore, means the encoding and sending of a message by using the right representation as well as a correct decoding of these representations upon reception. These representations may be verbal, written, nonverbal or musical. All of them contain a set of *unspoken rules* which can create both subtle and significant misunderstandings, if not understood. Thus, the danger of any decoding lies when the receiver comes from another culture with different rules and values.

Another important principle is that a message depends on the perception of the receiver, not what the presenter thinks has been expressed.

Unspoken rules to remember

German business conversation emphasizes content and downplays personal relationships. The unconscious desire is to appear *credible* and *objective*, making discussions

Table 4.8 Communication styles of Germans and Americans

Germans – need to be credible	Americans – need to be liked
More direct in expressing criticism, facts, commands	*More direct in expressing* pleasure, compliments, personal details
More use of upgraders – absolut, durchaus, bestimmt, total	*More use of downgraders –* sort of, kind of, well, maybe, somewhat
More use of modal verbs müssen, sollen – "Das muss so sein"	*More use of conditional* It would be good if we could do it that way
More use of imperative "Bringen Sie uns zwei Bier, bitte"	*More use of question format* "Could we have two beers, please?

fact-oriented and often academic. The inherent goal is to get at the truth (*Wahrheitssuche*). Germans aren't afraid to explore all sides of an issue, even if it means being unpleasant, confrontational and spending an excessive amount of time analyzing a problem.

Along with the Dutch, the Swiss and the Austrians, they're generally very direct when it comes to stating facts, offering criticism and giving orders. Because the personal element is marginalized, a German subordinate can confront his boss, flatly stating "No, you are wrong!" A heated discussion will then ensue, points being made aggressively, sometimes almost belligerently. An American observer would be very uncomfortable. But both Germans walk away unscathed, their relationship unchanged.

Americans, on the other hand, do nothing if not accentuate the personal: they want to *be liked* and *socially accepted*. In most situations, they're guided less by intrinsic values than by the opinion others may have of them. Being outgoing is the way to make friends, even in a business relationship.

Americans aren't shy when it comes to expressing pleasure or revealing personal details to people they don't know well. This is strongly related to the national mantra of upward mobility. Social acceptance is primordial; acquaintances are often referred to as "friends"; compliments are given freely and expected in return. Alexis de Tocqueville, in his 1835 work "*Democracy in America*," wrote "In dealing with strangers, Americans seem to be impatient with the slightest criticism and insatiable for praise." Germans see compliments as being somewhat redundant (a "job well done" is what it's supposed to be). Americans grin at a bad situation and say, "Let's make a positive out of a negative!" Germans are apt to answer, "That is a mathematical impossibility."

If these communication styles aren't appreciated and decoded correctly for what they are, Americans are bound to dismiss Germans as opinionated and argumentative know-it-alls while the latter will perceive Americans as naive and superficial!

A case history

The clash of styles was apparent a few years back when a large multinational German and American company held their first joint board meeting. The Germans began with a long introductory statement, including the history of the company, its various products and future prospects. They provided detailed background information and used lots of transparencies. Their need to be credible meant everything was communicated in an almost straight, humorless manner. What Americans called "a train-wreck of a presentation" lasted almost two hours.

The Americans presented their company in a simplistic fashion and basically went straight to presenting their products, using showy effects and easy-to-remember statements. The approach was that an of overly enthusiastic salesman, who wanted to be liked – lots of smiles and jokes –, and only 35 minutes long. All in all, for the Germans, it was an exercise in superficiality coupled with "optimism gone overboard."

And yet, somehow, both sides sincerely believed they'd done a good job. As mentioned earlier, the audience determines the message, not the speaker. The American CEO told a German reporter after the meeting, "The Germans have a penchant for coming to meetings armed with tons of overhead transparencies and colored charts. It's absolute information overkill."

Individuality versus collective risk-avoidance

In 1980, Dutch social scientist Geert Hofstede published a fascinating study of work-related cultural differences based on data collected from some 116,000 IBM employees in 50 countries. He identified 4 parameters by which to chart cultural perceptions. Two of them – "individuality vs. collectivism" and "uncertainty avoidance" – demonstrate how differently Americans and Germans see their working worlds.

People in individualistic cultures are mostly concerned for themselves and their families. Progress is seen as the result of individual effort; historical and socio-economic factors tend to be ignored. "Mobility" is the rule, both in terms of where one works and where one lives. Of the 50 countries, the U.S. showed the most pronounced sense of individualism.

Germans are more inclined to see themselves as part of a collectivity, subordinating individual needs to the common good. Opinions are often determined by the group and concepts like solidarity and harmony are extremely important. Relationships and "belonging" are emphasized. (Whenever I make a presentation to a German company, I'm asked "Which consulting group are you with?" It had never occurred to me that, working as a free-lance consultant, my "lone cowboy" attitude would come into conflict with German collective patterns.)

Adapting to change and coping with uncertainty is the second major area where Americans and Germans differ. The latter show a high degree of uncertainty-avoidance and behavioral rules, both written and unwritten, are rigid. Knowledge is respected and "experts" seldom questioned. Projects are thoroughly researched and risks are kept to a minimum. The more structure there is, the better. Americans, on the other hand, are more ambiguous, minimizing the rules and rituals that govern social conduct. Taking risks is seen as courageous and trying out new things is encouraged. "Common sense" is valued, as is general knowledge.

How these different approaches play out in the business world was evident when the Sarbanes-Oxley Act – which requires CEOs and the CFOs to swear their company's

Table 4.9 German collective risk-avoidance versus American militant individuality

Germans – group-oriented	Americans – self-actualization
"we" society	*"me" society*
strong attachment to group	*not much group identity*
little mobility	*enormous mobility*
experts and knowledge respected	*generalists and common sense valued*
loath to take risks	*risk-takers*
prefer careful analysis	*favor trial-and-error*

financial statements are truthful – was passed by the U.S. Congress. The entrepreneurial Americans were ready to sign on the dotted line from the start. In Germany, however, the law ignited debate in the press and in the boardrooms of companies doing business in the U.S. A popular reaction among risk-adverse Germans was to say, "We can't sign the statement because we didn't do the figures. They were done by the accounting department."

Problem-solving and German-American teams

In 1995, psychologist Sylvia Schroll-Machl examined the reasons American-German projects often fail. A German multinational brought her in to evaluate how American and German engineers and researchers interacted. It became clear early on that problems were due, in large part, to misunderstanding each other's way of problem-solving.

Schroll-Machl noticed that, at the outset of a project, Germans showed a greater need for detailed information and discussion. They tended to see the process from an engineering point of view, considering all of the difficulties that might arise, planning hypothetical solutions. The goal was to make sure everything would be done correctly, every element possible kept "under control." Avoiding uncertainty means avoiding anxiety.

The Germans expected all team members to share knowledge by sketching out their previous experiences. Reaching a consensus (which, they argued, permits the rapid implementation of any strategy) was essential. Schroll-Machl concluded that German decision-making concentrated on identifying problems, their history and components. Less emphasis was placed on results.

The action-oriented Americans found these discussions trying, often outright boring. The exchange of too much information felt like a waste of time, "paralysis through analysis." No matter how good a plan is, the thinking goes, it will be modified along the way. The Americans didn't speak up at this stage; by not saying anything, they hoped to speed up the process and get down to work. In their minds, problem-solving started out with a short brainstorming session to define goals and establish a series of approximate milestones.

Efficiency and creativity were the watchwords. The Americans wanted to "keep all options open," perceiving any project as a trial-and-error process. Schroll-Machl found their decision-making to be more open-ended, concentrating on a mission, a vision.

The Germans felt the Americans were acting without fully understanding the problem: "Shoot first and ask questions later." The Americans felt obsession with plans, and sticking to them, meant being locked into a rigid pattern, with no flexibility during the implementation-phase. Once a plan was established, German team members were able to work relatively independently. Americans expected further group meetings and informal communication throughout. The Germans complained that the Americans asked about issues which had already been discussed at length.

Basic philosophies – "going on a mission" vs "minding the shop" – were only part of the equation, though. Americans are often given tasks for which they have not been thoroughly trained. Frequent job-rotation leads to a learn-by-doing attitude. It goes without saying that one communicates more with superiors, as well as other team members. Germans are, on the whole, better trained. Mechanics, machinists and the like go through the famous *Dualsystem* but even engineers and executives receive a "holistic" mix of the practical and the theoretical. And, of course, the rules for doing business in Europe are stricter: whether it's cars or cosmetics or cold cuts, there are norms, guidelines, documentation which one actually has to read.

Germans also assume decisions made at group meetings are binding. Americans see them as guidelines which change when the need arises or a better solution presents itself. And Americans expect these changes to take place; it's part of the adventure!

Leadership, not unexpectedly, was also a major factor. The German leader is both an expert and a mediator (expected to convince, not order) who tends to vote with the group. During the implementation phase, there's little interaction with individual group members. "Distant" and "difficult to reach out to" was the way the Americans

Table 4.10 Summary of difference in joint German-American teams

Germans	Americans
See problems-solving from an engineering point of view; they consider all aspects by spending time on the problem and its history (and less on the ultimate solution)	*See problem-solving as more open-ended; they "brainstorm" on how to achieve a desired goal or vision.*
Decisions and plans are binding.	*Decisions and plans are guidelines.*
Find Americans have a "cowboy mentality"; "shoot first and ask questions later."	*Think long German discussions are boring, "paralysis through analysis."*
Due to active participation in discussions, can later work more autonomously and need less communication with colleagues.	*Don't say much in initial discussions, hoping to speed up process of getting to work, but expect more communication later.*
Think Americans ask redundant questions during implementation phase.	*Perceive the Germans as impersonal and inflexible during implementation phase.*
Group leader was seen as a mediator, expected to integrate differing views by persuasion.	*Group leader was seen as the decision-maker, expected to set goals in a top-down manner.*

put it. The American leader defines goals, makes decisions, distributes tasks and makes sure they're done. Motivation and coaching are part of the chain-of-command (or top-down) style. Communication is intense by European standards and continues in a "baseball team" atmosphere all the way through completion and out for celebratory drinks afterward.

Which brings us back to social psychology. Americans instinctively share more of their "personality" on the job. It's just another part of the same day. In fact, Americans don't act all that differently at work than they do when they're out bowling with the guys. Germans try to maintain a "work only" relationship with colleagues. They also don't invite relative strangers home for supper on the spur of the moment "to meet the wife and kids."

Schroll-Machl's study makes clear that if these differences are dealt with at the beginning, chances for success increase enormously. If not, German-American projects often fail, causing both financial loss and hurt feelings.

Concluding remarks

In an increasingly globalized world market, companies need to re-engineer organizational processes and equip personnel with "soft factor" skills. Global players must acquire effective intercultural competencies in order to forestall miscommunication, prevent misunderstandings and avert mistakes.

Understanding the complex behaviors of any culture is much like learning a foreign language: it takes practice and continual intellectual effort. By comprehending the sometimes obscure codes of another culture and their impact on behavior, you learn much more about yourself, become more conscious of your own national uniqueness. This, in the last analysis, is what makes intercultural learning so attractive. If this article encourages the reader to view and analyze cultural differences between Americans and Germans in terms of "why do I act the way I do?," then it will have bridged closer the gap between these two dynamic countries.

4.9.4 How to Merge German and American Talents to Achieve a Cross-Atlantic Culture of Understanding and Shared Success?

Bettina Palazzo, Craig DeForest and Bernhard K.F. Pelzer

This article examines the challenges of national culture within a merger context from three different view points. First, the roots and ramifications of US pragmatism and German Gründlichkeit are explored through Tocqueville's "habits of the heart." Second, the link between the essential nature of business groups and their cultures is investigated as well as the wisdom of valuing the culture rather than arbitrarily attempting to change it. Finally culture is explored from both its different perspectives and its different levels and layers. Specific recommendations and insights are offered to increase the effectiveness of post merger organizations.

A threefold approach by Dr. Bettina Palazzo of Basel Switzerland, Craig DeForest of Santa Fe, New Mexico, USA and Bernhard K.F. Pelzer of Hamburg, Germany

Bettina Palazzo

- After the merger of Daimler Benz and Chrysler the book "These strange German ways" by Susan Stern became a bestseller among Chrysler managers and employees. This was known because Amazon at that time published statistics of the buying decisions of certain identifiable groups – such as Chrysler employees. The book's title nicely illustrates that we tend to see our own culture as "normal" and universally valid, whereas the cultures of other countries (and companies) tend to be seen as strange and unreasonable.

Tocqueville called the shared cultural standardizations "habits of the heart," i.e., the common patterns of thinking, feeling and acting within a certain group or society. Since they are "habits of the heart" we are frequently unaware of their influence. They are taken for granted and only become conscious when put in contrast to other cultures with different tacit background assumptions. They then have the potential for intercultural misunderstandings and conflicts, mutual value violations, frustration, and, especially in the case of mergers & acquisitions, blocking communication and cooperation, and thereby risking the success of a merger. The Chrysler employees who bought the above mentioned book obviously had understood this dynamic and wanted to overcome this obstacle by trying to understand the other culture.

In this article we would like to explore how the different "habits of the heart" influence the respective intellectual styles and patterns of problem solving in Germany and the US. In general the US standards of thinking are referred to as pragmatism whereas Germans are famed for their meticulous and rigorous approach ("deutsche Gründlichkeit"). The German style is also called idealistic. There are – of course – many other cultural categories, that we could compare (e.g. notions of power). But we feel that the comparison of intellectual style is most enlightening – after all, the task to merge two companies from different national cultures is an ambitious and complex intellectual endeavor of problem solving.

On the basis of this analysis we will sketch how these intercultural differences can be transformed into an asset within transatlantic post-merger situations.

US Pragmatism

> The principle of the utopia come true explains the lack and even the uselessness of any metaphysics and imagination for the American life. It gives the Americans a perception of truth different from ours. The real is not linked to the impossible, no failure can make it questionable. What is thought in Europe gets realized in America – everything that vanishes in Europe reappears in San Francisco!
>
> **Jean Baudrillard**

The term "US Pragmatism" can mean many things to many people. When used within the United States (US), it is often a positive term. When used about the US it can be pejorative.

In its positive meaning "US Pragmatism" is often another way of saying "Yankee Ingenuity": a practical way to get the job done with whatever resources are available. The US prides itself on being able to complete a task even if the normally required materials, tools and people are not available. The emphasis is often on achieving an objective, getting to the finish line, completing a mission. The image of "Yankee Ingenuity" is a combination of tenacity, grit, and innovation with a strong measure of level-headed common sense. This image is very connected to the romanticized vision of the US as a place where anything can be accomplished regardless of education, social standing and quality of resources. It is a place where "getting it done" is often more important than how it gets done. This attitude is epitomized in Nike's slogan "Just do it!" The cultural root of US Pragmatism is among others the frontier experience, where settlers had to deal with shortages of resources, nonexistent infrastructure, and the absence of legal and societal frameworks.

Pragmatic cultures like the US break down bigger problems into smaller parts that can be dealt with subsequently. They strive for concrete results even if those do not add up to an overall solution of the fundamental problem.

One result is a specific kind of debating style: discussions are conducted to collect opinions (brainstorm) and thus statements do not have to be water-tight. Usually American-style discussions try to integrate as many opinions as possible. This agreement is possible because everybody believes in the existing empirical data without many theoretical underpinnings. Therefore adjustment to new material is easy.

The pragmatic style tends to stress the collecting of facts and the applicability of results. This style can be very appropriate and successful – especially in a fast-paced business situation and even more within a post-merger project.

On the other hand, "US Pragmatism" can be thought of as a defect in design, planning and execution – a sub-standard method. This pragmatism is often identified as the reason that a battle is won, but the war is lost. It can be anathema to rigorous engineering, methodical planning and flawless execution. Viewed from this perspective, the practicality of achieving a particular objective is only a short-term advantage that fades in the long-term. Viewed from a perspective of "Gründlichkeit," US Pragmatism can just look sloppy!

German Gründlichkeit

In comparison with US pragmatism the German intellectual style is more idealistic. In *idealistic* cultures, standards of thinking and communication have to adhere to a certain set of basic principles or ideas.

The idealistic, intellectual style in Germany concentrates on the development of theories and principles before dealing with facts.

The development of solutions or plans of action in the idealistic style could be compared to the building of a house of cards. Every little component of this complex building is vital for its stability. If you remove just one tiny part out of this tight structure the whole construction collapses. Therefore, it is important in discussions in the idealistic style that discussants criticize each other rather strictly to detect and avoid weak points from the very beginning. Differences in opinion are unavoidable, since different principles cannot be easily combined and integrated like facts can.

The German and the American approach constitute complementary styles: Americans start with the facts and work their way towards a theory (*inductive*), whereas Germans tend to develop their theories first and illustrate them with empirical data (*deductive*).

This different emphasis can also be seen in their different methods of *problem-solving*. Americans tend to spend most of the time for a project on its implementation phase and comparatively little time on the planning phase. It comes as no surprise that the German emphasis is exactly the other way around.

Nevertheless, the German style of problem-solving also aims at action and application. But, Germans do not start their activities because they *think* it might work, but because they have carefully analyzed every aspect of the problem and are sure that the solution they have come up with is the right one.

Especially when *bi-cultural teams* are working together these differences in intellectual style can cause conflicts: For an American it is very hard to participate in a German-style meeting. He or she is expecting decision-making and the assignment of tasks for the team members, whereas the Germans want to get to the bottom of things and analyze the cause of the problem. On the other hand, a German in an American meeting might be seen as ineffective since he or she is reluctant to quickly and convincingly propose pragmatic solutions. The German person is at the same time frustrated with the lack of thorough analysis she feels is necessary for any serious and successful solutions.

Instead of pragmatic little steps Germans want to tackle problems from the bottom up, from the root cause. On the one hand, this procedure helps to address many fundamental aspects of the problem. On the other hand, this kind of holistic method of problem-solving bears the danger of inflating the problem with the result that in the end it seems to be too big to solve at all.

In a nutshell the US and the German intellectual styles can be summarized in the following ironic remark of Bertrand Russell:

- "It may generally be said that the animals studied behaved in ways in which the experimenters believed before their investigation began. (...) animals studied by Americans rushed about with an incredible display of bustle and pep, before finally achieving the desired result by accident, while animals studied by Germans sat still and thought before finally evolving the solution out of their inner-consciousness."

Synthesis

The reality is that both approaches can be correct, or even required. There are situations where "US Pragmatism" is essential and others where "Deutsche Gründlichkeit" is required.

The merger of Chrysler and Daimler Benz is an oft-used example of just such a marriage of "US Pragmatism" and "Deutsche Gründlichkeit." The success of this merger is still being played out and will certainly rest on the ability of the two significantly different cultures being able to value and sustain each other. Chrysler's US Pragmatism was embodied in its former CEO Lee Iacocca. His role in the turnaround of Chrysler during the early 1980s made him a popular hero. His objective was to save the company, not build the "best" engineered car. The culture that permeated Chrysler at that time, and remains today, was one of getting the job done by whatever means possible. For Iacocca it meant government loans. For engineers it often meant searching through scrapped machinery to build anew a manufacturing line. While this culture may not have produced automobiles of the same engineering quality as Mercedes Benz, it accomplished the task of returning the company to profitability. Would a culture of engineering perfection have succeeded in the same circumstance?

Is the Chrysler way better than the Daimler Benz way? This is not a useful question. Rather, the question should be: How are the two cultures to be valued and used to sustain each other and the larger objective?

Here are some important requirements that are necessary to turn intercultural differences into an asset instead of letting them become barriers:

1. The identification of the different "habits of the heart" is a first necessary step for any kind of effective intercultural post-merger management, not only on the German-American front. Consequently, the Chrysler employees who ordered the book "These strange German Ways" were already at the right track. But of course they should not be left alone with their effort to understand the other culture. Intercultural training on all levels of both companies is absolutely necessary. When used early in a merger process they help to ease fears and misconceptions. Without them the intercultural learning curve is just too slow. An unsupported intercultural learning process unavoidably leads to frustration and costs too much in time and energy. It even runs the risk of continuous misunderstandings and

value violations eventually leading to a gridlock that prevents a mutual intercultural learning process.

2. As with any merger process, the creation of trust is vital. This is best achieved if international teams get to know each other early and on a personal basis. Experience shows that those teams and individuals who get to know each other personally are usually also more successful in their later cooperation. Thus, the investment in time and travel cost is returned.

3. The whole organization has to encourage the transatlantic flow of information. Travel, exchanges and relocations between both organizations are just some of the suggested tools to enhance mutual understanding. This should also happen in a systematic and strategic way. Future expatriates on both sides should participate in pre-departure training and should receive relocation support. Only if the experience in the other country is felt to be rewarding will the returning expatriate become an important multiplier of knowledge and appreciation for the other culture.

4. It is also helpful to start a process of a more explicit cultural integration by developing shared corporate values. This should not be additional work since a merged company will already need a new Mission, Vision, Values Statements as well as a Code of Conduct.

5. On a personal level and from the bottom-up it is very helpful to identify managers and employees who already have intercultural experience, such as members of minority groups, bi-linguals, etc. Their support on the micro-level and their intangible knowledge can be a precious resource. These people could form an informal network to exchange and develop ideas and support others.

All these are certainly measures that require a substantial amount of time, money, skill, and effort. But – as Nobel laureate Milton Friedman has said: There is no free lunch! You can not have the positive economic effects of a transatlantic merger without investing heavily in the intercultural management of values and processes. Nobody, for example, complains about the cost of migrating different computer software within a merger processes because it is accepted as unavoidable. A similar attitude should be adopted toward intercultural integration.

- Therefore, one final important requirement of a successful merger of cultures is that the top-management communicate and support the role and importance of the intercultural learning process to the merger on an equal level with all the other necessary processes and measures within the post-merger integration management.

In doing this the differing "habits of the heart" and the instability of cross-cultural business transactions can be seen as an opportunity for the innovative development of organizations and thus contribute to the merged company's economic success.

Craig DeForest

As Dr. Palazzo said, the culture of a business is more than just its way of doing things. Culture is about the very "being" of the business, and therefore about the "energy field" (or compelling atmosphere for thought, feeling, and behavior) it generates, sustains, and evolves over time. If sustained long enough, that being may even resemble a DNA-level phenomenon that requires generations to change.

The following more generalized beliefs about corporate mergers are intended to be additive to Dr. Palazzo's message without repeating it. When faced in the context of a German-American corporate merger, these challenges will almost certainly be exacerbated.

1. In a corporate merger, business cultures do not merge, no matter what senior management declares to be their intent. Virtually all mergers turn out to be acquisitions, with one management group in power and the other subordinated. Thus, one culture is usually required to change to adopt the culture of the other.

2. If a business organization has a long-standing and identifiable culture, to work to destroy it and change it to another company's culture is an inappropriate endeavor. Every established company has essence qualities that were planted at its inception and nurtured (consciously or unconsciously) as it grew and evolved. It is in these essence qualities that the strength of that company lived. To fail to recognize and honor those qualities is to kill something that is living in that company, with inevitable consequences to its people's spirit, commitment, and creative thrust.

3. The appropriate initial intention may be to help both cultures evolve to become more of their "true selves," and to restrict "cultural merger" activities to building the sort of mutual understanding and respect between them that will allow business and functional areas of commonality or complementarity to be well-managed and exploited for the good of both "wholes," the good of the (new) larger whole, and the benefit of those whom they serve through their products and services.

4. The core process of change for a company in a merger might therefore be called something like "Naturalizing Change." We as humans respond well to change as long as it engages our hearts and our "higher minds;" i.e., it is consistent with our own nature, consistent with the essence qualities of our company's culture, consistent with our country's nature, and aimed at something we believe is universally right and/or good for all. What can and should change initially, therefore, are needed changes to support business pursuits (e.g., increased value to customers, or responses to competitive threats) that any thoughtful person would see as directionally right to do and natural to pursue.

5. The wise restrain themselves from working hard on culture change too early in a merger process. People in business and industry in the US are not often familiar with the "world of being" that is the source of our energies, and are more comfortable working on the "world of function" (i.e, doing, knowledge, skills) alone.

- Beginning by aligning systems of communication, accounting, business planning, and so on is necessary following a legal merger.

- The next phase includes any intended shift in business purpose or direction for one or both entities, and the processes needed to generate collective will throughout the new (merged) business toward the new purpose.

- Third are needed shifts in "function" (what to do, how to work on it, etc.) and development of the knowledge and skills, support systems, etc. to support those shifts.

- Finally, work on "naturalizing culture" or "guided evolution of culture" will support both entities in a way that each becomes more of itself while they also become more of a unified whole.

Approaching mergers in this way can lead to a gradual merger of some of the desirable qualities of both entities into the other as people naturally work together in carrying out the work of the enterprise.

Bernhard K.F. Pelzer: Reconcile the different approaches

Differences

The approach to the differences of German-American cultures will initially start from different view points. Americans will like to talk about success, the people involved, their enthusiasm and what they have achieved. Germans, on the other hand, will like to describe the difficulties, the risks, the number of failures, the counter-forces involved and go deep into psychological and social science related analysis.

Culture as a concept

There are more cultural concepts than the ones individuals are conscious of themselves. These writings are, therefore, directly related to the culture concepts of the authors and will only disclose our understanding of the German-American cultural concepts.

By *concepts* we mean what people create out of their experiences. So the differences of German and American experiences have to be seriously looked at. Our approach to this is the so-called constructivist philosophy which posits that every society has their own construction rules that define their reality. To understand this further we will use a simple example of reality construction: Imagine an ancient Victorian chair and different individuals looking at it.

This chair, for example, triggers benevolent memories of my 80 year old aunt looking at the beauty of the chair and remembering Grandma Emma who used a similar one in her grand house.

Perhaps a New York investment banker sees new opportunities in investing in old furniture and is calculating his return after selling it within five years.

A German craftsman remembers his period of training and the wonderful crafted piece of furniture and he thinks about the enormous amount of time that is necessary to build such a piece of crafted art and he feels regret about the fact that nowadays nobody would pay him the money he would need to build such a chair.

Another point of view is an aboriginal bushman who has never used such a piece of furniture and is assessing this strange fragment of wood at its burning value for his warmth the next night.

As this example illustrates, it is absolutely essential to understand from which perspective we look at situations. One helpful perspective to start with in different cultures is the "extraterrestrial" point of view, i.e., I come from Mars as a "little green man" and everything is so new and beautifully colored here!; everything is interesting and what is at first seen as incomprehensible here is a problem to be worked out!

Culture as an excuse for failure

The concept of culture has become a general purpose excuse for the failure of mergers. The most frequent reasons are:

- It is easy to blame the culture because it is complex and influences all human and organizational relations.
- It accuses nobody personally, therefore everybody can accept it as the explanation.
- By the culture being blamed, there is no personal feeling of responsibility.
- Since culture is understood by everybody differently, the reason for the failure cannot be disproved (or even agreed upon).

Culture as a level

German-American culture is only one of many cultural levels we could examine. We could also look at:

- The national culture: It is usually the first framework to be examined within corporations for differences.
- Industries: Industries have industry-specific cultures and have created their own cultural behaviors (rules).
- The corporate culture: Each corporation has its own culture. Ideally this culture should be shaped by visions, values and personal convictions.
- Groups: Individual groups have a culture that determines in which way decisions are made and dilemmas are handled.

In addition to these examples there are also cultures with respect to religion, family, media, politics, fashion and other "rule sets."

Culture as a layer

Cultures are very complex and can't simply be described by check lists:

- Culture arises when people start to design their set of rules, either consciously or unconsciously, that creates their reality.
- And culture rebuilds itself by people behaving (living through their set of rules) in time, nature and relationships.
- Culture is a collective identity.
- Culture influences the development of identity and identity influences the culture.

Looking at German-American mergers and the cultural development in the related companies we must concede that up to now there is no consistently successful change program that has succeeded in any German or American company. Nevertheless looking at the largest German-American merger we can see that some management styles are better suited for German-American company success than others. This case shows us that an open minded, modest and highly skilled style can work toward changing nationally related cultures into a more intercultural behavior and can influence and change both the nationally related cultures so that a new, previously unseen culture (and set of rules) arises. Looking at the newly appointed CEO of Daimler-Chrysler we notice a new management style that has reshaped the American car builder Chrysler and will transform the global Daimler-Chrysler company to become even more successful.

Insights

Our experience has led to four insights:

Misunderstandings are part of everyday life!

The more we accept that misunderstandings are unavoidable in cultural contexts, the greater the ability of our teams to cooperate productively.

Misunderstandings often happen at the international level of cooperation in vicious circles. This frequently extends the effect of the misunderstanding. Dealing with employees is very different in Europe and America. Due to different national cultural behaviors, it is relatively easy for corporations in America to terminate employees; it is just as easy as an employee to find a new job. Therefore it is tempting not to invest in the long-term education of employees. Instead, corporations often rely on detailed work instructions (blue books) that are independent of the employee. A completely different approach has developed from ancient craftsmen and their professional group (Stände) from the middle ages in Europe. Social developments (social market economy) led to a fully developed protection of employees. Replacing employees against their wishes is very difficult. Because of this it becomes very important to invest in the training of the employees. The connection between the employees and the business can become close and strong. The employer may enjoy a high degree of loyalty and fewer turnovers of their employees.

If these cultural differences are only given superficial consideration then more serious misunderstandings are assured. If management actions and decisions are taken without a complete understanding of such differences they will inevitably lead to the deteriorating effectiveness of the organization.

Backgrounds determine the reality!

The more we have become conscious of the backgrounds of individuals and groups, the more we discovered how that reality is determined by acceptance of assumptions during past experiences and that knowledge can help change and design a better future.

Complexity isn't reducible!

The Moderation Method invented more than 25 years ago in Germany takes this key concept to heart. All of the various reductionistic techniques designed to reduce complexity to simplicity have repeatedly failed. Time and again complexity that is glossed over will appear again later in a change process and prevent continued progress until it is effectively dealt with.

By contrast, methods like *Open Space*, *Future Workshops* or *Real Time Strategic Change* use complexity as a way to speed up processes of change. Each of these methods does not rely on a concept of rigid control, focusing rather on the results of the process. This means that the requirements of the process itself can be unknown at the beginning! The end result of a process can be specified, yet the process itself is quite open and unpredictable. This is, of course not consistent with tightly controlled goal oriented systems. Leadership managers must rely on intrinsic motivation rather than explicit control. For example, if an explicit goal of a 15% cost reduction is set, perhaps opportunities to achieve a 35% reduction could be blocked because of conflicting motivational influences.

Variety stabilizes the system!

Our team became considerably more stable as it increased in cultural diversity (assuming we have adhered to the first three insights). This variety allows us to better cope with chaotic environments. In rigid and very uniform systems, such as government bureaucracies or labor unions, we experience initial extreme reactions to the introduction of diversity. Stability through variety is, however, one of the basic strategies that nature uses in dealing with changing environments. This simple risk management principle has the added advantage of storing the maximum quantity of organizational information and processing it with optimal speed by using its built-in parallel capabilities.

Summary

In summary, our experience has led to four insights about culture within organizations:

- Misunderstandings are part of everyday life! Expect them.
- Backgrounds determine the reality that we design for each other!
- Complexity isn't reducible!
- Variety stabilizes the system!

These basic insights, when used together, can help reconcile what at first appear to be irreconcilable differences in cultural attitudes and actions. This can lead to a cultural evolution in groups and corporations within a merger context and pave the way for the success of the whole.

5 Appendix

Large transatlantic M&A transactions from 1998 until 2005

Table 5.1 U.S.-German mergers and acquisitions over $1 billion by year (1998 to 2005)

Year	Value ($billion)	Acquired company	Host economy	Acquiring company	Home economy
1998	43.1	Chrysler Corp	US	DaimlerChrysler AG	Germany
1998	2.7	Trevira Polyester Unit	Germany	Koch/Saba	US
1998	2.6	Dupont Merck Pharmaceutical	Germany	Du Pont	US
1998	1.9	Brake & Chassis Business	US	Continental AG	Germany
1998	1.5	Power Generation Units	US	Siemens AG	Germany
1998	1.1	74 Interspar Warehouse Stores	Germany	Wal*mart	US
1998	1.1	Autobahn Tank & Rast AG	Germany	Investor Group	US
1998	1.1	In-Vitro Diagnostic Business	US	Bayer AG	Germany
1999	9.1	Bankers Trust New York Corp	US	Deutsche Bank AG	Germany
1999	1.9	Herberts Paints (Hoechst AG)	Germany	El du Pont de Nemours and Co	US
1999	1.1	Dover Corp-Elevator Business	US	Thyssen Aufzuege AG	Germany
1999	1.1	Cyprus Amax-US Coal Mining	US	RAG International Mining	Germany
1999	1.1	Lone Star Industries	US	Dyckerhoff AG	Germany
1999	1.1	Siemens Electromechanical	Germany	Tyco International Ltd	US
2000	9.2	E-plus Mobilfunk GMBH	Germany	Bellsouth Corp	US

Table 5.1 U.S.-German mergers and acquisitions over $1 billion by year (1998 to 2005)

Year	Value ($billion)	Acquired company	Host economy	Acquiring company	Home economy
2000	7.0	BASF Pharma	Germany	Abbott Laboratories	US
2000	4.1	AGA AB-B Shs	US	Linde AG	Germany
2000	3.8	Cyanamid Agricultural Products	US	Wyeth	Germany
2000	2.9	Land Rover	Germany	Ford Motor Co	US
2000	2.8	North Rhine & Westphalia	Germany	Callahan Associates Intl LLC	US
2000	2.5	Global Polyols Business	US	Bayer AG	Germany
2000	2.0	Siemens Medical Solutions	US	Siemens AG	Germany
2000	2.0	Mediaone International	US	Deutsche Telekom AG	Germany
2000	1.3	Fiber-optics Units	Germany	Corning Inc	US
2000	1.1	Air Express International	US	Deutsche Post AG	Germany
2001	29.4	VoiceStream Wireless Corp	US	Deutsche Telekom AG	Germany
2001	6.9	Knoll AG (BASF AG)	Germany	Abbott Laboratories	US
2001	2.2	Nicholas-Applegate Capt Mgmt	US	Allianz AG	Germany
2001	1.3	Sky Chefs Inc	US	LSG Lufthansa Service Holding	Germany
2001	1.3	Efficient Networks Inc	US	Siemens AG	Germany
2001	1.3	Wasserstein Perella Group Inc	US	Dresdner Bank AG	Germany
2001	1.1	Degussa Metals Catalysts AG	Germany	OM Group Inc	US
2002	8.3	AOL Europe, AOL Australia	Germany	America Online Inc	US
2002	2.5	Zurich Scudder Investments Inc	US	Deutsche Bank AG	Germany
2002	1.1	Schmalbach-Lubeca AG	Germany	Ball Corp	US

Table 5.1 U.S.-German mergers and acquisitions over $1 billion by year (1998 to 2005)

Year	Value ($billion)	Acquired company	Host economy	Acquiring company	Home economy
2003	7.7	American Water Works Co Inc	US	RWE AG	Germany
2003	4.5	Wella AG	Germany	Procter & Gamble	US
2003	1.7	MTU Aero Engines Holdings AG	Germany	Kohlberg Kravis Roberts & Co.	US
2003	1.5	Deutsche Bank – Securities Div	Germany	State Street Corp, Boston, MA	US
2003	1.2	Airborne Inc	US	Deutsche Post AG	Germany
2003	1.2	Deutsche Bank – Real Estate(51)	Germany	Blackstone Group LP	US
2004	4.3	GAGFAH Gemein-nuetzige AG	Germany	Fortress Investment LLC	US
2004	3.0	The Dial Corporation	US	Henkel KGAA-VORZUG	Germany
2004	2.7	Dynamit Nobel Chemicals Business	Germany	Rockwood Special-ties Group	US
2004	2.2	Celanese AG	Germany	Blackstone Group LP	US
2004	1.8	ATU Auto-Teile-Unger Group	Germany	Kohlberg Kravis Roberts & Co.	US
2004	1.7	Brenntag AG	Germany	Bain Capital LLC	US
2004	1.7	VWR International	Germany	Clayton Dubilier & Rice	US
2005	1.6	Kloeckner & Co	Germany	Linsday Goldberg & Bessemer	US
2005	1.0	Sirona Dental Systems GMBH	Germany	Madison Dearborn Partners LL	US

Source: UNCTAD and Bloomberg (Hamilton/Quinlan)

Table 5.2 Top 50 – Biggest international mergers and acquisitions by value
(2000 to 2005; grey: Transatlantic)

Value of transaction ($billion)	Year	Acquired company	Host economy	Acquiring company	Home economy
74.3	2004	Shell Transport & Trading Co	UK	Royal Dutch Petroleum Co	Netherlands
46.0	2000	Orange PLC	UK	France Telecom SA	France
40.4	2000	Seagram Co Ltd	Canada	Vivendi SA	France
34.0	2000	Beijing Mobile, 6 others	China	China Telecom Hong Kong Ltd	Hong Kong
29.4	2001	VoiceStream Wireless Corp	US	Deutsche Telekom AG	Germany
25.1	2000	Bestfoods	US	Unilever PLC	UK
19.4	2000	Allied Zurich PLC	UK	Zurich Allied AG	Switzerland
18.5	2005	Unocal Corp	US	China National Offshore Oil	China
18.3	2005	Bayerische Hypo- und Vereinsbank	Germany	UniCredit Italiano SpA	Italy
15.8	2004	Abbey National PLC	UK	Santander Central Hispano SA	Spain
14.4	2005	Allied Domecq PLC	UK	Goal Acquisitions Limited	Guernsey
14.4	2000	Airtel SA	Spain	Vodafone AirTouch PLC	UK
13.8	2001	Viag Interkom GmbH & Co	Germany	British Telecommunications PLC	UK
12.8	2001	Banacci	Mexico	Citigroup Inc	US
12.8	2005	Wind Telecomunicazioni SpA	Italy	Weather Investments Srl	Egypt
12.5	2001	Fortis (NL) NV	Netherlands	Fortis (B)	Belgium
12.2	2000	PaineWebber Group Inc	US	UBS AG	Switzerland
11.5	2001	Billiton PLC	UK	BHP Ltd	Australia
11.2	2001	AXA Financial Inc	US	AXA Group	France

Table 5.2 Top 50 – Biggest international mergers and acquisitions by value
(2000 to 2005; grey: Transatlantic)

Value of transaction ($billion)	Year	Acquired company	Host economy	Acquiring company	Home economy
11.1	2000	Credit Commercial de France	France	HSBC Holdings PLC {HSBC}	UK
11.1	2001	De Beers Con-solidated Mines	South Africa	DB Investments	UK
11.1	2004	John Hancock Finl Svcs Inc	US	Manulife Financial Corp	Canada
10.7	2002	USA Networks Inc-Ent Asts	US	Vivendi Universal SA	France
10.5	2001	Ralston Purina Co	US	Nestle SA	Switzerland
10.2	2000	Telecommuni-cacoes de Sao Paulo	Brazil	Telefonica SA	Spain
9.8	2001	AT&T Wireless Group	US	NTT DoCoMo Inc	Japan
9.6	2004	Amersham PLC	UK	General Electric Co	US
9.3	2001	CIT Group Inc	US	Tyco International Ltd	Bermuda
8.6	2005	Banca Nazio-nale del Lavoro SpA	Italy	BBVA	Spain
8.5	2001	Cable & Wire-less Optus Lt (C&W)	Australia	SingTel	Singapore
8.1	2005	Banca Anton-veneta SpA	Italy	ABN-AMRO Bank NV	Netherlands
7.8	2004	John Labatt Ltd	Canada	Ambev	Brazil
7.7	2003	American Water Works Co Inc	US	RWE AG	Germany
7.4	2002	Westcoast Energy Inc	Canada	Duke Energy Corp	US
7.4	2002	PowerGen PLC	UK	E.ON AG	Germany
6.9	2005	Gecina SA	France	Metrovacesa SA	Spain

Table 5.2 Top 50 – Biggest international mergers and acquisitions by value
(2000 to 2005; grey: Transatlantic)

Value of transaction ($billion)	Year	Acquired company	Host economy	Acquiring company	Home economy
6.9	2003	Hughes Electronics Corp	US	News Corp Ltd	Australia
6.6	2002	Aventis CropScience Hldg SA	France	Bayer AG	Germany
6.6	2005	IMS Health Inc	US	VNU NV	Netherlands
5.8	2001	GKN PLC-Support Services	UK	Brambles Industries Ltd	Australia
5.7	2005	Basell NV	Netherlands	Investor Group	US
5.7	2005	Hexal AG	Germany	Novartis AG	Switzerland
5.7	2001	Dao Heng Bank Group (Guoco)	Hong Kong	DBS Group Holdings Ltd	Singapore
5.5	2003	P&O Princess Cruises PLC	UK	Carnival Corp	US
5.5	2005	Amadeus Global Travel Distn	Spain	Wam Acquisition SA	Luxembourg
5.5	2005	Amalgamated Banks of S. Africa	South Africa	Barclays PLC	UK
5.5	2001	Japan Telecom, J-Phone	Japan	Vodafone Group PLC	UK
5.3	2003	Pechiney SA	France	Alcan Inc	Canada
5.0	2005	Intelsat Ltd	Bermuda	Investor Group	UK
4.9	2005	Edison SpA	Italy	Investor Group	France

Source: Thompson Financial, DB analysis (Griesser/Schwingeler)

Contributors

Dr. Lutz Angerer

Lutz Angerer is a partner of Lovells practicing in the Munich office. He specializes in corporate finance, M&A, corporate reorganizations and corporate law. Lutz Angerer has published a number of articles on corporate law and is co-author of the first commentary on the German Takeover Act.

Lutz Angerer graduated from the University of Hamburg in 1987 and received his doctorate degree from the University of Hamburg in 1990. In 1993 the University of Virginia (USA) bestowed on him his Master of Laws. He started his career by working as research assistant to the renowned corporate law professor Karsten Schmidt from 1988 to 1991. Since 1993 he has been practicing law. Lutz Angerer joined Lovells in 2001. In 2001 he was seconded to the Frankfurt office for 6 months. Lutz Angerer is a member of the German-American Lawyers Association (DAJV).

He can be reached at: *lutz.angerer@lovells.com*

Isabella Bach-Alexander

Isabella Bach-Alexander has been lawyer with Linklaters Oppenhoff & Rädler in the Litigation/Arbitration Department since 2000.

Education: After finalising law studies at University of Passau in 1998 she completed the I. Juristische Staatsexamen (First Legal State Examination) in 1998 and the II. Juristische Staatsexamen (Second Legal State Examination) in 2000. Subsequently, she successfully participated in the seminar to become a specialist (*Fachanwalt*) in insolvency law.

Experience: German civil, commercial, and corporate litigation, insolvency law and complex litigation; strategic advice and representation of creditors, shareholders and affiliated companies of debtors prior to and during insolvency proceedings, in particular the enforcement of security rights, the defence of claims arising from a breach of capital contribution and maintenance regulations, representation in all insolvency related court proceedings.

Thomas Bader

Thomas Bader has been lawyer with Linklaters Oppenhoff & Rädler in the Employment and Company Pension Department since 2004.

Education: After finalising law studies at University of Munich (LMU), he completed the I. Juristische Staatsexamen (First Legal State Examination) in 1999 and the II. Juristische Staatsexamen (Second Legal State Examination) in 2001. From 2002 to 2003 he worked as a research assistant at University Eichstätt-Ingolstadt.

Experience: General company pension issues (including closures and modification of pension plans, introduction of pension plans), individual and collective labour law (in particular transfer of business and outsourcing, advice on collective bargaining issues and industrial relations, employment litigation) as well as due diligence exercise.

Allison S. Bailey

Allison Bailey is a Vice President and Director in the Atlanta office of The Boston Consulting Group. She is a core group member of the firm's Worldwide Organization and Consumer Goods practices. Since joining in 1987, she has advised clients on both sides of the Atlantic on issues related to M&A growth strategies, portfolio restructuring, sales and marketing effectiveness, global corporate transformation, and post-merger integration. She holds a BA in mathematics from Dartmouth College, an MBA in finance from the Wharton School, an MA in international relations from SAIS of Johns Hopkins University, and an MA in public administration from the Kennedy School of Harvard University.

She can be reached at: *bailey.allison@bcg.com*

Rainer Bätz

Rainer Bätz is Director in the Corporate Finance Department of Deloitte & Touche, Munich. He joined the firm in 2002 after having worked as Manager for Arthur Andersen.

Rainer, born in 1966, is mainly focused in cross border deals involving financial investors and multinational conglomerates. He has nearly 10 years of experience in transaction and valuation advisory for media companies covering the whole value chain of film entertainment.

Prior to joining Arthur Andersen in 1996 he received his diploma in economics from the University of Heidelberg.

He can be reached at: *rbaetz@deloitte.de*

Steve Blum

Stephen Blum has forty years of solid and diversified management experience with broad and deep functional knowledge in strategic planning, corporate communications, investor and media relations, crisis management and marketing.

Blum was Senior Vice President of Investor Relations for the Dial Corporation and the integration officer for Dial following their acquisition by the Henkel Group. He is currently Adjunct Professor of Management at the W. P. Carey School of Business at Arizona State University.

His prior experience includes senior staff for Nelson A. Rockefeller during his term as Governor of the State of New York and Vice President of the United States of America and executive management positions at four major US based corporations. Blum earned a Bachelor of Science degree in Economics from New York University and a Masters of Business Administration Cum Laude from Fordham University.

Manfred Bögle

Manfred Bögle is Senior Partner at Deloitte & Touche GmbH. Manfred Bögle, born in 1956, is head of Corporate Finance Department at the Munich and Stuttgart office.

He is Member of the Valuation Board (Arbeitskreis Unternehmensbewertung) and of the Professional Insurance Committee of the Institute of Chartered Accountants (IDW). He has more than 20 years of experience in transaction and valuation advisory and has special experience in the financial and manufacturing industry (audit, corporate finance advisory, valuation and IFRS implementation). Manfred Bögle holds a degree in economics and is appointed as German Certified Public Accountant and German Tax Consultant.

He can be reached at: *mboegle@deloitte.de*

Russell J. DaSilva

Russell DaSilva is a partner in the New York office of Lovells, and is the head of the firm's United States banking practice. He handles secured and unsecured credit facilities, acquisition finance, project finance, asset-based lending, letters of credit and other trade financing arrangements, credit enhancement for public and private debt issuance, securitization and other sales of financial assets, derivatives and non-judicial restructurings. He is admitted to the bar of the State of New York.

DaSilva received his undergraduate degree from Princeton University (A.B., *summa cum laude*, 1976), and his law degree from Harvard University (J.D. 1979).

Craig DeForest

DeForest helps business leaders and groups learn to incorporate systemic approaches to change and development of their businesses, their operations, and their organizations. He has consulted to corporations across the U.S., Europe, and parts of Asia with small and large corporations. He is a senior member of the Institute for Developmental Processes of Carmel, California. The Institute has developed unique methodologies for building advanced business organizations which develop and apply the full potential of their employees to the delivery of superior customer value and remarkable business results. He can be reached at: *info@pelzerap.com*

Ingmar Dörr

Ingmar Dörr joined the Tax Team of Lovells Munich as Associate in 2003. He was admitted to the bar in 2004. The main focus of his practice is the consultation of German and international clients in M&A and private equity transactions as well as in international and European tax law issues. He is in the course of writing a doctoral thesis on the subject of European company taxation at the Max Planck Institute for Intellectual Property, Competition and Tax Law in Munich, department of accounting and tax law of Prof. Dr. Wolfgang Schön.

He can be reached at: *ingmar.doerr@lovells.com*

Jeanie Daniel Duck

Jeanie Daniel Duck is a Senior Vice President and Director in the Atlanta office of The Boston Consulting Group. She joined as a partner in 1988. She is the author of "The Change Monster: the Human Forces the Fuel and Foil Corporate Transformation and Change" and "Managing Change: the Art of Balancing" for the Harvard Business Review. For over twenty years she has focused on the emotional and behavioral impact of change on corporate performance. Jeanie has worked extensively with clients in multiple industries on post-merger integrations and major corporate transformations. She is BCG's guru on Change Management and a leader in their Organization practice group. She earned her BSAE degree from the University of Georgia and her MSAE at Pratt Institute.

She can be reached at: *duck.jeanie@bcg.com*

Markus Ebert

Markus Ebert has been lawyer with Linklaters Oppenhoff & Rädler in the Employment and Company Pension Department since 2003.

Education: After finalising law studies at University of Munich (LMU) he completed the I. Juristische Staatsexamen (First Legal State Examination) in 2000 and the II. Juristische Staatsexamen (Second Legal State Examination) in 2002. Subsequently, he continued with postgraduate studies in European and International commercial law (LL.M. Eur.) at University of Munich (LMU). In addition, he successfully participated in the seminar to become a specialist (*Fachanwalt*) in labour law.

Experience: Company pension (in particular legal assessments of pension schemes in connection with the acquisition of companies), individual and collective labour law (in particular day-to-day employment advice, drafting and review of employment and service contracts, dismissal and severance issues, employment litigation, co-determination), business closures and restructuring of companies as well as M&A-related labour law advice.

Fabian Ehlers

Fabian Ehlers is a partner of Linklaters Oppenhoff & Rädler. Practising in their Frankfurt office, he is specialized in corporate and securities laws. Fabian Ehlers has extensive experience in international and domestic capital markets transactions, in particular equity and equity-linked securities offerings, as well as takeovers and restructurings.

Fabian Ehlers is a graduate of Ruprecht-Karls-Universität Heidelberg and New York University School of Law (M.C.J.).

He can be reached at: *fabian.ehlers@linklaters.com*

Dr. Thomas Elser

Managing associate of Linklaters Oppenhoff & Rädler, Munich office.

Thomas Elser, born 1970, is mainly focused on corporate tax planning, structuring of national and international M&A transactions (including acquisition financing), and tax-efficient structuring of opportunity funds.

Elser, who joined the firm in 2001 after having worked since 1995 as assistant professor in tax law at the University of Stuttgart-Hohenheim, being managing associate since 2003, is known for his innovative tax solutions and is author of numerous professional publications and regular lecturer at conventions and seminars.

He can be reached at: *thomas.elser@linklaters.com*

Raymond J. Fisher

Raymond J. Fisher is a partner of Linklaters Oppenhoff & Rädler at the Frankfurt office. As head of the U.S. practice group in Frankfurt, he is specialized in U.S. aspects of equity and debt securities offerings including SEC registered transactions and U.S. aspects of cross-border mergers and acquisitions.

Raymond J. Fisher became partner at a New York law firm in 1998 and he joined Linklaters' Frankfurt office in 2002. He is a graduate of Harvard College and the New York University School of Law.

He can be reached at: *raymond.fisher@linklaters.com*

Alexander Geiser

Alexander Geiser is a Managing Partner at HERING SCHUPPENER Consulting and heads the German M&A business from the Frankfurt office. Over the past ten years he has advised management boards in over 75 corporate transactions and critical situations. He specialises in cross-border transactions and multi-market campaigns, drawing from a multi-local perspective – having worked in New York, London and Frankfurt.

In case of comments and questions, contact: *ageiser@heringschuppener.com*

Dr. Volker Geyrhalter

Volker Geyrhalter is a partner of Lovells practicing in the Munich office. He specializes in M&A and private equity transactions, including complex cross border transactions, corporate reorganizations and general corporate work. Volker Geyrhalter is well published and author of various articles on corporate law in legal journals. He is recommended in the JUVE Handbuch 2004/2005 as a specialist for M&A transactions.

Volker Geyrhalter graduated from the University of Regensburg in 1994 and received his doctorate degree from the University of Regensburg in 1995. He joined Lovells in 1997 and became a partner of the firm in May 2002. He was seconded to the Frankfurt office in 1999 and to the London office in 2000, in each case for 6 months.

He can be reached at: *volker.geyrhalter@lovells.com*

Dr. Kirsten Girnth

Kirsten Girnth was admitted as a lawyer to the Frankfurt bar in August 1997 and is a partner with the law firm DLA Piper Rudnick Gray Cary in the firm's Frankfurt office. She is a member of the firm's Corporate and IT practice. She provides commercial advice to international companies in the fields of IT law and cross-border mergers and acquisitions.

Kirsten Girnth is a graduate of Frankfurt university where she received her law degree as well as a degree in economics; she obtained her Ph.D. (Dr. rer. pol.) in February 1999. Her extensive work on the harmonization process of public procurement in the European Community was published in May 2000. Prior to working as a lawyer in 1997 she worked as a journalist for the *Frankfurter Allgemeine Zeitung* and for a radio station.

Stefan Griesser

Stefan Griesser is a Vice President in Deutsche Bank's M&A group in Frankfurt. He joined the Corporate and Investment Bank of Deutsche Bank in 2000. Between 1996 and 2000, he worked for the Group Investments Department which manages Deutsche Bank's own strategic M&A transactions. In both functions he worked on a number of US-German M&A transactions involving financial institutions and industrial companies. He holds a Diplom-Kaufmann from Westfälische Willhelms-Universität Münster.

Dr. Rüdiger Grube

Dr. Rüdiger Grube has been a member of the Board of Management of DaimlerChrysler AG since September 20, 2002, and is responsible for the Corporate Development which includes Corporate Strategy, Mergers & Acquisitions, Strategic Alliances, Industrial Participations and since October 1, 2004, responsible for all China-activities of DaimlerChrysler AG. In addition, he is a member of the Board of Directors of the Mitsubishi Motors Corporation (MMC), of the European Aeronautic Defence and Space Company (EADS N.V.) and Chairman of the Supervisory Board MTU Friedrichshafen GmbH as well as of the DaimlerChrysler-Off-Highway GmbH.

Dr. Grube was born in Hamburg on August 2, 1951. Following commercial/technical training in metal aircraft construction, he studied automotive engineering and aircraft construction at the University for Applied Sciences in Hamburg and graduated as a qualified engineer. He later studied vocational and business teaching at the University of Hamburg. He held a special teaching post in production and engineering at the University of Hamburg from 1981 to 1986. In 1986 he completed a doctorate at the Universities of Hamburg and Kassel in the areas of industrial science and polytechnology. Dr. Grube joined then Messerschmitt-Bölkow-Blohm GmbH in 1989, later Daimler-Benz Aerospace (DASA).

Prof. Dr. Daniel S. Hamilton

Daniel S. Hamilton is the Richard von Weizsäcker Professor and Director of the Center for Transatlantic Relations at the Paul H. Nitze School of Advanced International Studies, Johns Hopkins University. He also serves as Executive Director of the American Consortium on EU Studies, the EU Center Washington DC.

He is the publisher of the bimonthly magazine *Transatlantic: Europe, America & the World.* He served as Deputy Assistant Secretary of State for European Affairs; US Special Coordinator for Southeast European Stabilization, Associate Director of the Policy Planning Staff, Senior Associate at the Carnegie Endowment for International Peace, and Deputy Director of the Aspen Institute Berlin. He has also taught at the University of Innsbruck and the Free University of Berlin.

Recent publications include *The New Frontiers of Europe* (2005, ed.); *Partners in Prosperity: The Changing Geography of the Transatlantic Economy* (with Joseph P. Quinlan, 2004); *Transatlantic Transformations: Equipping NATO for the 21st Century* (2004, ed.).

Dirk Hoffmann

Dirk Hoffmann is Chief Financial Officer of Jamba! GmbH and Vice President of VeriSign.

He joined Jamba! in January 2001, shortly after the company had been founded. Today, he is responsible for finance and controlling for the Jamba! / Jamster group of companies. Before Jamba!, he had been a Senior Associate with Booz Allen Hamilton, working on international consulting assignments for the financial services and communications/media/ technology industry. Dirk Hoffmann holds a German Master's degree in Management (Dipl.-Kfm.) from WHU Koblenz, and an MBA from The University of Texas at Austin (USA).

Dirk Horcher

Dirk Horcher is a legal assistant in the M&A / Corporate department in Frankfurt am Main of Linklaters, in Germany operating under the name Linklaters Oppenhoff & Rädler. He studied law as well as economics in Bayreuth (Germany). In his legal traineeship he worked in the securities branch of the Federal Financial Supervisory Authority ("Bundesanstalt für Finanzdienstleistungsaufsicht") in Frankfurt am Main and in the Corporate department of Linklaters, London.

Reto Isenegger

Reto Isenegger is a Partner and Vice President of the global strategy and technology consulting firm Booz Allen Hamilton. He is a member of the firm's global Financial Services Group and member of the Swiss executive team, based in Zurich. His expertise lies in the area of strategic alliances as well as in designing and implementing efficiency improvement programs mainly with leading financial services companies.

Prior to joining the Financial Services Group of Booz Allen Hamilton, he worked several years for international management consulting firms in the area of performance improvement and corporate finance. Reto Isenegger holds a university degree in business administration and information management from the University of St. Gallen (Switzerland). During his university studies he worked in the business transformation and restructuring department for the headquarter of an international leading Swiss bank.

Contact: *isenegger_reto@bah.com*

Barbara S. Jeremiah

Barbara S. Jeremiah heads Alcoa's corporate development activities, which include corporate initiatives, supporting the business units as they look to expand through acquisitions and/or joint ventures, finding opportunities that cross business lines, and handling corporate divestitures. She was elected an executive vice president of Alcoa in July 2002 and is a member of the Alcoa Executive Council, the senior leadership group that provides strategic direction for the company. Ms Jeremiah serves on the Board of Directors of Equitable Resources Inc., the Women's Center and Shelter of Greater Pittsburgh and the Board of Trustees of the Pittsburgh Ballet Theatre. She is also a member of the Business Advisory Council of the University Of Virginia School Of Law and the Women's Center National Council at the University of Virginia. She holds a bachelor's degree in political science from Brown University and a Juris Doctor degree in law from the University of Virginia.

Ravin Jesuthasan, CFA

Ravin Jesuthasan is Managing Principal and Global Leader of Towers Perrin's Rewards and Performance Management Practice based in Chicago. He has extensive experience working with clients in North America, Europe, Asia and Latin America to align their people programs and policies with business strategy and shareholder value creation. As recognized thought leader, he is a frequent speaker at conferences and has been widely quoted by leading business media globally.

Nikolai Juchem

Nikolai Juchem is a Director at HERING SCHUPPENER Consulting and a member of the capital markets team in Frankfurt. He advises clients primarily on strategic IR and PR issues. Nikolai acquired his supra-disciplinary expertise among other things as Head of Financial Public Relations at TUI AG. Prior to that he was Vice President for Investor Relations at Stinnes AG, where he moved the company's equity story forwards and communicated it to the key international capital markets.

In case of comments and questions, contact: *njuchem@heringschuppener.com.*

Karoline Jung-Senssfelder

Karoline Jung-Senssfelder is a doctoral candidate at the Endowed Chair for Corporate Finance and Capital Markets at European Business School (ebs), Oestrich-Winkel and a research associate with the Center for Entrepreneurial and Small Business Finance. She is currently working as Summer Analyst with the investment banking division of Goldman Sachs.

She can be reached at: *karoline.jung-senssfelder@gs.com*

Dr. Michael Kaschke

Michael Kaschke is 48 years old, has a Ph.D. in physics and a degree in finance and marketing. He started his industrial career with IBM research in the USA. After joining Carl Zeiss in 1992, he was the General Manager of two business divisions and, before being appointed to the Executive Board, was head of the Medical Technology Group of Carl Zeiss. He is currently the CFO of Carl Zeiss and oversees the Medical, Consumer Optics and Asia/Pacific business of Carl Zeiss.

He can be reached at: *kaschke@zeiss.de*

Roland Klein

Roland Klein is a CNC Partner and head of CNC UK Ltd. London. Prior to joining CNC, he was as an Executive Board Member with Ericsson and responsible for Communications and Investor Relations.

From 1992 until 1999 he held various positions in the Communications department of Daimler-Benz AG / DaimlerChrysler AG, culminating in the post of Vice President Corporate Communications. Between 1980 and 1992, he worked as a financial journalist for the Frankfurter Allgemeine Zeitung, Börsen-Zeitung and Manager Magazin in Frankfurt am Main, Hamburg, New York and London.

Roland Klein studied Economics in Stuttgart and completed Post-Graduate Programs at the Harvard Business School and the University of Southern California.

Carsten Kratz

Carsten Kratz is a Senior Vice President and Director in the Frankfurt office of The Boston Consulting Group. He joined the Munich office of The Boston Consulting Group in 1990 and moved to the Frankfurt office in 1992. Since 1999 he leads the German Technology & Communications Practice Area. His assignments centered around strategy development and operational efficiency improvements, especially in supply chain management, customer relationship management and in sales an services, both for headquarters and country operations. Besides, he has a lot of experience in implementation issues, especially in turnaround and PMI situations. Mr. Kratz is a commercial engineer from the technical university of Darmstadt.

He can be reached at: *kratz.carsten@bcg.com*

de la Maza Foundation in 2000, she pursued an LL.M. in International Taxation from the New York University in 2001. Carolina Perez-Lopez joined Lovells in 2003 after acquiring some years of experience at a major US law firm in New York.

She can be reached at: *carolina.perez@lovells.com*

Udo Philipp

Udo Philipp is 41 years old, studied economics and politics in Paris, started his career in banking and consulting, worked for Bertelsmann as CFO of their Professional Information Business and became a founding partner of EQT Partners Munich in 2000. He was responsible partner for EQT's acquisitions of Leybold Optics, Symrise (Haarmann+ Reimer/ Dragoco), Sirona and Carl Zeiss Vision.

Dr. Gerhard Plaschka

Co-founder and managing partner of MindFolio, a concept development and decision-science based marketing consultancy.

MindFolio specializes in creating, quantifying and verifying choices, customer experiences and solutions for brands, products, properties and services. The business is based in Chicago, London, Salt Lake City and Düsseldorf. He has extensive experience in developing global product-market positioning and product-service optimization models for consumer and industrial market oriented companies and serves as Associate Professor of Strategy and Venture Management at The Charles H. Kellstadt Graduate School of Business, DePaul University, Chicago.

Prior to co-founding MindFolio he was principal at two boutique management consulting firms and Chairman of the Department of Management at DePaul University. He serves on the board of various for profit and non-for-profit organizations, and has written several books and journal articles on entrepreneurial venture management and customer driven growth strategies.

He can be reached at: *gplaschka@mindfolio.com*

Joseph P. Quinlan

Joseph P. Quinlan is a Fellow at the Center for Transatlantic Relations at the Paul H. Nitze School of Advanced International Studies, Johns Hopkins University. He specializes in global capital flows, international trade and multinational strategies. He has extensive experience on Wall Street and in the US corporate sector. He lectures at New York University and was appointed as an Eisenhower Fellow in 1998. His publications have appeared in such venues as Foreign Affairs, the Financial Times and the Wall Street Journal.

He is the author of the Center's 2003 study, *Drifting Apart or Growing Together? The Primacy of the Transatlantic Economy*; co-author (with Daniel S. Hamilton) of the Center's 2004 study, *Partners in Prosperity: The Changing Geography of the Transatlantic Economy*; and author of three other books, including *Global Engagement: How American Companies Really Compete in the Global Economy* (2000).

Dr. Wolfgang Reim

Dr. Wolfgang Reim is President & CEO of Dräger Medical, a global leader for acute-point-of-care medical equipment headquartered in Lübeck, Germany. He joined Dräger in 2000 with a turn-around task and moved the company to double-digit EBIT margin in 2003. Driven by strategic considerations, he started external growth at Dräger Medical with the integration of Siemens Monitoring in 2003 and the Air-Shields acquisition in 2004.
Dr. Reim has 15 years of experience in medical equipment industry and occupied positions with global responsibility in magnetic resonance, X-ray and ultrasound prior to Dräger Medical. Several years of his professional carreer he spent in the USA. Dr. Reim holds a PhD in Physics from ETH Zürich.

He can be reached at: *wolfgang.reim@draeger.com*

Julianne Reynolds

Julianne Reynolds is a partner in the New York office of Lovells. Her practice focuses on the US tax aspects of cross-border transactions, including mergers and acquisitions, capital markets, private equity funds, financial transactions, as well as in bound and outbound tax planning.

Julianne graduated from William & Mary law school in 1994. She joined Lovells in 2002 and became a partner in May 2003. Julianne is admitted to the bar in the states of New York and Virginia and in the District of Columbia.

She can be reached at *julie.reynolds@lovells.com*

Prof. Dr. Frank Richter

Frank Richter is consultant at Goldman Sachs & Co. oHG, Frankfurt, and holds the Chair of Strategic Management and Finance at University of Ulm.

Frank Richter joined Goldman Sachs in 2000. Since then he is working in the area of mergers & acquisitions, corporate finance and corporate strategy. Prior to joining Goldman Sachs, he worked nine years as a consultant for McKinsey & Company, also in the area of strategy and finance. In 2000 Frank Richter accepted a position as a professor at Private University Witten/Herdecke, and afterwards (in 2004) at University of Ulm. He is member of different supervisory boards and serves on the board of the Schmalenbach Foundation. Further information can be found on his website www.mathematik.uni-ulm.de/strategie/.

He can be reached at: *frank.richter@gs.com*

Robert Ripin

Robert Ripin practices in the New York office of Lovells and is the head of the US securities law team within Lovells' international capital market practice. He has a broad transactional practice in the field of international securities offerings and has represented issuers, underwriters, corporate trustees and depositary banks in both equity and debt offerings and also advises companies on US corporate law matters and SEC compliance.

Robert Ripin received his BA from Columbia University in 1985 and his JD from New York University School of Law in 1988. He was a visiting student at St. Ann's College, Oxford University in 1983-1984. After ten years with a Wall Street law firm he joined Lovells as a partner in 1999.

He can be reached at: *robert.ripin@lovells.com*

Dr. Jürgen Rothenbücher

Dr. Jürgen Rothenbücher leads the Engineering & Automation Industry Practice of A.T. Kearney. His major consulting areas are in growth – both organic growth as external growth and all related strategic and operational tasks.

Dr. Jürgen Rothenbücher has 16 years of consulting experience and worked also for several years as managing director of an industrial company. His academic background is in engineering and economics from TH Darmstadt, ECL Lyon and RWTH Aachen.

He can be reached at: *juergen.rothenbuecher@atkearney.com*

Dr. Jens Schädler

Dr. Jens Schädler is a Partner and Vice President of the global strategy and technology consulting firm Booz Allen Hamilton. He is a member of the firm's Organisation, Change Management & Leadership Group and Managing Partner of the Zurich office. In his consulting work he focuses on strategic and organizational issues in the telecommunication and transportation industries as well as the public sector.

Jens Schädler holds a Ph.D. in Law from the University of Hamburg and a Master's Degree in International Management from the Community of European Management Schools (CEMS). He received a bachelor's degree in business administration from the University of Cologne.

Contact: *schadler_jens@bah.com*

Dr. Marcus Schenck

Marcus Schenck is Co-Head of Goldman Sachs' investment banking business for Germany and Austria. He has predominantly worked on merger transactions, focusing mainly on large industrial companies. He was involved in various large-scale transactions such as Vodafone/ Mannesmann, Veba/Viag, EADS, and DaimlerChrysler/ Mitsubishi Motors/ Hyundai Motor.

Marcus Schenck joined Goldman Sachs from McKinsey in 1997. He became a Managing Director in 2001 and a Partner in 2002. He holds a master degree in economics from Bonn and Berkeley and earned a PhD at the University of Cologne.

He can be reached at: *marcus.schenck@gs.com*

Patrick Schmidt

Patrick Schmidt, author of "Understanding American and German Business Cultures," is a cross-cultural consultant and trainer, living in Düsseldorf. The focus of his seminars is international personnel work, cooperation in multinational teams and transfer of management methods. Further information about his work can be found on his website www.agcc.de.

For comments and questions, write to: *pschmidt.de@t-online.de*

Volker Schmidt

Volker Schmidt is Principal at the Munich office of The Riverside Company. Prior to joining Riverside in 2003 he worked eight years as a management consultant for The Boston Consulting Group. Volker Schmidt earned a Master of Industrial Engineering from the University of Karlsruhe and also holds an MBA from Stanford University.

He can be reached at: *vos@riversidecompany.com*

Susanne Schreiber

Susanne Schreiber is a senior associate of Lovells in Munich. She is specialized in corporate and tax law and joined Lovells in 2002 as lawyer after her bar exam. Her work primarily focuses on advising national and international clients on tax issues in domestic and cross-border M&A and private equity transactions, in particular on the development and implementation of acquisition finance structures. She further advises on tax aspects in business restructuring scenarios. After having successfully passed the exams required for attaining the tax specialist solicitor (*Fachanwalt für Steuerrecht*) qualification in 2003, she will qualify as tax advisor in 2005/2006.

She can be reached at: *susanne.schreiber@lovells.com*

Georg Christopher Schweiger

Georg Christopher Schweiger heads the Ernst & Young Transaction Advisory Services – Global Financial Services team in Germany and is responsible for the delivery of Corporate Finance services, including M&A to German financial services clients (e.g. banks, insurance companies, leasing companies, fund managers). Christopher has almost twenty years experience in investment banking assisting many clients with domestic and cross-border transactions.

Prior to joining Ernst & Young, Chris was Vice President – Head of Origination Western Europe at DZ BANK, London, where he was responsible for client relationships with corporates, financial institutions and sovereigns in Western Europe. Previously he worked in the Corporate Finance divisions of HypoVereinsbank and UBS Warburg.

Christopher holds degrees in business administration and law and has published a number of articles relating to mergers & acquisitions, banking, corporate finance and is author of a book on the European Central Bank.

He can be reached at: *christopher.schweiger@de.ey.com*

Thomas Schwingeler

Thomas Schwingeler is a Managing Director and Co-Head of Mergers & Acquisitions Germany of Deutsche Bank.

He began his M&A career at Goldman Sachs in London in 1991. After business school and some time at Merrill Lynch, Thomas Schwingeler rejoined Goldman Sachs in New York focussing on US and Latin American M&A, and moving to the Frankfurt office early 2000. Beginning in 2001 he spent three years at Dresdner Kleinwort Wasserstein as Co-Head of the Transactions Execution Group. He joined Deutsche Bank in January 2005 and is based in Frankfurt. Thomas has an MBA from Harvard Business School and a BA from Yale University.

Jörg Sellmann

Jörg Sellmann is Degussa's Global Head of M&A since the inception of the new degussa in 2001. His main recent responsibilities have been the formation and expansion of Degussa's M&A group in Düsseldorf, New York and Shanghai as well as the execution of the divestment program after the merger of Degussa-Hüls and SKW into today's degussa. This process resulted in some 20 transactions and the spin-off of approx. €7 bn in revenue.

Mr. Sellmann was also the Head of M&A of the predecessor companies Degussa-Hüls AG from 1999 to 2000 and Hüls AG from 1998 to 1999. Previously he spent approx. 5 years in cross-border Investmentbanking at West Merchant Bank in London and Düsseldorf from 1993 to 1997. Mr. Sellmann is a board member of Polymer Latex which is owned by TowerBrook Capital Partners LLC, as well as a member of the "M&A DAX 13" round.

He holds an MBA (Diplom Kaufmann) from Münster University and is a certified banking apprentice (Deutsche Bank).

Douglas Squeo

Director at MindFolio Chicago and responsible for the firm's activities in industrial, business-to-business and medical professional markets.

His entire 30-year professional career has focused on marketing and supporting the development of customer-focused business strategies. He has particular expertise in competitive positioning and product development and has been a key player and practitioner in the evolutionary development of computer-based data collection and market modeling methods. He consults with Fortune 500 or equivalent clients, divided evenly between Europe and North America; the majority of his extensive European experience is with German clients over the past 20 years.

Dr. Rainer Stadler

Partner of Linklaters Oppenhoff & Rädler, Munich office.

Rainer Stadler, born 1962, is mainly focused on the tax-oriented restructuring of groups, structuring of national and international M&A transactions, and tax-efficient structuring of opportunity funds and investments in such funds. Stadler, who joined the firm (then: Oppenhoff & Rädler) in 1994, being partner since 1999, has gained high recognition in the market for his efficient, targeted and client-oriented approach. He is regular lecturer at conventions and seminars.

He can be reached at: *rainer.stadler@linklaters.com*

Dr. Lothar Steinebach

Dr. Lothar Steinebach is Executive Vice President and Chief Financial Officer of Henkel KGaA (Düsseldorf, Germany) since July 2003 and General Counsel since January 2005.

He began his career with Henkel as an attorney in the Law Department in 1980 and moved into Finance being appointed Corporate Vice President Finance & Controlling in 1995 reporting to the CFO.

Before that, in 1979, he worked as an Assistant Professor at the Institute for International and Comparative Law of the University of Cologne. From 1977 to 1978, he attended a graduate law program at the University of Michigan, Ann Arbor, finishing with an LLM degree. From 1974 through 1977, he completed his legal education with the Second State Examination. From 1969 through 1974, he studied law at the University of Mainz, specializing in Conflicts of Law and Comparative Law and finishing with the First State Examination.

Lothar Steinebach is a German national born in Wiesbaden (Germany). At Henkel KGaA he was involved in many major transactions, acquisitions and joint ventures, particularly after 1985 when Henkel had issued preference shares which were traded at the stock exchange. Transactions involved parties in the United States, Japan and Brazil in addition to Germany and other European countries.

Dr. Martin Sura

Martin Sura leads Lovells' German competition law practice and is based in the firm's Dusseldorf office. He trained with the firm in 1994, qualified in 1995 and became a partner in 2001.

Martin Sura's main field of activity is merger control work, both before national authorities, in particular the German *Bundeskartellamt*, and the EC Commission. He is also regularly advising clients in cartel investigations and is involved in competition litigation both before the European Courts in Luxemburg and German courts.

He can be reached at: *martin.sura@lovells.com*